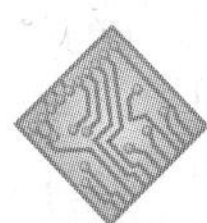

Pascal:

Understanding Programming and Problem Solving

Third Alternate Edition

Pascal:

Understanding Programming and Problem Solving

Third Alternate Edition

Douglas W. Nance
CENTRAL MICHIGAN UNIVERSITY

WEST PUBLISHING COMPANY
Minneapolis/St. Paul New York Los Angeles San Francisco

To "Mom" Johnson
Our sole surviving grandparent, beloved
matriarch of five generations.
Happy 100th birthday!
Doug and Helen

Copyeditor: Mary George
Interior and Cover design: Johnston Design Office
Illustrations: Miyake Illustration and Design
Composition: Carlisle Communications
Index: Schroeder Indexing Services
Production, Prepress, Printing and Binding: West Publishing Company

WEST'S COMMITMENT TO THE ENVIRONMENT

In 1906, West Publishing Company began recycling materials left over from the production of books. This began a tradition of efficient and responsible use of resources. Today, up to 95 percent of our legal books and 70 percent of our college and school texts are printed on recycled, acid-free stock. West also recycles nearly 22 million pounds of scrap paper annually—the equivalent of 181,717 trees. Since the 1960s, West has devised ways to capture and recycle waste inks, solvents, oils, and vapors created in the printing process. We also recycle plastics of all kinds, wood, glass, corrugated cardboard, and batteries, and have eliminated the use of Styrofoam book packaging. We at West are proud of the longevity and the scope of our commitment to the environment.

Printed in the United States of America
02 01 00 99 98 97 96 95 8 7 6 5 4 3 2 1 0

Library of Congress Cataloging-in-Publication Data

Nance, Douglas W.
Pascal: understanding programming and problem solving / Douglas W. Nance.—3rd alternate ed.
p. cm.
Includes index.
ISBN 0–314–04361–6 (soft)
1. Pascal (Computer program language) I. Title.
QA76.73.P2N35 1995
005.13′3—dc20 94–37681
CIP

Contents

Preface

Those who teach entry-level courses in computer science are familiar with the problems that beginning students encounter. Initially, students can get so involved in learning a language that they may fail to grasp the significance of using the language to solve problems. Conversely, it is possible to emphasize problem solving to the extent that using a particular language to solve problems becomes almost incidental. The intent of this text is to fall somewhere in between these two extremes. In addition to providing a complete, one-semester course in Pascal, the broader goals are for students to understand language concepts and subsequently be able to use them to solve problems.

Overview and Organization

The third edition of this text was intended to be a fine tuning of a well-accepted second edition. This goal has been accomplished. Without actually counting, an average of more than 10 changes per page appears to have been made throughout the text. Given the length of the text, this means more than 6000 changes have probably been made in the process of fine tuning the previous edition.

However, as always happens during a revision, more has been done than was originally intended when the process began. In addition to the fine tuning, I have increased the technical level of presentation, the emphasis on communication as part of computer science, the documentation for loops and selection, and the use of descriptive identifiers. All of these changes will be discussed in more detail later in this preface.

The material in Chapters 1 and 2 includes the basics of most programming languages: input, output, data types, arithmetic, and standard functions. Even if students are well versed in these mechanics from another programming language, they should not skip these two chapters. The fundamental issues of computer science as a science and program development by top-down design are contained in this material. I feel it is very important for students to have a broad perspective of the discipline of computer science and to use a problem-solving approach when designing solutions to solve problems. Chapters 1 and 2 set the stage for this kind of development.

Throughout the text, I have attempted to explain and develop concepts carefully. These are illustrated by frequent examples and diagrams. New concepts are then used in complete programs to show how they aid in solving problems. An early and consistent emphasis has been placed on good writing habits and on producing neat, attractive output. I firmly believe program documentation and readability are important. Thus, I frequently discuss them in the text, and I offer style tips where appropriate.

There are at least three general scenarios for which this text would be appropriate.

1. A deliberately paced, thorough presentation of concepts would allow you to get through records and/or files in a one-semester course.
2. An accelerated pace with students who have previous computing experience would allow you to get into Chapter 13 in a one-semester course.
3. A deliberate pace with a thorough presentation would allow you to present the material in Chapters 1–13 in a two-quarter sequence.

Subprograms are presented fairly early in this text. Procedures and user-defined functions are presented in their entirety in Chapter 3 before either selection statements (Chapter 4) or repetition statements (Chapter 5). This facilitates good problem solving habits in that a completely modular approach can be emphasized early in the course.

A completely interactive environment is assumed for the first five chapters. The first part of Chapter 6 introduces text files. From that point on, examples and programming problems use a combination of interactive and noninteractive environments. If you prefer, it would be possible to present the material on text files (Section 6.1) earlier in the course.

Chapters 7 and 8 develop arrays. Due to the significance of this concept, these chapters contain numerous examples, illustrations, and applications. Both the selection sort and bubble sort are presented in Chapter 7. Insertion sort and quick sort are discussed in Chapter 11. The insertion sort could be brought forward, but the quick sort requires the material on stacks to be covered before the sorting algorithm is presented. Records and files are discussed in Chapters 9 and 10, respectively. Their placement there is traditional. These chapters, combined with Chapters 7 and 8, present a detailed treatment of static data structures.

Chapter 11 is an optional chapter that discusses recursion and sorting. Recursion has been placed in this chapter so that an expanded presentation would be more appropriate. This also allows the quick sort to be developed. For advanced classes, material in this chapter could be used to motivate additional work with data structures.

Chapter 12, Sets, could be presented any time after Chapter 6. Although a full chapter has been devoted to this topic, a working knowledge could be given to students in one or two days. Dynamic variables and data structures are introduced in Chapter 13. A reasonable discussion and development of pointers, linked lists, and binary trees is included. However, a full development of these concepts would have to come from a second course with a different text.

T Pascal statements in this text conform to standard Pascal. Due to the increasing use of Turbo Pascal with personal computers, Turbo Pascal references are included in the margins to indicate where Turbo differs from standard Pascal.

Features

This text has a number of noteworthy pedagogical features.

- Objectives: A concise list of topics and learning objectives in each section.
- Communication and Style Tips: Suggestions for programming style, intended to enhance readability. A conscious attempt to emphasize the need for solid communication skills is developed in this text.
- Exercises: Short-answer questions at the end of each section.
- Programming Problems and Projects: Starting with Chapter 1, lengthy lists of suggestions for complete programs and projects at the end of each chapter.
- Communication in Practice: Beginning with Chapter 1, suggestions and problems at the end of each chapter to give students a variety of ways to improve their communication skills. Suggestions include program documentation, talking with software users, preparing reports, and giving reports.
- Module specifications: Specifications for all program modules.
- Structure charts: Charts that reflect modular development and include the use of data flow arrows to emphasize transmission of data to and/or from each module. These charts set the stage for understanding the use of value and variable parameters when procedures are introduced.
- Notes of Interest: Tidbits of information intended to create awareness of and interest in various aspects of computer science.

- Suggestions for test programs: Ideas included in exercises encourage students to use the computer to determine answers to questions and to see how to implement concepts in short programs.
- Focus on Program Design: When appropriate, a complete program at the end of the chapter that illustrates utilization of the concepts developed within the chapter.
- Running and Debugging Hints: Ideas preceding each Summary and programming problems set at the ends of chapters.
- New terms are italicized when first introduced.

In the back of the book there is a complete glossary, as well as appendixes on reserved words, standard identifiers, syntax diagrams, character sets, compiler error messages, Turbo Pascal references, the **GOTO** statement, and packing and unpacking. The final section of back matter provides answers to selected exercises.

Changes for the Third Alternate Edition

As the discipline of computer science evolves, there are two issues that its textbook authors must address. First, students of Pascal have an increasing level of experience and sophistication with computers. Second, the nature of an entry-level course should reflect current trends and meet current needs. These issues shaped the changes made in the second edition.

Three dominant themes have shaped the changes for this edition. First is the emphasis on communication as an integral part of learning about computer science. Changes made to reflect this emphasis include increased documentation for loops and selection statements and increased attention to descriptive identifiers. Communication in Practice problems at the end of each chapter contain suggestions that allow students to interact with users outside the classroom and then report their results to the class.

The second theme is to increase the technical level of the material presented. Changes made consistent with this theme include

- New material on numeric representation, including a discussion of representational and cancellation errors
- A discussion of the differences between type compatibility and assignment compatibility
- An emphasis on the difference between an expression and a statement
- Use of the phrase "field selector" when working with records
- Additional material on testing values for programs

Finally, programming in the large received additional emphasis. As previous users know, this has always been a feature of my textbooks. However, this edition contains more material and examples that contain reusable code. Also, several programming problems feature enhancements and subsequent development from previous chapters. These problems are denoted by a special symbol (■) when they appear in the problem set.

This edition maintains the philosophy that computer science is a dynamic discipline. Although Pascal is still the most-used language in entry-level courses, many concepts are presented in a language-independent manner. Thus, learning a language for the sake of learning the language is frequently deemphasized in favor of emphasizing concepts and problem-solving skills. Further, there is an increasing need for students to see both interactive and batch mode programs. These environments, coupled with popular nonstandard versions of Pascal (Turbo, for example), dictate greater flexibility in text preparation.

Consistent with the philosophy that Pascal is evolving as an introductory course in computer science, this third edition features

- Continuing emphasis on the design of solutions to problems
- Two sections on using assertions
- A section on software engineering and subsections throughout the text indicating how new concepts relate to software engineering
- A section on the software system life cycle
- Material on abstraction, including subsections on procedural abstraction, data abstraction, and abstract data types
- A high level of rigor in the development and use of the current terminology associated with subprograms, including discussions of cohesion, encapsulation, and interface
- Material emphasizing communication in computer science, including text references and exercises in every chapter designed to allow students to interview people, write reports, give oral reports, and write program specifications without writing code
- Graphic documentation of some algorithms to enable students to more easily understand code by using visual illustrations.
- Continuing use of interactive and batch mode examples in Chapters 1–8
- Occasional use of photographs to clarify and enhance presentations
- Comments about Turbo Pascal in the text and in Appendix 6 that are appropriate for all versions of Turbo
- A significant number of mathematical examples and programming problems
- Of the forty Notes of Interest, eleven are new and two have been updated since the last edition.

All of these changes have been made with two thoughts prevalent in my mind. It is essential that this edition reflect the current trends and future directions of computer science. It is also essential that concepts continue to be presented in such a manner that beginning students can understand a concept and how it is used to design a solution to some problem. In this regard, every attempt has been made to retain the pedogogical features that have proven to be trademarks of the first two editions, including frequent use of examples, clear exposition of new concepts, use of test programs, and varied exercises in every section.

Ancillaries

A broad-based teaching support package is essential for an introductory course in Pascal. The following ancillary materials are available from West Publishing Company:

1. Laboratory Manuals: In keeping with our intent to provide a modern approach and to meet the growing need for laboratory experience as put forth by the new ACM Curriculum Guidelines, two laboratory manuals are available (one for standard Pascal and one for Turbo users) that are tied closely to the pedagogy of the text. Authored by Carol Wilson (Western Kentucky University) and class-tested by students at two universities, both provide excellent sets of lab exercises to promote student understanding.
2. Student Solutions Manual: This manual contains solutions to all exercises at the end of each section. Appropriate problems are explained and developed. Complete solutions for two programming problems are included for each chapter.
3. Instructor's Manual: This manual contains the following for each chapter:
   a. outline
   b. teaching test questions
   c. chapter test questions
   d. answers to test questions

4. Transparency Masters: More than 75 transparency masters are available to adopters of the text. These include masters of figures, tables, and selected materials from the text.
5. Software with Machine-Readable Programming Problems: For each chapter, this software contains at least four complete programming problem solutions and the complete Focus on Program Design problem. This software will run on IBM-PCs and compatibles and DEC Vaxes. It is available in both standard and Turbo Pascal.
6. Computerized Test Bank: Adopters of this edition will receive a computerized test-generation system that allows instructors to edit, add, or delete questions as desired.

West Publishing Company recognizes the growing need for an integrated, full-year textbook for computer science students. Consequently, this text has been used as the basis for the first part of *Introduction to Computer Science: Programming, Problem Solving, and Data Structures,* Third Alternate Edition, which I coauthored with Tom Naps. The full-year text is appropriate for a two-semester or three-quarter course (with generic titles of CS1 and CS2) that presents Pascal as the programming language in the first term. Contact West Publishing Company for examination copies.

Each program and program segment in the text and all ancillaries have been compiled and run. Hence, original versions were all working. Unfortunately, the publication process does allow errors in code to occur after a program has been run. Every effort has been made to produce an error-free text, although this is virtually impossible. I assume full responsibility for all errors and omissions. If you detect any, please be tolerant and notify me or West Publishing Company so they can be corrected in subsequent printings and editions.

Acknowledgments

I would like to take this opportunity to thank those who in some way contributed to the completion of this text. Several reviewers have made significant constructive comments during various phases of manuscript development for this third edition. They include

Hamid R. Arabnia
University of Georgia

Clark B. Archer
Winthrop University

Anthony Q. Baxter
University of Kentucky

Kenneth D. Blaha
Pacific Lutheran University

Ronald J. Classen
Northeast Louisiana University

Lloyd D. Ellerbeck
Alabama A & M University

Ann R. Ford
University of Michigan

Linda Hayden
Elizabeth City State College

James Hester
California State University-Fullerton

Ronald A. Mann
University of Louisville

Robert Mercer
Middlesex College-University of Western Ontario

Kenneth Messa
Loyola University-New Orleans

Robert E. Norton
San Diego Mesa College

Matt Payne
University of Nebraska-Omaha

Ingrid Russell
University of Hartford

Terry Seethoff
Northern Michigan University

Ray Sunderraman
Wichita State University

Carol W. Wilson
Western Kentucky University

Betsy Friedman, Developmental Editor, coordinated the production of all ancillaries and prepared the analysis of reviewer responses. Jim Cowles (Ohio University at Lancaster) has done yeoman's work in preparing many of the ancillaries. Carol Wilson (Western Kentucky University) contributed two Notes of Interest and prepared a Laboratory Manual that can be used with this text. Tom Naps, (Lawrence University) contributed many helpful suggestions and recommendations.

Three other people deserve special mention because, without their expertise, this book would not exist. They are

Mary George, copyeditor. This is my third book with Mary. She continues to amaze me with her attention to detail. She is organized, efficient, and extremely competent. If you find this text readable, it is in large part due to her suggestions, changes, and rewordings.

Matt Thurber, Production Editor. This is my second book with Matt, and I am really impressed. He is highly motivated, well-organized, helpful, and responsive. He has done an excellent job of keeping everyone involved with the project on schedule. It was a pleasure to work with him.

Jerry Westby, Executive Editor. This is our fourteenth book together, and my respect for Jerry keeps increasing. He has an excellent sense for what makes a book useful. Most of the special features of this text are the result of Jerry's suggestions. He has offered constant support and invaluable suggestions.

My family and friends deserve special mention for their support and patience. For 10 years, most of my spare time and energy have been devoted to textbook writing. This would not have been possible without their encouragement and understanding.

Finally, there is one person without whose help this project would not have been possible. Helen, who was a student in my first Pascal class, has been of tremendous assistance since we started writing. She worked during every phase of the textbook-preparation process. She prepared tearsheets, read copyedited material, proofread galleys and pages, and made many helpful suggestions.

This is the fourteenth text for which Helen has done all of the above. Her unfailing patience and support have been remarkable. Fortunately for me, she has been my wife and best friend for more than 35 years.

Douglas W. Nance

CHAPTER 1

Computer Science: Architecture, Languages, Problem Solving, and Programs

CHAPTER OUTLINE

This chapter provides a quick introduction to computer science, computer languages, and computer programs. Section 1.1 is a preview of the study of computer science. Section 1.2 begins to explore the relationship between computers, computer languages, and computer programs. Section 1.3 lays the foundation for what many consider to be the most important aspect of entry-level courses in computer science: program development. The problem-solving theme of this section is continued throughout the text. The remainder of Chapter 1 focuses on writing complete programs as early as possible, which will enable you to use the computer and to be an active participant from the initial stages of your study of computer science.

As you read this chapter, do not be overly concerned about the introduction and early use of terminology. All terms will be subsequently developed. A good approach to an introductory chapter is to reread it periodically. This will help you maintain a good perspective of how new concepts and techniques fit in the broader picture of using computers. Finally, remember that learning a language that will make a computer work can be exciting; being able to control such a machine can lead to quite a sense of power.

1.1 Computer Science: A Preview

Computer science is a very young discipline. Electronic computers were initially developed in the 1940s. Those who worked with computers in the 1940s and 1950s often did so by teaching themselves about computers; most schools did not offer any instruction in computer science at that time. However, as these early pioneers in computers learned more about the machines they were using, a collection of principles

OBJECTIVES

- to understand that computer science is not computer literacy
- to understand that computer science is:
  - mathematics and logic
  - science
  - engineering
  - communication
  - interdisciplinary

began to evolve into the discipline we now call computer science. Because it emerged from the efforts of people who used computers in a variety of disciplines, the influence of these disciplines can often be seen in computer science. With that in mind, the next sections briefly discuss what computer science is (and what it is not).

Computer Science Is Not Computer Literacy

Computer literate people know how to use a variety of computer software to make their professional and home lives easier and more productive. This software includes, for instance, word processors for writing and data management systems for storing every conceivable form of information from address lists to recipes.

However, knowing how to use specific pieces of computer software is not the same as acquiring an understanding of computer science, just as being able to drive a car does not qualify someone to be an expert mechanic. The user of computer software needs only to be able to follow instructions about how to use the software, whereas, the modern computer scientist must, more than anything else, be a skillful problem solver. The collection of problems that computer science encompasses and the techniques used to solve those problems are the real substance of this rapidly expanding discipline.

Computer Science Is Mathematics and Logic

The problem-solving emphasis of computer science borrows heavily from the areas of mathematics and logic. Faced with a problem, the computer scientist must first formulate a solution. This method of solution, or *algorithm,* as it is often called in computer science, must be thoroughly understood before the computer scientist makes any attempt to implement the solution on the computer. Thus, at the early stages of problem solution, computer scientists work solely with their minds and do not rely upon the machine in any way.

Once the solution is understood, the computer scientist must then state the solution to this problem in a formal language called a *programming language.* This parallels the approach mathematicians or logicians take to develop a proof or argument in the formal language of mathematics. The formal solution stated in a programming language must then be evaluated in terms of its correctness, style, and efficiency. Part of this evaluation process involves entering the formally stated algorithm as a programmed series of steps for the computer to follow.

Another part of the evaluation process is distinctly separate from a consideration of whether or not the computer produces the "right answer" when the program is executed. Indeed, one of the main areas of emphasis throughout this text is on developing well-designed solutions to problems and recognizing the difference between such solutions and ones that work, but inelegantly. True computer scientists seek not just solutions to problems but the best possible solutions.

Computer Science Is Science

Perhaps nothing is as intrinsic to the scientific method as the formulation of hypotheses to explain phenomena and the careful testing of these hypotheses to prove them right or wrong. This same process plays an integral role in the way computer scientists work.

Upon observing a problem, such as a long list of names that needs to be arranged in alphabetical order, the computer scientist formulates a hypothesis in the form of an algorithm that he or she believes will effectively solve the problem. Using mathematical techniques, the computer scientist can make predictions about how such a proposed algorithm will solve the problem. But because the problems facing computer scientists arise from real-world applications, predictive techniques that rely solely upon mathematical theory are not sufficient to prove an algorithm correct. Ultimately, computer scientists must implement their solutions on computers and test them in the complex situations that originally gave rise to the problems. Only after such thorough testing can the hypothetical solutions be declared right or wrong.

Moreover, just as many scientific principles are not 100 percent right or wrong, the hypothetical solutions posed by computer scientists are often subject to limitations. An understanding of those limitations—of when the method is appropriate and when it is not—is a crucial part of the knowledge that computer scientists must have. This is analogous to the way in which any scientist must be aware of the particular limitations of a scientific theory in explaining a given set of phenomena.

Do not forget the experimental nature of computer science as you study this book. You must participate in computer science to truly learn it. Although a good book can help, *you* must solve the problems, implement those solutions on the computer, and then test the results. View each problem you are assigned as an experiment for which you are to propose a solution, and then verify the correctness of your solution by testing it on the computer. If the solution does not work exactly as you hypothesized, do not become discouraged. Instead, ask yourself why it did not work; by doing so, you will acquire a deeper understanding of the problem and your solution. In this sense, the computer represents the experimental tool of the computer scientist. Do not be afraid to use it for exploration.

Computer Science Is Engineering

Whatever the area of specialization, an engineer must neatly combine a firm grasp of scientific principles with implementation techniques. Without knowledge of the principles, the engineer's ability to creatively design problem-solving models is severely limited. Such model building is crucial to the engineering design process. The ultimate design of a bridge, for instance, results from the engineer's consideration of many possible models of the bridge and the selection of the best model. The transformation of abstract ideas into problem-solving models is central to the engineering design process. The ability to generate a variety of models that can be explored is the hallmark of creative engineering.

Similarly, the computer scientist is a model builder. Faced with a problem, the computer scientist must construct models for its solution. Such models take the form of an information structure to hold the data pertinent to the problem and the algorithmic method to manipulate that information structure to actually solve the problem. Just as an engineer must have an in-depth understanding of scientific principles to build a model, so must a computer scientist. Given these principles, the computer scientist can conceive models that are elegant, efficient, and appropriate to the problem at hand.

An understanding of principles alone is not sufficient for either the engineer or the computer scientist. Experience in the actual implementation of hypothetical models is also necessary. Without such experience, you can have only very limited intuition about what is feasible and how a large-scale project should be organized to reach a successful conclusion. Ultimately, computers are used to solve problems in the real world. There, you will need to design programs that come in on time, that are within (if not under) the budget, and that solve all aspects of the original problem. The experience you acquire in designing problem solutions and then implementing them is vital to your being a complete computer scientist. Remember you cannot actually study computer science without actively doing it. To merely read about computer science techniques will leave you with an unrealistic perspective of what is possible.

Computer Science Is Communication

As the discipline of computer science continues to evolve, communication is assuming a more significant role in the undergraduate curriculum. The Association for Comput-

A NOTE OF INTEREST

Ethics and Computer Science

Ethical issues in computer science are rapidly gaining public attention. As evidence, consider the following article from the Washington Post.

Should law-enforcement agencies be allowed to use computers to help them determine whether a person ought to be jailed or allowed out on bond? Should the military let computers decide when and on whom nuclear weapons should be used?

While theft and computer viruses have not gone away as industry problems, a group of 30 computer engineers and ethicists who gathered in Washington recently agreed that questions about the proper use of computers is taking center stage. At issue is to what degree computers should be allowed to make significant decisions that human beings normally make.

Already, judges are consulting computers that have been programmed to predict how certain personality types will behave. Judges are basing their decisions more upon what the computer tells them than upon their own analysis of the arrested person's history. Computers are helping doctors decide treatments for patients. They played a major role in the July 1988 shooting of the Iranian jetliner by the USS Vincennes, and they were the backbone of this country's former Strategic Defense Initiative.

Representatives from universities, IBM Corporation, the Brookings Institution, and several Washington theological seminaries recently discussed what they could do to build a conscience in the computer field.

The computer industry has been marked by "creativity and drive for improvement and advancement," not by ethical concerns, said Robert Melford, chairman of the computing-ethics subcommittee of the Institute of Electrical and Electronics Engineers.

Computer professionals, Melford said, often spend much of their time in solitude, separated from the people affected by their programs who could provide valuable feedback.

Unlike hospitals, computer companies and most organized computer users have no staff ethicists or ethics committees to ponder the consequences of what they do. Few businesses have written policies about the proper way to govern computers. But there is evidence that technical schools, at least, are beginning to work an ethical component into their curricula. For example, in recent years, all computer engineering majors at Polytechnic University in Brooklyn have been required to take a course in ethics. The Massachusetts Institute of Technology is considering mandating five years of study, instead of the current four, to include work in ethics.

Affirmation that such questions should be addressed by computer scientists is contained in the curriculum guidelines of the Association for Computing Machinery, Inc. These guidelines state that "Undergraduates should also develop an understanding of the historical, social, and ethical context of the discipline and the profession."

You will see further Notes of Interest on this area of critical concern later in this book.

ing Machinery, Inc., Curriculum Guidelines state, " . . . undergraduate programs should prepare students to . . . define a problem clearly; . . . document that solution; . . . and communicate that solution to colleagues, professionals in other fields, and the general public." [page 7]

It is no longer sufficient to be content that a program runs correctly. Extra attention should be devoted to the communication aspects associated with the program. For instance, you might be asked to submit a written proposal prior to designing a solution, to carefully and completely document a program as it is being designed, and/or to write a follow-up report after a program has been completed.

These are some ways in which communication can be emphasized as an integral part of computer science. Several opportunities are provided in the exercises and problems in this text to focus on the communication aspects associated with computer science.

Computer Science Is Interdisciplinary

The problems solved by computer scientists come from a variety of disciplines—mathematics, physics, chemistry, biology, geology, economics, business, engineering, linguistics, and psychology, to name a few. As a computer scientist working on a problem in one of these areas, you must be a quasi-expert in that discipline as well as in computer science. For instance, you cannot write a program to manage the checking account system of a bank unless you thoroughly understand how a bank works and how that bank runs its checking accounts. At minimum, you must be literate enough in other disciplines to converse with the people for whom you are writing programs and to learn precisely what it is they want the computer to do for them. Since such people are often very naive about the computer and its capabilities, you will have to possess considerable communication skills as well as a knowledge of that other discipline.

Are you beginning to think that a computer scientist must be knowledgeable about much more than just the computer? If so, you are correct. Too often, computer scientists are viewed as technicians, tucked away in their own little worlds and not thinking or caring about anything other than computers. Nothing could be further from the truth. The successful computer scientist must be able to communicate, to learn new ideas quickly, and to adapt to ever-changing conditions. Computer science is emerging from its early dark ages into a mature process—one that I hope you will find rewarding and exciting. In studying computer science, you will be developing many talents; this text can get you started on the road to that development process.

1.2 Computer Architecture and Language

OBJECTIVES

- to understand the historical development of computers
- to know what constitutes computer hardware
- to know what constitutes computer software
- to understand the various levels of computer languages
- to understand what a computer language is
- to understand the difference between a low-level language and a high-level language
- to understand the difference between a source program and an object program

This section is intended to provide you with a brief overview of what computers are and how they are used. Although there are various sizes, makes, and models of computers, you will see that they all operate in basically the same straightforward manner. Whether you work on a personal computer that costs a few hundred dollars or on a mainframe that costs in the millions, the principles of making the machine work are essentially the same.

In this section, we will look at the components of a computer and the idea of language for a computer. Also, we will continue to emphasize the notion of problem solving, which is independent of any particular language.

Modern Computers

The search for aids to perform calculations is almost as old as number systems. Early devices included the abacus, Napier's bones, the slide rule, and mechanical adding machines. More recently, scientific and graphing calculators have changed the nature of personal computing due to their availability, low cost, and high speed. The development of computers over time is highlighted in Figure 1.1. For more complete information, see John F. Vinsonhaler, Christian C. Wagner, and Castelle G. Gentry, *People and Computers, Partners in Problem Solving*, (Eagan, MN: West Publishing Company, 1989).

The last few decades have seen the most significant change in computing machines in the world's history as a result of improvements that have led to the modern computers. As recently as the 1960s, a computer required several rooms because of its size. However, the advent of silicon chips has reduced the size and increased the availability of computers to the point that parents are now able to purchase personal computers as presents for their children. These computers are more powerful than the early behemoths.

What is a computer? According to *Webster's New World Dictionary of the American Language* (2nd College Edition), a computer is "an electronic machine which, by means of stored instructions and information, performs rapid, often complex calculations or compiles, correlates, and selects data." These stored instructions can be altered by the user. Basically, a computer can be thought of as a machine that manipulates information in the form of numbers and characters. This information is referred to as *data.* What makes computers remarkable is the extreme speed and precision with which they can store, retrieve, and manipulate data.

Several types of computers are available. As recently as the early 1980s, computers were typically classified as mainframe computers, minicomputers, and microcomputers. In this grouping, *mainframe computers* were the large computers used

◆ FIGURE 1.1
Development of computers

Era	Early Computing Devices		Mechanical Computers	Electro-mechanical Computers
Year	1000 B.C.	A.D. 1614	1650 1900	1945
Development	Abacus	Napier's bones	Adding machine Slide rule Difference engine Analytic engine	Cogged wheels Instruction register Operation code Address Plug board Harvard Mark I Tabulating machine

by major companies, government agencies, and universities that could accommodate 100 or more users at the same time. *Minicomputers,* in a sense, were smaller versions of mainframe computers that could be used by several persons at once but that had less storage capacity and were much less expensive. *Microcomputers* (also called *personal computers*) had limited storage capacity, are generally used by one person at a time, and can be purchased for a few hundred dollars.

The current classification of computers is not as clear as it was in the early 1980s. We could place the computers that exist now into three categories: desk-top systems, mainframe systems, and super computers. *Desk-top systems* include single- and multiple-user personal computers and work stations; the operating speeds and storage capacities of some work stations exceed what was available on mainframe computers in the 1980s. *Mainframe systems* include both medium-scale and large-scale systems. The distinction between desk-top and mainframe systems is blurred because advances in technology occur so rapidly that the speed and storage capacity of a medium-scale mainframe system could soon become available in a desk-top system. *Super computers* are systems that are capable of enormous operating speeds due to a special method of processing information. All computers can execute only very simple, elementary instructions, but the speed at which the super computers operate sets them apart.

Two phrases that are used to describe the speed of computers are Million Instructions Per Second (MIPS) and Floating-point Operation Per Second (FLOPS). Currently, some Sun work stations are capable of operating at over 50 MIPS, and DEC Alpha systems (a medium-scale mainframe) operate at over 200 MIPS. Thanks to parallel processing, super computers are approaching operating speeds of 1000 MIPS, or 1 billion operations per second. Super computers are used mainly in situations that require massive computation. Examples of such situations include research projects at universities, research and development in industry, and government applications. For further information about the development of the speeds, information storage capabilities, and relative costs of computer systems, see the Note of Interest on page 8.

◆ FIGURE 1.1
(*continued*)

Noncommercial Electronic Computers	**Batch Processing**	**Time-Sharing Systems**	**Personal Computers**
1945 — 1950	1950 — 1965	1965 — 1975	1975 — Present
First-generation computers Vacuum tubes Machine language programming ENIAC	Second-generation computers Transistors Magnetic core memory Assemblers Compilers UNIVAC I IBM 704	Third-generation computers Integrated circuit technology Operating system software Teleprocessing	Fourth-generation computers Fifth-generation computers (supercomputers) Microprocessors Workstations

As you begin your work with computers, you will hear people talking about hardware and software. *Hardware* refers to the actual machine and its support devices. *Software* refers to programs that make the machine do something. Many software packages exist for today's computers. They include word processing, data-base programs, spreadsheets, games, operating systems, and compilers. You can (and will!) learn to create your own software. In fact, that is what this book is all about.

An *instruction* is a simple, elementary task to be performed by the computer. A *program* can be thought of as a set of instructions that tells the machine what to do. When you have written a program, the computer will behave exactly as you have instructed it. It will do no more or no less than what is contained in your specific instructions. For example, consider the following complete program.

```
PROGRAM ComputeAverage (input, output);

VAR
  Score1, Score2, Score3 : integer;
  Average : real;

BEGIN
  writeln ('Enter three scores and press <Enter>.');
  readln (Score1, Score2, Score3);
  Average := (Score1 + Score2 + Score3)/3;
  writeln (Average:20:3)
END.
```

This Pascal program gets three scores entered from the keyboard, computes their average, and then displays the result. Do not be concerned about specific parts of this program. It is intended only to illustrate the idea of a set of instructions. Very soon, you will be able to write significantly more sophisticated programs.

Learning to write programs requires two skills.

A NOTE OF INTEREST

Advances in Computing Technology

(This information was supplied by Dale Jarman, Manager, Computer Center, Central Michigan University.)

Computing technology has changed at an astounding rate during the last 20 years. One illustration of such change is the amount of memory available in a typical personal computer (PC). In 1975, less than 1K of memory was available; by 1985, available memory had increased to 512K. Eight years later, in 1993, PCs typically had 16 Meg (16,000K) of memory, and industry projections indicate 64 Meg of memory will be available on PCs by 1997. This growth is shown in the graph at right.

A second method of considering advances in computing technology is to compare cost to power. The graph below shows that the cost (in actual dollars) of a personal computer has decreased steadily since 1975. However, the power of the PC has grown tremendously. In this comparison, the Norton power rating, which assigns a power rating of 1 to the 64K machine of 1981 with an 8088 chip, has been used.

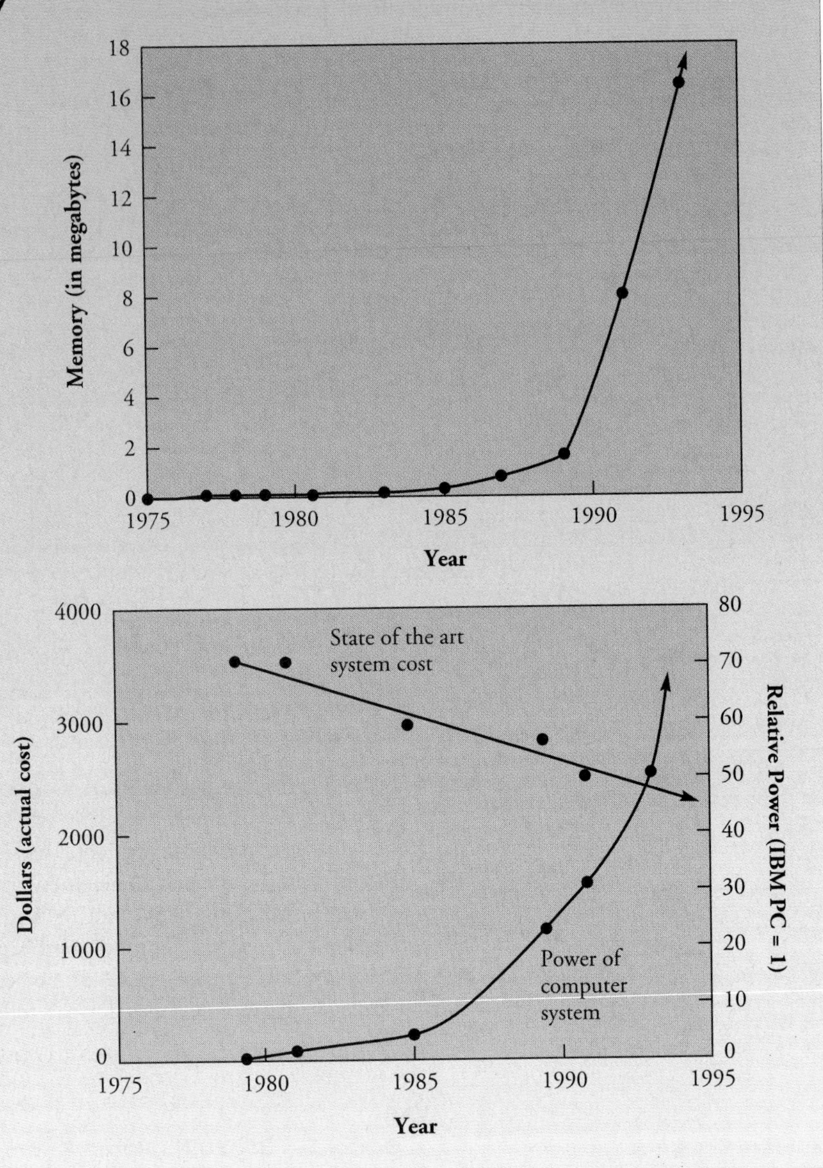

1. You need to be able to use specific terminology and punctuation that can be understood by the machine. In other words, you need to learn a programming language.
2. You need to be able to develop a plan for solving a particular problem. This plan, or algorithm, is a sequence of steps that, when followed, will lead to a solution of the problem.

Initially, you may think that learning a language is the more difficult task because your problems will have relatively easy solutions. Nothing could be further from the truth!

The single most important thing you can do as a student of computer science is to develop the skill to solve problems. Once you have this skill, you can learn to write programs in several different languages.

Computer Hardware

Let's take another look at the question, What is a computer? Our previous answer indicated it is a machine. Although there are several forms, names, and brands of computers, each consists of a *main unit* that is subsequently connected to peripheral devices. The main unit of a computer contains a *central processing unit (CPU)* and the *main (primary) memory*. The CPU is the "brain" of the computer. It contains an *arithmetic/logic unit (ALU)*, which is capable of performing arithmetic operations and evaluating expressions to see if they are true or false, and the *control unit*, which controls the action of the remaining components so your program can be followed step-by-step, or *executed.*

Main memory can be thought of as mailboxes in a post office. It is a sequence of locations where information representing instructions, numbers, characters, and so on can be stored. Main memory is usable while the computer is turned on. It is where the program being executed and the data it is manipulating are stored.

As you develop a greater appreciation of how the computer works, you might wonder how data are stored in memory. Each memory location has an address and is capable of holding a sequence of *binary digits* (0 or 1) which are commonly referred to as *bits.* Instructions, symbols, letters, numbers, and so on are translated into an appropriate pattern of binary digits and then stored in various memory locations. These data are retrieved, used, and changed according to instructions in your program. In fact, the program itself is similarly translated and stored in part of main memory. Main memory can be envisioned as shown in Figure 1.2, and the main unit can be envisioned as shown in Figure 1.3.

◆ FIGURE 1.2
Main memory

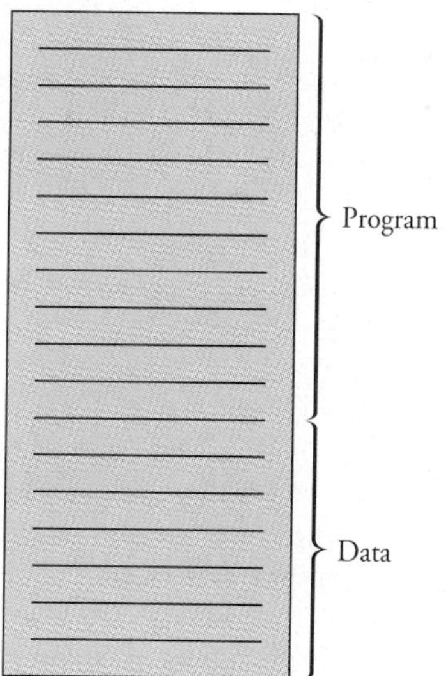

Peripherals can be divided into three categories: input devices, output devices, and secondary (auxiliary) memory devices. *Input devices* give information to a computer. Programs are entered through an input device, and program statements are then translated and stored as previously indicated. One input device (a typical keyboard) is shown in Figure 1.4.

◆ FIGURE 1.3
Main unit

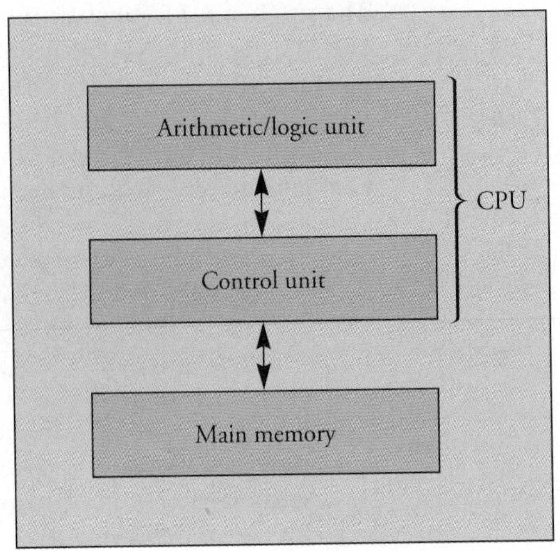

◆ FIGURE 1.4
Keyboard

Output devices show the results of a program. These devices are normally in the form of a screen, line printer, impact printer, or laser printer (Figure 1.5). Input and output devices are frequently referred to as *I/O devices.*

Secondary (auxiliary) memory devices are used if additional memory is needed. On small computers, these secondary memory devices could be floppy disks or hard disks (Figure 1.6), magnetic tapes, or magnetic bubbles. Programs and data waiting to be executed are kept "waiting in the wings" in secondary memory.

Communication between components of a computer is frequently organized around a group of wires called a *bus.* The relationship between a bus and various computer components can be envisioned as shown in Figure 1.7. A photograph of a bus is shown in Figure 1.8. What appear to be lines between the slots are actually wires imprinted upon the underlying board. Boards with wires connected to peripheral devices may be inserted into the slots.

◆ FIGURE 1.5
(a) Screen, (b) line printer (mainframe), (c) impact printer (microcomputer), and (d) laser printer

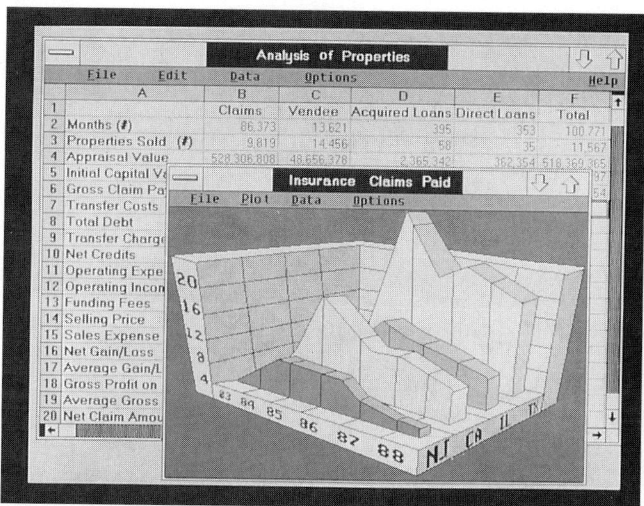

(a)

(b)

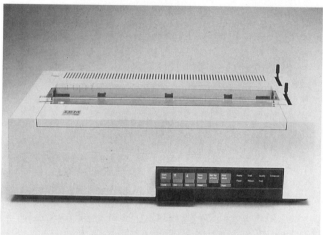

(c)

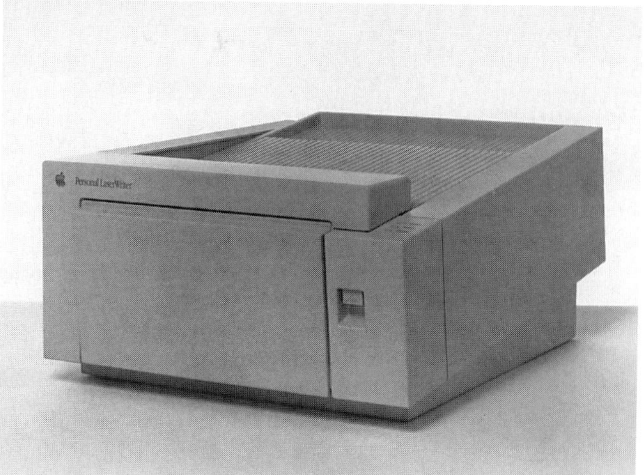

(d)

◆ FIGURE 1.6 Secondary memory devices
(a) Disk drive and (b) microcomputer with hard disk

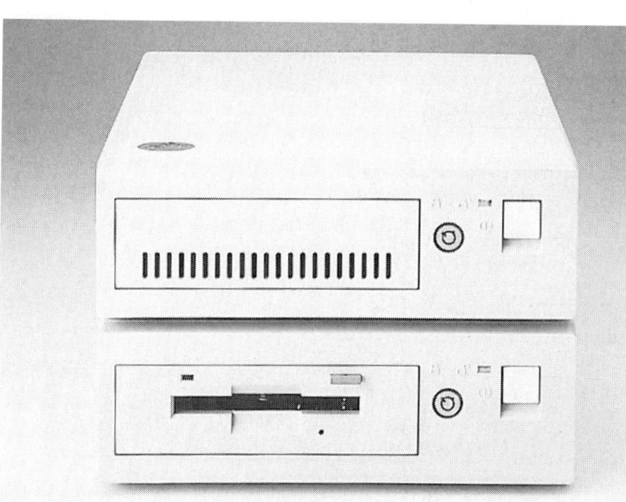

(a)

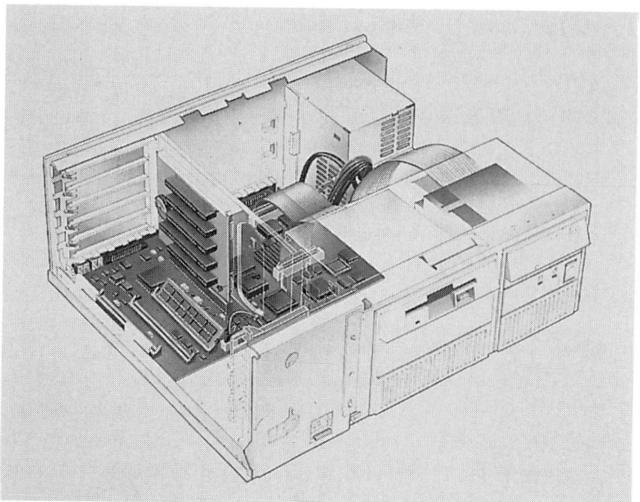

(b)

◆ **FIGURE 1.7**
Illustration of a bus

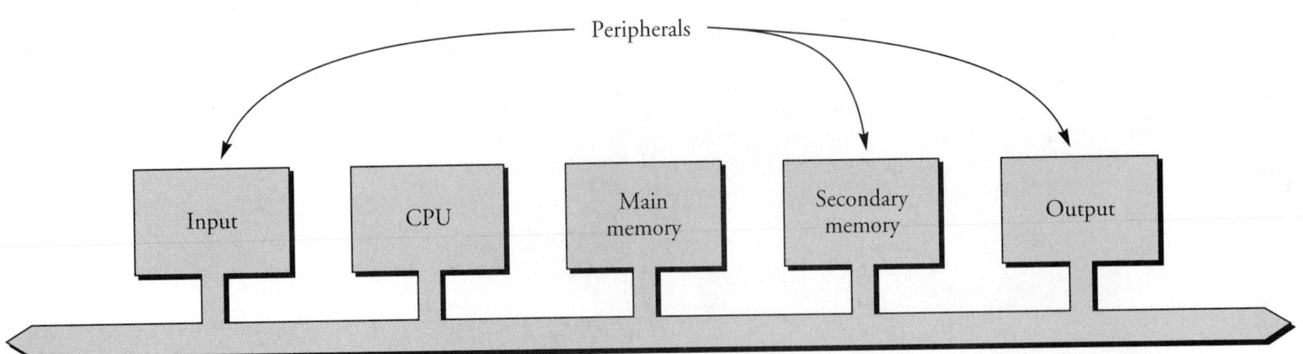

◆ **FIGURE 1.8**
Bus

A NOTE OF INTEREST

Data Loss on Floppy Disks

Why is it important to keep the dust covers on your diskettes? Look at the figure shown here. It illustrates how some very small particles look huge in comparison to the distance between the surface of a diskette and the read/write head. If these particles become lodged between the head and the surface of the diskette, the surface may be scratched, resulting in data loss. So consider yourself warned: handle your disks carefully.

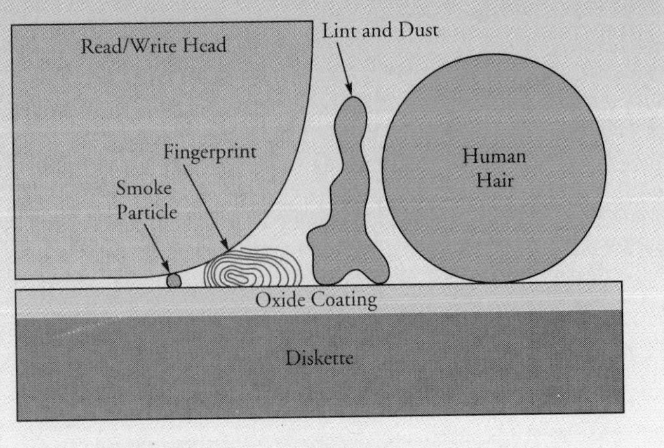

Computer Software

Software refers to programs that make the machine do something. Software consists of two kinds of programs: system software and applications software.

System software includes what is often called the *operating system*. (You may have heard a reference to DOS, which is an acronym for Disk Operating System.) The operating system for a computer is a large program and is usually supplied with a computer. This program allows the user to communicate with the hardware. More specifically, an operating system might control computer access (via passwords), allocate peripheral resources (perhaps with a printer queue), schedule shared resources (for CPU use), or control execution of other programs.

Applications software consists of programs designed for a specific use. Examples of applications software include programs for word processing, text editing, simulating spreadsheets, playing games, designing machinery, and figuring payrolls. Most computer users work with applications software and have little need for learning a computer language; the programs they require have already been written to accomplish their tasks.

Computer Languages

What is a computer language? All data transmission, manipulation, storage, and retrieval is actually done by the machine using electrical pulses generated by sequences of binary digits. If eight-digit binary codes are used, there would be 256 numbered instructions from 00000000 to 11111111. Instructions for adding two numbers would consist of a sequence of these eight-digit codes.

Instructions written in this form are referred to as *machine language*. It is possible to write an entire program in machine language. However, this process is very time consuming, the program is difficult to read and understand, and the language is hard to learn and susceptible to programmer errors.

Therefore, the next level of computer language allows words and symbols to be used in an unsophisticated manner to accomplish simple tasks. For example, the machine code for adding two integers might be

```
010000110011101000111101010000010010101101000010
```

which can be replaced by

```
LOAD A
ADD B
STORE C
```

These instructions cause the number in A to be added to the number in B and the result to be stored for later use in C. This computer language is an *assembly language*, which is generally referred to as a *low-level language*. What actually happens is that words and symbols are translated into appropriate binary digits and the machine uses the translated form.

Compared to machine language, assembly language improves readability and program development but is still a bit cumbersome. Consequently, many *high-level languages* have been developed, including Pascal, PL/I, FORTRAN, BASIC, COBOL, C, C++, Ada, Modula-2, Logo, and others. These languages simplify even further the terminology and symbolism necessary for directing the machine to perform various manipulations of data. For example, in these languages, the task of adding two integers would be written as

C := A + B	(Pascal)
C = A + B	(PL/I)
C = A + B	(FORTRAN)
C = A + B	(BASIC)
ADD A,B GIVING C	(COBOL)
C = A + B	(C)
C = A + B	(C++)
C := A + B	(Ada)
C := A + B	(Modula-2)
MAKE "C :A + :B	(Logo)

A high-level language makes it easier to read, write, and understand a program. This book develops the concepts, symbolism, and terminology needed to use Pascal as a programming language for solving problems. After you have become proficient in Pascal, you should find it relatively easy to learn the nuances of other high-level languages.

For a moment, let's consider how an instruction such as

C := A + B

gets translated into machine code. The actual bit pattern for this code varies according to the machine and software version, but it could be as previously indicated. In order for the translation to happen, a special program called a *compiler* "reads" this high-level instruction and translates it into machine code. This compiled version is then run using some appropriate data. The results are then presented through some form of output device. The special programs that activate the compiler, run the machine-code version, and cause output to be printed are examples of system programs (software). The written program is a *source program,* and the machine-code version generated by the compiler is an *object program* (also referred to as *object code*).

As you will soon see, the compiler does more than just translate instructions into machine code. It also detects certain errors in your source program and prints appropriate messages. For example, if you write the instruction

C := (A + B;

where the parentheses are not matched, when the compiler attempts to translate this line into machine code, it will detect that ")" is needed to close the parenthetical expression and will give you an error message, such as

```
ERROR IN VARIABLE
```

You will then need to correct the error (and any others) and recompile your source program before running it with the data.

To summarize:

1. An editor is used to key in a program (source program).
2. A compiler checks to see if the program is correct.
3. If the program is not correct, the user must go back to step 1 and correct the program.
4. The compiler translates the source program into machine code (object program).

Before leaving this section let's consider the question, Why study Pascal? Various languages have differing strengths and weaknesses. Pascal's strong features include the following.

1. It incorporates program structure in a reasonable approximation of English. For example, if a certain process is to be repeated until some condition is met, this could be written in the program as

```
REPEAT
    } (process here)
UNTIL (condition here)
```

2. It allows the use of descriptive words for variables and data types. Thus, programs for computing payrolls could use words like HoursWorked, StateTax, FICA, TotalDeductions, and GrossPay.
3. It provides a rich set of constructs and statements.
4. It facilitates good problem-solving habits; in fact, many people consider this to be Pascal's main strength. Acquiring the skill to solve a problem using a computer program is the most important trait to develop as a beginning programmer. Pascal is structured in such a manner that it encourages—indeed, almost requires—good problem-solving skills.

You are now ready to begin a detailed study of Pascal. You will undoubtedly spend much time and encounter some frustration during the course of your work. I hope your efforts result in an exciting and rewarding learning experience. Good luck.

1.3 Program Development: Top-Down Design

OBJECTIVES

- to understand what an algorithm is
- to understand what top-down design is
- to understand what stepwise refinement is
- to understand what modularity is
- to be able to develop algorithms

We are now ready to examine problems that computers can solve. First, we need to know how to solve a problem, and then we need to learn how to use a programming language to implement our solution on the computer. This section lays the foundation for what many consider to be the most important aspect of an entry-level course in computer science—program development. The problem-solving theme introduced here is continued throughout the text.

Before we look at problem solving and writing programs for the computer, we should consider some psychological aspects of working in computer science. Studying computer science can cause a significant amount of frustration for the following reasons.

1. Planning is a critical issue. First, you must plan to develop instructions to solve your problem, and then you should plan to translate these instructions into code before you sit down at the keyboard. You should not attempt to type in code "off the top of your head."
2. Time is a major problem. Writing programs is not like completing other assignments. You cannot expect to complete a programming assignment by staying up late the night before it is due. You must begin early and expect to make several revisions before your final version will be ready.
3. Successful problem solving and programming require extreme precision. Generally, concepts in computer science are not difficult. However, implementation of these concepts allows no room for error. For example, one misplaced semicolon in a 1000-line program could prevent the program from working.

In other words, you must be prepared to plan well, start early, be patient, handle frustration, and work hard to succeed in computer science. If you cannot do this, you will probably neither enjoy computer science nor be successful at it.

The key to writing a successful program is planning. Good programs do not just happen; they are the result of careful design and patience. Just as an artist commissioned to paint a portrait does not start out by shading in the lips and eyes, a good

A NOTE OF INTEREST

Why Learn Pascal?

From the point of view of many potential users, Pascal's major drawback is that it is a compiled rather than an interpreted language. This means that developing and testing a small Pascal program can take a lot longer and involve many more steps than it would with an interpreted language like BASIC. The effect of this drawback has been lessened recently with the development of interpreter programs for Pascal. [For example, some current versions of Pascal, such as Turbo Pascal, have quick compilation and are as easy to use as most interpreted languages.] Even so, most programs written by users of personal computers are small ones designed for quick solutions to particular problems, and the use of Pascal for such programs may be a form of overkill.

Ironically, the characteristics of Pascal that make it relatively unsuited for small programs are a direct consequence of its strengths as a programming language. The discipline imposed by the language makes it easier to understand large programs, but it may be more than a small program demands. For serious development of large programs or for the creation of tools that will be used over and over again (and require modifications from time to time), Pascal is clearly superior.

Experts generally consider Pascal an important language for people who are planning to study computer science or to learn programming. Indeed, the College Entrance Examination Board has designated Pascal as the required language for advanced-placement courses in computer science for high school students. Although it is true that an experienced programmer can write clearly structured programs in any language, learning the principles of structured programming is much easier in Pascal.

Is Pascal difficult to learn? We don't think so, but the question is relative and may depend upon which language you learn first. Programmers become accustomed to the first language they learn, making it the standard by which all others are judged. Even the poor features of the familiar language come to be seen as necessities, and a new language seems inferior. Don't let such subjective evaluations bar your way to learning Pascal, a powerful and elegant programming language.

computer programmer does not attack a problem by immediately trying to write code for a program to solve the problem. Writing a program is like writing an essay: an overall theme is envisioned, an outline of major ideas is developed, each major idea is subdivided into several parts, and each part is developed using individual sentences.

Six Steps to Good Programming Habits

You should follow six steps in developing a program to solve a problem: analyze the problem, develop an algorithm, write code for the program, run the program, test the results, and document the program. These steps will help develop good problem-solving habits and, in turn, solve programming problems correctly. A brief discussion of each of these steps follows.

Step 1. Analyze the Problem. This is not a trivial task. Before you can do anything, you must know exactly what it is you are to do. You must be able to formulate a clear and precise statement of what is to be done. You should understand completely what data are available to you and what assumptions you can make. You should also know exactly what output is desired and the form it should take.

Step 2. Develop an Algorithm. An algorithm is a finite sequence of effective statements that, when applied to the problem, will solve it. An *effective statement* is a clear, unambiguous instruction that can be carried out. Each algorithm you develop should (1) have a specific beginning; (2) at the completion of one step, have the next step uniquely determined; and (3) have an ending that is reached in a reasonable amount of time.

Step 3. Write Code for the Program. When the algorithm correctly solves the problem, you can think about translating your algorithm into a high-level language. An effective algorithm will significantly reduce the time you need to complete this step.

Step 4. Run the Program. After writing the code, you are ready to run the program. Using an editor, you type the program code into the computer, compile the program, and run the program. At this point, you may discover errors that can be as simple as typing errors or that may require a reevaluation of all or parts of your algorithm. The probability of having to make some corrections or changes at this stage is quite high.

Step 5. Test the Results. After your program has been run, you need to be sure that the results are correct, that they are in a form you like, and that your program produces the correct solution in all cases. To be sure the results are correct, you must look at them and compare them with what you expect. When using a program with arithmetic operations, this means checking some results with pencil and paper. If the program is complex, you will need to thoroughly test it by running it many times using data that you have carefully selected. Often you will need to make revisions and return to a previous step in the process.

Step 6. Document the Program. It is very important to completely document a working program. The writer knows how the program works. If others are to modify it, they must know the logic the writer used. As you develop the ability to write programs to solve more complex problems, you will find it helpful to include documentation in Step 3 as you write the code.

Developing Algorithms

An algorithm for solving a problem can be developed by stating the problem and then subdividing it into major subtasks. Each subtask can then be subdivided into smaller tasks. This process is repeated until each remaining task is one that is easily solved. This process is known as *top-down design,* and each successive subdivision is referred to as a *stepwise refinement.* Tasks identified at each stage of this process are called *modules.* The relationship between modules can be shown graphically in a *structure chart* (see Figure 1.9).

◆ FIGURE 1.9
Structure chart illustrating top-down design

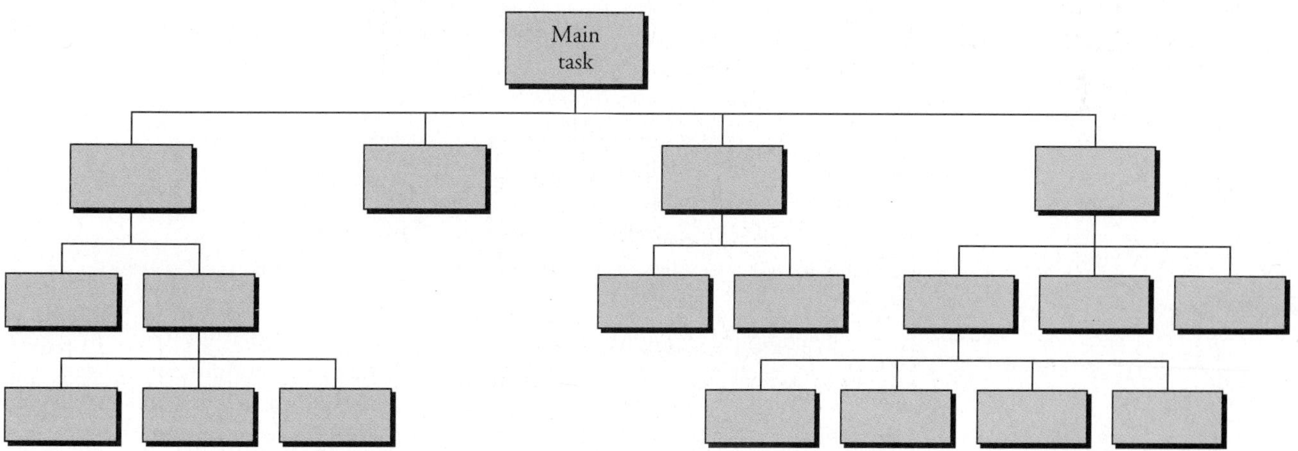

To illustrate developing an algorithm, we will use the problem of updating a checkbook after a transaction has been made. A first-level refinement is shown in Figure 1.10. An arrow pointing to a module means information is needed before the task can be performed. An arrow pointing from a module means the module task has been completed and the information required for subsequent work is available. Each of these modules could be further refined as shown in Figure 1.11. Finally, one of the last modules could be refined as shown in Figure 1.12.

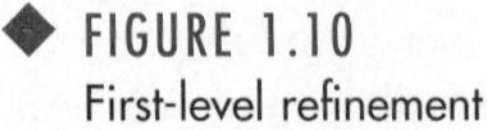

◆ FIGURE 1.10
First-level refinement

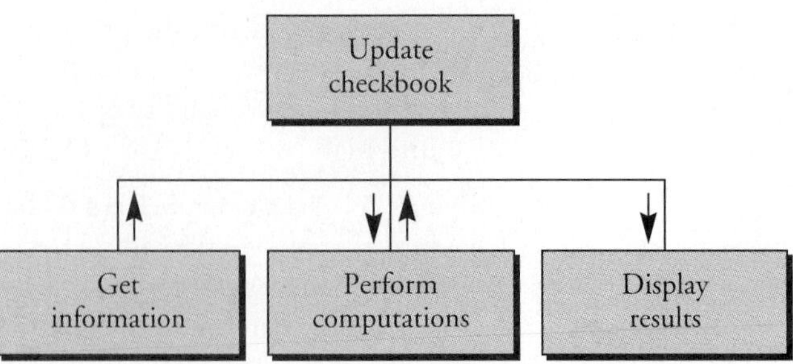

◆ FIGURE 1.11
Second-level refinement

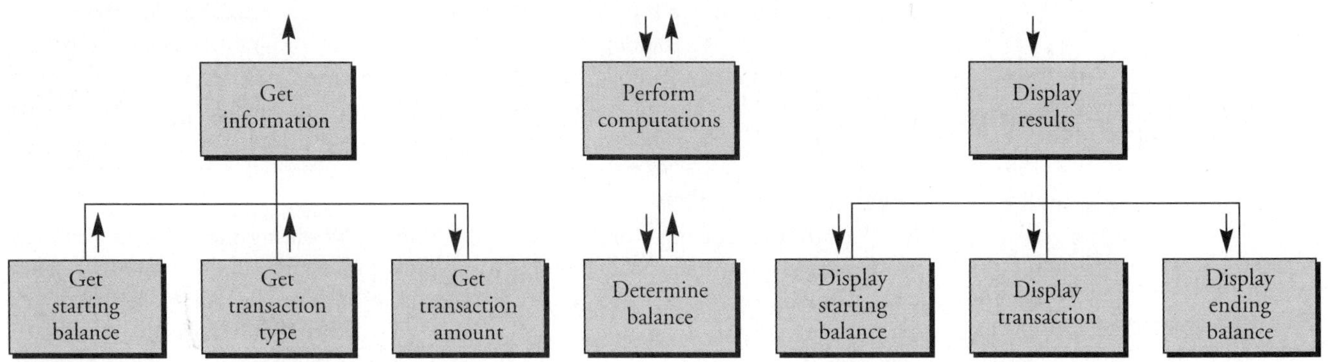

◆ FIGURE 1.12
Third-level refinement

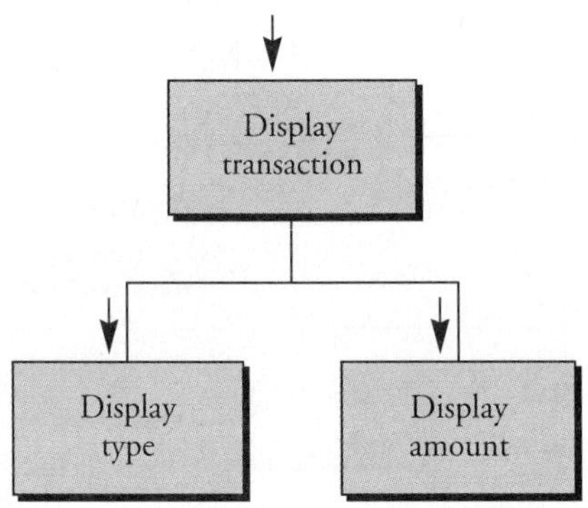

The complete top-down design could then be envisioned as illustrated in Figure 1.13. Notice each remaining task can be accomplished in a very direct manner.

As a further aid to understanding how data are transmitted, we will list *module specifications* for each main (first-level) module. Each module specification includes a description of data received, information returned, and logic used in the module. Module specifications for the Get Information module are

Get Information Module
Data received: None
Information returned: Starting balance
Transaction type
Transaction amount
Logic: Have the user enter information from the keyboard.

◆ FIGURE 1.13
Structure chart for top-down design

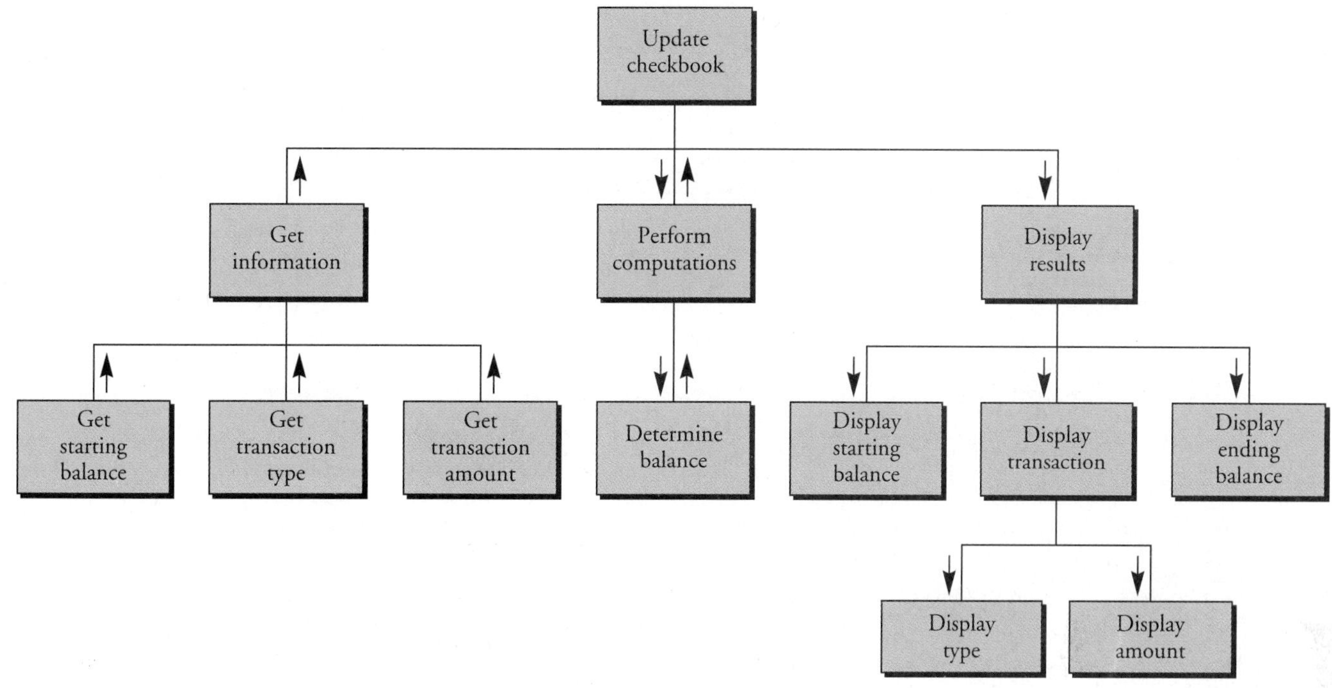

For the checkbook-balancing problem, complete module specifications are

1. Get Information Module
   Data received: None
   Information returned: Starting balance
   Transaction type
   Transaction amount
   Logic: Have the user enter information from the keyboard.
2. Perform Computations Module
   Data received: Starting balance
   Transaction type
   Transaction amount
   Information returned: Ending balance
   Logic: If transaction is a deposit, add it to the starting balance; otherwise, subtract it from the starting balance.
3. Display Results Module
   Data received: Starting balance
   Transaction type
   Transaction amount
   Ending balance
   Information returned: None
   Logic: Display results in a readable form.

At least two comments should be made about top-down design. First, different people can (and probably will) have different designs for the solution of a problem. However, each good design will have well-defined modules with functional subtasks. Second, the graphic method just used helps to formulate general logic for solving a problem but is somewhat awkward for translating to code. Thus, we will use a stylized,

A NOTE OF INTEREST

Software Verification

Sitting 70 kilometers east of Toronto on the shore of Lake Ontario, the Darlington Nuclear Generating Station looks much like any other large nuclear power plant of the Canadian variety. But behind its ordinary exteriors lies an unusual design feature.

Darlington is the first Canadian nuclear station to use computers to operate the two emergency shutdown systems that safeguard each of its four reactors. In both shutdown systems, a computer program replaces an array of electrically operated mechanical devices (switches and relays) designed to respond to sensors monitoring conditions critical to a reactor's safe operation, such as water levels in boilers.

Darlington's four reactors supply enough electricity to serve a city of 2 million people. Its Toronto-based builder, Ontario Hydro, opted for sophisticated software rather than old-fashioned hardware in the belief that a computer-operated shutdown system would be more economical, flexible, reliable, and safe than one under mechanical control.

But that approach carried unanticipated costs. To satisfy regulators that the shutdown software would function as advertised, Ontario Hydro engineers had to go through a frustrating but essential checking process that required nearly three years of extra effort.

"There are lots of examples where software has gone wrong with serious consequences," says engineer Glenn H. Archinoff of Ontario Hydro. "If you want a shutdown system to work when you need it, you have to have a high level of assurance."

The Darlington experience demonstrates the tremendous effort involved in establishing the correctness of even relatively short and straightforward computer programs. The 10,000 "lines" of instructions, or code, required for each shutdown system pale in comparison with the 100,000 lines that constitute a typical word-processing program or the millions of lines needed to operate a long-distance telephone network or a space shuttle.

half-English, half-code method called *pseudocode* to illustrate stepwise refinement in such a design. This pseudocode will be written in English, but the sentence structure and indentations will suggest Pascal code. Major tasks will be numbered with whole numbers; subtasks, with decimal numbers.

First-level pseudocode for the checkbook-balancing problem is

```
1. Get information
2. Perform computations
3. Display results
```

A second-level pseudocode development produces

```
1. Get information
   1.1 get starting balance
   1.2 get transaction type
   1.3 get transaction amount
2. Perform computations
   2.1 IF deposit THEN
          add to balance
       ELSE
          subtract from balance
3. Display results
   3.1 display starting balance
   3.2 display transaction
   3.3 display ending balance
```

Finally, Step 3.2 of the pseudocode is subdivided into

3.2 display transaction
  3.2.1 display transaction type
  3.2.2 display transaction amount

Two final comments are in order. First, each module developed should be tested with data for that module. Once you are sure each module does what you want it to do, the whole program should work when the modules are used together. Second, the process of dividing a task into subtasks is especially suited to writing programs in Pascal. As you will see, the language supports the development of subprograms for specific subtasks.

A Pascal program for the checkbook-balancing problem follows.

```
PROGRAM Checkbook (input, output);

VAR
  StartingBalance,
  EndingBalance,
  TransAmount : real;
  TransType : char;

BEGIN  {  Program  }

  {  Module for getting the data  }
  writeln ('Enter the starting balance and press <Enter>.');
  readln (StartingBalance);
  writeln ('Enter the transaction type (D) deposit or (W) withdrawal');   1*
  writeln ('and press <Enter>.');
  readln (TransType);
  writeln ('Enter the transaction amount and press <Enter>.');
  readln (TransAmount);

  {  Module for performing computations  }
  IF TransType = 'D' THEN
    EndingBalance := StartingBalance + TransAmount                         2
  ELSE IF TransType = 'W' THEN
    EndingBalance := StartingBalance - TransAmount;

  {  Module for displaying results  }
  writeln;
  writeln ('Starting Balance          $', StartingBalance:8:2);
  writeln ('Transaction               $', TransAmount:8:2, TransType:2);  3
  writeln ('---------':33);
  writeln ('Ending Balance            $', EndingBalance:8:2)
END.  {  of program  }
```

Notice how the sections of the program correspond to the module specifications.

Sample runs of the program produce the following output. Input from the keyboard is shown in color.

*These numbers refer to the modules previously developed with module specifications.

```
Enter the starting balance and press <Enter>.
235.16
Enter the transaction type (D) deposit or (W) withdrawal
and press <Enter>.
D
Enter the transaction amount and press <Enter>.
75.00

Starting Balance          $  235.16
Transaction               $   75.00 D
                          ---------
Ending Balance            $  310.16

Enter the starting balance and press <Enter>.
310.16
Enter the transaction type (D) deposit or (W) withdrawal
and press <Enter>.
W
Enter the transaction amount and press <Enter>.
65.75

Starting Balance          $  310.16
Transaction               $   65.75 W
                          ---------
Ending Balance            $  244.41
```

You probably would not use the power of a computer to solve something as simple as this program. You could just press a few calculator keys instead. However, as you will see, the language supports development of subprograms for specific subtasks. You will, for example, soon be able to enhance this program to check for overdrafts, save the new balance for later use, and repeat the process for several transactions. Learning to think in terms of modular development now will aid you not just in creating algorithms to solve problems but also in writing programs to solve problems.

Software Engineering

The phrase *software engineering* refers to the process of developing and maintaining very large software systems. Before becoming engrossed in the specifics of solving problems and writing relatively small programs, it is instructive to consider the broader picture faced by those who develop software for real-world use.

It is not unusual for software systems to be programs that, if written in this size type, would require between 100 and 150 pages of text. These systems must be reliable, economical, and subject to use by a diverse audience. Because of these requirements, software developers must be aware of and practice certain techniques.

As you might imagine, such large programs are not the work of a single individual but are developed by teams of programmers. Issues such as communication, writing style, and technique become as important as developing algorithms to solve particular parts of the problem. Management, coordination, and design are major considerations that need resolution very early in the process. Although you will not face these larger organizational issues in this course, you will see how some of what you learn here has implications for larger design issues.

Software engineering has been so titled because techniques and principles from the more established engineering disciplines are used to guide the large-scale development required in major software. To illustrate, consider the problems faced by an engineer who is to design and supervise construction of a bridge. This analysis was presented by Alfred Spector and David Gifford in an article entitled "A Computer Science Perspective on Bridge Design" published in *Communications of the ACM* (April 1986).

Engineers designing a bridge view it first as a hierarchy of substructures. This decomposition process continues on the substructures themselves until a level of very fundamental objects (such as beams and plates) ultimately is reached. This decomposition technique is similar to the stepwise refinement technique used by software designers, who break a complex problem down into a hierarchy of subproblems, each of which ultimately can be solved by a relatively simple algorithm.

Engineers build conceptual models before actually constructing a bridge. This model building allows them to evaluate various design alternatives in a way that eventually leads to the best possible design for the application being considered. This process is analogous to the way in which a skilled software designer builds models of a software system using structure charts and first-level pseudocode descriptions of modules. The designer then studies these conceptual models and eventually chooses the most elegant and efficient model for the application.

By the [way] in which engineers initially break down the bridge design, they insure that different aspects of the design can be addressed by different subordinate groups of design engineers working in a relatively independent fashion. This is similar to the goal of a software designer who oversees a program development team. The design of the software system must insure that individual components may be developed simultaneously by separate groups whose work will not have harmful side effects when the components are finally pulled together.

This overview is presented to give you a better perspective on how developments in this text are part of a greater whole. As you progress through your study of Pascal, you will see specific illustrations of how concepts and techniques can be viewed as part of the software engineering process.

Software System Life Cycle

Software engineering is the process by which large software systems are produced. As you might imagine, these systems need to be maintained and modified; ultimately, they are replaced with other systems. This entire process parallels that of an organism: there is a development, maintenance, and subsequent demise. Thus, this process is referred to as the *software system life cycle*. Specifically, a system life cycle is represented by six stages:

1. Analysis
2. Design
3. Coding
4. Testing/verification
5. Maintenance
6. Obsolescence

It probably comes as a surprise that computer scientists view this process as having a stage that precedes the design phase. However, it is extremely critical that a problem be completely understood before any attempt is made to design a solution to it. The analysis phase is complicated by the fact that potential users may not supply enough information when they describe the intended use of a system. Analysis requires careful attention to items such as exact form of input, exact form of output, how data entry errors (there will be some) should be handled, how large the data bases will become, how much training in using the system will be provided, and what possible modifications might be required as the intended audience increases/decreases. Clearly, the analysis phase requires an experienced communicator.

The design phase is what much of this text is about. At this stage, the solution is developed using a modular approach. Attention must be paid to the techniques involved, which include communication, algorithm development, writing style, and team work.

Coding closely follows design. Unfortunately, many beginning students want to write code too quickly. This can be a painful lesson if you have to scrap several days of work because your original design was not sufficient. You are encouraged to make sure your designs are complete before writing any code. In the real world, teams of designers work long hours before programmers ever get a chance to start writing code.

The testing/verification phase of a large system is a significant undertaking. Early testing is done on individual modules to get them running properly. Larger data sets must then be run on the entire program to make sure the modules interact properly with the main program. When the system appears ready to the designers, it is usually field tested by selected users. Each of these testing levels is likely to require changes in the design and coding of the system. The consequences of testing and verification can be much more significant than simply determining whether or not the software performs correctly. In radiation oncology, for example, computers control the machine that administers the radiation therapy. An error in the dosage or in the positioning of the machine could have fatal consequences; in such cases, the level of program verification can become a moral issue.

Finally, the system is released to the public and the maintenance phase begins. This phase lasts throughout the remainder of the useful life of the program. During this phase, the concern is to repair problems with the system that arise after it has been put into use. These problems are not necessarily bugs introduced during the coding phase. More often, they are the result of user needs that change over time. For instance, annual changes in the tax laws necessitate changes in even the best payroll programs. Or problems may be due to misinterpretation of user needs during the early analysis phase. Whatever the reason, we must expect a program to undergo numerous changes during its lifetime. During the maintenance phase, the time spent documenting the original program will be repaid many times over. One of the worst tasks imaginable in software development is to be asked to maintain an undocumented program. Undocumented code can quickly become virtually unintelligible, even to the program's original author. Indeed, one measure of a good program is how well it stands up to the maintenance phase.

Of course, no matter how good a program may be, it will eventually become obsolete. At that time, the system life cycle starts all over again with the development of a new system to replace the obsolete one. Hence, the system life cycle is never-ending, being itself part of a larger, repetitive pattern that continues to evolve with changing user needs and more powerful technology.

Effective communication is an important part of learning computer science. In recognition of this factor, this text contains two threads that consistently emphasize communication. First, several "Communication and Style Tips" contain notes about communication and suggestions for improving communication as it relates to developing programs.

The second thread is contained in the Programming Problems and Projects section, which appears at the end of each chapter. Each chapter also contains some "Communication in Practice" problems, which emphasize communication rather than program development. This approach is consistent with the Association for Computing Machinery, Inc., Curriculum Guidelines, which state, "Students should be encouraged to develop strong communication skills, both oral and written."

You are encouraged to discuss these ideas with your instructor and to incorporate them as part of your program development when appropriate.

EXERCISES 1.3

1. Which of the following can be considered effective statements—that is, clear, unambiguous instructions that can be carried out? Explain why each statement is effective or why it is not.
   a. Pay the cashier $9.15.
   b. Water the plants a day before they die.
   c. Determine all positive prime numbers less than 1,000,000.
   d. Choose X to be the smallest positive fraction.
   e. Invest your money in a stock that will increase in value.
2. What additional information must be obtained in order to understand each of the following problems?
   a. Find the largest number of a set of numbers.
   b. Alphabetize a list of names.
   c. Compute charges for a telephone bill.
3. Outline the main tasks required to solve each of the following problems.
   a. Write a good term paper.
   b. Take a vacation.
   c. Choose a college.
   d. Get a summer job.
   e. Compute the semester average for a student in a computer science course, and print all pertinent data.
4. Refine the main tasks in each part of Exercise 3 into a sufficient number of levels so the problem can be solved in a well-defined manner.
5. Use pseudocode to write a solution for each of the following problems. Indicate each stage of your development.
   a. Compute the wages for two employees of a company. The input information will consist of the hourly wage and the number of hours worked in one week. The output should contain a list of all deductions, gross pay, and net pay. For this problem, assume deductions are made for federal withholding taxes, state withholding taxes, social security, and union dues.
   b. Compute the average test score for five students in a class. Input for this problem will consist of five scores. Output should include each score and the average of these scores.
6. Develop an algorithm to find the total, average, and largest number in a given list of 25 numbers.
7. Develop an algorithm for finding the greatest common divisor (GCD) of two positive integers.
8. Develop an algorithm for solving the system of equations

   $ax + by = c$
   $dx + ey = f$
9. Develop an algorithm for each of the following problems.
   a. Find a specific book in the library.
   b. Withdraw money from an ATM machine.
   c. Find a telephone number in a telephone book.
10. Draw a structure chart and write module specifications for
    a. Exercise 5a.
    b. Exercise 5b.
    c. Exercise 6.
11. Discuss how the top-down design principles of software engineering are similar to the problems a construction engineer faces when designing a building. Be sure to include anticipated work with all subcontractors.

12. Using the construction analogy in Exercise 11, give an example of some specific communication required between electricians and the masons who finish the interior walls. Discuss why this information flow should be coordinated by a construction engineer.

13. State the phases of the software system life cycle.

14. Contact some company or major user of a software system to see what kinds of modifications might be required in a system after it has been released to the public. (Your own computer center might be sufficient.)

1.4 Writing Programs

OBJECTIVES

- to be able to recognize reserved words and predefined standard identifiers
- to be able to recognize and declare valid identifiers
- to know the three basic components of a program
- to understand the basic structure of a Pascal program
- to understand the difference between declaration statements and processing (executable) statements

Words in Pascal

Consider the following complete Pascal program.

```
PROGRAM Example (input, output);

CONST
  Skip = ' ';
  LoopLimit = 30;

VAR
  Index, Number, Sum : integer;
  Average : real;

BEGIN
  Sum := 0;
  FOR Index := 1 TO LoopLimit DO
    BEGIN
      writeln ('Enter a number and press <Enter>.');
      readln (Number);
      Sum := Sum + Number
    END;
  Average := Sum / LoopLimit;
  writeln;
  writeln (Skip:10, 'The average is', Average:8:2);
  writeln;
  writeln (Skip:10, 'The number of scores is', LoopLimit:3)
END.
```

This program, like most programming languages, requires the use of words when writing code. In Pascal, words that have a predefined meaning that cannot be changed are called *reserved words.* Some other predefined words (called *standard identifiers*) can have their meanings changed if the programmer has strong reasons for doing so. Other words (programmer-supplied *identifiers)* must be created according to a well-defined set of rules but can have any meaning subject to those rules.

In the body of this text, reserved words are capitalized and in bold type; standard identifiers are lowercase and in bold type. Reserved words used in the sample programs are capitalized; standard identifiers are lowercase. This convention is not required by the language.

Reserved Words

In Pascal, reserved words are predefined and cannot be used in a program for anything other than the purpose for which they are reserved. Some examples of reserved words are **AND, OR, NOT, BEGIN, END, IF,** and **FOR.** As you continue in Pascal, you will learn where and how these words are used. At this time, however, you need only become familiar with the reserved words in Table 1.1, which are also listed in Appendix 1. (*Note:* In this text, The symbol [T] appears in the margin to alert you to cases in which Turbo Pascal differs from standard Pascal. These differences are explained in Appendix 6.)

◇ TABLE 1.1
Reserved words

[T]

AND	**ELSE**	**IF**	**OR**	**THEN**
ARRAY	**END**	**IN**	**PACKED**	**TO**
BEGIN	**FILE**	**LABEL**	**PROCEDURE**	**TYPE**
CASE	**FOR**	**MOD**	**PROGRAM**	**UNTIL**
CONST	**FORWARD**	**NIL**	**RECORD**	**VAR**
DIV	**FUNCTION**	**NOT**	**REPEAT**	**WHILE**
DO	**GOTO**	**OF**	**SET**	**WITH**
DOWNTO				

Standard Identifiers

The meanings of standard identifiers, a second set of predefined words, can be changed by the programmer. For example, if a better algorithm could be developed for the trigonometric function **sin,** then it could be substituted in a program. However, a standard identifier should not be used in any way other than its intended application. Some standard identifiers are listed in Table 1.2 and in Appendix 2. The term *keywords* is used to refer to both reserved words and standard identifiers in subsequent discussions.

◇ TABLE 1.2
Standard identifiers

[T]

Data Types	Constants	Functions	Procedures	Files
boolean	**false**	**abs**	**dispose**	**input**
char	**maxint**	**arctan**	**get**	**output**
integer	**true**	**chr**	**new**	
real		**cos**	**pack**	
text		**eof**	**page**	
		eoln	**put**	
		exp	**read**	
		ln	**readln**	
		odd	**reset**	
		ord	**rewrite**	
		pred	**unpack**	
		round	**write**	
		sin	**writeln**	
		sqr		
		sqrt		
		succ		
		trunc		

A NOTE OF INTEREST

Object-Oriented Programming (OOP), Part 1

The concepts of top-down design and modular development are two essential ingredients for a rapidly growing method of developing programs called Object-Oriented Programming (OOP). Several OOP languages, such as Eiffel, Smalltalk, Object Pascal, and C++, have been developed with special features that facilitate modular development.

Two significant ramifications of the movement toward object-oriented programming are

1. The commercial aspect of using large OOP systems. The "objects" developed in OOP can be used in more than one system; thus, they become more valuable. The use of objects also simplifies the problems of maintenance and replacement that occur as systems evolve.
2. The introduction of OOP languages earlier in the computer science curricula of many colleges and universities. Object-oriented programming is currently the introductory programming course at several institutions.

For more information on object-oriented programming, see the *Note of Interest* on page 555.

Syntax and Syntax Diagrams

Syntax refers to the rules governing the construction of valid statements. Syntax includes the order in which statements occur, together with appropriate punctuation. *Syntax diagramming* is a method of formally describing the legal syntax of language structures. *Syntax diagrams* show the permissible alternatives for each part of each kind of sentence and where the parts may appear. The symbolism we will use is shown in Figure 1.14. A combined listing of syntax diagrams is contained in Appendix 3.

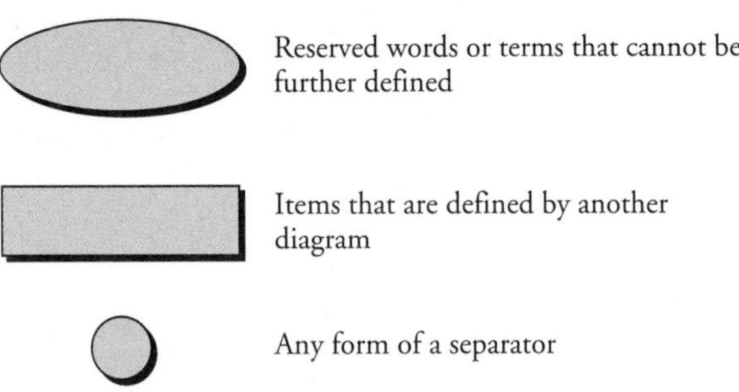

◆ FIGURE 1.14
Symbols used in syntax diagrams

Arrows are used to indicate possible alternatives. To illustrate, a syntax diagram for forming simple words in the English language is

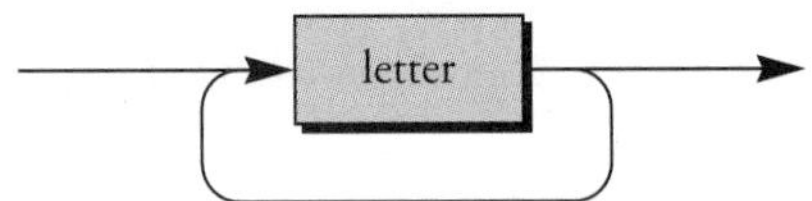

If the word must start with a vowel, this diagram becomes

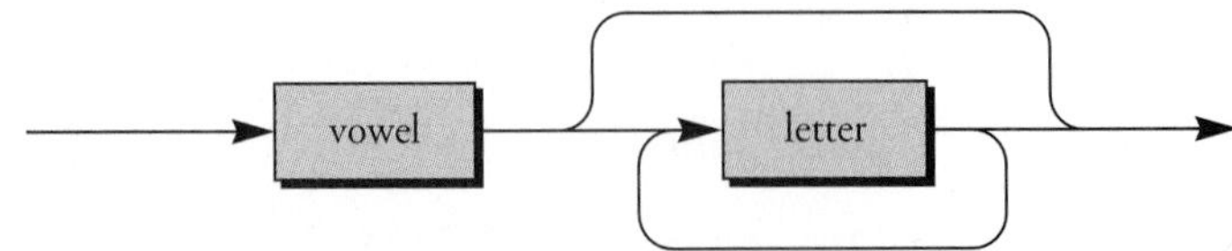

where vowel and letter are defined in a manner consistent with the English alphabet. Syntax diagrams are used throughout the text to illustrate formal constructs. You are encouraged to become familiar with them.

Identifiers

Reserved words and standard identifiers are restricted in their use. Most Pascal programs require other programmer-supplied identifiers; the more complicated the program is the more identifiers are needed. **A valid identifier must start with a letter of the alphabet and must consist of only letters and digits**. A syntax diagram for forming identifiers is

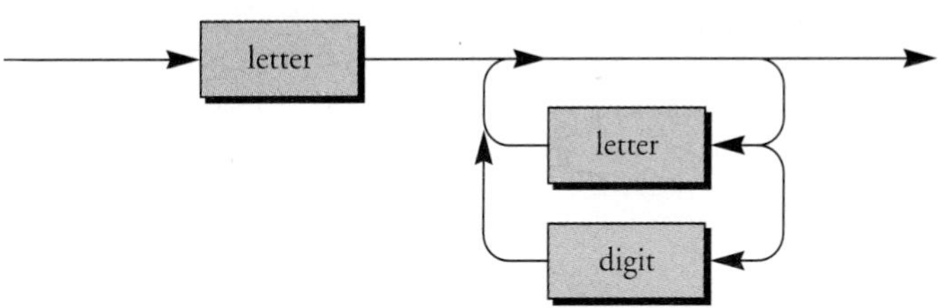

Table 1.3 lists some valid and invalid identifiers along with the reasons why an identifer is invalid. A valid identifier can be of any length. However, some versions of Pascal recognize only the first part of a long identifier (for example, the first eight or 10 characters). Therefore, identifiers such as MathTestScore1 and MathTestScore2 might be the same identifier to a computer and could not be used as different identifiers in a program. You should learn what restrictions are imposed by your compiler.

◇ TABLE 1.3
Valid and Invalid identifiers

Identifier	Valid	If Invalid, Reason
Sum	Yes	
X+Y	No	"+" is not allowed.
Average	Yes	
Text1	Yes	
1stNum	No	Must start with a letter.
X	Yes	
K mart	No	Spaces are not allowed.
ThisIsaLongOne	Yes	

The most common use of identifiers is to name the variables to be used in a program. Other uses for identifiers include the program name, symbolic constants, new data types, and subprogram names, all of which will be discussed later. Always use descriptive names for identifiers, even though single-letter identifiers are permitted; as you will soon discover, descriptive names make programs easier to follow.

Basic Program Components

A program in Pascal consists of three components: a program heading, an optional declaration section, and an executable section. These three components are illustrated in the program shown in Figure 1.15.

FIGURE 1.15
Components of a program

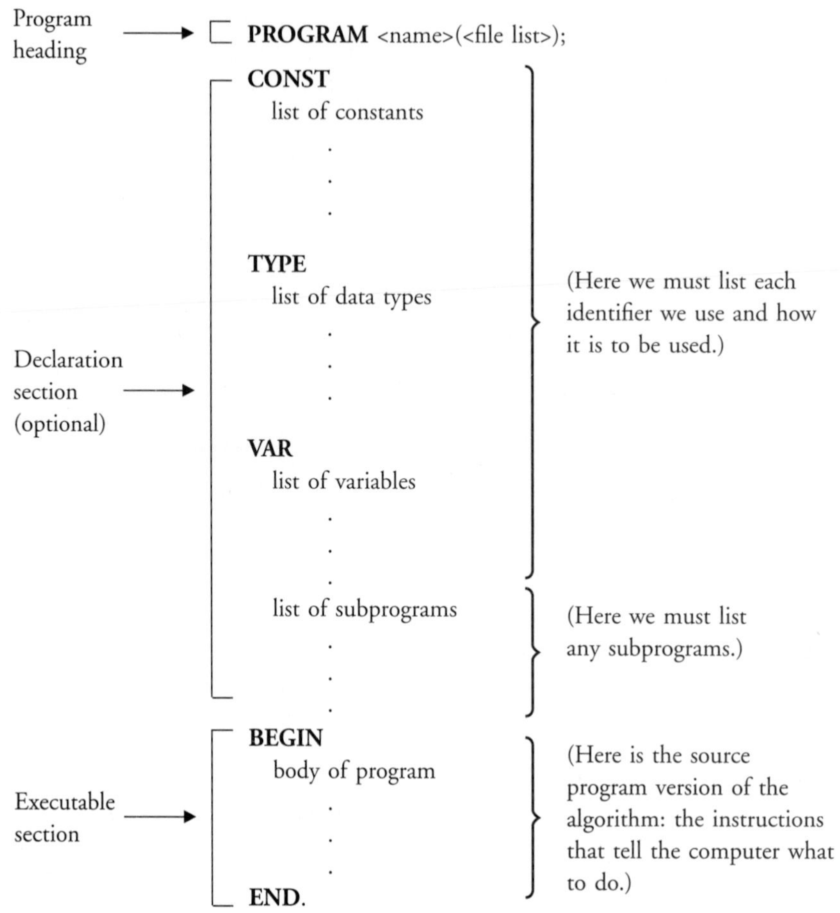
Program heading
PROGRAM <name>(<file list>);
CONST
list of constants
TYPE
list of data types
VAR
list of variables
(Here we must list each identifier we use and how it is to be used.)
Declaration section (optional)
list of subprograms
(Here we must list any subprograms.)
BEGIN
body of program
Executable section
END.
(Here is the source program version of the algorithm: the instructions that tell the computer what to do.)

The syntax diagram for a program is

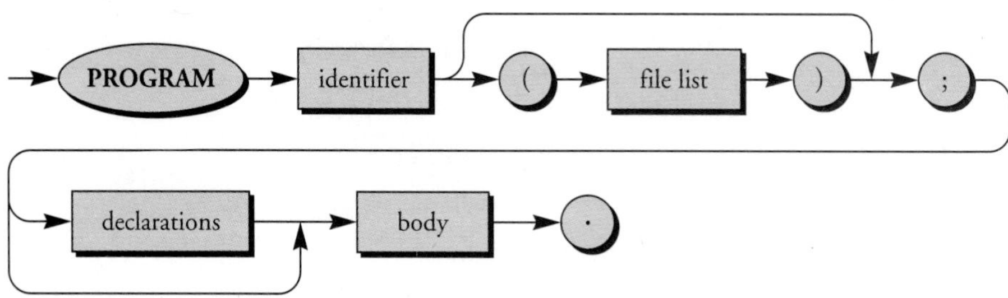
PROGRAM
identifier
(
file list
)
;
declarations
body
.

Figure 1.16 illustrates the program components of the sample program (**PROGRAM** Example) that started this section. Appropriate program parts are indicated.

The *program heading* is the first statement of any Pascal program. It is usually one line and must contain the reserved word **PROGRAM;** the program name, which must be a valid identifier; and a list of the files to be used. The semicolon at the end of the program heading is not considered part of the heading; it is used to separate the heading from the rest of the program. If the program receives input or produces output, the list of files must include the files **input** and/or **output.** Some other versions of Pascal (Turbo Pascal, for example) do not have this requirement. The respective parts of a program heading are

PROGRAM <name> (<file list>)

◆ FIGURE 1.16
Components of **PROGRAM** Example

Program heading →

```
PROGRAM Example (input, output);
```

Declaration section →

```
CONST
  Skip = ' ';
  LoopLimit = 30;

VAR
  Index, Number, Sum : integer;
  Average : real;
```

Executable section →

```
BEGIN
  Sum := 0;
  FOR Index := 1 TO LoopLimit DO
    BEGIN
      writeln ('Enter a number and press <Enter>.');
      readln (Number);
      Sum := Sum + Number
    END;
  Average := Sum / LoopLimit;
  writeln;
  writeln (Skip:10, 'The average is', Average:8:2);
  writeln;
  writeln (Skip:10, 'The number of scores is', LoopLimit:3)
END.
```

The template or fill-in-the-blanks form just presented is used throughout this text. Reserved words and standard identifiers are shown. You must use identifiers to replace the words in lowercase letters and enclosed in arrowheads "< >". Thus

PROGRAM <name> (<file list>)

could become

```
PROGRAM Rookie (input, output);
```

A syntax diagram for a program heading follows

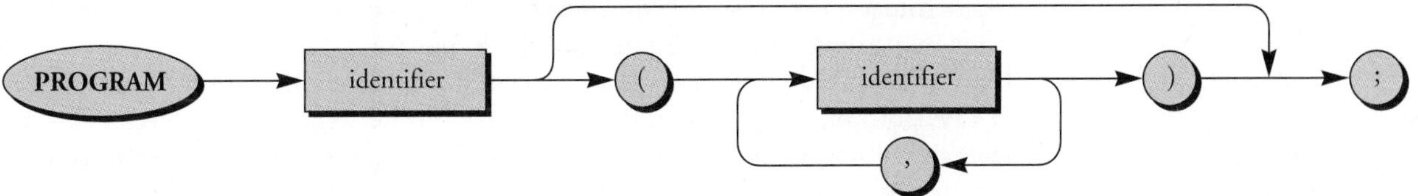

The remainder of the program is referred to as the *main block;* major divisions are the declaration section and the executable section. The *declaration section* is used to declare (name) all symbolic constants, data types, variables, and subprograms that are necessary to the program. All constants named in the declaration section are normally referred to as being defined. Thus, we generally say variables are declared and constants are defined.

When constants are defined, they appear in the *constant definition* portion of the declaration section after the reserved word **CONST.** The form for defining a constant is

```
CONST
  <identifier 1> = <value 1>;
  <identifier 2> = <value 2>;
       .
       .
       .
  <identifier n> = <value n>
```

The syntax diagram for this part is

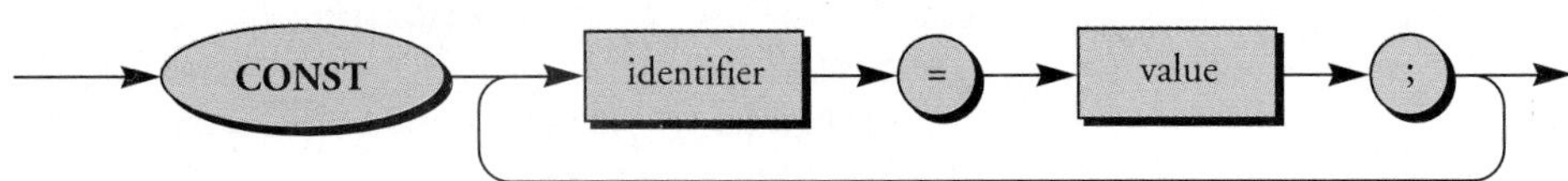

Values of constant identifiers cannot be changed during program execution.

If "value" is one character or a string of characters, it must be enclosed in single quotation marks (apostrophes). For example

```
CONST
  Date = 'July 4, 1776';
```

Any number of constants may be defined in this section. A typical constant definition portion of the declaration section could be

```
CONST
  Skip = ' ';
  Date = 'July 4, 1776';
  ClassSize = 35;
  SpeedLimit = 65;
  CmToInches = 0.3937;
  Found = true;
```

The **TYPE** portion of the declaration section will be explained in Section 6.2. For now, we assume data used in a Pascal program are one of the four *standard simple types*: **integer, real, char,** or **boolean.** Discussion of types **integer, real,** and **char** is in Section 1.5; discussion of **boolean** is in Section 4.1.

The *variable declaration* portion of the declaration section is listed after the **TYPE** portion, if present, and must begin with the reserved word **VAR.** This section contains all identifiers for variables to be used in the program; if a variable is used that has not been declared, an error will occur when the program is compiled.

The form required for declaring variables is somewhat different from that used for defining constants: it requires a colon instead of an equal sign and specific data types. The simplest correct form is

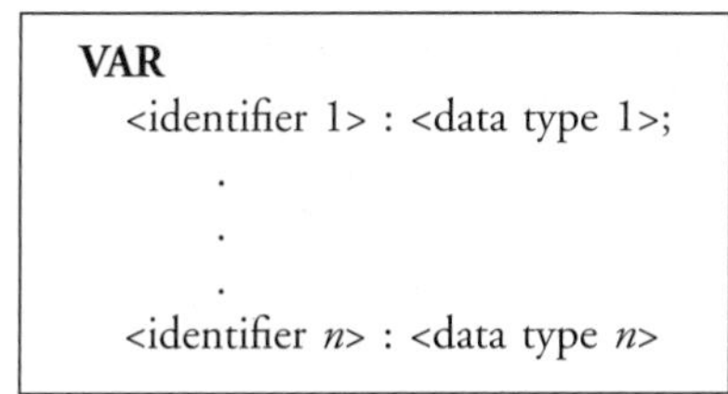

The syntax diagram is

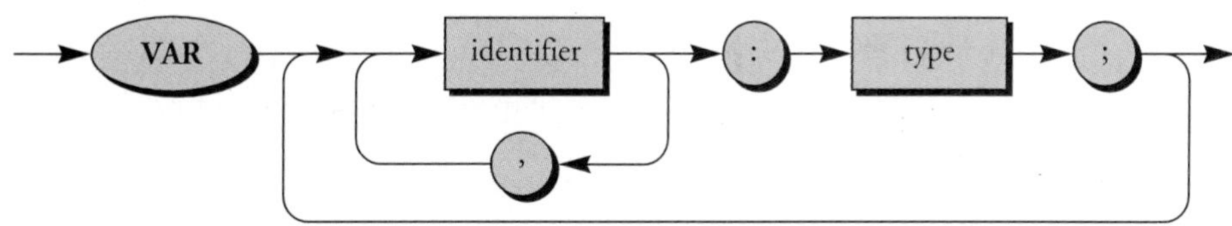

The reserved word **VAR** may appear only once in a program. Exceptions will be noted when subprograms are developed. If no variables are to be used, a variable declaration section is not needed; however, this seldom happens. A typical variable declaration section could look like this:

```
VAR
  Sum : integer;
  Average : real;
  Num1, Num2, Num3 : integer;
  Ch : char;
```

The third basic program component is the *executable section.* This section contains the statements that cause the computer to do something. It must start with the reserved word **BEGIN** and conclude with the reserved word **END.** Also, a period must follow the last **END** in the executable section. The syntax diagram is

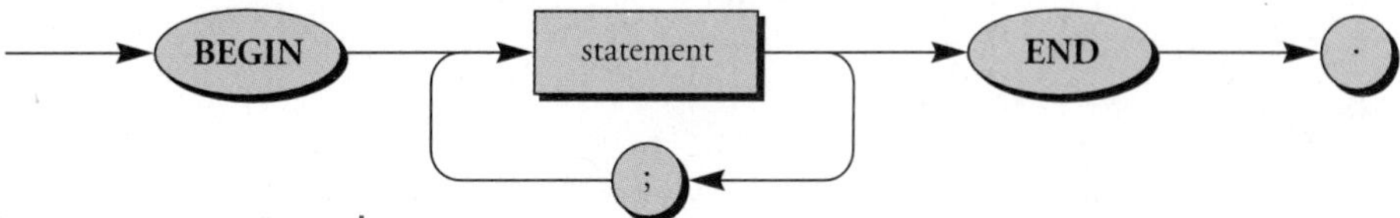

Statements in Pascal

In Pascal, the *statement* is the basic unit of expression. A program consists of a sequence of statements separated by semicolons. Statements perform two functions in a program: declarations and processing.

Declaration statements are used for the program heading and to define constants in the **CONST** section, define types in the **TYPE** section, and declare variables in the **VAR** section. Each of the following is an example of a declaration statement.

```
PROGRAM Rookie (input, output)
Date = 'July 4, 1976'
J, Number, Sum : integer
```

Processing statements cause the computer to take action when a program is run. The compiler creates machine-language instructions from processing statements. These instructions are then executed according to the sequence dictated by the program. Processing statements are often called *executable statements.* Referring to the sample program that appears in Figure 1.16, the following are processing statements.

```
Sum := 0
Average := Sum / LoopLimit
writeln
writeln (Skip:10, 'The average is ', Average:8:2)

FOR Index := 1 TO LoopLimit DO
  BEGIN
    readln (Number);
    Sum := Sum + Number
  END
```

The first four statements are *simple statements.* The last statement is a *compound statement.* Compound statements will be developed further in Section 4.2.

Writing Code in Pascal

We are now ready to examine the use of the executable section of a program. In Pascal, the basic unit of grammar is an executable statement, which consists of valid identifiers, standard identifiers, reserved words, numbers, and/or characters together with appropriate punctuation.

One of the main rules for writing code in Pascal is that a semicolon is used to separate executable statements. For example, if the statement

```
writeln ('The results are':20, Sum:8, ' and', Aver:6:2)
```

is to be used in a program, it will (almost always) require a semicolon between it and the next executable statement:

```
writeln ('The results are':20, Sum:8, ' and', Aver:6:2);
```

In one instance, an executable statement does not need to be followed by a semicolon: when a statement is followed by the reserved word **END.** A semicolon is not required here because **END** is not a statement by itself but part of a **BEGIN . . . END** pair. However, if a semicolon is included, it will not affect the program. You can visualize the executable section as shown in Figure 1.17.

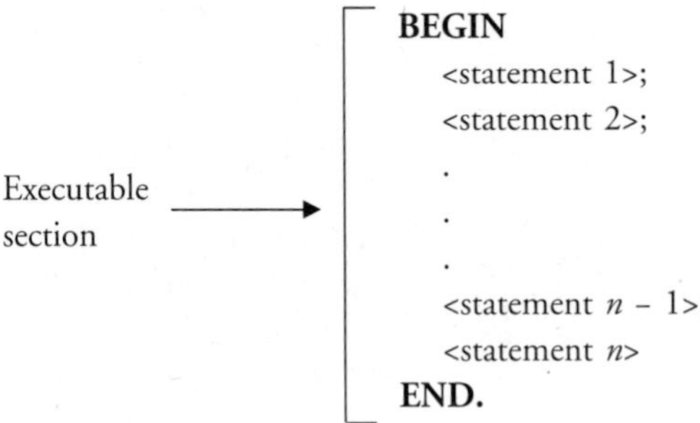

◆ FIGURE 1.17 Executable section

Pascal does not require that each statement be on a separate line. Actually, you could write a program as one long line (which may wrap around to fit the screen) if you wish; however, it would be difficult to read. Compare, for example, the readability of

```
PROGRAM ReadCheck (output); CONST Name = 'George';
Age = 26; VAR J, Sum : integer; BEGIN Sum := 0;
FOR J := 1 TO 10 DO Sum := Sum + J; writeln
('My name is ':28, Name); writeln ('My age is ':27, Age);
writeln; writeln ('The sum is ':28, Sum) END.
```

and of

```
PROGRAM ReadCheck (output);

CONST
  Name = 'George';
  Age = 26;

VAR
  J, Sum : integer;

BEGIN
  Sum := 0;
  FOR J := 1 TO 10 DO
    Sum := Sum + J;
    writeln ('My name is ':28, Name);
    writeln ('My age is ':27, Age);
    writeln;
    writeln ('The sum is ':28, Sum)
END.
```

You are not expected to know what the statements mean at this point, but it should be obvious that the second program is much more readable than the first. In addition, the second program is easier to change if corrections are necessary. However, these programs are executed identically because Pascal ignores extra spaces and line boundaries.

A NOTE OF INTEREST

Blaise Pascal

Blaise Pascal (1623–1662) began a spectacular, if short, mathematical career at a very early age. He was a brilliant child. As a youngster of 14, he attended meetings of senior French mathematicians. At age 16, he had so impressed the famous mathematician Descartes with his writings that Descartes refused to believe the author could be so young.

Two years later, Pascal invented a calculating machine, the Pascaline (shown at right), that stands as the very remote predecessor of the modern computer. The Pascaline could add and subtract; it functioned as a result of a series of eight rotating gears, similar to an automobile odometer. Pascal's machine was opposed by tax clerks of the era, who viewed it as a threat to their jobs. Pascal presented his machine to Queen Christina of Sweden in 1650; it is not known what she did with it.

In spite of his obvious talent for mathematics, Pascal devoted most of his adult life to questions of theology; his work in this area is still regularly studied. A man who often perceived omens in events around him, Pascal concluded that God's plan for him did not include mathematics and dropped the subject entirely. However, while experiencing a particularly nagging toothache when he was 35, Pascal let his thoughts wander to mathematics and the pain disappeared.

He took this as a heavenly sign and made a quick but intensive return to mathematical research. In barely a week, he managed to discover the fundamental properties of the cycloid curve. With that, Pascal again abandoned mathematics, and in 1662, at the age of 39, he died.

Program Comments

Programming languages typically include some provision for putting *comments* in a program. These comments are nonexecutable and are used only to document and explain various parts of the program. In Pascal, the form for including comments in a program is either

```
{ . . . <comment> . . . }

or

(* . . . <comment> . . . *)
```

COMMUNICATION AND STYLE TIPS

This text contains several suggestions for using program comments to make your programs more readable. One suggestion is to create an information section for inclusion in every program to be given to your instructor. The style and content of this section may vary according to your instructor's wishes. A sample for consideration is

```
{  Course Number          CPS-150  }
{  Assignment                 One  }
{  Due Date          September  20  }
{  Author               Mary Smith  }
{  Instructor            Dr. Jones  }
```

Typically, such a section would be placed at the beginning of the program.

EXERCISES 1.4

1. List the rules for forming valid identifiers.
2. Which of the following are valid identifiers? Give an explanation for each identifier that is invalid.

a. **7Up**	g. **1A**
b. **Payroll**	h. **Time&Place**
c. **Room222**	i. **CONST**
d. **Name List**	j. **X*Y**
e. **A**	k. **ListOfEmployees**
f. **A1**	l. **Lima,Ohio**

3. Which of the following are valid program headings? Give an explanation for each heading that is invalid.
   a. **PROGRAM Rookie (output)**
   b. **PROGRAM Pro (input, output);**
   c. **TestProgram (input, output);**
   d. **PROGRAM (output);**
   e. **PROGRAM GettingBetter (output);**
   f. **PROGRAM Have Fun (input, output);**
   g. **PROGRAM 2ndOne (output);**
4. Name the three main sections of a Pascal program.
5. Write constant definition statements for the following.

a. Your name	c. Your birth date
b. Your age	d. Your birthplace

6. Find all errors in the following definitions and declarations.

a.
```
CONST
  Company : 'General Motors';
VAR
  Salary : real;
```
b.
```
VAR
  Age = 25;
```
c.
```
VAR
  Days : integer;
  Ch : char;
CONST
  Name = 'John Smith';
```
d.
```
CONST
  Car : 'Cadillac';
```
e.
```
CONST
  Score : integer;
```
f.
```
VAR
  X, Y, Z : real;
  Score,
  Num : integer;
```

7. Discuss the significance of the use of semicolons in writing Pascal statements. Include an explanation of when semicolons are not required in a program.

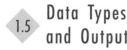

1.5 Data Types and Output

OBJECTIVES

- to understand and be able to use the data types **integer, real,** and **char**
- to understand the difference between the floating-point form and the fixed-point form of decimal numbers
- to understand the syntax for and the use of **write** and **writeln** statements for output
- to be able to format output

Data Type integer

Pascal requires that all data used in a program be given a *data type*. Since numbers of some form are used in computer programs, we will first look at numbers of data type **integer,** which are integers that are positive, negative, or zero. Some rules that must be observed when using integers are

1. Plus "+" signs do not have to be written before a positive integer.
2. Minus "–" signs must be written before a negative number.
3. Leading zeros are ignored.
4. Decimal points cannot be used when writing integers. Although 14 and 14.0 have the same value, 14.0 is not of type **integer.**
5. Commas cannot be used when writing integers: 271,362 is not allowed; it must be written as 271362.

The syntax diagram for an integer is

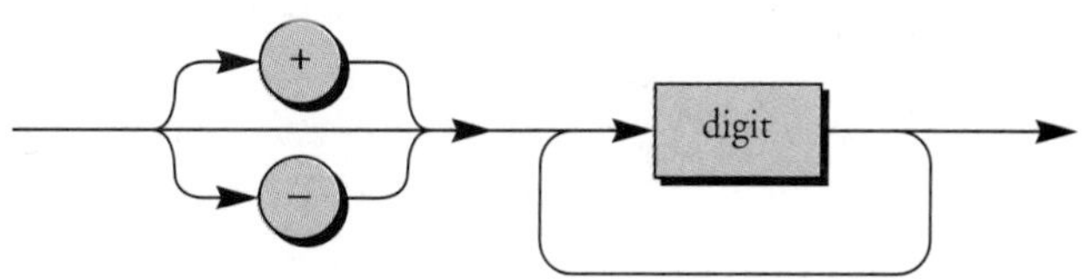

There are limits on the largest and the smallest integer constants. The largest such constant is **maxint;** the smallest is usually –**maxint** or (–**maxint**–1). The constants **maxint** and –**maxint** are recognized in every version of Pascal; however, different machines have different values for them. This section ends with a program that enables you to discover the value of **maxint** on your computer. Operations with integers will be examined in the next section, and integer variables will be discussed in Section 2.2.

T

Data Type **real**

T When using decimal notation, numbers of data type **real** must be written with a decimal point and have at least one digit on each side of the decimal. Thus, .2 is not a valid **real** but 0.2 is.

Plus "+" and minus "–" signs for data of type **real** are treated exactly as they are for data of type **integer.** When working with reals, however, both leading and trailing zeros are ignored. Thus, +23.45, 23.45, 023.45, 23.450, and 0023.45000 have the same value.

All reals seen thus far have been in *fixed-point form.* The computer will also accept reals in *floating-point* (exponential) *form,* an equivalent method for writing numbers in scientific notation to accommodate numbers that may have very large or very small values. The difference is that instead of writing the base decimal multiplied by some power of 10, the base decimal is followed by E and the appropriate power of 10. For example, 231.6 in scientific notation would be 2.316×10^2; in floating-point form, it would be 2.316E2. Table 1.4 lists several fixed-point decimal numbers and the equivalent scientific notation and floating-point form for each.

◇ TABLE 1.4
Forms for equivalent numbers

Fixed-point Form	Scientific Notation	Floating-point Form
46.345	4.6345×10	4.6345E1
59214.3	5.92143×10^4	5.92143E4
0.00042	4.2×10^{-4}	4.2E–4
36000000000.0	3.6×10^{10}	3.6E10
0.000000005	5.0×10^{-9}	5.0E–9
-341000.0	-3.41×10^5	-3.41E5

Floating-point form for real numbers does not require exactly one digit on the left of the decimal point. In fact, it can be used with no decimal points written. To illustrate, 4.16E1, 41.6, 416.0E-1, and 416E-1 have the same value and all are permissible. However, it is not a good habit to use floating-point form for decimal numbers unless exactly one digit appears to the left of the decimal. In most other cases, fixed-point form is preferable.

The syntax diagram for a floating-point number is

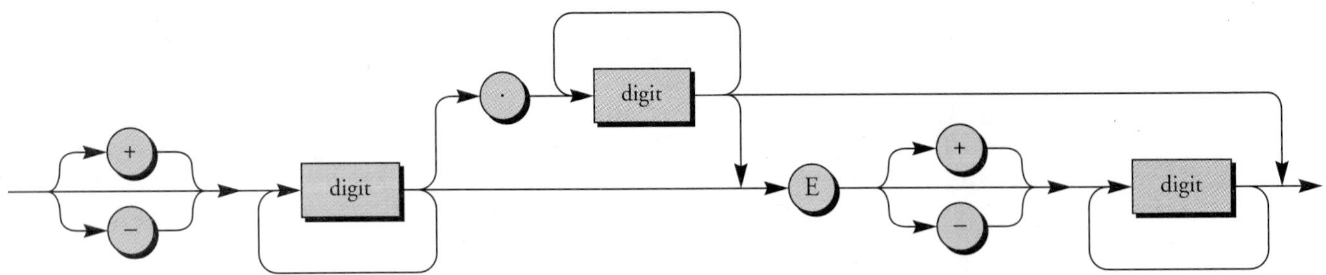

When using reals in a program, you may use either fixed-point or floating-point form. The computer will display reals in floating-point form unless you specify otherwise. Formatting of output is discussed later in this section.

Data Type **char**

Another data type available in Pascal is **char,** which is used to represent character data. Data of type **char** can be only a single character (which can even be a blank space).

These characters come from an available character set that differs somewhat from computer to computer but always includes the letters of the alphabet (uppercase and lowercase); the digits 0, 1, 2, 3, 4, 5, 6, 7, 8, and 9; and special symbols such as #, &, !, +, –, *, /. Two common character sets are given in Appendix 4.

Character constants of type **char** must be enclosed in single quotation marks when used in a program. Otherwise, they are treated as variables and subsequent use causes a compilation error. Thus, to use the letter A as a constant, you would type 'A'. The use of digits and standard operation symbols as characters is also permitted; for example, '7' is considered a character, but 7 is an integer.

If a word of one or more characters is used as a constant in a program, it is referred to as a *string constant.* String constants, generally called *strings,* may be defined in the **CONST** portion of the declaration section. The entire string must be enclosed in single quotation marks.

Students who have experience in BASIC usually expect the equivalent of a string variable for storing names and other information. A string is not a standard Pascal data type; standard Pascal does not have such a feature. An analogous feature, packed arrays of characters, is presented in Section 7.5.

When a single quotation mark is needed within a string, it is represented by two single quotation marks. For example, if the name desired is O'Malley, it would be represented by

```
'O''Malley'
```

When a single quotation mark is needed as a single character, it can be represented by placing two single quotation marks within single quotation marks. When typed, this appears as ''''. Note these are all single quotation marks; use of the double quotation mark character here will not produce the desired result.

Data Type **string** (Optional: nonstandard)

Standard Pascal does not provide for a **string** data type. However, since many versions of Pascal (particularly Turbo) do contain a **string** data type, we have decided to mention this data type here.

The data type **string** allows a programmer to design programs that are capable of using strings of characters as well as numeric data. This is particularly useful when a program is to process names of people and companies, for example. Later, we will see how such strings can be incorporated into a program; for now, it is sufficient that you be aware that several versions of nonstandard Pascal provide a **string** data type.

Output

The goal of most programs is to produce something. What gets displayed (either on a screen or on paper) is referred to as *output.* The two program statements that produce output are **write** and **writeln** (pronounced "write line"). They are usually followed by character strings, numbers, numeric expressions, or variable names enclosed in parentheses. The general form is

write (<expression 1>, <expression 2>, . . . , <expression *n*>)

or

writeln (<expression 1>, <expression 2>, . . . , <expression *n*>)

A simplified syntax diagram for **write** (applicable also for **writeln**) is

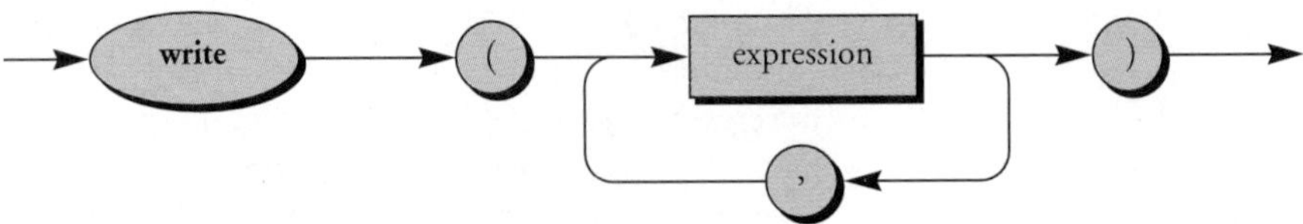

For more information on syntax diagrams for **write** and **writeln**, see Appendix 3.

A **writeln** statement can also be used as a complete statement; for example

```
writeln;
```

can cause a blank line to be displayed. This technique is frequently used to produce more readable output.

The **write** statement causes subsequent output to be printed on the same line, whereas the **writeln** statement causes subsequent output to be printed on the next line. This is because **writeln** is actually a **write** statement followed by a line feed. When output is to a monitor, **writeln** causes the cursor to move to the next line for the next I/O operation. To illustrate

```
write ('This is a test.');
writeln ('How many lines are printed?');
```

causes the output

```
This is a test.How many lines are printed?
```

whereas

```
writeln ('This is a test.');
writeln ('How many lines are printed?');
```

causes the output

```
This is a test.
How many lines are printed?
```

Some implementations require **writeln** to be the last output statement. Otherwise, output gathered in a buffer does not get printed.

When an output statement is executed, character strings can be printed by enclosing the string in single quotation marks within the parentheses. Numeric data can be printed by including the desired number or numbers within the parentheses. Thus

```
writeln (100)
```

produces

```
      100
```

EXAMPLE 1.1

Let's write a complete Pascal program to print the address

1403 South Drive
Apartment 3B
Pittsburgh, PA   15238

A complete program to print this output is

```
PROGRAM Address (output);

BEGIN
  writeln ('1403 South Drive');
  writeln ('Apartment 3B');
  writeln ('Pittsburgh, PA', 15238)
END.
```

When this program is run on a computer that uses a default field width of 10 positions, the output is

```
1403 South Drive
Apartment 3B
Pittsburgh, PA     15238
```

Formatting Integers

Output of integers can be controlled by *formatting.* Within a **write** or **writeln** statement, an integer, identifier, or integer expression can be followed by a colon and another integer to specify the field width. The value will then be printed on the right side of the specified field. Thus

```
writeln (100, 50:10, 25:10);
```

produces

```
100--------50--------25
```

where each "–" indicates a blank.

The general form for formating integers is

> **write** (<integer> : <*n*>)
> or
> **writeln** (<integer> : <*n*>)

Some illustrations for formatting integer output are

Program Statement	Output
`writeln (123:6);`	`___123`
`writeln (15, 10:5);`	`________15___10`
`writeln (-263:7, 21:3);`	`___-263_21`
`writeln (+5062:6);`	`__5062`
`writeln (65221:3);`	`65221`

In line five, an attempt is made to specify a field width smaller than the number of digits contained in the integer. Most versions of Pascal will automatically print the entire integer; however, some versions will print only within the specified width.

COMMUNICATION AND STYLE TIPS

Using **writelns** at the beginning and end of the executable section will separate desired output from other messages or directions. Thus, in Example 1.1, the program for printing an address could have been

```
PROGRAM Address (output);

BEGIN
  writeln;
  writeln ('1403 South Drive');
  writeln ('Apartment 3B');
  writeln ('Pittsburgh, PA', 15238);
  writeln
END.
```

Formatting Reals

Output of reals can also be controlled by formatting. The general form is

write (<real> : <*n*1> : <*n*2>)
or
writeln (<real> : <*n*1> : <*n*2>)

where *n*1 specifies the total field width and *n*2 specifies the number of positions to the right of the decimal. Thus

```
writeln (736.23:8:2);
```

produces

```
__736.23
```

Formatting reals causes the following to happen.

1. The decimal point uses one position in the specified field width.
2. Leading zeros are not printed.
3. Trailing zeros are printed to the specified number of positions to the right of the decimal.
4. Leading plus "+" signs are omitted.
5. Leading minus "–" signs are printed and use one position of the specified field.
6. Digits appearing to the right of the decimal are rounded rather than truncated.

As with integers, if a field width is specified that is too small, most versions of Pascal will default to the minimum width required to present all digits to the left of the decimal as well as the specified digits to the right of the decimal. Reals in floating-point form can also be used in a formatted **writeln** statement. The following table illustrates how output using data of type **real** can be formatted.

Program Statement	Output
`writeln (765.432:10:3)`	`___765.432`
`writeln (023.14:10:2)`	`_____23.14`
`writeln (65.50:10:2)`	`_____65.50`
`writeln (+341.2:10:2)`	`____341.20`
`writeln (-341.2:10:2)`	`____341.20`
`writeln (16.458:10:2)`	`_____16.46`
`writeln (0.00456:10:4)`	`____0.0046`
`writeln (136.51:4:2)`	`136.51`

Formatting Strings

Strings and string constants can be formatted using a colon followed by a positive integer "*n*" to specify field width. The general form for formatting strings is

write (<string> : <*n*>)
or
writeln (<string> : <*n*>)

The string will be right-justified in the field. Unlike reals, strings are truncated when necessary. Thus

```
writeln ('field', 'width':10, 'check':15);
```

will produce

```
field-----width----------check
     \___:10___/\____:15____/
```

COMMUNICATION AND STYLE TIPS

A constant consisting of a blank can be used as a formatting aid. For example, a constant section could include

```
CONST
  Skip = ' ';
  Indent = ' ';
```

Output statements can then use these constants as

```
writeln (Indent:6, message1, Skip:10, message2);
```

Test Programs

Programmers should develop the habit of using *test programs* to improve their knowledge and programming skills. A test program should be relatively short and written to provide an answer to a specific question. For example, in our earlier discussion of **maxint** in this section, it was mentioned that the value of **maxint** depended upon the machine being used. You could use a test program to discover what your computer uses for **maxint.** A complete program to accomplish this is

```
PROGRAM TestMax (output);

BEGIN
  writeln ('Maxint is ', maxint)
END.
```

Notice the brief message 'Maxint is ' is included to explain the output. Such a message or "output label" is almost always desirable.

Test programs allow you to experiment with the computer. You can answer "What if . . . " questions by adopting a "try it and see" attitude. This is an excellent way to become comfortable with your computer and with the programming language you are using. For example, you might change the previous test program to

```
PROGRAM TestMax (output);

BEGIN
  writeln ('Maxint is ', maxint);
  writeln ('TooMuch is ', maxint + 1)
END.
```

EXERCISES 1.5

1. Which of the following are valid integers? Explain why the others are invalid.
   a. 521
   b. -32.0
   c. 5,621
   d. +00784
   e. +65
   f. 6521492183
   g. -0
   h. 6E3
2. Which of the following are valid reals? Explain why the others are invalid.
   a. 26.3
   b. +181.0
   c. -.14
   d. 492.
   e. +017.400
   f. 43E2
   g. -0.2E-3
   h. 43,162.3E5
   i. -176.52E+1
   j. 1.43000E+2
3. Change the following fixed-point decimals to floating-point decimals with exactly one nonzero digit to the left of the decimal.
   a. 173.0
   b. 743927000000.0
   c. -0.000000023
   d. +014.768
   e. -5.2
4. Change the following floating-point decimals to fixed-point decimals.
   a. -1.0046E+3
   b. 4.2E-8
   c. 9.020E10
   d. -4.615230E3
   e. -8.02E-3
5. Indicate the data type for each of the following.
   a. -720
   b. -720.0
   c. 150E3
   d. 150
   e. '150'
   f. '23.4E2'
   g. 23.4E-2
6. Write and run test programs for each of the following.
   a. Examine the output for a decimal number without field width specified; for example

      ```
      writeln (2.31)
      ```

   b. Try to print a message without using quotation marks for a character string; for example

      ```
      writeln (Hello);
      ```

7. For each of the following, write a program that will produce the indicated output.
   a.

      ```
      Score
      -----
         86
         82
         79
      ```

      where "S" is in column 10.

   b.

      ```
      Price
      -------
      $ 19.94
      $100.00
      $ 58.95
      ```

      where "P" is in column 50.
8. Assume the hourly wages of five students are

   3.65
   4.10
   2.89
   5.00
   4.50

   Write a program that produces the following output, where the "E" in Employee is in column 20.

```
------------------------
Employee     Hourly Wage
------------------------
    1          $ 3.65
    2          $ 4.10
    3          $ 2.89
    4          $ 5.00
    5          $ 4.50
------------------------
```

9. What output does the following segment of code produce on your printer or terminal?

```
writeln ('My test average is', 87.5);
writeln ('My test average is':20, 87.5:10);
writeln ('My test average is':25, 87.5:10:2);
writeln ('My test average is':25, 87.5:6:2);
```

10. Write a program that produces the following output. Start Student in column 20 and Test in column 40.

```
Student Name             Test Score

Adams, Mike                   73
Conley, Theresa               86
Samson, Ron                   92
O'Malley, Colleen             81
```

11. The Great Lakes Shipping Company is going to use a computer program to generate billing statements for their customers. The heading of each bill is to be

```
          GREAT LAKES SHIPPING COMPANY
           SAULT STE. MARIE, MICHIGAN
-----------------------------------------------
  Thank you for doing business with our company.
  The information listed below was used to
  determine your total cargo fee. We hope you
  were satisfied with our service.
-----------------------------------------------
CARGO      TONNAGE         RATE/TON      TOTAL DUE
```

Write a complete Pascal program that produces this heading.

12. What output is produced by each of the following statements or sequence of statements when executed by the computer?

a. `writeln (1234, 1234:8, 1234:6);`

b. `writeln (12:4, -21:4, 120:4);`

c.
```
writeln ('FIGURE  AREA  PERIMETER');
writeln ('-----------------------');
writeln;
writeln ('SQUARE', 16:5, 16:12);
writeln;
writeln ('RECT ', 24:5, 20:12);
```

13. Write a complete program that produces the following table.

```
WIDTH       LENGTH       AREA
  4            2           8
 21            5         105
```

14. What output is produced when each of the following statements is executed?

a. `writeln (2.134:15:2);`

b. `writeln (423.73:5:2);`

c. `writeln (-42.1:8:3);`

d. `writeln (-4.21E3:6:2);`

e. `writeln (10.25);`

f. `writeln (1.25, 1.25:6:2, 1.25:6:1);`

15. Write a complete program that produces the following output.

```
Hourly Wage          Hours Worked          Total

    5.0                  20.0              100.00
    7.50                 15.25             114.375
```

16. What type of data would be used to print each of the following?

a. Your age

b. Your grade point average

c. Your name

d. A test score

e. The average test score

f. Your grade

SUMMARY

Key Terms

algorithm
applications software
arithmetic/logic unit (ALU)
assembly language
binary digits
bits
bus
central processing unit (CPU)
comments
compiler
compound statement
constant definition
control unit
data
data type
declaration section
declaration statement
desk-top system
effective statement
executable section
executable statement
executed
fixed-point form
floating-point form
formatting
hardware
high-level language
identifier
input device
instruction
I/O devices
keyword
low-level language
machine language
main block
main (primary) memory
main unit
mainframe computer
mainframe system
microcomputer (personal computer)
minicomputer
module
module specifications
object code
object program
operating system
output
output device
processing statement
program
program heading
programming language
pseudocode
reserved word
secondary (auxiliary) memory devices
simple statement
software
software engineering
software system life cycle
source program
standard identifier
standard simple type
statement
stepwise refinement
string
string constant
structure chart
super computer
syntax
syntax diagram
syntax diagramming
system software
test program
top-down design
variable declaration

Keywords

BEGIN	integer	VAR
char	maxint	write
CONST	output	writeln
END	PROGRAM	
input	real	

Keyword (Optional)

string

Key Concepts

- The six steps in problem solving include analyze the problem, develop an algorithm, write code for the program, run the program, test the results against answers manually computed with paper and pencil, and document the program.
- Top-down design is the process of dividing tasks into subtasks until each subtask can be readily accomplished.
- Stepwise refinement refers to refinements of tasks into subtasks.
- A structure chart is a graphic representation of the relationship between modules.
- Software engineering is the process of developing and maintaining large software systems.
- The software system life cycle consists of the following phases: analysis, design, coding, testing/verification, maintenance, and obsolescence.
- Valid identifiers must begin with a letter and can contain only letters and digits.
- The three components of a Pascal program are the program heading, the declaration section, and the executable section.
- Statements are the basic units of expression in Pascal.
- The two basic kinds of statements are declaration statements and executable (processing) statements.
- Semicolons are used to separate statements.
- Extra spaces and blank lines are ignored in Pascal.
- Output is generated by using **write** or **writeln** statements.
- Strings are formatted using a single colon followed by a positive integer that specifies the total field width; for example

```
writeln ('This is a string.':30);
```

- The following table summarizes the use of the data types **integer, real,** and **char.**

Data Type	Permissible Data	Formatting
integer	numeric	one colon; for example `writeln (25:6);`
real	numeric	two colons; for example `writeln (1234.5:8:2);`
char	character	one colon; for example `writeln ('A':6);`

PROGRAMMING PROBLEMS AND PROJECTS

Write and run a short program for each of the following.

1. Write a program to display your initials in block letters. Your output could look like

```
  JJJJJ           A           CC
    J            A A         C  C
    J           A   A       C
    J           AAAAA       C
 J  J           A   A        C  C
  JJ            A   A         CC
```

2. Design a simple picture and display it using **writeln** statements. If you plan the picture using a sheet of graph paper, it will be easier to keep track of spacing.
3. Write a program to display your mailing address.
4. Our Lady of Mercy Hospital prints billing statements for patients when they are ready to leave the hospital. Write a program that displays a heading for each statement as follows:

```
/////////////////////////////////////////
/                                       /
/      Our Lady of Mercy Hospital       /
/      --------------------------       /
/                                       /
/          1306 Central City            /
/         Phone (416) 333-5555          /
/                                       /
/////////////////////////////////////////
```

5. Your computer science instructor wants course and program information included as part of every assignment. Write a program that can be used to display this information. Sample output is

```
*************************************
*                                   *
*   Author:          Mary Smith     *
*   Course:          CPS-150        *
*   Assignment:      Program #3     *
*   Due Date:        September 18   *
*   Instructor:      Mr. Samson     *
*                                   *
*************************************
```

6. As part of a programming project that will compute and print grades for each student in your class, you have been asked to write a program that produces a heading for each student report. The column titles included in the heading should be as follows:
   - The border for the class name starts in column 30.
   - Student Name starts in column 20.
   - Test Average starts in column 40.
   - Grade starts in column 55.

   Write a program to print the following heading.

```
*************************
*                       *
*   CPS 150    Pascal   *
*                       *
*************************

Student Name          Test Average   Grade
------------          ------------   -----
```

COMMUNICATION IN PRACTICE

1. Exchange complete programs with a classmate, and critique the use of descriptive identifiers. Offer positive suggestions that would help others wishing to read and understand the program.
2. Discuss the issue of using descriptive identifiers with each of the following.
   a. Another student in your class
   b. A senior or graduate student in computer science
   c. A computer science instructor (not your own)
   d. A professional programmer

   Prepare a written report of your conversations with these people, and present the results to your class.

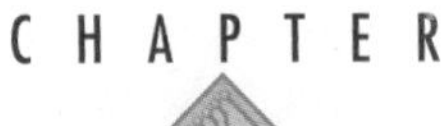

CHAPTER 2 Arithmetic, Variables, Input, Constants, and Standard Functions

CHAPTER OUTLINE

2.1 Arithmetic in Pascal

OBJECTIVES

- to understand what an expression is in Pascal
- to be able to evaluate arithmetic expressions using data of type **integer**
- to be able to evaluate arithmetic expressions using data of type **real**
- to understand the order of operations for evaluating expressions
- to be able to identify mixed-mode expressions
- to be able to distinguish between valid and invalid mixed-mode expressions
- to be able to evaluate mixed-mode expressions

In this chapter, we will discuss arithmetic operations, using data in a program, obtaining input, and using constants and variables. We will also discuss the use of functions to perform standard operations, such as finding the square root or absolute value of a number.

Expressions

An *expression* in Pascal occurs when two or more values are combined to produce a single value. Expressions can include constants, variables, and functions, and can be as elaborate as you choose to make them. Each of the following is an example of an expression:

```
2 + 3
TotalPoints / 5
sqrt(B * B - 4 * A * C)
```

Expressions can be used to form program statements. For example

```
Sum := 2 + 3
Average := TotalPoints / 5
Discriminant := sqrt(B * B - 4 * A * C)
```

are three executable statements that contain arithmetic expressions. In this chapter, we will examine expressions to see how they can be used in statements.

Basic Operations for Integers

Integer arithmetic in Pascal allows the operations of addition, subtraction, and multiplication to be performed. The notation for these operations is

Symbol	Operation	Example	Value
+	Addition	**3 + 5**	8
–	Subtraction	**43 - 25**	18
*	Multiplication	**4 * 7**	28

Noticeably absent from this list is a division operation. This is because *integer arithmetic operations* are expected to produce integer answers. Since division problems might not produce integers, Pascal provides two operations, **MOD** and **DIV,** to produce integer answers.

In a standard division problem, there is a quotient and a remainder. In Pascal, **DIV** produces the quotient and **MOD** produces the remainder when the first operand is positive. For example, in the problem 17 divided by 3, 17 **DIV** 3 produces 5 and 17 **MOD** 3 produces 2. Avoid using **DIV** 0 (zero) and **MOD** 0 (zero). A precise description of how **MOD** works is given on page 39 of the *Second Draft ANSI Standard for Pascal* as "A term of the form *i* mod *j* shall be an error if *j* is zero or negative; otherwise the value of *i* mod *j* shall be that value of $(i - (k * j))$ for integral *k* such that $0 <= i \bmod j < j$."

T

Several integer expressions and their values are shown in Table 2.1. Notice that when 3 is multiplied by –2, the expression is written as 3 * (–2) rather than 3 * –2. This is because consecutive operators cannot appear in an arithmetic expression. However, this expression could be written as –2 * 3.

◇ TABLE 2.1
Values of integer expressions

Expression	Value
`-3 + 2`	-1
`2 - 3`	-1
`-3 * 2`	-6
`3 * (-2)`	-6
`-3 * (-2)`	6
`17 DIV 3`	5
`17 MOD 3`	2
`17 DIV (-3)`	-5
`-17 DIV 3`	-5
`-17 MOD 3`	1
`-17 DIV (-3)`	5

Order of Operations for Integers

Expressions involving more than one operation are frequently used when writing programs. When this happens, it is important to know the order in which these operations are performed. This order of operations is referred to as the *precedence rule.* The priorities for these operations are:

1. All expressions within a set of parentheses are evaluated first. If there are parentheses within parentheses (if the parentheses are nested), the innermost expressions are evaluated first.
2. The operations *, **MOD,** and **DIV** are evaluated next, in order from left to right.
3. The operations + and – are evaluated last from left to right.

These are similar to algebraic operations; they are summarized in Table 2.2.

◇ TABLE 2.2
Integer arithmetic priority

Expression or Operation	Priority
`(   )`	1. Evaluate from inside out.
`*, MOD, DIV`	2. Evaluate from left to right.
`+, -`	3. Evaluate from left to right.

To illustrate how expressions are evaluated, consider the values of the expressions listed in Table 2.3.

◇ TABLE 2.3
Priority of operations

Expression	Value
`3 - 4 * 5`	–17
`3 - (4 * 5)`	–17
`(3 - 4) * 5`	–5
`3 * 4 - 5`	7
`3 * (4 - 5)`	–3
`17 - 10 - 3`	4
`17 - (10 - 3)`	10
`(17 - 10) - 3`	4
`-42 + 50 MOD 17`	–26

As expressions get more elaborate, it can be helpful to list partial evaluations in a manner similar to the order in which the computer performs the evaluations. For example, suppose the expression

```
(3 - 4) + 18 DIV 5 + 2
```

is to be evaluated. If we consider the order in which subexpressions are evaluated, we get

```
(3 - 4) + 18 DIV 5 + 2
   ↓
  -1    + 18 DIV 5 + 2
              ↓
  -1    +     3    + 2
        ↓
        2          + 2
              ↓
              4
```

Using MOD and DIV

MOD and **DIV** can be used when it is necessary to perform conversions within arithmetic operations. For example, consider the problem of adding two weights given in units of pounds and ounces. This problem can be solved by converting both weights to ounces, adding the ounces, and then converting the total ounces to pounds and ounces. The conversion from ounces to pounds can be accomplished by using **MOD** and **DIV.** If the total number of ounces is 243, then

243 **DIV** 16

yields the number of pounds (15), and

243 **MOD** 16

yields the number of ounces (3).

Representation of Integers

Computer representation of integers is different from what we see when we work with integers. Integers are stored and integer operations are performed in *binary notation.* Thus, the integer 19, which can be written as

$$\begin{aligned} 19 &= 16 + 0 + 0 + 2 + 1 \\ &= 1 \cdot 2^4 + 0 \cdot 2^3 + 0 \cdot 2^2 + 1 \cdot 2^1 + 1 \cdot 2^0 \end{aligned}$$

is stored as 1 0 0 1 1.

This binary number is actually stored in a *word* in memory, which consists of several individual locations called bits, as mentioned in Chapter 1. The number of bits used to store an integer is machine-dependent. If you use a 16-bit machine, then 19 is represented as

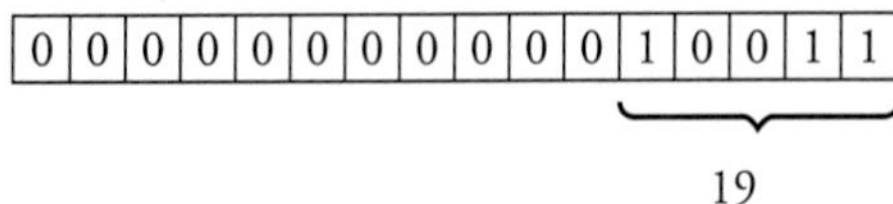

In this representation, the leftmost bit is reserved for the sign of the integer.

We can now make two observations regarding the storage and mechanics of the operation of integers. First, integer operations produce exact answers; numbers are stored exactly (up to the limits of the machine). Second, a maximum and a minimum number (**maxint** and **-maxint**-1, respectively) can be represented. In a 16-bit machine, **maxint** is

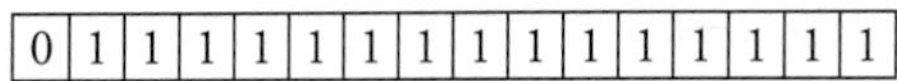

where the 0 represents a positive number. This number is

$$2^{15} + 2^{14} + 2^{13} + \cdots + 2^2 + 2^1 + 2^0$$

which equals 32,767. The lower bound for negative numbers is

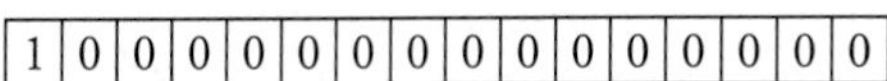

which represents $-2^{16} = -32{,}768$. This is **-maxint**-1.

If a program contains an integer operation that produces a number outside the range (**-maxint**-1, **maxint**), this is referred to as *integer overflow,* which means the number is too large or too small to be stored. Ideally, an error message is printed when such a situation arises. Some systems print a message such as **ARITHMETIC OVERFLOW** when this occurs; other systems merely assign a meaningless value and continue with the program. In Section 4.3, we will discuss how to protect a program against this problem.

Basic Operations for Reals

The operations of addition, subtraction, and multiplication are the same for data of type **real** as they are for data of type **integer.** Additionally, division is now permitted. Since **MOD** and **DIV** are restricted to data of type **integer,** the symbol for division of data of type **real** is "/". The *real arithmetic operations* are

Symbol	Operation	Example	Value
+	Addition	**4.2 + 19.36**	23.56
-	Subtraction	**19.36 - 4.2**	15.16
*	Multiplication	**3.1 * 2.0**	6.2
/	Division	**54.6 / 2.0**	27.3

Division is given the same priority as multiplication when arithmetic expressions are evaluated by the computer. The rules for order of operation are the same as those for evaluating integer arithmetic expressions. A summary of these operations is shown in Table 2.4.

◇ TABLE 2.4
Real arithmetic priority

Expression or Operation	Priority
( )	1. Evaluate from inside out.
*, /	2. Evaluate from left to right.
+, -	3. Evaluate from left to right.

Some example calculations using data of type **real** are

Expression	Value
`-1.0 + 3.5 + 2.0`	4.5
`-1.0 + 3.5 * 2.0`	6.0
`2.0 * (1.2 - 4.3)`	-6.2
`2.0 * 1.2 - 4.3`	-1.9
`-12.6 / 3.0 + 3.0`	-1.2
`-12.6 / (3.0 + 3.0)`	-2.1

As with integers, consecutive operations signs are not allowed. Thus, if you want to multiply 4.3 by -2.0, you can use -2.0 * 4.3 or 4.3 * (-2.0), but you cannot use 4.3 * -2.0. As expressions get a bit more complicated, it is again helpful to write out the expression and evaluate it step by step. For example

```
18.2 + (-4.3) * (10.1 + (72.3 / 3.0 - 4.5))
                              ↓
18.2 + (-4.3) * (10.1 +    (24.1     - 4.5))
                                    ↓
18.2 + (-4.3) * (10.1 +           19.6)
                         ↓
18.2 + (-4.3) *        29.7
                  ↓
18.2 +          -127.71
         ↓
     -109.51
```

Note that exponentiation has not been listed as an available operation for either integers or reals. Pascal does not have an exponentiation operator. A method of overcoming this problem is presented in Section 3.4.

Representation of Reals

As with integers, real numbers are stored and operations are performed using binary digits. Unlike integers, however, the storage and representation of real numbers frequently produces answers that are not exact. For example, an operation such as

```
1 / 3
```

produces the repeating decimal 0.3333. . . . At some point, this decimal must be truncated or rounded so that it can be stored. Such conversions produce *round-off errors*.

Now let's consider some errors that occur when working with real numbers. A value very close to zero may be stored as zero. Thus, you may think you are working with

$$1.23 \times 10^{-20} = 0.0000000000000000000123$$

but, in fact, this value may have been stored as 0. This condition is referred to as *underflow.* Generally, this would not be a problem because replacing numbers very close to zero with 0 does not affect the accuracy of most answers. However, sometimes this replacement can make a difference; therefore, you should be aware of the limitations of the system on which you are working.

Since operations with real numbers are not stored exactly, errors referred to as *representational errors* can be introduced. To illustrate, suppose we are using a machine that only yields three digits of accuracy (most machines exhibit much greater accuracy) and we want to add the three numbers 45.6, –45.5, and .215. The order in which we add these numbers makes a difference in the result we obtain. For example, –45.5 + 45.6 yields .1. Then, .1 + .215 yields .315. Thus, we have

$$(-45.5 + 45.6) + .215 = .315$$

However, if we consider 45.6 + .215 first, then the arithmetic result is 45.815. Since our hypothetical computer only yields three digits of accuracy, this result will be stored as 45.8. Then, –45.5 + 45.8 yields .3. Thus, we have

$$-45.5 + (45.6 + .215) = .3$$

This illustration produces a representational error.

Another form of representational error occurs when numbers of substantially different size are used in an operation. For example, consider the problem

$$2 + 0.0005$$

We would expect this total to be 2.0005, but stored to only three digits of accuracy, the result would be 2.00. In effect, the smaller of two numbers of substantially different size is canceled. Thus, this form of representational error is referred to as a *cancellation error.*

Although representational and cancellation errors cannot be avoided, their effects can be minimized. Operations should be grouped in such a way that numbers of approximately the same magnitude are used together before their resultant operand is used with another number. For example, all very small numbers should be summed before adding them to larger numbers.

One problem associated with how real numbers are stored and manipulated is that they should not be tested for equality. We will soon see how numbers can be compared and used to terminate certain conditions. In general, you should avoid using reals when strict checking for equality is required.

Attempting to store very large real numbers can result in *real overflow.* In principal, real numbers are stored with locations reserved for the exponents. An oversimplified illustration using base 10 digits is

	1	2	3	+	0	8

for the number 123×10^8. Different computers place different limits on the size of the exponent that can be stored. An attempt to use numbers outside the defined range causes overflow in much the same way that integer overflow occurs. When real overflow occurs, some machines halt execution and print an error message, such as **`FLOATING POINT OVERFLOW`**. Others assign a meaningless value and continue operations.

Mixed Expressions

Arithmetic expressions using data of two or more types are called *mixed-mode expressions.* When a mixed-mode expression involving both **integer** and **real** data types is evaluated, the result will be of type **real.** A real also results if division (/) is used with integers. When formatting the output of mixed expressions, always format for reals. (*Note:* Avoid using **MOD** and **DIV** with mixed-mode expressions.)

EXERCISES 2.1

1. Find the value of each of the following expressions.
   a. `17 - 3 * 2`
   b. `-15 * 3 + 4`
   c. `123 MOD 5`
   d. `123 DIV 5`
   e. `5 * 123 DIV 5 + 123 MOD 5`
   f. `-21 * 3 * (-1)`
   g. `14 * (3 + 18 DIV 4) - 50`
   h. `100 - (4 * (3 + 2)) * (-2)`
   i. `-56 MOD 3`
   j. `14 * 8 MOD 5 - 23 DIV (-4)`

2. Find the value of each of the following expressions.
   a. `3.21 + 5.02 / 6.1`
   b. `6.0 / 2.0 * 3.0`
   c. `6.0 / (2.0 + 3.0)`
   d. `-20.5 * (2.1 + 2.0)`
   e. `-2.0 * ((56.8 / 4.0 + 0.8) + 5.0)`
   f. `1.04E2 * 0.02E3`
   g. `800.0E-2 / 4.0 + 15.3`

3. Which of the following are valid expressions? For those that are, indicate whether they are of type **integer** or **real.**
   a. `18 - (5 * 2)`
   b. `(18 - 5) * 2`
   c. `18 - 5 * 2.0`
   d. `25 * (14 MOD 7.0)`
   e. `1.4E3 * 5`
   f. `28 / 7`
   g. `28.0 / 4`
   h. `10.5 + 14 DIV 3`
   i. `24 DIV 6 / 3`
   j. `24 DIV (6 / 3)`

4. Evaluate each of the valid expressions in Exercise 3.

5. What output is produced by the following program?

```
PROGRAM MixedMode (output);
BEGIN
  writeln;
  writeln ('    Expression     Value');
  writeln ('    ----------     -----');
  writeln;
  writeln ('    10 / 5' , 10/5:12:3);
  writeln ('    2.0+7*(-1)', 2.0 + 7 * (-1));
  writeln
END.
```

6. Find all errors in the following Pascal statements:
   a. `writeln (-20 DIV 4.0:8:3);`
   b. `writeln (-20 DIV 4:8:3);`

c. `writeln (-20 DIV 4:8);`
d. `writeln (8 - 3.0 * 5:6);`
e. `writeln (7 * 6 DIV 3 / 2:6:2);`
f. `writeln (-17.1 + 5 * 20.0:8:3);`

7. Write a test program to see what overflow message appears when real overflow occurs.

2.2 Using Variables

OBJECTIVES

- to understand utilization of storage area
- to distinguish between name of a memory location and value in a memory location
- to be able to use variables in assignment statements, expressions, and output statements

Memory Locations

It is frequently necessary to store values for later use. This is done by putting the value into a *memory location* by using a symbolic name to refer to this location. If the contents of the location are to be changed during a program, the symbolic name is referred to as a *variable;* if the contents are not to be changed, the name is referred to as a *constant.*

A graphic way to think about memory locations is to envision them as boxes; each box is named, and a value is stored inside. For example, suppose a program is written to add a sequence of numbers. If we name the memory location to be used Sum, initially we have

Sum

which depicts a memory location that has been reserved and can be accessed by a reference to Sum. If we then add the integers 10, 20, and 30 and store them in Sum, we have

60
Sum

It is important to distinguish between the name of a memory location (Sum) and the value or contents of a memory location (60). The name does not change during a program, but the contents can be changed as often as necessary. (Note that contents of memory locations that are referred to by constants cannot be changed.) If 30 were added to the contents in the previous example, the new value stored in Sum could be depicted as

90
Sum

Symbolic names representing memory locations containing values that will be changing must be declared in the **VAR** section of the program (as indicated in Section 1.4); for example

```
VAR
  Sum : integer;
```

Symbolic names that represent memory locations containing values that will not be changing must be declared in the **CONST** section.

Assignment Statements

Now let's examine how the contents of variables are manipulated. A value may be put into a memory location with an *assignment statement* in the form of

<variable name> := <value>
or
<variable name> := <expression>

where "variable name" is the name of the memory location. For example, if Sum were initially zero, then

```
Sum := 30;
```

changes

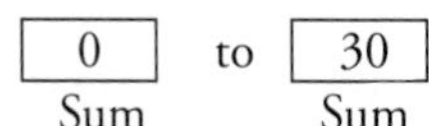

The syntax diagram for this is

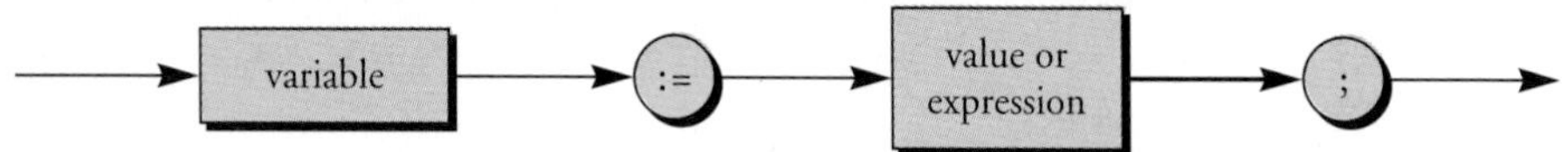

Some important rules concerning assignment statements are

1. The assignment is always made from right to left (←).
2. The syntax for assigning requires a colon followed immediately by an equal sign (:=).
3. Only one variable can be on the left side of the assignment symbol.
4. Constants cannot be on the left side of the assignment symbol.
5. The expression may be a constant, a constant expression, a variable that has previously been assigned a value, or a combination of variables and constants.
6. Values on the right side of the assignment symbol are not changed by the assignment.
7. The variable and expression must match in data type. An exception is that an integer expression can be assigned to a real variable, in which case the result of the expression evaluation gets converted to a real value.

Two common errors made by beginners are trying to assign from left to right and forgetting the colon when using an assignment statement.

Repeated assignments can be made. For example, if Sum is an integer variable, the statements

```
Sum := 50;
Sum := 70;
Sum := 100;
```

produce first 50, then 70, and finally 100 as shown.

~~50~~ ~~70~~ 100
Sum

In this sense, memory is destructive in that it retains only the last value assigned.

Pascal variables are symbolic addresses that can hold values. When a variable is declared, the type of values it will store must be specified (declared). Storing a value of the wrong type in a variable leads to a program error. This means that data types must match when assignment statements are used: reals must be assigned to **real** variables; integers, to **integer** variables; characters, to **char** variables. The only exception is that an integer can be assigned to a **real** variable; however, the integer is then converted to a real. If, for example, Average is a **real** variable and the assignment statement

```
Average := 21;
```

is made, the value is stored as the real 21.0.

The assignment of a constant to a character variable requires that the constant be enclosed in single quotation marks. For example, if Letter is of type **char** and you want to store the letter C in Letter, use the assignment statement

```
Letter := 'C';
```

This could be pictured as

C

Letter

Only one character can be assigned or stored in a character variable.

To illustrate working with assignment statements, assume that the variable declaration portion of the program is

```
VAR
  Sum : integer;
  Average : real;
  Letter : char;
```

Examples of valid and invalid assignment statements using the variables just declared are shown in Table 2.5.

◇ TABLE 2.5
Assignment statements

Statement	Valid	Reason If Invalid
`Sum := 50;`	Yes	
`Sum := 10.5;`	No	Data types do not match.
`Average := 15.6;`	Yes	
`Average := 33;`	Yes	
`Letter := 'A';`	Yes	
`Letter := 'HI';`	No	Is not a single character.
`Letter := 20;`	No	Data types do not match.
`Letter := 'Z';`	Yes	
`Letter := A;`	?	Valid if A is a variable or constant of type **char.**
`Sum := 7;`	Yes	
`Letter := '7';`	Yes	
`Letter := 7;`	No	Data types do not match.
`Sum := '7';`	No	Data types do not match.

Using Expressions

Actual use of variables in a program is usually more elaborate than what we have just seen. Variables may be used in any manner that does not violate their type declarations, including both arithmetic operations and assignment statements. For example, if Score1, Score2, Score3, and Average are **real** variables, then

```
Score1 := 72.3;
Score2 := 89.4;
Score3 := 95.6;
Average := (Score1 + Score2 + Score3) / 3.0;
```

is a valid fragment of code.

Now let's consider the problem of accumulating a total. Assuming NewScore and Total are integer variables, the following code is valid.

```
Total := 0;
NewScore := 5;
Total := Total + NewScore;
NewScore := 7;
Total := Total + NewScore;
```

As this code is executed, the values of memory locations for Total and NewScore could be depicted as

Statement	Total	NewScore
`Total := 0;`	0	
`NewScore := 5;`	0	5
`Total := Total + NewScore;`	5	5
`NewScore := 7;`	5	7
`Total := Total + NewScore;`	12	7

Output

Variables and variable expressions can be used when creating output. When used in a **writeln** statement, they perform the same function as a constant. For example, if the assignment statement

```
Age := 5;
```

has been made, the two statements

```
writeln (5);
writeln (Age);
```

produce the same output. If Age1, Age2, Age3, and Sum are integer variables and the assignments

```
Age1 := 21;
Age2 := 30;
Age3 := 12;
Sum := Age1 + Age2 + Age3;
```

are made, the three statements

```
writeln ('The sum is ', 21 + 30 + 12);
writeln ('The sum is ', Age1 + Age2 + Age3);
writeln ('The sum is ', Sum);
```

all produce the same output.

Formatting variables and variable expressions in **writeln** statements follows the same rules presented in Chapter 2 for formatting constants. The statements needed to write the sum of the previous example in a field width of four are

```
writeln ('The sum is ', (21 + 30 + 12):4);
writeln ('The sum is ', (Age1 + Age2 + Age3):4);
writeln ('The sum is ', Sum:4);
```

The next two examples illustrate the use of variables, assignment statements, and formatting.

A NOTE OF INTEREST

Herman Hollerith

Herman Hollerith (1860–1929) was hired by the United States Census Bureau in 1879 at the age of 19. Since the 1880 census was predicted to take a long time to complete (it actually took until 1887), Hollerith was assigned the task of developing a mechanical method of tabulating census data. He introduced his census machine in 1887. It consisted of four parts:

1. A punched paper card that represented data using a special code (Hollerith code)
2. A card punch apparatus
3. A tabulator that read the punched cards
4. A sorting machine with 24 compartments

The punched cards used by Hollerith were the same size as cards still in use today.

Using Hollerith's techniques and equipment, the 1890 census tabulation was completed in one-third the time required for the previous census tabulation. This included working with data for 12 million additional people.

Hollerith proceeded to form the Tabulating Machine Company (1896), which supplied equipment to census bureaus in the United States, Canada, and western Europe. After a disagreement with the census director, Hollerith began marketing his equipment in other commercial areas. Hollerith sold his company in 1911. It was later combined with 12 others to form the Computing-Tabulating-Recording Company, a direct ancestor of International Business Machines Corp.

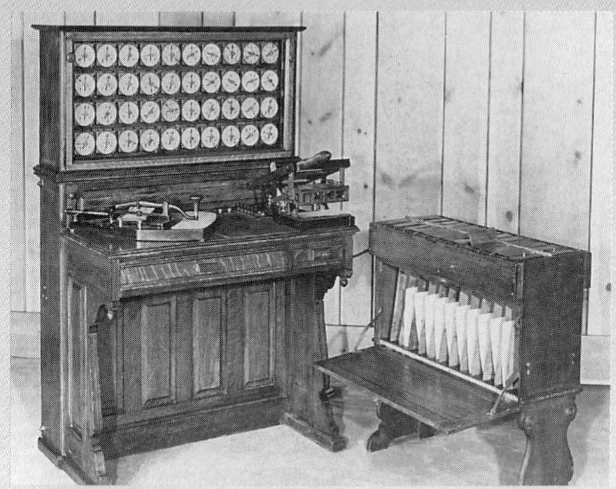

In the meantime, Hollerith's successor at the census bureau, James Powers, redesigned the census machines. He then formed his own company, which subsequently became Remington Rand and Sperry Univac.

EXAMPLE 2.1

Let's write a program to print data about the cost of three textbooks and the average price of the books. The variable declaration section could include

```
VAR
  MathText, BioText,
  CompSciText,
  Total, Average : real;
```

A portion of the program could be

```
  MathText := 23.95;
  BioText := 27.50;
  CompSciText := 19.95;
  Total := MathText + BioText + CompSciText;
  Average := Total / 3;
```

The output could be created by

```
  writeln ('Text                Price');
  writeln ('____                 ____');
  writeln;
  writeln ('Math', MathText:18:2);
```

```
writeln ('Biology', BioText:15:2);
writeln ('CompSci', CompSciText:15:2);
writeln;
writeln ('Total', Total:17:2);
writeln;
writeln ('The average price is', Average:7:2);
```

The output would then be

```
Text                Price
----                -----

Math                23.95
Biology             27.50
CompSci             19.95

Total               71.40

The average price is  23.80
```

EXAMPLE 2.2

Now let's see how we can use a variable of type **integer** to examine the problem of integer overflow. If we try to store an integer larger than **maxint** in a variable of type **integer,** we cause integer overflow. A test program to see what occurs is

```
PROGRAM IntOverFlow;

VAR
  Num : integer;

BEGIN
  Num := maxint + 1;
  writeln (Num)
END.
```

When this program is typed exactly as it appears here and then compiled, an error message such as

```
Error 76: Constant out of range.
```

may be given.

Software Engineering Implications

The communication aspect of software engineering can be simplified by judicious choices of meaningful identifiers. Systems programmers must be aware that others will need to read and analyze the code over time. Some extra time spent thinking about and using descriptive identifiers provides great time savings during the testing and maintenance phases. Using descriptive identifiers is part of the process referred to as writing *self-documenting code,* which will be discussed in the next chapter.

EXERCISES 2.2

1. Assume the variable declaration section of a program is

```
VAR
  Age, IQ : integer;
  Income : real;
```

Indicate which of the following are valid assignment statements. Give the reason why each of the remaining statements is invalid.

a. `Age := 21;`
b. `IQ := Age + 100;`
c. `IQ := 120.5;`
d. `Age + IQ := 150;`
e. `Income := 22000;`
f. `Income := 100 * (Age + IQ);`
g. `Age := IQ / 3;`
h. `IQ := 3 * Age;`

2. Write and run a test program to illustrate what happens when values of one data type are assigned to variables of another type.

3. Suppose A, B, and Temp have been declared as integer variables. Indicate the contents of A and B at the end of each sequence of statements.

a.
```
A := 5;
B := -2;
A := A + B;
B := B - A;
```
b.
```
A := 31;
B := 26;
Temp := A;
A := B;
B := Temp;
```
c.
```
A := 0;
B := 7;
A := A + B MOD 2 * (-3);
B := B + 4 * A;
```
d.
```
A := -8;
B := 3;
Temp := A + B;
A := 3 * B;
B := A;
Temp := Temp + A + B;
```

4. Suppose X and Y are real variables and the assignments

```
X := 121.3;
Y := 98.6;
```

have been made. What **writeln** statements would cause the following output?

a.
```
The value of X is  121.3
```
b.
```
The sum of X and Y is  219.9
```
c.
```
X =       121.3
Y =        98.6
          -----
Total = 219.9
```

5. Write a single assignment statement for each formula.

a. $d = rt$
b. $I = prt$
c. $S = n(n - 1) / 2$
d. $C = 5 / 9 (F - 32)$

6. If A and B are integer variables with values of 3 and 5, respectively, what are the values of the following expressions?

a. `A DIV B + A MOD B`
b. `B - A * A + B`
c. `B + A * B DIV 3 - A MOD 3`
d. `A + (A - B) / B + 4`

7. Assume the variable declaration section of a program is

```
VAR
  Age, Height : integer;
  Weight : real;
  Gender : char;
```

What output would be created by the following program fragment?

```
Age := 23;
Height := 73;
Weight := 186.5;
Gender := 'M';
```

```
writeln ('Gender', Gender:10);
writeln ('Age', Age:14);
writeln ('Height', Height:11, ' inches');
writeln ('Weight', Weight:14:1, ' lbs');
```

8. Write a complete program that allows you to add five integers and then display

a. the integers.

b. their sum.

c. their average.

9. Assume Ch and Age have been appropriately declared. What output is produced by the following?

```
Ch := 'M';
Age := 21;
writeln ('******************************':40);
writeln ('*':11, '*':29);
write ('*':11, 'Name':7, 'Age':9);
writeln ('Gender':6, '*':4);
writeln ('*':11, '____':7, '___':9, '___':9, '*':4);
writeln;
write ('*':11, 'Jones':8, Age:8, Ch:9, '*':4);
writeln;
writeln ('*':11, '*':29);
writeln ('****************************************':40);
```

10. Assume the variable declaration section of a program is

```
VAR
  Weight1, Weight2 : integer;
  AverageWeight : real;
```

and the following assignment statements have been made:

```
Weight1 := 165;
Weight2 := 174;
AverageWeight := (Weight1 + Weight2) / 2;
```

a. What output would be produced by the following section of code?

```
writeln ('Weight');
writeln ('______');
writeln;
writeln (Weight1);
writeln (Weight2);
writeln;
writeln ('The average weight is',
         (Weight1 + Weight2) / 2);
```

b. Write a segment of code to produce the following output (use AverageWeight).

```
                Weight
                ------


                  165
                  174
                  ---
Total             339

The average weight is 169.5 pounds.
```

11. Assume the variable declaration section of a program is

```
VAR
  Letter : char;
```

and the following assignment has been made:

```
Letter := 'A';
```

What output is produced from the following segment of code?

```
writeln ('This reviews string formatting,':40);
writeln ('When a letter', Letter, 'is used,');
writeln ('Oops!':14, 'I forgot to format.':20);
writeln ('When a letter':22, Letter:2, 'is used,':9);
writeln ('it is a string of length one.':38);
```

12. Modify Example 2.2 to be

```
PROGRAM IntOverFlow;

VAR
  Num : integer;

BEGIN
  Num := maxint;
  writeln (Num);
  writeln (Num + 1)
END.
```

Run this program, and discuss the results.

2.3 Input

OBJECTIVES

- to be able to use **read** and **readln** to get data for a program
- to understand the difference between interactive input and batch input
- to understand the concept of end-of-line markers
- to understand the concept of end-of-file markers

Earlier, "running a program" was subdivided into the three general categories of getting the data, manipulating it appropriately, and displaying the results. Our work thus far has centered on creating output and manipulating data. We are now going to focus on how to get data for a program.

Input Statements

Data for a program are usually obtained from an input device, which can be a keyboard, terminal, card reader, disk, or tape. When such data (*input*) are obtained, the standard file **input** must be included in the file list of the program heading. (Some interactive systems use a different method. Check with your instructor.) Your program heading will (probably) have the form

PROGRAM <program name> **(input, output)**

The Pascal statements used to get data are **read** and **readln.** These statements are analogous to **write** and **writeln** for output. General forms for these *input statements* are

read (<variable name>)
read (<variable 1>, <variable 2>, . . . , <variable *n*>)
readln (<variable name>)
readln (<variable 1>, <variable 2>, . . . , <variable *n*>)
readln

A simplified syntax diagram for **read** and **readln** statements is

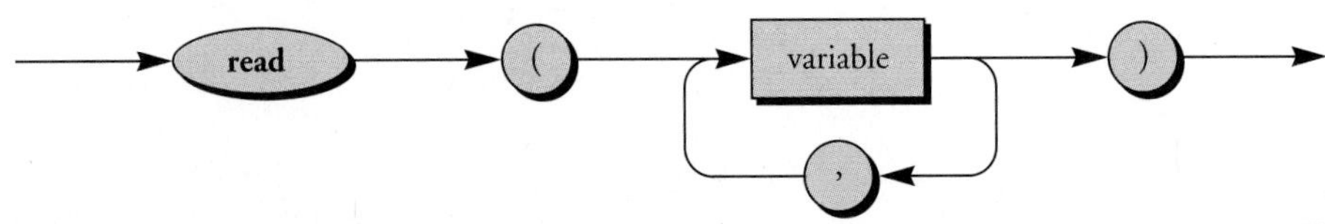

See Appendix 3 for a more detailed diagram.

When **read** or **readln** is used to get data, the value of the data item is stored in the indicated memory location. Data read into a program must match the type of variable in the variable list. To illustrate, if a variable declaration section includes

```
VAR
  Age : integer;
  Wage : real;
```

and the data items are

```
21          5.25
```

then

```
readln (Age, Wage);
```

results in

21	5.25
Age	Wage

Interactive Input

Interactive input refers to entering values from the keyboard while the program is running. Programs that get data from the keyboard are *interactive programs.* All interactive programs should use **readln** instead of **read** to get data. The **readln** statement causes the program to halt and wait for data items to be typed. A *prompt* will appear on the screen. For example, if you want to enter three-scores at some point in a program, you can use

```
readln (Score1, Score2, Score3);
```

as a program statement. At this point, you must enter at least three integers and press <Enter> (or some sequence of integers and <Enter> until at least three numbers are read as data items). The remaining part of the program is then executed. To illustrate, the following program reads in three integers and prints the integers and their average as output.

```
PROGRAM ComputeAverage (input, output);

CONST
  SKIP = ' ';

VAR
  Score1, Score2, Score3 : integer;
  Average : real;
```

```
BEGIN
  readln (Score1, Score2, Score3);
  Average := (Score1 + Score2 + Score3) / 3;
  writeln;
  writeln (Skip:10, 'The numbers are', Score1:4, Score2:4,
               Score3:4);
  writeln;
  writeln (Skip:10, 'Their average is', Average:8:2)
END.
```

When the program runs, if you type in

```
89 90 91
```

and press <Enter>, output is

```
The numbers are 89  90  91

Their average is  90.00
```

Interactive programs should have a prompting message to the user so the user knows what to do when a prompt appears. For example, the problem in the previous example can be modified by the lines

```
writeln ('Please enter 3 scores separated by spaces');
writeln ('and then press <Enter>.');
```

before the line

```
readln (Score1, Score2, Score3);
```

The screen will display the message

```
Please enter 3 scores separated by spaces
and then press <Enter>.
```

when the program is run.

Clearly stated screen messages to the person running a program are what make a program *user-friendly.* For long messages or several lines of output, you can use **readln** as a complete statement to halt execution. When you press <Enter>, the program will continue. When **readln** is used for input, <Enter> must be pressed before program execution will continue.

The next example is a complete interactive program that illustrates the use of screen messages.

EXAMPLE 2.3

Pythagorean triples are sets of three integers that satisfy the Pythagorean theorem. That is, integers a, b, and c such that $a^2 + b^2 = c^2$. The set of integers 3, 4, 5 is such a triple because $3^2 + 4^2 = 5^2$. Formulas for generating Pythagorean triples are $a = m^2 - n^2$, $b = 2mn$, and $c = m^2 + n^2$, where m and n are positive integers such that $m > n$. The following interactive program allows the user to enter values for m and n and then have the Pythagorean triple printed.

```
PROGRAM PythagoreanTriple (input, output);

VAR
  M, N, A, B, C : integer;
```

```
BEGIN
  writeln ('Enter a positive integer and press <Enter>.');
  readln (N);
  write ('Enter a positive integer greater than ', N);
  writeln (' and press <Enter>.');
  readln (M);
  A := (M * M) - (N * N);
  B := 2 * M * N;
  C := (M * M) + (N * N);
  writeln;
  writeln ('For M = ', M, ' and N = ', N);
  writeln ('the Pythagorean triple is ', A:5, B:5, C:5)
END.
```

Sample runs of this program (using data 1,2 and 2,5) produce

```
Enter a positive integer and press <Enter>.
1
Enter a positive integer greater than 1 and press <Enter>.
2

For M = 2 and N = 1
the Pythagorean triple is     3    4    5

Enter a positive integer and press <Enter>.
2
Enter a positive integer greater than 2 and press <Enter>.
5

For M = 5 and N = 2
the Pythagorean triple is    21   20   29
```

COMMUNICATION AND STYLE TIPS

A variable or expression may be used as a field-width specifier for formatting. When running interactive programs, this idea can be used to control desired accuracy as follows.

```
writeln ('How many places of accuracy?');
readln (Places):
    .
    .
    .
writeln ('Result is ', Result:Places+2:Places);
```

Reading Numeric Data

Reading numeric data into a program is reasonably straightforward. At least one blank must be used to separate numbers. The <Enter> character is read as a blank, so any sequence of numbers and spaces or <Enter> can be used to enter the required data.

Since the type of data items entered must match the data types for variables in an input statement, exercise some caution when using both reals and integers as input. To illustrate, if a variable declaration section is

```
VAR
  A : integer;
  X : real;
```

and we wish to enter the data items 97.5 and 86 respectively, **readln** (X,A) achieves the desired result. However, **readln** (A,X) results in an error. Since A is of type **integer,** only the 97 is read into A. The next character is a period, and when an attempt is made to read this period into the memory location for X, a type mismatch error occurs. One exception is that an integer can be read into a variable of type **real.** However, it is stored as a **real** and must be used accordingly.

Character Sets

Before we look at reading character data, we need to examine the way in which character data are stored. In the **char** data type, each character in the set of allowable characters is associated with an integer. Thus, the sequence of characters is associated with a sequence of integers. The particular sequence used by a machine for this purpose is referred to as the *collating sequence* for that *character set.* Two sequences currently in use are

1. American Standard Code for Information Interchange (ASCII)
2. Extended Binary Coded Decimal Interchange Code (EBCDIC)

Each collating sequence contains an ordering of the characters in a character set and is listed in Appendix 4. For programs in this text, we use the ASCII code. Fifty-two of the characters are letters, 10 are digits, and the rest are special characters, as shown in Table 2.6.

◇ TABLE 2.6
ASCII code

ƀ ! " # $ % & ' ( ) * + , - . / 0 1 2 3 4 5 6 7 8 9 : ; < = > ? @
A B C D E F G H I J K L M N O P Q R S T U V W X Y Z [\ ] ^ — '
a b c d e f g h i j k l m n o p q r s t u v w x y z { | } ~

Note: Of the special characters, ƀ is the symbol to denote a blank.

Reading Character Data

Reading characters is much different from reading numeric data. The following features apply to reading data of type **char.**

1. Only one character can be read at a time.
2. Each blank is a separate character.
3. The <Enter> character is read as a blank.
4. Each digit of a number is read as a separate character.

If you want to read in a student's initials followed by three test scores,

```
readln (FirstInitial, MiddleInitial, LastInitial);
readln (Score1, Score2, Score3);
```

accomplishes this. When program execution is halted, you would type in something like

```
JDK
```

and press <Enter>; then type in three integers, such as

```
89 90 91
```

and press <Enter> again.

Some errors are caused by not being careful with character data. For example, suppose you want to enter three test scores followed by a student's initials. You might try the program statements

```
read (Score1, Score2, Score3);
readln (FirstInitial, MiddleInitial, LastInitial);
```

When program execution halts for expected input, suppose you enter

```
89 90 91 JDK
```

When you try to print these values using

```
writeln (Score1, Score2:5, Score3:5);
writeln (FirstInitial, MiddleInitial, LastInitial);
```

the output is

```
89   90   91
 JD
```

because the blank following 91 is read as a character when an attempt is made to read FirstInitial. Note that the first three characters following 91 are a blank followed by "J" and "D". This problem can (and should) be avoided by entering the scores on one line and the initials on a separate line. In general, separate input lines should be used for separate data.

This topic of reading character data is expanded when text files are introduced in Chapter 6.

Reading Strings

Many current versions of Pascal—other than standard Pascal—permit reading textual data in strings as well as one character at a time. These versions allow some string data type. For example, in Turbo Pascal, strings of up to 20 characters can be declared by

```
VAR
  Name : string [20];
```

With this declaration, string names can be entered by

```
writeln ('Enter your name and press <Enter>.');
readln (Name);
```

A NOTE OF INTEREST

Communication Skills Needed

Emphasis on communication has been increasing in almost every area of higher education. Evidence of this is the current trend toward "writing across the curriculum" programs implemented in many colleges and universities in the 1980s. Indications that this emphasis is shared among computer scientists was given by Paul M. Jackowitz, Richard M. Plishka, and James R. Sidbury, University of Scranton, when they stated, "Make it possible to write programs in English, and you will discover that programmers cannot write in English."

All computer science educators are painfully aware of the truth of this old joke. We want our students to be literate. We want them to have well-developed writing skills and the capacity to read technical journals in our area. But too often we produce skilled programmers whose communication skills are poor and who have almost no research skills. We must alleviate this problem. Since the organizational techniques used to write software are the same ones that should be used to write papers, computing science students should have excellent writing skills. We should exploit this similarity in skills to develop better writers.

Further, Janet Hartman of Illinois State University and Curt M. White of Indiana-Purdue University at Fort Wayne noted: "Students need to practice written and oral communication skills, both in communications classes and computer classes. Students should write system specifications, project specifications, memos, users' guides or anything else which requires them to communicate on both a nontechnical and technical level. They should do presentations in class and learn to augment their presentations with audiovisual aids."

On a more general note, the need for effective communication skills in computer science has been acknowledged in the 1991 curriculum guidelines of the Association for Computing Machinery, Inc. These guidelines state that "undergraduate programs should prepare students to apply their knowledge to specific, constrained problems and produce solutions. This includes the ability to . . . communicate that solution to colleagues, professionals in other fields, and the general public."

A note of caution is in order. If you wish to enter a string and a numeric value, you must make sure that the number is not part of the string. For example, using the declaration for Name just given,

```
writeln ('Enter your name and age.  ');
readln (Name, Age);
```

could result in the user entering

```
Joan Smith 23
```

and then pressing <Enter>. Since the 23 is entered before column 20, it is considered part of the string of length 20. To avoid this problem, a separate question should be asked for each piece of information desired.

Batch Input

Batch input refers to a program getting data from a file that has previously been created. The beginning of this text is written assuming the reader will use an interactive mode. Development of batch input is deferred until Chapter 6. If you are working in a batch mode, you should read Chapter 6 at this time and check with your instructor.

EXERCISES 2.3

1. Discuss the difference between using **read** and **readln** to get data for a program.
2. Assume a variable declaration section is

```
VAR
  Num1, Num2 : integer;
  Num3 : real;
  Ch : char;
```

   and you wish to enter the data

```
15 65.3 -20
```

   Explain what results from each of the following statements. Also indicate what values are assigned to appropriate variables.

   a. `readln (Num1, Num3, Num2);`
   b. `readln (Num1, Num2, Num3);`
   c. `readln (Num1, Num2, Ch, Num3);`
   d. `readln (Num2, Num3, Ch, Num2);`
   e. `readln (Num2, Num3, Ch, Ch, Num2);`
   f. `readln (Num3, Num2);`
   g. `readln (Num1, Num3);`
   h. `readln (Num1, Ch, Num3);`
   i. `read (Num1, Num3, Num2);`
   j. `read (Num1, Num3, Ch, Num2);`
   k. `read (Num1, Num3, Ch, Ch, Num2);`
   l. `read (Num2, Num1, Ch, Num2);`
3. Write a program statement to be used to print a message to the screen directing the user to enter data in the form used for Exercise 2.
4. Write an appropriate program statement (or statements) to produce a screen message and write an appropriate input statement for each of the following.
   a. Desired input is number of hours worked and hourly pay rate.
   b. Desired input is three positive integers followed by –999.
   c. Desired input is price of an automobile and the state sales tax rate.

d. Desired input is the game statistics for one basketball player (check with a coach to see what must be entered).
e. Desired input is a student's initials, age, height, weight, and gender.
f. Desired input is a person's name and age.

5. Assume variables are declared as in Exercise 2. If an input statement is

```
readln (Num1, Num2, Ch, Num3);
```

indicate which lines of data do not result in an error message, and then indicate the values of the variables. For those that produce an error, explain what the error is.

a. 83 95 100
b. 83 95.0 100
c. 83 -72 93.5
d. 83 -72   93.5
e. 83.5
f. 70 73 -80.5
g. 91 92 93 94
h. -76 -81 -16.5

6. Why is it a good idea to print out values of variables that have been read into a program?

7. Suppose Price is a variable of type **real** and you have the program statement

```
read (Price);
```

a. What happens if you enter 17.95?
b. How does this input statement compare to **readln** (Price)?

8. Write a complete program that reads your initials and five test scores, computes your test average, and prints out all information in a reasonable form with suitable messages.

2.4 Using Constants

OBJECTIVES

- to be aware of appropriate use of constants
- to be able to use constants in programs
- to be able to format constants

The word "constant" has several interpretations. In this section, it will refer to values defined in the **CONST** definition subsection of a program. Recall that a Pascal program consists of a program heading, a declaration section, and an executable section. The declaration section can contain a variable declaration subsection (discussed in Section 1.4) and a constant definition subsection. When both are used, the **CONST** subsection must precede the **VAR** subsection. We will now examine uses for constants defined in the **CONST** subsection.

Rationale for Uses

There are many reasons to use constants in a program. If a number is to be used frequently, the programmer may wish to give it a descriptive name in the **CONST** definition subsection and then use the descriptive name in the executable section, thus making the program easier to read. For example, if a program includes a segment that computes a person's state income tax and the state tax rate is 6.25 percent of taxable income, the **CONST** section might include

```
CONST
   StateTaxRate = 0.0625;
```

This defines both the value and type for StateTaxRate. In the executable portion of the program, the statement

```
StateTax := Income * StateTaxRate;
```

omputes the state tax owed. Or suppose you want a program to compute areas of circles. Depending upon the accuracy you desire, you could define pi "π" as

```
CONST
   Pi = 3.14159;
```

You could then have a statement in the executable section such as

```
Area := Pi * Radius * Radius;
```

where Area and Radius are appropriately declared variables.

Perhaps the most important use of constants is for values that are currently fixed but subject to change for subsequent runs of the program. If such a value is defined in the **CONST** section, it can be used throughout the program. If the value changes later, only one change has to be made to keep the program current. This prevents the need to locate all uses of a constant in a program. Some examples might be

```
CONST
  MinimumWage = 4.25;
  SpeedLimit = 65;
  Price = 0.75;
  StateTaxRate = 0.0625;
```

Constants can also be used to name character strings that occur frequently in program output. Suppose a program needs to print two different company names. Instead of typing the names each time they are needed, the following definition could be used:

```
CONST
  Company1 = 'First National Bank of America';
  Company2 = 'Metropolitan Bank of New York';
```

Company1 and Company2 could then be used in **writeln** statements.

Constants can also be defined for later repeated use in making output more attractive. Included could be constants for underlining and for separating sections of output. Some definitions could be

```
CONST
  Underline = '_________________________________';
  Splats = '**********************************';
```

To separate the output with asterisks, the statement

```
writeln (Splats, Splats);
```

could be used. In a similar fashion

```
writeln (Underline);
```

could be used for underlining.

A NOTE OF INTEREST

Defined Constants and Space Shuttle Computing

An excellent illustration of the utilization of defined constants in a program was given by J. F. ("Jack") Clemons, former manager of avionics flight software development and verification for the space shuttle on-board computers. In an interview with David Gifford, editor for *Communications of the ACM*, Clemons was asked, "Have you tried to restructure the software so that it can be changed easily?"

His response was, "By changing certain data constants, we can change relatively large portions of the software on a mission-to-mission basis. For example, we've designed the software so that characteristics like atmospheric conditions on launch day or different lift-off weights can be loaded as initial constants into the code. This is important when there are postponements or last-minute payload changes that invalidate the original inputs."

Software Engineering Implications

The appropriate use of constants is consistent with principles of software engineering. Communication between teams of programmers is enhanced when program constants have been agreed upon. Each team should have a list of these constants for use as members work on their part of the system.

The maintenance phase of the software system life cycle is also aided by use of defined constants. Clearly, a large payroll system is dependent upon being able to perform computations that include deductions for federal tax, state tax, FICA, Medicare, health insurance, retirement options, and so on. If appropriate constants are defined for these deductions, system changes are easily made as necessary. For example, the current salary limit for deducting FICA taxes is $57,600. Since this amount changes regularly, we could define

```
CONST
  FICALimit = 57600.00;
```

Program maintenance is then simplified by changing the value of this constant as the law changes.

Formatting Constants

Formatting numeric constants is identical to formatting reals and integers, as discussed in Section 1.5. Real constants are formatted as reals; integer constants, as integers. When a character string is defined as a constant, a single positive integer can be used for formatting. This integer establishes the field width for the character string and right justifies the character string in the output field.

EXERCISES 2.4

1. One use of constants is for values that are used throughout a program but are subject to change over time (minimum wage, speed limit, and so on). List at least five items in this category that were not mentioned in this section.
2. Assume the **CONST** definition section of a program is

```
CONST
  CourseName = 'CPS 150';
  TotalPts = 100;
  Underline = '___________________________________';
```

and you want to obtain the following output:

```
COURSE:             CPS 150     TEST #1
-----------------------------------
TOTAL POINTS        100
```

Fill in the appropriate formatting positions in the following **writeln** statements to produce the indicated output.

```
writeln ('COURSE:':7, CourseName:    , 'TEST #1':13);
writeln (Underline:     );
writeln;
writeln ('TOTAL POINTS':12, TotalPts:    );
```

3. Using the **CONST** definition section in Exercise 2, what output is produced by the following segment of code?

```
writeln;
writeln (CourseName:10, 'TEST #2':20);
writeln (Underline);
writeln;
writeln ('Total points':16, TotalPts:15);
writeln ('My score':12, 93:19);
writeln ('Class average':17, 82.3:14:1);
```

4. Use the constant definition section to define appropriate constants for the following:
   a. Your name
   b. Today's date
   c. Your social security number
   d. Your age
   e. The name of your school
   f. The number of students in your class
   g. The average age of students in your class
   h. The average hourly wage of steelworkers
   i. The price of a new car

2.5 Standard Functions

OBJECTIVES

- to understand reasons for having standard functions
- to be able to use standard functions in a program
- to be able to use appropriate data types for arguments of standard functions

Some standard operations required by programmers are squaring numbers, finding square roots of numbers, rounding numbers, and truncating numbers. Because these operations are so basic, all versions of Pascal provide *standard (built-in) functions* for them. Various versions of Pascal and other programming languages have different standard functions available, so you should always check on which functions can be used with a particular version. Appendix 2 lists the standard functions available in most versions.

A function can be used in a program if it appears in the form

<function name> (<argument>)

where *argument* is a value or variable with an assigned value. When a function is listed in this manner, it is said to be *invoked* or *called.* A function is invoked by using its name and argument in an expression or statement. If, for example, you want to square the integer 5,

```
sqr(5)
```

produces this result, which can then be used as desired.

The syntax diagram for this is

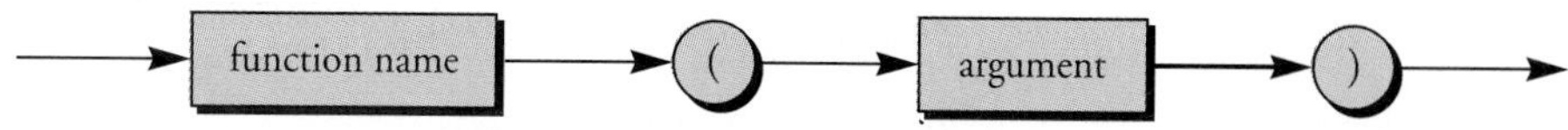

Many functions operate on numbers, starting with a given number and returning some associated value. Table 2.7 shows five standard functions, each with its argument type, data type produced, and an explanation of the value returned.

Several examples of specific function expressions together with the value returned by each expression are depicted in Table 2.8.

◇ TABLE 2.7
Numeric function calls and return types

Function Call	Argument Type	Type of Return	Function Value
sqr(argument)	**real** or **integer**	Same as argument	Returns the square of the argument
sqrt(argument)	**real** or **integer** (nonnegative)	**real**	Returns the square root of the argument
abs(argument)	**real** or **integer**	Same as argument	Returns the absolute value of the argument
round(argument)	**real**	**integer**	Returns the value rounded to the nearest integer
trunc(argument)	**real**	**integer**	Returns the value truncated to an integer

◇ TABLE 2.8
Values of function expressions

Expression	Value
`sqr(2)`	4
`sqr(2.0)`	4.0
`sqr(-3)`	9
`sqrt(25.0)`	5.0
`sqrt(25)`	5.0
`sqrt(0.0)`	0.0
`sqrt(-2.0)`	Not permissible
`abs(5.2)`	5.2
`abs(-3.4)`	3.4
`abs(-5)`	5
`round(3.78)`	4
`round(8.50)`	9
`round(-4.2)`	–4
`round(-4.7)`	-5
`trunc(3.78)`	3
`trunc(8.5)`	8
`trunc(-4.2)`	–4
`trunc(-4.7)`	–4

Using Functions

When a function is invoked, it produces a value in much the same way that 3 + 3 produces 6. Thus, use of a function should be treated similarly to use of a constant or value of an expression. Since function calls are not complete Pascal statements, they must be used within some statement. Typical uses are in assignment statements

```
X := sqrt(16.0);
```

in output statements

```
writeln (abs(-8):20);
```

or in arithmetic expressions

```
X := round(3.78) + trunc(-4.1);
```

Arguments of functions can be expressions, variables, or constants. However, be sure the argument is always appropriate. For example

```
A := 3.2;
X := sqrt(trunc(A));
```

is appropriate, but

```
A := -3.2;
X := sqrt(trunc(A));
```

produces an error since **trunc**(–3.2) has the value –3 and **sqrt**(–3) is not a valid expression.

The following example illustrates how functions can be used in expressions.

EXAMPLE 2.4

Let's find the value of the following expression:

```
4.2 + round(trunc(2.0 * 3.1) + 5.3) - sqrt(sqr(-4.1));
```

The solution is

```
4.2 + round(trunc(2.0 * 3.1) + 5.3) - sqrt(sqr(-4.1))
                     ↓                        ↓
4.2 +    round(trunc(6.2)      + 5.3) - sqrt(16.81)
                  ↓                           ↓
4.2 +       round(6.0          + 5.3) -      4.1
                          ↓
4.2 +            round(11.3)          -      4.1
                     ↓
                     ↓
4.2 +                 11.0            -      4.1
          ↓
         15.2                         -      4.1
                           ↓
                          11.1
```

Character Functions

Ordering a character set requires associating an integer with each character. Data types ordered in some association with the integers are known as *ordinal data types.* Each integer is the ordinal of its associated character. Integers are therefore considered to be an ordinal data type. Character sets are also considered to be an ordinal data type, as shown in Table 2.9. In each case, the ordinal of the character appears to the left of the character. Real numbers are not an ordinal data type.

Using ASCII, as shown in Table 2.9, the ordinal of a capital a ('A') is 65, the ordinal of the character representing the arabic number one ('1') is 49, the ordinal of a blank (ƀ) is 32, and the ordinal of a lowercase a ('a') is 97.

Pascal provides several standard functions that have arguments of ordinal type. They are listed in Table 2.10 together with a related function **chr** that returns a character when called.

Again using the ASCII collating sequence shown in Table 2.9, we can determine the value of these functions, as shown in Table 2.11.

Variables and variable expressions can be used as arguments for functions. For example, if Ch is a **char** variable and the assignment statement

```
Ch := 'D';
```

is made, then **ord**(Ch) has the value 68.

◇ **TABLE 2.9**
ASCII ordering of a character set

Ordinal	Character	Ordinal	Character	Ordinal	Character
32	b̸	64	@	96	'
33	!	65	A	97	a
34	"	66	B	98	b
35	#	67	C	99	c
36	$	68	D	100	d
37	%	69	E	101	e
38	&	70	F	102	f
39	'	71	G	103	g
40	(	72	H	104	h
41	)	73	I	105	i
42	*	74	J	106	j
43	+	75	K	107	k
44	,	76	L	108	l
45	-	77	M	109	m
46	.	78	N	110	n
47	/	79	O	111	o
48	0	80	P	112	p
49	1	81	Q	113	q
50	2	82	R	114	r
51	3	83	S	115	s
52	4	84	T	116	t
53	5	85	U	117	u
54	6	86	V	118	v
55	7	87	W	119	w
56	8	88	X	120	x
57	9	89	Y	121	y
58	:	90	Z	122	z
59	;	91	[	123	{
60	<	92	\	124	|
61	=	93	]	125	}
62	>	94	^	126	~
63	?	95	_		

Note: Codes 00–31 and 127 are nonprintable control characters.

◇ **TABLE 2.10**
Function calls with ordinal arguments or character values

Function Call	Argument Type	Type of Result	Function Value
ord(argument)	Any ordinal type	**integer**	Ordinal corresponding to argument
pred(argument)	Any ordinal type	Same as argument	Predecessor of the argument
succ(argument)	Any ordinal type	Same as argument	Successor of the argument
chr(argument)	**integer**	**char**	Character associated with the ordinal of the argument

◇ TABLE 2.11
Values of character functions

Expression	Value
`ord('E')`	69
`ord('9')`	57
`ord(9)`	9
`ord('>')`	62
`pred('N')`	'M'
`pred('A')`	'@'
`succ('(')`	')'
`succ('!')`	'"'
`chr(74)`	'J'
`chr(32)`	'b̸'
`chr(57)`	'9'
`chr(59)`	';'
`chr(114)`	'r'

Now let's consider a short program that allows the use of the standard functions **ord, pred, succ,** and **chr.**

```
PROGRAM FunctionTest (output);

VAR
  Num : integer;
  Ch : char;

BEGIN
  Ch := 'C';
  writeln ('Ord of C is', ord(Ch):5);
  writeln ('Succ of C is', succ(Ch):4);
  writeln ('Pred of C is', pred(Ch):4);
  writeln ('Chr of 67 is', chr(67):4);
  Num := 0;
  writeln ('The ordinal of Num is ', ord(Num))
END.
```

When this program is run, the output is

```
Ord of C is   67
Succ of C is   D
Pred of C is   B
Chr of 67 is   C
The ordinal of Num is    0
```

You should obtain a complete list of the characters available and their respective ordinals for your local system. Note particular features, such as **succ**('R') is not 'S' when using EBCDIC and **chr**(n) is nonprintable for $n < 32$ or $n > 126$ when using ASCII.

One of the uses for functions **chr** and **ord** is to convert between uppercase and lowercase letters. Closely related is the conversion of a digit (entered as a **char** value) to its integer value. The next example shows how to convert an uppercase letter to lowercase. Other conversions are deferred to the exercises.

A NOTE OF INTEREST

Debugging or Sleuthing?

Investigating why programs don't work as expected requires ingenuity. The reason can be quite bizarre. To illustrate, consider two situations reported by Jon Bentley in *Communications of the ACM*.

1. "When a programmer used his new computer terminal, all was fine when he was sitting down, but he couldn't log in to the system when he was standing up. That behavior was 100 percent repeatable: he could always log in when sitting and never when standing."
2. "A banking system had worked for quite some time, but halted the first time it was used on international data. Programmers spent days scouring the code, but they couldn't find any stray command that would return control to the operating system."

What do you think are possible solutions? The answers are set forth in the programming problems for this chapter.

EXAMPLE 2.5

To show how functions **chr** and **ord** can be used to convert an uppercase letter to lowercase, let's assume our task is to convert the letter 'H' into the letter 'h'. Using the ASCII chart shown in Table 2.9, we first note that the ordinal of 'H' is 72. We subtract the ordinal of 'A' from this to obtain

```
ord('H') - ord('A')
```

which is

```
72 - 65 = 7
```

We now add the ordinal of 'a' to get

```
ord('H') - ord('A') + ord('a')
```

which yields

```
72 - 65 + 97 = 104
```

This is the ordinal of 'h'. It can be converted to the letter by using **chr.** Thus

```
chr(ord('H') - ord('A') + ord('a'))
```

produces the letter 'h'. In general, the following is sufficient for converting from uppercase to lowercase:

```
Lowercase := chr(ord(Uppercase) - ord('A') + ord('a'));
```

Note that if you always use the same ASCII ordering, –ord('A') + ord('a') could be replaced by the constant 32. If you choose to do this, it should be done in the **CONST** section. A typical definition is

```
CONST
  UpperToLowerShift = 32;
```

You would then write the Lowercase conversion as

```
Lowercase := chr(ord(Uppercase) + UpperToLowerShift);
```

EXERCISES 2.5

1. Find the value of each of the following expressions.
   a. `abs(-11.2) + sqrt(round(15.51))`
   b. `trunc(abs(-14.2))`
   c. `4 * 11 MOD (trunc(trunc(8.9) / sqrt(16)))`
   d. `sqr(17 DIV 5 * 2)`
   e. `-5.0 + sqrt(5 * 5 - 4 * 6) / 2.0`
   f. `3.1 * 0.2 - abs(-4.2 * 9.0 / 3.0)`

2. Write a test program that illustrates what happens when an inappropriate argument is used with a function. Be sure to include something like **ord**(15.3).

3. Two standard algebraic problems come from the Pythagorean theorem and the quadratic formula. Assume variables *a, b,* and *c* have been declared in a program. Write Pascal expressions that allow you to evaluate

a. the length of the hypotenuse of a right triangle

$(\sqrt{a^2 + b^2})$

b. both solutions to the quadratic formula

$$\frac{-b \pm \sqrt{b^2 - 4ac}}{2a}$$

4. Indicate whether the following are valid or invalid expressions. Find the value of each valid expression; explain why the others are invalid.

a. `-6 MOD (sqrt(16))`
b. `8 DIV (trunc(sqrt(65)))`
c. `sqrt(63 MOD 2)`
d. `abs(-sqrt(sqr(3) + 7))`
e. `sqrt(16 DIV (-3))`
f. `sqrt(sqr(-4))`
g. `round(14.38 * 10) / 10`

5. The standard function **round** permits you to round to the nearest integer. Write an expression that permits you to round the real number X to the nearest tenth.

6. Using ASCII, find the values of each of the following expressions.

a. `ord(13 + 4 MOD 3)`
b. `pred(succ('E'))`
c. `succ(pred('E'))`
d. `ord(5)`
e. `ord('5')`
f. `chr(ord('+'))`
g. `ord(chr(40))`

7. Assume the variable declaration section of a program is

```
VAR
  X : real;
  A : integer;
  Ch : char;
```

What output is produced by each of the following program fragments?

a.
```
X := -4.3;
writeln (X:6:2, abs(X):6:2, trunc(X):6, round(X):6);
```

b.
```
X := -4.3;
A := abs(round(X));
writeln (ord(A));
writeln (ord('A'));
```

c.
```
Ch := chr(76);
writeln (Ch:5, pred(Ch):5, succ(Ch):5);
```

8. Write a complete program to print each uppercase letter of the alphabet and its ordinal in the collating sequence used by your machine's version of Pascal.

9. Using ASCII, show how each of the following conversions can be made.

a. A lowercase letter converted to its uppercase equivalent.

b. A digit entered as a **char** value converted to its indicated numeric value.

10. For each of the following formulas, write the Pascal statement or statements necessary to produce the desired result.

a. Hypotenuse = $\sqrt{A^2 + B^2}$
(Pythagorean Theorem)

b. volume = $\frac{1}{3}\pi\, r^2 h$ (volume of a cone)

c. volume = $\frac{4}{3}\pi\, r^3$ (volume of a sphere)

The *Communication and Style Tips* following provides a quick reference to writing styles and suggestions. Such tips are intended to stimulate rather than terminate your imagination.

COMMUNICATION AND STYLE TIPS

1. Use descriptive identifiers. Words (Sum, Score, Average) are easier to understand than letters (A, B, C or X, Y, Z).
2. Constants can be used to create neat, attractive output. For example,

```
CONST
  Splats = '**************************************';
  Underline = '_________________________';
  Border = '*                            *';
```

3. Use the constant definition section to define an appropriately named blank, and use it to control line spacing for output. Thus, you could have

```
CONST
  Skip = ' ';
  Indent = ' ';
```

and then output statements could be

```
writeln (Skip:20, <message>, Skip:10, <message>);
```

or

```
writeln (Indent:20, <message>, Skip:10, <message>);
```

4. As you write Pascal statements, use blanks for line spacing within the program. Spacing between words and expressions should resemble typical English usage. Thus

```
PROGRAM EarlyBird (input, output);
```

is preferable to

```
PROGRAM    EarlyBird    (     input,      output    );
```

5. Output of a column of reals should have decimal points in a line.

```
 14.32
181.50
 93.63
```

6. Output can be made more attractive by using columns, left and right margins, underlining, and blank lines.
7. Extra **writelns** at the beginning and end of the executable section will separate desired output from other messages.

```
BEGIN
  writeln;
          .
          . (program body here)
          .
  writeln
END.
```

The *Focus on Program Design* sections contain complete programs to illustrate concepts developed in the chapter. In each case, a typical problem is stated, a solution is developed in pseudocode and illustrated with a structure chart, and module specifications are written for appropriate modules.

FOCUS ON PROGRAM DESIGN

Let's write a complete program to find the unit price for a pizza. Input for the program consists of the price and size of the pizza. Size is the diameter of the pizza ordered. Output consists of the price per square inch. A first-level development is

1. Get the data
2. Perform the computations
3. Print the results

A structure chart for this problem is given in Figure 2.1.

◆ FIGURE 2.1
Structure chart for the pizza problem

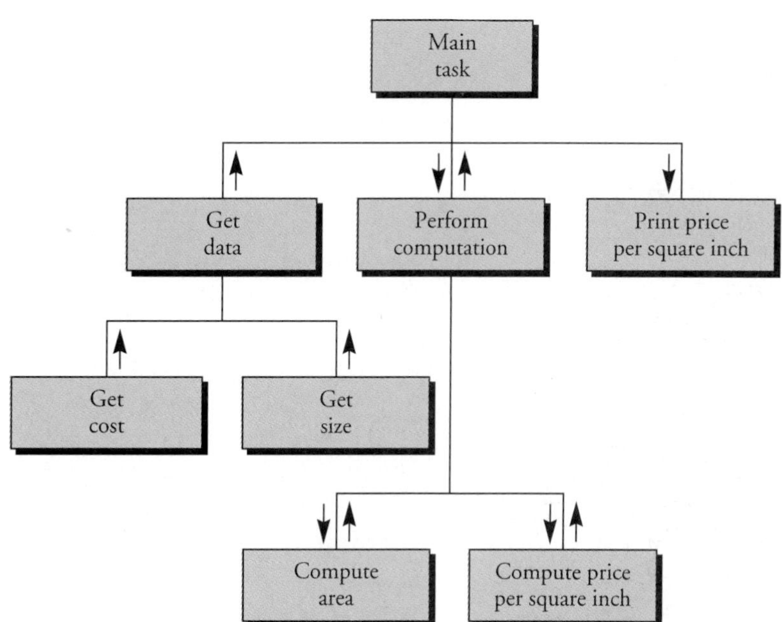

Module specifications for the main modules are

1. Get Data Module
Data received: None
Information returned: Price
Size
Logic: Have the user enter price and size.

2. Perform Computation Module
Data received: Price
Size
Information returned: Price per square inch
Logic: Given the diameter, find the radius.
Compute the area using Area = Pi * Radius * Radius.
Price per square inch is found by dividing Price by Area.

3. Print Results Module
   Data received: PricePerSquareInch
   Information returned: None
   Logic: Print the price per square inch.

A further refinement of the pseudocode produces

1. Get the data
   1.1 get price
   1.2 get size
2. Perform the computations
   2.1 compute area
   2.2 calculate unit price

Step 3 of the pseudocode, "Print the results" only requires printing the price per square inch, so no further development is required.

A complete program for this is

```
PROGRAM PizzaCost (input, output);

CONST
  Pi = 3.14;

VAR
  Size, Radius, Cost, Area,
  PricePerSquareInch : real;

BEGIN

  {  This module gets the data.  }
  writeln ('Enter the pizza price and press <Enter>.');
  readln (Cost);                                              1
  writeln ('Enter the pizza size and press <Enter>.');
  readln (Size);

  {  This module computes the unit price.  }
  Radius := Size / 2;                                         2
  Area := Pi * sqr(Radius);
  PricePerSquareInch := Cost / Area;

  {  This module prints the results.  }
  writeln ('The price per square inch is $',                  3
           PricePerSquareInch:4:2)
END.
```

A sample run of this program yields

```
Enter the pizza price and press <Enter>.
10.50
Enter the pizza size and press <Enter>.
16
The price per square inch is $0.05
```

SUMMARY

Key Terms

argument
assignment statement
batch processing
batch input
binary notation
cancellation error
character set
collating sequence: ASCII, EBCDIC
constant
expression
input
input statement
integer arithmetic operations: +, −, *, **MOD, DIV**
integer overflow
interactive input
interactive program
invoke (call)
memory location
mixed-mode expression
ordinal data type
overflow
precedence rule
prompt
real arithmetic operations: +, −, *, /
real overflow
representational error
round-off error
self-documenting code
standard (built-in) function
underflow
user-friendly
variable
word

Keywords

abs
chr
DIV
MOD
ord
pred
read
readln
round
sqr
sqrt
succ
trunc

Key Concepts

- Operations and priorities for data of types **integer** and **real** are summarized as follows:

Data Type	Operations	Priority
integer	*, **MOD, DIV**	1. Evaluate in order from left to right.
	+, −,	2. Evaluate in order from left to right.
real	*, /	1. Evaluate in order from left to right.
	+, −	2. Evaluate in order from left to right.

- Mixed-mode expressions return values of type **real.**
- Priority for order of operations on mixed-mode expressions is
  1. *, /, **MOD, DIV** in order from left to right
  2. +, − in order from left to right
- Real overflow is caused by a value too large for computing on a particular machine.
- Underflow is caused by a value too small (close to zero) for computing. These numbers are automatically replaced by zero.
- Round-off errors, representational errors, and cancellation errors are possible when working with data of type **real.**
- A memory location can have a name that can be used to refer to the contents of the location.
- The name of a memory location is different from the contents of the memory location.
- Self-documenting code includes the use of descriptive identifiers.
- Assignment statements are used to assign values to memory locations; for example

```
Sum := 30 + 60;
```

- Variables and variable expressions can be used in output statements.
- The **read(ln)** statement is used to get data; correct form is

  read(ln) (<variable name>);
  read(ln) (<variable 1>, <variable 2>, . . . , <variable *n*>);
- The **read(ln)** (<variable name>) statement causes a value to be transferred to the variable location.
- Interactive input expects data items to be entered from the keyboard at appropriate times during execution of the program.
- Data types for variables in a **read** or **readln** statement should match data items read as input.
- Appropriate uses for constants in the **CONST** definition section include frequently used numbers, current values subject to change over time (for example, MinimumWage = 4.25), and character strings for output.
- Character strings are formatted using a single colon.
- Five standard numeric functions available in Pascal are **abs**, **round**, **sqr**, **sqrt** and **trunc**.
- Functions can be used in assignment statements

  ```
  X := sqrt(16.0);
  ```
  in output statements
  ```
  writeln (abs(-8):20);
  ```
  and in arithmetic expressions
  ```
  round(3.78) + trunc(-4.1);
  ```
- Four standard character functions available in Pascal are **chr**, **ord**, **pred**, and **succ**.

A NOTE OF INTEREST

Debugging or Sleuthing: Answers

1. "The problem was in the terminal's keyboard: the tops of two keys were switched. When the programmer was seated, he was a touch-typist and the problem went unnoticed, but when he stood, he was led astray by hunting and pecking."

2. "When [the programmers] observed the behavior more closely, they found that the problem occurred as they entered data for the country of Ecuador: when the user typed the name of the capital city (Quito), the program interpreted that as a request to quit the run!"

PROGRAMMING PROBLEMS AND PROJECTS

Write a complete Pascal program for each of the following problems. Each program should use one or more **readln** statements to obtain necessary values. Input statements should be preceded by an appropriate prompting message.

1. Susan purchases a computer for $985. The sales tax on the purchase is 5.5 percent. Compute and print the total purchase price.
2. Find and print the area and perimeter of a rectangle that is 4.5 feet long and 2.3 feet wide. Print both rounded to the nearest tenth of a foot.
3. Compute and print the number of minutes in a year.
4. Light travels at $3 * 10^8$ meters per second. Compute and print the distance that a light beam would travel in one year. (This is called a light year.)
5. The 1927 New York Yankees won 110 games and lost 44. Compute their winning percentage, and print it rounded to three decimal places.

6. A 10-kilogram object is traveling at 12 meters per second. Compute and print its momentum. (Momentum is mass times velocity.)
7. Convert 98.0 degrees Fahrenheit to degrees Celsius.
8. Given a positive number, print its square and square root.
9. The Golden Sales Company pays its salespeople \$0.27 for each item they sell. Given the number of items sold by a salesperson, print the amount of pay due.
10. Given the length and width of a rectangle, print its area and perimeter.
11. The kinetic energy of a moving object is given by

$$KE = \frac{1}{2}mv^2$$

Given the mass m and the speed v of an object, find its kinetic energy.
12. Miss Lovelace wants you to write a program to enable her to balance her checkbook. She wishes to enter a beginning balance, five letters for an abbreviation for the recipient of the check, and the amount of the check. Given this information, write a program that will find the new balance in her checkbook.
13. Write an interactive program that allows the user to enter three real numbers and then have the output display the numbers, their sum, and their average.
14. A supermarket wants to install a computerized weighing system in its produce department. Input to this system will consist of a three-letter identifier for the type of produce, the weight of the produce purchase (in pounds), and the cost per pound of the produce. A typical input screen would be

```
Enter each of the following:

Description <Enter>
ABC
Weight <Enter>
2.0
Cost/lb. <Enter>
1.98
```

Print a label showing the input information along with the cost of the purchase. The label should appear as follows:

```
%%%%%%%%%%%%%%%%%%%%%%%%%%%%%%%%%%%%%%%%%%%

          Penny Spender Supermarket
              Produce Department

  ITEM       WEIGHT        COST/lb      COST
   ABC       2.0 lb         $1.98       $3.96

                  Thank You!

%%%%%%%%%%%%%%%%%%%%%%%%%%%%%%%%%%%%%%%%%%%
```

15. The New-Wave Computer Company sells its product, the NW-PC, for \$675. In addition, it sells memory-expansion cards for \$69.95, disk drives for \$198.50, and software for \$34.98 each. Given the number of memory cards, disk drives, and software packages desired by a customer purchasing an NW-PC, print out a bill of sale that appears as follows:

```
****************************
     New Wave Computers

   ITEM                COST
1  NW-PC            $675.00
2  Memory card       139.90
1  Disk drive        198.50
4  Software          139.92
                    -------
      TOTAL        $1153.32
```

16. Write a test program that allows you to see the characters contained within the character set of your computer. Given a positive integer, you can use the **chr** function to determine the corresponding character. On most computers, only integers less than 255 are valid. Also, remember that most character sets contain some unprintable characters, such as ASCII values less than 32. Print your output in the form

```
Character number nnn is x.
```

17. Mr. Vigneault, a coach at Shepherd High School, is working on a program that can be used to assist cross-country runners in analyzing their times. As part of the program, a coach enters elapsed times for each runner, given in units of minutes, seconds, and hundredths. In a 5000 meter (5K) race, elapsed times are entered at the one-mile and two-mile marks. These elapsed times are then used to compute "splits" for each part of the race (that is, how long it takes a runner to run each of the three race segments).

    Write a complete program that will accept as input three times, given in units of minutes, seconds, and hundredths, and then produce output that includes the split for each segment. A typical input screen would be

```
Runner number              234
Mile times: 1              5:34.22
            2             11:21.67
Finish time:              17:46.85
```

Typical output would be

```
Runner number              234
Split one                  5:34.22
Split two                  5:47.45
Split three                6:25.18
Finish time               17:46.85
```

18. The Swim-More Pool Installation Company installs rectangular swimming pools surrounded by a cement edge that extends three feet from each side of the pool. The cement is poured to a uniform depth of four inches. Write a program that accepts as input the dimensions of the pool and then provides as output the number of cubic yards of cement needed along with the total cost of the cement. Use the constant definition section to define the price per yard. Contact a local cement company to obtain the current price.

COMMUNICATION IN PRACTICE

1. Modify one of the programs you have written for this chapter by changing all constant and variable identifiers to single-letter identifiers. Exchange your modified program with another student who has done the same thing. After reading

the exchanged program, discuss the use of meaningful identifiers with the other student. Suggest identifiers for the program you are reading.

2. Remove all documentation from a program you have written for this chapter. Exchange this version with another student who has done the same thing. Write documentation for the exchanged program. Compare your documentation with that originally written for the program. Discuss the differences and similarities with the other student.
3. Many (but not all) instructors in beginning computer science courses encourage their students to use meaningful identifiers when writing code. It is natural to wonder to what extent this practice is followed outside the educational world. Investigate this issue by contacting several programmers who work for nearby companies. Prepare a complete written report of your conversations for distribution to class members. Include charts that summarize your findings.

CHAPTER

3 Subprograms: Procedures and Functions for Problem Solving

CHAPTER OUTLINE

Recall from Section 1.3 the process of solving a problem by stepwise refinement of tasks into subtasks. This top-down design method is especially suitable for writing Pascal programs to solve problems using subprograms.

This concept is not difficult to understand. A *subprogram* is a program within a program and is provided by most programming languages. Each subprogram should complete some task, the nature of which can range from simple to complex.

3.1 Program Design

OBJECTIVES

- to understand the concepts of modularity and bottom-up testing
- to be aware of the use of structured programming

Modularity

We have previously discussed and illustrated the process of solving a problem by top-down design. Using this method, we divide the main task into major subtasks and then continue to divide the subtasks (stepwise refinement) into smaller subtasks until all subtasks can be easily performed. Once an algorithm for solving a problem has been developed using top-down design, the programmer then writes code to translate the general solution into a Pascal program.

Code written to perform one well-defined subtask is referred to as a module. The programmer should be able to design, code, and test each module in a program independently from the rest of the program. In this sense, a module is a subprogram containing all definitions and declarations needed to perform the indicated subtask. Everything required for the subtask (but not needed in other parts of the program) can be created in the subprogram. Consequently, the definitions and declarations have meaning only when the module is being used.

A program that has been created using modules to perform various tasks is said to possess *modularity.* In general, modular programs are easier to test, debug, and correct than programs that are not modular because each independent module can be tested by running it from a test driver. Then, once the modules are running correctly, they can become part of a longer program. This independent testing of modules is referred to as *bottom-up testing.*

Structured Programming

Structured programming is the process of developing a program in which emphasis is placed upon the communication between independent modules. Connections between these modules are specified in parameter lists and are usually controlled by the main

A NOTE OF INTEREST

Structured Programming

From 1950 to the early 1970s, programs were designed and written on a linear basis. A program written and designed on such a basis can be called an unstructured program. Structured programming, on the other hand, organizes a program around separate, semi-independent modules that are linked together by a single sequence of simple commands.

In 1964, mathematicians Corrado Bohm and Guiseppe Jacopini proved that any program logic, regardless of complexity, can be expressed by using sequence, selection, and iteration. This result is termed the structure theorem. Combined with the efforts of Edger W. Dijkstra, this result led to a significant move toward structured programming and away from the use of **GOTO** statements.

In fact, in a letter to the editor of *Communications of the ACM* (Volume 11, March 1968), Dijkstra stated that the **GOTO** statement "should be abolished from all 'higher level' programming languages . . . . [The **GOTO** statement] is just too primitive; it is too much an invitation to make a mess of one's program."

The first time structured programming concepts were applied to a large-scale data processing application was the IBM Corporation's "New York Times Project" from 1969 to 1971. Using these techniques, programmers posted productivity figures four to six times higher than those of the average programmer. In addition, the error rate was a phenomenally low 0.0004 per line of coding.

program. Structured programming is especially suitable for large programs that are worked on by teams. By carefully designing the modules and specifying what information is to be received by and returned from each module, a team of programmers can independently develop their module and then connect it to the complete program.

The remainder of this chapter is devoted to an examination of how subprograms can be written to accomplish specific tasks. There are two types of subprograms in standard Pascal: procedures and functions. First, we will examine the writing and use of procedures. Then we will learn how to write user-defined functions. (We discussed built-in functions in Section 2.5).

3.2 Procedures as Subprograms

OBJECTIVES

- to be aware of some uses of procedures
- to be aware of differences in procedures
- to understand the form of a procedure
- to be able to use a procedure in a program
- to be able to use correct form and syntax when writing a procedure
- to understand the difference between variable and value parameters
- to understand the difference between formal and actual parameters
- to be able to use a procedure in a program

A *procedure* can be used as a subprogram for many purposes. Two significant uses are to facilitate the top-down design philosophy of problem solving and to avoid having to write repeated segments of code.

Procedures facilitate problem solving. Recall the Focus on Program Design problem in Chapter 2. In that problem, you were asked to compute the unit cost for a pizza. The main modules were

1. Get the data
2. Perform the computations
3. Print the results

A procedure can be written for each of these tasks, and the program can then call each procedure as needed. Thus, the main portion of the program would have the form

```
BEGIN  {  Main program  }
  GetData (<parameter list>);
  PerformComputations (<parameter list>);
  PrintResults (<parameter list>)
END.  {  of main program  }
```

This makes it easy to see and understand the main tasks of the program.

Before you learn how to write procedures and recognize the significance of the "parameter list" in the previous program segment, a few comments are in order. First, once you develop the ability to write and use subprograms, you will usually write programs by writing the main program first. Your main program should be written so it can be easily read by a nonprogrammer but still contains enough structure to enable a programmer to know what to do if asked to write code for the tasks. In this sense, it is not necessary for a person reading the main program to understand *how* a subprogram accomplishes its task; it need only be apparent *what* the subprogram does.

Second, we should briefly consider the problem of data flow. The most difficult aspect of learning to use subprograms is handling the transmission of data. Recall from the structure charts used earlier that arrows indicate if data are received by and/or sent from a module. Also, each module specification indicates if data are received by that module and if information is sent from it. Since a subprogram will be written to accomplish the task of each module, we must be able to transmit data as indicated. Once you have developed this ability, using procedures and functions becomes routine.

Form and Syntax

Procedures are placed in the declaration section of the main program. The form for a procedure is

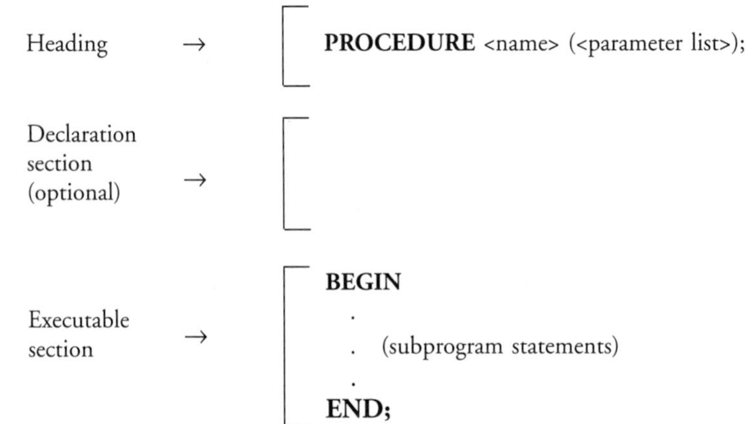

The syntax diagram is

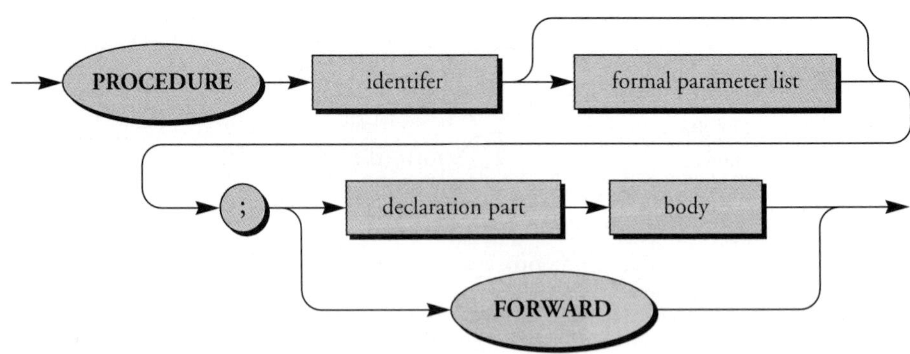

Procedures without Parameters

Some procedures are written without parameters because they require no data transmission to or from the main program or any other subprogram. Typically, these procedures print headings or closing messages for output. For example, suppose you are writing a program for Our Lady of Mercy Hospital and you wish the billing statement for each patient to have the heading

```
////////////////////////////////////////
/                                      /
/       Our Lady of Mercy Hospital     /
/       --------------------------     /
/                                      /
/           1306 Central City          /
/          Phone (416) 333-5555        /
/                                      /
////////////////////////////////////////
```

A procedure DisplayHeading can be written to print this message, and you can then call it from the main program when needed by

```
  DisplayHeading;
```

The procedure to perform this task follows.

```
PROCEDURE DisplayHeading;

  CONST
    Marks = '////////////////////////////////////////';
    Edge = '/                                      /';
    Skip = ' ';

  BEGIN
    writeln;
    writeln (Skip:10, Marks);
    writeln (Skip:10, Edge);
    writeln (Skip:10, '/', Skip:7,
             'Our Lady of Mercy Hospital', Skip:6, '/');
    writeln (Skip:10, '/', Skip:7,
             '--------------------------', Skip:6, '/');
    writeln (Skip:10, Edge);
    writeln (Skip:10, '/', Skip:11, '1306 Central City',
             Skip:11, '/');
    writeln (Skip:10, '/', Skip:10, 'Phone (416) 333-5555',
             Skip:9, '/');
    writeln (Skip:10, Edge);
    writeln (Skip:10, Marks);
    writeln
  END;  {  of PROCEDURE DisplayHeading  }
```

Parameters

Parameters are used so values of variables may be transmitted (or passed) from the main program to the procedure and from the procedure to the main program. If values are to be passed only from the main program to the procedure, the parameters are called *value parameters.* If values are to be changed in the procedure and passed back from the procedure to the main program, the parameters are called *variable parameters.*

When using parameters with procedures, the following should be noted.

1. The number and order of parameters in the parameter list contained in the procedure heading must match the number and order of variables or values used when calling the procedure from the main program.
2. The type of parameters must match the corresponding type of variables or values used when calling the procedure.
3. The parameter types are declared in the procedure heading.

Parameters contained in a procedure are *formal parameters.* Formal parameters can be thought of as blanks in the heading of the procedure waiting to receive values from the parameters in a calling program. Parameters contained in the procedure call from the main program are *actual parameters.* Actual parameters are also referred to as arguments.

To illustrate formal and actual parameters used with procedures, consider the following complete program.

```
PROGRAM ProcDemo (output);

VAR
  Num1, Num2 : integer;
  Num3 : real;

{*************************************************}

PROCEDURE PrintNum (N1, N2 : integer; N3 : real);
  BEGIN
    writeln;
    writeln ('Number 1 = ', N1:3);
    writeln ('Number 2 = ', N2:3);
    writeln ('Number 3 = ', N3:6:2)
  END;  {  of PROCEDURE PrintNum  }

{*************************************************}

BEGIN  {  Main program  }
  Num1 := 5;
  Num2 := 8;
  Num3 := Num2 / Num1;
  PrintNum (Num1, Num2, Num3)
END.  {  of main program  }
```

When this program is run, the output is

```
Number 1 =    5
Number 2 =    8
Number 3 =    1.60
```

In this program, N1, N2, and N3 are formal parameters and Num1, Num2, and Num3 are actual parameters. Now let's examine the relationship between the parameter list in the procedure

```
PROCEDURE PrintNum (N1, N2 : integer; N3 : real);
```

and the procedure call in the main program

```
PrintNum (Num1, Num2, Num3)
```

In this case, Num1 corresponds to N1, Num2 corresponds to N2, and Num3 corresponds to N3. Notice both the number and type of variables in the parameter list correspond to the number and type of variables listed in the procedure call.

Value Parameters

The preceding procedure demonstrates the use of value parameters or of one-way transmission of values. Different memory areas have been set aside for the variables Num1, Num2, and Num3 and for N1, N2, and N3. Thus, initially we have

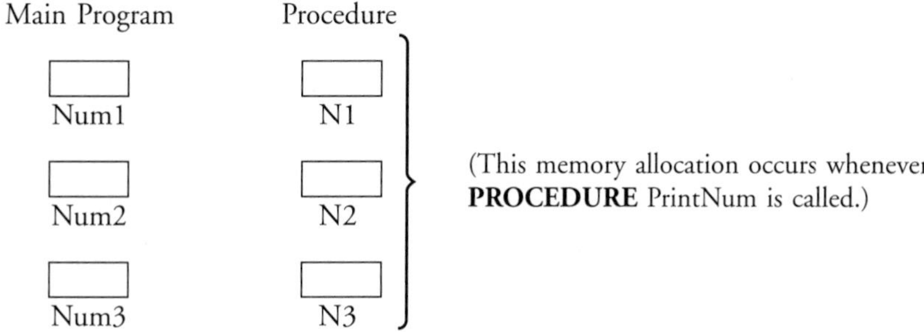

The assignment statements

```
Num1 := 5;
Num2 := 8;
Num3 := Num2 / Num1;
```

produce

Main Program	Procedure
5	
Num1	N1
8	
Num2	N2
1.6	
Num3	N3

When the procedure PrintNum is called from the main program by

```
PrintNum (Num1, Num2, Num3)
```

the values are transmitted to N1, N2, and N3, respectively, as follows:

Main Program	Procedure
5	5
Num1	N1
8	8
Num2	N2
1.6	1.6
Num3	N3

At this stage, **PROCEDURE** PrintNum can use N1, N2, and N3 in any appropriate manner.

These parameters are value parameters because values are passed from the main program to the procedure only. If the procedure changes the value of N1, N2, or N3, the corresponding value of Num1, Num2, or Num3 will not be changed. For example, suppose the procedure is changed to

```
PROCEDURE PrintNum (N1, N2 : integer; N3 : real);
  BEGIN
    writeln;
    writeln (N1:10, N2:10, N3:10:2);
```

```
    N1 := 2 * N1;
    N2 := 2 * N2;
    N3 := 2 * N3;
    writeln (N1:10, N2:10, N3:10:2);
    writeln
  END;  { of PROCEDURE PrintNum  }
```

Furthermore, suppose the main program is changed to

```
BEGIN  {  Main program  }
  Num1 := 5;
  Num2 := 8;
  Num3 := Num2 / Num1;
  writeln;
  writeln (Num1:10, Num2:10, Num3:10:2);
  PrintNum (Num1, Num2, Num3);
  writeln (Num1:10, Num2:10, Num3:10:2);
  writeln
END.  {  of main program  }
```

When this program is run, the output is

```
         5         8      1.60      (from main program)
         5         8      1.60      (from procedure)
        10        16      3.20      (from procedure)
         5         8      1.60      (from main program)
```

The first line of this output is produced by the first

```
writeln (Num1:10, Num2:10, Num3:10:2);
```

of the main program. The next two lines of output result from the procedure. The last line of output is produced by the second

```
writeln (Num1:10, Num2:10, Num3:10:2);
```

of the main program. You should carefully note that although the procedure changes the values of N1, N2, and N3, the values of Num1, Num2, and Num3 in the main program do not change. Thus, we have

Main Program	Procedure
5 Num1	10 N1
8 Num2	16 N2
1.6 Num3	3.2 N3

Variable Parameters

You will frequently want a procedure to change values in the main program. This can be accomplished by using variable parameters in the parameter list. Variable parameters are declared by placing the reserved word **VAR** before appropriate formal parameters in the procedure heading. This causes all of the formal parameters listed between **VAR** and the subsequent data type to be variable parameters. If value parameters of the same type are needed, they must be listed elsewhere. A separate **VAR** declaration is needed for each data type used when listing variable parameters. The use of **VAR** in a parameter list is slightly different than its use in the declaration of variables, but it is the same reserved word.

When variable parameters are declared, transmission of values appears to be two-way rather than one-way; that is, values are sent from the main program to the procedure and from the procedure to the main program. Actually, when variable parameters are used, values are not transmitted at all. Variable parameters in the procedure heading are merely aliases for actual variables used in the main program. Thus, variables are said to be *passed by reference* rather than by value. When variable parameters are used, any change of values in the procedure produces a corresponding change of values in the main program.

To illustrate the declaration of variable parameters, consider the procedure heading

```
PROCEDURE PrintNum (VAR N1, N2 : integer; N3 : real);
```

In this case, N1 and N2 are variable parameters corresponding to integer variables in the main program; N3 is a value parameter corresponding to a real variable. This procedure can be called from the main program by

```
PrintNum (Num1, Num2, Num3);
```

To illustrate the passing of values, assume the procedure is

```
PROCEDURE PrintNum (VAR N1, N2 : integer; N3 : real);
  BEGIN
    writeln (N1:5, N2:5, N3:10:2);
    N1 := 2 * N1;
    N2 := 2 * N2;
    N3 := 2 * N3;
    writeln (N1:5, N2:5, N3:10:2)
  END;  {  of PROCEDURE PrintNum  }
```

If the corresponding variables in the main program are Num1, Num2, and Num3, respectively, we initially have

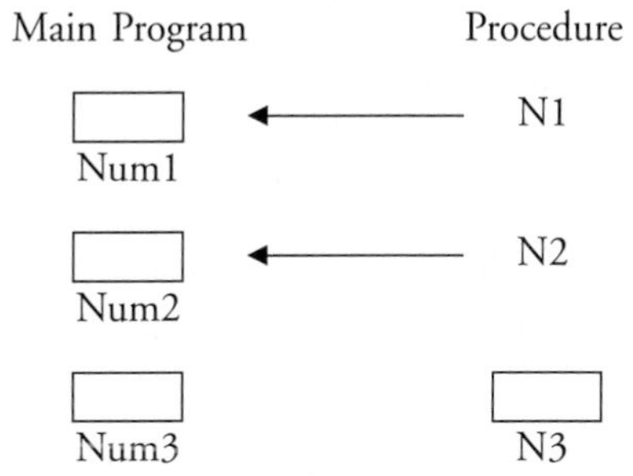

Main Program		Procedure
[ ] Num1	←	N1
[ ] Num2	←	N2
[ ] Num3		[ ] N3

Technically, N1 and N2 do not exist as variables. They contain pointers to the same memory locations as Num1 and Num2, respectively. Thus, a statement in the procedure such as

```
N1 := 5;
```

causes the memory location reserved for Num1 to receive the value 5; that is, it causes the net action

```
Num1 := 5;
```

Constants cannot be used when calling a procedure with variable parameters. For example

```
PrintNum (3, 4, 5);
```

produces an error because 3 and 4 correspond to variable parameters.

If the main program makes the assignment statements

```
Num1 := 5;
Num2 := 8;
Num3 := Num2 / Num1;
```

we have

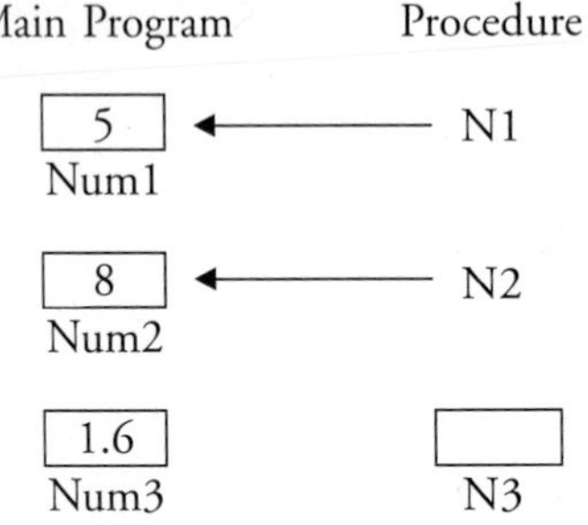

When the procedure is called by

```
PrintNum (Num1, Num2, Num3);
```

we have

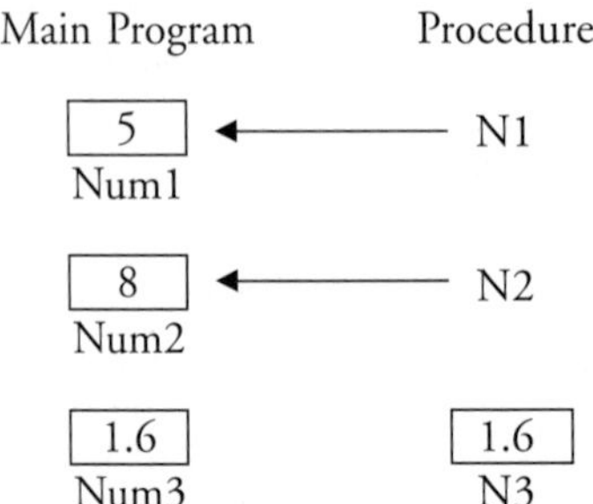

When the statements from the procedure

```
N1 := 2 * N1;
N2 := 2 * N2;
N3 := 2 * N3;
```

are executed, we have

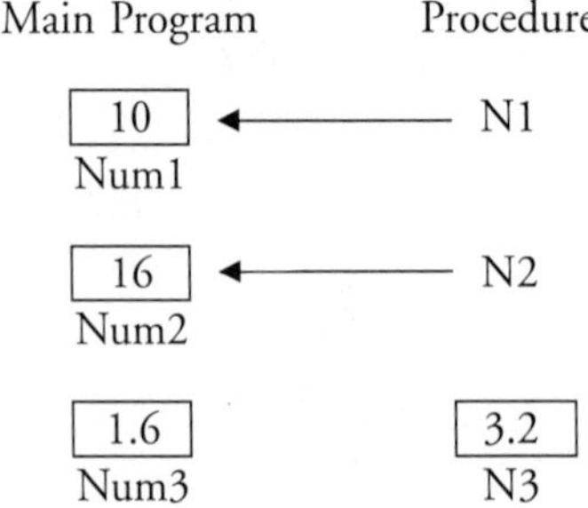

Notice the variable parameters N1 and N2 produce changes in the corresponding variables in the main program but the value parameter N3 does not.

Now let's consider a short, complete program that illustrates the difference between variable and value parameters. In this program (and throughout the text), the graphic documentation that accompanies the program highlights the way in which parameters are passed between the main program and the procedure.

```
PROGRAM ProcDemo2 (output);

VAR
  X, Y : real;
  Ch : char;

{*********************************************}

PROCEDURE DemonstrateVAR (VAR X1 : real;
                          Y1 : real;
                          VAR Ch1 : char);
  BEGIN
    writeln (X1:10:2, Y1:10:2, Ch1:5);
    X1 := 2 * X1;
    Y1 := 2 * Y1;
    Ch1 := '*';
    writeln (X1:10:2, Y1:10:2, Ch1:5)
  END;  {  of PROCEDURE DemonstrateVAR  }

{*********************************************}

BEGIN  {  Main program  }
  X := 3.6;
  Y := 5.2;
  Ch := 'A';
  writeln (X:10:2, Y:10:2, Ch:5);
  DemonstrateVAR (X, Y, Ch);
  writeln (X:10:2, Y:10:2, Ch:5)
END.  {  of main program  }
```

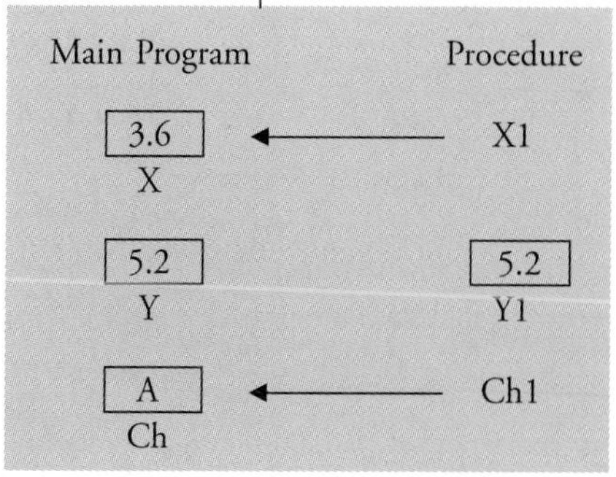

Main Program		Procedure
[3.6] X	←	X1
[5.2] Y		[5.2] Y1
[A] Ch	←	Ch1

The output from the program is

```
3.60      5.20    A      (from main program)
3.60      5.20    A      (from procedure)
7.20     10.40    *      (from procedure)
7.20      5.20    *      (from main program)
```

The variables can be depicted as

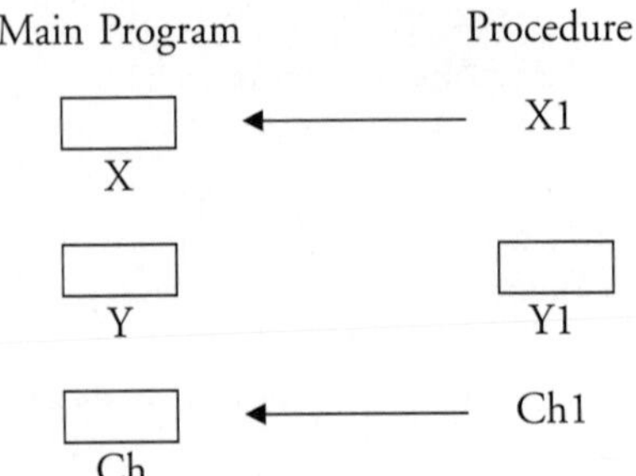

The assignment statements

```
X := 3.6;
Y := 5.2;
Ch := 'A';
```

then produce

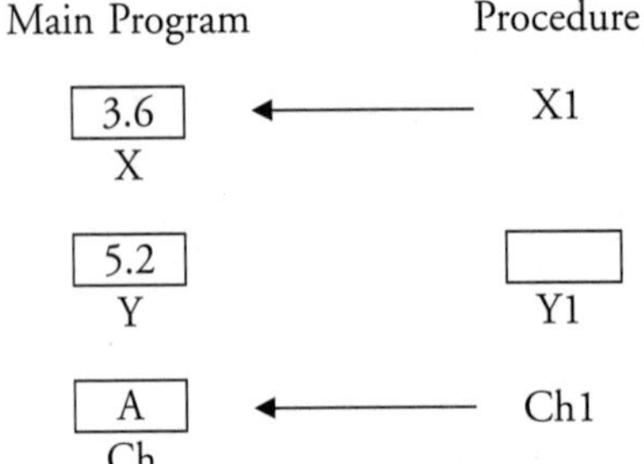

When the procedure is called by

```
DemonstrateVAR (X, Y, Ch);
```

the contents can be envisioned as

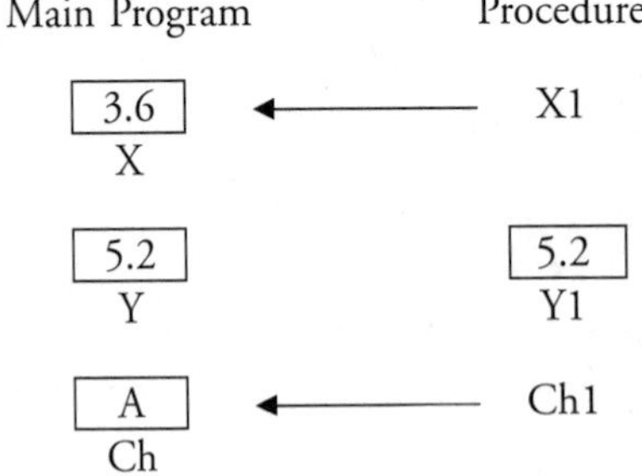

When the procedure assignment statements

```
X1 := 2 * X1;
Y1 := 2 * Y1;
Ch1 := '*';
```

are executed, the variables become

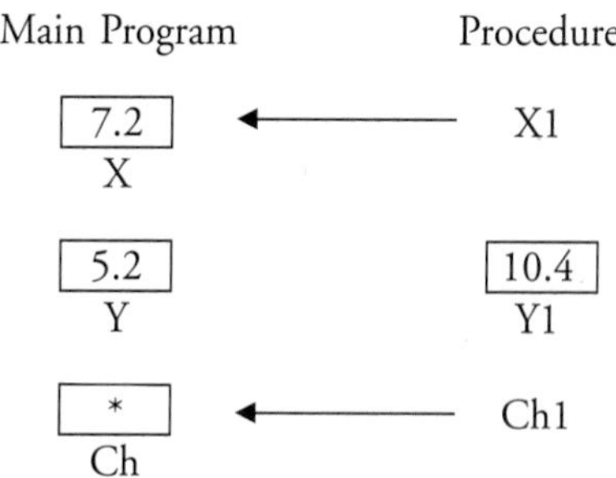

Notice changes in the variable parameters X1 and Ch1 produce corresponding changes in X and Ch but a change in the value parameter Y1 does not produce a change in Y.

Side Effects

A *side effect* is an unintentional change in a variable that results from some action taken in a program. Side effects are frequently caused by the misuse of variable parameters. Since any change in a variable parameter causes a change in the corresponding actual parameter in the calling program or procedure, you should use variable parameters only when your intent is to produce such changes. In all other cases, use value parameters.

To illustrate how a side effect can occur, suppose you are working with a program that computes the midterm and final grades for students in a class. For the midterm grade, Quiz 1 and Quiz 2 are doubled and then added to Test 1. Using variable parameters in a procedure for this yields

```
PROCEDURE ComputeMidTerm (VAR Q1, Q2, T1 : integer);
  BEGIN
    Q1 := 2 * Q1;
    Q2 := 2 * Q2;
     .
     .      (rest of procedure)
     .
```

When this procedure is called from the main program by

```
ComputeMidTerm (Quiz1, Quiz2, Test1);
```

the values in Quiz1 and Quiz2 will be changed. This was probably not the intent when ComputeMidTerm was called. This unwanted side effect can be avoided by making Q1 and Q2 value parameters. The procedure heading then becomes

```
PROCEDURE ComputeMidTerm (Q1, Q2, T1 : integer);
```

Cohesive Subprograms

The cohesion of a subprogram is the degree to which the subprogram performs a single task. A subprogram that is developed in such a way is called a *cohesive subprogram.* As you use subprograms to implement designs based on modular development, you should always try to write cohesive subprograms.

The property of cohesion is not well defined. Subtask complexity varies in the minds of different programmers. In general, if the task is unclear, the corresponding subprogram will not be cohesive. When this happens, you should subdivide the task until a subsequent development allows cohesive subprograms.

To briefly illustrate the concept of cohesion, consider the first-level design of a problem to compute grades for a class. Step 3 of this design could be

3. Process grades for each student

Clearly, this is not a well-defined task. Thus, a subprogram written for this task would not be cohesive. When we look at the subsequent development of this step

3. Process grades for each student
   - 3.1 get a line of data
   - 3.2 compute average
   - 3.3 compute letter grade
   - 3.4 print data
   - 3.5 compute totals

we see that the procedures to accomplish subtasks 3.1, 3.2, 3.3, and 3.4 will be cohesive because each subtask consists of a single task. Subtask 3.5, compute totals, may or may not result in a cohesive subprogram. More information is needed before we can decide what is to be done at this step.

Procedural Abstraction

The purpose of using procedures is to simplify reasoning. During the design stage, as a problem is subdivided into tasks, the problem solver (you) should have to consider only "what" a procedure is to do and not "how" the procedure accomplishes the task. The name and comments at the beginning of the procedure should be sufficient to inform the user as to what the procedure does. Developing procedures in this manner is referred to as *procedural abstraction.*

Procedural abstraction is the first step in designing and writing a procedure. The list of parameters and comments about the action of the procedure should be written before the procedure body. This forces clarity of thought and facilitates program design. Using this method may cause you to discover your design is not sufficient to solve the task and redesign is necessary. Therefore, you could reduce design errors and save time when writing code.

Procedural abstraction becomes especially important when teams work on a project. Each member of the writing team should be able to understand the purposes and uses of procedures written by other team members without having to analyze the body of each procedure. This is analogous to the situation in which you use a predefined function without really understanding how the function works.

Procedural abstraction is perhaps best formalized in terms of preconditions and postconditions. A *precondition* is a comment that states precisely what is true before a certain action is taken. A *postcondition* states what is true after the action has been taken. Carefully written preconditions and postconditions used in conjunction with procedures enhance the concept of procedural abstraction. (Additional uses of preconditions and postconditions are discussed in Sections 4.6 and 5.4.)

In summary, procedural abstraction means that when writing or using procedures, you should think of them as single, clearly understood units, each of which accomplishes a specific task.

Encapsulation

Encapsulation is the process of placing all implementation details in a distinct physical package. This process is closely related to the use of procedural abstraction in designing a problem solution. Procedural abstraction separates what a procedure does from how it is done. Developing the implementation details of a procedure, including everything necessary to accomplish the task of the procedure as part of the procedure, is referred to as encapsulation.

Encapsulation is a key concept in object-oriented programming (OOP). Programming languages that support object-oriented programming enforce encapsulation to differing degrees. Standard Pascal does not support object-oriented programming. See *A Note of Interest* features on pages 28, 555, and 573.

Interface and Documentation

Independent subprograms, whether they are procedures or functions, need to communicate with the main program and with other subprograms. A formal statement about how such communication occurs is called the *interface* of the subprogram. An interface usually consists of comments at the beginning of a subprogram and includes all the documentation the reader will need to use the subprogram. This information typically consists of

1. What is received by the subprogram when it is called
2. What task the subprogram performs
3. What is returned after the subprogram performs its task
4. How the subprogram is called

This information aids in debugging programs. In this text, our interface consists of the three-part documentation section

```
{  Given:   <Statement of information sent from the program>  }
{  Task:    <Statement of task(s) to be performed>             }
{  Return:  <Statement of value(s) returned to the program>    }
```

The headings of subprograms in complete programs are given in this manner. When subprograms are separately developed and illustrated, this documentation is not included; instead, text development immediately preceding the subprogram serves the same purpose. How a subprogram is called is usually apparent from the identifiers listed in the subprogram heading.

Software Engineering Implications

Perhaps the greatest difference between beginning students in computer science and real-world programmers is how the need for documentation is perceived. Typically, beginning students want to make a program run; they view anything that delays this process as an impediment. Thus, some students consider using descriptive identifiers, writing variable dictionaries, describing a problem as part of program documentation, and using appropriate comments throughout a program as bothersome. In contrast, system designers and programmers, who write code for a living, often spend up to 50 percent of their time and effort on documentation.

There are at least three reasons for this difference in perspective. First, real programmers work on large, complex systems with highly developed logical paths. Without proper documentation, even the person who develops an algorithm will have difficulty following its underlying logic six months later. Second, communication between and among teams is required as systems are developed. Complete, clear statements about what the problems are and how they are being solved are essential communication tools. And third, programmers are trained to develop algorithms and write subsequent code; to them, problems of searching, sorting, and file manipulation are routine. Knowing they can solve a problem allows them to devote more time and energy to documenting how to achieve the problem solution.

We close this section with a revision of the program in Chapter 2 that finds the unit cost for a pizza. The structure chart is shown in Figure 3.1.

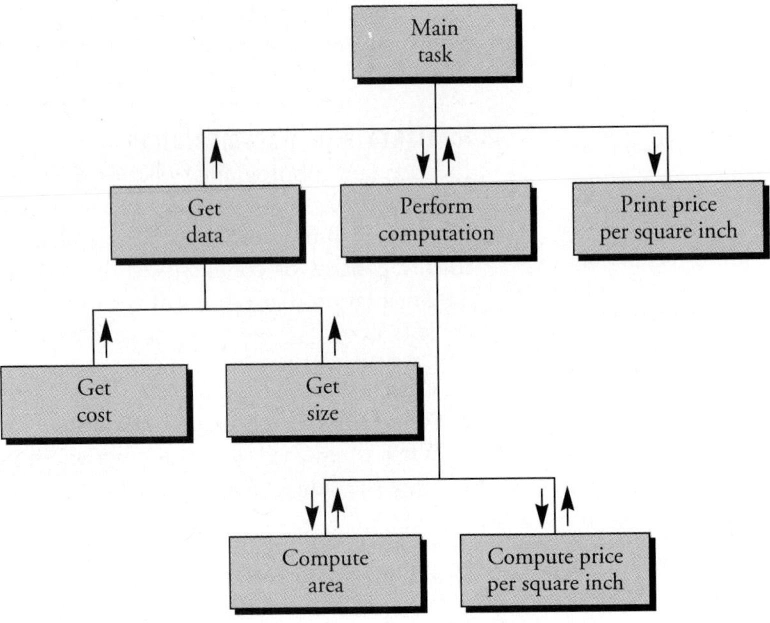

◆ **FIGURE 3.1**
Structure chart for the pizza problem

The module specifications are

1. GetData Module
   Data received: None
   Information returned: Cost
   Size
   Logic: Have the user enter cost and size.
2. PerformComputations Module
   Data received: Cost
   Size
   Information returned: Price per square inch
   Logic: Given the diameter, find the radius.
   Compute the area using Area = Pi * sqr(Radius).
   Price per square inch is found by dividing Cost by Area.
3. PrintResults Module
   Data received: PricePerSquareInch
   Information returned: None
   Logic: Print the price per square inch.

A procedure for getting the data requires two variable parameters—one for the size and one for the cost—since these values will be returned to the main program. This procedure is

```
PROCEDURE GetData (VAR PizzaCost : real;
                   VAR PizzaSize : integer);
  BEGIN
    writeln ('Enter the pizza price and press <Enter>.');
    readln (PizzaCost);
    writeln ('Enter the pizza size and press <Enter>.');
    readln (PizzaSize)
  END;  {  of PROCEDURE GetData  }
```

Now let's write a procedure for performing the desired computations. (Later we will learn how this task can be done with a function instead of a procedure.) This procedure receives the Cost and Size and then returns the PricePerSquareInch. Thus, Cost and Size are value parameters and PricePerSquareInch is a variable parameter. This procedure also requires the variables Radius and Area to be declared in the declaration section of the procedure. Assuming Pi has been defined as a constant, the procedure is

```
PROCEDURE PerformComputations (PizzaCost : real;
                               PizzaSize : integer;
                               VAR PricePerSqInch : real);
  VAR
    Radius, Area : real;
  BEGIN
    Radius := PizzaSize / 2;
    Area := Pi * sqr(Radius);
    PricePerSqInch := PizzaCost / Area
  END;  {  of PROCEDURE PerformComputations  }
```

Finally, a procedure to print the results receives the unit cost. Thus, a value parameter is declared and the procedure is

```
PROCEDURE PrintResults (PricePerSqInch : real);
  BEGIN
    writeln;
    write ('The price per square inch is $');
    writeln (PricePerSqInch:6:2)
  END;  {  of PROCEDURE PrintResults  }
```

With these procedures written, the main program becomes

```
BEGIN  {  Main program  }
  GetData (Cost, Size);
  PerformComputations (Cost, Size, PricePerSquareInch);
  PrintResults (PricePerSquareInch)
END.  {  of main program  }
```

The complete program for this problem follows.

```
PROGRAM Pizza (input, output);

CONST
  Pi = 3.14159;

VAR
  Cost, PricePerSquareInch : real;
  Size : integer;

{*********************************************************}

PROCEDURE GetData (VAR PizzaCost : real;
                   VAR PizzaSize : integer);
  BEGIN
    writeln;
    writeln ('Enter the pizza price and press <Enter>.');     1
    readln (PizzaCost);
    writeln ('Enter the pizza size and press <Enter>.');
    readln (PizzaSize)
  END;  {  of PROCEDURE GetData  }
```

```
{*************************************************************}

PROCEDURE PerformComputations (PizzaCost : real;
                               PizzaSize : integer;
                               VAR PricePerSqInch : real);
  VAR
    Radius, Area : real;
  BEGIN
    Radius := PizzaSize/2;
    Area := Pi * sqr(Radius);
    PricePerSqInch := PizzaCost/Area
  END;  {  of PROCEDURE PerformComputations  }
```

2

```
{*************************************************************}

PROCEDURE PrintResults (PricePerSqInch : real);
  BEGIN
    writeln;
    write ('The price per square inch is $');
    writeln (PricePerSqInch:6:2)
  END;  {  of PROCEDURE PrintResults  }
```

3

```
{*************************************************************}

BEGIN  {  Main program  }
  GetData (Cost, Size);
```

Main Program	PROCEDURE GetData
10.5 ← Cost	PizzaCost
16 ← Size	PizzaSize

```
  PerformComputations (Cost, Size, PricePerSquareInch);
```

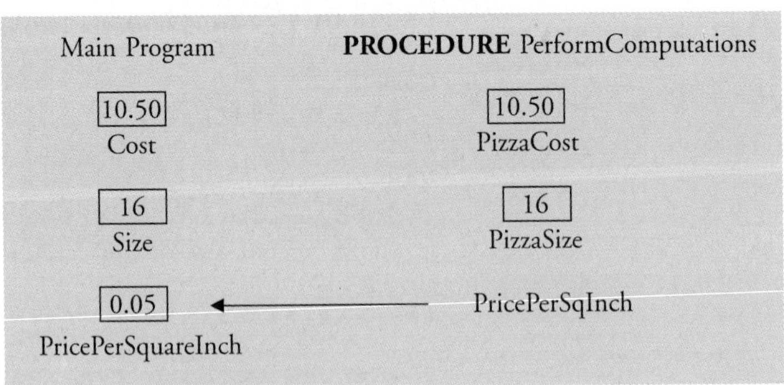


```
  PrintResults (PricePerSquareInch)
```

Main Program	PROCEDURE PrintResults
0.05	0.05
PricePerSquareInch	PricePerSqInch

```
END.  {  of main program  }
```

Sample runs of this program produce

```
Enter the pizza price and press <Enter>.
10.50
Enter the pizza size and press <Enter>.
16

The price per square inch is $  0.05

Enter the pizza price and press <Enter>.
8.75
Enter the pizza size and press <Enter>.
14

The price per square inch is $  0.06
```

EXERCISES 3.2

1. Explain the difference between value parameters and variable parameters. Between formal parameters and actual parameters.
2. Write a test program to find out what happens if the parameter lists do not match when a procedure is called from the main program. Investigate each of the following.
   a. Correct number of parameters in wrong order
   b. Incorrect number of parameters
3. Indicate which of the following parameters are variable parameters and which are value parameters.

   a.
   ```
   PROCEDURE Demo1 (VAR A, B : integer;
                    X : real);
   ```
   b.
   ```
   PROCEDURE Demo2 (VAR A : integer;
                    B : integer;
                    VAR X : real;
                    Ch : char);
   ```
   c.
   ```
   PROCEDURE Demo3 (A, B : integer;
                    VAR X, Y, Z : real;
                    Ch : char);
   ```
4. Indicate which of the following are appropriate procedure headings. Explain what is wrong with those that are inappropriate.

   a.
   ```
   PROCEDURE Prac1 (A : integer : Y : real);
   ```
   b.
   ```
   PROCEDURE Error? (Ch1, Ch2 : char);
   ```
   c.
   ```
   PROCEDURE Prac2 (A, VAR B : integer);
   ```
   d.
   ```
   PROCEDURE Prac3 (A, B, C : integer
                    VAR X, Y : real
                    Ch : char);
   ```
   e.
   ```
   PROCEDURE Prac4 (VAR A : integer,
                    X : real);
   ```
5. Indicate how each of the following procedures would be called from the main program.

   a.
   ```
   PROCEDURE Prob5 (A, B : integer;
                    Ch : char);
   ```
   b.
   ```
   PROCEDURE PrintHeader;
   ```

c.
```
PROCEDURE FindMax (N1, N2 : integer;
                   VAR NewMax : integer);
```
d.
```
PROCEDURE Switch (VAR X, Y : real);
```

6. Suppose a program contains the following procedure.

```
PROCEDURE Switch (VAR A, B : integer);
  VAR
    Temp : integer;
  BEGIN
    Temp := A;
    A := B;
    B := Temp
  END;  { of PROCEDURE Switch  }
```

Indicate what output is produced by each of the following fragments of code in the main program.

a.
```
Num1 := 5;
Num2 := 10;
writeln (Num1, Num2);
Switch (Num1, Num2);
writeln (Num1, Num2);
Switch (Num1, Num2);
writeln (Num1, Num2);
```
b.
```
N := 3;
M := 20;
Switch (M, N);
writeln (M, N);
Switch (N, M);
writeln (N, M);
```

7. Write a procedure for each of the following, and indicate how it would be called from the main program.

a. Print the heading for the output.

```
Acme National Electronics
   Board of Directors
     Annual Meeting
```

b. Find the maximum and the average of three reals. Both values are to be returned to the main program.

c. Convert Fahrenheit temperature to Celsius temperature.

8. Assume a program contains the variable declaration section

```
VAR
  Num1, Num2 : integer;
  X, Y : real;
  Ch1, Ch2 : char;
```

Further suppose the same program contains the procedure heading

```
PROCEDURE Demo (VAR N1, N2 : integer;
                X1 : real;
                Ch : char);
```

Indicate which of the following are appropriate calls to **PROCEDURE** Demo. Explain why the others are inappropriate.

a. `Demo (Num1, Num2);`
b. `Demo (Num1, Num2, X);`
c. `Demo (Num1, Num2, X, Ch1);`
d. `Demo (X, Y, Num1, Ch2);`
e. `Demo (Num2, X, Y, Ch1);`
f. `Demo (Num1, Num2, Ch2);`
g. `Demo;`
h. `Demo (Num2, Num1, Y, Ch1);`

3.3 Scope of Identifiers

OBJECTIVES

- to understand what is meant by local identifiers
- to understand what is meant by global identifiers
- to understand the scope of an identifier
- to recognize appropriate and inappropriate uses of global identifiers
- to be able to use appropriate names for local and global identifiers

Global and Local Identifiers

Identifiers that declare variables in the declaration section of a program can be used throughout the entire program. For the purposes of this discussion, we will think of the program as a *block* and of each subprogram as a *subblock* or block for the subprogram. Each block may contain a parameter list, a local declaration section, and the body of the block. A program block for **PROGRAM** ShowScope may be envisioned as shown in Figure 3.2. Furthermore, if X1 is a variable in ShowScope, we indicate this as shown in Figure 3.3, where an area in memory has been set aside for X1. When a program contains a subprogram, a separate memory area within the memory area for the program is set aside for the subprogram to use during execution. Thus, if ShowScope contains a procedure named Subprog1, we can envision this as shown in Figure 3.4. If Subprog1 contains the variable X2, we have the program shown in Figure 3.5.

FIGURE 3.2
Program heading and main block

FIGURE 3.3
Variable location in main block

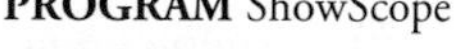
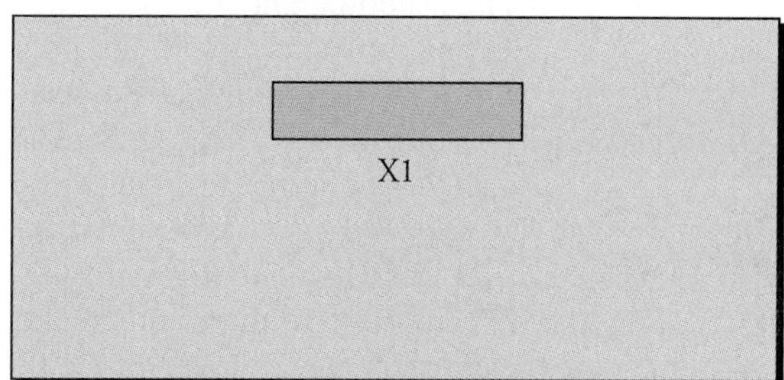

FIGURE 3.4
Illustration of a subblock

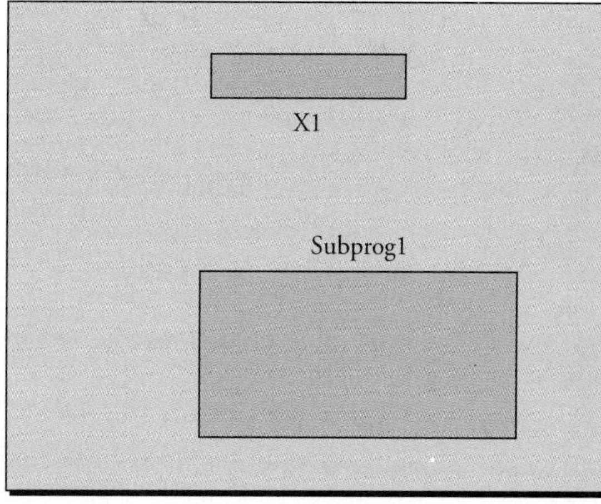

◆ **FIGURE 3.5**
Variable location within a subblock

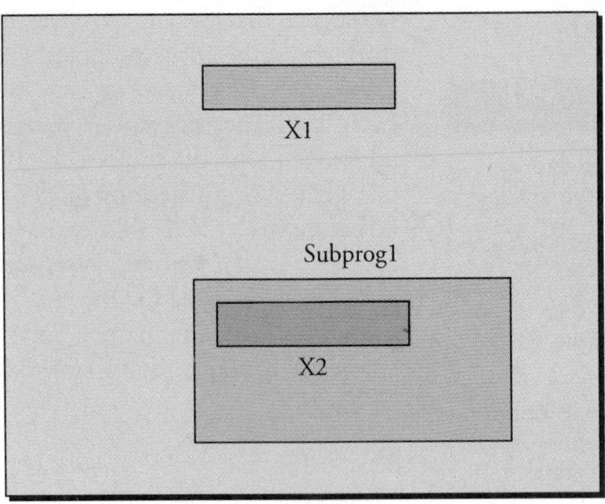

This could be indicated in the program by

```
PROGRAM ShowScope (input, output);

VAR
  X1 : real;

PROCEDURE Subprog1 (X2 : real);
```

The *scope of an identifier* refers to the block in which it is declared or defined. When subprograms are used, each identifier is available only to the block in which it is declared; this includes all subprograms contained within the block of the subprogram. Identifiers are not available outside their blocks.

Identifiers that are declared in the main block are called *global identifiers* (or *global variables*); identifiers that are restricted to use within a subblock are called *local identifiers* (or *local variables*). Variable X1 in Figure 3.5 can be used in the main program and in **PROCEDURE** Subprog1; therefore, it is a global identifier. On the other hand, variable X2 can be used only within the procedure where it is declared; it is a local identifier. Any attempt to reference X2 outside the procedure will result in an error. Identifiers used in blocks in which they are not declared are said to be *nonlocal* to the block.

Figure 3.6 illustrates the scope of identifiers. In this figure, the scope of X3 is **PROCEDURE** Inner, the scope of X2 is **PROCEDURE** Outer, and the scope of X1 is **PROGRAM** ShowScope. When procedures are nested like this, the scope of an identifier is the largest block in which it is declared.

Now let's examine an illustration of local and global identifiers. Consider the program and procedure declaration

```
PROGRAM ScopePrac (output);

VAR
  A, B : integer;

PROCEDURE Subprog (A1 : integer);
  VAR
    X : real;
```

Blocks for this program can be envisioned as shown in Figure 3.7.

◆ FIGURE 3.6
Scope of identifiers

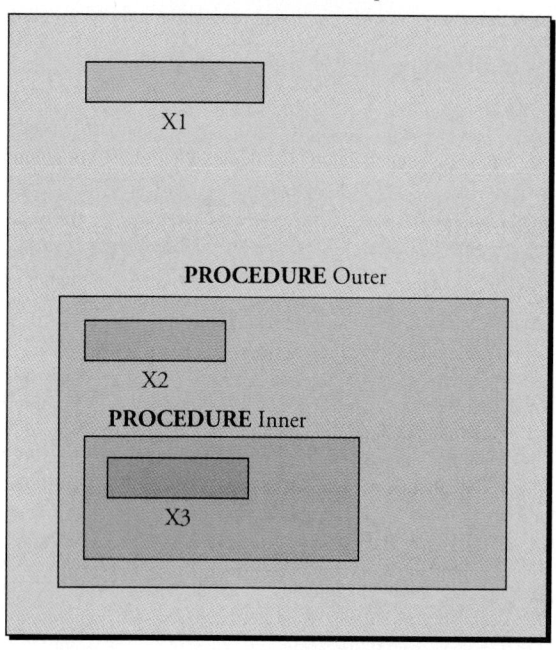

◆ FIGURE 3.7
Relation of identifiers for **PROGRAM** ScopePrac

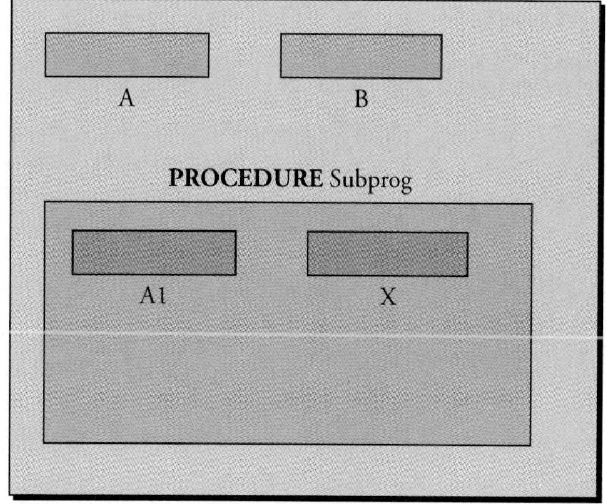

Since A and B are global identifiers, the statement

```
writeln (A, B, A1, X:10:2);
```

could be used in **PROCEDURE** Subprog even though A and B are not specifically declared there. However, this statement could not be used in the main program because A1 and X are local to **PROCEDURE** Subprog.

A NOTE OF INTEREST

Computer Ethics: Hacking and Other Intrusions

A famous sequence of computer intrusions was originally detailed by Clifford Stoll. The prime intruder came to Stoll's attention in August 1986, when he attempted to penetrate a computer at Lawrence Berkeley Laboratory (LBL). Instead of denying the intruder access, management at LBL went along with Stoll's recommendation that they attempt to unmask the intruder, even though the risk was substantial because the intruder had gained system-manager privileges.

Markus H., a member of a small group of West Germans, was an unusually persistent intruder but no computer wizard. He made use of known deficiencies in the half-dozen or so operating systems, including UNIX, VMS, VM-TSO, and EMBOS, with which he was familiar, but he did not invent any new modes of entry. He penetrated 30 of the 450 computers then on the network system at LBL.

After Markus H. was successfully traced, efforts were instituted to make LBL's computers less vulnerable. To insure high security, it would have been necessary to change all passwords overnight and recertify each user. This and other demanding measures were deemed impractical. Instead, deletion of all expired passwords was instituted; shared accounts were eliminated; monitoring of incoming traffic was extended, with alarms set in key places; and education of users was attempted.

The episode was summed up by Stoll as a powerful learning experience for those involved in the detection process and for all those concerned about computer security. That the intruder was caught at all is a testimony to the ability of a large number of concerned professionals to keep the tracing effort secret.

In a later incident, an intruder left the following embarrassing message in the computer file assigned to Clifford Stoll: "The cuckoo has egg on his face." The reference is to Stoll's book, *The Cuckoo's Egg*, which tracks the intrusions of the West German hacker just described. The embarrassment was heightened by the fact that the computer, owned by Harvard University, with which astronomer Stoll is now associated, is on the Internet network. The intruder, or intruders, under the name of Dave, also attempted to break into dozens of other computers on the same network—and succeeded.

The "nom de guerre" Dave was used by one or more of three Australians recently arrested by the federal police down under. The three, who at the time of the arrest were 18, 20, and 21 years of age, successfully penetrated computers in both Australia and the United States.

The three Australians went beyond browsing to damage data in computers in their own nation and in the United States. At the time they began their intrusions in 1988 (when the youngest was only 16), there was no law in Australia under which they could be prosecuted. It was not until legislation making such intrusions prosecutable was passed that the police began to take action.

Using Global Variables and Constants

In general, it is not good practice to refer to global variables within procedures. Using locally defined variables helps to avoid unexpected side effects and protects your programs. In addition, locally defined variables facilitate debugging and top-down design and enhance the portability of procedures. These factors are especially important if a team is developing a program and different people are working on different procedures.

Using global constants is different. Since constant values cannot be changed by a procedure, it is preferable that constants be defined in the **CONST** section of the main program and then be used whenever needed by any subprogram. This is especially important if the constant is subject to change over time (for example, StateTaxRate). When a change is necessary, one change in the main program is all that is needed to make all subprograms current. If a constant is used in only one procedure (or function), some programmers prefer to define it near the point of use (in the subprogram in which it is used).

Name of Identifiers

Since separate areas in memory are set aside when subprograms are used, it is possible to have identifiers with the same name in both the main program and a subprogram. Thus

```
PROGRAM Demo (input, output);

VAR
  Age : integer;

PROCEDURE Subprog (Age : integer);
```

can be envisioned as shown in Figure 3.8.

◆ FIGURE 3.8
Using identifiers in subprograms

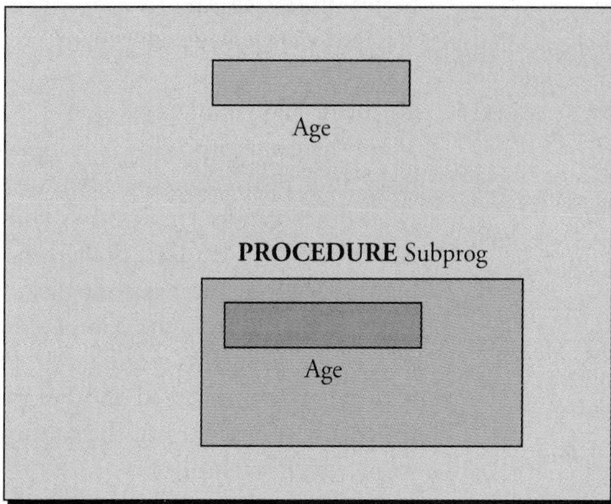

When the same name is used in this manner, any reference to this name results in action being taken as locally as possible. Thus, the assignment statement

```
Age := 20;
```

made in **PROCEDURE** Subprog assigns 20 to Age in the procedure but not to Age in the main program (see Figure 3.9).

◆ FIGURE 3.9
Assigning a value to a subprogram

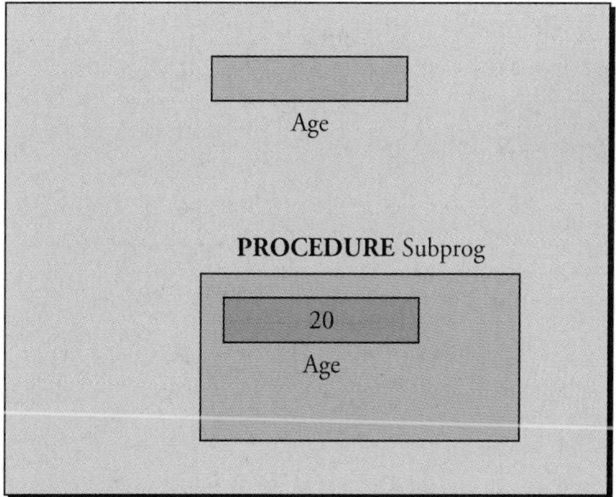

Now that you know you can use the same name for an identifier in a subprogram and in the main program, the question is, "Should you?" There are two schools of thought regarding this issue. If you use the same name in the procedures as you do in the main program, it facilitates matching parameter lists and independent development of procedures. However, this practice can be confusing when you first start working with subprograms. Thus, some instructors prefer using different, but related, identifiers. For example

```
GetData (Score1, Score2);
```

in the main program could have a procedure heading of

```
PROCEDURE GetData (VAR PScore1, PScore2 : integer);
```

where the letter P denotes an identifier in the procedure. Although this may facilitate better understanding in early work with subprograms, it is less conducive to portability and independent development of procedures. Both styles are used in this text.

Multiple Procedures

More than one procedure can be used in a program. When this occurs, all the previous uses and restrictions of identifiers apply to each procedure. Blocks for multiple procedures can be depicted as shown in Figure 3.10. Identifiers in the main program can be accessed by each procedure. However, local identifiers in the procedures cannot be accessed outside their blocks.

When a program contains several procedures, they can be called from the main part of the program in any order. Procedures can be called from the main program only if they are not nested in another procedure. If one procedure contains a call to another procedure (or function), the subprogram being called must appear before the procedure from which it is called.

The same names for identifiers can be used in different procedures. Thus, if the main program uses the variables Wage and Hours and both of these variables are used as arguments in calls to different procedures, we have the situation shown in Figure 3.11.

◆ **FIGURE 3.10**
Blocks for multiple subprograms

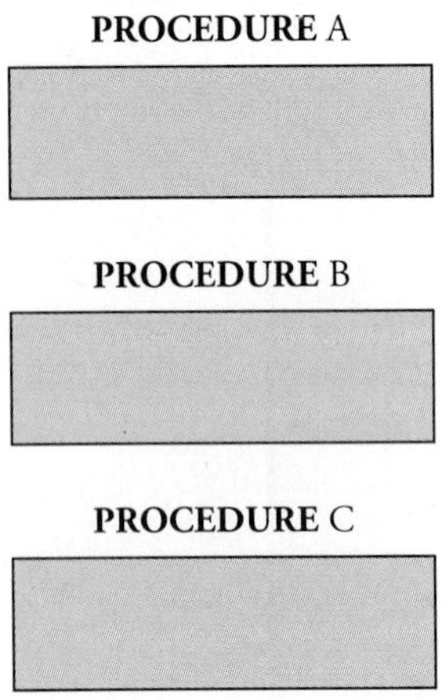

PROCEDURE A

PROCEDURE B

PROCEDURE C

◆ **FIGURE 3.11**
Identifiers in multiple subprograms

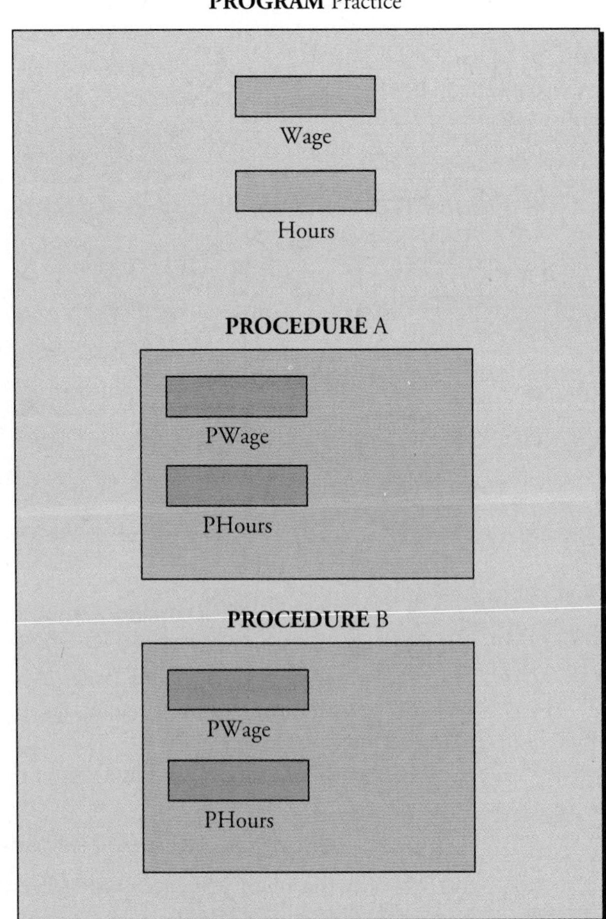

Using the same names for identifiers in different procedures makes it easier to keep track of the relationship among variables in the main program and their associated parameters in each subprogram.

EXERCISES 3.3

1. Explain the difference between local identifiers and global identifiers.
2. State the advantages of using local identifiers.
3. Discuss some appropriate uses of global identifiers. List several constants that would be appropriate global definitions.
4. What is meant by the scope of an identifier?
5. Write a test program that will enable you to see:
   a. What happens when an attempt is made to access an identifier outside its scope.
   b. How the values change as a result of assignments in the subprogram and in the main program when the same identifier is used in the main program and in a procedure.
6. Review the following program.

```
PROGRAM Practice (input, output);

VAR
  A, B : integer;
  X : real;
  Ch : char;

PROCEDURE Sub1 (A1 : integer);
  VAR
    B1 : integer;
  BEGIN
    .
    .
    .
  END;  {  of PROCEDURE Sub1  }

PROCEDURE Sub2 (A1 : integer;
                VAR B1 : integer);
  VAR
    X1 : real;
    Ch1 : char;
  BEGIN
    .
    .
    .
  END;  {  of PROCEDURE Sub2  }
```

   a. List all global variables.
   b. List all local variables.
   c. Indicate the scope of each identifier.
7. Provide a schematic representation of the program and all subprograms and variables in Exercise 6.

8. Using the program with the variables and subprograms depicted in Figure 3.12, state the scope of each identifier.

◆ FIGURE 3.12

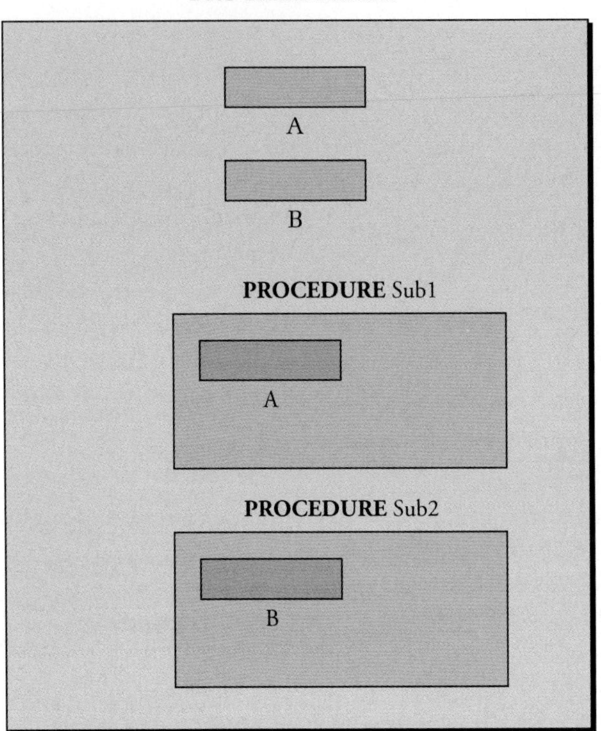

9. What output is produced from the following program?

```
PROGRAM Exercise9 (output);

VAR
  A : integer;

PROCEDURE Sub1 (A : integer);
  BEGIN
    A := 20;
    writeln (A)
  END;  {  of PROCEDURE Sub1  }

PROCEDURE Sub2 (VAR A : integer);
  BEGIN
    A := 30;
    writeln (A)
  END;  {  of PROCEDURE Sub2  }

BEGIN  {  Main program  }
  A := 10;
  writeln (A);
  Sub1 (A);
  writeln (A);
  Sub2 (A);
  writeln (A)
END.  {  of main program  }
```

10. Review the following program.

```
PROGRAM ExerciseTen (output);

VAR
  Num1, Num2, : integer;

PROCEDURE Change (X : integer;
                  VAR Y : integer);
  VAR
    Num2 : integer;
  BEGIN
    Num2 := X;
    Y := Y + Num2;
    X := Y
  END;

BEGIN
  Num1 := 10;
  Num2 := 7;
  Change (Num1, Num2);
  writeln (Num1, Num2)
END.
```

a. What output is produced by the program as written?

Determine the output of the program if the following procedure headings are substituted.

b. `PROCEDURE Change (VAR X : integer; Y : integer);`

c. `PROCEDURE Change (X, Y : integer);`

d. `PROCEDURE Change (VAR X, Y : integer);`

11. Assume the variable declaration section of a program is

```
VAR
  Age, Hours : integer;
  Average : real;
  Initial : char;
```

Further assume procedure headings and declaration sections for procedures in this program are as follows. Find all errors in each.

a.
```
PROCEDURE Average (Age1, Hrs : integer;
                   VAR Aver : real);
```

b.
```
PROCEDURE Sub1 (Hours : integer;
                VAR Average : real);
  VAR
    Age : integer;
    Init : char;
```

c.
```
PROCEDURE Compute (Hrs : integer;
                   VAR Aver : real);
  VAR
    Age : real;
```

12. Write appropriate headings and declaration sections for the program and subprograms illustrated in Figure 3.13.

◆ FIGURE 3.13

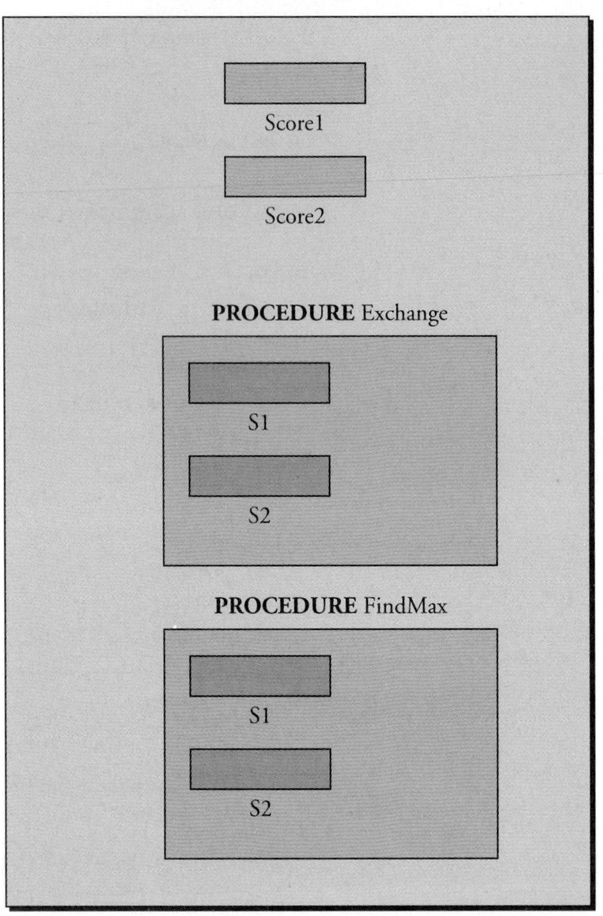

13. Find all errors in the following program.

```
PROGRAM Exercise13 (output);

VAR
  X, Y : real;

PROCEDURE Sub1 (VAR X1 : real);
  BEGIN
    writeln (X1:20:2);
    writeln (X:20:2);
    writeln (Y:20:2)
  END;  {  of PROCEDURE Sub1  }

BEGIN  {  Main program  }
  X := 10.0;
  Y := 2 * X;
  writeln (X:20:2, Y:20:2);
  Sub1 (X);
  writeln (X1:20:2);
  writeln (X:20:2);
  writeln (Y:20:2)
END.  {  of main program  }
```

14. Discuss the advantages and disadvantages of using the same name for an identifier in a subprogram and an identifier in the main program.

3.4 User-Defined Functions

OBJECTIVES

- to be able to use the correct form and syntax for writing a function
- to be able to call a function from the main program
- to be able to write a function to perform a specific task

The standard functions **sqr, sqrt, abs, round,** and **trunc** were introduced in Section 2.5. To briefly review, some concepts to note when using these functions are

1. An argument is required for each; thus, **sqrt**(Y) and **abs**(−21) are appropriate.
2. Standard functions can be used in expressions; for example

```
X := sqrt(Y) + sqrt(Z);
```

3. Standard functions can be used in output statements; for example

```
writeln (sqr(3):8);
```

Need for User-Defined Functions

It is relatively easy to envision the need for functions that are not on the list of standard functions available in Pascal. For example, if you must frequently cube numbers, it would be convenient to have a function Cube so you could make an assignment such as

```
X := Cube(Y);
```

Other examples from mathematics include an exponential function (x^Y) and computing a factorial ($n!$), computing a discriminant ($b^2 - 4ac$), and finding the roots of a quadratic equation $\left(\frac{-b \pm \sqrt{b^2-4ac}}{2a}\right)$.

In business, a motel manager might need to have a function available to determine a customer's bill given the number in the party, the length of stay, and any telephone charges. Similarly, a hospital administrator might need a function to compute the room charge for a patient given the type of room (private, ward, and so on) and various other options, including telephone (yes or no) and television (yes or no). Functions such as these are not standard functions. However, in Pascal, we can create *user-defined functions* to perform these tasks.

Form of User-Defined Functions

A user-defined function is a subprogram and, as such, is part of the declaration section of the main (or calling) program. It has the components

Heading →

Declaration section →

Executable section →

The general form of a function heading is

FUNCTION <function name> (<parameter list>) : <return type>

A syntax diagram for a function is

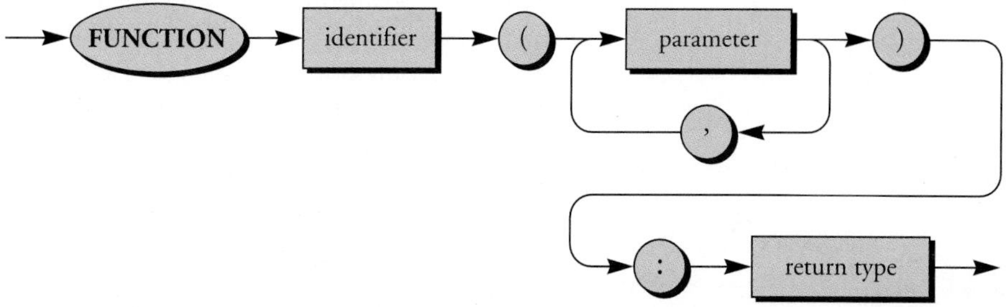

As with procedures, the list of formal parameters (variables in the function heading) must match the number and corresponding types of actual parameters (variables in the function call) used when the function is called from the main program. Thus, if you are writing a function to compute the area of a rectangle and you want to call the function from the main program by

```
RectArea := Area(Width, Length);
```

the function Area might have

```
FUNCTION Area (W, L : integer) : integer;
```

as a heading. The two formal parameters W and L correspond to the actual parameters Width and Length, assuming Width and Length are of type **integer**. In general, you should make sure the formal parameter list and the actual parameter list match up as indicated:

```
(W, L : integer)
(Width, Length)
```

One exception is that an actual parameter of type **integer** may be associated with a formal parameter of type **real.**

A function to compute the cube of an integer could have the heading

```
FUNCTION Cube (X : integer) : integer;
```

Several additional comments on the general form of a function heading are now in order.

1. **FUNCTION** is a reserved word and must be used only as indicated.
2. The term "function name" is any valid identifier.
   a. The function name should be descriptive.
   b. Some value must be assigned to the function name in the executable section of the function. The last assigned value is the value returned to the main program; for example, in the function Cube, we have

      ```
      Cube := X * X * X;
      ```

   c. The function name can be used only on the left side of an assignment statement within the function. For example

      ```
      Cube := Cube + 1;
      ```

      produces an error. (An exception to this rule involves recursion and is discussed in Section 11.1.)
3. The term "return type" declares the data type for the function name. This indicates what type of value will be returned to the main program.
4. A function can return a single value of any of the data types **integer, real, char,** or **boolean.**

As in the main program, there does not have to be a declaration section for a function. When there is one, only variables needed in the function are declared. Further, the section is usually not very elaborate because the purpose of a function is normally a small, single task.

Finally, the executable section for a function must perform the desired task, assign a value to the function name, terminate with a semicolon rather than a period, and have the general form

```
BEGIN
  .
  .  (work of function here)
  .
END
```

We will now illustrate user-defined functions with several examples.

EXAMPLE 3.1

Let's write a function to compute the cube of an integer. Since the actual parameter from the main program will be of type **integer,** we have

```
FUNCTION Cube (X : integer) : integer;
  BEGIN
    Cube := X * X * X
  END;
```

A typical call to this function from the main program is

```
A := Cube(5);
```

EXAMPLE 3.2

Now let's write a function to perform the task of computing the unit cost for pizza. (We used a procedure to do this in Section 3.2.) Data sent to the function are size and cost; the function returns the unit cost. Formal parameters are Cost and Size. Using the function name PricePerSquareInch, we have

```
FUNCTION PricePerSquareInch (Cost, Size : real) : real;
  VAR
    Radius, Area : real;
  BEGIN
    Radius := Size / 2;
    Area := Pi * sqr(Radius);
    PricePerSquareInch := Cost / Area
  END;  {  of FUNCTION PricePerSquareInch  }
```

This function can be called from the main program by

```
UnitCost := PricePerSquareInch(Cost, Size);
```

EXAMPLE 3.3

Standard Pascal does not provide a power function. However, now that you know how to write a function, you can use the built-in functions **ln** and **exp** to write a power function. Before you do this, however, let's consider how these functions can be used to produce the desired result.

First, **exp** and **ln** are inverse functions in the sense that

$$\mathbf{exp}(\mathbf{ln}(X)) = X$$

for all positive X. Thus, we have

$$3^{2.5} = \mathbf{exp}(\mathbf{ln}(3^{2.5}))$$

Using properties of logarithms

$$\mathbf{ln}(a^b) = b * \mathbf{ln}(a)$$

Hence

$$\exp(\mathbf{ln}(3^{2.5})) = \mathbf{exp}(2.5 * \mathbf{ln}(3))$$

Since each of these operations can be performed in standard Pascal, we can compute $3^{2.5}$ by

$$3^{2.5} = \mathbf{exp}(2.5 * \mathbf{ln}(3))$$

or more generally

$$A^X = \mathbf{exp}(X * \mathbf{ln}(A))$$

If we let Base denote the base A and Exponent denote the exponent X, we can now write a function Power as

```
FUNCTION Power (Base, Exponent : real) : real;
  BEGIN
    Power := exp(Exponent * ln(Base))
  END;  {  of FUNCTION Power  }
```

This function can be called from the main program by

```
Base := 3;
Exponent := 2.5;
Num := Power(Base, Exponent);
```

Use in a Program

Now that you have seen several examples of user-defined functions, let's consider their use in a program. Once they are written, user-defined functions can be used in the same manner as standard functions, usually in one of the following forms.

1. Assignment statements:

```
A := 5;
B := Cube(A);
```

2. Arithmetic expressions:

```
A := 5;
B := 3 * Cube(A) + 2;
```

3. Output statements:

```
A := 5;
writeln (Cube(A):17);
```

Multiple Functions

Programs can contain more than one function. When several user-defined functions are needed in a program, each one should be developed and positioned in the program as previously indicated.

When a program calls several functions, they can generally be positioned above the main program body in any order. However, if one function contains a call to another function, the function being called must appear before the function from which it is called.

A NOTE OF INTEREST

Program Documentation—EDS Style

(The following information was provided by Patrick J. Goss, Systems Engineer Supervisor for EDS (Electronic Data Systems). He is employed at the Lansing (MI) Regional Support Center. His primary function is to supervise support of the Sales, Service, and Marketing systems of the Oldsmobile Division of General Motors.)

Program documentation plays a significant part in the training and subsequent work efforts of the systems engineering group at EDS, as it does in any software development group. To illustrate the importance of documentation in software systems developed and maintained by EDS, consider the emphasis at EDS on documentation standards, reasons for stressing documentation, training for and enforcement of coding standards, and specific examples of using documentation.

Documentation Standards

Standards for documentation by systems engineers include

- The use of "flower boxes" (enclosure by asterisks) to physically separate and identify elements
- Strict naming conventions for variables, data sets, and programs
- Emphasis on structured, modularized code
- Complete documentation of the purpose of each routine within the program
- Complete documentation of the overall function of the total program, with particular emphasis on the business function it serves
- Complete documentation of the subsystem interfaces
- The use of descriptive and standard variable names that are consistent throughout the program, system, and related subsystems
- The consistent use of indentation and alignment to improve program readability

Reasons for Stressing Documentation

EDS has several reasons for placing a heavy emphasis on program documentation. First, well-documented systems are easier to maintain; the work can be streamlined when changes need to be made. Second, the use of personnel is more flexible, so staff members can be moved in and out of assignments with little or no decline in productivity. Third, the learning curve on systems support is reduced. Fourth, stress on production support/abend resolutions (system stop) is also reduced. Finally, on-call responsibilities can be rotated because it is easier to solve problems with well-documented systems.

Training and Enforcement

Systems engineers at EDS receive uniform and intensive training in program development and the use of documentation. Initial training occurs during a 10-week course in Plano, Texas. It is not unusual for program participants to work 12–15 hours per day, seven days a week. Approximately 20 percent of their time is spent on documentation-related issues. The successful completion rate by participants is sometimes less than 50 percent.

After the training session, maintenance of documentation skills and in-service training is provided by "walk-throughs" on every system change. These inspections involve a team of at least three peers and a secretary to record comments. During these sessions, developers are told to "check your ego at the door." Graduates from recent Technical Training sessions are often used as peers in order to guarantee adherence to current standards. (The *Note of Interest* on page 340 elaborates on inspections.)

Some Current Examples

The result of EDS's emphasis on program documentation is perhaps best illustrated by examining some current programs.

A recent capstone project from the Technical Training session is a program that contains 1934 lines, of which 670 (35 percent) are comment lines. When the systems engineers return to their jobs, they put their practice to work. Three programs in use in 1993 consist of length and documentation as follows:

Program Length	Comment Lines	Percent Documentation
1213	397	33
1236	247	20
3234	854	26

EXERCISES 3.4

1. Explain the difference between a procedure and a function.
2. Write a test program to see what happens when the function name is used on the right side of an assignment statement. For example

```
FUNCTION Total (OldSum, NewNum : integer) : integer;
  BEGIN
    Total := OldSum;
    Total := Total + NewNum
  END;
```

3. Indicate which of the following are valid function headings. Explain what is wrong with those that are invalid.

   a. `FUNCTION RoundTenth (X : real);`

   b. `FUNCTION MakeChange (X, Y) : real;`

c. `FUNCTION Max (M1, M2, M3 : integer) : integer;`

d. `FUNCTION Sign (Num : real) : char;`

e. `FUNCTION Truth (Ch : char, Num : real) : boolean;`

4. Find all errors in each of the following functions.

a.
```
FUNCTION AvOf2 (N1, N2 : integer) : integer;
  BEGIN
    AvOf2 := (N1 + N2) / 2
  END;
```

b.
```
FUNCTION Total (L1, L2 : integer) : integer;
  VAR
    Sum : integer;
  BEGIN
    Total := 0;
    Sum := L1 + L2
  END;
```

5. Write a function for each of the following.
   a. Round a real to the nearest tenth.
   b. Round a real to the nearest hundredth.
   c. Convert degrees Fahrenheit to degrees Celsius.
   d. Compute the charge for cars at a parking lot; the rate is $0.75 per hour or a fraction thereof.
6. Write a program that uses the function you wrote in Exercise 5(d) to print a ticket for a customer who parks in the parking lot. Assume the input is in minutes.
7. The factorial of a positive integer n is defined as

   $n! = n * (n - 1) * \cdots * 2 * 1$ for $n > 1$

   Write a function (Factorial) that will compute and return $n!$.
8. Write a complete program using Cube and Factorial that will produce a table of the integers 1 to 10 together with their squares, cubes, and factorials.
9. Use the functions **sqr** and Cube to write a program to print a chart of the integers 1 to 5 together with their squares and cubes. Output from this program should be

```
Number     Number Squared     Number Cubed
------     --------------     ------------

  1              1                  1
  2              4                  8
  3              9                 27
  4             16                 64
  5             25                125
```

10. Write a program that allows the user to enter a Base (a) and an Exponent (x), and then have the program print the value of a^x.
11. Write a function (Arithmetic) that will receive a sign (+ or $*$) and two integers (N1, N2) and then compute and return either N1 + N2 or N1 $*$ N2, depending upon the sign received.
12. Algebra teachers often have students play "guess the rule." In this game, the first person writes down a rule (function), such as $y = x^2 + 1$. A second person then assigns a value to x. The first person indicates the function value associated with the input. Thus, for $x = 3$, y would be 10 if $y = x^2 + 1$. The game continues until the second person guesses the rule.

    Write a program that allows you to play this game with another student. Write it in such a way that it can be easily modified to use different functions.

3.5 Using Subprograms

OBJECTIVES

- to understand how subprograms can be used as reusable code
- to understand when to use functions instead of procedures in a program
- to understand when to use variable parameters instead of value parameters in a procedure

The use of subprograms facilitates writing programs for problems that have solutions that have been developed using top-down design. A procedure or function can be written for each main task. Each subprogram can contain its own subprograms if needed.

How complex should a procedure or function be? In general, functions should be relatively short and should perform a specific task. Procedures can be longer but probably should not be more than one page of printout. Some programmers prefer to limit procedures to no more than one full screen. If a procedure is longer than a page or screen, you might consider subdividing the task into smaller procedures or functions.

Reusable Code

A significant use of subprograms is for the development of procedures and functions that can be used in subsequent programs. To illustrate, let's develop a procedure called Swap that interchanges the values in two variables.

```
PROCEDURE Swap (VAR Num1, Num2 : integer);
  VAR
    Temp : integer;
  BEGIN
    Temp := Num1;
    Num1 := Num2;
    Num2 := Temp
  END;  {  of PROCEDURE Swap  }
```

We can now use this procedure to exchange the values of two variables by a call to Swap such as

```
Swap (Number1, Number2);
```

We will use **PROCEDURE** Swap in the text whenever it is necessary to interchange values of variables. This technique is often used in sorting algorithms.

Functions Versus Procedures

When should you use a function instead of a procedure in a program? A general rule is to think of a function as a construct that returns only one value. Thus, a function should be used when a single value is required in the main program. Variable parameters can be used with functions, but this is discouraged in good programming practices.

A NOTE OF INTEREST

Niklaus Wirth

Niklaus Wirth began his work in the computing field by taking a course in numeric analysis at Laval University in Quebec, Canada. However, the computer (Alvac III E) was frequently out of order and the hexadecimal code programming exercises went untested. Wirth received his doctorate from the University of California, Berkeley in 1963.

After other early experiences in programming, it became apparent to Wirth that computers of the future had to be more effectively programmable. Consequently, he joined a research group that worked on developing a compiler for an IBM 704. This language was NELIAC, a dialect of ALGOL 58. In rapid succession, he developed or contributed to the development of Euler, ALGOL W, and PL360. In 1967, he returned to Switzerland and established a team of three assistants with whom he developed and implemented the language Pascal.

Pascal was the first major programming language to implement the ideas and methodology of structured programming and was initially developed to teach programming concepts. It is particularly successful as a teaching language because it allows the instructor to focus on structures and concepts rather than on features and peculiarities. However, Pascal has rapidly expanded beyond its initial purpose and has found increasing acceptance in business and scientific applications.

What Kind of Parameters Should Be Used?

Use variable parameters when information is going to be returned to the main program; otherwise, use value parameters. The choices will be apparent if you use data flow arrows or module specifications when designing the solution to the problem.

Using Stubs

As programs get longer and incorporate more subprograms, a technique frequently used to get the program running is *stub programming.* A stub program is a no-frills, simple version of what will be a final program. It does not contain details of output and full algorithm development. It does contain a rough version of each subprogram and all parameter lists. When the stub version runs, you know your logic is correct and values are being passed to and from subprograms appropriately. Then you can fill in the necessary details to get a complete program.

Using Drivers

The main program is sometimes referred to as the *main driver.* When subprograms are used in a program, this driver can be modified to check them in a sequential fashion. For example, suppose a main driver is

```
BEGIN  {  Main driver  }
  Initialize (Sum, Count);
  GetData (Sum, Count);
  PerformComputations (Sum, Count);
  PrintResults (Sum, Count)
END.  {  of main driver  }
```

Procedures can be checked by putting comment indicators around the remainder of the program and temporarily adding a statement to print the values of the variables. Thus, you could run the version

```
BEGIN  {  Main driver  }
  Initialize (Sum, Count);
  GetData (Sum, Count);
  writeln ('Sum is ', Sum, 'Count is ', Count);
{ PerformComputations (Sum, Count);
  PrintResults (Sum, Count)  }
END.  {  of main driver  }
```

Once you are sure a subprogram is running, you can remove the comment indicators and continue through the main driver to check successive subprograms.

FOCUS ON PROGRAM DESIGN

To encourage people to shop downtown, the Downtown Businesses Association partially subsidizes parking. They have established the E-Z Parking parking lot, where customers are charged $0.75 for each full hour of parking. There is no charge for part of an hour; thus, if someone uses the lot for less than an hour, there is no charge.

The E-Z Parking parking lot is open from 9:00 A.M. until 11:00 P.M. When a vehicle enters, the driver is given a ticket with the entry time printed in military style: if a car enters the lot at 9:30 A.M., the ticket will read 0930; if a vehicle enters the lot at 1:20 P.M., the ticket will read 1320. When the vehicle leaves, the driver presents the ticket to the attendant and the amount due is computed.

Now let's develop a solution and write a program to assist the attendant. Input consists of a starting time and an ending time. Output should be a statement to the customer indicating the input information, the total amount due, a heading, and a closing message. Sample output for the data 1050 (10:50 A.M.) and 1500 (3:00 P.M.) is

```
Please enter the time in and press <Enter>.
1050
Please enter the time out and press <Enter>.
1500

                E - Z Parking
                -------------

    Time in:    1050
    Time out:   1500

    Amount due      $  3.00

 Thank you for using E - Z Parking

                  BUCKLE UP
                     and
                DRIVE SAFELY
```

A first-level development for this problem is

1. Get the data
2. Compute amount
3. Print results

A structure chart for this problem is given in Figure 3.14. (Recall an arrow pointing to a module indicates data are being received by the module and an arrow pointing from a module indicates data are being sent from the module.)

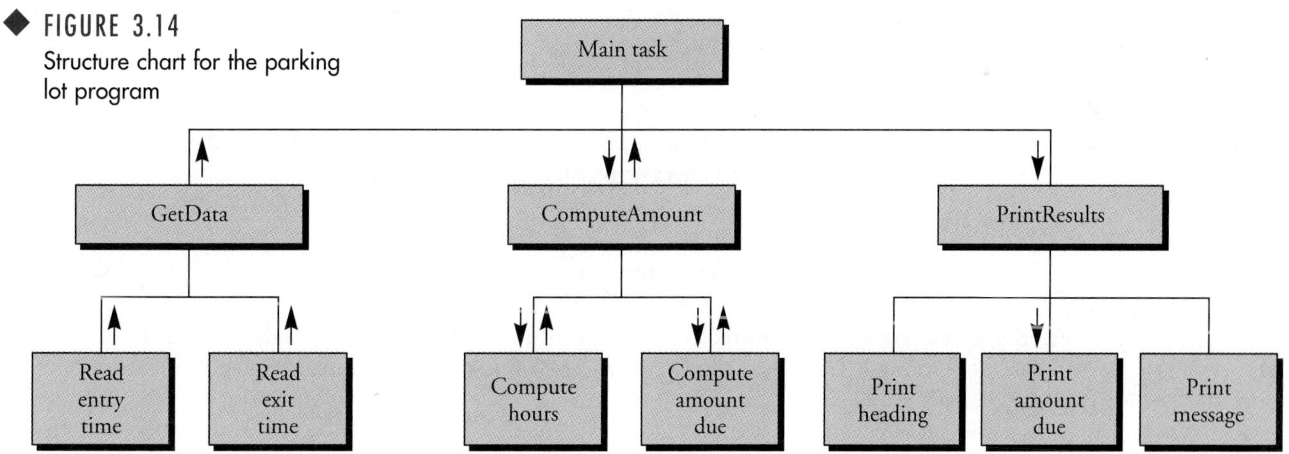

◆ FIGURE 3.14
Structure chart for the parking lot program

Module specifications for the three main modules are

1. GetData Module
   Data received: None
   Information returned: Entry time
   Exit time
   Logic: Have the user enter information from the keyboard.

2. ComputeAmount Module
Data received: Entry time
Exit time
Information returned: Amount due
Logic: Subtract the entry time from the exit time and use **DIV** 100 to get the number of full hours.

3. PrintResults Module
Data received: Entry time
Exit time
Amount due
Information returned: None
Logic: Print the heading, entry time, exit time, amount due, and closing message.

If we examine the module specifications, we see that two variable parameters are needed for GetData. ComputeAmount needs two value parameters and one variable parameter, and PrintResults needs three value parameters.

A second-level pseudocode development is

1. Get the data
   1.1 read time entered
   1.2 read time exited
2. Compute amount
   2.1 compute number of hours
   2.2 compute amount due
3. Print results
   3.1 print a heading
   3.2 print amount due
   3.3 print a closing message

The main driver is

```
BEGIN  {  Main program  }
  GetData (Entrytime, ExitTime);
  AmountDue := ComputeAmount(EntryTime, ExitTime);
  PrintResults (EntryTime, ExitTime, AmountDue)
END.  {  of main program  }
```

A complete program for this problem follows.

```
PROGRAM Parking (input, output);

{  This program prints statements for customers of the E-Z    }
{  Parking parking lot.  Interactive input consists of entry  }
{  time and exit time from the lot.  Output consists of a     }
{  customer statement.  Emphasis is placed on using           }
{  procedures and a function to develop the program.          }

CONST
  HourlyRate = 0.75;
  Indent = ' ';

VAR
  EntryTime,                  {  Time of entry into parking lot  }
  ExitTime : integer;         {  Time of exit from parking lot   }
  AmountDue : real;           {  Cost of parking in lot          }
```

```
{************************************************************}

PROCEDURE GetData (VAR EntryTime, ExitTime : integer);

  {  Given:    Nothing                                       }
  {  Task:     Enter EntryTime and ExitTime from the keyboard  }
  {  Return:   EntryTime, ExitTime                           }

  BEGIN                                                          1
    writeln ('Please enter the time in and press <Enter>.');
    readln (EntryTime);
    writeln ('Please enter the time out and press <Enter>.');
    readln (ExitTime)
  END;  {  of PROCEDURE GetData  }

{************************************************************}

FUNCTION ComputeAmount (EntryTime, ExitTime : integer) : real;

  {  Given:    EntryTime and ExitTime                        }
  {  Task:     Find full hours and multiply by HourlyRate    }
  {  Return:   AmountDue                                     }

  VAR                                                            2
    NumberOfHours : integer;
  BEGIN
    NumberOfHours := (ExitTime - EntryTime) DIV 100;
    ComputeAmount := NumberOfHours * HourlyRate
  END;  {  of FUNCTION ComputeAmount  }

{************************************************************}

PROCEDURE PrintHeading;

  {  Given:    Nothing                                       }
  {  Task:     Print a suitable heading for the ticket       }
  {  Return:   Nothing                                       }

  BEGIN
    writeln;
    writeln (Indent:11, 'E - Z Parking');
    writeln (Indent:11, '-------------');
    writeln
  END;  {  of PROCEDURE PrintHeading  }

{************************************************************}

PROCEDURE PrintMessage;

  {  Given:    Nothing                                       }
  {  Task:     Print a closing message for the ticket        }
  {  Return:   Nothing                                       }
```

```
  BEGIN
    writeln;
    writeln (Indent:1, 'Thank you for using E - Z Parking');
    writeln;
    writeln (Indent:13, 'BUCKLE UP');
    writeln (Indent:16, 'and');
    writeln (Indent:11, 'DRIVE SAFELY');
    writeln
  END;  {  of PROCEDURE PrintMessage  }

{**************************************************************}

PROCEDURE PrintResults (EntryTime, ExitTime : integer;
                        AmountDue : real);

  {  Given:   EntryTime, ExitTime, AmountDue                   }
  {  Task:    Print a customer receipt;  calls both            }
  {                PrintHeading and PrintMessage               }
  {  Return:  Nothing                                          }

  BEGIN
    PrintHeading;
    writeln (Indent:4, 'Time in: ', EntryTime:6);
    writeln (Indent:4, 'Time out:', ExitTime:6);
    writeln;
    writeln (Indent:4, 'Amount due     $', AmountDue:6:2);
    PrintMessage
  END;  {  of PROCEDURE PrintResults  }

{**************************************************************}

BEGIN  {  Main program  }
  GetData (EntryTime, ExitTime);
  AmountDue := ComputeAmount(EntryTime, ExitTime);
  PrintResults (EntryTime, ExitTime, AmountDue)
END.  {  of main program  }
```

3

A sample run using the data 0930 as entry time and 1320 as exit time produces

```
Please enter the time in and press <Enter>.
0930
Please enter the time out and press <Enter>.
1320

          E - Z Parking
          -------------

    Time in:    0930
    Time out:   1320

    Amount due      $  2.25

Thank you for using E - Z Parking

             BUCKLE UP
                and
           DRIVE SAFELY
```

RUNNING AND DEBUGGING HINTS

1. Each subprogram can be tested separately to see if it is producing the desired result. This is accomplished by a main program that calls and tests only the subprogram in question.
2. You can use related or identical variable names in the parameter lists. For example

   ```
   PROCEDURE Compute (N1, N2 : integer;
                      VAR Av : real);
   ```

   or

   ```
   PROCEDURE Compute (Number1, Number2 : integer;
                      VAR Average : real);
   ```

   could be called by

   ```
   Compute (Number1, Number2, Average);
   ```

3. Be sure the type and order of actual parameters and formal parameters agree. You can do this by listing them one below the other. For example

   ```
   PROCEDURE GetData (VAR Init1, Init2:char; Sc:integer);
   ```

   could be called by

   ```
   GetData (Initial1, Initial2, Score);
   ```

4. Carefully distinguish between value parameters and variable parameters. If a value is to be returned to the main program, it must be passed by reference using a variable parameter. This means it must be declared with **VAR** in the procedure heading.

SUMMARY

Key Terms

actual parameter
block
bottom-up testing
cohesive subprogram
encapsulation
formal parameter
global identifier (variable)
interface
local identifier (variable)
main driver
modularity
nonlocal identifier
passed by reference
postcondition
precondition
procedural abstraction
procedure
scope of an identifier
side effect
structured programming
stub programming
subblock
subprogram
user-defined function
value parameter
variable parameter

Keywords

FUNCTION
PROCEDURE
ln
exp

Key Concepts

- A subprogram is a program within a program; procedures and functions are subprograms.
- Subprograms can be utilized to perform specific tasks in a program. Procedures are often used to initialize variables (variable parameters), get data (variable parameters), print headings (no variables needed), perform computations (value and/or variable parameters), and print data (value parameters).
- The general form of a procedure heading is

  PROCEDURE <name> (<parameter list>)

- Value parameters are used when values are passed only from the main program to the procedure; a typical parameter list is

```
PROCEDURE PrintData (N1, N2 : integer;
                     X, Y : real);
```

- Variable parameters are used when values are to be returned to the main program; a typical parameter list is

```
PROCEDURE GetData (VAR Init1, Init2 : char;
                   VAR N1 : integer);
```

- A formal parameter is a parameter listed in the subprogram heading; it is like a blank waiting to receive a value from the calling program.

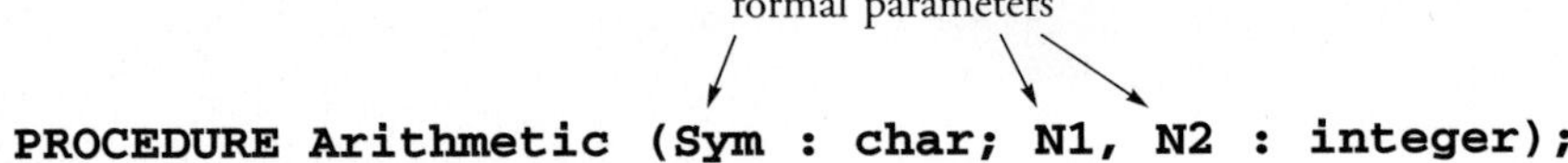


```
PROCEDURE Arithmetic (Sym : char; N1, N2 : integer);
```

- An actual parameter is a variable listed in the subprogram call in the calling program.

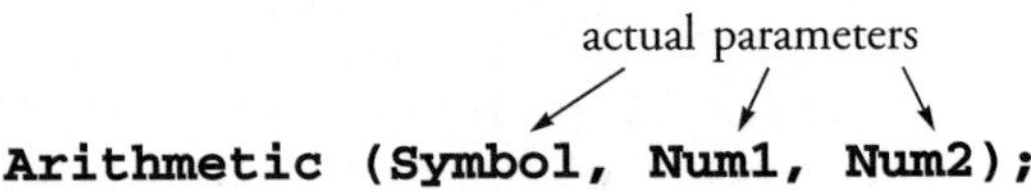


```
Arithmetic (Symbol, Num1, Num2);
```

- The formal parameter list in the subprogram heading must match the number and types of actual parameters used in the main program when the subprogram is called.

```
PROCEDURE Arithmetic (Sym : char; N1, N2 : integer);
Arithmetic (Symbol, Num1, Num2);
```

- Global identifiers can be used by the main program and all subprograms.
- Local identifiers are available only to the subprogram in which they are declared.
- Each identifier is available to the block in which it is declared; this includes all subprograms contained within the block.
- Identifiers are not available outside their blocks.
- The scope of an identifier refers to the block or blocks in which the identifier is available.
- Understanding the scope of identifiers is aided by the graphic illustration of blocks in a program; thus

```
PROGRAM Practice (input, output);

VAR
  X, Y, Z : real;

PROCEDURE Sub1 (X1 : real);
  VAR
    X2 : real;
  BEGIN
    .
    .
    .
  END;  { of PROCEDURE Sub1 }

PROCEDURE Sub2 (X1 : real);
  VAR
    Z2 : real;
```

can be visualized as shown in Figure 3.15.

◆ FIGURE 3.15

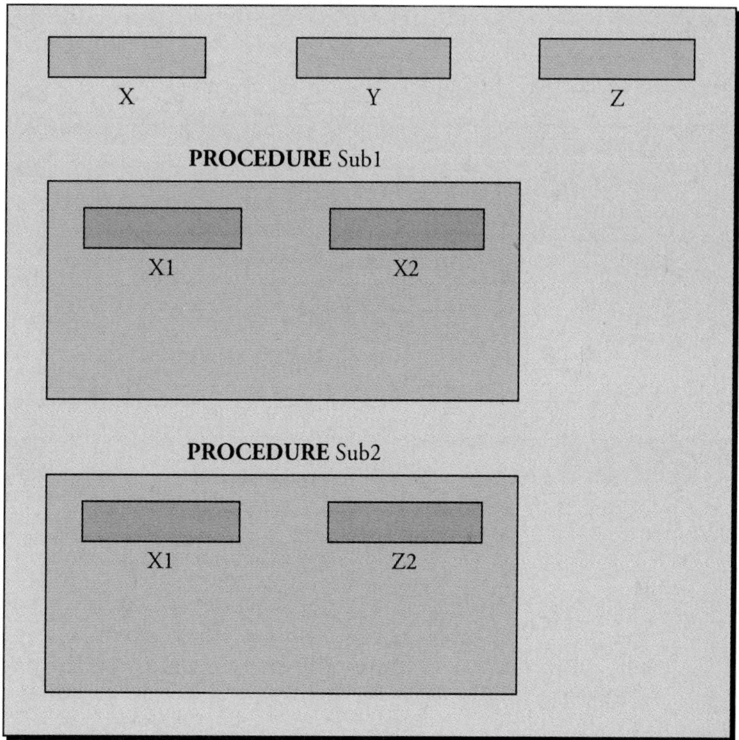

- A user-defined function is a subprogram that performs a specific task.
- The form of a user-defined function is

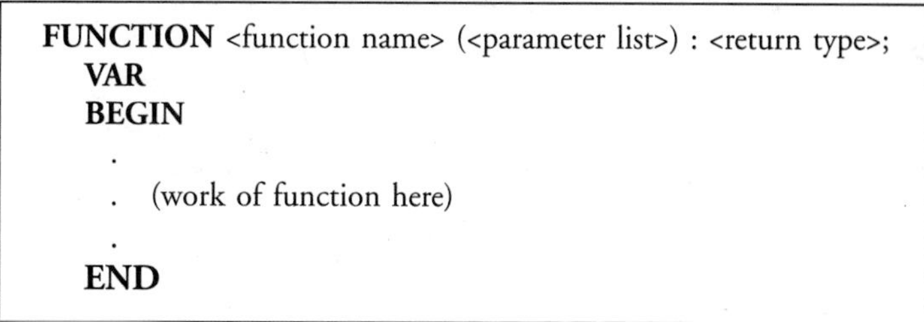

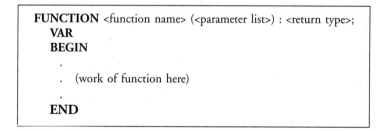

```
FUNCTION <function name> (<parameter list>) : <return type>;
   VAR
   BEGIN
     .
     .  (work of function here)
     .
   END
```

- An assignment must be made to the function name in the body of the function.
- Within a function, the function name can be used only on the left side of an assignment statement.
- A function returns exactly one value; a procedure may return no values or several values.

PROGRAMMING PROBLEMS AND PROJECTS

The following programming problems will be run on a very limited set of data. In later chapters, as you build your programming skills, you will run these problems with larger data bases and subprograms for various parts. Problems marked with a box to the left of the number are referred to and used repeatedly; carefully choose the ones on which to work and then develop them completely.

1. Write a program to get the coefficients of a quadratic equation

$$ax^2 + bx + c = 0$$

from the keyboard and then print the value of the discriminant

$$b^2 - 4ac$$

A sample display for getting input is

```
Enter coefficients a, b, and c for the quadratic equation

   ax^2 + bx + c = 0

 a = 1
 b = 2
 c = 3
```

Run this program at least three times using test data that result in $b^2 - 4ac = 0$, $b^2 - 4ac > 0$, and $b^2 - 4ac < 0$.

2. Write a program to compute the cost of carpeting a room. Input should consist of the room length, room width, and carpet price per square yard. Use constants for the pad charge and installation charge. Include a heading as part of the output.

   A typical input screen would be

```
What is the room length in feet? <Enter>?
What is the room width in feet?  <Enter>?
What is the carpet price/square yard? <Enter>?
```

Output for a sample run of this program (without a heading) could be

```
Dimensions of the room (in feet) are 17 x 22.
The area to be carpeted is 41.6 square yards.
The carpet price is $11.95 per square yard.

    Room dimensions                     17 x 22
    Carpet required                     41.6 square yards
    Carpet price/square yard             $11.95
    Pad price/square yard                $ 2.95
    Installation cost/square yard        $  .95
                                         ------
    Total cost/square yard               $15.85
    Total cost                                      $659.36
```

3. Williamson's Paint and Papering store wants you to develop a computer program to help them determine how much paint is needed to paint a room. Assuming a room is to have four walls and the ceiling painted, input for the program should be the length, width, and height of the room. Use a constant for the wall height (usually eight feet). One gallon of paint should cover 250 square feet. Cost of paint for the walls and ceiling should be entered by the user. Output should be the amount and cost for each kind of paint and the total cost.

4. The Fairfield College faculty recently signed a three-year contract that included salary increments of 7 percent, 6 percent, and 5 percent, respectively, for the next three years. Write a program that allows a user to enter the current salary and then prints out the compounded salary for each of the next three years.

5. Several instructors use various weights (percentage of the final grade) for test scores. Write a program that allows the user to enter three test scores and the weight for each score. Output should consist of the input data, the weighted score for each test, and the total score (sum of the weighted scores).

6. The Roll-Em Lanes Bowling Team would like you to develop a computer program that prints the team results for one series of games. The team consists of four members, whose names are Weber, Fazio, Martin, and Patterson. Each person on the team bowls three games during the series; thus, the input will contain three lines, each with four integer scores. Output should include all input data, individual series totals, game average for each member, team total, and team average. Sample output is

```
NAME          GAME 1    GAME 2    GAME 3    TOTAL    AVERAGE

Weber           212       220       190      622      207.3
Fazio           195       235       210      640      213.3
Martin          178       190       206      574      191.3
Patterson       195       215       210      620      206.7

Team Total:   2456

Team Average:   818.7
```

■ 7. The Natural Pine Furniture Company has recently hired you to help them convert their antiquated payroll system to a computer-based model. They know you are still learning, so all they want right now is a program that will print a one-week pay report for three employees. You should use the constant definition section for the following.

(1) Federal withholding tax rate 18%
(2) State withholding tax rate 4.5%
(3) Hospitalization $25.65
(4) Union dues $7.85

Each line of input will contain the employee's initials, the number of hours worked, and the employee's hourly rate. Output should include a report for each employee and a summary report for the company files. A sample employee form follows.

```
Employee:        JIM
Hours Worked:  40.00
Hourly Rate:    9.75

     Total Wages:                                390.00

     Deductions:
          Federal Withholding       70.20
          State Withholding         17.55
          Hospitalization           26.65
          Union Dues                 7.85
                                   ------
               Total Deductions    122.25

     Net Pay                                    $267.75
```

Output for a summary report could be

```
                 Natural Pine Furniture Company
                        Weekly Summary

     Gross Wages:

     Deductions:
          Federal Withholding
          State Withholding
          Hospitalization
          Union Dues

               Total Deductions

     Net Wages
```

8. The Child-Growth Encyclopedia Company wants a computer program that will print a monthly sales chart. Products produced by the company, prices, and sales commissions for each are

(1) Basic encyclopedia	$325.00	22%
(2) Child educational supplement	$127.50	15%
(3) Annual update book	$ 18.95	20%

Monthly sales data for one region consist of a two-letter region identifier (such as MI) and three integers representing the number of units sold for each product listed above. A typical input screen would be

```
What is your sales region?
MI
How many Basic Encyclopedia were sold?
150
How many Child Supplements were sold?
120
How many Annual Updates were sold?
105
```

Write a program that will get the monthly sales data for two sales regions and produce the desired company chart. The prices may vary from month to month and should be defined in the constant definition section. The commissions are not subject to change. Typical output could be

```
                         MONTHLY SALES CHART

                               Basic            Child          Annual
            Region          Encyclopedia      Supplement       Update

Units sold     MI               150               120            105
(by region)    TX               225               200            150
                               -----             -----          -----
Total units sold:               375               320            255

  Price/unit                  $325.00           $127.50         $18.95

Gross Sales:                $121,875.00        $40,800.00      $4,832.25

  Commission rate               22%               15%            20%

Commissions paid:            $26,812.50         $6,120.00       $966.45
```

9. The Village Variety Store is having its annual Christmas sale. They would like you to write a program to produce a daily report for the store. Each item sold is identified by a code consisting of one letter followed by one digit. Your report should include data for three items. Each of the three lines of data will include item code, number of items sold, original item price, and reduction percentage. Your report should also include a chart with the input data, sale price per item, and total amount of sales per item. In addition, you should print a daily summary. Sample input is

```
A1 13 5.95 15
A2 24 7.95 20
A3 80 3.95 50
```

Typical output could be

```
Item Code  # Sold  Original Price  Reduction   Sale Price  Income
---------  ------  --------------  ----------  ----------  ------
   A1        13        $5.95          15%         $5.06    $65.78

Daily Summary
-------------
   Gross Income:
```

10. The Holiday-Out Motel Company, Inc., wants a program that will print a statement for each overnight customer. Each line of input will contain room number (integer), room rate (real), number of nights (integer), telephone charges (real), and restaurant charges (real). You should use the constant definition section for the date and current tax rate. Each customer statement should include all input data, the date, tax rate and amount, total due, appropriate heading, and appropriate closing message. Test your program by running it for two customers. The tax rate applies only to the room cost. A typical input screen is

```
Room number?
135
Room rate?
39.95
Number of nights?
3
Telephone charges?
3.75
Meals?
57.50
```

A customer statement form is

```
       Holiday-Out Motel Company, Inc.
       ----------- ----- -------- ---
Date: XX-XX-XX
Room #                         135
Room Rate:                  $39.95
Number of Nights:                3

Room Cost:                 $119.85
Tax:  XXX%                    4.79
     Subtotal:                       $124.64
```

```
Telephone:                                      3.75
Meals:                                         57.50

     TOTAL DUE                               $185.89

        Thank you for staying at Holiday-Out
                    Drive safely
                  Please come again
```

■ **11.** As a part-time job this semester, you are working for the Family Budget Assistance Center. Your boss has asked you to write and execute a program that will analyze data for a family. Input for each family will consist of

Family ID number	(**integer**)
Number in family	(**integer**)
Income	(**real**)
Total debts	(**real**)

Your program should output the following.

(1) An appropriate header

(2) The family's identification number, number in family, income, and total debt

(3) Predicted family living expenses ($3000 × the size of the family)

(4) The monthly payment necessary to pay off the debt in one year

(5) The amount the family should save [family size × 2% of income – debt, or family size * 0.02 * (income – debt)].

(6) Your service fee (0.5 percent of the income)

Run your program for the following two families.

Identification Number	Size	Income	Debt
51	4	$18,000.00	$2000.00
72	7	26,000.00	4800.00

Output for the first family could be

```
      Family Budget Assistance Center
                March 1995
         Telephone: (800)555-1234

Identification number               51
Family size                          4
Annual income                 $ 18000.00
Total debt                    $  2000.00
Expected living expenses      $ 12000.00
Monthly payment               $   166.67
Savings                       $  1280.00
Service fee                   $    90.00
```

■ **12.** The Caswell Catering and Convention Service has asked you to write a computer program to produce customers' bills. The program should read in the following data.

(1) The number of adults to be served
(2) The number of children to be served
(3) The cost per adult meal
(4) The cost per child meal (60 percent of the cost of the adult meal)
(5) The cost for dessert (same for adults and children)
(6) The room fee (no room fee if catered at the person's home)
(7) A percentage for tip and tax (not applied to the room fee)
(8) A deduction from the bill of any prior deposit

Write a program and test it using data sets 2, 3, and 4 from the table shown.

Data Set	Adult Count	Child Count	Adult Cost	Dessert Cost	Room Rate	Tip/Tax	Deposit
1	23	7	$12.75	$1.00	$45.00	18%	$50.00
2	54	3	13.50	1.25	65.00	19%	40.00
3	24	15	12.00	0.00	45.00	18%	75.00
4	71	2	11.15	1.50	0.00	6%	0.00

Data set 1 produces the following sample output.

```
         Caswell Catering and Convention Service
                        Final Bill

                  Number of adults:          23
                Number of children:           7
    Cost per adult without dessert:   $   12.75
    Cost per child without dessert:   $    7.65
                  Cost per dessert:   $    1.00
                          Room fee:   $   45.00
                  Tip and tax rate:        0.18

        Total cost for adult meals:   $  293.25
        Total cost for child meals:   $   53.55
            Total cost for dessert:   $   30.00
                   Total food cost:   $  376.80
                  Plus tip and tax:   $   67.82
                     Plus room fee:   $   45.00
                      Less deposit:   $   50.00

                       Balance due:   $  439.62
```

13. The Maripot Carpet Store has asked you to write a computer program to calculate the amount a customer should be charged. The president of the company has given you the following information to help in writing the program.

(1) The carpet charge is equal to the number of square yards purchased multiplied by the carpet cost per square yard.

(2) The labor cost is equal to the number of square yards purchased multiplied by the labor cost per square yard. A fixed fee for floor preparation is added to some customers' bills.

(3) Large-volume customers are given a percentage discount, but the discount applies only to the carpet charge and not to the labor costs.

(4) All customers are charged 4 percent sales tax on the carpet: there is no sales tax on the labor cost.

Write the program and test it for customers 2, 3, and 4.

Customer	Sq. yds.	Cost per sq. yd.	Labor per sq. yd.	Prep. Cost	Discount
1	17	$18.50	$3.50	$38.50	0.02
2	40	24.95	2.95	0.00	0.14
3	23	16.80	3.25	57.95	0.00
4	26	21.25	0.00	80.00	0.00

The data for customer 1 produces the following sample output.

```
Square yards purchased:          17
  Cost per square yard:   $   18.50
 Labor per square yard:   $    3.50
Floor preparation cost:   $   38.50
       Cost for carpet:   $  314.50
        Cost for labor:   $   98.00
    Discount on carpet:   $    6.29
         Tax on carpet:   $   12.33
    Charge to customer:   $  418.54
```

14. The manager of the Croswell Carpet Store has asked you to write a program to print customers' bills. The manager has given you the following information.

(1) The store expresses the length and width of a room in terms of feet and tenths of a foot. For example, the length might be reported as 16.7 feet.

(2) The amount of carpet purchased is expressed in square yards. It is found by dividing the area of the room (in square feet) by nine.

(3) The store does not sell a fraction of a square yard. Thus, square yards must always be rounded up.

(4) The carpet charge is equal to the number of square yards purchased multiplied by the carpet cost per square yard. Sales tax equal to 4 percent of the carpet cost must be added to the bill.

(5) All customers are sold a carpet pad at $2.25 per square yard. Sales tax equal to 4 percent of the pad cost must be added to the bill.

(6) The labor cost is equal to the number of square yards purchased multiplied by $2.40, which is the labor cost per square yard. No tax is charged on labor.

(7) Large-volume customers may be given a discount. The discount may apply only to the carpet cost (before sales tax is added), only to the pad cost (before sales tax is added), only to the labor cost, or to any combination of the three charges.

(8) Each customer is identified by a five-digit number; that number should appear on the bill. The sample output follows.

```
          Croswell Carpet Store
                 Invoice

        Customer number:            26817

                  Carpet :          574.20
                     Pad :           81.00
                   Labor :           86.40

                Subtotal :          741.60
           Less discount :           65.52

                Subtotal :          676.08
                Plus tax :           23.59
                   Total :          699.67
```

Write the program and test it for the following three customers.

a. Mr. Wilson (customer 81429) ordered carpet for his family room, which measures 25 feet long and 18 feet wide. The carpet sells for $12.95 per square yard, and the manager agreed to give him a discount of 8 percent on the carpet and 6 percent on the labor.

b. Mr. and Mrs. Adams (customer 04246) ordered carpet for their bedroom, which measures 16.5 feet by 15.4 feet. The carpet sells for $18.90 per square yard, and the manager granted a discount of 12 percent on everything.

c. Ms. Logan (customer 39050) ordered carpet that cost $8.95 per square yard for her daughter's bedroom. The room measures 13.1 by 12.5 feet. No discounts were given.

15. Each week Abduhl's Flying Carpets pays its salespeople a base salary plus a bonus for each carpet they sell. In addition, the company pays a commission of 10 percent of the total sales by each salesperson.

Write a program to compute a salesperson's salary for the month by inputting Base, Bonus, Quantity, and Sales and making the necessary calculations. Use the following test data.

Salesperson	Base	Bonus	Quantity	Commission	Sales
1	$250.00	$15.00	20	10%	$1543.69
2	280.00	19.50	36	10%	2375.90

The commission figure is 10 percent. Be sure you can change this easily if necessary. Sample output follows.

```
      Salesperson :    1
             Base :  250.00
            Bonus :   15.00
         Quantity :   20
      Total Bonus :  300.00
       Commission :   10%
            Sales : 1543.69
 Total Commission :  154.37
              Pay :  704.37
```

COMMUNICATION IN PRACTICE

1. Modify one of your programs from this section by saving *only* the documentation, constant definitions, variable declaration section, subprogram headings, and main driver. Exchange your modified version with a student who has prepared a similar version. Using the modified version, reconstruct the tasks of the program. Discuss your results with the student who wrote the program.
2. Modify one of your programs from this section by deleting all documentation. Exchange your modified version with a student who has prepared a similar version. Using the modified version, write documentation for the program. Compare your results with the other student's original version.
3. "Think Metric" is the preferred way of having members of a nonmetric society become familiar with the metric system. Unfortunately, during the transition, many people are forced to rely on converting from their present system to the metric system. Develop a solution and write a program to help people convert their height and weight from inches and pounds to centimeters and kilograms. The program should get input of a person's height (in feet and inches) and weight (rounded to the nearest pound) from a keyboard. Output should consist of the height and weight in metric units.
4. Discuss the issue of documenting subprograms with instructors of computer science, upper-level students majoring in computer science, and some of your classmates. Prepare a report for the class on this issue. Your report should contain information about different forms of documentation, the perceived need for documentation by various groups, the significance of documenting data transmission, and so forth. If possible, use specific examples to illustrate good versus poor documentation of subprograms.
5. Reread the material in Section 3.2 concerning procedural abstraction. Then, from Problems 5, 7, 8, and 11, select one that you have not yet worked. Develop a structure chart and write module specifications for each module required in the problem you have chosen. Also, write a main driver for your program and write complete documentation for each subprogram, including comments about all parameters.

CHAPTER

4 Selection Statements

CHAPTER OUTLINE

The previous chapters set the stage for using computers to solve problems. You have seen how programs in Pascal can be used to get data, perform computations, and print results. You should be able to write complete, short programs, so it is now time to examine other aspects of programming.

A major feature of a computer is its ability to make decisions. For example, a condition is examined and a decision is made as to which program statement is next executed. Statements that permit a computer to make decisions are called *selection statements.* Selection statements are examples of *control structures* because they allow the programmer to control the flow of execution of program statements.

4.1 Boolean Expressions

OBJECTIVES

- to be able to use the data type **boolean**
- to be able to use relational operators
- to understand the hierarchy for simple Boolean expressions
- to be able to use the logical connectives **AND, OR,** and **NOT**
- to be able to use compound Boolean expressions
- to understand the hierarchy for compound Boolean expressions

Before we take a look at how a computer makes decisions, we need to examine the logical constructs in Pascal, which include a new data type called **boolean.** This data type allows you to represent something as true or false. Although this sounds relatively simple (and it is), this is a very significant feature of computers.

The boolean Data Type

Thus far we have used the three data types **integer, real,** and **char;** a fourth data type is **boolean.** A typical declaration of a Boolean variable is

```
VAR
  Flag : boolean;
```

In general, Boolean variables are declared by

VAR
<variable 1>,
<variable 2>,
.
.
.
<variable *n*> : **boolean**

There are only two values for variables of the **boolean** data type: **true** and **false.** These are both constant standard identifiers and can be used only as Boolean values. When these assignments are made, the contents of the designated memory locations will be the assigned values. For example, if the declaration

```
VAR
  Flag1, Flag2 : boolean;
```

is made, then

```
Flag1 := true;
Flag2 := false;
```

produces

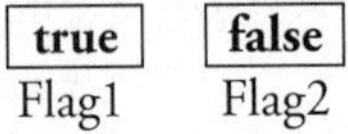

As with other data types, if two variables are of type **boolean,** the value of one variable can be assigned to another variable as

```
Flag1 := true;
Flag2 := Flag1;
```

and can be envisioned as

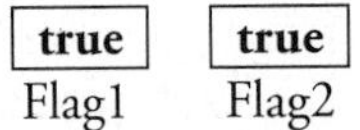

Note quotation marks are not used when assigning the values **true** or **false** since these are Boolean constants, not strings.

The **boolean** data type is an ordinal type. Thus, there is an order relationship between **true** and **false: false** < **true**. Furthermore, the **ord** function can be applied to the **boolean** values: **ord**(**false**) = 0 and **ord**(**true**) = 1.

Output of boolean

Boolean variables can be used as arguments for **write** and **writeln.** Thus

```
Flag := true;
writeln (Flag);
```

produces

```
TRUE
```

However, some versions will not support the output of Boolean variables.

The field width for Boolean output can be controlled by formatting with a colon followed by a positive integer to designate the field width. The Boolean value will appear right-justified in the field.

Although Boolean variables and constants can be assigned and used in output statements, they cannot be used in input statements. Thus, if Flag is a Boolean variable, a statement such as

```
read (Flag);
```

produces an error. Instead, the user typically reads some value and then uses this value to assign an appropriate Boolean value to a Boolean variable. This technique will be illustrated later in this chapter.

Relational Operators and Simple Boolean Expressions

In arithmetic, integers and reals can be compared by using equalities (=) and inequalities (<, >, ≠, and so on). Pascal also provides for the comparison of numbers or values of variables. The operators used for comparison are called *relational operators,* and there are six of them. Their arithmetic notation, Pascal notation, and meanings are given in Table 4.1.

◇ TABLE 4.1
Relational operators

Arithmetic Operation	Relational Operator	Meaning
$=$	**=**	Is equal to
$<$	**<**	Is less than
$>$	**>**	Is greater than
$\leq$	**<=**	Is less than or equal to
$\geq$	**>=**	Is greater than or equal to
$\neq$	**<>**	Is not equal to

When two numbers or variable values are compared using a single relational operator, the expression is referred to as a *simple Boolean expression.* Each simple Boolean expression has the Boolean value **true** or **false,** according to the arithmetic validity of the expression. In general, only data of the same type can be compared; thus, integers must be compared to integers, reals must be compared to reals, and characters must be compared to characters. The usual exception can be applied here: reals can be compared to integers. When comparing reals, however, the computer representation of a real number might not be the exact real number intended. Therefore, the equality (=) comparison should be avoided; instead, the absolute value of the difference should be checked to see if it is smaller than a given value.

Table 4.2 sets forth several Boolean expressions and their respective Boolean values, assuming the assignment statements A := 3 and B := 4 have been made.

◇ TABLE 4.2
Values of simple Boolean expressions

Simple Boolean Expression	Boolean Value
`7 = 7`	**true**
`-3.0 = 0.0`	**false**
`4.2 > 3.7`	**true**
`-18 < -15`	**true**
`13 < 100`	**true**
`13 <= 100`	**true**
`13 <= 13`	**true**
`0.012 > 0.013`	**false**
`-17.32 <> -17.32`	**false**
`A <= B`	**true**
`B > A`	**true**

Arithmetic expressions can also be used in simple Boolean expressions. Thus

```
4 < (3 + 2)
```

has the value **true.** When the computer evaluates this expression, the parentheses dictate that (3 + 2) be evaluated first and the relational operator be evaluated second. Sequentially, this becomes

```
4 < (3 + 2)
4 <    5
true
```

If the parentheses are not used, can the expression be evaluated? This type of expression requires that a priority level be set for the relational operators and the arithmetic operators. A summary of the priorities of these operations is

Expression	Priority
`( )`	1
`*, /, MOD, DIV`	2
`+, -`	3
`=, <, >, <=, >=, <>`	4

Thus, we see the relational operators are evaluated last. Like arithmetic operators, relational operators are evaluated in order from left to right. Thus, the expression

```
4 < 3 + 2
```

without parentheses will have the same Boolean value.

The following example illustrates the evaluation of a somewhat more complex Boolean expression.

EXAMPLE 4.1

Let's indicate the successive steps in the evaluation of the Boolean expression

```
10 MOD 4 * 3 - 8 <= 18 + 30 DIV 4 - 20
```

The steps in this evaluation are

```
10 MOD 4 * 3 - 8 <= 18 + 30 DIV 4 - 20  ┐
   ↓                                    │
   2     * 3 - 8 <= 18 + 30 DIV 4 - 20  ├ first pass
           ↓                            │
           6 - 8 <= 18 + 30 DIV 4 - 20  ┘
                            ↓
           6 - 8 <= 18 +      7    - 20 ┐
             ↓        ↓                 ├ second pass
             - 2 <=   25           - 20 ┘
                                     ↓
             - 2 <=                  5  ┐
                   ↓                    ├ third pass
                  true                  ┘
```

As shown in Example 4.1, parentheses are not required when arithmetic expressions are used with relational operators. It is usually a good idea to use them to enhance the readability of the expression and to avoid the use of an incorrect expression.

Logical Operators and Compound Boolean Expressions

Boolean values may also be generated by using *logical operators* with simple Boolean expressions. The logical operators used by Pascal are **AND**, **OR**, and **NOT**. The operators **AND** and **OR** are used to connect two Boolean expressions. The operator **NOT** is used to negate the Boolean value of an expression; hence, it is sometimes referred to as *negation.* When these connectives or negation are used to generate Boolean values, the complete expression is referred to as a *compound Boolean expression.*

If **AND** is used to join two simple Boolean expressions, the resulting compound expression is **true** only when both simple expressions are **true.** If **OR** is used, the result is **true** if either or both of the expressions are **true.** These rules are summarized as follows:

Expression 1 (E1)	Expression 2 (E2)	E1 **AND** E2	E1 **OR** E2
true	true	true	true
true	false	false	true
false	true	false	true
false	false	false	false

As previously indicated, **NOT** merely produces the logical complement of an expression, as follows:

Expression (E)	**NOT** E
true	false
false	true

When using these operators with relational expressions, parentheses are required because logical operators are evaluated before relational operators. Illustrations of the Boolean values generated using logical operators are given in Table 4.3.

◇ TABLE 4.3
Values of compound Boolean expressions

Expression	Boolean Value
`(4.2 >= 5.0) AND (8 = (3 + 5))`	false
`(4.2 >= 5.0) OR (8 = (3 + 5))`	true
`(-2 < 0) AND (18 >= 10)`	true
`(-2 < 0) OR (18 >= 10)`	true
`(3 > 5) AND (14.1 = 0.0)`	false
`(3 > 5) OR (14.1 = 0.0)`	false
`NOT (18 = 10 + 8)`	false
`NOT (-4 > 0)`	true

Complex Boolean expressions can be generated by using several logical operators in an expression. The priority for evaluating these operators follows.

Operator	Priority
NOT	1
AND	2
OR	3

When complex expressions are being evaluated, the logical operators, arithmetic expressions, and relational operators are evaluated during successive passes through the expression. The priority list is then as follows:

Expression or Operation	Priority
`(   )`	1. Evaluate from inside out.
`NOT`	2. Evaluate from left to right.
`*, /, MOD, DIV, AND`	3. Evaluate from left to right.
`+, -, OR`	4. Evaluate from left to right.
`<, >, <=, >=, =, <>`	5. Evaluate from left to right.

A NOTE OF INTEREST

George Boole

George Boole was born in 1815 in Lincoln, England. Boole was the son of a small shopkeeper, and his family belonged to the lowest social class. In an attempt to rise above his station, Boole spent his early years teaching himself Latin and Greek. During this period, he also received elementary instruction in mathematics from his father.

At the age of 16, Boole worked as a teacher in an elementary school. He used most of his wages to help support his parents. At the age of 20 (after a brief, unsuccessful attempt to study for the clergy), he opened his own school. As part of his preparation for running his school, he had to learn more mathematics. This activity led to the development of some of the most significant mathematics of the nineteenth century.

Boole's major contributions were in the field of logic. An indication of his genius is given by the fact that his early work included the discovery of invariants. The mathematical significance of this is perhaps best explained by noting that the theory of relativity developed by Albert Einstein would not have been possible without the previous work on invariants.

Boole's first published contribution was *The Mathematical Analysis of Logic*, which appeared in 1848 while he was still working as an elementary teacher and the sole support for his parents. In 1849, he was appointed Professor of Mathematics at Queen's College in Cork, Ireland. The relative freedom from financial worry and time constraints the college appointment provided allowed him to pursue his work in mathematics. His masterpiece, *An Investigation of the Laws of Thought, on which Are Founded the Mathematical Theories of Logic and Probabilities*, was published in 1854. Boole was then 39, relatively old for such original work. According to Bertrand Russell, pure mathematics was discovered by Boole in this work.

The brilliance of Boole's work laid the foundation for what is currently studied as formal logic. The data type, Boolean, is named in honor of Boole because of his contribution to the development of logic as part of mathematics. Boole died in 1864. His early death resulted from pneumonia contracted by keeping a lecture engagement when he was soaked to the skin.

Thus, an expression like

```
0 < X AND X < 2
```

produces an error. The expression must be written as

```
(0 < X) AND (X < 2)
```

The following examples illustrate the evaluation of some complex Boolean expressions.

EXAMPLE 4.2

```
(3 < 5) OR (21 <> 18) AND (-81 > 0)   ┐
   ↓                                  │
  true  OR (21 <> 18) AND (-81 > 0)   │ first pass
               ↓                      │ (parentheses first)
  true  OR    true    AND (-81 > 0)   │
                              ↓       ┘
  true  OR    true    AND   false     } second pass
                       ↓
  true  OR           false            ┐
         ↓                            │ third pass
        true                          ┘
```

EXAMPLE 4.3

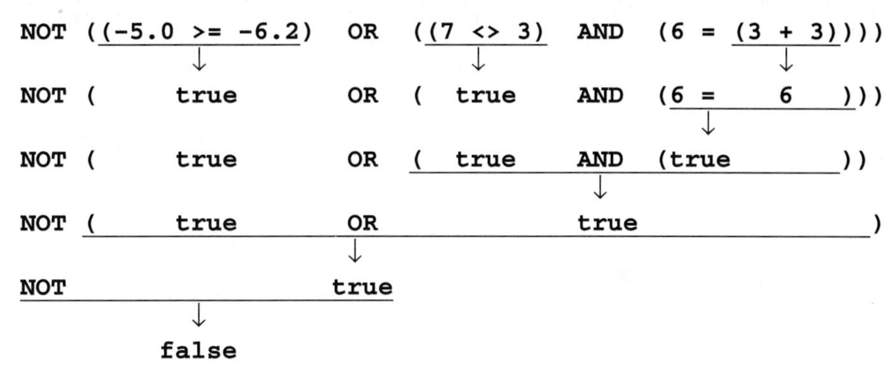

EXERCISES 4.1

1. Assume the variable declaration section of a program is

```
VAR
  Flag1, Flag2 : boolean;
```

What output is produced by the following segment of code?

```
Flag1 := true;
Flag2 := false;
writeln (Flag1, true:6, Flag2:8);
Flag1 := Flag2;
writeln (Flag2:20);
```

2. Write a test program that illustrates what happens when Boolean expressions are not enclosed in parentheses. For example

```
3 < 5 AND 8.0 <> 4 * 3
```

3. Assume the variable declaration section of a program is

```
VAR
  Ch : char;
  Flag : boolean;
```

Indicate if the following assignment statements are valid or invalid.

a. `Flag := 'true';`
b. `Flag := T;`
c. `Flag := true;`
d. `Ch := Flag;`
e. `Ch := true;`
f. `Ch := 'T';`

4. Evaluate each of the following expressions.

a. `(3 > 7) AND (2 < 0) OR (6 = 3 + 3)`
b. `((3 > 7) AND (2 < 0)) OR (6 = 3 + 3)`
c. `(3 > 7) AND ((2 < 0) OR (6 = 3 + 3))`
d. `NOT ((-4.2 <> 3.0) AND (10 < 20))`
e. `(NOT (-4.2 <> 3.0)) OR (NOT (10 < 20))`

5. Indicate whether each of the following simple Boolean expressions is **true, false,** or invalid.

a. `-3.01 <= -3.001`
b. `-3.0 = -3`
c. `25 - 10 <> 3 * 5`
d. `42 MOD 5 < 42 DIV 5`
e. `-5 * (3 + 2) > 2 * (-10)`
f. `10 / 5 < 1 + 1`
g. `3 + 8 MOD 5 >= 6 - 12 MOD 2`

6. Indicate whether each of the following expressions is valid or invalid. Evaluate those that are valid.

   a. `3 < 4 OR 5 <> 6`

   b. `NOT 3.0 = 6 / 2`

   c. `NOT (true OR false)`

   d. `NOT true OR false`

   e. `NOT true OR NOT false`

   f. `NOT (18 < 25) AND OR (-3 < 0)`

   g. `8 * 3 < 20 + 10`

7. Assume the variable declaration section of a program is

```
VAR
  Int1, Int2 : integer;
  Rl1, Rl2 : real;
  Flag1, Flag2 : boolean;
```

and the values of the variables are

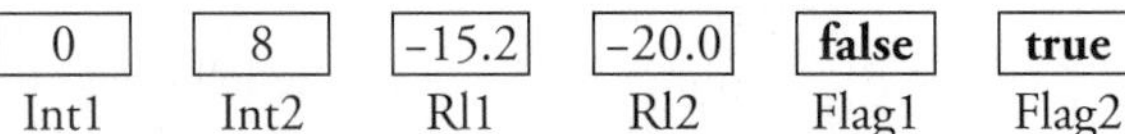

0	8	-15.2	-20.0	**false**	**true**
Int1	Int2	Rl1	Rl2	Flag1	Flag2

Evaluate each of the following expressions.

   a. `(Int1 <= Int2) OR NOT (Rl2 = Rl1)`

   b. `NOT (Flag1) OR NOT (Flag2)`

   c. `NOT (Flag1 AND Flag2)`

   d. `((Rl1 - Rl2) < 100 / Int2) AND ((Int1 < 1) AND NOT (Flag2))`

   e. `NOT ((Int2 - 16 DIV 2) = Int1) AND Flag1`

8. DeMorgan's Laws state the following.

   a. **NOT** (A **OR** B) is equivalent to (**NOT** A) **AND** (**NOT** B).

   b. **NOT** (A **AND** B) is equivalent to (**NOT** A) **OR** (**NOT** B).

   Write a test program that demonstrates the validity of each of these equivalent statements.

4.2 IF . . . THEN Statements

OBJECTIVES

- to learn the form and syntax of an **IF . . . THEN** statement
- to understand the flow of control when using an **IF . . . THEN** statement
- to be able to use an **IF . . . THEN** statement in a program
- to understand why compound statements are needed
- to understand how **BEGIN . . . END** is used to write compound statements
- to be able to use correct syntax in writing a compound statement
- to be able to design programs using **IF . . . THEN** statements

The first decision-making statement we will examine is the **IF . . . THEN** statement. **IF . . . THEN** is used to make a program do something only when certain conditions are met. The form and syntax of an **IF . . . THEN** statement are

> **IF** <Boolean expression> **THEN**
>   <statement>

where <statement> represents any Pascal statement.

The Boolean expression can be any valid expression that is either **true** or **false** at the time of evaluation. If the expression is **true,** the statement following the reserved word **THEN** is executed. If it is **false,** control is transferred to the first program statement following the complete **IF . . . THEN** statement. In general, code has the form

> <statement 1>;
> **IF** <Boolean expression> **THEN**
>   <statement 2>;
> <statement 3>

as illustrated in Figure 4.1.

◆ FIGURE 4.1
IF . . . THEN flow diagram

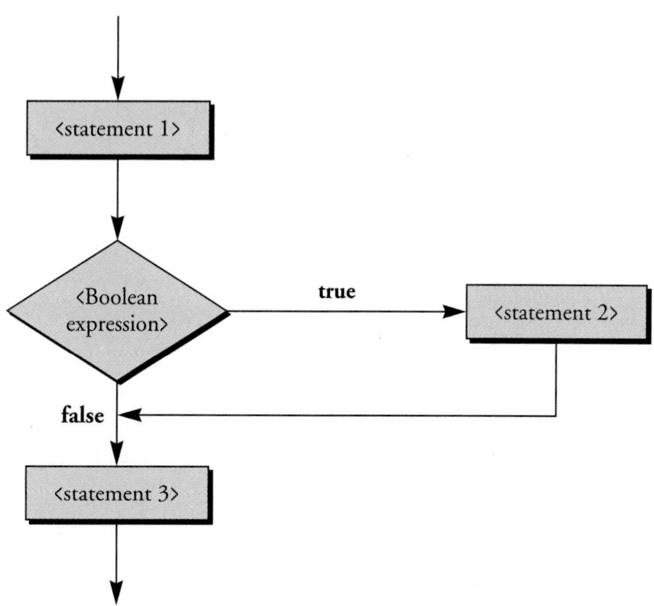

As a further illustration of how an **IF . . . THEN** statement works, consider the program fragment

```
Sum := 0.0;
read (Num);
IF Num > 0.0 THEN
  Sum := Sum + Num;
writeln (Sum:10:2);
```

If the value read is 75.85, then prior to execution of the **IF . . . THEN** statement, the contents of Num and Sum are

75.85	0.0
Num	Sum

The Boolean expression Num > 0.0 is now evaluated. Since it is **true,** the statement

```
Sum := Sum + Num;
```

is executed and we have

75.85	75.85
Num	Sum

The next program statement is executed and produces the output

```
      75.85
```

However, if the value read is –25.5, the variable values are

–25.5	0.0
Num	Sum

The Boolean expression Num > 0.0 is **false,** and control is transferred to the line

```
writeln (Sum);
```

Thus, the output is

```
0.00
```

Now, let's suppose you want one objective of a program to be to count the number of zeros in the input. Assuming suitable initialization and declaration, a program fragment for this task could be

```
readln (Num);
IF Num = 0 THEN
  ZeroCount := ZeroCount + 1;
```

One writing style for an **IF . . . THEN** statement calls for indenting the program statement to be executed if the Boolean expression is **true.** This, of course, is not required.

```
IF Num = 0 THEN
  ZeroCount := ZeroCount + 1;
```

could be written

```
IF Num = 0 THEN ZeroCount := ZeroCount + 1;
```

However, the indenting style for simple **IF . . . THEN** statements is consistent with the style used with more elaborate conditional statements.

Compound Statements

The last concept we need to consider before looking further at selection in Pascal is the *compound statement.* Simple statements conform to the syntax diagram for statements shown in Appendix 3. In a Pascal program, simple statements are separated by semicolons. Thus

```
readln (A, B);
A := 3 * B;
writeln (A);
```

are three simple statements.

In some instances, it is necessary to perform several simple statements when some condition is true. For example, you may want the program to do certain things if a condition is true. In this situation, several simple statements that can be written as a single compound statement would be helpful. In general, several Pascal constructs require compound statements. A *compound statement* is created by using the reserved words **BEGIN** and **END** at the beginning and end of a sequence of simple statements. Correct syntax for a compound statement is

```
BEGIN
  <statement 1>;
  <statement 2>;
      .
      .
      .
  <statement n>
END
```

Statements within a compound statement are separated by semicolons. The last statement before **END** does not require a semicolon; however, if a semicolon is used here, it will not affect the program.

A NOTE OF INTEREST

New Legal Research Uses Plain English

In October 1992, West Publishing introduced WIN® (WESTLAW is Natural™), a Natural Language search method that allows legal researchers to describe their issue in plain English when using WESTLAW®, West's computer-assisted legal research service. This Natural Language search method offers researchers an alternative to the traditional Boolean language format, which uses terms and connectors query formulation. For example, suppose an attorney wanted to submit DNA profiling as significant evidence in a criminal case. The attorney would need to research whether the results of such testing would be admissible in court. WIN allows the WESTLAW user to simply pose the question in plain English; for example:

```
Is DNA profiling evidence admissible in a
criminal trial?
```

Using Boolean methods, the attorney would have to enter the query in the following format:

```
D.N.A. /p profil! /p evidence /p admiss! admit!
inadmiss! /p criminal /s trial
```

WIN works by identifying the key concepts within a question and then comparing the concepts with documents in its databases. Through sophisticated statistical methods, WIN retrieves documents based on how frequently a concept occurs in a document, and how infrequently it occurs in a database. The results retrieved most closely match the search description.

When a compound statement is executed within a program, the entire segment of code between **BEGIN** and **END** is treated as a single action. This is referred to as a ***BEGIN . . . END** block.* It is important that you develop a consistent, acceptable style for writing compound statements. What you use will vary according to your instructor's wishes and your personal preferences. In examples in this text, each simple statement within a compound statement will be indented two spaces. Thus

```
BEGIN
  read (A, B);
  A := 3 * B;
  writeln (A)
END;
```

is a compound statement in a program. What it does is easily identified.

Using Compound Statements

As you might expect, compound statements can be (and frequently are) used as part of an **IF . . . THEN** statement. They are required if more than one simple statement is to be executed. The form and syntax of this are

```
IF <Boolean expression> THEN
  BEGIN
    <statement 1>;
    <statement 2>;
         .
         .
         .
    <statement n>
  END
```

Program control is exactly as before, depending upon the value of the Boolean expression. For example, suppose you are writing a procedure to keep track of and compute fees for vehicles in a parking lot where separate records are kept for senior citizens. A segment of code in the procedure could be

```
IF Customer = 'S' THEN
  BEGIN
    SeniorCount := SeniorCount + 1;
    AmountDue := SeniorCitizenRate
  END;
```

IF . . . THEN Statements with Procedures

The following example designs a program to solve a problem using an **IF . . . THEN** statement with procedures.

EXAMPLE 4.4

Let's write a program that reads two integers and prints them in the following order: larger first, smaller second. The first-level pseudocode solution is

1. Read numbers
2. Determine larger
3. Print results

A structure chart for this problem is given in Figure 4.2.

◆ FIGURE 4.2
Structure chart for integer problem

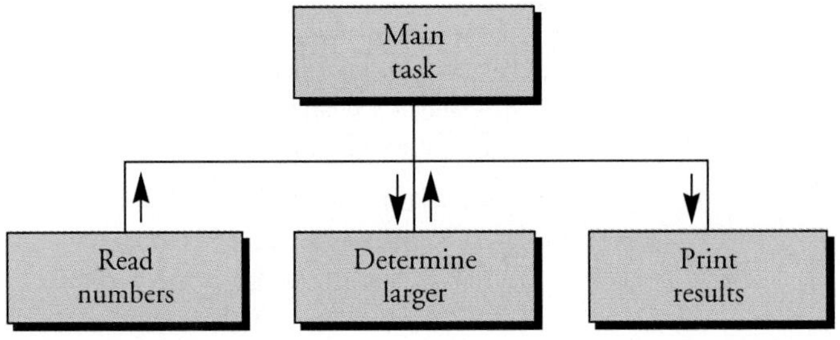

The procedures for ReadNumbers and PrintResults are similar to those used previously, so let's consider the module DetermineLarger. Data sent to this procedure will be two integers. Information returned will be the same two integers in the following order: larger, smaller. Code for this is

```
IF Num1 < Num2 THEN
  Switch (Num1, Num2);
```

where Switch is a procedure as follows:

```
PROCEDURE Switch (VAR Num1, Num2 : integer);
  VAR
    Temp : integer;
  BEGIN
    Temp := Num1;
    Num1 := Num2;
    Num2 := Temp
  END;  {  of PROCEDURE Switch  }
```

Note an additional variable Temp is needed to temporarily hold the value of Num1. This type of exchange is used frequently throughout the text.

The main program for this problem is

```
    BEGIN  {  Main program  }
      ReadNumbers (Num1, Num2);
      IF Num1 < Num2 THEN
        Switch (Num1, Num2);
      PrintResults (Num1, Num2)
    END.  {  of main program  }
```

A complete program for this problem follows.

```
PROGRAM UseIFTHEN (input, output);

{  This short program illustrates using an IF...THEN       }
{  statement; two numbers are read, then printed in        }
{  order, larger first.                                    }

CONST
  Skip = ' ';

VAR
  Num1, Num2 : integer;     {  Two numbers to be arranged  }

{*********************************************************}

PROCEDURE ReadNumbers (VAR Num1, Num2 : integer);

  {  Given:   Nothing                                      }
  {  Task:    Read two numbers entered from the keyboard   }
  {  Return:  Two integers                                 }   1

  BEGIN
    writeln ('Enter two integers and press <Enter>.');
    readln (Num1, Num2)
  END;  {  of PROCEDURE ReadNumbers  }

{*********************************************************}

PROCEDURE Switch (VAR Num1, Num2 : integer);

  {  Given:   Two integers, Num1 and Num2                  }
  {  Task:    Use variable parameters to switch values     }
  {  Return:  Two integers, Num1 and Num2, with values     }
  {                   switched, if in wrong order          }

  VAR                                                          2
    Temp : integer;
  BEGIN
    Temp := Num1;
    Num1 := Num2;
    Num2 := Temp
  END;  {  of PROCEDURE Switch  }

{*********************************************************}
```

```
PROCEDURE PrintResults (Num1, Num2 : integer);

  {  Given:   Two integers                                    }
  {  Task:    Print the integers with a suitable heading      }
  {  Return:  Nothing                                         }

  BEGIN
    writeln;                                                      3
    writeln (Skip:19, 'Larger number',
             Skip:10, 'Smaller number');
    writeln (Skip:19, '-------------',
             Skip:10, '--------------');
    writeln;
    writeln (Num1:26, Num2:23)
  END;  {  of PROCEDURE PrintResults  }

{************************************************************}

BEGIN  {  Main program  }
  ReadNumbers (Num1, Num2);
  IF Num1 < Num2 THEN
    Switch (Num1, Num2);
  PrintResults (Num1, Num2)
END.  {  of main program  }
```

Sample runs of this program produce the following output.

```
Enter two integers and press <Enter>.
35 115

                   Larger number          Smaller number
                   -------------          --------------

                        115                     35

Enter two integers and press <Enter>.
85 26

                   Larger number          Smaller number
                   -------------          --------------

                         85                     26
```

Note two runs of this program are required to test the logic of the **IF . . . THEN** statement.

EXERCISES 4.2

1. What output is produced by each of the following program fragments? Assume the assignment statements

   ```
   A := 10;
   B := 5;
   ```

   precede each fragment.

```
a. IF A <= B THEN
     B := A;
   writeln (A, B);
b. IF A <= B THEN
     BEGIN
       B := A;
       writeln (A, B)
     END;
c. IF A < B THEN
     Temp := A;
   A := B;
   B := Temp;
   writeln (A, B);
d. IF A < B THEN
     BEGIN
       Temp := A;
       A := B;
       B := Temp
     END;
   writeln (A, B);
e. IF (A < B) OR (B - A < 0) THEN
     BEGIN
       A := A + B;
       B := B - 1;
       writeln (A, B)
     END;
   writeln (A, B);
f. IF (A < B) AND (B - A < 0) THEN
     BEGIN
       A := A + B;
       B := B - 1;
       writeln (A, B)
     END;
   writeln (A, B);
```

2. Write a test program to illustrate what happens when a semicolon is inadvertently inserted after **THEN** in an **IF . . . THEN** statement. For example

```
IF A > 0 THEN;
  Sum := Sum + A;
```

3. Find and explain the errors in each of the following program fragments. Assume all variables have been suitably declared.

```
a. IF A := 10 THEN
     writeln (A);
b. X := 7;
   IF 3 < X < 10 THEN
     BEGIN
       X := X + 1;
       writeln (X)
     END;
```

```
c. Count := 0;
   Sum := 0;
   A := 50;
   IF A > 0 THEN
     Count := Count + 1;
     Sum := Sum + A;
d. read (Ch);
   IF Ch = 'A' OR 'B' THEN
     writeln (Ch:10);
```

4. What output is produced by each of the following program fragments? Assume all variables have been suitably declared.

a.
```
J := 18;
IF J MOD 5 = 0 THEN
  writeln (J);
```

b.
```
A := 5;
B := 90;
B := B DIV A - 5;
IF B > A THEN
  B := A * 30;
writeln (A, B);
```

5. Can a simple statement be written using a **BEGIN . . . END** block? Write a short program that allows you to verify your answer.

6. Discuss the differences in the following programs. Predict the output for each program using sample values for Num.

a.
```
PROGRAM Exercise6a (input, output);

VAR
  Num : integer;

BEGIN
  writeln ('Enter an integer and press <Enter>.');
  readln (Num);
  IF Num > 0 THEN
    writeln;
    writeln ('The number is':22, Num:6);
    writeln;
    writeln ('The number squared is':30, Num * Num:6);
    writeln ('The number cubed is':28, Num * Num *
              Num:6);
    writeln
END.
```

b.
```
PROGRAM Exercise6b (input, output);

VAR
  Num : integer;

BEGIN
  writeln ('Enter an integer and press <Enter>.');
  readln (Num);
  IF Num > 0 THEN
    BEGIN  {  Start output  }
      writeln;
      writeln ('The number is':22, Num:6);
      writeln;
      writeln ('The number squared is':30, Num *
                Num:6);
      writeln ('The number cubed is':28, Num * Num *
                Num:6);
      writeln
    END  {  output for one number  }
END.
```

7. Discuss the writing style and readability of compound statements.

8. Find all errors in the following compound statements.
   a.
```
BEGIN
  read (A)
  writeln (A)
END;
```
   b.
```
BEGIN
  Sum := Sum + Num
END;
```
   c.
```
BEGIN
  readln (Size1, Size2);
  writeln (Size1:8, Size2:8)
END.
```
   d.
```
BEGIN
  readln (Age, Weight);
  TotalAge := TotalAge + Age;
  TotalWeight := TotalWeight + Weight;
  writeln (Age:8, Weight:8)
```
9. Write a single compound statement that does the following.
   (1) Reads three integers from the keyboard.
   (2) Adds them to a previous total.
   (3) Prints the numbers on one line.
   (4) Skips a line (output).
   (5) Prints the new total.
10. Write a program fragment that reads three reals, counts the number of positive reals, and accumulates the sum of positive reals.
11. Write a program fragment that reads three characters and then prints them only if they have been read in alphabetical order. (For example, print "boy" but do not print "dog".)
12. Given two integers A and B, A is a divisor of B if B **MOD** A = 0. Write a complete program that reads two positive integers, A and B, and if A is a divisor of B,
    a. Prints A
    b. Prints B
    c. Prints the result of B divided by A

    For example, the output could be
```
A is 14
B is 42
B divided by A is 3
```

4.3 IF . . . THEN . . . ELSE Statements

Form and Syntax

In Section 4.2, we discussed the one-way selection statement **IF . . . THEN.** The second selection statement we will examine is the two-way selection statement **IF . . . THEN . . . ELSE.** The correct form and syntax of the **IF . . . THEN . . . ELSE** statement are

> **IF** <Boolean expression> **THEN**
>   <statement>
> **ELSE**
>   <statement>

OBJECTIVES

- to learn the form and syntax of an **IF . . . THEN . . . ELSE** statement
- to understand the flow of control when using an **IF . . . THEN . . . ELSE** statement
- to be able to use an **IF . . . THEN . . . ELSE** statement in a program
- to be able to design programs using **IF . . . THEN . . . ELSE** statements

Flow of control when using an **IF . . . THEN . . . ELSE** statement is as follows:

1. The Boolean expression is evaluated.
2. If the Boolean expression is **true,** the statement following **THEN** is executed and control is transferred to the first program statement following the complete **IF . . . THEN . . . ELSE** statement.
3. If the Boolean expression is **false,** the statement following **ELSE** is executed and control is transferred to the first program statement following the **IF . . . THEN . . . ELSE** statement.

A flow diagram for this statement is given in Figure 4.3.

◆ FIGURE 4.3
IF . . . THEN . . . ELSE flow diagram

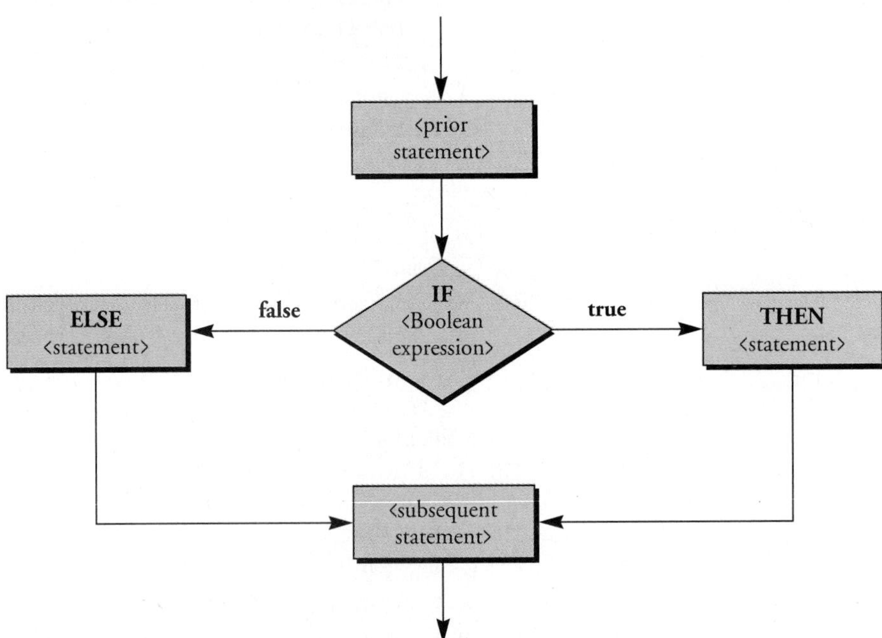

A few points to remember concerning **IF . . . THEN . . . ELSE** statements follow.

1. The Boolean expression can be any valid expression that has a value of **true** or **false** at the time it is evaluated.
2. The complete **IF . . . THEN . . . ELSE** statement is one program statement and is separated from other complete statements by a semicolon whenever appropriate.
3. No semicolon precedes the reserved word **ELSE.** A semicolon preceding the reserved word **ELSE** causes the compiler to treat the **IF . . . THEN** portion as a complete program statement and the **ELSE** portion as a separate statement. This produces an error message indicating that **ELSE** is being used without **IF . . . THEN.**
4. Writing style should include indenting in the **ELSE** option in a manner consistent with indenting in the **IF . . . THEN** option.

EXAMPLE 4.5

Let's write a program fragment to keep separate counts of the negative and nonnegative numbers entered as data. Assuming all variables have been suitably declared and initialized, an **IF . . . THEN . . . ELSE** statement could be used as follows:

```
writeln ('Please enter a number and press <Enter>.');
readln (Num);
IF Num < 0 THEN
  NegCount := NegCount + 1
ELSE
  NonNegCount := NonNegCount + 1;
```

Using Compound Statements

Program statements in both the **IF . . . THEN** option and the **ELSE** option can be compound statements. When using compound statements in these options, you should employ a consistent, readable indenting style. Remember to use **BEGIN . . . END** for each compound statement, and do not put a semicolon before **ELSE.** Next, we will consider some examples that require the use of compound statements within **IF . . . THEN . . . ELSE** statements.

EXAMPLE 4.6

Suppose you want a program to read a number, count it as negative or nonnegative, and print it in either a column of negative numbers or a column of nonnegative numbers. Assuming all variables have been suitably declared and initialized, the fragment might be

```
writeln ('Please enter a number and press <Enter>.');
readln (Num);
IF Num < 0 THEN
  BEGIN
    NegCount := NegCount + 1;
    writeln (Num:15)
  END  {  of IF...THEN option  }
ELSE
  BEGIN
    NonNegCount := NonNegCount + 1;
    writeln (Num:30)
  END;  {  of ELSE option  }
```

EXAMPLE 4.7

Let's write a function that computes gross wages for an employee of the Florida OJ Canning Company. Input includes hours worked and the hourly rate. Overtime (more than 40 hours) pay is computed at "time-and-a-half." A function would be

```
FUNCTION ComputeWages (Hours, PayRate : real) : real;
  VAR
    Overtime : real;
  BEGIN
    IF Hours <= 40.0 THEN
      ComputeWages := Hours * PayRate
    ELSE
```

```
      BEGIN
        Overtime := 1.5 * (Hours - 40.0) * PayRate;
        ComputeWages := 40 * PayRate + Overtime
      END
  END;  {  of FUNCTION ComputeWages  }
```

Robust Programs

If a program is completely protected against all possible crashes that can be caused by bad data and unexpected values, it is said to be *robust.* The preceding examples all assume the desired data is accurately entered from the keyboard. In actual practice, this is seldom the case. **IF . . . THEN . . . ELSE** statements can be used to guard against bad data entries. For example, if a program is designed to use positive numbers, you could guard against negatives and zero by

```
writeln ('Enter a positive number and press <Enter>.');
readln (Number);
IF Number <= 0 THEN
  writeln ('You entered a nonpositive number.');
ELSE
    .
    .   (code for expected action here)
    .
```

This protection can be used anywhere in a program. For example, if you are finding the square roots of numbers, you could avoid a program crash by

```
IF Num < 0 THEN
  writeln ('The number ', Num, ' is negative.')
ELSE
    .
    .   (rest of action here)
    .
```

In actual practice, students need to balance robustness against length and efficiency of code. An overemphasis on making a program robust can detract from time spent learning new programming concepts. Discuss this with your instructor, and determine the best course of action to follow. Generally, there should be an agreement between the programmer and the customer regarding the level of robustness required. For most programs and examples in this text, it is assumed that valid data are entered when requested.

Guarding against Overflow

As we discussed in Chapter 2, integer overflow occurs when the absolute value of an integer exceeds **maxint** and real overflow occurs when a value is obtained that is too large to be stored in a memory location. The maximum value of an integer is stored in **maxint**. Unfortunately, there is no convenient analogue for reals.

One method used to guard against integer overflow is based upon the principle of checking a number against some function of **maxint**. Thus, if you want to multiply a number by 10, you would first compare it to **maxint DIV** 10. A typical segment of code could be

```
IF Num > maxint DIV 10 THEN
  .
  .   (overflow message here)
  .
ELSE
  BEGIN
    Num := Num * 10;
      .
      .   (rest of action here)
      .
  END;
```

We can now use this same idea with a Boolean-valued function. For example, consider the function

```
FUNCTION NearOverflow (Num : integer) : boolean;
  BEGIN
    NearOverflow := (Num > maxint DIV 10)
  END;
```

which could be used in the following manner.

```
IF NearOverflow (Num) THEN
  .
  .   (overflow message here)
  .
ELSE
  BEGIN
    Num := Num * 10;
      .
      .   (rest of action here)
      .
  END;
```

A NOTE OF INTEREST

Artificial Intelligence

Artificial intelligence (AI) research seeks to understand the principles of human intelligence and apply those principles to the creation of smarter computer programs. The original goal of AI research was to create programs with humanlike intelligence and capabilities. Yet after many years of research, little progress has been made toward this goal.

In recent years, however, AI researchers have pursued much more modest goals with much greater success. Programs based upon AI techniques are playing increasingly important roles in such down-to-earth areas as medicine, education, recreation, business, and industry. Such programs nowhere nearly achieve human levels of intelligence, but they often have capabilities not easily achieved with non-AI programs.

The main principles of AI can be summarized as follows:

Search: The computer solves a problem by searching through all logically possible solutions.

Rules: Knowledge about what actions to take in particular circumstances is stored as rules; each rule has the form

IF <situation> **THEN** <action or conclusion>

Reasoning: Programs can use reasoning to draw conclusions from the facts and rules available to the program.

Planning: The control program plans the actions that must be taken to accomplish a particular goal and then modifies the plan if unexpected obstacles are encountered; this is most widely used in robot control.

Pattern recognition: This is important for rule-based systems, the ***IF*** part of a rule specifies a particular pattern of facts; the rule is to be applied when that pattern is recognized in the facts known to the program.

Knowledge bases: Locations where the facts and rules that govern the operation of an AI program are stored.

EXERCISES 4.3

1. What output is produced by each of the following program fragments? Assume all variables have been suitably declared.

a.
```
A := -14;
B := 0;
IF A < B THEN
  writeln (A, abs(A))
ELSE
  writeln (A * B);
```

b.
```
A := 50;
B := 25;
Count := 0;
Sum := 0;
IF A = B THEN
  writeln (A, B)
ELSE
  BEGIN
    Count := Count + 1;
    Sum := Sum + A + B;
    writeln (A, B)
  END;
writeln (Count, Sum);
```

c.
```
Temp := 0;
A := 10;
B := 5;
IF A > B THEN
  writeln (A, B)
ELSE
  Temp := A;
  A := B;
  B := Temp;
writeln (A, B);
```

2. Write a test program that illustrates what error message occurs when a semicolon precedes **ELSE** in an **IF . . . THEN . . . ELSE** statement. For example

```
PROGRAM SyntaxError (output);

VAR
  A, B : integer;

BEGIN
  A := 10;
  B := 5;
  IF A < B THEN
    writeln (A);
  ELSE
    writeln (B)
END.
```

3. Find all errors in the following program fragments.

a.
```
IF Ch <> '.' THEN
  CharCount := CharCount + 1;
  writeln (Ch)
ELSE
  PeriodCount := PeriodCount + 1;
```

b.
```
IF Age < 20 THEN
  BEGIN
    YoungCount := YoungCount + 1;
    YoungAge := YoungAge + Age
  END;  {  of IF...THEN option  }
ELSE
  BEGIN
    OldCount := OldCount + 1;
    OldAge := OldAge + Age
  END;  {  of ELSE option  }
```

c.
```
IF Age < 20 THEN
  BEGIN
    YoungCount := YoungCount + 1;
    YoungAge := YoungAge + Age
  END  {  of IF...THEN option  }
ELSE
  OldCount := OldCount + 1;
  OldAge := OldAge + Age;
```

4. Assume the declaration section

```
VAR
  MaxValue,
  X, Y, Z : real;
```

is part of a program and X, Y, and Z have values assigned to them.

a. Write a segment of code that uses **IF . . . THEN** statements to assign the largest value to MaxValue.

b. Write a segment of code that uses **IF . . . THEN . . . ELSE** statements to assign the largest value to MaxValue.

5. Write a program to balance your checkbook. Your program should get an entry from the keyboard, keep track of the number of deposits and checks, and maintain a running balance. The data consist of a character, D (deposit) or C (check), followed by an amount.

6. Write an interactive program that determines the slopes of two lines. Input consists of two points (X1,Y1) and (X2,Y2) on each line. The slope of each nonvertical line is to be computed. A special message should be printed if the line is vertical (X1 = X2). Output for other lines should indicate if they are parallel ($m_1 = m_2$), perpendicular $\left(m_1 = -\frac{1}{m_2}\right)$, or neither.

4.4 Nested and Extended IF Statements

OBJECTIVES

- to learn the form and syntax of nested **IF** statements
- to know when to use nested **IF** statements
- to be able to use extended **IF** statements
- to be able to trace the logic when using nested **IF** statements
- to develop a consistent writing style for nested **IF** statements

Multiway Selection

In Sections 4.2 and 4.3, we examined one-way (**IF . . . THEN**) selection and two-way (**IF . . . THEN . . . ELSE**) selection. Since each of these is a single Pascal statement, either one can be used as part of a selection statement to achieve multiple selection. In this case, the multiple selection statement is referred to as a *nested **IF** statement.* Nested statements can be any combination of **IF . . . THEN** or **IF . . . THEN . . . ELSE** statements.

To illustrate, let's write a program fragment to issue interim progress reports to students in a class. If a student's score is below 50, the student is failing. If the score is between 50 and 69 inclusive, the progress is unsatisfactory. If the score is 70 or above, the progress is satisfactory. The first decision to be made is based upon whether the score is below 50 or not; the design is

```
IF Score >= 50 THEN
   .
   .   (progress report here)
   .
ELSE
  writeln ('You are currently failing.':34);
```

We now use a nested **IF . . . THEN . . . ELSE** statement for the progress report to students who are not failing. The complete fragment is

```
IF Score >= 50 THEN
  IF Score > 69 THEN
    writeln ('Your progress is satisfactory.':38)
  ELSE
    writeln ('Your progress is unsatisfactory.':40)
ELSE
  writeln ('You are currently failing.':34);
```

One particular instance of nesting selection statements requires special development. When additional **IF . . . THEN . . . ELSE** statements are used in the **ELSE** option, we call this an *extended **IF** statement* and use the form

```
IF <condition 1> THEN
    .
    .     (action 1 here)
    .
ELSE IF <condition 2> THEN
    .
    .     (action 2 here)
    .
ELSE IF <condition 3> THEN
    .
    .     (action 3 here)
    .
ELSE
    .
    .     (action 4 here)
    .
```

Using this form, we can redesign the previous fragment that prints progress reports as follows:

```
IF Score > 69 THEN
  writeln ('Your progress is satisfactory.':38)
ELSE IF Score > 50 THEN
  writeln ('Your progress is unsatisfactory.':40)
ELSE
  writeln ('You are currently failing.':34);
```

If you trace through both fragments with scores of 40, 60, and 80, you will find they produce identical output.

Another method of writing the nested fragment is to use sequential selection statements as follows:

```
IF Score > 69 THEN
  writeln ('Your progress is satisfactory.':38);
IF (Score <= 69) AND (Score >= 50) THEN
  writeln ('Your progress is unsatisfactory.':40);
IF Score < 50 THEN
  writeln ('You are currently failing.':34);
```

However, this method is less efficient because each **IF . . . THEN** statement is executed each time through the program. You should generally avoid using sequential **IF . . . THEN** statements if a nested statement can be used; this reduces execution time for a program.

Tracing the flow of logic through nested or extended **IF** statements can be tedious. However, it is essential that you develop this ability. For practice, let's trace through the following example.

EXAMPLE 4.8

Let's consider the nested statement

```
IF A > 0 THEN
  IF A MOD 2 = 0 THEN
    Sum1 := Sum1 + A
  ELSE
    Sum2 := Sum2 + A
ELSE IF A = 0 THEN
  writeln ('A is zero':18)
ELSE
  NegSum := NegSum + A;
writeln ('All done':17);
```

We will trace through this statement and discover what action is taken when A is assigned the values of 20, 15, 0, and –30. For A := 20, the statement A > 0 is **true;** hence

```
A MOD 2 = 0
```

is evaluated. This is **true,** so

```
Sum1 := Sum1 + A
```

is executed and control is transferred out of the nested statement to

```
writeln ('All done':17);
```

For A := 15, A > 0 is **true** and

```
A MOD 2 = 0
```

is evaluated. This is **false,** so

```
Sum2 := Sum2 + A
```

is executed and control is again transferred out of the nested statement to

```
writeln ('All done':17);
```

For A := 0, A > 0 is **false;** thus

```
A = 0
```

is evaluated. Since this is **true,** the statement

```
writeln ('A is zero':18)
```

is executed and control is transferred to

```
writeln ('All done':17);
```

Finally, for A := –30, A > 0 is **false;** thus

```
A = 0
```

is evaluated. This is **false,** so

```
NegSum := NegSum + A;
```

is executed and control is then transferred to

```
writeln ('All done':17);
```

This example traces through all possibilities involved in the nested statement. It is essential to do this to guarantee that your statement is properly constructed.

Designing solutions to problems that require multiway selection can be difficult. A few guidelines can help. If a decision has two courses of action and if one is complex and the other is fairly simple, nest the complex part in the **IF . . . THEN** option and the simple part in the **ELSE** option. This method is frequently used to check for bad data. An example of the program design for this is

```
     .
     .  (get the data)
     .
IF DataOK THEN
     .
     .  (complex action here)
     .
ELSE
   (message about bad data here)
```

This method can also be used to guard against dividing by zero in computation. For instance, we can have

```
Divisor := <value>;
IF Divisor <> 0 THEN
    .
    .  (proceed with action)
    .
ELSE
  writeln ('Division by zero');
```

When there are several courses of action that can be considered sequentially, an extended **IF . . . THEN . . . ELSE** statement should be used. To illustrate, consider the program fragment in the following example.

EXAMPLE 4.9

Let's write a program fragment that allows you to assign letter grades based upon students' semester averages. Grades are to be assigned according to the scale

$100 \geq X \geq 90$	A
$90 > X \geq 80$	B
$80 > X \geq 70$	C
$70 > X \geq 55$	D
$55 > X$	E

Extended **IF** statements can be used to accomplish this as follows:

```
IF Average >= 90 THEN
  Grade := 'A'
ELSE IF Average >= 80 THEN
  Grade := 'B'
ELSE IF Average >= 70 THEN
  Grade := 'C'
ELSE IF Average >= 55 THEN
  Grade := 'D'
ELSE
  Grade := 'E';
```

Since any Average greater than 100 or less than zero would be a sign of some data or program error, this example could be protected with the following statement.

```
IF (Average <= 100) AND (Average >= 0) THEN
   .
   . (compute letter grade)
   .
ELSE
  writeln ('There is an error. Average is':38,
           Average:8:2);
```

Protecting parts of a program in this manner will help you avoid unexpected results or program crashes. It also allows you to identify the source of an error.

Form and Syntax

The rule for matching **ELSE** statements in nested selection statements is

> *When an* **ELSE** *statement is encountered, it is matched with the most recent* **THEN** *statement that has not yet been matched.*

Matching **IF . . . THEN** statements with **ELSE** statements is a common source of errors. When you design programs, you should be very careful to match them correctly.

A situation that can lead to an error is an **IF . . . THEN . . . ELSE** statement such as

IF <condition 1> **THEN**
   .
   . (action 1)
   .
ELSE
   .
   . (action 2)
   .

where action 1 consists of an **IF . . . THEN** statement. Specifically, suppose we want a fragment of code to read a list of positive integers and print the ones that are perfect squares. A way to protect against negative integers and zero could be

```
readln (Num);
IF Num > 0 THEN
   .
   . (action 1 here)
   .
ELSE
  writeln (Num, ' is not positive.');
```

If we now develop action 1 so it prints only the positive integers that are perfect squares, it is

```
IF abs(sqrt(Num) - trunc(sqrt(Num))) < 0.0001 THEN
  writeln (Num)
```

Nesting this selection statement in our design, we have

```
readln (Num);
IF Num > 0 THEN
  IF abs(sqrt(Num) - trunc(sqrt(Num))) < 0.0001 THEN
    writeln (Num)
ELSE
  writeln (Num, ' is not positive.');
```

If we now use this segment with input of 20 for Num, the output is

```
20 is not positive.
```

Thus, this fragment is not correct to solve the problem. The indenting is consistent with our intent, but the actual execution of the fragment treated the code as

```
readln (Num);
IF Num > 0 THEN
  IF abs(sqrt(Num) - trunc(sqrt(Num))) < 0.0001 THEN
    writeln (Num)
  ELSE
    writeln (Num, ' is not positive.');
```

because the **ELSE** is matched with the most recent **THEN**. This problem can be resolved in several ways. We can use an **ELSE** option with an *empty (null) statement*. We would then have

```
readln (Num);
IF Num > 0 THEN
  IF abs(sqrt(Num) - trunc(sqrt(Num))) < 0.0001 THEN
    writeln (Num)
  ELSE  {  Do nothing  }
ELSE
  writeln (Num, ' is not positive.');
```

The second **IF . . . THEN** statement can be isolated by enclosing it in a **BEGIN . . . END** block. Thus, we would have

```
readln (Num);
IF Num > 0 THEN
  BEGIN
    IF abs(sqrt(Num) - trunc(sqrt(Num))) < 0.0001 THEN
      writeln (Num)
  END  {  of IF...THEN option  }
ELSE
  writeln (Num, ' is not positive.');
```

Or we can redesign the fragment as follows:

```
readln (Num);
IF Num <= 0 THEN
  writeln (Num,' is not positive.');
ELSE IF abs(sqrt(Num) - trunc(sqrt(Num))) < 0.0001 THEN
  writeln (Num);
```

COMMUNICATION AND STYLE TIPS

It is very important to use a consistent, readable writing style when using nested or extended **IF** statements. The style used here for nested **IF** statements is to indent each nested statement two spaces. Also, each **ELSE** of an **IF . . . THEN . . . ELSE** statement is in the same column as the **IF** of that statement. This allows you to see at a glance where the **ELSE**s match with the **IF . . . THEN**s. For example

```
IF . . . THEN
  IF . . . THEN
  ELSE
ELSE
```

In an extended IF statement, all the **ELSE**s are on the same indenting level as the first **IF**. This reinforces the concept of extended **IF**. For example

```
IF . . . THEN
ELSE IF . . . THEN
ELSE IF . . . THEN
ELSE
```

We conclude this section with an example that uses nested **IF** statements.

EXAMPLE 4.10

Let's write a program that computes the gross pay for an employee of the Clean Products Corporation of America. The corporation produces three products: A, B, and C. Supervisors earn a commission of 7 percent of sales, and representatives earn 5 percent. Bonuses of $100 are paid to supervisors whose commission exceeds $300 and to representatives whose commission exceeds $200. Typical input consists of an S for supervisor or an R for representative followed by three integers representing the number of units of each of the products sold. A sample input screen is

```
Enter S or R for classification.
S
Enter ASales, BSales, CSales
1100 990 510
```

Since product prices may vary over time, the constant definition section will be used to indicate the current prices. The section for this problem will be

```
CONST
  SuperRate = 0.07;
  RepRate = 0.05;
  APrice = 13.95;
  BPrice = 17.95;
  CPrice = 29.95;
```

A first-level pseudocode development for this problem is

1. Get the data
2. Compute commission and bonus
3. Print heading
4. Print results

The structure chart for this problem is shown in Figure 4.4.

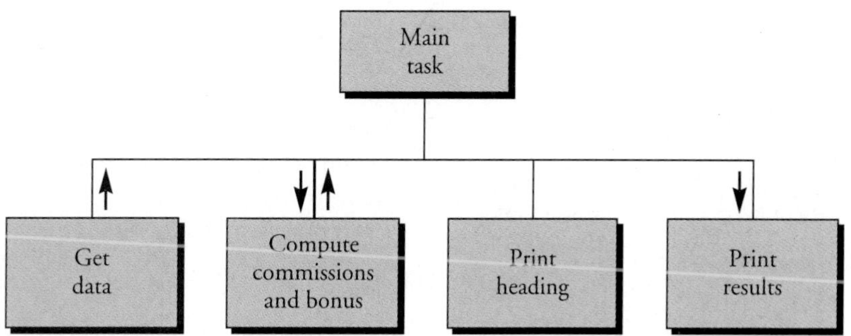

◆ FIGURE 4.4
Structure chart for the Clean Products Corporation of America problem

Module specifications for each of the main modules are

1. GetData Module
Data received: None
Information returned: Employee classification
Sales of products A, B, and C
Logic: Read input data from the keyboard.

2. ComputeCommAndBonus Module
   Data received: Classification
   ASales
   BSales
   CSales
   Information returned: ACommission
   BCommission
   CCommission
   TotalCommission
   Bonus
   Logic: **IF** a supervisor **THEN**
   compute total commission
   compute bonus
   ELSE
   compute total commission
   compute bonus
3. PrintHeading Module
   Data received: None
   Information returned: None
   Logic: Use **writeln** statements to print a heading for the report.
4. PrintResults Module
   Data received: Classification
   ASales
   BSales
   CSales
   ACommission
   BCommission
   CCommission
   TotalCommission
   Bonus
   Information returned: None
   Logic: Use **writeln** statements to print the employee's report.

Modules for GetData, PrintHeading, and PrintResults are similar to those previously developed. The module ComputeCommAndBonus requires some development. Step 2 of the pseudocode becomes

```
2. Compute commission and bonus
   2.1 IF employee is supervisor THEN
         compute supervisor's earnings
       ELSE
         compute representative's earnings
```

where "compute supervisor's earnings" is refined to

```
2.1.1 compute commission from sales of A
2.1.2 compute commission from sales of B
2.1.3 compute commission from sales of C
2.1.4 compute total commission
2.1.5 compute supervisor's bonus
      2.1.5.1 IF total commission > 300 THEN
                bonus is 100.00
              ELSE
                bonus is 0.00
```

A similar development is used for computing a representative's earnings.

Step 3 will be an appropriate procedure to print a heading. Step 4 will contain whatever you feel is appropriate for output. Minimum output should be number of sales, amount of sales, commissions, bonuses, and total compensation.

The main program for this problem is

```
BEGIN  {  Main program  }
  GetData (Classification, ASales, BSales, CSales);
  ComputeCommAndBonus (Classification, ASales, BSales,
                       CSales, AComm, BComm, CComm,
                       TotalCommission, Bonus);
  PrintHeading;
  PrintResults (Classification, ASales, BSales, CSales,
                AComm, BComm, CComm, TotalCommission,
                Bonus)
END.  {  of main program  }
```

A complete program for this problem follows.

```
PROGRAM ComputeEarnings (input, output);

{  This program computes gross pay for an employee.  Note the    }
{  use of constants and selection.                               }

CONST
  CompanyName = 'Clean Products Corporation of America';
  Line = '-------------------------------------';
  SuperRate = 0.07;
  RepRate = 0.05;
  APrice = 13.95;
  BPrice = 17.95;
  CPrice = 29.95;
  Month = 'June';
  Skip = ' ';

VAR
  ASales, BSales,
  CSales : integer;        {  Sales of products A, B, C           }
  AComm, BComm, CComm,     {  Commission on sales of A, B, C      }
  Bonus,                   {  Bonus, if earned                    }
  TotalCommission : real;  {  Commission on all products          }
  Classification : char;   {  S-Supervisor or R-Representative    }

{*************************************************************}

PROCEDURE GetData (VAR Classification : char;
                   VAR ASales, BSales, CSales : integer);

  {  Given:   Nothing                                          }
  {  Task:    Have classification and sales amounts entered    }
  {               from the keyboard                            }  1
  {  Return:  Classification, ASales, BSales, CSales           }
```

```
 BEGIN
   writeln ('Enter S or R for classification.');
   readln (Classification);
   writeln ('Enter ASales, BSales, CSales');
   readln (ASales, BSales, CSales)
 END;  {  of PROCEDURE GetData  }

{***************************************************************}

PROCEDURE ComputeCommAndBonus (Classification : char;
                               ASales, BSales, CSales : integer;
                               VAR AComm, BComm, CComm,
                               TotalCommission, Bonus : real);

  {  Given:   Employee classification and sales for products    }
  {               A, B, and C                                    }
  {  Task:    Compute commission and bonus                       }
  {  Return:  Commission for each of products A, B, and C;       }
  {               TotalCommission; and Bonus                     }

  BEGIN
    IF Classification = 'S' THEN          {  Supervisor  }
      BEGIN
        AComm := ASales * APrice * SuperRate;
        BComm := BSales * BPrice * SuperRate;
        CComm := CSales * CPrice * SuperRate;
        TotalCommission := AComm + BComm + CComm;                    2
        IF TotalCommission > 300.0 THEN
          Bonus := 100.0
        ELSE
          Bonus := 0.0
      END
    ELSE
      BEGIN
        AComm := ASales * APrice * RepRate;
        BComm := BSales * BPrice * RepRate;
        CComm := CSales * CPrice * RepRate;
        TotalCommission := AComm + BComm + CComm;
        IF TotalCommission > 200.0 THEN
          Bonus := 100.0
        ELSE
          Bonus := 0.0
      END  {  of ELSE option  }
  END;  {  of PROCEDURE ComputeCommAndBonus  }

{***************************************************************}

PROCEDURE PrintHeading;

  {  Given:   Nothing                                            }
  {  Task:    Print a heading for the output                     }
  {  Return:  Nothing                                            }
```

```
  BEGIN
    writeln;
    writeln (Skip:10, CompanyName);
    writeln (Skip:10, Line);
    writeln;
    writeln (Skip:10, 'Sales Report for:', Skip:3, Month);     3
    writeln;
    write (Skip:10, 'Classification:');
    IF Classification = 'S' THEN
      writeln (Skip:5, 'Supervisor')
    ELSE
      writeln (Skip:5, 'Representative');
    writeln;
    writeln (Skip:12, 'Product     Sales     Commission');
    writeln (Skip:12, '-------     -----     ----------');
    writeln
  END;  {  of PROCEDURE PrintHeading  }

{***********************************************************}

PROCEDURE PrintResults (Classification : char;
                        ASales, BSales, CSales : integer;
                        AComm, BComm, CComm,
                        TotalCommission, Bonus : real);

  {  Given:   Employee classification;  sales of products A,     }
  {                B, and C; commissions for products A, B,      }
  {                and C; total commission; and bonus            }
  {  Task:    Print the results in a readable form              }
  {  Return:  Nothing                                           }
                                                                    4
  BEGIN
    writeln (Skip:15, 'A', ASales:13, AComm:14:2);
    writeln (Skip:15, 'B', BSales:13, BComm:14:2);
    writeln (Skip:15, 'C', CSales:13, CComm:14:2);
    writeln;
    writeln ('Subtotal':31, '$':3, TotalCommission:9:2);
    writeln;
    writeln ('Your bonus is:':31, '$':3, Bonus:9:2);
    writeln ('-------':43);
    writeln ('Total Due':31, '$':3, (TotalCommission + Bonus):9:2)
  END;  {  of PROCEDURE PrintResults  }

{***********************************************************}

BEGIN  {  Main program  }
  GetData (Classification, ASales, BSales, CSales);
  ComputeCommAndBonus (Classification, ASales, BSales, CSales,
                       AComm, BComm, CComm, TotalCommission, Bonus);
  PrintHeading;
  PrintResults (Classification, ASales, BSales, CSales, AComm,
                BComm, CComm, TotalCommission, Bonus)
END.  {  of main program  }
```

A sample run produces the following output.

```
Enter S or R for classification.
S
Enter ASales, BSales, CSales
1100 990 510

          Clean Products Corporation of America
          -------------------------------------

          Sales Report for:    June

          Classification:      Supervisor

            Product      Sales       Commission
            -------      -----       ----------

               A          1100          1074.15
               B           990          1243.93
               C           510          1069.21

                       Subtotal  $   3387.29

                 Your bonus is:  $    100.00
                                     -------

                      Total Due  $   3487.29
```

Program Testing

In actual practice, a great deal of time is spent testing programs in an attempt to make them run properly when they are installed for some specific purpose. Formal program verification is discussed in Section 4.6 and is developed more fully in subsequent course work. However, examining the issue of which data are minimally necessary for program testing is appropriate when working with selection statements.

As you might expect, test data should include information that tests every logical branch in a program. Whenever a program contains an **IF . . . THEN . . . ELSE** statement of the form

```
IF <condition> THEN
  .
  .    (action 1 here)
  .
ELSE
  .
  .    (action 2 here)
  .
```

the test data should guarantee that both the **IF . . . THEN** and the **ELSE** options are executed.

A bit more care is required when selecting test data for nested and extended **IF** statements. In general, a single **IF . . . THEN . . . ELSE** statement requires at least two data items for testing. If an **IF . . . THEN . . . ELSE** statement is nested within the **IF . . . THEN** option, at least two more data items are required to test the nested selection statement.

For the purposes of illustration, let's reexamine the program in Example 4.10. This procedure contains the logic

```
IF Classification = 'S' THEN
  .
  .
  .
  IF TotalCommission > 300.00 THEN
     .
     .
     .
  ELSE
     .
     .
     .
ELSE
  .
  .
  .
  IF TotalCommission > 200.00 THEN
     .
     .
     .
  ELSE
     .
     .
     .
```

To see what data should minimally be used to test this procedure, consider the following table.

Classification	Total Commission
S	$400.00
S	250.00
R	250.00
R	150.00

It is a good idea to include boundary conditions in the test data. Thus, the table could also list 300.00 as the total commission for S and 200.00 as the total commission for R.

In summary, you should always make sure every logical branch is executed when running the program with test data.

EXERCISES 4.4

1. Consider the program fragment

```
IF X >= 0.0 THEN
  IF X < 1000.00 THEN
    BEGIN
      Y := 2 * X;
      IF X <= 500 THEN
        X := X / 10
    END
  ELSE
    Y := 3 * X
ELSE
  Y := abs(X);
```

Indicate the values of X and Y after this fragment is executed for each of the following initial values of X.

a. `X := 381.5;`

b. `X := -21.0;`

c. `X := 600.0;`

d. `X := 3000.0;`

2. Write a nested **IF . . . THEN . . . ELSE** statement that has separate branches for positive integers, zero, and negative integers. The branch for positive integers should distinguish between even and odd integers. Write and run a test program that checks each of these branches.

3. Rewrite each of the following program fragments using nested or extended **IF** statements without compound conditions.

a.
```
IF (Ch = 'M') AND (Sum > 1000) THEN
  X := X + 1;
IF (Ch = 'M') AND (Sum <= 1000) THEN
  X := X + 2;
IF (Ch = 'F') AND (Sum > 1000) THEN
  X := X + 3;
IF (Ch = 'F') AND (Sum <= 1000) THEN
  X := X + 4;
```

b.
```
read (Num);
IF (Num > 0) AND (Num <= 10000) THEN
  BEGIN
    Count := Count + 1;
    Sum := Sum + Num
  END
ELSE
  writeln ('Value out of range':27);
```

c.
```
IF (A > 0) AND (B > 0) THEN
  writeln ('Both positive':22)
ELSE
  writeln ('Some negative':22);
```

d.
```
IF ((A > 0) AND (B > 0)) OR (C > 0) THEN
  writeln ('Option one':19)
ELSE
  writeln ('Option two':19);
```

4. Consider each of the following program fragments.

a.
```
IF A < 0 THEN
  IF B < 0 THEN
    A := B
ELSE
  A := B + 10;
writeln (A, B);
```

b.
```
IF A < 0 THEN
  BEGIN
    IF B < 0 THEN
      A := B
  END  {  of IF...THEN option  }
ELSE
  A := B + 10;
writeln (A, B);
```

c.
```
IF A >= 0 THEN
  A := B + 10
ELSE IF B < 0 THEN
  A := B;
writeln (A, B);
```

d.
```
IF A >= 0 THEN
  A := B + 10;
IF B < 0 THEN
  A := B;
writeln (A, B);
```

Indicate the output of each fragment for each of the following assignment statements.

i.
```
A := -5;
B := 5;
```

ii.
```
A := -5;
B := -3;
```

iii.
```
A := 10;
B := 8;
```

iv.
```
A := 10;
B := -4;
```

5. Refer to Example 4.9, in which we assigned grades to students, and rewrite the grade assignment fragment using a different nesting. Could you rewrite this fragment without using any nesting? Should you?

6. Many nationally based tests report scores and indicate in which quartile each score lies. Assuming the quartile designation

Score	Quartile
100–75	1
74–50	2
49–25	3
24–0	4

write a program to read a score from the keyboard and report in which quartile the score lies.

7. What are the values of A, B, and C after the following program fragment is executed?

```
A := -8;
B := 21;
C := A + B;
IF A > B THEN
  BEGIN
    A := B;
    C := A * B
  END  {  of IF...THEN option  }
ELSE IF A < 0 THEN
  BEGIN
    A := abs(A);
    B := B - A;
    C := A * B
  END  {  of ELSE option  }
ELSE
  C := 0;
```

8. Create minimal sets of test data for each part of Exercise 4 and for Exercise 7. Explain why each data item has been included.
9. Discuss a technique that could be used as a debugging aid to guarantee that all possible logical paths of a program have been used.

4.5 CASE Statements

OBJECTIVES

- to know the form and syntax of **CASE** statements
- to understand how **CASE** statements can be used as an alternate method of multiway selection
- to be able to use **CASE** statements when designing programs to solve problems

Thus far, this chapter has examined one-way selection, two-way selection, and multiway selection. Section 4.4 illustrates how multiple selection can be achieved using nested and extended **IF** statements. Since multiple selection can sometimes be difficult to follow, Pascal provides an alternative method of handling this concept: the **CASE** statement.

Form and Syntax

CASE statements are often used when several options depend upon the value of a single variable or expression. The general structure for a **CASE** statement is

```
CASE <selector> OF
    <label list 1> : <statement 1>;
    <label list 2> : <statement 2>;
         .               .
         .               .
         .               .
    <label list n> : <statement n>
END
```

which is shown graphically in Figure 4.5.

◆ FIGURE 4.5
CASE flow diagram

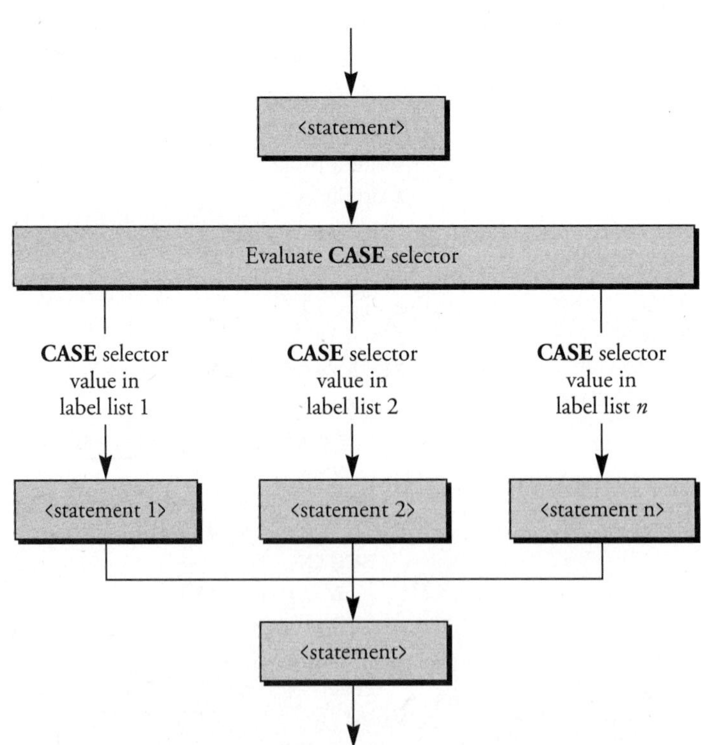

The selector can be any variable or expression with a value of any data type we have studied previously except **real.** (Only ordinal data types can be used.) Values of the selector constitute the label list. Thus, if Age is an integer variable with values restricted to 18, 19, and 20, we can have

```
CASE Age OF
  18 : <statement 1>;
  19 : <statement 2>;
  20 : <statement 3>
END;  {  of CASE Age  }
```

When this program statement is executed, the value of Age will determine to which statement control is transferred. More specifically, the program fragment

```
Age := 19;
CASE Age OF
  18 : writeln ('I just became a legal voter.');
  19 : writeln ('This is my second year to vote.');
  20 : writeln ('I am almost twenty-one.')
END;  {  of CASE Age  }
```

produces the output

```
This is my second year to vote.
```

Before considering more examples, several comments are in order.

1. The flow of logic within a **CASE** statement is as follows:
   a. The value of the selector is determined.
   b. The value is found in the label list.
   c. The statement following the value in the list is executed.
   d. Control is transferred to the first program statement following the **CASE** statement **END.**
2. The selector can have a value of any type previously studied except **real.** Only ordinal data types may be used.
3. Several values, separated by commas, may appear on one line. For example, if Age can have any integer value from 15 to 25 inclusive, the **CASE** statement can appear as

```
CASE Age OF
  15, 16, 17     : <statement 1>;
  18, 19, 20, 21 : <statement 2>;
  22, 23, 24     : <statement 3>;
  25             : <statement 4>
END;  {  of CASE Age  }
```

4. All possible values of the **CASE** selector do not have to be listed. However, if a value that is not listed is used, most versions of Pascal produce a run-time error message and execution is terminated. Consequently, it is preferable to list all values of the **CASE** selector. If certain values require no action, they should be listed on the same option with a null statement; for example

```
CASE Age OF
  18 : <statement 1>;
  19 : ; {  Do nothing  }
  20 : <statement 2>
END;  {  of CASE Age  }
```

5. Values for the selector can appear only once in the list. Thus

```
CASE Age OF
  18        : <statement 1>;
  18, 19    : <statement 2>;   {  error  }
  20        : <statement 3>
END;  {  of CASE Age  }
```

produces an error since it is not clear which statement should be executed when the value of Age is 18.

6. Proper syntax for using **CASE** statements includes
   a. A colon separates each label from its respective statement.
   b. A semicolon follows each statement option except the statement preceding **END.**
   c. Commas are placed between labels on the same option.

7. For the first time, **END** is used without a **BEGIN.** An appropriate program comment should indicate the end of a **CASE** statement. Therefore, our examples will include

```
END;  {  of CASE  }
```

8. Statements for each option can be compound. If they are, they must be in a **BEGIN . . . END** block.

COMMUNICATION AND STYLE TIPS

Writing style for a **CASE** statement should be consistent with your previously developed style. The lines containing options should be indented, the colons should be lined up, and **END** should start in the same column as **CASE.** Thus, a typical **CASE** statement is

```
CASE Score OF
  10, 9, 8       : writeln ('Excellent');
  7, 6, 5        : writeln ('Fair');
  4, 3, 2, 1, 0 : writeln ('Failing')
END;  {  of CASE Score  }
```

At this stage, let's consider several examples that illustrate various uses of **CASE** statements. Since these examples are for purposes of illustration, they will be somewhat contrived. Later examples will serve to illustrate how these statements are used in solving problems.

EXAMPLE 4.11

The selector can have a value of type **char,** and the ordinal of the character determines the option. Thus, the label list must contain the appropriate characters in single quotation marks. If Grade has values 'A', 'B', 'C', 'D', or 'E', a **CASE** statement can be

```
CASE Grade OF
  'A' : Points := 4.0;
  'B' : Points := 3.0;
  'C' : Points := 2.0;
  'D' : Points := 1.0;
  'E' : Points := 0.0
END;  {  of CASE Grade  }
```

EXAMPLE 4.12

To avoid inappropriate values for the **CASE** selector, the entire **CASE** statement may be protected by using an **IF . . . THEN . . . ELSE** statement. For example, suppose you are using a **CASE** statement for number of days worked. You expect the values to be 1, 2, 3, 4, or 5, so you can protect the statement by

```
IF (NumDays > 0) AND (NumDays < 6) THEN
  CASE NumDays OF
    1 : <statement 1>;
    2 : <statement 2>;
    3 : <statement 3>;
    4 : <statement 4>;
    5 : <statement 5>
  END  {  of CASE NumDays  }
ELSE
  writeln ('Value of NumDays', NumDays,
           'is out of range.');
```

A good debugging technique is to print the value of the selector in your **ELSE** statement.

EXAMPLE 4.13

Compound statements are required if more than one simple statement is to be executed as part of a selector option. The following general form is appropriate.

```
CASE Age OF
  18 : BEGIN
         .
         .
         .
       END;
  19 : BEGIN
         .
         .
         .
       END;
  20 : BEGIN
         .
         .
         .
       END
END;  {  of CASE Age  }
```

OTHERWISE Option

T

Some versions of Pascal provide an additional reserved word and option, **OTHERWISE,** which can be used with **CASE** statements. The general structure of this option is

```
CASE <selector> OF
    <label 1> : <statement 1>;
    <label 1> : <statement 2>;
        .           .
        .           .
        .           .
    <label n> : <statement n>
OTHERWISE
    <statement 1>;
    <statement 2>;
        .
        .
        .
    <statement n>
END  {  of CASE  }
```

This option can be used if the same action is to be taken for several values of the **CASE** selector. It can also be used to protect against a **CASE** selector that is out of range. Note the statements following **OTHERWISE** are executed sequentially and do not have to be in a **BEGIN** . . . **END** block. You should check your version of Pascal to see if this option is available to you.

Equivalent of Extended **IFs**

As previously indicated, **CASE** statements can sometimes be used instead of extended **IF** statements when multiple selection is required to solve a problem. The following example illustrates this use.

EXAMPLE 4.14

Let's rewrite the following program fragment using a **CASE** statement.

```
IF (Score = 10) OR (Score = 9) THEN
  Grade := 'A'
ELSE IF (Score = 8) OR (Score = 7) THEN
  Grade := 'B'
ELSE IF (Score = 6) OR (Score = 5) THEN
  Grade := 'C'
ELSE
  Grade := 'E';
```

If we assume Score is an integer variable with values 0, 1, 2, . . . , 10, we can use a **CASE** statement as follows:

```
CASE Score OF
  10, 9          : Grade := 'A';
  8, 7           : Grade := 'B';
  6, 5           : Grade := 'C';
  4, 3, 2, 1, 0 : Grade := 'E'
END;  {  of CASE Score  }
```

Use in Problems

CASE statements should not be used in relational tests that involve large ranges of values. For example, if we want to examine a range from 0 to 100 to determine test

A NOTE OF INTEREST

A Software Glitch

The software glitch that disrupted AT&T's long-distance telephone service for nine hours in January 1990 dramatically demonstrates what can go wrong even in the most reliable and scrupulously tested systems. Of the roughly 100 million telephone calls placed with AT&T during that period, only about half got through. The breakdown cost the company more than $60 million in lost revenues and caused considerable inconvenience and irritation for telephone-dependent customers.

The trouble began at a "switch"—one of 114 interconnected, computer-operated electronic switching systems scattered across the United States. These sophisticated systems, each a maze of electronic equipment housed in a large room, form the backbone of the AT&T long-distance telephone network.

When a local exchange delivers a telephone call to the network, it arrives at one of these switching centers, which can handle up to 700,000 calls an hour. The switch immediately springs into action. It scans a list of 14 different routes it can use to complete the call; at the same time, it hands off the telephone number to a parallel, signaling network, invisible to any caller. This private data network allows computers to scout the possible routes and to determine whether the switch at the other end can deliver the call to the local company it serves.

If the answer is no, the call is stopped at the original switch to keep it from tying up a line and the caller gets a busy signal. If the answer is yes, a signaling-network computer makes a reservation at the destination switch and orders the original switch to pass along the waiting call—after that switch makes a final check to insure that the chosen line is functioning properly. The whole process of passing a call down the network takes 4–6 seconds. Because the switches must keep in constant touch with the signaling network and its computers, each switch has a computer program that handles all the necessary communications between the switch and the signaling network.

AT&T's first indication that something might be amiss appeared on a giant video display at the company's network control center in Bedminster, New Jersey. At 2:25 P.M. on Monday, January 15, 1990, network managers saw an alarming increase in the number of red warning signals appearing on many of the 75 video screens that show the status of various parts of AT&T's worldwide network. The warnings signaled a serious collapse in the network's ability to complete calls within the United States.

To bring the network back up to speed, AT&T engineers first tried a number of standard procedures that had worked in the past. This time, the methods failed. The engineers realized they had a problem never seen before. Nonetheless, within a few hours, they managed to stabilize the network by temporarily cutting back on the number of messages moving through the signaling network. They cleared the last defective link at 11:30 that night.

Meanwhile, a team of more than 100 telephone technicians tried frantically to track down the fault. Because the problem involved the signaling network and seemed to bounce from one switch to another, they zeroed in on the software that permits each switch to communicate with the signaling-network computers.

The day after the slowdown, AT&T personnel removed the apparently faulty software from each switch, temporarily replacing it with an earlier version of the communications program. A close examination of the flawed software turned up a single error in one line of the program. Just one month earlier, network technicians had changed the software to speed the processing of certain messages, and the change had inadvertently introduced a flaw into the system.

From that finding, AT&T could reconstruct what had happened.

scores, it is better to use nested selection than a **CASE** statement. We close this section with some examples that illustrate how **CASE** statements can be used in solving problems.

EXAMPLE 4.15

Let's write a program for a gasoline station owner who sells four grades of gasoline: regular, unleaded, unleaded plus, and super unleaded. The program reads a character (R, U, P, S) that designates which kind of gasoline was purchased and then takes subsequent action. The outline for this fragment is

```
readln (GasType);
CASE GasType OF
   'R' : <action for regular>;
   'U' : <action for unleaded>;
   'P' : <action for unleaded plus>;
   'S' : <action for super unleaded>
END;  {  of CASE GasType  }
```

EXAMPLE 4.16

An alternative method of assigning letter grades based upon integer scores between 0 and 100 inclusive is to divide the score by 10 and assign grades according to some scale. This idea can be used in conjunction with a **CASE** statement as follows:

```
NewScore := Score DIV 10;
CASE NewScore OF
  10, 9          : Grade := 'A';
  8              : Grade := 'B';
  7              : Grade := 'C';
  6, 5           : Grade := 'D';
  4, 3, 2, 1, 0  : Grade := 'E'
END;  {  of CASE NewScore  }
```

EXERCISES 4.5

1. Discuss the need for program protection when using a **CASE** statement.
2. Write a test program to see whether or not the **OTHERWISE** option is available on your system.
3. Show how the following **CASE** statement could be protected against unexpected values.

```
CASE Age DIV 10 OF
  10,9,8,7 : writeln ('These are retirement years':40);
     6,5,4 : writeln ('These are middle age years':40);
       3,2 : writeln ('These are mobile years':40);
         1 : writeln ('These are school years':40)
END;  {  of CASE Age  }
```

4. Find all errors in the following statements.

a.
```
CASE A OF
    1        :  ;
    2        : A := 2 * A
    3        ; A := 3 * A;
    4; 5; 6  : A := 4 * A
  END;  {  of CASE A  }
```

b.
```
CASE Num OF
    5              : Num := Num + 5;
    6, 7           ; Num := Num + 6;
    7, 8, 9, 10    : Num := Num + 10
  END;  {  of CASE Num  }
```

c.
```
CASE Age OF
    15, 16, 17 : YCount := YCount + 1;
                 writeln (Age, YCount);
    18, 19, 20 : MCount := MCount + 1;
    21         : writeln (Age)
  END;  {  of CASE Age  }
```

d.
```
CASE Ch OF
    A : Points := 4.0;
    B : Points := 3.0;
    C : Points := 2.0;
    D : Points := 1.0;
    E : Points := 0.0
  END;  {  of CASE Ch  }
```

e.
```
CASE Score OF
  5       : Grade := 'A';
  4       : Grade := 'B';
  3       : Grade := 'C';
  2, 1, 0 : Grade := 'E';
```

f.
```
CASE Num / 10 OF
  1 : Num := Num + 1;
  2 : Num := Num + 2;
  3 : Num := Num + 3
END;  {  of CASE Num  }
```

5. What output is produced by each of the following program fragments?

a.
```
A := 5;
Power := 3;
CASE Power OF
  0 : B := 1;
  1 : B := A;
  2 : B := A * A;
  3 : B := A * A * A
END;  {  of CASE Power  }
writeln (A, Power, B);
```

b.
```
GasType := 'S';
write ('You have purchased ');
CASE GasType OF
  'R' : write ('Regular');
  'U' : write ('Unleaded');
  'P' : write ('Unleaded Plus');
  'S' : write ('Super Unleaded')
END;  {  of CASE GasType  }
writeln (' gasoline');
```

c.
```
A := 6;
B := -3;
CASE A OF
  10, 9, 8 : CASE B OF
               -3, -4, -5 : A := A * B;
                0, -1, -2 : A := A + B
             END;
   7, 6, 5 : CASE B OF
               -5, -4 : A := A * B;
               -3, -2 : A := A + B;
               -1,  0 : A := A - B
             END
END;  {  of CASE A  }
writeln (A, B);
```

d.
```
Symbol := '-';
A := 5;
B := 10;
CASE Symbol OF
  '+' : Num := A + B;
  '-' : Num := A - B;
  '*' : Num := A * B
END;  {  of CASE Symbol  }
writeln (A, B, Num);
```

6. Rewrite each of the following program fragments using a **CASE** statement.

a.
```
IF Power = 1 THEN
  Num := A;
IF Power = 2 THEN
  Num := A * A;
IF Power = 3 THEN
  Num := A * A * A;
```

b. Assume Score is an integer between 0 and 10.

```
IF Score > 9 THEN
  Grade := 'A'
ELSE IF Score > 8 THEN
  Grade := 'B'
ELSE IF Score > 7 THEN
  Grade := 'C'
ELSE IF Score > 5 THEN
  Grade := 'D'
ELSE
  Grade := 'E';
```

c. Assume Measurement is either M or N.

```
IF Measurement = 'M' THEN
  BEGIN
    writeln ('This is a metric measurement.':37);
    writeln ('It will be converted to nonmetric.':42);
    Length := Num * CMToInches
  END  {  of IF...THEN option  }
ELSE
  BEGIN
    writeln ('This is a nonmetric measurement.':40);
    writeln ('It will be converted to metric.':39);
    Length := Num * InchesToCM
  END;  {  of ELSE option  }
```

7. Show how a **CASE** statement can be used in a program to compute college tuition fees. Assume there are different fee rates for undergraduates (U), graduates (G), foreign students (F), and special students (S).

8. Write an interactive program that allows the user to convert Celsius to Fahrenheit temperatures and vice versa. The program should present the user with a menu such as

```
MENU CHOICES

F - Celsius to Fahrenheit
C - Fahrenheit to Celsius
Q - Quit

Enter your choice and press <Enter>.
```

A **CASE** statement should be used to provide the options listed.

9. Use nested **CASE** statements to design a program fragment to compute postage for domestic (nonforeign) mail. Your design should provide for four weight categories for both letters and packages. Each can be sent first, second, third, or fourth class.

4.6 Assertions (Optional)

OBJECTIVES

- to know how to use assertions as preconditions
- to know how to use assertions as postconditions

An *assertion* is a program comment in the form of a statement about what we expect to be true at the point in the program where the assertion is placed. For example, if you wish to compute a test average by dividing SumOfScores by NumberOfStudents, you could use an assertion in the following manner.

```
{  Assertion: NumberOfStudents <> 0  }
ClassAverage := SumOfScores / NumberOfStudents;
```

Assertions are usually Boolean-valued expressions and typically concern a particular program action. Assertions frequently come in pairs: one preceding the program action and one following the action. In this format, the first assertion is a precondition and the second is a postcondition.

To illustrate preconditions and postconditions, let's consider the segment of code

```
IF Num1 < Num2 THEN
  BEGIN
    Temp := Num1;
    Num1 := Num2;
    Num2 := Temp
  END;  {  of IF...THEN  }
```

The intent of this code is to have Num1 be greater than or equal to Num2. If we intend for both Num1 and Num2 to be positive, we can write

```
{  Assertion: Num1 >= 0 AND Num2 >= 0  }     ←— precondition

IF Num1 < Num2 THEN
  BEGIN
    Temp := Num1;
    Num1 := Num2;
    Num2 := Temp
  END;  {  of IF...THEN  }

{  Assertion: Num1 >= Num2 >= 0  }           ←— postcondition
```

In practice, you may choose to label preconditions and postconditions, as the following comments illustrate.

```
{  Precondition: Num1 >= 0 and Num2 >= 0  }

IF Num1 < Num2 THEN
  BEGIN
    Temp := Num1;
    Num1 := Num2;
    Num2 := Temp
  END;  {  of IF...THEN  }

{  Postcondition: Num1 >= Num2 >= 0  }
```

As a second example, consider a **CASE** statement used to assign grades based upon quiz scores.

```
CASE Score OF
  10          : Grade := 'A';
  9, 8        : Grade := 'B';
  7, 6        : Grade := 'C';
  5, 4        : Grade := 'D';
  3, 2, 1, 0 : Grade := 'E'
END;  {  of CASE Score  }
```

Assertions can be used as preconditions and postconditions in the following manner.

```
{  Precondition:  Score is an integer between 0 and 10
                  inclusive  }

CASE Score OF
  10          : Grade := 'A';
  9, 8        : Grade := 'B';
  7, 6        : Grade := 'C';
  5, 4        : Grade := 'D';
  3, 2, 1, 0 : Grade := 'E'
END;  {  of CASE Score  }

{  Postcondition:  Grade has been assigned a letter grade
                   according to the scale
              10          -> A
              9, 8        -> B
              7, 6        -> C
              5, 4        -> D
              3, 2, 1, 0 -> E  }
```

Assertions can be used in program proofs. Simply put, a *program proof* is an analysis of a program that attempts to verify the correctness of the program results. A detailed study of program proofs is beyond the scope of this text. If, however, you use assertions as preconditions and postconditions now, you will better understand them in subsequent courses. If you do choose to use assertions in this manner, be aware that the postcondition of one action is the precondition of the next action.

FOCUS ON PROGRAM DESIGN

The Gas-N-Clean Service Station sells gasoline and has a car wash. Fees for the car wash are $1.25 with a gasoline purchase of $10.00 or more and $3.00 otherwise. Three kinds of gasoline are available: regular at $1.149, unleaded at $1.199, and super unleaded at $1.289 per gallon. Let's write a program that prints a statement for a customer. Input consists of number of gallons purchased, kind of gasoline purchased (R, U, S, or, for no purchase, N), and car wash desired (Y or N). We use the constant definition section for gasoline prices. Our output should include appropriate messages. Sample output for this data follows.

```
Enter number of gallons and press <Enter>.
9.7
Enter gas type (R, U, S, or N) and press <Enter>.
R
Enter Y or N for car wash and press <Enter>.
Y
             ****************************************
             *                                      *
             *     Gas-N-Clean Service Station      *
             *                                      *
             *            July 25, 1994             *
             *                                      *
             ****************************************
```

```
Amount of gasoline purchased:     9.700 gallons
Price per gallon:               $ 1.149

Total gasoline cost                    $ 11.15
Car wash cost                          $  1.25
                                       -------
              Total due                $ 12.40

           Thank you for stopping
             Please come again

   Remember to buckle up and drive safely
```

A first-level pseudocode development is

1. Get data
2. Compute charges
3. Print results

A structure chart for this problem is given in Figure 4.6.

◆ FIGURE 4.6
Structure chart for the Gas-N-Clean Service Station problem

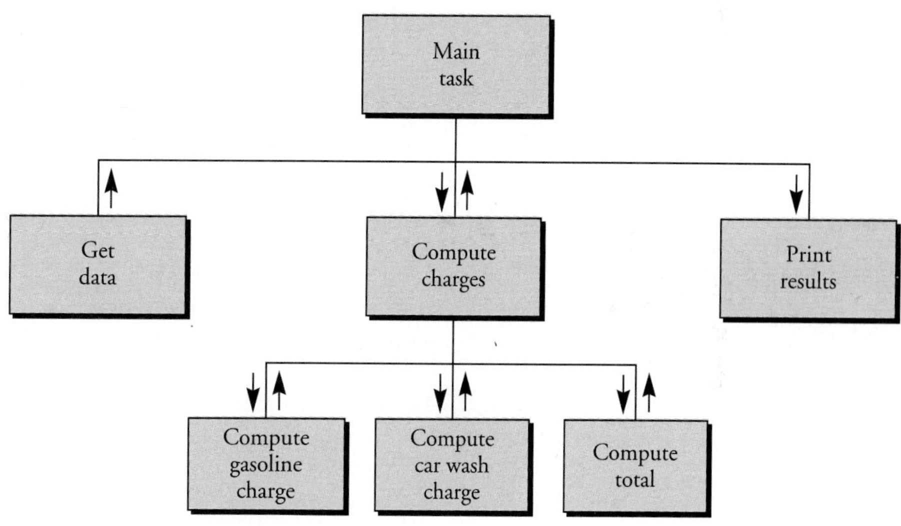

Module specifications for the main modules are

1. GetData Module
   Data received: None
   Information returned: Number of gallons purchased
   Type of gasoline
   Whether or not a car wash is desired
   Logic: Get information interactively from the keyboard.
2. ComputeCharges Module
   Data received: NumGallons
   GasType
   WashOption

Information returned: GasCost
WashCost
TotalCost

Logic: Use a **CASE** statement to compute the GasCost.
Use nested selection to determine the WashCost.
Sum GasCost and WashCost to get TotalCost.

3. PrintResults Module

Data received: NumGallons
GasType
WashOption
GasCost
WashCost
TotalCost

Information returned: None

Logic: Use a procedure for the heading.
Use several **writeln** statements.

Further refinement of the pseudocode produces

```
1. Get data
   1.1 read number of gallons
   1.2 read kind of gas purchased
   1.3 read car wash option
2. Compute charges
   2.1 compute gasoline charge
   2.2 compute car wash charge
   2.3 compute total
3. Print results
   3.1 print heading
   3.2 print information in transaction
   3.3 print closing message
```

Module 2 consists of three subtasks. A refined pseudocode development of this step is

```
2. Compute charges
   2.1 compute gasoline charge
       2.1.1 CASE GasType OF
                R
                U
                S
                N
   2.2 compute car wash charge
       2.2.1 IF WashOption is yes THEN
                compute charge
             ELSE
                charge is 0.0
   2.3 compute total
       2.3.1 Total is GasCost plus WashCost
```

A Pascal program for this problem follows.

```
PROGRAM GasNClean (input, output);

{  This program is used to compute the amount due from a        }
{  customer of the Gas-N-Clean Service Station.  Constants are  }
{  used for gasoline prices.  Note the use of nested selection  }
{  to compute cost of the car wash.                             }

CONST
  Skip = ' ';
  Date = 'July 25, 1994';
  RegularPrice = 1.149;
  UnleadedPrice = 1.199;
  SuperUnleadedPrice = 1.289;

VAR
  GasType,               {  Type of gasoline purchased (R,U,S,N)  }
  WashOption : char;     {  Character designating option (Y, N)   }
  NumGallons,            {  Number of gallons purchased           }
  GasCost,               {  Computed cost of gasoline             }
  WashCost,              {  Car wash cost                         }
  TotalCost : real;      {  Total amount due                      }

{*************************************************************}

PROCEDURE GetData (VAR NumGallons : real;
                   VAR GasType, WashOption : char);

  {  Given:   Nothing                                           }
  {  Task:    Have NumGallons, GasType, and WashOption entered  }
  {               from the keyboard                             }
  {  Return:  NumGallons, GasType, and WashOption               }

  BEGIN                                                             1
    writeln ('Enter number of gallons and press <Enter>.');
    readln (NumGallons);
    writeln ('Enter gas type (R, U, S, or N) and press <Enter>.');
    readln (GasType);
    writeln ('Enter Y or N for car wash and press <Enter>.');
    readln (WashOption)
  END;  {  of PROCEDURE GetData  }

{*************************************************************}

PROCEDURE ComputeCharges (VAR GasCost, WashCost, TotalCost : real;
                              NumGallons : real;
                              GasType, WashOption : char);

  {  Given:   NumGallons, GasType, and WashOption               }
  {  Task:    Compute GasCost, WashCost, and TotalCost          }
  {  Return:  GasCost, WashCost, and TotalCost                  }
```

```
  BEGIN

    {  Compute gas cost  }
    CASE GasType OF
      'R' : GasCost := NumGallons * RegularPrice;
      'U' : GasCost := NumGallons * UnleadedPrice;
      'S' : GasCost := NumGallons * SuperUnleadedPrice;          2
      'N' : GasCost := 0.0
    END;  {  of CASE GasType  }

    {  Compute car wash cost  }
    IF WashOption = 'Y' THEN
      IF GasCost >= 10.0 THEN
        WashCost := 1.25
      ELSE
        WashCost := 3.0
    ELSE
      WashCost := 0.0;
    TotalCost := GasCost + WashCost
  END;  {  of PROCEDURE ComputeCharges  }

{*****************************************************************}

PROCEDURE PrintHeading;

  {  Given:   Nothing                                        }
  {  Task:    Print a heading for the output                 }
  {  Return:  Nothing                                        }

  BEGIN
    writeln (Skip:13, '****************************************');
    writeln (Skip:13, '*                                      *');
    writeln (Skip:13, '*     Gas-N-Clean Service Station      *');
    writeln (Skip:13, '*                                      *');
    writeln (Skip:13, '*', Skip:12, Date, Skip:13, '*');
    writeln (Skip:13, '*                                      *');
    writeln (Skip:13, '****************************************');
    writeln
  END;  {  of PROCEDURE PrintHeading  }

{*****************************************************************}

PROCEDURE PrintMessage;

  {  Given:   Nothing                                        }
  {  Task:    Print an appropriate closing message           }
  {  Return:  Nothing                                        }

  BEGIN
    writeln;
    writeln (Skip:21, 'Thank you for stopping');
```

```
    writeln (Skip:23, 'Please come again');
    writeln;
    writeln (Skip:13, 'Remember to buckle up and drive safely');
    writeln
  END;  {  of PROCEDURE PrintMessage  }

{*************************************************************}

PROCEDURE PrintResults (NumGallons : real;
                        GasType, WashOption : char;
                        GasCost, WashCost, TotalCost : real);

  {  Given:   NumGallons, GasType, WashOption, computed costs   }
  {               for GasCost, WashCost, and TotalCost          }
  {  Task:    Print customer statement                          }
  {  Return:  Nothing                                           }

  BEGIN
    PrintHeading;

    writeln (Skip:10, 'Amount of gasoline purchased:', Skip:3,
             NumGallons:6:3, ' gallons');
    write (Skip:10, 'Price per gallon:', Skip:13, '$');

    CASE GasType OF
      'R' : writeln (RegularPrice:7:3);
      'U' : writeln (UnleadedPrice:7:3);
      'S' : writeln (SuperUnleadedPrice:7:3);
      'N' : writeln (0.0:7:3)
    END;  {  of CASE GasType  }

    writeln;
    writeln (Skip:10, 'Total gasoline cost', Skip:19, '$',
             GasCost:6:2);
    IF WashCost > 0 THEN
      writeln (Skip:10, 'Car wash cost', Skip:25, '$',
               WashCost:6:2);
    writeln (Skip:48, '-------');
    writeln (Skip:25, 'Total due', Skip:14, '$', TotalCost:6:2);

    PrintMessage
  END;  {  of PROCEDURE PrintResults  }

{*************************************************************}

BEGIN  {  Main program  }
  GetData (NumGallons, GasType, WashOption);
  ComputeCharges (GasCost, WashCost, TotalCost, NumGallons,
                  GasType, WashOption);
  PrintResults (NumGallons, GasType, WashOption, GasCost,
                WashCost, TotalCost)
END.  {  of main program  }
```

3

A sample run of this program produces

```
Enter number of gallons and press <Enter>.
11.3
Enter gas type (R, U, S, or N) and press <Enter>.
S
Enter Y or N for car wash and press <Enter>.
N
                 ****************************************
                 *                                      *
                 *     Gas-N-Clean Service Station      *
                 *                                      *
                 *            July 25, 1994             *
                 *                                      *
                 ****************************************

          Amount of gasoline purchased:   11.300 gallons
          Price per gallon:              $ 1.289

          Total gasoline cost                    $ 14.57
                                                 -------
                         Total due               $ 14.57

                     Thank you for stopping
                       Please come again

                Remember to buckle up and drive safely
```

RUNNING AND DEBUGGING HINTS

1. **IF . . . THEN . . . ELSE** is a single statement in Pascal. Thus, a semicolon before **ELSE** creates an **IF . . . THEN** statement and **ELSE** appears incorrectly as a reserved word.
2. A misplaced semicolon used with an **IF . . . THEN** statement can also be a problem. For example

Incorrect	*Correct*
`IF A > 0 THEN;` `  writeln (A);`	`IF A > 0 THEN` `  writeln (A);`

3. Be careful when using compound statements as options in an **IF . . . THEN . . . ELSE** statement; they must be in a **BEGIN . . . END** block.

Incorrect

```
IF A >= 0 THEN
  writeln (A);
  A := A + 10
ELSE
  writeln ('A is negative');
```

Correct

```
IF A >= 0 THEN
  BEGIN
    writeln (A);
    A := A + 10
  END
ELSE
  writeln ('A is negative');
```

4. Your test data should include values that will check both options of an **IF . . . THEN . . . ELSE** statement.

5. **IF . . . THEN . . . ELSE** can be used to check for other program errors. In particular
   a. Check for bad data by using
      read (<data>);
      IF <good data> **THEN**
         .
         . (proceed with program)
         .
      ELSE
         .
         . (error message here)
         .
   b. Check for reasonable computed values by using
      IF <reasonable value> **THEN**
         .
         . (proceed with program)
         .
      ELSE
         .
         . (error message here)
         .

   For example, if you were computing a student's test average, you could have
      IF (TestAverage <= 100) **AND** (TestAverage >= 0) **THEN**
         .
         . (proceed with program)
         .
      ELSE
         .
         . (error message here)
         .
6. Be careful with Boolean expressions. You should always keep expressions reasonably simple, use parentheses, and minimize the use of **NOT.**
7. Be careful to properly match **ELSE** with **IF** statements in nested **IF . . . THEN . . . ELSE** statements. Indenting levels for writing code are very helpful.

   IF <condition 1> **THEN**
      IF <condition 2> **THEN**
         .
         . (action here)
         .
      ELSE
         .
         . (action here)
         .
   ELSE
      .
      . (action here)
      .
8. The form for using extended **IF** statements is

   IF <condition 1> **THEN**
      .
      . (action 1 here)
      .
   ELSE IF <condition 2> **THEN**
      .
      . (action 2 here)
      .
   ELSE
      .
      . (final option here)
      .
9. Be sure to include the **END** of a **CASE** statement.

Key Terms

BEGIN . . . END block
compound Boolean expression
compound statement
control structure
empty (null) statement
extended **IF** statement
logical operators: **AND, OR, NOT**
negation
nested **IF** statement
relational operator
robust
selection statement
simple Boolean expression

Key Terms (optional)

assertion
program proof

Keywords

AND
boolean
CASE
ELSE
false
IF
NOT
OF
OF
OTHERWISE (nonstandard)
THEN
true

Key Concepts

- Relational operators are =, <, >, <=, >=, =, <>.
- Relational operators are always evaluated last.
- Logical operators **AND, OR,** and **NOT** are used as operators on Boolean expressions.
- Variables of type **boolean** may only have values of **true** or **false.**
- A complete priority listing of arithmetic operators, relational operators, and logical operators is

Expression or Operation	Priority
`(   )`	1. Evaluate from inside out.
`NOT`	2. Evaluate from left to right.
`*, /, MOD, DIV, AND`	3. Evaluate from left to right.
`+, -, OR`	4. Evaluate from left to right.
`<, >, <=, >=, =, <>`	5. Evaluate from left to right.

- A selection statement is a program statement that transfers control to various branches of the program.
- A compound statement is sometimes referred to as a **BEGIN . . . END** block; when it is executed, the entire segment of code between **BEGIN** and **END** is treated like a single statement.
- **IF . . . THEN . . . ELSE** is a two-way selection statement.
- A semicolon should not precede the **ELSE** portion of an **IF . . . THEN . . . ELSE** statement.
- If the Boolean expression in an **IF . . . THEN . . . ELSE** statement is **true,** the command following **THEN** is executed; if the expression is **false,** the command following **ELSE** is executed.
- Multiple selections can be achieved by using decision statements within decision statements; this is termed multiway selection.

- An extended **IF** statement has the form

  IF <condition 1> **THEN**
  .
  . (action 1 here)
  .
  ELSE IF <condition 2> **THEN**
  .
  . (action 2 here)
  .
  ELSE IF <condition 3> **THEN**
  .
  . (action 3 here)
  .
  ELSE
  .
  . (action 4 here)
  .

- Program protection can be achieved by using selection statements to guard against unexpected results.
- **CASE** statements sometimes can be used as alternatives to multiple selection.
- **CASE** statements use an **END** without any **BEGIN.**
- **OTHERWISE,** a reserved word in some versions of Pascal, can be used to handle values not listed in the **CASE** statement.

PROGRAMMING PROBLEMS AND PROJECTS

The first 13 problems listed here are relatively short, but to complete them you must use concepts presented in this chapter. Some of the remaining programming problems are used as the basis for writing programs for subsequent chapters as well as for this chapter. In this chapter, each program is run on a very limited set of data. Material in later chapters will permit us to run the programs on larger data bases. Since the problems marked by a color square are referred to and used repeatedly, you should carefully choose which ones you want to work on and then develop them completely.

1. A three-minute telephone call to Scio, NY, costs $1.15. Each additional minute costs $0.26. Given the total length of a call in minutes, print the cost.
2. When you first learned to divide, you expressed answers using a quotient and a remainder rather than a fraction or a decimal quotient. For example, if you divided 7 by 2, your answers would have been given as 3 r. 1. Given two integers, divide the larger by the smaller and print the answer in this form. Do not assume the numbers are entered in any order.
3. Revise Problem 2 so that if there is no remainder, you print only the quotient without a remainder or the letter r.
4. Given the coordinates of two points on a graph, find and print the slope of a line passing through them. Remember the slope of a line can be undefined.
5. ■ Dr. Lae Z. Programmer wishes to computerize his grading system. He gives five tests and then averages only the four highest scores. An average of 90 or better earns a grade of A; 80–89, a grade of B; and so on. Write a program that accepts five test scores and prints the average and grade according to this method.
6. Given the lengths of three sides of a triangle, print whether the triangle is scalene, isosceles, or equilateral.

7. Given the lengths of three sides of a triangle, use the Pythagorean theorem to determine whether or not the triangle is a right triangle. Do not assume the sides are entered in any order.
8. Given three integers, print only the largest.
9. The island nation of Babbage charges its citizens an income tax each year. The tax rate is based upon the following table

Income	Tax Rate
$0–5000	0.0
5001–10,000	3.0%
10,001–20,000	5.5%
20,001–40,000	10.8%
more than $40,000	23.7%

   Write a program that when given a person's income, prints the tax owed rounded to the nearest dollar.
10. Many states base the cost of car registration upon the weight of the vehicle. Suppose the fees are as follows:

Weight	Cost
0–1500 pounds	$23.75
1501–2500 pounds	27.95
2501–3000 pounds	30.25
more than 3000 pounds	37.00

   Given the weight of a car, find and print the cost of registration.
11. The Mapes Railroad Corporation pays an annual bonus as a part of its profit-sharing plan. This year, all employees who have been with the company for 10 years or more receive a bonus of 12 percent of their annual salary, and those who have worked at Mapes from five through nine years receive a bonus of 5.75 percent. Those who have been with the company less than five years receive no bonus. Given the initials of an employee, the employee's annual salary, and the number of years employed with the company, find and print the bonus. All bonuses are rounded to the nearest dollar. Output should be in the following form.

```
        MAPES RAILROAD CORP.

Employee xxx    Years of service nn
     Bonus earned: $ yyyy
```

12. A substance floats in water if its density (mass/volume) is less than 1 g/cc (1 gram per cubic centimeter) and sinks if its density is 1 g/cc or more. Given the mass and volume of an object, print whether it will sink or float.
13. Mr. Arthur Einstein, your high school physics teacher, wants you to develop a program for English-to-metric conversions. You are given a letter indicating whether the measurement is in pounds (P), feet (F), or miles (M). Such measures are to be converted to newtons, meters, or kilometers, respectively. (There are 4.9 newtons in a pound, 3.28 feet in a meter, and 1.61 kilometers in a mile.) Given an appropriate identifying letter and the size of the measurement, convert it to metric units. Print the answer in the form

```
3.0 miles = 4.83 kilometers.
```

■ **14.** The Caswell Catering and Convention Service (Chapter 3, Problem 12) has decided to revise its billing practices and is in need of a new program to prepare bills. The changes Caswell wishes to make follow.

a. For adults, the deluxe meals will cost $15.80 per person and the standard meals will cost $11.75 per person, dessert included. Children's meals will cost 60 percent of adult meals. Everyone within a given party must be served the same meal type.

b. There are five banquet halls. Room A rents for $55.00, room B rents for $75.00, room C rents for $85.00, room D rents for $100.00, and room E rents for $130.00. The Caswells are considering increasing the room fees in about six months, and this should be taken into account.

c. A surcharge (currently 7 percent) is added to the total bill if the catering is to be done on the weekend (Friday, Saturday, or Sunday).

d. All customers will be charged the same rate for tip and tax (currently 18 percent). It is applied only to the cost of food.

e. To induce customers to pay promptly, a discount is offered if payment is made within 10 days. This discount depends upon the amount of the total bill. If the bill is less than $100.00, the discount is 0.5 percent; if the bill is at least $100.00 but less than $200.00, the discount is 1.5 percent; if the bill is at least $200.00 but less than $400.00, the discount is 3 percent; if the bill is at least $400.00 but less than $800.00, the discount is 4 percent; and if the bill is at least $800.00, the discount is 5 percent.

Test your program on each of the following three customers.

Customer A: This customer is using room C on Tuesday night. The party includes 80 adults and six children. The standard meal is being served. The customer paid a $60.00 deposit.
Customer B: This customer is using room A on Saturday night. Deluxe meals are being served to 15 adults. A deposit of $50.00 was paid.
Customer C: This customer is using room D on Sunday afternoon. The party includes 30 children and 2 adults, all of whom are served the standard meal.

Output should be in the same form as that for Problem 12 in Chapter 3.

■ **15.** State University charges $90.00 for each semester hour of credit, $200.00 per semester for a regular room, $250.00 per semester for an air-conditioned room, and $400.00 per semester for food. All students are charged a $30.00 matriculation fee. Graduating students must also pay a $35.00 diploma fee. Write a program to compute the fees that must be paid by a student. Your program should include an appropriate warning message if a student is taking more than 21 credit hours or fewer than 12 credit hours. A typical line of data for one student should include room type (R or A), student number (in four digits), credit hours, and graduating (T or F).

16. Write a program to determine the day of the week a person was born, given his or her birth date. You should use the following steps to find the day of the week corresponding to any date in this century.

a. Divide the last two digits of the birth year by 4. Put the quotient (ignoring the remainder) in Total. For example, if the person was born in 1983, divide 83 by 4 and store 20 in Total.

b. Add the last two digits of the birth year to Total.

c. Add the last two digits of the date of birth to Total.

d. Using the following table, find the "month number" and add it to Total.

January = 1	July = 0
February = 4	August = 3
March = 4	September = 6
April = 0	October = 1
May = 2	November = 4
June = 5	December = 6

e. If the year is a leap year and if the month you are working with is either January or February, then subtract 1 from the Total.

f. Find the remainder when Total is divided by 7. Look up the remainder in the following table to determine the day of the week the person was born. Do not use this procedure if the person's year of birth is earlier than 1900.

1 = Sunday	5 = Thursday
2 = Monday	6 = Friday
3 = Tuesday	0 = Saturday
4 = Wednesday	

Typical input is

5-15 78

where the first entry (5-15) represents the birthdate (May 15) and the second entry (78) represents the birth year. An appropriate error message should be printed if a person's year of birth is before 1900.

■ **17.** Community Hospital needs a program to compute and print a statement for each patient. Charges for each day are as follows:

Room charges:

Private room—$125.00
Semiprivate room—$95.00
Ward—$75.00

Telephone charge—$1.75
Television charge—$3.50

Write a program to get a line of data from the keyboard, compute the patient's bill, and print an appropriate statement. Typical input is

5PNY

where 5 indicates the number of days spent in the hospital, P represents the room type (P, S, or W), N represents the telephone option (Y or N), and Y represents the television option (Y or N). A statement for the data given follows.

```
              Community Hospital

           Patient Billing Statement

Number of days in hospital:       5
Type of room:                   Private

Room charge                $625.00
Telephone charge           $  0.00
Television charge          $ 17.50
                           -------

      TOTAL DUE            $642.50
```

18. Write a program that converts degrees Fahrenheit to degrees Celsius and degrees Celsius to degrees Fahrenheit. In the input, the temperature is followed by a designator (F or C).

■ **19.** The city of Mt. Pleasant bills its residents for sewage, water, and sanitation every three months. The combined sewer and water charge is figured according to how much water is used by the resident. The scale is

Amount (gallons)	Rate
0–1000	\$0.03 per gallon
1001–2000	\$30 + \$0.02 for each gallon over 1000
more than 2000	\$50 + \$0.015 for each gallon over 2000

The sanitation charge is \$7.50 per month.

Write a program to read the number of months for which a resident is being billed (1, 2, or 3) and how much water was used; then print a statement with appropriate charges and messages. Use the constant definition section for all rates, and include an error check for incorrect number of months. Typical input is

3 2175

■ **20.** Al Derrick, owner of the Lucky Wildcat Well Corporation, wants you to develop a program to help him decide whether or not a well is making money. Data for a well will consist of one or two lines. The first line will contain a single character (D for a dry well, O for oil found, or G for gas found) followed by a real number for the cost of the well. If an O or G is detected, the cost will be followed by an integer indicating the volume of oil or gas found. In this case, there will also be a second line containing an N or S indicating whether or not sulfur is present. If there is sulfur, the S will be followed by the percentage of sulfur present in the oil or gas.

Unit prices are \$5.50 for oil and \$2.20 for gas. These prices should be defined as constants. Your program should compute the total revenue for a well (reduce output for sulfur present) and print all pertinent information with an appropriate message to Mr. Derrick. A gusher is defined as a well with profit in excess of \$50,000. Typical input is

G 8000.00 20000
S 0.15

21. The Mathematical Association of America hosts an annual summer meeting. Each state sends one official delegate to the Section Officer's meeting at this summer session. The national organization reimburses the official state delegates according to the following scale.

Round-trip Mileage	Rate
0–500 miles	15 cents per mile
501–1000 miles	\$75.00 + \$0.12 for each mile over 500
1001–1500 miles	\$135.00 + \$0.10 for each mile over 1000
1501–2000 miles	\$185.00 + \$0.08 for each mile over 1,500
2001–3000 miles	\$225.00 + \$0.06 for each mile over 2000
more than 3000 miles	\$285.00 + \$0.05 for each mile over 3000

Write a program that will accept as input the number of round-trip miles for a delegate and compute the amount of reimbursement.

■ **22.** Dr. Lae Z. Programmer (Problem 5) wants you to write a program to compute and print out the grade for a student in his class. The grade is based upon three examinations (worth a possible 100 points each), five quizzes (10 points each), and a 200-point final examination. Your output should include all scores, the percentage grade, and the letter grade. The grading scale is

90	≤	average	≤	100	A
80	≤	average	<	90	B
70	≤	average	<	80	C
60	≤	average	<	70	D
0	≤	average	<	60	E

Typical input is

80 93 85	(examination scores)
9 10 8 7 10	(quiz scores)
175	(final examination)

■ **23.** Dr. Lae Z. Programmer now wants you to modify Problem 22 by adding a check for bad data. Any time an unexpected score occurs, you are to print an appropriate error message and terminate the program.

24. A quadratic equation has the form

$ax^2 + bx + c = 0$

where $a \neq 0$. Solutions to this equation are given by

$$x = \frac{-b \pm \sqrt{b^2 - 4ac}}{2a}$$

where the quantity $(b^2 - 4ac)$ is referred to as the discriminant of the equation. Write a program to read three integers as the respective coefficients *a, b,* and *c,* compute the discriminant, and print out the solutions. The following rules apply.

(1) Discriminant = 0 → single root

(2) Discriminant < 0 → no real number solution

(3) Discriminant > 0 → two distinct real solutions

25. Write a program that receives as input the lengths of three sides of a triangle. Output should first identify the triangle as scalene, isosceles, or equilateral. The program should use the Pythagorean theorem to determine whether or not scalene or isosceles triangles are right triangles. An appropriate message should be part of the output.

■ **26.** The sign on the attendant's booth at the Pentagon parking lot is

PENTAGON VISITOR PARKING

Cars:	
First 2 hours	No charge
Next 3 hours	$0.50/hour
Next 10 hours	$0.25/hour
Trucks:	
First 1 hour	No charge
Next 2 hours	$1.00/hour
Next 12 hours	$0.75/hour
Senior Citizens:	No charge

Write a program that will accept as input a one-character designator (C, T, or S) followed by the number of minutes a vehicle has been in the lot. The program should then compute the appropriate charge and print a ticket for the customer. Any part of an hour is to be counted as a full hour.

27. Some businesses use attention-getting telephone numbers with an 800 prefix (for example, 1-800-STARTUP) so more customers will become familiar with their telephone numbers. Write a program that allows the user to enter a seven-letter telephone message and then have the corresponding telephone number printed. Typical input will consist of seven letters. Typical output will consist of the message and the associated telephone number.

28. Write a program that will add, subtract, multiply, and divide fractions. Input will consist of a single line representing a fraction arithmetic problem as follows:

integer / integer operation integer / integer

For example, a line of input might be
2/3 + 1/2
Your program should

(1) Check for division by zero.

(2) Check for proper operation symbols.

(3) Print the problem in its original form.

(4) Print the answer.

(5) Print all fractions in horizontal form.

Your answer need not be in lowest terms. For the sample input

2/3 + 1/2

sample output is

```
2   1   7
- + - = -
3   2   6
```

29. Write a program that permits the user to print various recipes. Write a procedure for each recipe. After the user enters a one-letter identifier for the desired recipe, a **CASE** statement should be used to call the appropriate procedure. Part of the code could be

```
readln (Selection);
CASE Selection OF
  'J'  :  Jambalaya;
  'S'  :  Spaghetti;
  'T'  :  Tacos
END;  {  of CASE Selection  }
```

30. The force of gravity is different for each of the nine planets in our solar system. For example, on Mercury it is only 0.38 times as strong as on Earth. Thus, if you weigh 100 pounds (on Earth), you would weigh only 38 pounds on Mercury. Write a program that allows you to enter your (Earth) weight and your choice of the planet to which you would like your weight converted. Output should be your weight on the desired planet together with the planet name. The screen message for input should include a menu for the choice of planet. Use a **CASE** statement in the program for computation and output. The relative forces of gravity are

Earth	1.00	Pluto	0.05
Jupiter	2.65	Saturn	1.17
Mars	0.39	Uranus	1.05
Mercury	0.38	Venus	0.78
Neptune	1.23		

■ **31.** Cramer's Rule is a method for solving a system of linear equations. If you have two equations with variables x and y written as

$ax + by = c$
$dx + ey = f$

then the solution for x and y can be given as

$$x = \frac{\begin{vmatrix} c & b \\ f & e \end{vmatrix}}{\begin{vmatrix} a & b \\ d & e \end{vmatrix}} \qquad y = \frac{\begin{vmatrix} a & c \\ d & f \end{vmatrix}}{\begin{vmatrix} a & b \\ d & e \end{vmatrix}}$$

Using this notation

$$\begin{vmatrix} a & b \\ d & e \end{vmatrix}$$

is the determinant of the matrix

$$\begin{bmatrix} a & b \\ d & e \end{bmatrix}$$

and is equal to $ae - bd$.

Write a complete program that will solve a system of two equations using Cramer's Rule. Input will be all coefficients and constants in the system. Output will be the solution to the system. Typical output is

```
For the system of equations

     x  +  2y  =  5
    2x  -   y  =  0

we have the solution

     x  =  1
     y  =  2
```

Use an **IF . . . THEN . . . ELSE** statement to guard against division by zero.

COMMUNICATION IN PRACTICE

1. Using a completed program from this chapter, remove all documentation pertaining to selection statements. Exchange this version with another student who has prepared a similar version. Write documentation for all selection statements in the other student's program. Compare your results with the program author's original version. Discuss the differences and similarities with your class.
2. Contact a programmer and discuss the concept of robustness in a program. Prepare a report of your conversation for class. Include a list of specific instances of how programmers make programs robust.
3. Conduct an unscientific survey of at least two people from each of the following groups: students in upper-level computer science courses, instructors of computer science, and programmers working in industry. Your survey should attempt to determine the importance of and use of robustness at each level. Discuss the similarities and differences of your findings with those of other class members.
4. Selecting appropriate test data for a program that uses nested selection is a nontrivial task. Create diagrams that allow you to trace the flow of logic when nested selection is used. Use your diagrams to draw conclusions about the minimal test data required to test all branches of a program that uses nested selection to various levels.

CHAPTER 5 Repetition Statements

CHAPTER OUTLINE

The previous chapter on selection introduced you to a programming concept that takes advantage of a computer's ability to select. A second major concept designed to utilize the speed of a computer is repetition. Many problems require a process to be repeated. When this is the case, some form of controlled repetition is needed.

This chapter examines the different methods Pascal permits for performing some process repeatedly. For example, we still cannot conveniently write a program that solves the simple problem of adding the integers from 1 to 100 or processing the grades of 30 students in a class. By the end of this chapter, you will be able to solve these problems in three different ways. The three forms of repetition (loops) are

1. **FOR . . . TO . . . DO**
2. **WHILE . . . DO**
3. **REPEAT . . . UNTIL**

[T] Each of these three loops contains the basic constructs necessary for repetition: a variable is assigned some value, the variable value changes at some point in the loop, and repetition continues until the value reaches some predetermined value. When the predetermined value (or Boolean condition) is reached, repetition is terminated and program control moves to the next executable statement.

5.1 Classifying Loops

OBJECTIVES

- to understand the difference between a pretest loop and a posttest loop
- to understand what a fixed repetition loop is
- to understand when to use a fixed repetition loop
- to understand what a variable control loop is

Pretest and Posttest Loops

A loop that uses a condition to control whether or not the body of the loop is executed before going through the loop is a *pretest* or *entrance controlled loop*. The testing condition is the *pretest condition*. If the condition is **true**, the body of the loop is executed. If the condition is **false**, the program skips to the first line of code following the loop. The **FOR** loops and the **WHILE . . . DO** loop are pretest loops.

A loop that examines a Boolean expression after the loop body is executed is a *posttest* or *exit controlled loop*. This is the **REPEAT . . . UNTIL** loop.

Fixed Repetition versus Variable Condition Loops

Fixed repetition (iterated) loops are used when it can be determined in advance how often a segment of code needs to be repeated. For instance, you might have a predetermined number of repetitions of a segment of code for (1) a program to add the integers from 1 to 100 or (2) a program using a fixed number of data lines (for example, game statistics for a team of 12 basketball players). The number of repetitions need not be constant. For example, a user might enter information during execution of a program that would determine how often a segment should be repeated. **FOR** loops are fixed repetition loops.

Variable condition loops are needed to solve problems in which conditions change within the body of the loop. These conditions involve sentinel values, Boolean flags, arithmetic expressions, or end-of-line and end-of-file markers (see Chapter 6). A variable condition loop uses a control feature that provides more power than is available in many early languages, such as BASIC and FORTRAN. **WHILE . . . DO** and **REPEAT . . . UNTIL** are variable condition loops.

5.2 FOR Loops

OBJECTIVES

- to understand how the loop control variable is used in a loop
- to understand the flow of control when using a fixed repetition loop in a program
- to be able to use a **FOR . . . TO . . . DO** loop in a program
- to be able to use a **FOR . . . DOWNTO . . . DO** loop in a program

There are two kinds of **FOR** loops: the **FOR . . . TO . . . DO** loop and the **FOR . . . DOWNTO . . . DO** loop. These loops are pretest and fixed repetition loops.

FOR . . . TO . . . DO Loops

The form necessary for using a **FOR . . . TO . . . DO** loop is

```
    FOR <index> : = <initial value> TO <final value> DO
      <statement>;
or
    FOR <index> := <initial value> TO <final value> DO
      BEGIN
        <statement 1>;
        <statement 2>;
            .
            .
            .
        <statement n>
      END
```

A **FOR . . . TO . . . DO** loop is considered to be a single executable statement. The actions performed in the loop are referred to as the body of the loop. The *index* is an identifier that is assigned values for each repetition of the loop. The internal logic of a **FOR . . . TO . . . DO** loop is

1. The index is assigned the initial value.
2. The index value is compared to the final value.
3. If the index value is less than or equal to the final value:
   a. The body of the loop is executed.
   b. The index value is incremented by 1.
   c. Another check with the final value is made.
4. If the index value exceeds the final value:
   a. The index may revert to an unassigned status.
   b. Control of the program is transferred to the first statement following the loop.

A flow diagram for a **FOR . . . TO . . . DO** loop is given in Figure 5.1.

◆ FIGURE 5.1
FOR . . . TO . . . DO
flow diagram

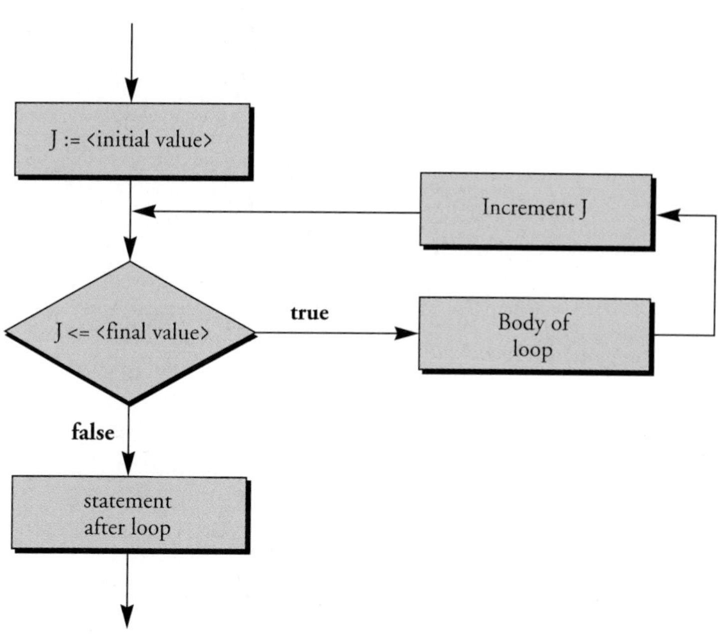

Accumulators

The problem of adding the integers from 1 to 100 needs only one statement in the body of the loop. This problem can be solved by code that constructs an *accumulator,* which merely sums the values of some variable. In the following code, the index variable Number successively assumes the values 1, 2, 3, . . . , 100.

```
Sum:= 0;
FOR Number := 1 TO 100 DO
  Sum := Sum + Number;
```

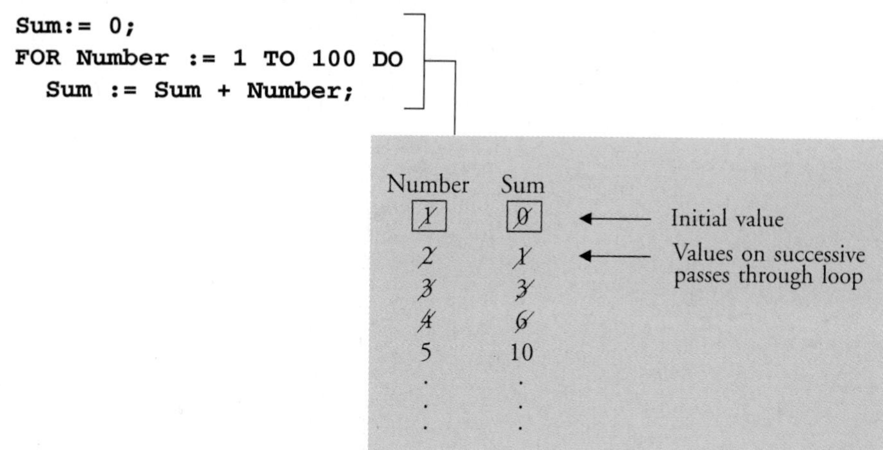

This program segment contains an example of graphic documentation. Throughout the text, these insets will be used to help illustrate what the code is actually doing. The insets are not part of the program; they merely show what some specific code is trying to accomplish.

To see how Sum accumulates these values, let's trace through the code for several values of Number. Initially, Sum is set to zero by

```
Sum := 0;
```

When Number is assigned the value 1

```
Sum := Sum + Number;
```

produces

~~0~~ 1

1	~~0~~ 1
Number	Sum

For Number = 2, we get

2	~~1~~ 3
Number	Sum

Number = 3 yields

3	~~3~~ 6
Number	Sum

Note Sum has been assigned a value equal to 1 + 2 + 3. The final value of Number is 100. Once this value has been assigned to Sum, the value of Sum will be 5050, which is the sum 1 + 2 + 3 + · · · + 100.

Accumulators are frequently used in loops. The general form is

```
Accumulator := 0;  {  Before loop  }
FOR Number := <initial value> TO <final value> DO
  BEGIN
    .
    .  (loop body here)
    .
    Accumulator := Accumulator + <new value>
  END;  {  of FOR loop  }
```

Some comments concerning the syntax and form of **FOR . . . TO . . . DO** loops are now necessary.

1. The words **FOR, TO,** and **DO** are reserved and must be used only in the order **FOR . . . TO . . . DO.**
2. The index must be declared as a variable. Although it can be any ordinal data type, we will use mostly integer examples.
3. The index variable can be any valid identifier.
4. The index can be used within the loop just like any other variable. The value of the index variable should never be changed by the statements in the body of the loop.
5. The initial and final values may be constants or variable expressions with appropriate values.
6. If either the initial value or the final value is a variable expression, it should not be changed by statements in the body of the loop. If either of these values is changed, unexpected results will be produced.
7. The loop will be repeated for each value of the index in the range indicated by the initial and final values.
8. T The index may not retain the last value it had during the last time through the loop. When the loop is finished, the index variable may revert to a state of having no assigned value.

At this point you might try writing some test programs to see what happens if you don't follow these rules. Then consider the following examples, which illustrate the features of **FOR . . . TO . . . DO** loops.

EXAMPLE 5.1

Let's write a segment of code to list the integers from 1 to 10 together with their squares and cubes. This can be done by

```
FOR Index := 1 TO 10 DO
  writeln (Index, Index * Index, Index * Index * Index);
```

This segment produces

```
     1         1         1
     2         4         8
     3         9        27
     4        16        64
     5        25       125
     6        36       216
     7        49       343
     8        64       512
     9        81       729
    10       100      1000
```

EXAMPLE 5.2

Write a **FOR . . . TO . . . DO** loop to produce the following design.

Assuming the first asterisk is in column 20, the following loop will produce the desired result. Note carefully how the output is formatted.

```
FOR J := 1 TO 5 DO
  writeln ('*':21-J, '*':2*J-1);
```

EXAMPLE 5.3

When computing compound interest, it is necessary to evaluate the quantity $(1 + R)^N$ where R is the interest rate for one time period and N is the number of time periods. A **FOR. . .TO. . .DO** loop can be used to perform this computation. If we declare a variable Base, this can be solved by

```
{  Initialize Base  }

Base := 1;
FOR J := 1 TO N DO
  Base := Base * (1 + R);
```

Base

1 ← Initial value

$(1 + R)^1$ ← Values on successive passes through loop

$(1 + R)^2$

$(1 + R)^3$

.

.

.

$(1 + R)^N$

FOR ... DOWNTO ... DO Loops

A second pretest, fixed repetition loop is the **FOR . . . DOWNTO . . . DO** loop. This loop does exactly what you expect; it is identical to a **FOR . . . TO . . . DO** loop except the index variable is decreased by 1 instead of increased by 1 each time it passes through the loop. This is referred to as a *decrement.* The test is index value >= final value. The loop terminates when the index value is less than the final value. Proper form and syntax of a loop of this type are

```
FOR <index> := <initial value> DOWNTO <final value> DO
   <statement>
or
FOR <index> := <initial value> DOWNTO <final value> DO
   BEGIN
      <statement 1>;
      <statement 2>;
          .
          .
          .
      <statement n>
   END
```

The conditions for **FOR . . . DOWNTO . . . DO** loops are the same as those for **FOR . . . TO . . . DO** loops. We will now consider an example of a **FOR . . . DOWNTO . . . DO** loop.

EXAMPLE 5.4

Let's illustrate the index values of a **FOR . . . DOWNTO . . . DO** loop by writing the index value during each pass through the loop. The segment of code for this could be

```
FOR Index := 20 DOWNTO 15 DO
  writeln ('Index =', Index:4);
```

and the output is

```
Index =  20
Index =  19
Index =  18
Index =  17
Index =  16
Index =  15
```

From this point on, both **FOR . . . TO . . . DO** and **FOR . . . DOWNTO . . . DO** loops will be referred to as **FOR** loops. The form intended should be clear from the context.

Writing Style for Loops

As you can see, writing style is an important consideration when writing code using loops. There are three features to consider. First, the body of the loop should be indented. Compare

```
FOR Index := 1 TO 10 DO
  BEGIN
    read (Num, Amt);
    Total1 := Total1 + Amt;
    Total2 := Total2 + Num;
    writeln ('The number is', Num:6)
  END;  {  of FOR loop  }
writeln ('The total amount is', Total1:8:2);
Average := Total2 / 10;
```

and

```
FOR Index := 1 TO 10 DO
BEGIN
read (Num, Amt);
Total1 := Total1 + Amt;
Total2 := Total2 + Num;
writeln ('The number is', Num:6)
END;  {  of FOR loop  }
writeln ('The total amount is', Total1:8:2);
Average := Total2 / 10;
```

The indenting in the first segment makes it easier to determine what is contained in the body of the loop. In the second segment, without any indenting, the beginning and the end of the body of the loop are not as easy to see.

The fact that lines of code are indented under a **FOR** statement does not mean that they are part of the loop. If a compound statement is the body of a loop, **BEGIN** and **END** must be included as part of the statement. Thus

```
FOR Index := 1 TO 5 DO
  read (Number);
  Sum := Sum + Number;
```

does not accomplish the desired task. It should be coded as

```
FOR Index := 1 TO 5 DO
  BEGIN
    read (Number);
    Sum := Sum + Number
  END;  {  of FOR loop  }
```

Second, blank lines can be used before and after a loop for better readability. Compare

```
readln (X, Y);
writeln (X:6:2, Y:6:2);
writeln;

FOR Index := -3 TO 5 DO
  writeln (Index:3, '*':5);

Sum := Sum + X;
writeln (Sum:10:2);
```

and

```
readln (X, Y);
writeln (X:6:2, Y:6:2);
writeln;
FOR Index := -3 TO 5 DO
  writeln (Index:3, '*':5);
Sum := Sum + X;
writeln (Sum:10:2);
```

Again, the first segment is clearer because it emphasizes that the entire loop is a single executable statement and makes it easy to locate the loop.

Third, appropriate comments make loops more readable. Comments that state the purpose of a loop and the condition for entering the loop should be given prior to entering the loop. A comment should always accompany the **END** of a compound statement that is the body of a loop. The general form is

```
{  Get a test score; there are 50 scores.  }
FOR Index := 1 TO 50 DO
  BEGIN
     .
     . (body of the loop)
     .
  END;  {  of FOR loop  }
```

COMMUNICATION AND STYLE TIPS

There are three features you may wish to incorporate as you work with **FOR** loops. First, loop limits can be defined as constants or declared as variables and then assigned values. Thus, you could have

```
CONST
  LoopLimit = 50;
```

Second, the loop control variable can be declared as

```
VAR
  LCV : integer;
```

The loop could then be written as

```
FOR LCV := 1 TO LoopLimit DO
       .
       . (body of the loop here)
       .
```

Third, a loop limit can be declared as a variable and the user can then enter a value during execution.

```
VAR
  LoopLimit : integer;
     .
     .
     .
  writeln ('How many entries?');
  readln (LoopLimit);
  FOR LCV := 1 TO LoopLimit DO
     .
     .
     .
```

A NOTE OF INTEREST

Charles Babbage

The first person to propose the concept of the modern computer was Charles Babbage (1791–1871), a man truly ahead of his time. Babbage was a professor of mathematics at Cambridge University, as well as an inventor. As a mathematician, he realized the time-consuming and boring nature of constructing mathematical tables (squares, logarithms, sines, cosines, and so on). Since the calculators developed by Pascal and Gottfried Wilhelm Leibniz (1646–1716) could not provide the calculations required for these more complex tables, Babbage proposed the idea of building a machine that could compute the various properties of numbers, accurate to 20 digits.

With a grant from the British government, he designed and partially built a simple model of the difference engine. However, the lack of technology in the 1800s prevented him from making a working model. Discouraged by his inability to materialize his ideas, Babbage imagined a better version, which would be a general-purpose, problem-solving machine—the analytical engine.

The similarities between the analytical engine and the modern computer are amazing. Babbage's analytical engine, which was intended to be a steam-powered device, had four components:

1. A "mill" that manipulated and computed the data
2. A "store" that held the data
3. An "operator" of the system that carried out instructions
4. A separate device that entered data and received processed information via punched cards.

After spending many years sketching variations and improvements for this new model, Babbage received some assistance in 1842 from Ada Augusta Byron (see the next *Note of Interest*).

Example 5.5 uses a **FOR** loop to solve a problem.

EXAMPLE 5.5

Let's write a segment of code to compute the test average for each of 30 students in a class and the overall class average. Data for each student consist of the student's initials and four test scores.

A first-level pseudocode development is

1. Print a heading
2. Initialize Total
3. Process data for each of 30 students
4. Compute class average
5. Print a summary

A **FOR** loop can be used to implement step 3. The step can first be refined to

3. Process data for each of 30 students
   3.1 get data for a student
   3.2 compute average
   3.3 add to Total
   3.4 print student data

   The code for this step is

```
FOR Student := 1 TO ClassSize DO
  BEGIN
    writeln ('Enter three initials and press <Enter>.');
    readln (Init1, Init2, Init3);
    writeln ('Enter four test scores and press <Enter>.');
    readln (Score1, Score2, Score3, Score4);
    Average := (Score1 + Score2 + Score3 + Score4) / 4;
    Total := Total + Average;
    writeln;
    write (Init1:4; Init2, Init3);
    write (Score1:6, Score2:6, Score3:6, Score4:6);
    writeln (Average:10:2)
  END;  {  of FOR loop  }
```

EXERCISES 5.2

1. What output is produced by each of the following segments of code?
   a. `FOR LCV := 3 TO 8 DO`
      `writeln ('*':LCV);`
   b. `FOR LCV := 1 TO 10 DO`
      `writeln (LCV:4, ' :', (10 - LCV):5);`
   c. `A := 2;`
      `FOR LCV := (3 * 2 - 4) TO 10 * A DO`
      `writeln ('**', LCV:4);`
   d. `FOR LCV := 50 DOWNTO 30 DO`
      `writeln (51 - LCV:5);`
2. Write a test program for each of the following.
   a. Illustrate what happens when the loop control variable is assigned a value inside the loop.
   b. Demonstrate how an accumulator works. For this test program, sum the integers from 1 to 10. Your output should show each partial sum as it is assigned to the accumulator.
3. Write segments of code using **FOR . . . TO . . . DO** or **FOR . . . DOWNTO . . . DO** loops to produce the following designs.

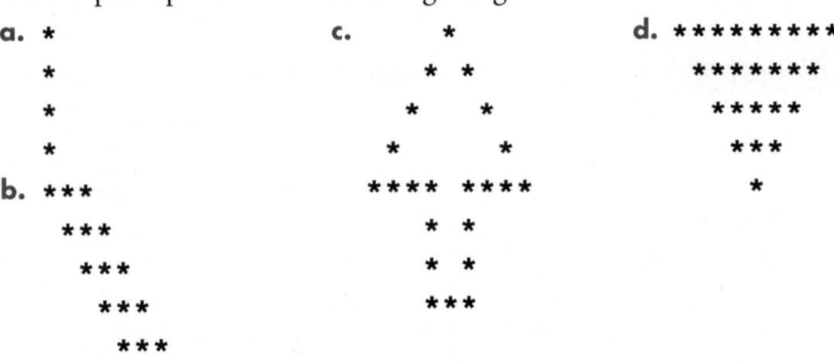

4. Which of the following segments of code do you think accomplish their intended tasks? For those that do not, what changes would you suggest?

a.
```
FOR K := 1 TO 5 DO;
  writeln (K);
```

b.
```
Sum := 0;
FOR J := 1 TO 10 DO
  read (A);
  Sum := Sum + A;
writeln (Sum:15);
```

c.
```
Sum := 0;
FOR J = -3 TO 3 DO
  Sum := Sum + J;
```

d.
```
A := 0;
FOR Index := 1 TO 10 DO
  BEGIN
    A := A + Index;
    writeln (Index:5, A:5, A + Index:5)
  END;  {  of FOR loop  }
writeln (Index:5, A:5, A + Index:5);
```

5. Produce each of the following outputs using both a **FOR . . . TO . . . DO** loop and a **FOR . . . DOWNTO . . . DO** loop.

a.
```
1  2  3  4  5
```

b.
```
*
 *
  *
   *
    *
```

6. Rewrite the following segment of code using a **FOR . . . DOWNTO . . . DO** loop to produce the same result.

```
Sum := 0;
FOR Index := 1 TO 4 DO
  BEGIN
    writeln ('*':21+Index);
    Sum := Sum + Index
  END;  {  of FOR loop  }
```

7. Rewrite the following segment of code using a **FOR . . . TO . . . DO** loop to produce the same result.

```
FOR J := 10 DOWNTO 2 DO
  writeln (J:J);
```

8. Write a complete program that produces a table showing the temperature equivalents in degrees Fahrenheit and degrees Celsius. Let the user enter the starting and ending values. Use the formula

$$\text{CelsTemp} = \frac{5}{9} * (\text{FarenTemp} - 32)$$

9. Write a complete program to produce a chart consisting of the multiples of 5 from -50 to 50 together with the squares and cubes of these numbers. Use a procedure to print a suitable heading and user-defined functions for square and cube.

10. The formula $A = P(1 + R)^N$ can be used to compute the amount due A when a principal P has been borrowed at a monthly rate R for a period of N months. Write a complete program that will read in the principal, annual interest rate (divide by 12 for monthly rate), and number of months and then produce a chart that shows how much will be due at the end of each month.

5.3 WHILE . . . DO LOOPS

OBJECTIVES

- to understand when variable repetition should be used in a program
- to understand why **WHILE . . . DO** is a variable repetition loop
- to understand the flow of control when using a **WHILE . . . DO** loop
- to be able to use a counter in a **WHILE . . . DO** loop
- to be able to use a **WHILE . . . DO** loop in a program

FOR loops (loops in which the body of the loop is repeated a fixed number of times) were presented in Section 5.2. However, the FOR loop is inappropriate for some problems since a segment of code may need to be repeated an unknown number of times. The condition controlling the loop must be an expression rather than a constant. Recall Pascal provides two repetition statements with variable control conditions: one with a pretest condition, and one with a posttest condition.

The pretest loop with variable conditions in Pascal is the **WHILE . . . DO** loop. The condition controlling the loop is a Boolean expression written between the reserved words **WHILE** and **DO.** The correct form and syntax of such a loop are

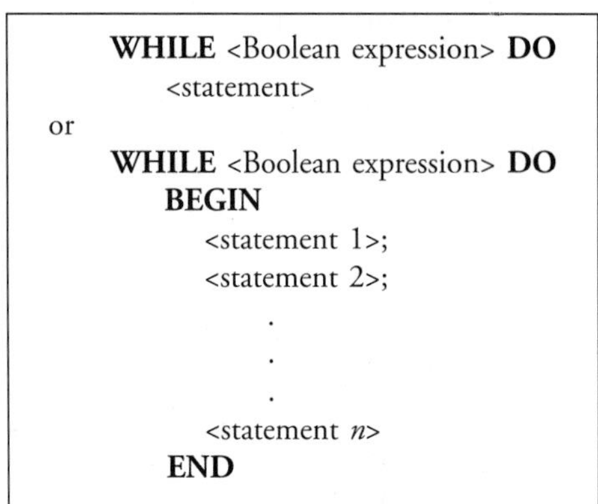

```
    WHILE <Boolean expression> DO
       <statement>
or
    WHILE <Boolean expression> DO
       BEGIN
         <statement 1>;
         <statement 2>;
              .
              .
              .
         <statement n>
       END
```

The flow diagram for a **WHILE . . . DO** loop is given in Figure 5.2.

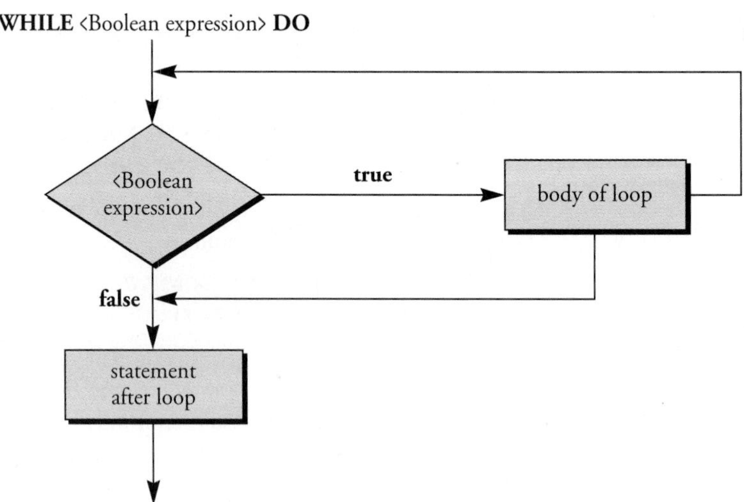

◆ FIGURE 5.2 **WHILE . . . DO** flow diagram

Program control when using a **WHILE . . . DO** loop is in the following order.

1. The loop condition is examined.
2. If the loop condition is **true,** the entire body of the loop is executed before another check is made.

3. If the loop condition is **false,** control is transferred to the first line following the loop. For example

```
A := 1;
WHILE A < 0 DO
  BEGIN
    Num := 5;
    writeln (Num);
    A := A + 10
  END;  {  of WHILE loop  }
writeln (A);
```

produces the single line of output

```
1
```

Before we analyze the components of the **WHILE . . . DO** statement, let's consider a short example.

EXAMPLE 5.6

This example prints some powers of 2.

```
Power2 := 1;
WHILE Power2 < 100 DO
  BEGIN
    writeln (Power2);
    Power2 := Power2 * 2
  END;  {  of WHILE loop  }
```

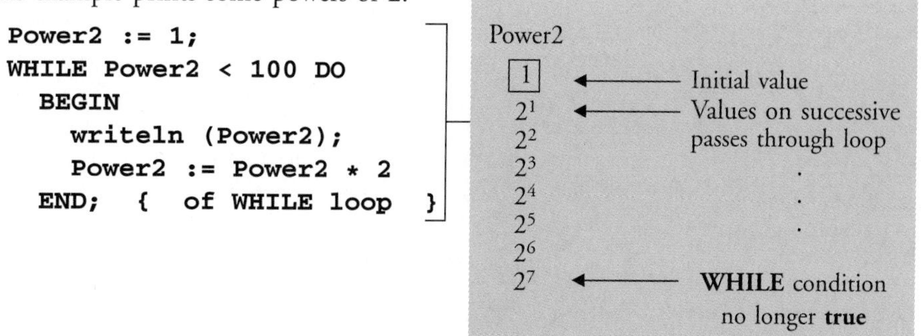

The output from this segment of code is

```
 1
 2
 4
 8
16
32
64
```

Keeping this example in mind, let's examine the general form for using a **WHILE . . . DO** loop.

1. The Boolean expression can be any expression that has Boolean values. Standard examples include relational operators and Boolean variables; thus, each of the following would be appropriate.

```
WHILE J < 10 DO
WHILE A <> B DO
WHILE Done = false DO
WHILE Continue DO
```

2. The Boolean expression must have a value prior to entering the loop.

3. The body of the loop can be a single statement or a compound statement.
4. Provision must be made for appropriately changing the loop control condition in the body of the loop. If no such change is made, the following could happen.
   a. If the loop condition is **true** and no changes are made, a condition called an *infinite loop* is caused. For example

```
A := 1;
WHILE A > 0 DO
  BEGIN
    Num := 5;
    writeln (Num)
  END;  {  of WHILE loop  }
writeln (A);
```

   The condition A > 0 is **true,** the body is executed, and the condition is retested. However, since the condition is not changed within the loop body, A > 0 will always be **true.** This causes the loop to be repeated with no provision for termination, thereby creating an infinite loop. It will not produce a compilation error, but when the program is run the output will be a list of 5s.
   b. If the loop condition is **true** and changes are made but the condition never becomes **false,** an infinite loop again results. For example

```
Power3 := 1;
WHILE Power3 <> 100 DO
  BEGIN
    writeln (Power3);
    Power3 := Power3 * 3
  END;  {  of WHILE loop  }
```

   Since the variable Power3 never is assigned the value 100, the condition Power3 <> 100 is always **true** and the loop is never exited.

The best way to avoid an infinite loop is to be sure the loop control variable eventually reaches the terminating condition, which causes loop execution to cease. An alternative, less efficient method is to put a *counter* inside the loop and add a Boolean condition to the loop control statement. Thus, if we want the loop to terminate after at most 100 repetitions, the general form can be

```
Counter := 0;
WHILE <condition> AND (Counter < 100) DO
  BEGIN
    .
    .
    .
    Counter := Counter + 1  {  Guard against infinite loop  }
  END;  {  of WHILE loop  }
```

Sentinel Values

The Boolean expression of a variable control loop is frequently controlled by a *sentinel value.* For example, a program might require the user to enter numeric data. When there are no more data, the user will be instructed to enter a special (sentinel) value, which signifies the end of the process. The following example illustrates the use of such a sentinel.

EXAMPLE 5.7

Let's write a segment of code that allows the user to enter a set of test scores and then print the average score.

```
NumScores := 0;
Sum := 0;
writeln ('Enter a score and press <Enter>, -999 to quit.');
readln (Score);
WHILE Score <> -999 DO
  BEGIN
    NumScores := NumScores + 1;
    Sum := Sum + Score;
    writeln ('Enter a score and press <Enter>, -999 to quit.');
    readln (Score)
  END;  {  of WHILE loop  }
IF NumScores > 0 THEN
  BEGIN
    Average := Sum / NumScores;
    writeln;
    writeln ('The average of', NumScores:4, ' scores is',
             Average:6:2);
  END  {  of IF...THEN option  }
ELSE
  writeln ('Division by zero!');
```

Writing Style

The writing style for **WHILE . . . DO** loops should be similar to that adopted for **FOR** loops. Indenting, skipping lines, and comments should all be used to enhance readability.

Using Counters

Since **WHILE . . . DO** loops may be repeated a variable number of times, it is common practice to count the number of times the loop body is executed. This is accomplished by declaring an appropriately named integer variable, initializing it to zero before the loop, and then incrementing it by one each time through the loop. For example, if you use Count for your variable name, Example 5.6 (in which we printed some powers of 2) can be modified to

```
Count := 0;
Power2 := 1;

{  Display powers less than 100  }
WHILE Power2 < 100 DO
  BEGIN
    writeln (Power2:10);
    Power2 := Power2 * 2;
    Count := Count + 1
  END;  {  of WHILE loop  }

writeln ('There are', Count:4,
         ' powers of 2 less than 100.');
```

A NOTE OF INTEREST

Ada Augusta Byron

Ada Augusta Byron, Countess of Lovelace (1815–1852), became interested in Charles Babbage's efforts when she was translating a paper on the analytical engine from French to English. Upon meeting Babbage, she began the task of writing an original paper. Through the process, she documented Babbage's ideas and made it possible to understand Babbage's original intentions. Over time, she became a full collaborator on the project, correcting some errors and suggesting the use of the binary system of storage rather than the decimal system.

Lady Lovelace's most important contribution was her concept of a loop. She observed that a repetition of a sequence of instructions often was necessary to perform a single calculation. Thus, she discovered that by using a single set of cards and a conditional jump facility, the calculation could be performed with a fraction of the effort. This idea has earned her the distinction of being the first programmer.

In honor of her role as the first computer programmer, the United States Department of Defense named its newly designed computer language Ada.

The output from this segment of code is

```
              1
              2
              4
              8
             16
             32
             64
There are    7 powers of 2 less than 100.
```

Although the process is tedious, it is instructive to trace the values of variables through a loop where a counter is used. Therefore, let's consider the segment of code we have just seen. Before the loop is entered, we have

0	1
Count	Power2

The loop control expression is Power2 < 100 (1 < 100). Since this is **true,** the loop body is executed and the new values become

1	2
Count	Power2

Prior to each successive pass through the loop, the condition Power2 < 100 is checked. Thus, the loop produces the sequence of values

Count	Power2
1	2
2	4
3	8
4	16
5	32
6	64
7	128

Although Power2 = 128, the remainder of the loop is executed before checking the loop condition. Once a loop is entered, it is executed completely before the loop control condition is reexamined. Since 128 < 100 is **false,** control is transferred to the statement following the loop.

Compound Conditions

All previous examples and illustrations of **WHILE . . . DO** loops have used simple Boolean expressions. However, since any Boolean expression can be used as a loop control condition, compound Boolean expressions can also be used. For example

```
read (A, B);
WHILE (A > 0) AND (B > 0) DO
  BEGIN
    writeln (A, B);
    A := A - 5;
    B := B - 3
  END;  {  of WHILE loop  }
```

will go through the body of the loop only when the Boolean expression (A > 0) **AND** (B > 0) is **true.** Thus, if the values of A and B obtained from the keyboard are

17 8

the output from this segment of code is

```
17        8
12        5
 7        2
```

Compound Boolean expressions can be as complex as you wish to make them. However, if several conditions are involved, the program can become difficult to read and debug. Therefore, you may wish to redesign your solution to avoid this problem.

EXERCISES 5.3

1. Compare and contrast **FOR** loops with **WHILE . . . DO** loops.
2. Write a test program that illustrates what happens when you have an infinite loop.
3. What output is produced by each of the following segments of code?

a.
```
K := 1;
WHILE K <= 10 DO
  BEGIN
    writeln (K);
    K := K + 1
  END;  {  of WHILE loop  }
```

b.
```
A := 1;
WHILE 17 MOD A <> 5 DO
  BEGIN
    writeln (A, 17 MOD A);
    A := A + 1
  END;  {  of WHILE loop  }
```

c.
```
A := 2;
B := 50;
WHILE A < B DO
  A := A * 3;
writeln (A, B);
```

d.
```
Count := 0;
Sum := 0;
WHILE Count < 5 DO
  BEGIN
    Count := Count + 1;
    Sum := Sum + Count;
    writeln ('The partial sum is', Sum:4)
  END;  {  of WHILE loop  }
writeln ('The count is', Count:4);
```
e.
```
X := 3.0;
Y := 2.0;
WHILE X * Y < 100 DO
  X := X * Y;
writeln (X:10:2, Y:10:2);
```

4. Indicate which of the following are infinite loops, and explain why they are infinite.

a.
```
J := 1;
WHILE J < 10 DO
  writeln (J);
  J := J + 1;
```
b.
```
A := 2;
WHILE A < 20 DO
  BEGIN
    writeln (A);
    A := A * 2
  END;  {  of WHILE loop  }
```
c.
```
A := 2;
WHILE A <> 20 DO
  BEGIN
    writeln (A);
    A := A * 2
  END;  {  of WHILE loop  }
```
d.
```
B := 15;
WHILE B DIV 3 = 5 DO
  BEGIN
    writeln (B, B DIV 5);
    B := B - 1
  END;  {  of WHILE loop  }
```

5. Write a **WHILE . . . DO** loop for each of the following tasks.
   a. Print a positive real number (Num), and then print successive values where each value is 0.5 less than the previous value. The list should continue as long as values to be printed are positive.
   b. Print a list of squares of positive integers as long as the difference between consecutive squares is less than 50.
6. Write a segment of code that reads a positive integer and prints a list of powers of the integer that are less than 10,000.

5.4 REPEAT . . . UNTIL Loops

In the previous two sections, we discussed two kinds of repetition. We looked at fixed repetition using **FOR** loops and at variable repetition using **WHILE . . . DO** loops. Pascal provides a second form of variable repetition, a **REPEAT . . . UNTIL** loop, which is a posttest or exit controlled loop.

OBJECTIVES

- to understand that a **REPEAT . . . UNTIL** loop is a posttest loop
- to understand the flow of control using a **REPEAT . . . UNTIL** loop
- to be able to use a **REPEAT . . . UNTIL** loop in a program
- to be able to use **REPEAT . . . UNTIL** loops with multiple conditions

The basic form and syntax of a **REPEAT . . . UNTIL** loop is

```
REPEAT
   <statement 1>;
   <statement 2>;
        .
        .
        .
   <statement n>
UNTIL <Boolean expression>
```

A flow diagram for a **REPEAT . . . UNTIL** loop is given in Figure 5.3.

◆ FIGURE 5.3
REPEAT . . . UNTIL flow diagram

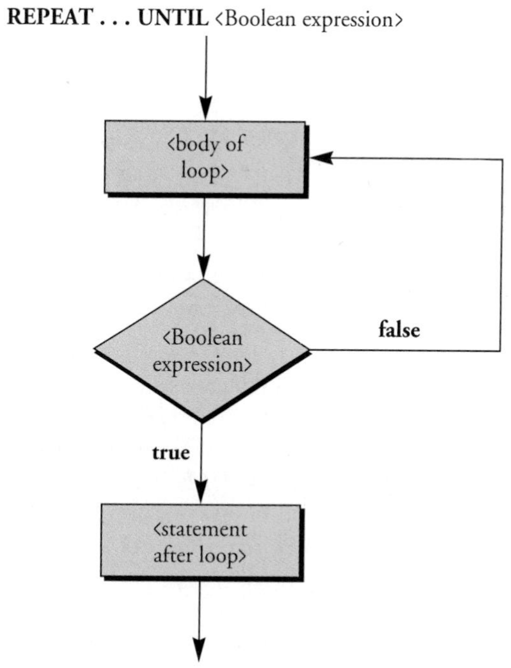

Prior to examining this form, let's consider the fragment of code

```
Count := 0;
REPEAT
  Count := Count + 1;
  writeln (Count:8)
UNTIL Count = 5;
writeln ('All done':10);
```

The output for this fragment is

```
       1
       2
       3
       4
       5
All done
```

Keeping this example in mind, the following comments concerning the use of a **REPEAT . . . UNTIL** loop are in order.

T

1. All simple statements in the body of a **REPEAT . . . UNTIL** loop are executed in the order in which they appear. Thus, a compound statement is not needed when multiple actions are desired within the loop.
2. A semicolon is not required between the last statement in the body of the loop and the reserved word **UNTIL.**
3. The Boolean expression must have a value before it is used at the end of the loop.
4. The loop must be entered at least once because the Boolean expression is not evaluated until after the loop body has been executed.
5. When the Boolean expression is evaluated, if it is **false,** control is transferred back to the top of the loop; if it is **true,** control is transferred to the next program statement.
6. Provision must be made for changing values inside the loop so the Boolean expression used to control the loop will eventually be **true.** If this is not done, an infinite loop will result, as shown in the code

```
J := 0;
REPEAT
  J := J + 2;
  writeln (J)
UNTIL J = 5;
```

7. The writing style for using **REPEAT . . . UNTIL** loops should be consistent with the style for using other loop structures.

There are two important differences between **WHILE . . . DO** and **REPEAT . . . UNTIL** loops. First, a **REPEAT . . . UNTIL** loop must be executed at least once, but a **WHILE . . . DO** loop will be skipped if the initial value of the Boolean expression is **false.** For this reason, **REPEAT . . . UNTIL** loops are generally used less frequently than **WHILE . . . DO** loops. The second difference is that a **REPEAT . . . UNTIL** loop is repeated until the Boolean expression becomes **true.** In a **WHILE . . . DO** loop, repetition continues until the Boolean expression becomes **false.**

EXAMPLE 5.8

An early method of approximating square roots, the Newton–Raphson method, consisted of starting with an approximation and then getting successively better approximations until the desired degree of accuracy was achieved. Writing code for this method, each NewGuess is defined to be

```
NewGuess := 1/2 * (OldGuess + Number / OldGuess)
```

Thus, if the number entered is 34 and the first approximation is 5, the second approximation will be

```
1/2 * (5 + 34 / 5)        (5.9)
```

and the third approximation will be

```
1/2 * (5.9 + 34 / 5.9)        (5.83135593)
```

Let's see how a **REPEAT . . . UNTIL** loop can be used to obtain successively better approximations until a desired degree of accuracy is reached. Assume we wish to approximate the square root of the value contained in Number. OldGuess contains a first approximation, and DesiredAccuracy is a defined constant. A loop used in the solution of this problem is

```
writeln (NewGuess:12:8);

{  Compute and list approximations  }
REPEAT
  OldGuess := NewGuess;
  NewGuess := 1/2 * (OldGuess + Number / OldGuess);
  writeln (NewGuess:12:8)
UNTIL abs(NewGuess - OldGuess) < DesiredAccuracy;
```

If DesiredAccuracy is 0.0001, Number is 34, and NewGuess is originally 5, the output from this segment is

```
5.00000000
5.90000000
5.83135593
5.83095191
5.83095189
```

EXAMPLE 5.9

Interactive programming frequently requires the use of a menu to give the user a choice of options. For example, suppose you want a menu to be

```
Which of the following recipes do you wish to see?

  (T)acos
  (J)ambalaya
  (G)umbo
  (Q)uit

Enter the first letter and press <Enter>.
```

This screen message can then be written as the procedure Menu and the main program can use a **REPEAT . . . UNTIL** loop as follows:

```
REPEAT
  Menu;
  readln (Selection);
  CASE Selection OF
    'T' : Tacos;
    'J' : Jambalaya;
    'G' : Gumbo;
    'Q' : GoodbyeMessage
  END  {  of CASE Selection  }
UNTIL Selection = 'Q';
```

where Tacos, Jambalaya, Gumbo, and GoodbyeMessage are separate procedures with appropriate messages.

Compound Conditions

The Boolean expression used with a **REPEAT . . . UNTIL** loop can be as complex as you choose to make it. However, as with **WHILE . . . DO** loops, if the expression gets too complicated, you might enhance program readability and design by redesigning the algorithm to use simpler expressions.

Choosing the Correct Loop

"Which loop should I use?" is a question often faced by programmers. A partial answer is easy. If a loop is to be repeated a predetermined number of times during execution, a **FOR** loop is preferable. If the number of repetitions is not known, one of the variable control loops should be used.

The more difficult part of the answer is deciding which variable control loop is appropriate. Simply stated, if a control check is needed before the loop is executed, use a **WHILE . . . DO** loop. If a control check is needed at the end of the loop, use a **REPEAT . . . UNTIL** loop. Remember, however, a **REPEAT . . . UNTIL** loop must always be executed at least once. If there is a possibility that the loop will never be executed, a **WHILE . . . DO** loop must be used. For example, when reading data (especially from files; see Chapter 10), if there is a possibility of no data, a **WHILE . . . DO** loop must be used with a prompting read or other control check prior to the loop. Thus, you could have

```
writeln ('Enter a score, -999 to quit.');
readln (Score);
MoreData := (Score <> -999);
WHILE MoreData DO
  BEGIN
    .
    .  (process data)
    .
    writeln ('Enter a score, -999 to quit.');
    readln (Score);
    MoreData := (Score <> -999)
  END;  {  of WHILE loop  }
```

If the three lines of code required to get a score are written as a procedure, this would appear as

```
GetData (Score, MoreData);
WHILE MoreData DO
  BEGIN
    .
    .  (process data)
    .
    GetData (Score, MoreData)
  END;  {  of WHILE loop  }
```

In the event either variable control loop can be used, the problem itself may help with the decision. Does the process need to be repeated until something happens, or does the process continue as long as (while) some condition is true? If either of these is apparent, use the code that most accurately reflects the solution to the problem.

Data Validation

Variable condition loops can be used to make programs more robust. In particular, suppose you are writing an interactive program that expects positive integers to be entered from the keyboard, with a sentinel value of –999 to be entered when you wish to quit. You can guard against bad data by using

```
REPEAT
  writeln ('Enter a positive integer; <-999> to quit.');
  readln (Num)
UNTIL (Num > 0) OR (Num = -999);
```

This process of examining data prior to its use in a program is referred to as *data validation.* Loops are useful for such validation. A second example of using a loop for this purpose follows.

EXAMPLE 5.10

One problem associated with interactive programs is guarding against keyboard errors. This example illustrates how a **REPEAT . . . UNTIL** loop can be used to prevent the user from entering something other than the anticipated responses. Specifically, suppose users of an interactive program are asked to indicate whether or not they wish to continue by entering either a Y or N. The screen message could be

```
Do you wish to continue? <Y or N>
```

You wish to allow any of Y, y, N, or n to be used as an appropriate response. Any other entry is considered an error. This can be accomplished by

```
{  Read one of Y, y, N, or n  }
REPEAT
  writeln ('Do you wish to continue? <Y or N>');
  readln (Response);
  GoodResponse := (Response = 'Y') OR (Response = 'y') OR
                  (Response = 'N') OR (Response = 'n')
UNTIL GoodResponse;
{  A valid response has been read  }
```

Any response other than those permitted as good data (Y, y, N, n) results in GoodResponse being **false** and the loop being executed again.

EXERCISES 5.4

1. Explain the difference between a pretest loop and a posttest loop.
2. Write a test program that illustrates what happens when the initial condition for a **REPEAT . . . UNTIL** loop is **false.** Compare this with a similar condition for a **WHILE . . . DO** loop.
3. Indicate what output is produced by each of the following.

a.
```
A := 0;
B := 10;
REPEAT
  A := A + 1;
  B := B - 1;
  writeln (A, B)
UNTIL A > B;
```

b.
```
Power := 1;
REPEAT
  Power := Power * 2;
  writeln (Power)
UNTIL Power > 100;
```

c.
```
J := 1;
REPEAT
  writeln (J);
  J := J + 1
UNTIL J > 10;
```

d.
```
A := 1;
REPEAT
  writeln (A, 17 MOD A);
  A := A + 1
UNTIL 17 MOD A = 5;
```

4. Indicate which of the following are infinite loops, and explain why.

a.
```
J := 1;
REPEAT
  writeln (J)
UNTIL J > 10;
J := J + 1;
```

b.
```
A := 2;
REPEAT
  writeln (A);
  A := A * 2
UNTIL A > 20;
```

c.
```
A := 2;
REPEAT
  writeln (A);
  A := A * 2
UNTIL A = 20;
```

d.
```
B := 15;
REPEAT
  writeln (B, B DIV 5);
  B := B - 1
UNTIL B DIV 3 <> 5;
```

5. Write a **REPEAT . . . UNTIL** loop for each of the following tasks.
   a. Print a positive real number (Num), and then print successive values where each value is 0.5 less than the previous value. The list should continue as long as values to be printed are positive.
   b. Print a list of squares of positive integers as long as the difference between consecutive squares is less than 50.
6. Discuss whether or not a priming read (a read before the loop is entered) is needed before a **REPEAT . . . UNTIL** loop that is used to get data.
7. Give an example of a situation that would require a predetermined number of repetitions.
8. In mathematics and science, many applications require that a certain level or degree of accuracy be obtained by successive approximations. Explain how the process of reaching the desired level of accuracy relates to loops in Pascal.
9. Write a program that utilizes the algorithm for approximating a square root as shown in Example 5.8. Let the defined accuracy be 0.0001. Input should consist of the number for which the square root is desired. Your program should guard against bad data entries (negatives and zero). Output should include a list of approximations and a check of your final approximation.
10. Compare and contrast the three repetition structures previously discussed in this chapter.

5.5 Loop Verification (Optional)

OBJECTIVES

- to understand how input assertions and output assertions can be used to verify loops
- to understand how loop invariants and loop variants can be used to verify loops

Loop verification is the process of guaranteeing that a loop performs its intended task. Such verification is part of program testing and correctness, which we referred to in Chapter 4.

Some work has been done on constructing formal proofs that loops are "correct." We will now examine a modified version of loop verification. A complete treatment of the issue will be the topic of subsequent course work.

Preconditions and Postconditions with Loops

Preconditions and postconditions can be used with loops. Loop preconditions are referred to as *input assertions*. They are comments that indicate what can be expected to be true before the loop is entered. Loop postconditions are referred to as *output assertions*. They are comments that indicate what can be expected to be true when the loop is exited.

To illustrate input and output assertions, let's consider the mathematical problem of summing the proper divisors of a positive integer; for example

Integer	Proper Divisors	Sum
6	1, 2, 3	6
9	1, 3	4
12	1, 2, 3, 4, 6	16

Consider a program with a positive integer as input and the following as output: a determination of whether the integer is perfect (Sum = integer), abundant (Sum > integer), or deficient (Sum < integer). As part of the program, it is necessary to sum the divisors. A loop to perform this task is

```
DivisorSum := 0;
FOR TrialDivisor := 1 TO Num DIV 2 DO
  IF Num MOD TrialDivisor = 0 THEN
    DivisorSum := DivisorSum + TrialDivisor;
```

An input assertion for this loop is

```
{  Precondition: 1. Num is a positive integer.          }
{                2. DivisorSum = 0.                      }
```

An output assertion is

```
{  Postcondition: DivisorSum is the sum of all proper  }
{                 divisors of Num.                      }
```

When these assertions are placed with the previous code, we have

```
DivisorSum := 0;

 {  Precondition: 1. Num is a positive integer.         }
 {                2. DivisorSum = 0.                     }

FOR TrialDivisor := 1 TO Num DIV 2 DO
  IF Num MOD TrialDivisor = 0 THEN
    DivisorSum := DivisorSum + TrialDivisor;

{  Postcondition: DivisorSum is the sum of all proper  }
{                 divisors of Num.                      }
```

Invariant and Variant Assertions

A *loop invariant* is an assertion that expresses a relationship between variables that remains constant throughout all iterations of the loop. In other words, it is a statement that is true both before the loop is entered and after each pass through the loop. An invariant assertion for the preceding code segment could be

```
{  DivisorSum is the sum of proper divisors of Num that  }
{  are less than or equal to TrialDivisor.               }
```

A *loop variant* is an assertion that changes in terms of its truth between the first and final execution of the loop. The loop variant expression should be stated in such a way that it guarantees the loop is exited. Thus, it should contain some statement about the loop variable being incremented (or decremented) during execution of the loop. A variant assertion for the preceding code, could be

```
{  TrialDivisor is incremented by 1 each time through the  }
{  loop. It eventually exceeds the value Num DIV 2, at     }
{  which point the loop is exited.                          }
```

Variant and invariant assertions usually occur in pairs.

We will now use four kinds of assertions—input, output, variant, and invariant—to produce the formally verified loop that follows.

```
DivisorSum := 0;

{  Precondition: 1. Num is a positive integer.  }   (input
{                2. DivisorSum = 0.             }   assertion)

FOR TrialDivisor := 1 TO Num DIV 2 DO

{  TrialDivisor is incremented by 1 each time   }   (variant
{  through the loop. It eventually exceeds the  }   assertion)
{  value Num DIV 2, at which point the loop is  }
{  exited.                                      }

  IF Num MOD TrialDivisor = 0 THEN
    DivisorSum := DivisorSum + TrialDivisor;

{  DivisorSum is the sum of proper divisors     }   (invariant
{  of Num that are less than or equal to        }   assertion)
{  TrialDivisor.                                }

{  Postcondition: DivisorSum is the sum of      }   (output
{  all proper divisors of Num.                  }   assertion)
```

In general, code that is presented in this text does not include formal verification of the loops. This issue is similar to that of robustness. In an introductory course, a decision must be made as to the trade-off between learning new concepts and writing robust programs with formal verification of loops. The practice is encouraged, but space and time considerations make it inconvenient to include such documentation at this level. We close this discussion with another example illustrating loop verification.

EXAMPLE 5.11

Let's consider the problem of finding the greatest common divisor (GCD) of two positive integers. To illustrate, we have

Num1	Num2	GCD (Num 1, Num2)
8	12	4
20	10	10
15	32	1
70	40	10

A segment of code to produce the GCD of two positive integers after they have been ordered as Small, Large is

```
TrialGCD := Small;
GCDFound := false;
WHILE NOT GCDFound DO
  IF (Large MOD TrialGCD = 0) AND
     (Small MOD TrialGCD = 0) THEN
```

```
      BEGIN
        GCD := TrialGCD;
        GCDFound := true
      END  {  of IF...THEN option  }
  ELSE
    TrialGCD := TrialGCD - 1;
```

Using assertions as previously indicated, this code would appear as

```
TrialGCD := Small;
GCDFound := false;

{  Precondition: 1. Small <= Large                        }
{                2. TrialGCD (Small) is the first         }
{                   candidate for GCD.                    }
{                3. GCDFound is false.                    }

WHILE NOT GCDFound DO

{  TrialGCD assumes integer values ranging from Small  }
{  to 1. It is decremented by 1 each time through the  }
{  loop. When TrialGCD divides both Small and Large,   }
{  the loop is exited. Exit is guaranteed since 1      }
{  divides both Small and Large.                       }

IF (Large MOD TrialGCD = 0) AND
   (Small MOD TrialGCD = 0) THEN
  BEGIN

    {  When TrialGCD divides both Large and Small,          }
    {  GCD is assigned that value.                          }

    GCD := TrialGCD;
    GCDFound := true
  END  {  of IF...THEN option  }
ELSE
  TrialGCD := TrialGCD - 1;

{  Postcondition: GCD is the greatest common divisor   }
{                 of Small and Large.                  }
```

EXERCISES 5.5 (OPTIONAL)

1. Write appropriate input and output assertions for each of the following loops.

   a.
   ```
   readln (Score);
     WHILE Score <> -999 DO
       BEGIN
         NumScores := NumScores + 1;
         Sum := Sum + Score;
         writeln ('Enter a score; -999 to quit.');
         readln (Score)
       END;  {  of WHILE loop  }
   ```

b.
```
Count := 0;
Power2 := 1;
WHILE Power2 < 100 DO
  BEGIN
    writeln (Power2);
    Power2 := Power2 * 2;
    Count := Count + 1
  END;  {  of WHILE loop  }
```

c. (From Example 5.8)

```
REPEAT
  OldGuess := NewGuess;
  NewGuess := 1/2 * (OldGuess + Number / OldGuess);
  writeln (NewGuess:12:8)
UNTIL abs(NewGuess - OldGuess) < DesiredAccuracy;
```

2. Write appropriate loop invariant and loop variant assertions for each of the loops in Exercise 1.
3. The following loop comes from a program called HiLo. The first player enters a target number, and the second player enters a number (Guess). The computer then displays a message indicating whether the guess is correct, too high, or too low. Add appropriate input, output, loop invariant, and loop variant assertions to the following code.

```
Correct := false;
Count := 0;
WHILE (Count < MaxTries) AND (NOT Correct) DO
  BEGIN
    Count := Count + 1;
    writeln ('Enter choice number ', Count);
    readln (Guess);
    IF Guess = TargetNumber THEN
      BEGIN
        Correct := true;
        writeln ('Congratulations!')
      END  {  of IF...THEN option  }
    ELSE IF Guess < TargetNumber THEN
      writeln ('Your guess is too low')
    ELSE
      writeln ('Your guess is too high')
  END;  {  of WHILE loop  }
```

5.6 Nested Loops

OBJECTIVES

- to be able to use nested loops
- to understand the flow of control when using nested loops
- to be able to employ a consistent writing style when using nested loops

In this chapter, we have examined three loop structures. Each of them has been discussed with respect to syntax, semantics, form, writing style, and use in programs. But remember each loop is treated as a single statement in Pascal. In this sense, it is possible for a loop to be one of the statements in the body of another loop. When this happens, the loops are said to be *nested loops.*

Loops can be nested to any depth; that is; a loop can be within a loop within a loop, and so on. Also, any of the three types of loops can be nested within any type of loop. However, a programmer should be careful not to design a program with nesting that is too complex. If program logic becomes too difficult to follow, it is better to redesign the program.

Flow of Control

As a first example of using a loop within a loop, consider

```
FOR K := 1 TO 5 DO
  FOR J := 1 TO 3 DO
    writeln (K + J);
```

When this fragment is executed

(1) K is assigned a value.
(2) For each value of K, the following loop is executed.

```
FOR J := 1 TO 3 DO
  writeln (K + J);
```

Thus, for K := 1, the "inside" or nested loop produces the output

```
2
3
4
```

At this point, K := 2, and the next portion of the output produced by the nested loop is

```
3
4
5
```

The complete output from these nested loops is

```
2 }
3 } from K := 1
4 }
3 }
4 } from K := 2
5 }
4 }
5 } from K := 3
6 }
5 }
6 } from K := 4
7 }
6 }
7 } from K := 5
8 }
```

As you can see, for each value assigned to the index of the outside loop, the inside loop is executed completely. Suppose you want the output to be printed in the form of a chart as follows:

```
2    3    4
3    4    5
4    5    6
5    6    7
6    7    8
```

The pseudocode design to produce this output is

1. **FOR** K := 1 **TO** 5 **DO**
   produce a line

A refinement of this is

1. **FOR** K := 1 **TO** 5 **DO**
   1.1 print on one line
   1.2 advance the printer

The code for this development becomes

```
FOR K := 1 TO 5 DO
  BEGIN
    FOR J := 1 TO 3 DO
      write ((K + J):4);
    writeln
  END;  {  of FOR loop  }
```

Our next example shows how nested loops can be used to produce a design.

EXAMPLE 5.12

Let's use nested **FOR** loops to produce the output

```
*
**
***
****
*****
```

where the left vertical row of asterisks is in column 10. The first-level pseudocode to solve this problem could be

1. **FOR** Line := 1 **TO** 5 **DO**
   produce a line

A refinement of this could be

1. **FOR** Line := 1 **TO** 5 **DO**
   1.1 print on one line
   1.2 advance the printer

Step 1.1 is not yet sufficiently refined, so our next level could be

1. **FOR** Line := 1 **TO** 5 **DO**
   1.1 print on one line
      1.1.1 put a blank in column 9
      1.1.2 print Line asterisks
   1.2 advance the printer

We can now write a program fragment to produce the desired output as follows:

```
FOR Line := 1 TO DO
  BEGIN
    write (' ':9);
    FOR J := 1 TO Line DO
      write ('*');
    writeln
  END;  {  of outer loop  }
```

A significant feature has been added to this program fragment. Note the loop control for the inner loop is the index of the outer loop.

Thus far, nested loops have been used only with **FOR** loops, but any of the loop structures may be used in nesting. Our next example illustrates a **REPEAT . . . UNTIL** loop nested within a **WHILE . . . DO** loop.

EXAMPLE 5.13

Let's trace the flow of control and indicate the output for the following program fragment.

```
A := 10;
B := 0;
WHILE A > B DO
  BEGIN
    writeln (A:5);
    REPEAT
      writeln (A:5, B:5, (A + B):5);
      A := A - 2
    UNTIL A <= 6;
    B := B + 2
  END;  {  of WHILE loop  }
writeln;
writeln ('All done':20);
```

The assignment statements produce

10	0
A	B

and A > B is **true;** thus, the **WHILE . . . DO** loop is entered. The first time through this loop, the **REPEAT . . . UNTIL** loop is used. Output for the first pass is

```
10
10    0   10
```

and the values for A and B are

8	0
A	B

The Boolean expression A <= 6 is **false.** The **REPEAT . . . UNTIL** loop is executed again to produce the next line of output

```
 8    0    8
```

and the values for A and B become

6	0
A	B

At this point, A <= 6 is **true** and control transfers to the line of code

```
B := B + 2;
```

Thus, the variable values are

6	2
A	B

and the Boolean expression A > B is **true.** This means the **WHILE . . . DO** loop will be repeated. The output for the second time through this loop is

```
 6
 6    2    8
```

and the values for the variables are

4	4
A	B

Now A > B is **false** and control transfers to the line following the **WHILE . . . DO** loop. Output for the complete fragment is

```
10
10    0   10
 8    0    8
 6
 6    2    8

          All done
```

Example 5.13 is a bit contrived, and tracing the flow of control is somewhat tedious. However, it is important for you to be able to follow the logic involved in using nested loops.

COMMUNICATION AND STYLE TIPS

When working with nested loops, use line comments to indicate the effect of each loop control variable. For example

```
FOR K := 1 TO 5 DO       {  Each value produces a line  }
  BEGIN
    write (' ':9);
    FOR J := 1 TO K DO   {  This moves across one line  }
      write ('*');
    writeln
  END;  {  of outer loop }
```

Writing Style

As usual, you should be aware of the significance of employing a consistent, readable style of writing when using nested loops. There are at least three features you should consider.

1. **Indenting.** Each loop should have its own level of indenting. This makes it easier to identify the body of the loop. If the loop body consists of a compound statement, **BEGIN** and **END** should start in the same column. Using our previous indenting style, a typical nesting might be

```
FOR K := 1 TO 10 DO
  BEGIN
    WHILE A > 0 DO  {  Start WHILE loop  }
      BEGIN
        REPEAT  {  Start REPEAT loop  }
          .
          .
          .
        UNTIL <condition>;  {  End of REPEAT loop  }
        <statement>
      END;  {  of WHILE loop  }
    <statement>
  END;  {  of FOR loop  }
```

If the body of a loop becomes very long, it is sometimes difficult to match the **BEGIN**s with the proper **END**s. In this case, you should either redesign the program (for example, write a separate subprogram) or be especially careful.

2. **Using comments.** A comment can precede a loop to explain what the loop will do, or it can be used with a statement inside the loop to explain what the statement does. A comment should be used to indicate the end of a loop when the loop body is a compound statement.
3. **Skipping lines.** This is an effective way to isolate loops within a program and to make nested loops easier to identify.

A note of caution is in order with respect to writing style. Program documentation is important; however, excessive use of comments and skipped lines can detract from readability. You should develop a happy medium.

Statement Execution in Nested Loops

The use of nested loops can significantly increase the number of times statements are executed in a program. Suppose a program contains a **REPEAT . . . UNTIL** loop that gets executed six times before it is exited. This is illustrated by

If one of the statements inside this loop is another loop, the inner loop will also be executed six times. Suppose this inner loop is repeated five times whenever it is entered. This means each statement within the inner loop will be executed 6 × 5 = 30 times when the program is run. This is illustrated by

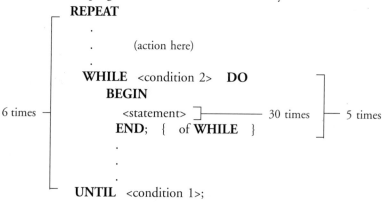

```
        REPEAT
          .
          .      (action here)
          .
          WHILE <condition 2> DO
            BEGIN
6 times       <statement> ]———— 30 times     5 times
            END; { of WHILE }
          .
          .
          .
        UNTIL <condition 1>;
```

When a third level of nesting is used, the number of times a statement is executed can be determined by the product of three factors, $n_1 * n_2 * n_3$, where n_1 represents the number of repetitions for the outside loop, n_2 represents the number of repetitions for the first level of nesting, and n_3 represents the number of repetitions for the innermost loop.

We close this section with an example of a program that uses nested loops to print a multiplication table.

EXAMPLE 5.14

This example presents a complete program that outputs the multiplication table from 1 × 1 to 10 × 10. A suitable heading is part of the output.

```
PROGRAM MultTable (input, output);

CONST
  Indent = ' ';

{*********************************************************************}

PROCEDURE PrintHeading;

  {  Given:    Nothing                                              }
  {  Task:     Print a heading for the multiplication table         }
  {  Return:   Nothing                                              }

  BEGIN
    writeln;
    writeln (Indent:22, 'Multiplication Table');
    writeln (Indent:22, '--------------------');
    writeln (Indent:15, '( Generated by nested FOR loops )');
    writeln
  END;  {  of PROCEDURE PrintHeading  }

{*********************************************************************}

PROCEDURE PrintTable;

  {  Given:    Nothing                                              }
  {  Task:     Use nested loops to print a multiplication table     }
  {  Return:   Nothing                                              }

  VAR
    Row, Column : integer;
  BEGIN

    {  Print the column heads  }
    writeln (Indent:11, '    1    2    3    4    5    6    7    8    9   10');
    writeln (Indent:8, '---!--------------------------------------------');

    {  Now start the loop for printing rows  }
    FOR Row := 1 TO 10 DO
      BEGIN  {  Print one row  }
        write (Row:10, ' !');
```

```
        FOR Column := 1 TO 10 DO
          write (Row * Column:4);
        writeln;
        writeln (Indent:11, '!')
      END  { of each row  }
  END;  { of PROCEDURE PrintTable  }

{***********************************************************************}

BEGIN  { Main program  }
  PrintHeading;
  PrintTable
END.  { of main program  }
```

The output from this program is

```
                    Multiplication Table
                    --------------------

              ( Generated by nested FOR loops )

          1   2   3   4   5   6   7   8   9  10
      ---!-----------------------------------------
       1 !   1   2   3   4   5   6   7   8   9  10
         !
       2 !   2   4   6   8  10  12  14  16  18  20
         !
       3 !   3   6   9  12  15  18  21  24  27  30
         !
       4 !   4   8  12  16  20  24  28  32  36  40
         !
       5 !   5  10  15  20  25  30  35  40  45  50
         !
       6 !   6  12  18  24  30  36  42  48  54  60
         !
       7 !   7  14  21  28  35  42  49  56  63  70
         !
       8 !   8  16  24  32  40  48  56  64  72  80
         !
       9 !   9  18  27  36  45  54  63  72  81  90
         !
      10 !  10  20  30  40  50  60  70  80  90 100
         !
```

EXERCISES 5.6

1. Write a program fragment that uses nested loops to produce each of the following designs.

a.
```
*****
 ****
  ***
   **
    *
```

b.
```
   *
  ***
 *****
*******
 *****
  ***
   *
```

c.
```
***
***
***
***
******
******
******
```

A NOTE OF INTEREST

IBM and Apple = Pinstripes and T-Shirts

After signing the Treaty of Amiens in 1802, Napolean said, "What a beautiful fix we are in now; peace has been declared." In July 1991, representatives of IBM and Apple announced an alliance that similarly shocked many industry analysts. IBM has long been positioned in the mainstream of the computer industry, gaining its reputation more from selling the reliability of its corporate image than from technological innovation. Apple, on the other hand, has based its claim to fame on bold new technologies developed by computer enthusiasts with a distinct bent toward "hacking." For instance, the window-based environment of the first Apple Macintosh in 1983 established a new and exciting mode of human–computer interaction. When IBM and Microsoft later "copied" the "look and feel" of the Mac environment to an IBM-compatible operating system, Apple promptly took them to court. The effects of this case on the software industry are still being debated.

Small wonder that eyebrows have been raised by the agreement between these two corporate antagonists. What are the underlying reasons for the move? According to joint press releases, the companies will cooperate on four fronts:

1. IBM will take steps to better integrate the Mac into IBM-based computer networks.
2. Apple will build future machines using IBM's RISC architecture chip technology.
3. The companies will work together to develop data standards for multimedia.
4. There will be a joint endeavor to produce a new, object-oriented operating system that will eventually be marketed for both IBM and Apple computers.

The last of these ventures is the one that seems to be generating the most excitement on an industry-wide basis. The two companies had been working individually on object-oriented operating systems. Apple had been calling their exploratory system Pink; IBM had called its system Metaphor. It now appears that the Pink and Metaphor research groups will combine their efforts, with the long-range goal that users and third-party software developers will only have to deal with one common interface for a variety of different machines from the two companies. By taking advantage of the abstraction emphasized by the object-oriented approach, the details of the particular machine will be completely hidden.

It all sounds good in theory, but can researchers from two such historically different companies really define a common set of goals? If they can, will it destroy their own individual initiatives? Only time will tell.

2. What output is produced by each of the following fragments?

a.
```
FOR K := 2 TO 6 DO
  BEGIN
    FOR J := 5 TO 10 DO
      write (K + J);
    writeln
  END;  {  of outer FOR loop  }
```

b.
```
FOR K := 2 TO 6 DO
  BEGIN
    FOR J := 5 TO 10 DO
      write (K * J);
    writeln
  END;  {  of outer FOR loop  }
```

c.
```
Sum := 0;
A := 7;
WHILE A < 10 DO
  BEGIN
    FOR K := A TO 10 DO
      Sum := Sum + K;
    A := A + 1
  END;  {  of WHILE loop  }
writeln (Sum);
```

d.
```
Sum := 0;
FOR K := 1 TO 10 DO
  FOR J := (10 * K - 9) TO (10 * K) DO
    Sum := Sum + J;
writeln (Sum);
```

3. What output is produced by the following segment of code?

```
A := 4;
B := 7;
REPEAT
  Num := A;
  WHILE Num <= B DO
    BEGIN
      FOR K := A TO B DO
        write (Num:4);
      writeln;
      Num := Num + 1
    END;  {  of WHILE loop  }
  writeln;
  A := A + 1
UNTIL A = B;  {  End of REPEAT loop  }
```

4. Write a program fragment that uses nested loops to produce the output

```
2    4    6    8   10
3    6    9   12   15
4    8   12   16   20
5   10   15   20   25
```

5. Write an interactive program that generates a pyramid of asterisks. Input will consist of a positive integer *N* from 1 to 20. Output will consist of a pyramid of asterisks with *N* layers. For example, for *N* = 3, the output would be

```
  *
 * *
* * *
```

5.7 Repetition and Selection

OBJECTIVES

- to be able to use a selection statement within the body of a loop
- to be able to use a loop within an **IF . . . THEN** option of a selection statement

Selection within Repetition (Loops)

In Chapter 4 we discussed the use of selection statements. In this chapter, we have discussed the use of three different types of loops. It is now time to see how these elements are used together. We will first examine selection statements contained within the body of a loop.

EXAMPLE 5.15

Let's write a program fragment that computes gross wages for employees of the Florida OJ Canning Company. The data consist of three initials, the total hours worked, and the hourly rate; for example

JHA 44.5 12.75

Overtime (more than 40 hours) is computed at time-and-a-half. The output should include all input data and a column of gross wages. A first-level pseudocode development for this program is

1. **WHILE** MoreEmployees **DO**
   1.1 process one employee
   1.2 print results

which can be refined to

```
1. WHILE MoreEmployees DO
   1.1 process one employee
       1.1.1 get data
       1.1.2 compute wage
   1.2 print results
```

Step 1.1.2 can be refined to

```
       1.1.2 compute wage
             1.1.2.1 IF Hours <= 40.0 THEN
                        compute regular time
                     ELSE
                        compute time-and-a-half
```

The final algorithm for the fragment is then

```
1. WHILE MoreEmployees DO
   1.1 process one employee
       1.1.1 get data
       1.1.2 compute wage
             1.1.2.1 IF Hours <= 40.0 THEN
                        compute regular time
                     ELSE
                        compute time-and-a-half
   1.2 print results
```

The code for this fragment is

```
writeln ('Any employees?  <Y> or <N>');
readln (Choice);
MoreEmployees := (Choice = 'Y') OR (Choice = 'y');
WHILE MoreEmployees DO
  BEGIN
    writeln;
    writeln ('Enter initials, hours, and payrate.');
    readln (Init1, Init2, Init3, Hours, PayRate);
    IF Hours <= 40.0 THEN
      TotalWage := Hours * PayRate
    ELSE
      BEGIN
        Overtime := 1.5 * (Hours - 40.0) * PayRate;
        TotalWage := 40 * PayRate + Overtime
      END;  {  of ELSE option  }
    writeln;
    write (Init1:5, Init2, Init3);
    write (Hours:10:2, PayRate:10:2);
    writeln ('$':10, TotalWage:7:2);
    writeln;
    writeln ('Any more employees?  <Y> or <N>');
    readln (Choice);
    MoreEmployees := (Choice = 'Y') OR (Choice = 'y')
  END;  {  of WHILE loop  }
```

Repetition (Loops) within Selection

The next example illustrates the use of a loop within an **IF . . . THEN** statement.

EXAMPLE 5.16

Let's write a program fragment that allows you to read an integer from the keyboard. If the integer is between 0 and 50, you are to print a chart containing all positive integers less than the integer and their squares and cubes. Thus, if 4 is read, the chart is

```
1    1    1
2    4    8
3    9   27
```

The design for this problem has a first-level pseudocode development of

1. **readln** Num
2. **IF** (Num > 0) **AND** (Num < 50) **THEN**
   2.1 print the chart

Step 2.1 can be refined to

2.1 print the chart
  2.1.1 **FOR** K := 1 **TO** Num – 1 **DO**
    2.1.1.1 print each line

We can now write the code for this fragment as follows:

```
readln (Num);
IF (Num > 0) AND (Num < 50) THEN
  FOR K := 1 TO Num - 1 DO
    writeln (K, K * K, K * K * K);
```

EXERCISES 5.7

1. Find and explain the errors in each of the following program fragments. Assume all variables have been suitably declared.

a.
```
A := 25;
Flag := true;
WHILE Flag = true DO
  IF A >= 100 THEN
    BEGIN
      writeln (A);
      Flag := false
    END;  {  of WHILE loop  }
```

b.
```
FOR K := 1 TO 10 DO
  writeln (K, K * K);
IF K MOD 3 = 0 THEN
  BEGIN
    write (K);
    writeln (' is a multiple of three')
  END;  {  of IF...THEN  }
```

2. What output is produced by each of the following program fragments? Assume variables have been suitably declared.

a.
```
FOR K := 1 TO 100 DO
  IF K MOD 5 = 0 THEN
    writeln (K);
```

b.
```
J := 20;
IF J MOD 5 = 0 THEN
  FOR K := 1 TO 100 DO
    writeln (K);
```
c.
```
A := 5;
B := 90;
REPEAT
  B := B DIV A - 5;
  IF B > A THEN
    B := A + 30
UNTIL B < 0;
writeln (A, B);
```
d.
```
Count := 0;
FOR K := -5 TO 5 DO
  IF K MOD 3 = 0 THEN
    BEGIN
      write ('K =  ' , K:4, '  output  ');
      WHILE Count < 10 DO
        BEGIN
          Count := Count + 1;
          writeln (Count:4)
        END;  {  of WHILE loop  }
      Count := 0;
      writeln
    END;  {  of IF...THEN  }
```
e.
```
A := 5;
B := 2;
IF A < B THEN
  FOR K := A TO B DO
    writeln (K)
ELSE
  FOR K := A DOWNTO B DO
    writeln (K);
```
f.
```
FOR K := -5 TO 5 DO
  BEGIN
    write ('K =  ', K:4, '  output  ');
    A := K;
    IF K < 0 THEN          {  K = -5, -4, -3, -2, -1  }
      REPEAT
        writeln (-2 * A:5);
        A := A + 1
      UNTIL A > 0
    ELSE                   {  K = 0, 1, 2, 3, 4, 5  }
      WHILE (A MOD 2 = 0) DO
        BEGIN
          writeln (A);
          A := A + 1
        END;  {  of WHILE loop  }
    writeln
  END;  {  of FOR loop  }
```

3. Write a program fragment that reads reals from the keyboard, counts the number of positive reals, and accumulates their sum.

4. Given two integers, *A* and *B*, *A* is a divisor of *B* if *B* **MOD** *A* = 0. Write a complete program that reads a positive integer *B* and then prints all the positive divisors of *B*.

5. Write a fragment of code to find the smallest and/or largest value in a list of numbers. The numbers will be entered from the keyboard. Use a sentinel value to indicate when there are no more numbers to be entered.

FOCUS ON PROGRAM DESIGN

The problem for this chapter-ending program was chosen because it illustrates several concepts studied in this chapter. Specifically, the problem is to write a program that allows a positive integer to be entered from the keyboard and then lists all primes less than or equal to that number. The program should include a check for bad data and the use of a sentinel value to terminate the process.

Typical output for the integer 17 is

```
Enter a positive integer; <-999> to quit.
17
                    ----------------------------------------------
                                The number is 17.  The prime numbers
                                less than or equal to 17 are:

                                           2
                                           3
                                           5
                                           7
                                          11
                                          13
                                          17

Enter a positive integer; <-999> to quit.
-999
```

Note the mathematical property that a number K is prime if it has no divisors (other than 1) less than its square root. For example, since 37 is not divisible by 2, 3, or 5, it is prime. Thus, when we check for divisors, it is only necessary to check up to **sqrt** (K). Also note 1 is not prime by definition.

The solution to this problem requires the combined use of repetition and selection. Nested repetition with different kinds of loops is also employed. The algorithmic development utilizes several mathematical properties of divisors of integers. This particular problem can be used to stimulate a discussion of algorithmic efficiency.

A first-level pseudocode development for this problem is

1. Get a number
WHILE MoreData **DO**
2. Process the number
    2.1 Examine the number
    2.2 Get a number

A structure chart for this problem is shown in Figure 5.4.

◆ **FIGURE 5.4**
Structure chart for **PROGRAM** ListPrimes

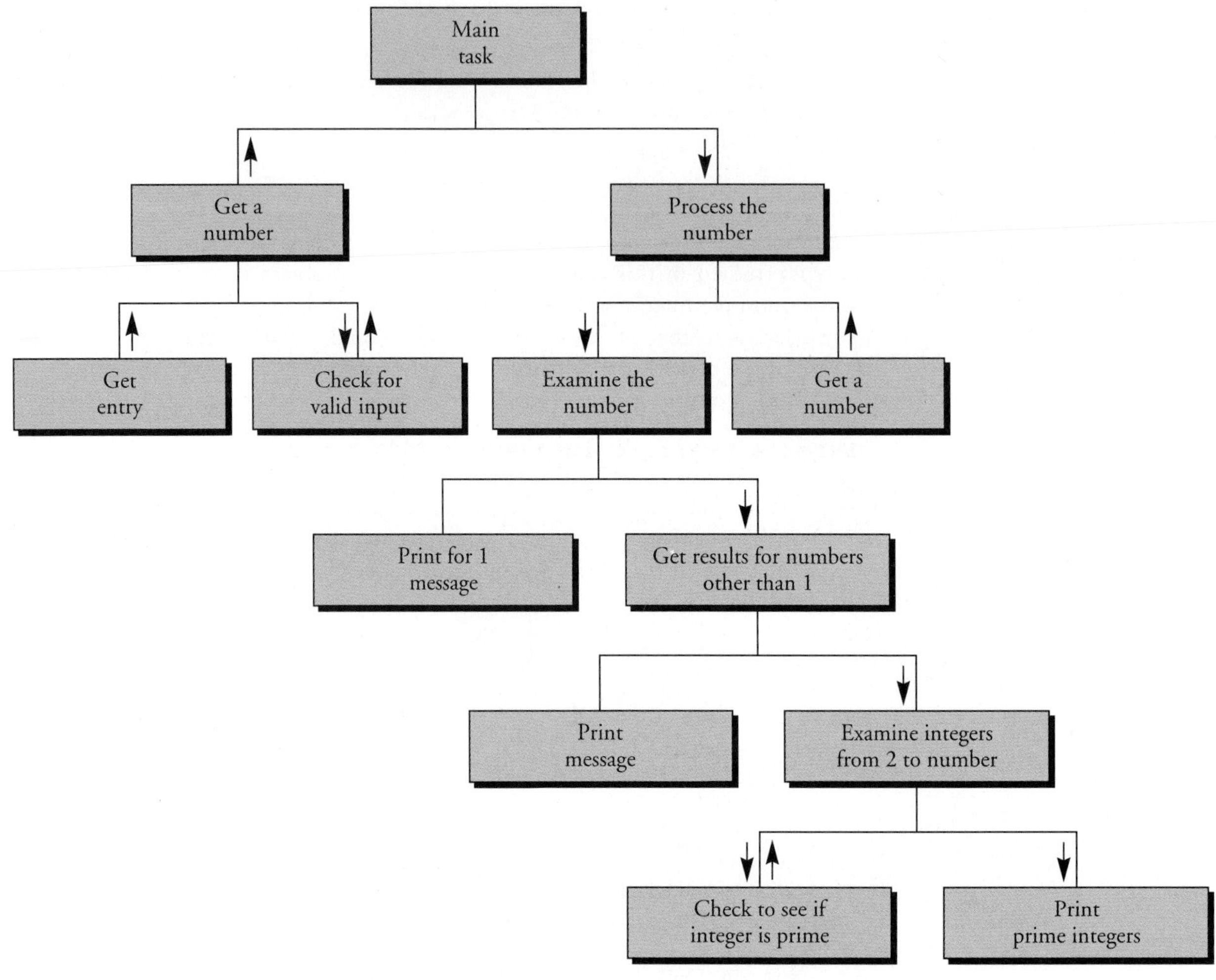

The module specifications for the main modules are

1. GetANumber Module
   Data received: None
   Information returned: Number
   Boolean flag MoreData
   Logic: Get an entry from the keyboard.
   Make sure it is a valid entry or the sentinel value for terminating the process.
   If it is the sentinel value, set the Boolean variable MoreData to **false**.
2. ProcessTheNumber Module
   Data received: The integer read
   Information returned: None

```
Logic: IF the number is 1 THEN print a message
       ELSE
         Print a heading.
         FOR K := 2 TO Number DO
           Check K for a prime number.
           IF K is prime THEN print it.
```

A second-level development is

```
1. Get a number
   1.1 Get entry from the keyboard
   1.2 Check for valid entry
WHILE MoreData DO
2. Process the number
   2.1 Examine the number
   IF Number is 1 THEN
        2.1.1 print a message for 1
   ELSE list the primes
        2.1.2 print a message
        2.1.3 check for primes less than or equal to Number
   2.2 Get a number
        2.2.1 Get entry from the keyboard
        2.2.2 Check for valid entry
```

Step 2.1.3 can be refined to

```
        2.1.3 check for primes less than or equal to Number
              FOR K := 2 TO Number DO
              2.1.3.1 check to see if K is prime
              2.1.3.2 IF K is prime THEN
                        print K in a list of primes
```

Thus, the complete pseudocode development is

```
1. Get a number
   1.1 Get entry from the keyboard
   1.2 Check for valid entry
WHILE MoreData DO
2. Process the number
   2.1 Examine the number
   IF Number is 1 THEN
        2.1.1 print a message for 1
   ELSE list the primes
        2.1.2 print a message
        2.1.3 check for primes less than or equal to Number
              FOR K := 2 TO Number DO
              2.1.3.1 check to see if K is prime
              2.1.3.2 IF K is prime THEN
                        print K in a list of primes
   2.2 Get a number
        2.2.1 Get entry from the keyboard
        2.2.2 Check for valid entry
```

Given this pseudocode development, the main program is

```
BEGIN  {  Main program  }
  GetANumber (Number, MoreData);
  WHILE MoreData DO
    BEGIN
      ExamineTheNumber (Number);
      GetANumber (Number, MoreData)
    END  {  of WHILE loop  }
END.  {  of main program  }
```

A complete program for this problem follows.

```
PROGRAM ListPrimes (input, output);

CONST
  Skip = ' ';
  Dashes = '------------------------------------------------';

VAR
  Number : integer;
  MoreData : boolean;

{*****************************************************************}

PROCEDURE GetANumber (VAR Number : integer;
                      VAR MoreData : boolean);

  {  Given:   Nothing                                            }
  {  Task:    Read an integer entered from the keyboard           }
  {  Return:  The integer read                                    }

  BEGIN
                                                                      1
    {  Get valid input from the keyboard  }
    REPEAT
      writeln;
      writeln ('Enter a positive integer; <-999> to quit.');
      readln (Number);
      MoreData := Number <> -999
    UNTIL (Number > 0) OR (Number = -999)  {  Assumes valid data  }
  END;  {  of PROCEDURE GetANumber  }

{*****************************************************************}

PROCEDURE PrintOneMessage;

  {  Given:   Nothing                                            }
  {  Task:    Print a message for 1                              }
  {  Return:  Nothing                                            }

  BEGIN
    writeln;
    writeln (Skip:10, Dashes);
```

```
    writeln;
    writeln (Skip:20, '1 is not prime by definition.')
  END;  {  of PROCEDURE PrintOneMessage  }

{******************************************************************}

PROCEDURE PrintMessage (Number : integer);

  {  Given:   The integer read                                     }
  {  Task:    Print a heading for the output                       }
  {  Return:  Nothing                                              }

  BEGIN
    writeln;
    writeln (Skip:10, Dashes);
    writeln;
    writeln (Skip:20, 'The number is ', Number,
             '.  The prime numbers');
    writeln (Skip:20, 'less than or equal to ', Number, ' are:');
    writeln
  END;  {  of PROCEDURE PrintMessage  }

{******************************************************************}

PROCEDURE ListAllPrimes (Number : integer);
                                                                      2
  {  Given:   The integer read                                     }
  {  Task:    List all primes less than or equal to the integer    }
  {               read                                             }
  {  Return:  Nothing                                              }

  VAR
    Prime:  boolean;
    Candidate, Divisor : integer;
    LimitForCheck : real;
  BEGIN

    {  Check all integers from 2 to Number  }
    FOR Candidate := 2 TO Number DO
      BEGIN
        Prime := true;
        Divisor := 2;
        LimitForCheck := sqrt(Candidate);

        {  See if Candidate is prime  }
        WHILE (Divisor <= LimitForCheck) AND Prime DO
          IF Candidate MOD Divisor = 0 THEN
            Prime := false            {  Candidate has a divisor  }
          ELSE
            Divisor := Divisor + 1;
```

```
        IF Prime THEN                   {  Print in list of primes  }
          writeln (Candidate:35)
      END  {  of FOR loop  }
  END;  {  of PROCEDURE ListAllPrimes  }

{*****************************************************************}

PROCEDURE ExamineTheNumber (Number : integer);

  {  Given:   The integer read                                    }
  {  Task:    Print primes less than or equal to Number           }
  {  Return:  Nothing                                             }

  BEGIN
    IF Number = 1 THEN
      PrintOneMessage
    ELSE
      BEGIN
        PrintMessage (Number);
        ListAllPrimes (Number)
      END  {  of ELSE option  }
  END;  {  of PROCEDURE ExamineTheNumber  }

{*****************************************************************}

BEGIN  {  Main program  }
  GetANumber (Number, MoreData);
  WHILE MoreData DO
    BEGIN
      ExamineTheNumber (Number);
      GetANumber (Number, MoreData)
    END  {  of WHILE loop  }
END.  {  of main program  }
```

Sample runs of this program produce the output

```
Enter a positive integer; <-999> to quit.
10

          -----------------------------------------------

                    The number is 10.  The prime numbers
                    less than or equal to 10 are:

                                  2
                                  3
                                  5
                                  7

Enter a positive integer; <-999> to quit.
17
```

```
          -----------------------------------------------

                    The number is 17.  The prime numbers
                    less than or equal to 17 are:

                                  2
                                  3
                                  5
                                  7
                                 11
                                 13
                                 17

Enter a positive integer; <-999> to quit.
1
          -----------------------------------------------

                    1 is not prime by definition.

Enter a positive integer; <-999> to quit.
25

          -----------------------------------------------

                    The number is 25.  The prime numbers
                    less than or equal to 25 are:

                                  2
                                  3
                                  5
                                  7
                                 11
                                 13
                                 17
                                 19
                                 23

Enter a positive integer; <-999> to quit.
-3
Enter a positive integer; <-999> to quit.
2

          -----------------------------------------------

                    The number is 2.  The prime numbers
                    less than or equal to 2 are:

                                  2

Enter a positive integer; <-999> to quit.
-999
```

More efficient algorithms than the one we used here do exist. However, the purpose of this program is to see how loops can be used to solve a problem.

RUNNING AND DEBUGGING HINTS

1. Most errors involving loops are not compilation errors. Thus, you will not be able to detect most errors until you try to run your program.
2. Remember to include **BEGIN** and **END** as part of a compound statement in the body of **FOR . . . TO . . . DO** and **WHILE . . . DO** loops.
3. A syntax error that will not be detected by the compiler is a semicolon after **WHILE . . . DO.** The fragment

```
WHILE MoreData DO;
  BEGIN
    readln (A);
    writeln (A)
  END;
```

is incorrect and will not get past

```
WHILE MoreData DO;
```

The misplaced semicolon causes repetition of the null statement. Note that this is an infinite loop.
4. Carefully check entry conditions for each loop.
5. Carefully check exit conditions for each loop. Make sure that the loop is exited (not infinite) and that you have the correct number of repetitions.
6. Loop entry, execution, and exit can be checked by:
   a. Pencil and paper check on initial and final values
   b. Count of the number of repetitions
   c. Use of debugging **writeln**s
      i. Boolean condition prior to loop
      ii. Variables inside loop
      iii. Values of the counter in loop
      iv. Boolean values inside loop
      v. Values after loop is exited

SUMMARY

Key Terms

accumulator
counter
data validation
decrement
fixed repetition (iterated) loop
index
infinite loop
nested loop
posttest (exit controlled) loop
pretest condition
pretest (entrance controlled) loop
sentinel value
variable condition loop

Key Terms (optional)

input assertion
loop invariant
loop variant
loop verification
output assertion

Keywords

DO
DOWNTO
FOR
REPEAT
TO
UNTIL
WHILE

Key Concepts

◆ The following table provides a comparison summary of the three repetition structures discussed in this chapter.

Traits of Loops	FOR . . . TO . . . DO Loop	WHILE . . . DO Loop	REPEAT . . . UNTIL Loop
Pretest loop	Yes	Yes	No
Posttest loop	No	No	Yes
BEGIN . . . END for compound statements	Required	Required	Not required
Repetition	Fixed	Not fixed	Not fixed
Loop index	Yes	No	No
Index automatically incremented	Yes	No	No
Boolean expression used	No	Yes	Yes

- A fixed repetition loop (**FOR . . . TO . . . DO**) is to be used when you know exactly how many times something is to be repeated. The basic form for a **FOR . . . TO . . . DO** loop is

```
FOR <index> := <initial value> TO <final value> DO
   <statement>
```

or

```
FOR <index> := <initial value> TO <final value> DO
   BEGIN
      <statement 1>;
      <statement 2>;
         .
         .
         .
      <statement n>
   END
```

After the loop is finished, the value of the index variable may become unassigned. Program control is transferred to the first executable statement following the loop.

- A **WHILE . . . DO** loop is a pretest loop that can have a variable loop control; a typical loop is

```
Score := 0;
Sum := 0;
MoreData := true;
WHILE MoreData DO
  BEGIN
    Sum := Sum + Score;
    writeln ('Enter a score; -999 to quit.');
    readln (Score);
    MoreData := (Score <> -999)
  END;
```

- A counter is a variable that indicates how often the body of a loop is executed.
- An accumulator is a variable that sums values.
- An infinite **WHILE . . . DO** loop results if a **true** loop control condition is never changed to **false.**
- A posttest loop checks a Boolean condition after the loop body has been completed.
- A **REPEAT . . . UNTIL** loop is a posttest loop; a typical loop is

```
REPEAT
  writeln ('Enter a positive integer; <-999> to quit .');
  readln (Num)
UNTIL (Num < 0) OR (Num = -999);
```

- **REPEAT . . . UNTIL** and **WHILE . . . DO** are variable control loops; **FOR** is a fixed control loop.
- **WHILE . . . DO** and **FOR** are pretest loops; **REPEAT . . . UNTIL** is a posttest loop.
- Any one of these loops can be nested within any other type of loop.
- Indenting each loop is important for program readability.
- Several levels of nesting make the logic of a program difficult to follow.
- Loops and conditionals are frequently used together. Careful program design will facilitate writing code in which these concepts are integrated; typical forms are

```
WHILE <condition1> DO
   BEGIN
     .
     .
     .
     IF <condition2> THEN
       .
       .
       .
     ELSE
       .
       .
       .
     .
     .
     .
   END;  {  of WHILE loop  }
```

and

```
IF <condition> THEN
  BEGIN
    .
    .
    .
    FOR Index := <initial value> TO <final value> DO
      BEGIN
        .
        .
        .
      END;  {  of FOR loop  }
    .
    .
    .
  END  {  of IF . . . THEN option  }
ELSE
  .
  .
  .
```

PROGRAMMING PROBLEMS AND PROJECTS

1. The Caswell Catering and Convention Service (Problem 12, Chapter 3; Problem 14, Chapter 4) wants you to upgrade its program so the program can be used for all of its customers.
2. Modify your program for a service station owner (Focus on Program Design, Chapter 4) so it can be used for an unknown number of customers. Your output should include the number of customers and all other pertinent items in a daily summary.
3. Modify the Community Hospital program (Problem 17, Chapter 4) so it can be run for all patients leaving the hospital in one day. Include appropriate bad data checks and daily summary items.
4. The greatest common divisor (GCD) of two integers *a* and *b* is a positive integer *c* such that *c* divides *a*, *c* divides *b*, and for any other common divisor *d* of *a* and *b*, *d* is less than or equal to *c*. (For example, the GCD of 18 and 45 is 9.)

   One method of finding the GCD of two positive integers (*a*, *b*) is to begin with the smaller (*a*) and see if it is a divisor of the larger (*b*). If it is, then the smaller is the GCD. If it is not, find the next largest divisor of *a* and see if it is a divisor of *b*. Continue this process until you find a divisor of both *a* and *b*. This is the GCD of *a* and *b*.

   Write an interactive program that will accept two positive integers as input and then print out their GCD. Enhance your output by printing all divisors of *a* that do not divide *b*. A sample run could produce

```
Enter two positive integers.
42 72

The divisors of 42 that do not divide 72 are:
      42
      21
      14
       7

The GCD of 42 and 72 is 6.
```

5. The least common multiple (LCM) of two positive integers *a* and *b* is a positive integer *c* such that *c* is a multiple of both *a* and *b* and for any other multiple *m* of *a* and *b*, *c* is a divisor of *m*. (For example, the LCM of 12 and 8 is 24.)

   Write a program that allows the user to enter two positive integers and then print the LCM. The program should guard against bad data and should allow the user the option of "trying another pair" or quitting.
6. A perfect number is a positive integer such that the sum of the proper divisors equals the number. Thus, $28 = 1 + 2 + 4 + 7 + 14$ is a perfect number. If the sum of the divisors is less than the number, it is deficient. If the sum exceeds the number, it is abundant.

   a. Write a program that allows the user to enter a positive integer and then displays the result indicating whether the number entered is perfect, deficient, or abundant.

   b. Write another program that allows the user to enter a positive integer *N* and then displays all perfect numbers less than or equal to *N*.

   Your programs should guard against bad data and should allow the user the option of entering another integer or quitting.

■ **7.** In these days of increased awareness of automobile mileage, more motorists are computing their miles per gallon (mpg) than ever before. Write a program that will perform these computations for a traveler. Data for the program will be entered as indicated by the following table.

Odometer Reading	Gallons of Fuel Purchased
18828(start)	—
19240	9.7
19616	10.2
19944	8.8
20329	10.1
20769(finish)	10.3

The program should compute the mpg for each tank and the cumulative mpg each time the tank is filled up. Your output should produce a chart with the headings

```
Odometer   Odometer   Fuel    Miles   Fuel    Miles   mpg     mpg
(start)    (finish)   (tank)  (tank)  (trip)  (trip)  (tank)  (trip)
```

8. Parkside's Other Triangle is generated from two positive integers: one for the size and one for the seed. For example

```
Size 6, Seed 1      Size 5, Seed
1 2 4 7 2 7         3 4 6 9 4
  3 5 8 3 8           5 7 1 5
    6 9 4 9             8 2 6
      1 5 1               3 7
        6 2                 8
          3
```

Size gives the number of columns. Seed specifies the starting value for column 1. Column *n* contains *n* values. Each successive value is obtained by adding 1 to the previous value, reading down by column. When 9 is reached, the next value becomes 1.

Write a program that reads pairs of positive integers and produces Parkside's Other Triangle for each pair. The check for bad data should include checking for seeds between 1 and 9, inclusive.

9. Modify the sewage, water, and sanitation problem (Problem 19, Chapter 4) so it can be used with data containing appropriate information for all residents of the community.

■ **10.** Modify the program for the Lucky Wildcat Well Corporation (Problem 20, Chapter 4) so it can be run with data containing information about all of Al Derrick's wells.

11. Modify the program concerning the Mathematical Association of America (Problem 21, Chapter 4). There will now be 50 official state delegates attending the next summer national meeting. The new data will be the two-letter state abbreviation for each delegate. Output should include one column listing the state abbreviation and another listing the amount reimbursed.

12. In Fibonacci's sequence

0, 1, 1, 2, 3, 5, 8, 13, . . .

the first two terms are 0 and 1 and each successive term is formed by adding the previous two terms. Write a program that will read positive integers and then print the number of terms indicated by each integer read. Be sure to test your program with data that includes the integers 1 and 2.

■ **13.** Dr. Lae Z. Programmer is at it again. Now that you have written a program to compute the grade for one student in his class (Problems 5, 22, and 23, Chapter 4), he wants you to modify this program so it can be used for the entire class. He will help you by making the first entry be a positive integer that represents the number of students in the class. Your new version should compute an overall class average and the number of students receiving each letter grade.

■ **14.** Modify the Pentagon Parking Lot problem (Problem 26, Chapter 4) so it can be used for all customers in one day. In the new program, time should be entered in military style as a four-digit integer. The lot opens at 0600 (6:00 A.M.) and closes at 2200 (10:00 P.M.). Your program should include appropriate summary information.

■ **15.** The Natural Pine Furniture Company (Problem 7, Chapter 3) now wants you to refine your program so it will print a one-week pay report for each employee. You do not know how many employees there are, but you do know that all information for each employee is on a separate line. Each line of input will contain the employee's initials, the number of hours worked, and the hourly rate. You are to use the constant definition section for

Federal withholding tax rate	18%
State withholding tax rate	4.5%
Hospitalization	$25.65
Union dues	$ 7.85

Your output should include a report for each employee and a summary report for the company files.

16. Orlando Tree Service, Incorporated, offers the following services and rates to its customers.

a. Tree removal	$500 per tree
b. Tree trimming	$80 per hour
c. Stump grinding	$25 plus $2 per inch for each stump with a diameter exceeding 10 inches. The $2 charge is only for the diameter inches in excess of 10.

Write a complete program to allow the manager, Mr. Sorwind, to provide an estimate when he bids on a job. Your output should include a listing of each separate charge and a total. A 10-percent discount is given for any job with a total that exceeds $1000. Typical data for one customer are

```
R 7
T 6.5
G 8
8 10 12 14 15 15 20 25
```

where R, T, and G are codes for removal, trimming, and grinding, respectively. The integer following G represents the number of stumps to be ground. The next line of integers represents the diameters of stumps to be ground.

17. A standard science experiment is to drop a ball and see how high it bounces. Once the "bounciness" of the ball has been determined, the ratio gives a bounciness index. For example, if a ball dropped from a height of 10 feet bounces 6 feet high, the index is 0.6 and the total distance traveled by the ball is 16 feet after one bounce. If the ball continues to bounce, the distance after two bounces would be 10 ft + 6 ft + 6 ft + 3.6 ft = 25.6 ft. Note the distance traveled for each successive bounce is the distance to the floor plus 0.6 of that distance as the ball comes back up.

Write a program that lets the user enter the initial height of the ball and the number of times the ball is allowed to continue bouncing. Output should be the total distance traveled by the ball. At some point in this process, the distance traveled by the ball becomes negligible. Use the **CONST** section to define a "negligible" distance (for example, 0.00001 inches). Terminate the computing when the distance becomes negligible. When this stage is reached, include the number of bounces as part of the output.

18. Write a program that prints a calendar for one month. Input consists of an integer specifying the first day of the month (1 = Sunday) and an integer specifying how many days are in a month.

■ **19.** An amortization table shows the rate at which a loan is paid off. It contains entries indicating the interest paid, the principal paid, and the remaining balance for each month. Given the amount of money borrowed (the principal), the annual interest rate, and the amount the person is to repay each month, print an amortization table. (Make sure the amount of the monthly payment is larger than the first month's interest.) Your table should stop when the loan is paid off and should be printed with the following heads.

```
MONTH NUMBER   INTEREST PAID   PRINCIPAL PAID   BALANCE
```

20. Computers work in the binary system, which is based upon powers of 2. Write a program that prints out the first 15 powers of 2, beginning with 2 to the zero power (2^0). Print your output in headed columns.

21. Print a list of the positive integers less than 500 that are divisible by either 5 or 7. When the list is complete, print a count of the number of integers found.

22. Write a program that reads in 20 real numbers and then prints the average of the positive numbers and the average of the negative numbers.

■ **23.** In 1626, the Dutch settlers purchased Manhattan Island from the Native Americans. According to legend, the purchase price was $24. Suppose the Native Americans had invested this amount at 3 percent annual interest compounded quarterly. If the money had earned interest from the start of 1626 to the end of last year, how much money would the Native Americans have in the bank today? (*Hint:* Use nested loops for the compounding.)

24. Write a program to print the sum of odd integers from 1 to 99.

25. The theory of relativity holds that as an object moves, it gets smaller. The new length of the object can be determined from the formula

$$\textit{New Length} = \textit{Original Length} * \sqrt{1 - B^2}$$

where B^2 is the percentage of the speed of light at which the object is moving, entered in decimal form. Given the length of an object, print its new length for speeds ranging from 0 to 99 percent of the speed of light. Print the output in the columns

```
Percent of Light Speed        Length
----------------------        ------
```

■ **26.** Mr. Christian uses a 90-, 80-, 70-, 60-percent grading scale. Given a list of test scores, print out the number of As, Bs, Cs, Ds, and Fs on the test. Terminate the list of scores with a sentinal value.

27. The mathematician Gottfried Leibniz determined the following formula for estimating the value of π.

$$\frac{\pi}{4} = 1 - \frac{1}{3} + \frac{1}{5} - \frac{1}{7} + \frac{1}{9} - \frac{1}{11} + \ldots$$

Evaluate the first 200 terms of this formula, and print its approximation of π.

28. In a biology experiment, Carey finds that a sample of an organism doubles in population every 12 hours. If she starts with 1000 organisms, in how many hours will she have 1 million?

29. Pascal does not have a mathematical operator that permits raising a number to a power. We can easily write a program to perform this function, however. Given an integer to represent the base number and a positive integer to represent the power desired, write a program that prints the number raised to that power.

30. Mr. Thomas has negotiated a salary schedule for his new job. He will be paid \$0.01 the first day, with the daily rate doubling each day. Write a program to find his total earnings for 30 days. Print your results in a table set up as follows:

```
Day Number   Daily Salary   Total Earned
     1            .01            .01
     2            .02            .03
     3             .              .
     .             .              .
     .             .              .
     .
    30
```

31. Write a program to print the perimeters and areas of rectangles using all combinations of lengths and widths running from 1 to 10 ft, in increments of 1 ft. Print the output in headed columns.

32. Teachers in most school districts are paid on a salary schedule that provides a salary based upon their number of years of teaching experience. Suppose a beginning teacher in the Babbage School District is paid \$19,000 the first year. For each year of experience after this up to 12 years, a 4-percent increase over the preceding year's salary is received. Write a program that prints a salary schedule for teachers in this district. The output should appear as follows:

```
Years Experience       Salary
----------------       ------
       0              $19,000
       1              $19,760
       2              $20,550
       3              $21,372
       .                 .
       .                 .
       .                 .
      12
```

(Actually, most teacher's salary schedules are more complex than this one. As an additional problem, you might like to find out how the salary schedule is determined in your school district and write a program to print that salary schedule.)

33. The Euclidean Algorithm can be used to find the greatest common divisor (GCD) of two positive integers (n_1, n_2). For example, if $n_1 = 72$ and $n_2 = 42$, you can use this algorithm in the following manner.

(1) Divide the larger (72) by the smaller (42):

$72 = 42 * 1 + 30$

(2) Divide the divisor (42) by the remainder (30):

$42 = 30 * 1 + 12$

(3) Repeat this process until you get a remainder of zero:

$30 = 12 * 2 + 6$
$12 = 6 * 2 + 0$

The last nonzero remainder is the GCD of n_1 and n_2.

Write a program that lets the user enter two integers and then prints out each step in the process of using the Euclidean Algorithm to find their GCD.

34. Cramer's Rule for solving a system of equations was given in Problem 31, Chapter 4. Add an enhancement to your program by using a loop to guarantee that the coefficients and constants entered by the user are precisely the ones intended.

35. Gaussian Elimination is another method used to solve systems of equations. To illustrate, if the system is

$$\begin{aligned} x - 2y &= 1 \\ 2x + y &= 7 \end{aligned}$$

Gaussian Elimination starts with the augmented matrix

$$\left[\begin{array}{cc|c} 1 & -2 & 1 \\ 2 & 1 & 7 \end{array}\right]$$

and produces the identity matrix on the left side

$$\left[\begin{array}{cc|c} 1 & 0 & 3 \\ 0 & 1 & 1 \end{array}\right]$$

At this stage, the solution to the system is $x = 3$ and $y = 1$.

Write a program in which the user enters coefficients for a system of two equations containing two variables. The program should then solve the system and display the answer. Your program should include the following.

(1) A check for bad data

(2) A solvable system check

(3) A display of partial results as the matrix operations are performed

36. Reexamine the output for the Focus on Program Design problem in this chapter. In particular, note the prime numbers less than 10 are 2, 3, 5, and 7. Using this list, 10 can be written as the sum of primes 3 + 7. It is conjectured that this is possible for all even positive integers greater than 2. (For example, 24 = 17 + 7.)

a. Write an interactive program that accepts an even positive integer as input and then displays that number as the sum of two primes. Your program should validate input and supply an appropriate message for invalid data. The program should also allow the user the option of repeating the process if desired.

b. Enhance the program you wrote in (a) by displaying a list of consecutive even positive integers written as the sum of primes. Input should consist of the number of lines desired. Thus, for input of $N = 5$, output would be

```
 4 = 2 + 2
 6 = 3 + 3
 8 = 3 + 5
10 = 3 + 7
12 = 5 + 7
```

37. A Pythagorean triple consists of three integers *A*, *B*, and *C* such that $A^2 + B^2 = C^2$. For example, 3, 4, 5 is such a triple because $3^2 + 4^2 = 5^2$. These triples can be generated by positive integers *m* and *n* ($m > n$), where $a = m^2 - n^2$, $b = 2mn$, and $c = m^2 + n^2$. These triples will be primitive (no common factors) if *m* and *n* have no common factors and are not both odd.

Write a program that allows the user to enter a value for *m* and then prints out all possible primitive Pythagorean triples such that $m > n$. Use one function to find the greatest common factor of *m* and *n*, another to see if *m* and *n* are both odd, and another to guard against overflow. For the input value of $m = 5$, typical output would be

```
m    n    a    b    c    a*a    b*b     c*c
----------------------------------------------
2    1    3    4    5      9     16      25
3    2    5   12   13     25    144     169
4    1   15    8   17    225     64     289
4    3    7   24   25     49    576     625
5    2   21   20   29    441    400     841
5    4    9   40   41     81   1600    1681
```

38. The Focus on Program Design problem in this chapter determines whether or not an integer is prime by checking for divisors less than or equal to the square root of the number. The check starts with 2 and increments trial divisors by 1 each time, as seen by the code

```
Prime := true;
Divisor := 2;
LimitForCheck := sqrt(Candidate);
WHILE (Divisor <= LimitForCheck) AND Prime DO
  IF Candidate MOD Divisor = 0 THEN
    Prime := false
  ELSE
    Divisor := Divisor + 1;
```

Other methods can be used to determine whether or not an integer *N* is prime. For example, you may

a. Check divisors from 2 to $N - 1$, incrementing by 1.

b. Check divisors from 2 to $(N - 1) / 2)$, incrementing by 1.

c. Check divisor 2, 3, 5, . . . $(N - 1) / 2)$, incrementing by 2.

d. Check divisor 2, 3, 5, . . . sqrt(*N*), incrementing by 2.

Write a program that allows the user to choose between these options in order to compare the relative efficiency of different algorithms. Use a function for each option.

39. The prime factorization of a positive integer is the positive integer written as the product of primes. For example, the prime factorization of 72 is

$$72 = 2 * 3 * 3 * 4$$

Write a program that allows the user to enter a positive integer and then displays the prime factorization of the integer. A minimal main program could be

```
BEGIN  {  Main program  }
  GetANumber (Num);
  NumberIsPrime := PrimeCheck(Num);
  IF NumberIsPrime THEN
    writeln (Num, ' is prime.')
  ELSE
    PrintFactorization(Num)
END.  {  of main program  }
```

Enhancements to this program could include an error trap for bad data and a loop for repeated trials.

40. Several interesting mathematical properties can be determined by looking at multiplication tables in modular number systems with bases of <10. The product of two numbers in a system is defined to be the remainder when the normal product (base 10) is divided by the new base. To illustrate, the multiplication table in base 4 is

	0	1	2	3
0	0	0	0	0
1	0	1	2	3
2	0	2	0	2
3	0	3	2	1

Write a program that allows the user to choose a base between 2 and 9, inclusive, and then displays the multiplication table for that base. Have the program guard against bases entered that are less than 2 or greater than 9.

COMMUNICATION IN PRACTICE

1. Using a completed program from this chapter, remove all documentation and replace all identifiers with one- or two-letter identifiers. Exchange this version with another student who has prepared a similar version of a different program. Add documentation and change identifiers to meaningful identifiers. Compare your results with the text version of the program. Discuss the similarities and differences with your class.

2. As you might expect, instructors of computer science do not agree as to whether a **REPEAT . . . UNTIL** loop or a **WHILE . . . DO** loop is the preferred variable control loop in Pascal. Interview several computer science instructors at your college or university to determine what preference (if any) they have regarding these two forms of repetition. Prepare a class report based upon your interviews. Include advantages and disadvantages of each form of repetition.

3. Examine the repetition constructs of at least five other programming languages. Prepare a report that compares and contrasts repetition in each of the languages. Be sure to include information such as which languages provide for both fixed and variable repetition and which languages have more than one kind of variable repetition. Which language appears to have the most desirable form of repetition? Include your rationale for this decision in your report.

4. Examine some old computer science texts and talk to some computer science instructors who worked with the first languages to see how repetition was achieved in the "early days." Prepare a brief chronological chart for class display that depicts the various stages in the development of repetition in computer programming.

CHAPTER

6 Text Files and Enumerated Data Types

CHAPTER OUTLINE

Now that you have completed five chapters, you have made a significant step in the process of learning to use a programming language for the purpose of solving problems. We have covered the essential elements of arithmetic, variables, input/output, selection, repetition, and subprograms and are now ready to look at a somewhat different area of Pascal.

Thus far, you have been unable to work with large amounts of data. In order to write programs that solve problems using large data bases, it is necessary to be able to store, retrieve, and manage the data. In this chapter, we first look at the storage and retrieval of data (text files) and then study a feature of Pascal (enumerated data types) that facilitates handling the data.

These topics are not closely related, but since both are useful when working with data structures which are examined in Chapter 7, we present them together. As you study this material, remember that we are "setting the stage" for working with large amounts of data.

6.1 Text Files

T

OBJECTIVES

- to understand how data can be stored in text files
- to be able to **read** from a text file
- to be able to **write** to a text file
- to understand the difference between internal and external files

The implementation of concepts presented in this section depends upon the computer you are using; it is very system-dependent. Your instructor will probably supplement this material with examples and explanations suitable for your particular environment. At the very least, you should be able to use the manual for your system for reference.

Consider the relatively simple problem of using a computer to compute and print water bills for a community of 30,000 customers. If the data needed consist of a customer name, address, and amount of water used, you can imagine that entering this information interactively every billing period would involve an enormous amount of time and expense and would probably result in errors in the data. Furthermore, it is often desirable to save information between runs of a program for other uses.

To serve these needs, we can store data in some secondary storage device, usually magnetic tapes or disks. Data can be created separately from a program, stored on these devices, and then accessed by programs when necessary. It is also possible to update and save information for other runs of the same program or for running another program using this same data. For now, we will store all data in *text files.* (Other kinds of files are examined in Chapter 10.)

Creating a Text File

Text files can be created by a text editor or by a program. Often the editor you use to create your program can be used to create a text file. The use of text editors varies significantly, and you should consult your instructor and/or manual before using this method. This, however, is how your instructor may create data files for you to use with subsequent programming problems.

Each line in a data file has an *end-of-line* ***(eoln)*** *marker,* which has an ASCII representation. For text writing purposes, we use the symbol ▌ to represent this. Thus, two lines of integer data could be envisioned as

18 26 17 21▌

19 23 18 22▌

Each data file has an *end-of-file* ***(eof)*** *marker* after the last end-of-line marker. As with the end-of-line marker, an end-of-file marker also has an ASCII representation. For text writing purposes, we use the symbol ■ to represent end-of-file. For example, suppose a text file is used to store data for students in a class. If each line consists of an identification number for each student followed by three scores, a typical file can be envisioned as

00723 85 93 100▌

00131 78 91 85▌

00458 82 75 86▌ ■

Technically, these lines are stored as one continuous stream, with end-of-line markers used to differentiate between lines and the end-of-file marker used to signify the end of one file:

00723 85 93 100▌00131 78 91 85▌00458 82 75 86▌ ■

However, we frequently use separate lines to illustrate lines in a text file. Both end-of-line and end-of-file markers are appropriately placed by the computer at the time a file is created. When characters are read, **eoln** markers are read as blanks. Later in this text, we see how special functions can be used to detect when end-of-line and end-of-file symbols have been reached when reading data from a data file.

When a text file in secondary storage is to be used by a program, a file variable (or symbolic file name) must be included in the file list, along with the standard files **input** and **output,** as part of the program heading. Thus, if ClassList is the file variable, a heading might be

```
PROGRAM ClassRecordBook (input, output, ClassList);
```

This file variable must be declared in the variable declaration section and is of type **text.** Thus, the declaration section would be

```
VAR
  ClassList : text;
```

The file variable ClassList must be associated with the text file, which is stored externally. This may be done by creating a procedure file prior to compiling and running the program. It may also be accomplished within the program; for example, in

T Turbo Pascal, an **assign** statement is used for this purpose. Thus, if the data needed in a program are stored on a disk under the name Data1, the statement

```
assign (ClassList, 'Data1');
```

establishes the desired relationship between the file variable ClassList and the data stored externally in the text file Data1.

Reading from a Text File

Before data can be read from a file, the file must be *opened for reading.* This is done by the statement

```
reset (<file variable>);
```

which moves a data pointer to the first position of the first line of the data file to be read. Thus

```
reset (ClassList);
```

positions the pointer as follows:

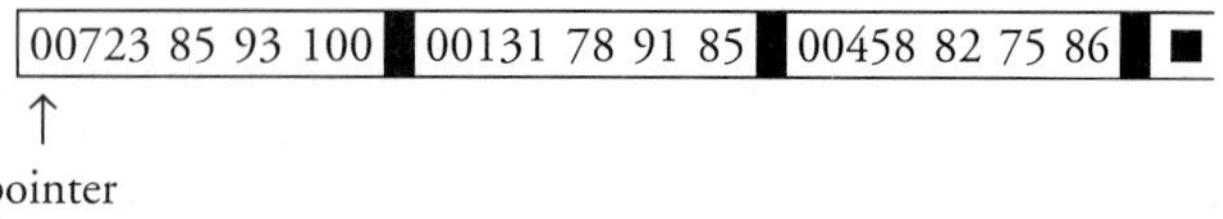

```
|00723 85 93 100█00131 78 91 85█00458 82 75 86█ ■
↑
pointer
```

Reading from a text file is very similar to getting input interactively or reading from a standard input file. The standard procedures **read** and **readln** are used with appropriate variables as arguments in either format, as shown.

> **read** (<file variable>, <input list>)
> or
> **readln** (<file variable>, <input list>)

If the file variable is not specified, the standard file **input** is assumed. Thus, data from one line of the file of student test scores, ClassList, can be obtained by

```
readln (ClassList, IDNumber, Score1, Score2, Score3);
```

As data items are read using **readln,** values are stored in the designated variables and the pointer is moved to the first position past the end-of-line marker. Thus

```
reset (ClassList);
readln (ClassList, IDNumber, Score1, Score2, Score3);
```

results in

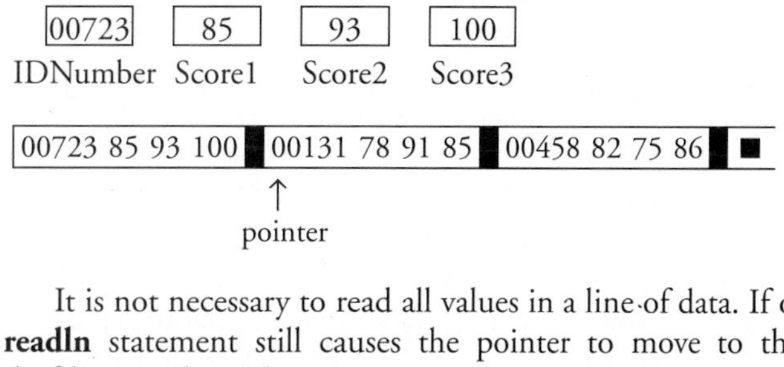

00723	85	93	100
IDNumber	Score1	Score2	Score3

```
|00723 85 93 100█00131 78 91 85█00458 82 75 86█ ■
                 ↑
                 pointer
```

It is not necessary to read all values in a line of data. If only some values are read, a **readln** statement still causes the pointer to move to the first position past the end-of-line marker. Thus

```
reset (ClassList);
readln (ClassList, IDNumber, Score1);
```

results in

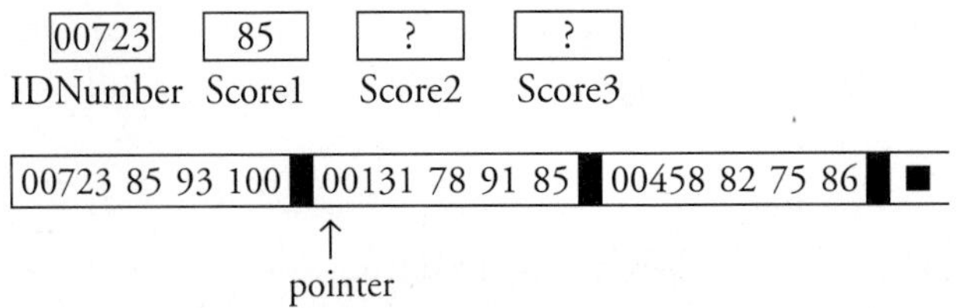

However, when data items are read using **read,** the pointer moves to the first position past the last data item read. Thus, the statement

```
read (ClassList, IDNumber, Score1);
```

results in

00723 85
IDNumber Score1

00723 85 93 100 | 00131 78 91 85 | 00458 82 75 86

pointer

Variables in the variable list of **read** and **readln** can be listed one at a time or in any combination that does not result in a type conflict. For example

```
readln (ClassList, IDNumber, Score1);
```

can be replaced by

```
read (ClassList, IDNumber);
readln (ClassList, Score1);
```

However, unnecessary procedure calls are inefficient.

Pascal has two Boolean-valued functions that may be used when working with text files: **eoln** (for end-of-line) and **eof** (for end-of-file). Only if the data pointer is at an end-of-line or end-of-file marker is the Boolean function **eoln**(<file variable>) true. Similarly, **eof** (<file variable>) is true only when the data pointer is positioned at the end-of-file marker. This allows both **eoln**(<file variable>) and **eof**(<file variable>) to be used as Boolean conditions when designing problem solutions. Thus, part of a solution might be

```
WHILE NOT eof(<file variable>) DO
  process a line of data
```

In this loop, data from one line of the text file would typically be read by a **readln** statement. This allows the end-of-file condition to become **true** after the last data line has been read.

Text files can contain any character available in the character set being used. When numeric data are stored, the system converts a number to an appropriate character representation. When this number is retrieved from the file, another conversion takes place to change the character representation to a number.

EXAMPLE 6.1

Now let's write a short program that uses the text file ClassList and the end-of-file (**eof**) condition. If the problem is to print a listing of student identification numbers, test scores, and test averages, a first-level pseudocode development is

1. Open the file
2. Print a heading
3. **WHILE NOT eof** (<file variable>) **DO**

3.1 process a line of data

Step 3.1 can be refined to

3.1 process a line of data
  3.1.1 get the data
  3.1.2 compute test average
  3.1.3 print the data

A short program to accomplish this task follows.

```
PROGRAM ClassRecordBook (input, output, ClassList);

{  This program uses data from a text file.  Data for each      }
{  student are on a separate line in the file.  Lines are       }
{  processed until there are no more lines.                     }

VAR
  Score1, Score2, Score3,               {  Test scores           }
  IDNumber : integer;                   {  Student number        }
  TestAverage : real;                   {  Average of three tests }
  ClassList : text;                     {  Text file             }

{*************************************************************}

FUNCTION Average (Score1, Score2, Score3 : integer) : real;

  {  Given:   Three integers                                    }
  {  Task:    Compute their average                             }
  {  Return:  The average of three integers                     }

  BEGIN
    Average := (Score1 + Score2 + Score3) / 3
  END;  {  of FUNCTION Average  }

{*************************************************************}

PROCEDURE PrintHeading;

  {  Given:   Nothing                                           }
  {  Task:    Print the heading                                 }
  {  Return:  Nothing                                           }

  CONST
    Skip = ' ';
  BEGIN
    writeln ('Identification Number', Skip:5, 'Test Scores',
             Skip:5, 'Average');
    writeln ('---------------------', Skip:5, '-----------',
             Skip:5, '-------');
    writeln
  END;  {  of PROCEDURE PrintHeading  }

{*************************************************************}
```

```
BEGIN  {  Main program  }
  reset (ClassList);
  PrintHeading;
  WHILE NOT eof(ClassList) DO
    BEGIN
      readln (ClassList, IDNumber, Score1, Score2, Score3);
      TestAverage := Average(Score1, Score2, Score3);
      writeln (IDNumber:10, Score1:18, Score2:4, Score3:4,
               TestAverage:12:2)
    END  {  of WHILE NOT eof DO loop  }
END.  {  of main program  }
```

When this program is run using the text file ClassList with values

00723 85 93 100 ▮ 00131 78 91 85 ▮ 00458 82 75 86 ▮ ■

the output produced is

```
Identification Number      Test Scores      Average
---------------------      -----------      -------

         723               85  93 100        92.67
         131               78  91  85        84.67
         458               82  75  86        81.00
```

A note of caution is in order. Any attempt to **read** beyond the end of a file results in an error. To illustrate, if

```
read (ClassList, IDNumber, Score1, Score2, Score3);
```

had been used in the previous example instead of

```
readln (ClassList, IDNumber, Score1, Score2, Score3);
```

an error would have occurred because when **read** is used with the last line of data, the data pointer is positioned as

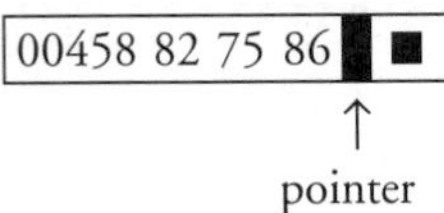

At this point, **eoln** (ClassList) is **true** but **eof** (ClassList) is still **false,** and the loop for processing a line of data would be entered one more time. Using **readln,** however, positions the data pointer as

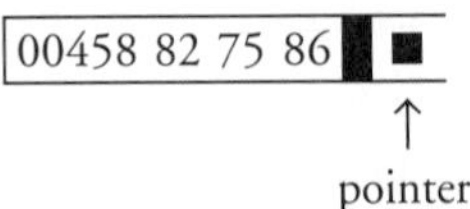

which causes the end-of-file condition to be **true** when expected.

Writing to a Text File

It is also possible to write to a text file. If the file is to be saved for later use, a file variable must be included in the file list as part of the program heading, just as is done when reading from files. The file variable must be declared to be of type **text.** Before writing a file, the new file must be *opened for writing* by

```
rewrite (<file variable>);
```

This standard procedure creates an empty file with the specified name. Any values previously in the file are erased by this statement. Data are then written to the file by using the standard procedures **write** and **writeln.** The general form is

> **write** (<file variable>, <list of values>)
> or
> **writeln** (<file variable>, <list of values>)

Either statement causes the list of values to be written on one line in the file. The difference is that **writeln** causes an end-of-line marker to be placed after the last data item. Using **write** allows the user to continue entering data items on the same line with subsequent **write** or **writeln** statements. If desired

```
writeln (<file variable>);
```

can be used to place an end-of-line marker at the end of a data line.

Formatting can be used to control the spacing of data items in a line of text. For example, since numeric items must be separated, the user might choose to put test scores in a file by

```
writeln (ClassList, Score1:4, Score2:4, Score3:4);
```

If the scores are 85, 72, and 95, the line of data created is

85 72 95 ▌

and each integer is allotted four columns. Let's now illustrate writing to a file with an example.

EXAMPLE 6.2

Let's write a program that allows you to create a text file containing data for students in a class. Each line in the file will have a student identification number followed by three test scores. A first-level pseudocode development is

1. Open the file
2. **WHILE** more data **DO**
   2.1 process a line

Step 2.1 can be refined to

2.1 process a line
    2.1.1 get data from the keyboard
    2.1.2 write data to text file

A complete program for this problem follows.

```
PROGRAM CreateFile (input, output, ClassList);

{  This program creates a text file.  Each line of the file     }
{  contains data for one student.  Data are entered inter-       }
{  actively from the keyboard and then written to the file.     }

VAR
  Score1, Score2, Score3,        {  Scores for three tests       }
  IDNumber : integer;            {  Student number               }
  Response : char;               {  Indicator for continuation   }
  MoreData : boolean;            {  Loop control variable        }
  ClassList : text;              {  External text file           }
```

```
{***************************************************************}

PROCEDURE GetStudentData (VAR IDNumber, Score1, Score2,
                              Score3 : integer);

  {  Given:   Nothing                                          }
  {  Task:    Get IDNumber and three test scores from the      }
  {                keyboard                                    }
  {  Return:  IDNumber, Score1, Score2, Score3                 }

  BEGIN
    write ('Please enter a student ID number.  ');
    readln (IDNumber);
    writeln ('Please enter three test scores.');
    readln (Score1, Score2, Score3)
  END;  {  of PROCEDURE GetStudentData  }

{***************************************************************}

BEGIN  {  Main program  }
  rewrite (ClassList);                    {  Open for writing  }
  MoreData := true;
  WHILE MoreData DO
    BEGIN
      GetStudentData (IDNumber, Score1, Score2, Score3);
      writeln (ClassList, IDNumber, Score1:4, Score2:4,
               Score3:4);

      {  Check for more data  }
      writeln;
      writeln ('Any more students?  Y or N');
      readln (Response);
      IF (Response = 'N') OR (Response = 'n') THEN
        MoreData := false
    END  {  of WHILE loop  }
END.  {  of main program  }
```

External and Internal Files

All files used thus far have been *external files,* which are files that are stored in secondary memory and are external to the main memory. If a program is to use an external file, a file variable must be included in the file list portion of the program heading. The file variable must then be declared in the variable declaration section as being of type **text.**

On some occasions, it is desirable to use a file only while the program is running and it is not necessary to save the contents for later use. In such cases, an *internal file* (also called a *temporary* or *scratch file*) can be created by declaring a file variable of type **text** in the variable declaration section but not including it in the file list of the program heading. Internal files are normally used during file processing when it is desirable to temporarily save the contents of a file that is being altered. Our next example illustrates the use of an internal file.

EXAMPLE 6.3

Let's write a program that allows you to update the text file ClassList by adding one more test score to each line of data. We need two text files in this program: ClassList (external) and TempFile (internal). With these two files, we can create new lines in

TempFile by reading a line from ClassList and getting a score from the keyboard. When all lines have been updated, we copy TempFile to ClassList. A first-level pseudocode solution for this problem is

1. Open the files (**reset** ClassList, **rewrite** TempFile)
2. **WHILE NOT eof** (ClassList) **DO**
   2.1 read one line
   2.2 get new score
   2.3 write one line to TempFile
3. Open files (**reset** TempFile, **rewrite** ClassList)
4. Update file
   WHILE NOT eof (TempFile) **DO**
   4.1 read one line from TempFile
   4.2 write one line to ClassList

A complete program for this problem follows.

```
PROGRAM UpdateClassList (input, output, ClassList);

{  This program updates an existing text file.  The process      }
{  requires a second file.  Contents of the external file are    }
{  copied to a temporary internal file and the external file is  }
{  then updated one line at a time.                              }

VAR
  Score1, Score2,                       {  Scores for four tests  }
  Score3, Score4,
  IDNumber : integer;                   {  Student number         }
  ClassList, TempFile : text;           {  Text files             }

BEGIN  {  Program  }
  reset (ClassList);
  rewrite (TempFile);

  WHILE NOT eof(ClassList) DO
    BEGIN
      readln (ClassList, IDNumber, Score1, Score2, Score3);
      writeln ('Enter a new test score for student ', IDNumber);
      readln (Score4);
      writeln (TempFile, IDNumber, Score1:4, Score2:4,
               Score3:4, Score4:4)
    END;  {  of lines in ClassList  }

  reset (TempFile);
  rewrite (ClassList);  {  Contents of old ClassList are erased  }

  WHILE NOT eof(TempFile) DO
    BEGIN
      readln (TempFile, IDNumber, Score1, Score2, Score3, Score4);
      writeln (ClassList, IDNumber, Score1:4, Score2:4,
               Score3:4, Score4:4)
    END  {  of copying TempFile to ClassList  }
END.  {  of program  }
```

EXAMPLE 6.4

As an illustration of the use of **eoln,** let's write a program that replaces all blanks in a text file with asterisks. Output is directed to the monitor, and a new text file is created for the purpose of saving the altered form of the original text file. Note that reading a character advances the data pointer only one character position unless **readln** is used. A first-level pseudocode development is

1. Open the files
WHILE NOT eof (FileWithBlanks) **DO**
2. Process one line
3. Prepare for the next line

A second-level pseudocode development is

1. Open the files
   1.1 open FileWithBlanks
   1.2 open FileWithoutBlanks
WHILE NOT eof (FileWithBlanks) **DO**
2. Process one line
   2.1 read a character
   2.2 **IF** character is a blank **THEN**
      2.2.1 replace with an asterisk
   2.3 write character to FileWithoutBlanks
   2.4 write character to the screen
3. Prepare for the next line
   3.1 insert end-of-line marker in FileWithoutBlanks
   3.2 end-of-line marker to screen
   3.3 advance pointer in FileWithBlanks

A complete program for this problem follows.

```
PROGRAM DeleteBlanks (input, output, FileWithBlanks,
                      FileWithoutBlanks);

{  This program illustrates using eof and eoln with a text   }
{  file.  It replaces blanks with asterisks.                 }

VAR
  FileWithBlanks,            {  Existing text file           }
  FileWithoutBlanks : text;  {  Altered text file            }
  Ch : char;                 {  Used for reading characters  }

BEGIN  {  Program  }
  reset (FileWithBlanks);                  {  Open the files    }
  rewrite (FileWithoutBlanks);

  WHILE NOT eof(FileWithBlanks) DO
    BEGIN                                 {  Process one line   }
      WHILE NOT eoln(FileWithBlanks) DO
        BEGIN
          read (FileWithBlanks, Ch);
          IF Ch = ' ' THEN
            Ch := '*';
          write (FileWithoutBlanks, Ch);
          write (Ch)                    {  Write to the screen  }
        END;  {  of reading one line  }
```

```
      writeln (FileWithoutBlanks);      { Insert end-of-line   }
      writeln;
      readln (FileWithBlanks)          {  Advance the pointer  }
    END  {  of lines in text file  }
END.  {  of program  }
```

On the final time through the loop, **readln** changes the pointer from

last line	■	■

↑ pointer

to

last line	■	■

↑ pointer

Hence, **eof**(FileWithBlanks) becomes **true.**

When this program is run using the text file

```
This is a text file with normal blanks.
After it has been processed by
PROGRAM DeleteBlanks, every blank will
be replaced with an asterisk ''*''.
```

the output to the screen is

```
This*is*a*text*file*with*normal*blanks.
After*it*has*been*processed*by
PROGRAM*DeleteBlanks,*every*blank*will
be*replaced*with*an*asterisk*''*''.
```

The external text file FileWithoutBlanks also contains the version shown as output.

Reading Mixed Data

It is often necessary to include data of more than one type in a text file. For example, each line of a data file might contain a person's age and gender:

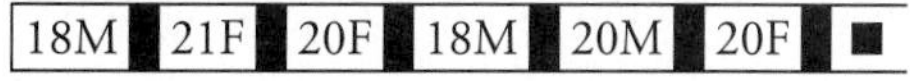

When reading data from such a file, you must guard against reading data into a variable that is not consistent with the type of data being read. The data from the data file here can be read by

```
WHILE NOT eof(Data) DO
  BEGIN
    readln (Data, Age, Gender);
      .
      .  (process data here)
      .
  END;
```

The material in this section allows us to make a substantial change in our approach to writing programs. We can now proceed assuming that data files exist for a program. This somewhat simplifies program design and also allows us to design

A NOTE OF INTEREST

Inspections: Debugging in the 1990s

(The following information was provided at the author's request by Franco E. Mau, Development Engineer at Tandem Computers Incorporated. Cupertino, California.)

The process of debugging software has become multifaceted. One form of finding code defects currently used by Tandem Computers Incorporated is the use of "inspections." This inspection process was pioneered by Bill Fagan at IBM in the late 1970s and was introduced at Tandem Computers Incorporated in 1989.

Simply stated, an inspection is a team process of finding defects, particularly in software packages and smaller segments of computer code. An inspection team consists of a least five members: the author (code writer), a moderator, a reader, and two inspectors, one of whom also serves as a recorder. A typical session is about two hours long; many sessions are required to inspect a single software package.

Prior to an inspection session, the reader and both inspectors spend about two hours examining the package or code to be reviewed. At the beginning of the inspection process for a document, initial rules are established concerning what kinds of defects (logical, syntactic, and so on) are being sought. Subsequently, all defects are related to these initial rules.

During a session, authors are available only to make clarifications and otherwise are not involved in the discussion. All members of the inspection team are active participants in the inspection. The moderator sets the pace, makes sure all participants are prepared, inspects code, and generally coordinates the session. The reader provides an oral description of what the code is attempting to accomplish. The recorder records code defects on forms. The code line numbers are listed with respective references to how the lines relate to the defects being sought.

All participants in an inspection are encouraged to stress professionalism. They must be willing to communicate and share their technical expertise. When discussing defects in the code or algorithms, they are expected to make technical comments and to avoid personal references. Inspections focus on the work—not on the author. The style of the code or algorithms are not criticized; the sole purpose of an inspection is to find defects. Consistent with this philosophy, managers are not present at inspections and inspection results may not be used to evaluate employee performance.

Inspections are typically conducted before the code is run. Particular importance is paid to the boundary conditions associated with the software package. This helps to identify defects that may not be apparent because "the program runs." A defect can be something that is incorrect or something that is missing. All defects identified in the inspection become part of a data base. If no defects are found, it is assumed the inspection is not sufficient.

The primary positive result of an inspection is that it does identify defects. In a typical two-hour session, while inspecting 200–300 lines of code, four to six defects may be identified. However, a second, but important, byproduct of inspections is the training of personnel. Authors of code learn more about how to avoid defects in the future; readers and inspectors learn how to improve their own work. Finally, all involved learn from the shared expertise of the inspection team. This is especially helpful when the team consists of members with diverse backgrounds.

In summary, inspections have proved to be very valuable. They result in improved communication, higher morale, in-service training, and better software packages.

programs for large sets of data. Consequently, most programs developed in the remainder of this text use text files for input. If you wish to continue with interactive programs, you should be able to make appropriate modifications.

EXERCISES 6.1

1. Explain the difference between an external file and an internal file. Give appropriate uses for each.
2. Write a test program that allows the user to print a line of text from a file to the output file.
3. Explain what is wrong with using

```
writeln (ClassList, Score1, Score2, Score3);
```

   if you want to write three scores to the text file ClassList.
4. Write a program that allows the user to display a text file line by line.
5. Assume that the text file InFile is

18	▮	19M	▮	-14.3	▮	JO	▮	142.1F	▮	■

For each question, also assume the pointer is positioned at the beginning of the file and the variable declaration section of a program is

```
VAR
  A, B : integer:
  X, Y : real;
  Ch : char;
  InFile : text;
```

What output is produced from each of the following segments of code?

a.
```
read (InFile, A);
read (Infile, B, Ch);
writeln (A:5, B:5, Ch:5);
```

b.
```
read (Infile, Ch);
write (Ch:10);
readln (InFile, Ch);
writeln (Ch);
read (InFile, Ch);
writeln (Ch:10);
```

c.
```
read (InFile, A, B, Ch, X);
writeln (A, B, Ch, X);
writeln (A:5, B:5, Ch:5, X:10:2);
read (InFile, Ch);
writeln (Ch:5);
```

d.
```
readln (InFile);
read (InFile, Ch, Ch);
readln (InFile, Y);
writeln (Ch:5, Y:10:2);
```

6. Using the text file and variable declaration section in Exercise 5, indicate the contents of each variable location and the position of the pointer after the segment of code is executed. Assume the pointer is positioned at the beginning for each problem.

a. `read (InFile, Ch, A);`

b. `readln (InFile, Ch, A);`

c. `readln (InFile);`

d.
```
readln (InFile);
readln (InFile);
```

e. `readln (InFile, A, B, Ch, X);`

f. `read (InFile, A, B, Ch, Y);`

g.
```
readln (InFile, A, Ch);
readln (InFile, Ch, Ch, B);
```

h. `read (InFile, A, B, Ch, X, Ch);`

7. Again, use the text file and variable declaration section in Exercise 5. For each of the following segments of code, indicate if the exercise produces an error and, if so, explain why an error occurs.

a. `read (InFile, X, Y);`

b.
```
readln (InFile, A);
read (InFile, B);
```

c.
```
readln (InFile, Ch);
readln (InFile, Ch);
readln (InFile, Ch);
```

d. `read (InFile, X , A, Ch, B, Ch);`

e.
```
readln (InFile);
read (InFile, Ch, Ch, A, Ch, B);
```

8. Write a complete Pascal program that reads your three initials and five test scores from a text file. Your program should then compute your test average and print out all information in a reasonable form with suitable messages.
9. Write a program that allows you to create a text file that contains your name, address, social security number, and age. Reset the file, and have the information printed as output. Save the file in secondary storage for later use.
10. Show what output is produced from the following program. Also indicate the contents of each file after the program is run.

```
PROGRAM Exercise10 (input, output, F2);

VAR
  Ch : char;
  F1, F2 : text;

BEGIN
  rewrite (F1);
  rewrite (F2);
  writeln (F1, 'This is a test.');
  writeln (F1, 'This is another line.');
  reset (F1);
  WHILE NOT eof(F1) DO
    BEGIN
      WHILE NOT eoln(F1) DO
        BEGIN
          read (F1, Ch);
          IF Ch = ' ' THEN
            writeln ('*')
          ELSE
            write (F2, Ch)
        END;  {  of WHILE NOT eoln  }
        readln (F1)
    END
END.
```

11. Write a program that deletes all blanks from a text file. Your program should save the revised file for later use.
12. Write a program using a **CASE** statement to scramble a text file by replacing all blanks with an asterisk (*) and interchanging all As and Us and Es with Is. Your program should print out the scrambled file and save it for subsequent use.
13. Write a program to update a text file by numbering the lines consecutively as 1, 2, 3, ...
14. Write a program to count the number of words in a text file. Assume each word is followed by a blank or a period.
15. Write a program to find the longest word in a text file. Output should include the word and its length.
16. Write a program to compute the average length of words in a text file.

6.2 TYPE Definitions in Pascal

Ordinal Data Types

Of the data types we have previously used, **integer, char,** and **boolean** are called ordinal data types. Recall, a data type is ordinal if values of that type have an immediate predecessor and an immediate successor. The exceptions are that the first listed element has only a successor and the last listed element has only a predecessor. For example,

OBJECTIVES

- to understand what is meant by ordinal data type
- to be able to declare enumerated data types
- to be able to use enumerated data types in a program
- to understand why enumerated data types are of value in writing programs

data of type **integer** are ordinal and can be listed as **-maxint,** . . . , -1, 0, 1, 2, . . . , **+maxint.** The Boolean values **false** and **true** and data of type **char** are listed according to the collating sequence shown in Appendix 4. Data of type **real** are not ordinal because a given real has neither an immediate predecessor nor an immediate successor. Permissible values for data of the three ordinal data types are summarized as follows:

Data Type	Values
integer	**-maxint** to **maxint**
char	Character set in a collating sequence
boolean	**true, false**

The four data types **integer, char, boolean,** and **real** used thus far are standard data types. We are now ready to see how Pascal allows us to define other data types called enumerated data types.

Simple Enumerated Data Types

The declaration section of a program can contain a **TYPE** definition section that can be used to define a data type. In this section, an *enumerated data type* is defined by the programmer and allows a discrete number of values for that data type. For example

```
TYPE
  Weekday = (Mon, Tues, Wed, Thur, Fri);
```

After such a definition has been made, the variable declaration section can contain identifiers of the type Weekday. Thus, we could have

```
VAR
  Day : Weekday;
```

Values in an enumerated data type can have any legal identifier. Several comments are now in order concerning the **TYPE** definition.

1. Simple enumerated data types are also referred to as *user-defined data types.* (Other user-defined data types include subranges and structured data types, which will be studied later.)
2. This defined type will be an ordinal data type with the first defined constant having ordinal zero. Ordinal values increase by 1 in order from left to right. Every constant except the first has a predecessor, and every constant except the last has a successor. Using the previously defined **TYPE** Weekday, we have

```
Mon    Tues    Wed    Thur    Fri
 ↕      ↕       ↕      ↕       ↕
 0      1       2      3       4
```

3. Variables can be declared to be of the new type.
4. The values defined in the **TYPE** definition section are constants that can be used in the program. These values must be valid identifiers.
5. No identifier can belong to more than one enumerated data type.
6. Identifiers that are defined values cannot be used as operands in arithmetic expressions.
7. Enumerated data types are for internal use only; you cannot **read** or **write** values of these variables.

Thus, given the previous **TYPE** definition of Weekday and the variable declaration of Day, each of the following would be an appropriate program statement.

```
1. Day := Tues;
2. Day := pred(Day);
3. IF Day = Mon THEN
     .
     .
     .
   ELSE
     .
     .
     .
4. FOR Day := Mon TO Fri DO
     BEGIN
       .
       .
       .
     END;
```

Now that we have seen an example of an enumerated data type and some typical related program statements, let's look at a more formal method of definition. In general, we have

> **TYPE**
> <type identifier> = (<constant1>, <constant2>, . . . <constant*n*>);
> **VAR**
> <identifier> : <type identifier>;

The **TYPE** definition section is part of the declaration section of a program. It follows the constant definition section (**CONST**) and precedes the variable declaration section (**VAR**), as shown in Figure 6.1.

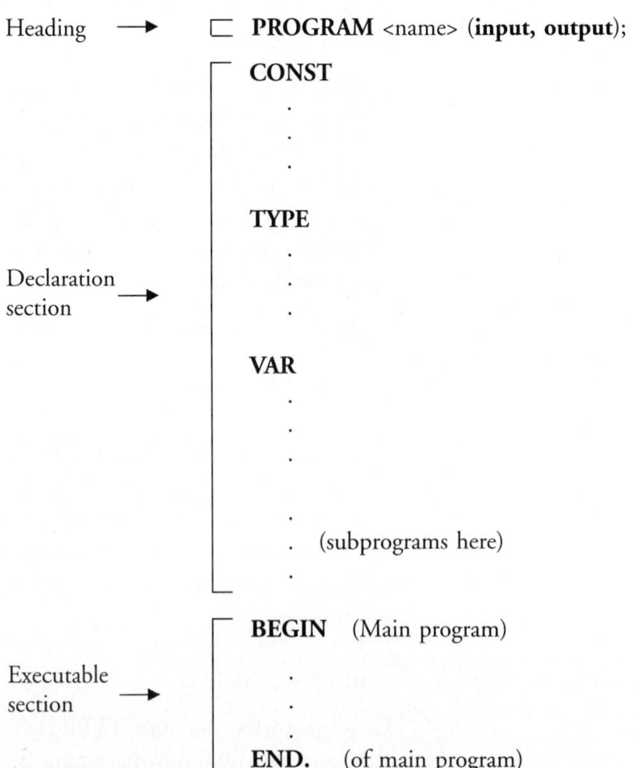

◆ FIGURE 6.1
Placement of **TYPE** definition section

The following short program illustrates the placement and use of enumerated data types.

```
PROGRAM TypePrac (output);

CONST
  Skip = ' ';

TYPE
  Weekday = (Mon, Tues, Wed, Thur, Fri);

VAR
  Day : Weekday;

BEGIN
  Day := Wed;
  IF Day < Fri THEN
    writeln (Skip:20, 'Not near the weekend.')
  ELSE
    writeln (Skip:20, 'The weekend starts tomorrow.')
END.
```

The output from this program is

```
                    Not near the weekend.
```

Reasons for Using Enumerated Data Types

At first, it may seem like a lot of trouble to define new types for use in a Pascal program, but there are several reasons for doing so. In fact, being able to create enumerated data types is one of the advantages of using Pascal as a programming language. Why? With enumerated data types, you can express the logical structure of data clearly, enhance the readability of your program, provide program protection against bad data values, and declare parameters in subprograms.

Suppose you are working on a program to count the number of days in the month of a certain year. Enumerated data types allow you to use the following definition and subsequent declaration.

```
TYPE
  AllMonths = (Jan, Feb, March, April, May, June,
               July, Aug, Sept, Oct, Nov, Dec);
VAR
  Month : AllMonths;
```

Given this definition, it is easier to understand what the code does. It could contain statements such as

```
FOR Month := Jan TO April DO
      .
      .
      .
```

or

```
IF (Month = Feb) AND (Year MOD 4 = 0) THEN
  NumDays := 29;
```

A NOTE OF INTEREST

Career Opportunities in Computer Science

The list "Fastest Growing Occupations, 1990–2005," published by the Bureau of Labor Statistics, includes computer programmers and computer system analysts. During this time period, the number of these jobs is expected to increase by 78.9 percent. If this job grouping is broadened to include all computer and data processing professionals, 24,000 workers joined the employment rolls between December 1991 and December 1992. Employment grew 4 percent in this area, compared to 0.5 percent for total nonagricultural employment (*Forecasts: Cahners Economics*). Employment of computer professionals is expected to grow much faster than the average of all occupations through the year 2005 (*Occupational Outlook Handbook*).

In 1992, a total of 751 employers were surveyed to determine which academic disciplines were of greatest interest to employers. Of these, 60 percent mentioned computer science.

The relative ranking of the disciplines has remained very stable since 1980 when they were first compiled. The same three disciplines—computer science, electrical engineering, and mechanical engineering—have been on the top of the list, sought after by about two-thirds of the responding companies. (Peterson, *Job Opportunities*).

Unemployment among computer specialists is traditionally exceptionally low, and almost all who enter the work force find jobs. In 1990, the median annual income was about $38,700 for a system analyst and about $34,000 for a computer programmer (*Occupational Outlook Handbook*).

All able students—particularly women and minorities, who have been traditionally under-represented in the sciences—are encouraged to consider computer science as a career.

This second segment of code clearly indicates that the extra day in February is counted for a leap year. (This is an oversimplification of checking for a leap year; see Exercise 7 at the end of this section.)

Enumerated data types can be used in **CASE** statements. For example, movie ticket prices are frequently broken into three categories: youth, adult, and senior citizen. If the definition and declaration

```
TYPE
  Categories = (Youth, Adult, Senior);
VAR
  Patron : Categories;
```

is made, a program statement can be something like

```
CASE Patron OF
  Youth  : Price := YouthPrice;
  Adult  : Price := AdultPrice;
  Senior : Price := SeniorPrice
END;  {  of CASE Patron  }
```

Once an enumerated data type has been defined at the global level, it is available to all subprograms. Thus, if we have a function for counting the days, a typical function heading might be

```
FUNCTION NumDays (Month : AllMonths;
                  Year : integer) : integer;
```

This aspect of user-defined data types will become more significant when we examine structured data types, including arrays and records.

Recall the limitation imposed on variables that are of an enumerated type: they are for internal use only; you cannot **read** or **write** values of these variables. Thus, in the earlier example using months of the year, we could have the statement

```
Month := June;
```

but not

```
writeln (Month);
```

However (as we saw in Section 4.5), use of a **CASE** statement allows translation procedures to be written with relative ease.

We close this section with some typical definitions for enumerated data types that are intended to improve program readability. You are encouraged to incorporate enumerated data types into subsequent programs. In general, you are limited only by your imagination.

```
TYPE
  SoftDrinks = (Pepsi, Coke, SevenUp, Orange, RootBeer);
  Seasons = (Winter, Spring, Summer, Fall);
  Colors = (Red, Orange, Yellow, Green, Blue, Indigo, Violet);
  ClassStanding = (Freshman, Sophomore, Junior, Senior);
  Fruits = (Apple, Orange, Banana);
  Vegetables = (Corn, Peas, Broccoli, Spinach);
```

Given these type definitions, each of the following would be a reasonable variable declaration.

```
VAR
  Pop, Soda : SoftDrinks;
  Season : Seasons;
  Hue : Colors;
  Class : ClassStanding;
  Appetizer : Fruits;
  SideDish : Vegetables;
```

EXERCISES 6.2

1. Explain what is meant by an ordinal data type.
2. Write a test program to see what happens in each of the following instances.
   a. Try to **write** the value of a variable that is an enumerated data type.
   b. Try to find the predecessor (**pred**) of a defined constant which has zero as its ordinal in an enumerated type.
3. Find all errors in the following definitions.
   a.
   ```
   TYPE
     Names = (John, Joe, Mary, Jane);
     People = (Henry, Sue, Jane, Bill);
   ```
   b.
   ```
   TYPE
     Colors = (Red, Blue, Red, Orange);
   ```
   c.
   ```
   TYPE
     Letters = A, C, E;
   ```
4. Assume the **TYPE** definition
   ```
   TYPE
     Colors = (Red, Orange, Yellow, Blue, Green);
   ```
   has been given. Indicate whether each of the following is **true** or **false**.
   a. `Orange < Blue`
   b. `(Green <> Red) AND (Blue > Green)`
   c. `(Yellow < Orange) OR (Blue >= Red)`
5. Assume the **TYPE** definition and variable declaration
   ```
   TYPE
     AllDays = (Sun, Mon, Tues, Wed, Thur, Fri, Sat);
   VAR
     Day, Weekday, Weekend : AllDays;
   ```

have been given. Indicate which of the following are valid program statements. For those that are not, give an explanation.

a. `Day := Tues;`

b. `Day := Tues + Wed;`

c. `Weekday := Sun;`

d.
```
IF Day = Sat THEN
  writeln ('Clean the garage.':30);
```

e.
```
IF (Day < Sat) AND (Day > Sun) THEN
  writeln ('It is a workday.':30)
ELSE
  writeln ('It is the weekend.':30);
```

f.
```
FOR Day := Mon TO Fri DO
  writeln (Day);
```

g.
```
read (Day);
IF Day < Sat THEN
  Weekday := Day;
```

h. `Wed := Tues + 1;`

6. Assume the following definitions and declarations have been made in a program.

```
TYPE
  Cloth = (Flannel, Cotton, Rayon, Orlon);
VAR
  Material : Cloth;
  NumberOfYards, Price : real;
```

What output is produced by the following segment of code?

```
Material := Cotton;
NumberOfYards := 3.5;
IF (Material = Rayon) OR (Material = Orlon) THEN
  Price := NumberOfYards * 4.5
ELSE IF Material = Cotton THEN
  Price := NumberOfYards * 2.75
ELSE
  Price := NumberOfYards * 2.5;
writeln (Price:30:2);
```

7. Find the complete definition of a leap year in the Gregorian calendar. Define appropriate data types, and write a segment of code that would indicate whether or not a given year is a leap year.

6.3 Subrange as a Data Type

OBJECTIVES

- to be able to define a subrange as a data type
- to be able to use subrange data types in a program
- to understand compatibility of data types
- to understand why subrange data types are used in a program

Defining Subranges

In Section 6.2, we learned how to define new data types by using the **TYPE** definition section. Now we will investigate another way to define new data types.

A *subrange* of an existing ordinal data type may be defined as a data type by

```
TYPE
  <identifier> = <initial value>. .<final value>
```

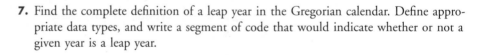

where the initial value and the final value are separated by two periods. For example, a subrange of the integers could be defined by

```
TYPE
  USYears = 1776..1995;
```

When defining a subrange, the following items should be noted.

1. The original data type must be an ordinal type.
2. Any valid identifier may be used for the name of the type.
3. The initial and final values must be of the original data type.
4. The underlying data type is ordered. In this ordering, the initial value of a defined subrange must occur before the final value.
5. Only values in the indicated subrange (endpoints included) may be assigned to a variable of the type defined by the subrange.
6. The same value may appear in different subranges.

Some of these points are illustrated in the following example.

EXAMPLE 6.5

Consider the subranges Weekdays and Midweek of the enumerated ordinal Days.

```
TYPE
  Days = (Sun, Mon, Tues, Wed, Thur,
          Fri, Sat);                 { Enumerated }
  Weekdays = Mon..Fri;               { Subrange   }
  Midweek = Tues..Thur;              { Subrange   }
VAR
  SchoolDay : Weekdays;
  Workday : Midweek;
```

In this case, Days is defined first and we can then define appropriate subranges. Because the variable SchoolDay is declared to be of type Weekdays, we can use any of the values Mon, Tues, Wed, Thur, or Fri with SchoolDay. However, we cannot assign either Sat or Sun to SchoolDay.

Notice Tues, Wed, and Thur are values that appear in different type definitions. However, since these values are in subranges, this will not produce an error. Furthermore

```
Workday := Tues;
```

and

```
SchoolDay := Workday;
```

are both acceptable statements.

COMMUNICATION AND STYLE TIPS

The **CONST** and **TYPE** definition sections can be used together to enhance readability and facilitate program design. For example, rather than use the subrange

```
TYPE
  USYears = 1776..1995;
```

you could define an ending constant and then use it as indicated.

```
CONST
  CurrentYear = 1995;
TYPE
  USYears = 1776..CurrentYear;
```

Some other subrange definitions are

```
TYPE
  Grades = 'A'..'E';
  Alphabet = 'A'..'Z';
  ScoreRange = 0..100;
  Months = (Jan, Feb, Mar, Apr, May, June,
            July, Aug, Sept, Oct, Nov, Dec);
  Year = Jan..Dec;
  Summer = June..Aug;
```

Months is not a subrange here. However, once Months is defined, an appropriate subrange, such as Summer, can be defined. With these subranges defined, each of the following declarations would be appropriate.

```
VAR
  FinalGrade : Grades;
  Letter : Alphabet;
  TestScore : ScoreRange;
  SumMonth : Summer;
```

Subrange limits may be ignored by some compilers. Thus, the assignment of a value outside the specified range may not cause a compilation error. Since the value that will be stored cannot be predicted, subranges should not be used as a form of program protection because program crashes can be caused by inappropriate values.

Compatibility of Variables

Now that we know how to define subranges of existing ordinal data types, we need to look carefully at the compatibility of variables. Variables are *type compatible* if they have the same base type. Thus, in

```
TYPE
  AgeRange = 0..110;
VAR
  Age : AgeRange;
  Year : integer;
```

the variables Age and Year are type compatible because they both have **integer** as the base type (AgeRange is a subrange of integers). If variables are type compatible, assignments can be made between them or they can be manipulated in any manner that variables of that base type can be manipulated.

Even when variables are type compatible, caution should be exercised when making assignment statements. To illustrate, using Age and Year as previously declared, consider the statements

```
Age := Year;
Year := Age;
```

Since Age is of type AgeRange and AgeRange is a subrange of **integer,** any value in Age is acceptable as a value that can be assigned to Year. Thus

```
Year := Age;
```

is permissible. However, since values in Age are restricted to the defined subrange, it is possible that

```
Age := Year;
```

will produce an error. Since Age and Year are type compatible, there will not be a compilation error, but consider

```
Year := 150;
Age := Year;
```

Since 150 is not in the subrange for Age, execution could be halted; an error message would then be printed.

Two variables are said to be *type identical* if—and only if—they are declared with the same type identifier. It is important to distinguish between variables of compatible and identical types when using subprograms. A value parameter and its argument must be type compatible; a variable parameter and its argument must be type identical. A type-compatibility error will be generated if these rules are not followed. To illustrate, consider

```
TYPE
  GoodScore = 60..100;
VAR
  Score1, Score2 : GoodScore;
PROCEDURE Compute (HS1 : integer;
                   VAR HS2 : GoodScore);
```

This procedure may be called by

```
Compute (Score1, Score2);
```

Note HS1 is a value parameter and must only be compatible with Score1 whereas HS2 is a variable parameter and must be identical in type to Score2. However, if the procedure heading is

```
PROCEDURE Compute (VAR HS1 : integer;
                   HS2 : GoodScore);
```

then an attempt to call the procedure by

```
Compute (Score1, Score2);
```

will result in an error because Score1 and HS1 are not type identical.

An expression is considered *assignment compatible* with a variable if at least one of the following is true.

1. The variable and the expression are type identical.
2. They are compatible ordinal types such that the value of the expression is contained in the range of the variable.
3. The variable is of type **real,** and the expression is of type **integer.**

When used as data types for parameters, **TYPE** definitions must be defined in the main program since they cannot be defined in a subprogram heading. However, **TYPE** definitions can be defined internally for subprograms.

Software Engineering Implications

Enumerated types and subranges are features of Pascal that are consistent with principles of software engineering. As previously stated, communication, readability, and maintenance are essential when developing large systems. The use of enumerated types and subranges is important in all of these areas. To illustrate, suppose a program includes working with a chemical reaction that normally occurs at approximately 180° Fahrenheit. If the definition section includes

```
TYPE
  ReactionRange = 150..210;
```

subsequent modules could use a variable such as

```
VAR
  ReactionTemp : ReactionRange;
```

In Chapter 7, you will see how the use of enumerated or user-defined data types is even more essential to maintaining principles of software engineering. Specifically, defining data structures becomes an important design consideration.

EXERCISES 6.3

1. Indicate whether the following **TYPE** definitions, subsequent declarations, and uses are valid or invalid. Explain what is wrong with those that are invalid.

   a.
   ```
   TYPE
     Reverse = 10..1;
   ```
   b.
   ```
   TYPE
     Bases = (Home, First, Second, Third);
     Double = Home..Second;
     Score = Second..Home;
   ```
   c.
   ```
   TYPE
     Colors = (Red, White, Blue);
     Stripes = Red..White;
   VAR
     Hue : Stripes;
   BEGIN
     Hue := Blue;
   ```
   d.
   ```
   TYPE
     Weekdays = Mon..Fri;
     Days = (Sun, Mon, Tues, Wed, Thur, Fri, Sat);
   ```
   e.
   ```
   TYPE
     ScoreRange = 0..100;
     HighScores = 70..100;
     Midscores = 50..69;
     LowScores = 20..49;
   VAR
     Score1 : Midscores;
     Score2 : HighScores;
   BEGIN
     Score1 := 60;
     Score2 := Score1 + 70;
   ```

2. Write a test program to see what happens when you try to use (assign, read, and so on) a value for a variable that is not in the defined subrange.

3. Explain why each of the following subrange definitions might be used in a program.

   a. `Dependents = 0..20;`

   b. `HoursWorked = 0..60;`

   c. `QuizScores = 0..10;`

   d. `TotalPoints = 0..700;`

4. Indicate reasonable subranges for each of the following. Explain your answers.
   a. `TwentiethCentury =`
   b. `Digits =`
   c. `JuneTemp =`
   d. `WinterRange =`
   e. `Colors = (Black, Brown, Red, Pink, Yellow, White);`
      `LightColors =`
5. Assume the declaration section of a program contains

```
TYPE
  ChessPieces = (Pawn, Knight, Bishop, Rook, King, Queen);
  Expendable = Pawn..Rook;
  Valuable = King..Queen;
  LowRange = 0..39;
  Midrange = 40..80;
VAR
  Piece1 : Valuable;
  Piece2 : Expendable;
  Piece3 : ChessPieces;
  Score1 : LowRange;
  Score2 : Midrange;
  Score3 : integer;
```

   Indicate which of the following pairs of variables are type compatible.
   a. `Piece1 and Piece2`
   b. `Piece2 and Piece3`
   c. `Piece3 and Score1`
   d. `Score1 and Score2`
   e. `Score1 and Score3`
   f. `Piece2 and Score3`
6. Assume the declaration section of a program contains

```
TYPE
  PointRange = 400..700;
  FlowerList = (Rose, Iris, Tulip, Begonia);
  Sublist = Rose..Tulip;
VAR
  TotalPts : PointRange;
  Total : integer;
  Flower : Sublist;
  OldFlower : FlowerList;
```

   and the procedure heading is

```
PROCEDURE TypePrac (A : PointRange;
                    VAR B : integer;
                    Fl : Sublist);
```

   Indicate which of the following are valid calls to this procedure.
   a. `TypePrac (TotalPts, Total, Flower);`
   b. `TypePrac (Total, TotalPts, Flower);`
   c. `TypePrac (TotalPts, Total, OldFlower);`
   d. `TypePrac (Total, Total, Flower);`
   e. `TypePrac (Total, Total, OldFlower);`

6.4 Operations on Ordinal Data Types

OBJECTIVES

- to be able to use functions **ord, pred,** and **succ** with enumerated data types
- to be able to use ordinal data types in Boolean expressions
- to be able to use ordinal data types in **CASE** statements
- to be able to use ordinal data types as loop indices

Functions for Ordinal Data Types

Earlier, we characterized ordinal data types as types in which there is a first and last listed element and each element other than the first and last has an immediate predecessor and an immediate successor. Of the standard data types, only **real** is not ordinal. Since the enumerated data types are all ordinal, the functions **ord, pred,** and **succ** may be used on them. Thus, if we have the definition

```
TYPE
  Days = (Sun, Mon, Tues, Wed, Thur, Fri, Sat);
  Weekdays = Mon..Fri;
```

the function calls have the following values.

Function Call	Value
ord(Sun)	0
ord(Wed)	3
pred(Thur)	Wed
succ(Fri)	Sat
ord(**pred**(Fri))	4

When using functions on enumerated ordinals, the following should be noted.

1. The first-listed identifier has ordinal zero.
2. Successive ordinals are determined by the order in which identifiers are listed.
3. The function call **pred** should not be used on the first identifier; **succ** should not be used on the final identifier.
4. If a subrange data type is defined, the functions return values consistent with the underlying base type; for example, **ord**(Wed) = 3.

Using Ordinal Values of Enumerated Data Types

Now that we are somewhat familiar with ordinal data types and the functions that use them as arguments, let's consider some ways in which they can be incorporated into programs. One typical use is in Boolean expressions. Suppose you are writing a program to compute the payroll for a company that pays time-and-a-half for working on Saturday. Assume the definition and declaration

```
TYPE
  Workdays = (Mon, Tues, Wed, Thur, Fri, Sat);
VAR
  Day : Workdays;
```

have been made. A typical segment of code is

```
Day := <some value>;
IF Day = Sat THEN
  ComputeOvertime(<calculation>)
ELSE
  ComputeRegularPay(<calculation>)
```

A second use is with **CASE** statements. As previously explained, one limitation of enumerated data types is that they have no external representation (you cannot **read** or **write** their values). However, this limitation can be circumvented by the appropriate use of a **CASE** statement. For example, suppose we have the definition and declaration

A NOTE OF INTEREST

Computer Ethics: Viruses

Tiny programs that deliberately cause mischief are epidemic among computers and are causing nervousness among those who monitor them. Written by malicious programmers, the "computer viruses" are sneaked into computer systems by piggybacking them on legitimate programs and messages. There, they may be passed along or instructed to wait until a prearranged moment to burst forth and destroy data.

At NASA headquarters in Washington, several hundred computers had to be resuscitated after being infected. NASA officials have taken extra precautions and reminded their machines' users to follow routine computer hygiene: Don't trust foreign data or strange machines.

Viruses have the eerie ability to perch disguised among legitimate data, just as biological viruses hide among genes in human cells, and then spring out unexpectedly, multiplying and causing damage. Experts say that even when they try to study viruses under controlled conditions, the programs can get out of control and erase everything in a computer. The viruses can be virtually impossible to stop if their creators are determined enough.

"The only way to protect everybody against them is to do something much worse than the viruses: stop talking to one another with computers," says William H. Murray, an information-security specialist at Ernst and Whinney, financial consultants in Hartford, Conn.

Hundreds of programs and files have been destroyed by the viruses, and thousands of hours of repair or prevention time have been logged. Programmers have quickly produced antidote programs with such titles as "Vaccine," "Flu Shot," "Data Physician," and "Syringe."

Experts say known damage is minimal compared to the huge, destructive potential. They express the hope that the attacks will persuade computer users to minimize access to programming and data.

Viruses are the newest of evolving methods of computer mayhem. One type of virus is the "Trojan horse": it looks and acts like a normal program but contains hidden commands that eventually take effect, ordering mischief. The "time bomb" explodes at a set time; the "logic bomb" goes off when the computer arrives at a certain result during normal computation. The "salami attack" executes barely noticeable acts, such as shaving a penny from thousands of accounts.

A virus typically is written as perhaps only a few hundred characters in a program containing tens of thousands of characters. When the computer reads legitimate instructions, it encounters the virus, which instructs the computer to suspend normal operations for a fraction of a second.

During that time, the virus instructs the computer to check for other copies of itself and, if none are found, to make and hide copies. Instruction to commit damage may be included.

Is Your Machine at Risk?

1. Computer viruses are actually miniature computer programs. Most were written by malicious programmers intent on destroying information in computers for fun.
2. Those who write virus programs often conceal them on floppy disks that are inserted in the computer.
3. A malicious programmer makes the disk available to others, saying it contains a useful program or game. These programs can be lent to others or put onto computerized "bulletin boards," where anyone can copy them for personal use.
4. A computer receiving the programs will "read" the disk and the tiny virus program at the same time. The virus may then order the computer
   - To read the virus and follow instructions.
   - To make a copy of the virus and place it on any disk inserted in the machine today.
   - To check the computer's clock and, on a certain date, to destroy all information that tells where data is stored on any disk: if an operator has no way of retrieving information, it is destroyed.
   - Not to list the virus programs when the computer is asked for an index of programs.
5. In this way, the computer will copy the virus onto many disks—perhaps all or nearly all the disks used in the infected machine. The virus may also be passed over the telephone, when one computer sends or receives data from another.
6. Ultimately, hundreds or thousands of people may have infected disks and potential time bombs in their systems.

```
TYPE
  Colors = (Red, White, Blue);
VAR
  Hue : Colors;
```

If we wish to print the value of Hue, we can do so by

```
CASE Hue OF
  Red   : writeln ('Red':20);
  White : writeln ('White':20);
  Blue  : writeln ('Blue':20)
END;  {  of CASE Hue  }
```

A third use is as a loop index. For example, consider

```
TYPE
  AllDays = (Sun, Mon, Tues, Wed, Thur, Fri, Sat);
VAR
  Day : AllDays;
```

Each of the following would be an appropriate loop.

```
1. FOR Day := Mon TO Fri DO
     BEGIN
       .
       .
       .
     END;
2. Day := Mon;
   WHILE Day < Sat DO
     BEGIN
       Day := succ(Day);
         .
         .
         .
     END;
3. Day := Sun;
   REPEAT
     Day := succ(Day);
       .
       .
       .
   UNTIL Day = Fri;
```

The loop control in a **FOR** loop is based upon the ordinals of the values of the loop index. Thus, the statement

```
FOR Day := Mon TO Fri DO
```

is treated like the statement

```
FOR J := 1 TO 5 DO
```

because **ord**(Mon) is 1 and **ord**(Fri) is 5.

In the **WHILE . . . DO** and **REPEAT . . . UNTIL** loops, the user must be sure to increment (increase the ordinal of) the variable. One method of doing this is to use the function **succ**.

EXERCISES 6.4

1. Suppose the following **TYPE** definition is given.

```
TYPE
  Trees = (Oak, Ash, Maple, Pine);
  SlackType = (Denim, Cotton, Polyester);
```

Give the value of each of the following expressions. Indicate any expression that is invalid.

a. **pred**(Ash)
b. **succ**(Denim)
c. **ord**(Polyester)
d. **ord**(**pred**(Oak))
e. **ord**(**succ**(Maple))
f. **succ**(Polyester)
g. **ord**(**pred**(**succ**(Oak)))

2. Write a test program that lists the ordinals of values in a subrange of an enumerated data type.
3. The character set for some computers is such that **ord**('A') = 65 and **ord**('Z') = 90. Assuming such a sequence, what is the value of each of the following expressions? Indicate any expression that is invalid.
   a. **chr(ord('D'))**
   b. **ord(chr(75))**
   c. **chr(3 + ord('E'))**
   d. **ord(chr(200 DIV 3) + chr(70))**
   e. **ord(pred('K') + 3)**
   f. **succ(chr(ord('Z') - 1))**
4. Write a program that will list the letters of the alphabet and their respective ordinals for the character set used with your machine.
5. Assume the **TYPE** definition and variable declaration

```
TYPE
  AllDays = (Sun, Mon, Tues, Wed, Thur, Fri, Sat);
VAR
  Day : AllDays;
```

   are made.
   a. What output is produced from the following **REPEAT . . . UNTIL** loop?

```
Day := Sun;
REPEAT
  CASE Day OF
    Sat, Sun                       : writeln ('Weekend':20);
    Mon, Tues, Wed, Thur, Fri : writeln ('Weekday':20)
  END;  { of CASE Day }
  Day := succ(Day)
UNTIL Day = Sat;
```

   b. Rewrite the previous loop as both a **WHILE . . . DO** loop and a **FOR** loop.
   c. Find another method to control the loop variable. (For example, replace

```
Day := succ(Day)
```

   and make any other necessary changes.)
   d. Revise the loop so that all seven days are considered.
6. A standard programming problem is to convert an integer character to its corresponding numeric value (for example, the character '2' to the number 2). Since the digits are listed sequentially in every character set, this could be accomplished by

```
ord('2') - ord('0');
```

   a. Write a function to convert a single character digit ('0', '1', . . . , '9') to its corresponding numeric value.
   b. Write a function to convert a two-digit number read as consecutive characters to the corresponding numeric value.
7. Suppose you are working with a program that reads an integer representing a month of the year (Jan = 1). Write a function to convert the integer to the appropriate month.

FOCUS ON PROGRAM DESIGN

The summary program for this chapter computes the number of days in your birth year from your birthday to the end of the year. Sample input (if you were born on March 16, 1975) would be

```
3 16 75
```

We want the output to be

```
During your birth year, 1975,
you were alive  291 days.
```

Features of this program include enumerated data types and subranges. In particular, note the data type

```
AllMonths = (Jan, Feb, March, April, May, June,
             July, Aug, Sept, Oct, Nov, Dec);
```

A reasonable first-level pseudocode design for this program is

1. Get data
2. Assign month
3. Compute days
4. Print results

A structure chart for this program is given in Figure 6.2.

◆ FIGURE 6.2
Structure chart for **PROGRAM** Birthday

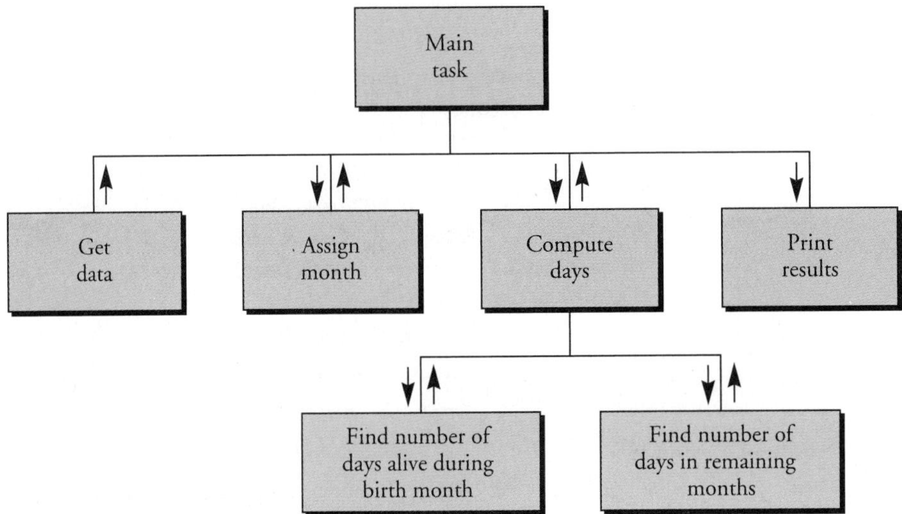

Module specifications for this problem are

1. GetData Module
   Data received: None
   Information returned: Day
   Month
   Year of birth
   Logic: Have the user enter his/her birth date.
2. AssignMonth Module
   Data received: A numeric equivalent of the birth month
   Information returned: The name of the birth month
   Logic: A **CASE** statement assigns the name of the birth month to BirthMonth, which is an enumerated data type.
3. ComputeDays Module
   Data received: Month
   Day
   Year of birth
   Information returned: The number of days alive during the year of birth

Logic: Compute the number of days alive during the month of birth.
Compute the number of days in the remaining months.

4. PrintResults Module
Data received: Number of days alive during the year of birth
Information returned: None
Logic: Use **write(ln)** statements to print the results in a readable form.

GetData merely consists of a **readln** statement; AssignMonth is a procedure using a **CASE** statement (a function could be used here instead), and PrintResults prints the information in a readable form. A function for computing the number of days is further developed as

3. Compute days
   3.1 compute days alive during birth month
   3.2 compute total of days in remaining months

This could be refined to

3. Compute days
   3.1 compute days alive during birth month
      3.1.1 compute for months with 31 days
      3.1.2 compute for months with 30 days
      3.1.3 compute for February
         IF leap year **THEN** use 29 days
         ELSE use 28 days
   3.2 compute total of days in remaining months
      IF NOT December **THEN**
         FOR rest of months **DO**
            add number of days in month

The complete program to solve this problem follows.

```
PROGRAM Birthday (input, output);

{  This program determines how many days you were alive during   }
{  your birth year.  Input is your birth date.  Later, you can   }
{  use this program as the basis for a biorhythm program.        }
{  Note the use of enumerated data types and subranges.          }

TYPE
  AllMonths = (Jan, Feb, March, April, May, June,
               July, Aug, Sept, Oct, Nov, Dec);
  DayRange = 1..31;
  MonthRange = 1..12;
  YearRange = 0..99;

VAR
  BirthMonth : AllMonths;        {  Literal form of birth month    }
  DayNum : DayRange;             {  The day you were born          }
  Month : MonthRange;            {  Birth month                    }
  TotalDays : integer;           {  Days alive in birth year       }
  Year : YearRange;              {  Representation of birth year   }

{*****************************************************************}
```

```
PROCEDURE GetData  (VAR Month : MonthRange;
                    VAR Day : DayRange;
                    VAR Year : YearRange);

  {  Given:   Nothing                                            }
  {  Task:    Enter your birth date in the form 3 16 75          }
  {  Return:  Month, day, and year of birth                      }  1

  BEGIN
    writeln ('Please enter your birth date in the form 3 16 75.');
    writeln ('Press <Enter> when finished.');
    readln (Month, Day, Year)
  END;  {  of PROCEDURE GetData  }

{*****************************************************************}

PROCEDURE AssignMonth (Month : MonthRange;
                       VAR BirthMonth : AllMonths);

  {  Given:   A numeric equivalent of the birth month            }
  {  Task:    Convert to literal BirthMonth                      }
  {  Return:  Literal BirthMonth                                 }

  BEGIN
    CASE Month OF
       1 : BirthMonth := Jan;
       2 : BirthMonth := Feb;
       3 : BirthMonth := March;                                     2
       4 : BirthMonth := April;
       5 : BirthMonth := May;
       6 : BirthMonth := June;
       7 : BirthMonth := July;
       8 : BirthMonth := Aug;
       9 : BirthMonth := Sept;
      10 : BirthMonth := Oct;
      11 : BirthMonth := Nov;
      12 : BirthMonth := Dec
    END   {  of CASE Month  }
  END;  {  of PROCEDURE AssignMonth  }

{*****************************************************************}

FUNCTION ComputeDays (BirthMonth : AllMonths;
                      DayNum : DayRange;
                      Year : YearRange) : integer;

  {  Given:   Month, day, and year of birth                      }
  {  Task:    Compute the days alive during the year of birth    }
  {  Return:  Number of days alive during the year of birth      }

  VAR
    Days : integer;
    Mon : AllMonths;
```

```
  BEGIN

    {  Compute days alive in birth month  }
    CASE BirthMonth OF
      Jan, March, May,
           July, Aug, Oct, Dec : Days := 31 - DayNum + 1;
      April, June, Sept, Nov   : Days := 30 - DayNum + 1;
      Feb                      : IF Year MOD 4 = 0 THEN
                                   Days := 29 - DayNum + 1        3
                                 ELSE
                                   Days := 28 - DayNum + 1
    END;  {  of CASE BirthMonth  }

    {  Now compute days in remaining months  }
    IF BirthMonth <> Dec THEN
      FOR Mon := succ(BirthMonth) TO Dec DO
        CASE Mon OF
          Jan, March, May,
               July, Aug, Oct, Dec : Days := Days + 31;
          April, June, Sept, Nov   : Days := Days + 30;
          Feb                      : IF Year MOD 4 = 0 THEN
                                       Days := Days + 29
                                     ELSE
                                       Days := Days + 28
        END;  {  of CASE Mon  }

    {  Assign total days to function's name  }
    ComputeDays := Days
  END;  {  of FUNCTION ComputeDays  }

{*******************************************************************}

PROCEDURE PrintResults (TotalDays : integer;
                        Year : YearRange);

  {  Given:   Birth year and total days alive during that year   }
  {  Task:    Print a message indicating the year of birth and   }
  {               number of days alive during that year          }
  {  Return:  Nothing                                            }

  BEGIN                                                              4
    writeln ('During your birth year,', (Year + 1900):5, ',');
    writeln ('you were alive', TotalDays:5, ' days.');
    writeln
  END;  {  of PROCEDURE PrintResults  }

{*******************************************************************}

BEGIN  {  Main program  }
  GetData (Month, DayNum, Year);
  AssignMonth (Month, BirthMonth);
  TotalDays := ComputeDays(BirthMonth, DayNum, Year);
  PrintResults (TotalDays, Year)
END.  {  of main program  }
```

A sample run of this program produces

```
Please enter your birth date in the form 3 16 75.
Press <Enter> when finished.
3 16 75
During your birth year, 1975,
you were alive  291 days.
```

RUNNING AND DEBUGGING HINTS

1. An end-of-line marker is read as a blank. Thus, when reading data of type **char,** you must remember to read past the end-of-line marker so that the end-of-file marker will be recognized.
2. Permanent text files must be listed in the program heading file list as well as in the variable declaration section.
3. Be aware of the possibility of extra blanks at the beginning or end of lines in a text file. Some implementations cause these blanks to be inserted when creating a text file.
4. The end-of-line marker is read as a blank. Thus, when working with character data in a text file, it may appear that extra blanks are in the file. However, the **eoln** function still returns **true** when the pointer is positioned at an end-of-line marker.
5. Subranges should be used if the bounds of a variable are known.
6. Enumerated data types should be used to enhance readability.
7. Be careful not to use **pred** with the first element in a list or **succ** with the last element.
8. Make sure variable parameters passed to subprograms are type identical. For example, using the declaration

   ```
   TYPE
     Weekdays = (Mon, Tues, Wed, Thur, Fri);
   VAR
     Day : Weekdays;
   ```

   if a procedure call is

   ```
   PrintChart (Day);
   ```

   a procedure heading could be

   ```
   PROCEDURE PrintChart (VAR Wkday : Weekdays);
   ```

9. A value parameter and its argument must be type compatible.

SUMMARY

Key Terms

assignment compatible
end-of-file (**eof**) marker
end-of-line (**eoln**) marker
enumerated data type
external file
internal file
opened for reading
opened for writing
scratch file
subrange
temporary file
text file
type compatible
type identical
user-defined data type

Keywords

eof
eoln
reset
rewrite
text
TYPE

Key Concepts

- Text files can be used to store data between runs of a program.
- An end-of-line marker (▮) is placed at the end of each line in a text file.

- An end-of-file marker (■) is placed after the last character in a text file.
- A text file can be declared by

```
VAR
  <file name> : text;
```

- An external file exists outside the program block in secondary storage. When used, it must be included in the file list as part of the program heading.
- An internal file exists within the program block. Values stored there will be lost when the program is no longer running.
- Text files must be opened before they can be written to or read from. Before reading from a file, it can be opened by

  reset (<file variable>);

  Before writing to a file, it can be opened by

  rewrite (<file variable>);

- Reading from a text file can be accomplished by

  read (<file variable>, <list of variables>);
  or
  readln (<file variable>, <list of variables>);

  If no file variable is given, the procedures apply to the standard file **input**.

- Writing to a text file can be accomplished by

  write (<file variable>, <list of values>);
  or
  writeln (<file variable>, <list of values>);

  If no file variable is given, the procedures apply to the standard file **output**.

- A data type is ordinal if data of that type have a first and last listed element and each element other than the first and last has an immediate predecessor and an immediate successor.
- Enumerated data types can be defined by using the **TYPE** definition section. Typical syntax and form are

```
TYPE
  Weekdays = (Mon, Tue, Wed, Thur, Fri);
```

- When a simple enumerated data type has been defined:
  1. The newly defined type will be an ordinal data type.
  2. Variables can be declared to be of the new type.
  3. The identifiers declared in the **TYPE** definition section are constants that can be used in the program.
  4. No identifier can belong to more than one data type.
  5. Identifiers that are defined values cannot be used as operands in expressions.
- You cannot **read** or **write** values of an enumerated data type.
- A subrange of an existing ordinal data type can be defined by

  TYPE
  <identifier> = <initial value>..<final value>;

  Examples are

```
TYPE
  ScoreRange = 0..100;
  Alphabet = 'A'..'Z';
```

- Type-compatible variables must have the same base type.

- Type-identical variables must have the same type identifier.
- An expression can be assigned to a variable only if the expression is assignment compatible with the variable.
- Two significant reasons for using subranges are program protection and program readability.
- The functions **pred, succ,** and **ord** can be used with enumerated data types and subranges of existing ordinal data types.
- When one of the functions **pred, succ,** or **ord** is used with an argument that contains a value in a subrange, reference is to the base data type, not to the subrange. Thus, in

```
TYPE
  Letters = 'J'..'O';
```

  ord('J') does not have the value 0. Rather, it yields the appropriate ordinal for the collating sequence being used. In the ASCII collating sequence, **ord**('J') yields 74; in EBCDIC it yields 209.

PROGRAMMING PROBLEMS AND PROJECTS

1. Write a program to compute the payroll for a company. Data for each employee is to be on two lines. Line 1 contains an employee number followed by the hourly wage rate. Line 2 contains seven integer entries indicating the hours worked each day. Wages are to be computed at time-and-a-half for anything over eight hours on a weekday and double time for any weekend work. Deductions should be withheld as follows:

(1) State income tax	4.6%
(2) Federal income tax	21.0%
(3) Social Security (FICA)	6.2%
(4) Medicare tax	1.45%

   Employee numbers are the subrange 0001..9999. You should define and use a data type for the days of the week.

2. The Caswell Catering and Convention Service (Problem 12, Chapter 3; Problem 14, Chapter 4; Problem 1, Chapter 5) wants to upgrade its existing computer program. Use the **TYPE** definition section for each of the following, and revise the program you developed previously as appropriate.
   (1) The room names are now color-coded as follows:

Room A	RedRoom
Room B	BlueRoom
Room C	YellowRoom
Room D	GreenRoom
Room E	BrownRoom

   (2) Use a subrange for the room rents.
   (3) Use defined constants for the low value and high value of the room rents.

■ 3. State University (Problem 15, Chapter 4) wants you to upgrade its computer program by using the **TYPE** definition section for each of the following.
   (1) The room types are Regular or AirConditioned.
   (2) Student numbers are between 0001 and 9999. (Use **CONST** for end values.)
   (3) Credit hours taken must be between 1 and 25.
   (4) The GoodRange for credit hours is 12 to 21.

   The university should be able to use your new version on a data file that contains information on several students.

4. Al Derrick (Problem 20, Chapter 4; Problem 10, Chapter 5) wants you to revise his program by using the **TYPE** definition section to enhance readability and ensure protection against bad data. Your new version should run for several wells and include types of wells (Dry, Oil, and Gas), volume for gas (between 10,000 and 100,000), and volume for oil (between 2000 and 50,000).

■ 5. Dr. Lae Z. Programmer is relentless. He wants you to modify your latest version of the grading program (Problems 5, 22, and 23, Chapter 4; Problem 13, Chapter 5) by using the **TYPE** definition section. Your new version should include a range for test scores (from 0 to 100), a range for quiz scores (from 0 to 10), and a range for the final examination (from 0 to 200).

6. Upgrade your most recent version of the Pentagon parking lot program (Problem 26, Chapter 4; Problem 14, Chapter 5) by using the **TYPE** definition section. Time in and time out will be between 0600 and 2200 (6:00 A.M. and 10:00 P.M.). Vehicle type should be denoted by Car, Truck, or Senior.

7. Read a text file containing a paragraph of text. Count the number of words in the paragraph. Assume consecutive words are separated by at least one blank.

8. Write a program that will print the contents of a text file and omit any occurrences of the letter "e" from the output.

9. A text file contains a list of integers in order from lowest to highest. Write a program to read and print the text file with all duplications eliminated.

10. Mr. John Napier, a professor at Lancaster Community College, wants you to develop a program to compute grade point averages. Each line of a text file contains three initials followed by an unknown number of letter grades. These grades are A, B, C, D, or E. Write a program that reads the file and prints a list of the students' initials and their grade point averages. (Assume an A is 4 points, a B is 3 points, and so on.) Print an asterisk next to any grade point average greater than 3.75.

11. An amortization table (Problem 19, Chapter 5) shows the rate at which a loan is paid off. It contains monthly entries that indicate interest paid, principal paid, and remaining balance. Given the amount of money borrowed (the principal), the annual interest rate, and the amount the person wishes to repay each month, print an amortization table. (The desired payment must be larger than the first month's interest.) Your table should stop when the loan is paid off and should be printed with the heads

```
MONTH NUMBER    INTEREST PAID    PRINCIPAL PAID    BALANCE
```

Create an enumerated data type for the month number. Limit this to require that the loan be paid back within 60 months.

12. In 1626, the Dutch settlers purchased Manhattan Island from the Native Americans (Problem 23, Chapter 5). According to legend, the purchase price was $24. Suppose the Indians had invested this amount at 3 percent annual interest compounded quarterly. If the money had earned interest from the start of 1626 to the end of last year, how much money would the descendants of these Native Americans have in the bank today? (*Hint:* Use nested loops for the compounding.) Create an enumerated data type for the range of years (1626 to last year) that will be used.

13. Mr. Christian (Problem 26, Chapter 5) uses a 90-percent, 80-percent, 70-percent, 60-percent grading scale on his tests. Given a list of test scores, print the number of As, Bs, Cs, Ds, and Es on the test. Terminate the list of scores with a sentinel value. Use a subrange of the integers for the input grades.

14. Write a program to print the perimeter and area of rectangles. Use all combinations of lengths and widths from 1 foot to 10 feet in increments of 1 foot. Print the output in headed columns. Use a subrange to restrict the lengths and widths from 1 to 10.

15. Write a program that can serve as a "triangle analyzer". Each line of input should consist of three positive integers representing the lengths of the sides of a triangle. Initially, your program should determine whether or not a triangle with the indicated side lengths is possible. (The length of the longest side cannot exceed the sum of the lengths of the other two sides.) Permissible triangles should then be identified as scalene, isosceles, or equilateral, according to the number of sides of equal length. Finally, all right triangles should be identified. Your program should utilize a user-defined data type for the triangle types Scalene, Isosceles, and Equilateral.

COMMUNICATION IN PRACTICE

1. Select a problem that you have not done from the Programming Problems and Projects section in this chapter. For that problem, write documentation that includes a complete description of
   a. Required input
   b. Required output
   c. Required processing and computation

   Exchange your documentation with another student who has been given the same assignment. Compare your results.
2. Remove all documentation from a program you have written for this chapter. Exchange this version with another student who has done the same thing. Write documentation for the exchanged program. Compare your documentation with that originally written for the program. Discuss the differences and similarities in documentation with the other student.
3. Contact a programmer, graduate student, or upper-division major in computer science, and discuss the issue of using enumerated and other user-defined data types. Among other things, find out how often (or even if) that person uses such data types, how important he or she considers such data types to be as part of a programming language, and some specific examples of how he or she uses enumerated data types. Give an oral report of your findings to your class.
4. Enumerated and other user-defined data types are one advantage of using Pascal as a programming language. Examine several other programming languages to see if they include a comparable feature. Prepare a chart that summarizes your findings.
5. Select a team of three or four students, and contact businesspeople who use computers for data storage. Find out exactly how they enter, store, and retrieve data. Discuss how they use their data bases and how large the data bases are. Ask them what they like and dislike about data entry and retrieval and if they have suggestions for modifying any aspect of working with their data bases. Prepare a report for class that summarizes your team's findings.

CHAPTER

7 One-Dimensional Arrays

CHAPTER OUTLINE

This chapter begins a significant new stage of programming. Until now, we have been unable to manipulate and store large amounts of data in a convenient way. For example, if we wanted to work with a long list of numbers or names, we had to declare a separate variable for each number or name. Fortunately, Pascal and all other programming languages provide several structured variables to facilitate solving problems that require working with large amounts of data. Simply put, a structured variable uses one identifier to reserve a large amount of memory. This memory is capable of holding several individual values. The structured variables included in this text are arrays, records, files, and sets.

Arrays (the topic of this chapter) are designed to handle large amounts of data of the same type in an organized manner. Arrays are used whenever there is a need to store data for subsequent use in a program. Using arrays permits us to set aside a group of memory locations that we can then manipulate either as a single entity or as separate components. Some very standard applications for array variables include creating tabular output (tables), alphabetizing a list of names, analyzing a list of test scores, manipulating character data, and keeping an inventory.

7.1 Arrays

OBJECTIVES

- to understand the basic concept of an array
- to use correct notation for arrays
- to be able to declare arrays with variable declarations and with type definitions
- to be able to use array components with appropriate arithmetic operations
- to be able to use array components with appropriate **read** and **write** statements

Basic Idea and Notation

In many instances, several variables of the same data type are required. At this point, let's work with a list of five integers: 18, 17, 21, 18, and 19. Prior to this chapter, we would have declared five variables (A, B, C, D, and E) and assigned them appropriate values or read them from an input file. This would have produced five values in memory, each accessed by a separate identifier:

18	17	21	18	19
A	B	C	D	E

If the list is very long, however, this would be an inefficient way to work with these data. An alternative is to use an array. In Pascal, we declare a variable as an array variable by using either of the following methods:

```
1. VAR
     List : ARRAY [1..5] OF integer;
2. TYPE
     Numbers = ARRAY [1..5] OF integer;
   VAR
     List : Numbers;
```

Given either of these declarations, we now have five integer variables with which to work. They are denoted by

List[1]	List[2]	List[3]	List[4]	List[5]

and each is referred to as a *component,* or *element, of the array.* A good way to visualize these variables is to assume memory locations are aligned in a column on top of each other and the name of the column is List. If we then assign the five values of our list to these five variables, we have in memory

List	
18	List[1]
17	List[2]
21	List[3]
18	List[4]
19	List[5]

The components of an array are referred to in terms of their relative position in the array. This relative position is called the *index,* or *subscript,* of the component. In the array of our five values, the component List[3] has an index of 3 and value of 21.

For the sake of convenience, you may choose to depict an array by listing only the index beside its appropriate component. Thus, List could be shown as

List	
	1
	2
	3
	4
	5

If you choose this method, remember that the array elements are referenced by the array name and the index (for example, List[3] for the third component). Whichever method you use, it is important to remember that each array component is a variable and can be treated exactly as any other declared variable of that base type in the program.

Declaring an Array

An array type can be defined as a user-defined type, and then an appropriate variable can be declared to be of this type. An earlier declaration was

```
TYPE
  Numbers = ARRAY [1..5] OF integer;
VAR
  List : Numbers;
```

Now let's examine this declaration more closely. Several comments are in order.

1. The data type Numbers is a user-defined data type.
2. **ARRAY** is a reserved word and is used to indicate that an array type is being defined.
3. [1 . . 5] is the syntax that indicates the array consists of five memory locations that can be accessed by specifying each of the numbers 1, 2, 3, 4, and 5. We would say this array is "of length five". The information inside the brackets is the

index type and is used to refer to the components of an array. This index type can be any ordinal data type that specifies a beginning value and an ending value. However, subranges of data type **integer** are the most easily read and frequently used index types.

4. The reserved word **OF** refers to the data type for the components of the array.
5. The key word **integer** indicates the data type for the components. This can, of course, be any valid data type.
6. The identifier List can be any valid identifier. As always, it is good practice to use descriptive names to enhance readability.

The general form for defining an array type is

```
TYPE
  <name> = ARRAY [<index type>] OF <component type>
```

where "name" is any valid identifier, "index type" is any ordinal data type that specifies both an initial value and a final value, and "component type" is any predefined or user-defined data type (except files). The syntax diagram for defining an array is

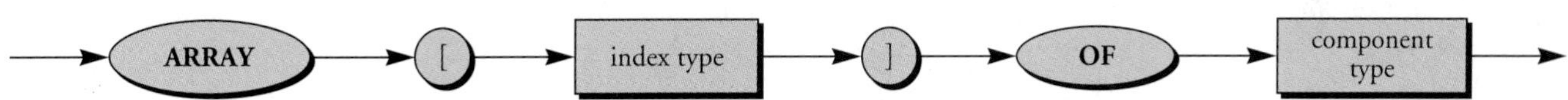

The following example illustrates another declaration of an array variable.

EXAMPLE 7.1

Suppose you want to create a list of 10 integer variables for the hours worked by 10 employees as follows:

Employee Number	Hours Worked
1	35
2	40
3	20
4	38
5	25
6	40
7	25
8	40
9	20
10	45

Let's declare an array that has 10 components of type **integer,** and show how it can be visualized. A descriptive name could be Hours. There are 10 items, so we will use **ARRAY** [1 . . 10] in the definition. Since the data consist of integers, the component type will be **integer**. An appropriate definition and subsequent declaration could be

```
TYPE
  HourList = ARRAY [1..10] OF integer;
VAR
  Hours : HourList;
```

At this stage, the components can be visualized as

Hours	
	Hours[1]
	Hours[2]
	Hours[3]
	Hours[4]
	Hours[5]
	Hours[6]
	Hours[7]
	Hours[8]
	Hours[9]
	Hours[10]

After making appropriate assignment statements, Hours can be visualized as

Hours	
35	Hours[1]
40	Hours[2]
20	Hours[3]
38	Hours[4]
25	Hours[5]
40	Hours[6]
25	Hours[7]
40	Hours[8]
20	Hours[9]
45	Hours[10]

Other Indices and Data Types

The previous two arrays use index types that are subranges of the **integer** data type. Although this is a common way to specify the index to an array, we can use subranges of any ordinal type for this definition. The following examples illustrate some array definitions with other indices and data types.

EXAMPLE 7.2

Suppose you want to declare an array to allow you to store the hourly price for a share of IBM stock. A descriptive name could be StockPrice. A price is quoted at each hour from 9:00 A.M. to 3:00 P.M., so **ARRAY** [9 . . 15] should be used in the declaration section. Since the data consist of reals, the component type must be **real**. A possible declaration could be

```
TYPE
  StockPriceList = ARRAY [9..15] OF real;
VAR
  StockPrice : StockPriceList;
```

This will allow you to store the 9:00 A.M. price in StockPrice[9], the 1:00 P.M. price in StockPrice[13], and so on.

EXAMPLE 7.3

The declaration

```
TYPE
  AlphaList = ARRAY [-2..3] OF char;
VAR
  Alpha : AlphaList;
```

will reserve components, which can be depicted as

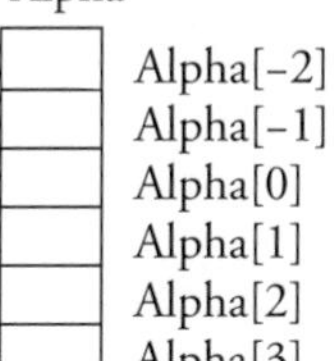

Each component is a character variable.

EXAMPLE 7.4

The declaration

```
TYPE
  TotalHoursList = ARRAY ['A'..'E'] OF integer;
VAR
  TotalHours : TotalHoursList;
```

will reserve components which can be depicted as

TotalHours

'A'
'B'
'C'
'D'
'E'

Components of this array are integer variables.

EXAMPLE 7.5

The declaration

```
TYPE
  FlagValues = ARRAY [1..4] OF boolean;
VAR
  Flag : FlagValues;
```

will produce an array with components that are **boolean** variables.

It is important to note that in each example, the array components have no assigned values until the program specifically makes some kind of assignment. Declaring an array does not assign values to any of the components.

Two additional array definitions and subsequent declarations follow.

```
1. TYPE
     Days = (Mon, Tues, Wed, Thur, Fri, Sat, Sun);
     Workdays = ARRAY [Mon..Fri] OF real;
   VAR
     HoursWorked : Workdays;
2. TYPE
     List50 = ARRAY [1..50] OF real;
     List25 = ARRAY [1..25] OF integer;
     String20 = ARRAY [1..20] OF char;
   VAR
     PhoneCharge : List50;
     Score : List25;
     Word : String20;
     A, B, C, D : List50;
```

(Note: a more efficient method of manipulating character data than the strings just used will be presented in Section 7.5 when we discuss packed arrays.)

COMMUNICATION AND STYLE TIPS

Descriptive constants and type identifiers should be utilized when working with arrays. For example, if you are working with an array of test scores for a class of 35 students, you could have

```
CONST
  ClassSize = 35;
TYPE
  TestScores = 0..100;
  ScoreList = ARRAY [1..ClassSize] OF TestScores;
VAR
  Score : ScoreList;
```

Assignment Statements

Suppose we have declared an array

```
A : ARRAY [1..5] OF integer;
```

and we want to put the values 1, 4, 9, 16, and 25 into the respective components. We can accomplish this with the assignment statements

```
A[1] := 1;
A[2] := 4;
A[3] := 9;
A[4] := 16;
A[5] := 25;
```

If variables B and C of type **integer** are declared in the program, then the following are also appropriate assignment statements.

```
A[3] := B;
C := A[2];
A[2] := A[5];
```

If we want to interchange the values of two components (for example, exchange A[2] with A[3]), we can use a third integer variable:

```
B := A[2];
A[2] := A[3];
A[3] := B;
```

This exchange is frequently used in sorting algorithms, so let's examine it more closely. Assume B contains no previously assigned value and A[2] and A[3] contain 4 and 9, respectively, as follows:

B	A[2]	A[3]
	4	9

The assignment statement

```
B := A[2];
```

then produces

B	A[2]	A[3]
4	4	9

The assignment statement

```
A[2] := A[3];
```

produces

B	A[2]	A[3]
4	9	9

and the assignment statement

```
A[3] := B;
```

produces

B	A[2]	A[3]
4	9	4

in which the original values of A[2] and A[3] are interchanged.

The next example illustrates the use of a **TYPE** definition and a subsequent assignment statement.

EXAMPLE 7.6

Given the definitions and declarations

```
TYPE
  Seasons = (Fall, Winter, Spring, Summer);
  TemperatureList = ARRAY [Seasons] OF real;
VAR
  AvTemp : TemperatureList;
```

an assignment statement such as

```
  AvTemp[Fall] := 53.2;
```

is appropriate. The array is then

AvTemp	
53.2	Fall
	Winter
	Spring
	Summer

Arithmetic

Components of an array can also be used in any appropriate arithmetic operation. For example, suppose A is the array of integers

A	
1	A[1]
4	A[2]
9	A[3]
16	A[4]
25	A[5]

and the values of the components of the array are to be added. This can be accomplished by the statement

```
Sum := A[1] + A[2] + A[3] + A[4] + A[5];
```

Each of the following is also a valid use of an array component.

```
B := 3 * A[2];
C := A[4] MOD 3;
D := A[2] * A[5];
```

For the array A given, these assignment statements produce

55	12	1	100
Sum	B	C	D

Some invalid assignment statements and the reasons they are invalid follow.

`A[0] := 7;`	(0 is not a valid subscript.)
`A[2] := 3.5;`	(Component A[2] is not of type **real**.)
`A[2.0] := 3;`	(A subscript of type **real** is not allowed.)

Reading and Writing

Since array components are names for variables, they can be used with **read, readln, write,** and **writeln**. For example, if Score is an array of five integers and we want to input the scores 65, 43, 98, 75, and 83 from a data file, we could use the code

```
readln (Data, Score[1], Score[2], Score[3], Score[4], Score[5]);
```

which produces the array

Score	
65	Score[1]
43	Score[2]
98	Score[3]
75	Score[4]
83	Score[5]

If we want to print the scores above 80, we could use the code

A NOTE OF INTEREST

Monolithic Idea: Invention of the Integrated Circuit

One of the most significant breakthroughs in the history of technology occurred in the late 1950s. Prior to 1958, computer circuitry was limited because transistors, diodes, resistors, and capacitors were separate units that had to be wired together and soldered by hand. Although designers could design intricate computer supercircuits using 500,000 transistors, they were almost impossible to build because of the extensive handwork involved. For example, a circuit with 100,000 components could require over 1,000,000 soldered connections. It was virtually impossible to assemble that many components without human error. Thus, the electronics industry was faced with an apparently insurmountable limit.

About this time, Jack St. Clair Kilby developed what has come to be known as the Monolithic Idea. He decided to put the components of an entire circuit in a monolithic block of silicon. The idea, together with Robert Noyce's work on interconnecting circuits, allowed electronics engineers to overcome the obstacle presented by separate components. Kilby and Noyce's work resulted in the integrated circuit, the most important new product in the history of electronics. For their efforts, both men were awarded the National Medal of Science.

```
writeln (Score[3]:10, Score[5]:10);
```

to produce

```
        98        83
```

It is important to note that we cannot **read** or **write** values into or from an entire array by referencing the array name. (An exception will be explained in Section 7.5.) Statements such as

```
read (A);
writeln (A);
```

are invalid if A is an array.

Out-of-range array references should be avoided. For example, if the array A has index values 1 . . 5, a reference to A[6] or A[0] will produce an error. This will become more of a problem when we start to process arrays with loops in the next section.

EXERCISES 7.1

1. Using descriptive names, define an array type and declare subsequent variables for each of the following.
   a. A list of 35 test scores
   b. The prices of 20 automobiles
   c. The answers to 50 true-or-false questions
   d. A list of letter grades for the classes you are taking this semester
2. Write a test program in which you declare an array of three components, read values into each component, sum the components, and print out the sum and value of each component.
3. Find all errors in the following definitions of array types.
   a.
   ```
   TYPE
     Time = ARRAY [1..12] OF Hours;
   ```
   b.
   ```
   TYPE
     Scores = ARRAY [1..30] OF integer;
   ```
   c.
   ```
   TYPE
     Alphabet = ARRAY OF char;
   ```
   d.
   ```
   TYPE
     List = ARRAY [1 TO 10] OF real;
   ```

e.
```
TYPE
  Answers = ARRAY [OF boolean];
```
f.
```
TYPE
  X = ARRAY [1...5] OF real;
```

4. Assume the array List is declared as

```
TYPE
  Scores = ARRAY [1..100] OF integer;
VAR
  List : Scores;
```

and all other variables have been appropriately declared. Label the following as valid or invalid. Include an explanation for any statement that is invalid.

a. `read (List[3]);`
b. `A := List[3] + List[4];`
c. `writeln (List);`
d. `List[10] := 3.2;`
e. `Max := List[50];`
f. `Average := (List[1] + List[8]) / 2;`
g. `write (List[25, 50, 75, 100]);`
h. `write ((List[10] + List[90]):25);`
i.
```
FOR J := 1 TO 100 DO
  read (List);
```
j. `List[36] := List[102];`
k. `Scores[47] := 92;`
l. `List[40] := List[41] / 2;`

5. Change each of the following so that the **TYPE** definition section is used to define the array type.

a.
```
VAR
  LetterList : ARRAY [1..100] OF 'A'..'Z';
```
b.
```
VAR
  CompanyName : ARRAY [1..30] OF char;
```
c.
```
VAR
  ScoreList : ARRAY [30..59] OF real;
```

6. Consider the array declared by

```
TYPE
  ListOfSizes = ARRAY [1..5] OF integer;
VAR
  WaistSize : ListOfSizes;
```

a. Sketch how the array should be envisioned in memory.
b. After assignments

```
WaistSize[1] := 34;
WaistSize[3] := 36;
WaistSize[5] := 32;
WaistSize[2] := 2 * 15;
WaistSize[4] := (WaistSize[1] + WaistSize[3]) DIV 2;
```

are made, sketch the array and indicate the contents of each component.

7. Let the array Money be declared by

```
TYPE
  List3 = ARRAY [1..3] OF real;
VAR
  Money : List3;
```

Let Temp, X, and Y be real variables, and assume Money has the values

Money	
19.26	Money[1]
10.04	Money[2]
17.32	Money[3]

If Money contains these initial values before each segment is executed, what does the array contain after each of the following sections of code?

a.
```
Temp := 173.21;
X := Temp + Money[2];
Money[1] := X;
```

b.
```
IF Money[2] < Money[1] THEN
  BEGIN
    Temp := Money[2];
    Money[2] := Money[1];
    Money[1] := Temp
  END;
```

c.
```
Money[3] := 20 - Money[3];
```

8. Let the array List be declared by

```
TYPE
  Scores = ARRAY [1..5] OF real;
VAR
  List : Scores;
```

Write a program segment to initialize all components of List to 0.0.

7.2 Using Arrays

OBJECTIVES

- to be able to use loops to read data into an array from an input file
- to be able to use loops to write data from an array
- to be able to assign array values by aggregate assignment and by component assignment
- to be able to use loops with arrays to solve programming problems

Loops for Input and Output

One advantage of arrays is the small amount of code needed when loops are used to manipulate array components. For example, suppose a list of 100 scores stored in a data file is to be used in a program. If an array is declared by

```
TYPE
  List100 = ARRAY [1..100] OF integer;
VAR
  Score : List100;
  J : integer;
```

the data file can be read into the array using a **FOR** loop:

```
FOR J := 1 TO 100 DO
  read (Data, Score[J]);
```

Remember, a statement such as **read** (Data, Score) is invalid. Data may only be read into individual components of the array.

Loops can be similarly used to produce output of array components. For example, if the array of test scores just given is to be printed in a column, then

```
FOR J := 1 TO 100 DO
  writeln (Score[J]);
```

will accomplish this. If the components of Score contain the values

```
Score
78    Score[1]
93    Score[2]
 .       .
 .       .
 .       .
82    Score[100]
```

the loop for writing produces

```
78
93
.
.
.
82
```

Note that we cannot cause the array components to be printed by a statement such as **write** (Score) or **writeln** (Score). These statements are invalid. We must refer to the individual components.

Loops for output are seldom this simple. Usually, we are required to format the output in some manner. For example, suppose the array Score is as declared and we wish to print these scores 10 to a line, each with a field width of five spaces. The following segment of code would accomplish this.

```
FOR J := 1 TO 100 DO
  BEGIN
    write (Score[J]:5);
    IF J MOD 10 = 0 THEN
      writeln
  END;
```

Loops for Assigning

Loops can also be used to assign values to array components. At certain times, we might want an array to contain values that are not read from an input file. The following examples show how loops can be used in such instances.

EXAMPLE 7.7

Recall array A in Section 7.1 in which we made the following assignments.

```
A[1] := 1;
A[2] := 4;
A[3] := 9;
A[4] := 16;
A[5] := 25;
```

These assignments could have been made with the loop

```
FOR J := 1 TO 5 DO
  A[J] := J * J;
```

EXAMPLE 7.8

Suppose the components of an array must contain the letters of the alphabet in order from A to Z. Using the ASCII character set, the desired array could be declared by

```
TYPE
  Letters = ARRAY [1..26] OF char;
VAR
  Alphabet : Letters;
```

The array Alphabet could then be assigned the desired characters by the statement

```
FOR J := 1 TO 26 DO
  Alphabet[J] := chr(J-1 + ord('A'));
```

If

```
J := 1;
```

we have

```
Alphabet[1] := chr(ord('A'));
```

Thus

```
Alphabet[1] := 'A';
```

Similarly, for

```
J := 2;
```

we have

```
Alphabet[2] := chr(1 + ord('A'));
```

Eventually, we obtain

Alphabet

'A'	Alphabet[1]
'B'	Alphabet[2]
'C'	Alphabet[3]
.	.
.	.
.	.
'Z'	Alphabet[26]

Assignment of values from components of one array to corresponding components of another array is a frequently encountered problem. For example, suppose the arrays A and B are declared as

```
TYPE
  List50 = ARRAY [1..50] OF real;
VAR
  A, B : List50;
```

If B has been assigned values and we want to put the contents of B into A, component by component, we could use the loop

```
FOR J := 1 TO 50 DO
  A[J] := B[J];
```

However, for problems of this type, Pascal allows the entire array to be assigned by

```
A := B;
```

This aggregate assignment actually causes 50 assignments to be made at the component level. The arrays must type identical to do this.

Processing with Loops

Loops are especially suitable for reading, writing, and assigning array components and can be used in conjunction with arrays to process data. For example, suppose the arrays A and B are declared as

```
TYPE
  List100 = ARRAY [1..100] OF real;
VAR
  A, B : List100;
```

If we want to add the values of components of B to the respective values of components of A, we could use the loop

```
FOR J := 1 TO 100 DO
  A[J] := A[J] + B[J];
```

It would appear that since

```
A := B;
```

is valid, this could be accomplished by

```
A := A + B;
```

Not true. Pascal does not allow the aggregate addition of A + B if A and B are arrays.

The following examples illustrate additional uses of loops for processing data contained in array variables.

EXAMPLE 7.9

Earlier in this section, we read 100 test scores into an array. Assume the scores have been read and we now wish to find the average score and the largest score. Assume variables Sum, Max, and Average have been appropriately declared. The following segment will compute the average.

```
Sum := 0;
FOR J := 1 TO 100 DO
  Sum := Sum + Score[J];
Average := Sum / 100;
```

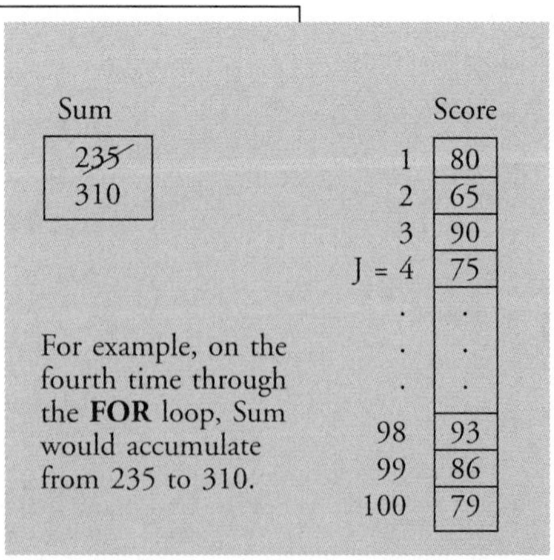

The maximum score can be found by using the following segment of code.

```
Max := Score[1];
FOR J := 2 TO 100 DO
  IF Score[J] > Max THEN
    Max := Score[J];
```

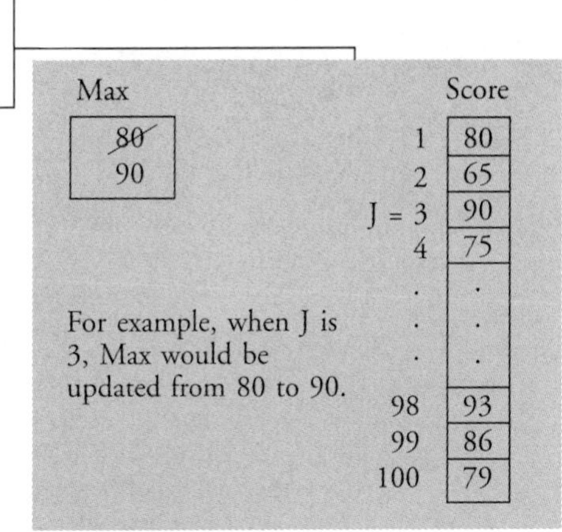

EXAMPLE 7.10

Let's write a segment of code to find the smallest value of array A and the index of the smallest value. Assume the variables have been declared as

```
TYPE
  Column100 = ARRAY [1..100] OF real;
VAR
  A : Column100;
  Min : real;
  Index : integer;
```

and the values have been read into components of A. The following algorithm will solve the problem.

1. Assign 1 to Index
2. **FOR** J := 2 **TO** 100 **DO**
   IF A[J] < A[Index] **THEN** assign J to Index
3. Assign A[Index] to Min

The segment of code is

```
Index := 1;
FOR J := 2 TO 100 DO
  IF A[J] < A[Index] THEN
    Index := J;
Min := A[Index];
```

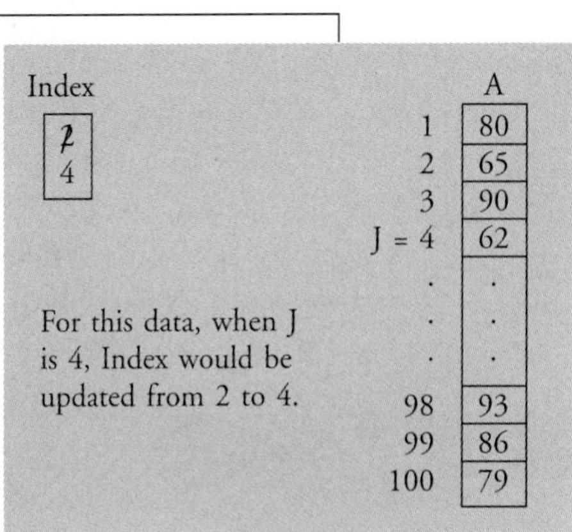

A NOTE OF INTEREST

Impact of Computers on Art

Dana J. Lamb recently discussed the impact of computers on the arts in an article appearing in *Academic Computing.* Among other things, she reported part of a conversation held with Alice Jones, a freelance graphic designer and a member of a summer arts program studying developments in full-color graphics on personal computers. When Jones was asked about the use of computers in her professional pursuits, she indicated her study led her to believe the time required to produce a typical paste-up could be reduced by as much as 75 percent, depending upon the proficiency of the graphic artist. She pointed out that the traditional means of producing art required the teamwork of a graphic artist, typesetter, copy camera operator, photographer, and/or illustrator. The logistics of even the simplest paste-up of a few black and white photographs often required days in transit as copy was typeset at one location and photos and illustrations were created and then reduced or enlarged at two other locations—all traveling from each place of business to another while the graphic designer sat waiting. Jones observed that this dispersion of design components has been suddenly unified and put into the hands of the designer.

Later in the article, Lamb addressed the issue of how artists perceive the computer. According to Lamb, the opinions of those in the art world can be divided into three major groups:

1. Those who deny the computer has any legitimate place in the creation of art
2. Those who believe the computer should be included in the realm of traditional and/or nontraditional tools in the creation of art
3. Those who believe the computer, together with its fundamental structure, is an art medium unto itself

Lamb concludes her article with the following paragraph:

It is easy to forget that we are witnessing the infancy of this medium in relationship to the arts because of its phenomenal growth in eight years. Artists have been using computers since the 1950s but up to the last decade were viewed as oddities with few arenas to exhibit or share their work. Those days are over, and as the image of these machines becomes less a philosophical issue and simply another tool in the creative process, we can move on to develop the "clear path" between the visual concept and final product espoused.

A very standard problem encountered when working with arrays is what to do when we don't know exactly how many components of an array will be needed. In such instances, we must select some upper limit for the length of the array. A standard procedure is to declare a reasonable limit, keeping two points in mind.

1. The length must be sufficient to store all the data.
2. The amount of storage space must not be excessive; do not set aside excessive amounts of space that will not be used.

To guard against the possibility of not reading all the data into array elements, an **IF . . . THEN** statement, such as

```
IF NOT eof(Data) THEN
  writeln ('There are more data.');
```

could be included in the procedure used to get data from the data file. These points are illustrated in the following example. The array will be partially filled when the number of checks is less than the array length. This information can be retained by including a program statement such as

```
NumberOfChecks := J;
```

after the loop is exited.

EXAMPLE 7.11

Suppose an input file contains an unknown number of dollar amounts from personal checks. We want to write a segment of code to read them into an array and output the number of checks. Since the data are in dollars, we use real components and the identifier Check as follows:

```
TYPE
  List = ARRAY [1..?] OF real;
VAR
  Check : List;
```

If we think there are fewer than 50 checks, we can define a constant by

```
CONST
  MaxChecks = 50;
```

and then define List by

```
List = ARRAY [1..MaxChecks] OF real;
```

The data can then be accessed using a **WHILE . . . DO** loop:

```
J := 0;
WHILE NOT eof AND (J < MaxChecks) DO
  BEGIN
    J := J + 1;
    readln (Check[J])
  END;
IF NOT eof THEN
  writeln ('There are more data.');
NumberOfChecks := J;
```

Now we have the data in the array, we know the number of data items, and we can use NumberOfChecks as a loop limit. Then the loop

```
FOR J := 1 TO NumberOfChecks DO
  BEGIN
    writeln;
    writeln ('Check number':20, J:4, '$':5, Checks[J]:7:2)
  END;
```

will print the checks on every other line.

COMMUNICATION AND STYLE TIPS

Indices with semantic meanings can be useful when working with arrays. For example, suppose you are writing a program that includes the inventory for shoe styles in a shoe store. If the styles are loafer, wing tip, docksider, high pump, low pump, and plain tie, you would define

```
TYPE
  Style = (Docksider, HighPump, Loafer, LowPump,
           PlainTie, WingTip);
  ShoeInventory = ARRAY [Docksider..WingTip] OF integer;
VAR
  Stock : ShoeInventory;
  ShoeType : Style;
```

Typical program statements could be

```
Stock[WingTip] := 25;
Stock[Loafer] := Stock[Loafer] - 3;
FOR ShoeType := Docksider TO WingTip DO
  writeln (Stock[ShoeType]);
```

EXERCISES 7.2

1. Assume the following array declarations.

```
TYPE
  NumList = ARRAY [1..5] OF integer;
  AnswerList = ARRAY [1..10] OF boolean;
  NameList = ARRAY [1..20] OF char;
VAR
  List, Score : NumList;
  Answer : AnswerList;
  Name : NameList;
```

Indicate the contents of the arrays after each segment of code.

a.
```
FOR J := 1 TO 5 DO
  List[J] := J DIV 3;
```

b.
```
FOR J := 2 TO 6 DO
  BEGIN
    List[J-1] := J + 3;
    Score[J-1] := List[J-1] DIV 3
  END;
```

c.
```
FOR J := 1 TO 10 DO
  IF J MOD 2 = 0 THEN
    Answer[J] := true
  ELSE
    Answer[J] := false;
```

d.
```
FOR J := 1 TO 20 DO
  Name[J] := chr(J + 64);
```

2. Write a test program to illustrate what happens when you try to use an index that is not in the defined subrange for an array. For example, try to use the loop

```
FOR J := 1 TO 10 DO
  read (Data, A[J]);
```

when A has been declared as

```
TYPE
  NumList = ARRAY [1..5] OF integer;
VAR
  A : NumList;
```

3. Let the array Best be declared by

```
TYPE
  List30 = ARRAY [1..30] OF integer;
VAR
  Best : List30;
```

and assume test scores have been read into Best. What does the following section of code do?

```
Count := 0;
FOR J := 1 TO 30 DO
  IF Best[J] > 90 THEN
    Count := Count + 1;
```

4. Declare an array and write a segment of code to
   a. Read 20 integer test scores into the array.
   b. Count the number of scores ≥ 55.

5. Declare an array using the **TYPE** definition section and write a section of code to read a name of 20 characters from a line of input.
6. Let the array List be declared as

```
TYPE
  Numbers = ARRAY [11..17] OF integer;
VAR
  List : Numbers;
```

and assume the components have values of

List	
-2	List[11]
3	List[12]
0	List[13]
-8	List[14]
20	List[15]
14	List[16]
-121	List[17]

Show what the array components would be after the following program segment is executed.

```
FOR J := 11 TO 17 DO
  IF List[J] < 0 THEN
    List[J] := 0;
```

7. Assume the array A is declared as

```
TYPE
  List100 = ARRAY [1..100] OF real;
VAR
  A : List100;
```

Write a segment of code that uses a loop to initialize all components to zero.
8. The following segment of code can be used to input the values in Example 7.11.

```
FOR J := 1 TO 50 DO
  IF NOT eof THEN
    readln (Check[J]);
```

Discuss the differences between this code and the code in the example.
9. Let the array N be declared as

```
TYPE
  String10 = ARRAY [1..10] OF char;
VAR
  N : String10;
```

and assume the array components have been assigned the values

J	O	H	N		S	M	I	T	H
N[1]	N[2]	N[3]	N[4]	N[5]	N[6]	N[7]	N[8]	N[9]	N[10]

What output is produced by the following?

a.
```
FOR J := 1 TO 10 DO
  write (N[J]);
writeln;
```

b.
```
FOR J := 1 TO 5 DO
  write (N[J+5]);
write (', ');
FOR J := 1 TO 4 DO
  write (N[J]);
writeln;
```
c.
```
FOR J := 10 DOWNTO 1 DO
  write (N[J]);
```

10. Let arrays A, B, and C be declared as

```
TYPE
  FirstList = ARRAY [21..40] OF real;
  SecondList = ARRAY [-4..15] OF real;
VAR
  A, B : FirstList;
  C : Secondlist;
```

Indicate if the following segments of code are valid or invalid. Include an explanation for those that are invalid.

a.
```
FOR J := 21 TO 40 DO
  A[J] := C[J-25];
```
b. `A := B;`

c. `A := C;`

d.
```
FOR J := 1 TO 10 DO
  B[J+20] := C[J+10];
```
e.
```
FOR J := 11 TO 20 DO
  B[J+20] := A[J+20];
```

11. Assume an array has been declared as

```
TYPE
  List50 = ARRAY [1..50] OF integer;
VAR
  TestScore : List50;
```

Write a segment of code to print a suitable heading (assume this is a list of test scores) and then output a numbered list of the array components.

12. Write a program segment to read 100 real numbers from a data file, compute the average, and find the largest and smallest values.

7.3 Selection and Bubble Sorts

OBJECTIVE

- to understand the algorithm for a selection sort
- to be able to sort an array using the selection sort
- to understand the algorithm for a bubble sort
- to be able to use a bubble sort in a program

A common problem involving arrays is sorting the components of the array in either ascending or descending order. Several sorting algorithms are given in Chapter 11, but here let's consider two of the easier methods, the selection sort and the bubble sort.

Selection Sort

Suppose we have an array A of five integers that we wish to sort from smallest to largest. The values currently in A are depicted in the left array below; we wish to end up with the values arranged as shown in the right array.

A		A	
6	A[1]	1	A[1]
4	A[2]	4	A[2]
8	A[3]	6	A[3]
10	A[4]	8	A[4]
1	A[5]	10	A[5]

The basic steps in a *selection sort* are:

1. Find the smallest number in the array, and exchange it with A[1].
2. Find the smallest number among A[2] through A[5], and exchange it with A[2].
3. Continue this process until the array is sorted.

The first step produces

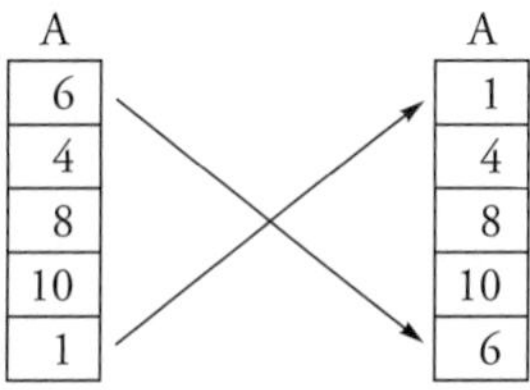

The second, third, and fourth steps produce

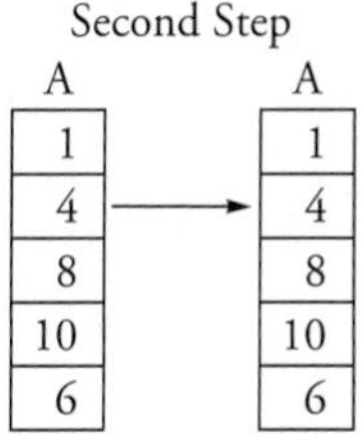

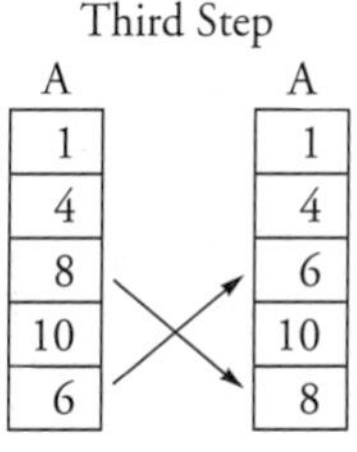

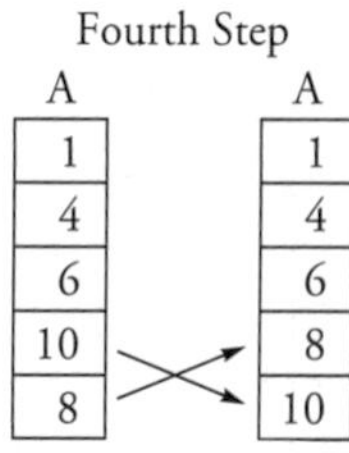

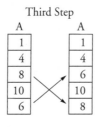

Notice that in the second step, since the second smallest number was already in place, we do not need to exchange anything.

Before writing the algorithm for this sorting procedure, note the following.

1. If the array is of length *n,* we need *n* – 1 steps.
2. We must be able to find one of the smallest remaining numbers.
3. We need to exchange appropriate array components.

When searching for one of the smallest remaining numbers, it is not necessary to exchange values. Thus, note strict inequality (<) rather than weak inequality (<=) is used when looking for the smallest remaining value. The algorithm to sort by selection is

1. **FOR** J := 1 **TO** N – 1
   1.1 find the smallest value among A[J], A[J+1], . . . , A[N], and store the index of the smallest value in Index
   1.2 exchange the values of A[J] and A[Index], if necessary

In Example 7.10, we wrote a segment of code to find the smallest value of array A. With suitable changes, we can incorporate this in the segment of code for a selection sort:

```
Index := 1;
FOR J := 2 TO ArrayLength DO
  IF A[J] < A[Index] THEN
    Index := J;
```

Let A be an array of length *n,* and assume all variables have been appropriately declared. Then the following segment of code will sort A from low to high.

```
FOR J := 1 TO N - 1 DO      {  Find the minimum N - 1 times  }
  BEGIN
    Index := J;
    FOR K := J + 1 TO N DO
      IF A[K] < A[Index] THEN
        Index := K;         {  Find index of smallest number  }
    IF Index <> J THEN
      BEGIN
        Temp := A[Index];
        A[Index] := A[J];
        A[J] := Temp
      END  {  of exchange  }
  END;  {  of FOR J loop  }
```

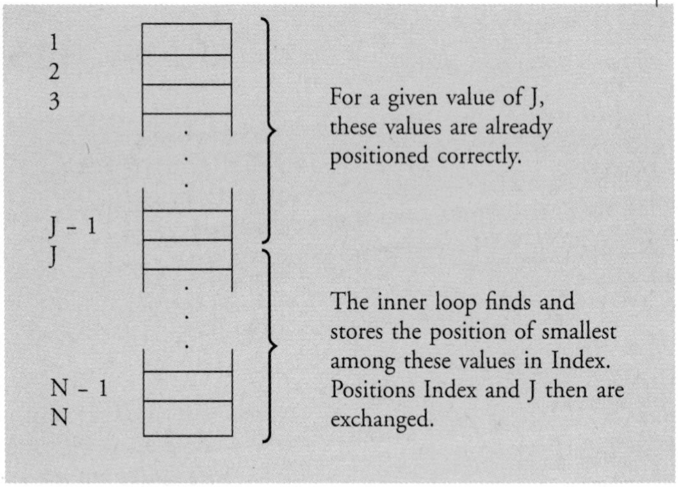

1
2
3
.
.
.
J - 1
J
.
.
.
N - 1
N

For a given value of J, these values are already positioned correctly.

The inner loop finds and stores the position of smallest among these values in Index. Positions Index and J then are exchanged.

Now let's trace this sort for the five integers in the array we sorted at the beginning of this section:

A	
6	A[1]
4	A[2]
8	A[3]
10	A[4]
1	A[5]

For J := 1, Index := 1. This produces

1
Index

For the loop **FOR** K := 2 **TO** 5, we get successive assignments:

K	Index
2	2
3	2
4	2
5	5

The statements

```
Temp := A[Index];
A[Index] := A[J];
A[J] := Temp;
```

produce the partially sorted array

A	
1	A[1]
4	A[2]
8	A[3]
10	A[4]
6	A[5]

Each successive J value continues to partially sort the array until J := 4. This pass produces a completely sorted array.

A NOTE OF INTEREST

Too Few Women in the Computer Science Pipeline?

Studies show that women in computer science programs in U.S. universities terminate their training earlier than men do. Between 1983 and 1986 (the latest year for which we have such figures), the percentage of bachelor's degrees in computer science awarded to women was in the range of 36–37 percent and the percentage of master's degrees was in the range of 28–30 percent. During the same time span, the percentage of doctoral degrees awarded to women was in the range of only 10–12 percent, and it has remained at that level, with the exception of a slight increase in 1989.

If we look at the people who are training the future computer scientists, we may find a clue as to why this discrepancy exists. Women currently hold only 6.5 percent of the faculty positions in the computer science and computer engineering departments in the 158 Ph.D-granting institutions included in the 1988–1989 Taulbee Survey. In fact, a third of these departments have no female faculty members at all. This pattern of decreasing representation is often described as pipeline shrinkage: as women move along the academic pipeline, their percentages continue to shrink.

The ACM Committee on the Status of Women has made a number of recommendations to promote change. These recommendations include

- Ensure equal access to computers for young girls and boys and develop educational software appealing to both.
- Establish programs (such as science fairs, scouting programs, and conferences in which women speak about their careers in science and engineering) to encourage high school girls to continue with math and science.
- Develop programs to pair undergraduate women with women graduate students or faculty members who serve as role models, providing encouragement and advice.
- Provide women with opportunities for successful professional experiences (such as involvement in research projects), beginning as early as the undergraduate years.
- Establish programs that make women computer scientists visible to undergraduates and graduate students. Women can be invited to campuses to give talks or to serve as visiting faculty members (as, for example, in the National Science Foundation's Visiting Professorships for Women).
- Encourage men and women to serve as mentors for young women in the field.
- Maintain lists of qualified women computer scientists to increase the participation of women in influential positions, such as program committees, editorial boards, and policy boards.
- Establish more reentry programs that enable women who have stopped their scientific training prematurely to retrain as computer scientists.
- Increase awareness of and sensitivity to subtle discrimination and its effects.
- Develop and enforce safety procedures on campus. Provide safe access at all hours to public terminal areas, well-lit routes from offices to parking lots, and services to escort those walking on campus after dark.
- Provide affordable, quality childcare.

To provide support for women computer professionals, several organizations have been established that focus on networking, including Systers, the Association for Women in Computing (AWC), and the International Network of Women in Technology (WITI).

EXAMPLE 7.12

Our concluding example:

1. Inputs real numbers from a data file.
2. Echo prints the numbers in a column with a width of six spaces, with two places to the right of the decimal (:6:2).
3. Sorts the array from low to high.
4. Prints the sorted array using the same output format.

An expanded pseudocode development for this is

1. Print header—prints a suitable explanation of the program and includes a heading for the unsorted list
2. Get data (echo print)—uses a **WHILE** loop to read the data and prints them in the same order in which they are read
3. Sort list—uses the selection sort to sort the array from low to high
4. Display sorted list—uses a **FOR** loop to display the sorted list

The complete program for this problem follows.

```
PROGRAM ArraySample (input, output, DataFile);

{  This program illustrates the use of a sorting algorithm with  }
{  an array of reals.  Output includes data in both an unsorted  }
{  list and a sorted list.  The data are formatted and numbered  }
{  to enhance readability.                                       }

CONST
  Skip = ' ';
  ListMax = 20;

TYPE
  NumList = ARRAY [1..ListMax] OF real;

VAR
  Index : integer;        {  Stores position of an element        }
  J, K : integer;         {  Indices                              }
  NumReals : integer;     {  Length of the list                   }
  Temp : real;            {  Temporary storage for array elements }
  List : NumList;         {  Array of reals                       }
  DataFile : text;        {  File of data                         }

{*****************************************************************}

PROCEDURE PrintHeading;

  {  Given:    Nothing                                            }
  {  Task:     Print a heading for the output                     }
  {  Return:   Nothing                                            }

  BEGIN
    writeln;
    writeln ('This sample program does the following:');
    writeln;
    writeln (Skip:2, '<1> Gets reals from a data file.');
    writeln (Skip:2, '<2> Echo prints the data.');
    writeln (Skip:2, '<3> Sorts the data from low to high.');
    writeln (Skip:2, '<4> Prints a sorted list of the data.');
    writeln
  END;  {  of PROCEDURE PrintHeading  }
```

```
{***********************************************************}

BEGIN  {  Main program  }

  {  Print the heading  }
  PrintHeading;

  {  Get the data and echo print it  }
  reset (DataFile);
  writeln ('The original data are as follows:');
  writeln;
  NumReals := 0;
  WHILE NOT eof(DataFile) AND (NumReals < ListMax) DO
    BEGIN
      NumReals := NumReals + 1;
      readln (DataFile, List[NumReals]);
      writeln (Skip:2, '<', NumReals:2, '>', List[NumReals]:6:2)
    END;  {  of WHILE NOT loop  }
  IF NOT eof(DataFile) THEN
    writeln ('There are more data.');

  {  Now sort the list  }
  FOR J := 1 TO NumReals - 1 DO
    BEGIN
      Index := J;
      FOR K := J + 1 TO NumReals DO
        IF List[K] < List[Index] THEN
          Index := K;
      IF Index <> J THEN
        BEGIN
          Temp := List[Index];
          List[Index] := List[J];
          List[J] := Temp
        END  {  of exchange  }
    END;  {  of FOR loop (selection sort)  }

  {  Now print the sorted list  }
  writeln;
  writeln ('The sorted list is as follows:');
  writeln;
  FOR J := 1 TO NumReals DO
    writeln (Skip:2, '<', J:2, '>', List[J]:6:2)
END.  {  of main program  }
```

The output for this program is

```
This sample program does the following:

  <1> Gets reals from a data file.
  <2> Echo prints the data.
  <3> Sorts the data from low to high.
  <4> Prints a sorted list of the data.
```

```
The original data are as follows:

  < 1> 34.56
  < 2> 78.21
  < 3> 23.30
  < 4> 89.90
  < 5> 45.00
  < 6> 56.80
  < 7> 39.01
  < 8> 45.56
  < 9> 34.40
  <10> 45.10
  <11> 98.20
  <12>  5.60
  <13>  8.00
  <14> 45.00
  <15> 99.00
  <16> 56.78
  <17> 56.78
  <18> 45.00

The sorted list is as follows:

  < 1>  5.60
  < 2>  8.00
  < 3> 23.30
  < 4> 34.40
  < 5> 34.56
  < 6> 39.01
  < 7> 45.00
  < 8> 45.00
  < 9> 45.00
  <10> 45.10
  <11> 45.56
  <12> 56.78
  <13> 56.78
  <14> 56.80
  <15> 78.21
  <16> 89.90
  <17> 98.20
  <18> 99.00
```

Bubble Sort

The sorting algorithm commonly referred to as a *bubble sort* rearranges the elements of an array until they are in either ascending or descending order. Like the selection sort, an extra array is not used. Basically, a bubble sort starts at the beginning of an array and compares two consecutive elements of the array. If they are in the correct order, the next pair of elements is compared. If they are not in the correct order, they are switched and the next pair compared. When this has been done for the entire array, the correct element will be in the last position.

Starting at the top (the beginning) each time, successive passes through the array are made until the array is sorted. Two items should be noted here.

1. A flag is needed to indicate whether or not an exchange was made during a given pass through the array. If none was made, the array is sorted.
2. Since each pass filters the largest (or smallest) element to the bottom, the length of what remains to be sorted can be decreased by one after each pass.

To illustrate how this algorithm works, assume the array is

A
12
0
3
2
8

The first pass through the array produces

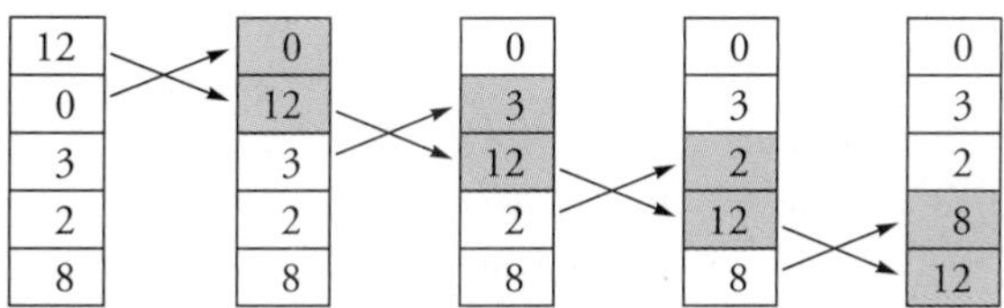

Since an exchange was made, we need to make at least one more pass through the array. However, the length is decreased by one because there is no need to compare the last two elements since the largest element is in its correct position. A second pass produces

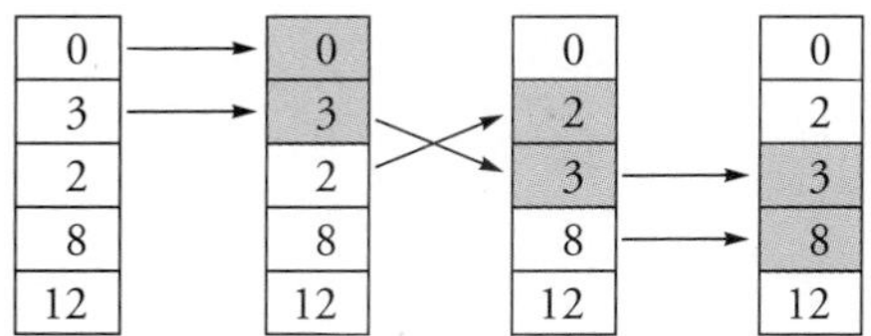

At this stage, the array is sorted, but since an exchange was made, the length is decreased by one and another pass is made. Since no exchange is made during this third pass, the sorting process is terminated.

Assuming the variable declaration section includes

```
VAR
 ExchangeMade : boolean;
 J, Length, Last, Temp : integer;
```

values to be sorted are in the array A, and Length has been assigned a value, an algorithm for a bubble sort could be

```
Last := Length - 1;
REPEAT
  ExchangeMade := false;
  FOR J := 1 TO Last DO
    IF A[J] > A[J+1] THEN
      BEGIN          {  Exchange values  ]
        Temp := A[J];
        A[J] := A[J+1];
        A[J+1] := Temp;
        ExchangeMade := true
      END;
  Last := Last - 1          {  Decrement length  ]
UNTIL (NOT ExchangeMade) OR (Length = 1);
```

EXERCISES 7.3

1. Assume the following array Column is to be sorted from low to high using the selection sort.

   Column

-20
10
0
10
8
30
-2

   a. Sketch the contents of the array after each of the first two passes.
   b. How many exchanges are made during the sort?
2. Write a test program that prints the partially sorted arrays after each pass during a selection sort.
3. Change the code for the selection sort so it sorts an array from high to low.
4. Write a complete program to
   a. Read 10 reals into an array from an input file.
   b. Sort the array from high to low if the first real is positive; sort the array from low to high if the first real is negative.
   c. Print a numbered column containing the sorted reals using the format :10:2.
5. The array

17
0
3
2
8

   requires five exchanges of elements when sorted using a bubble sort. Since each exchange requires three assignment statements, there are 15 assignments for elements in the array. Sort the same array using the selection sort and determine the number of assignments made.
6. Modify the selection sort by including a counter that counts the number of assignments of array elements made during a sort.
7. Using the modification in Exercise 6, sort lists of differing lengths that contain randomly generated numbers. On a graph similar to the one at the top of the next page, display the number of assignments made for each sort. Use lists with lengths of multiples of 10.

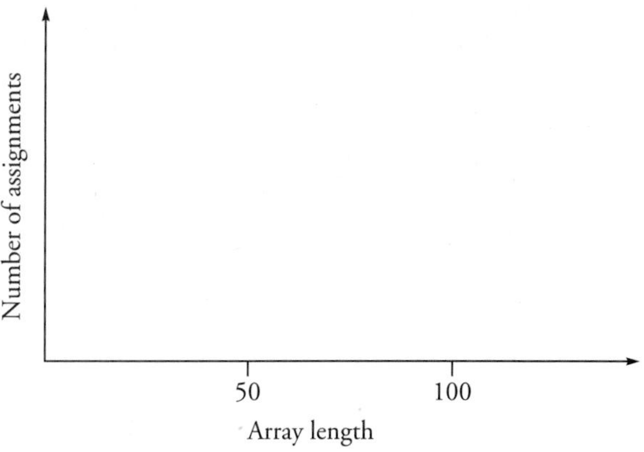

8. Modify the bubble sort to include a counter for the number of assignments made during a sort.
9. Use the modified versions of both sorts to examine their relative efficiency; that is, run them on arrays of varying lenegths and plot the results on a graph. What are your conclusions?
10. Modify the bubble sort to sort from high to low rather than low to high.
11. Sorting parallel arrays is a common practice (for example, an array of names and a corresponding array of scores on test). Modify both sorts so that you can sort a list of initials and associated test scores.

7.4 Arrays and Subprograms

OBJECTIVE

- to be able to use arrays with subprograms correctly

Basic Idea and Syntax

Procedures and functions should be used with arrays to maintain the structured design philosophy. Before we look at specific examples, let's examine the method and syntax required to pass an array to a procedure. Remember to pass either a value parameter or a variable parameter to a procedure, we must declare an actual parameter of exactly the same type as the formal parameter in the procedure heading. In addition, if more than one parameter is passed, there must be a one-for-one ordered matching of the actual parameters with the formal parameters in the heading of the procedure.

First, let's consider how a procedure can be used to read data into an array. Suppose the definitions and declarations include

```
CONST
  ListMax = 20;
TYPE
  NumList = ARRAY [1..ListMax] OF real;
```

We use two variable parameters in the procedure heading, List and ListLength. Thus, the heading is

```
PROCEDURE GetData (VAR List : Numlist;
                   VAR ListLength : integer);
```

Within **PROCEDURE** GetData, we can now read values into the array List by the code

```
ListLength := 0;          {  Initialize  }
WHILE NOT eof(Data) AND ListLength < ListMax DO
  BEGIN
    ListLength := ListLength + 1;
    readln (Data, List[ListLength])
  END;  {  of WHILE loop  }
IF NOT eof(Data) THEN
  writeln ('There are more data.');
```

The complete procedure is

```
PROCEDURE GetData (VAR List : NumList;
                   VAR ListLength : integer);

  {  Given:   Nothing                              }
  {  Task:    Read integers into the array List    }
  {  Return:  The array of integers List and the   }
  {                 length of the list ListLength  }

  BEGIN
    ListLength := 0;          {  Initialize  }
    WHILE NOT eof(Data) AND ListLength < ListMax DO
      BEGIN
        ListLength := ListLength + 1;
        readln (Data, List[ListLength])
      END;  {  of WHILE loop  }
    IF NOT eof(Data) THEN
      writeln ('There are more data.');
  END;  {  of PROCEDURE GetData  }
```

This procedure is called by

```
GetData (List, ListLength);
```

Notice the procedure call and the procedure heading

```
PROCEDURE GetData (VAR List : NumList;
                   VAR ListLength : integer);
```

exhibit the desired matching of variables. Since variable parameters are used, both List and ListLength are passed by reference and are available to the rest of the program.

Let's briefly consider the heading for **PROCEDURE** GetData. Note that we use the data type NumList when declaring the variable parameter List. A common mistake is to attempt to build a data type inside the procedure heading. This does not work. The heading

```
PROCEDURE GetData (VAR List : ARRAY [1..ListMax] OF real;
                   VAR ListLength : integer);
```

produces an error message because Pascal compilers check for name equivalence rather than structure equivalence. To illustrate, we could have two arrays

```
Position : ARRAY [1..3] OF real;
Nutrition : ARRAY [1..3] OF real;
```

where Position is used to represent coordinates of a point in space and Nutrition is used to represent the volume, weight, and caloric content of a serving of food. Although

Position and Nutrition have the same structure, they have significantly different meanings. Thus, requiring name equivalence decreases the chances of inadvertent or meaningless uses of structured variables. Also, compiler implementation of name equivalence is easier than compiler implementation of structure equivalence.

Next, we consider passing an array to a function. Suppose we want to find the average of an array of integers. Using the previous definitions and declarations, the data are obtained by

```
GetData (List, ListLength);
```

where the array List contains ListLength integers. A function to find the average of the numbers in the array List is

```
FUNCTION CalculateAverage (Scores : NumList;
                           NumScores : integer) : real;
  VAR
    Index, Sum : integer;
  BEGIN
    Sum := 0;
    FOR Index := 1 TO NumScores DO
      Sum := Sum + Scores[Index];
    CalculateAverage := Sum / NumScores
  END;  {  of FUNCTION CalculateAverage  }
```

This function can be called by

```
Average := CalculateAverage(List, ListLength);
```

The next example is a complete program that features the use of an array with subprograms.

EXAMPLE 7.13

Let's develop a program that reads data from a data file into an array, computes the average of the array elements, and uses two procedures to display the results.

```
PROGRAM TestScores (input, output, ScoreFile);

{  This program illustrates the use of arrays and sub-       }
{  programs.  Specifically, subprograms are used to          }
{     1.  read data into an array                            }
{     2.  compute the average of array elements              }
{     3.  print contents of the array                        }

CONST
  MaxLength = 100;

TYPE
  List = ARRAY [1..MaxLength] OF integer;

VAR
  Scores : List;                    {  Array of scores      }
  Average : real;                   {  Average score        }
  Length : integer;                 {  Length of the array  }
  ScoreFile : text;                 {  Data file            }

{***********************************************************}
```

```
PROCEDURE GetData (VAR Scores : List;
                   VAR Length : integer);

  {  Given:   Nothing                                          }
  {  Task:    Read integers into the array Scores              }
  {  Return:  The array of integers Scores and the             }
  {                length of the list Length                   }

  BEGIN
    Length := 0;                            {  Initialize  }
    WHILE NOT eof(ScoreFile) AND (Length < MaxLength) DO
      BEGIN
        Length := Length + 1;
        readln (ScoreFile, Scores[Length])
      END;  {  of WHILE loop  }
    IF NOT eof(ScoreFile) THEN
      writeln ('There are more data.')
  END;  {  of PROCEDURE GetData  }

{*************************************************************}

FUNCTION ComputeAverage (Scores : List;
                         Length : integer) : real;

  {  Given:   A list of scores                                 }
  {  Task:    Compute the average score                        }
  {  Return:  The average score                                }

  VAR
    Index, Sum : integer;
  BEGIN
    Sum := 0;
    FOR Index := 1 TO Length DO
      Sum := Sum + Scores[Index];
    ComputeAverage := Sum / Length
  END;  {  of FUNCTION ComputeAverage  }

{*************************************************************}

PROCEDURE PrintHeader;

  {  Given:   Nothing                                          }
  {  Task:    Print a heading for the output                   }
  {  Return:  Nothing                                          }

  BEGIN
    writeln;
    writeln ('Test Scores');
    writeln ('---- ------');
    writeln
  END;  {  of PROCEDURE PrintHeader  }

{*************************************************************}
```

```
PROCEDURE PrintResults (Scores : List;
                         Average : real;
                         Length : integer);

  {  Given:    Array of scores and average score              }
  {  Task:     Print the scores in a list and print the       }
  {                  average score                            }
  {  Return:   Nothing                                        }

  VAR
    J : integer;
  BEGIN
    FOR J := 1 TO Length DO
      writeln (Scores[J]:5);
    writeln;
    writeln ('The average score on this test was',
             Average:6:2, '.')
  END;  {  of PROCEDURE PrintResults  }

{*****************************************************}

BEGIN  {  Main program  }
  reset (ScoreFile);
  GetData (Scores, Length);
  Average := ComputeAverage(Scores, Length);
  PrintHeader;
  PrintResults (Scores, Average, Length)
END.  {  of main program  }
```

Sorting arrays is a standard problem for programmers. Now that we can pass arrays to procedures and functions, let's consider a problem in which an unknown number of reals are to be read from an input file and a sorted list (high to low) is to be printed as output. A first-level pseudocode design is

1. Get data (**PROCEDURE** GetData)
2. Sort list (**PROCEDURE** Sort)
3. Print header (**PROCEDURE** PrintHeader)
4. Print sorted list (**PROCEDURE** PrintData)

Since the number of data items is unknown, we will have to declare an array that is of sufficient length to store all the data but that does not use an unreasonable amount of memory. The nature of the problem should provide sufficient information for this declaration. For now, assume we know there are at most 50 data items. Then the following declaration is sufficient.

```
CONST
  MaxLength = 50;
TYPE
  NumList = ARRAY [1..MaxLength] OF real;
VAR
  List : NumList;
  Length : integer;
```

The procedure to sort the array uses a version of the selection sort in Section 7.3. Both the array and the number of data items need to be passed to the procedure. An appropriate procedure is

```
PROCEDURE Sort (VAR List : NumList;
                Length : integer);
  VAR
    J, K, Index : integer;
    Temp : real;
  BEGIN
    FOR J := 1 TO Length - 1 DO
      BEGIN
        Index := J;
        FOR K := J + 1 TO Length DO
          IF List[K] > List[Index] THEN
            Index := K;
        IF Index <> J THEN
          BEGIN
            Temp := List[Index];
            List[Index] := List[J];
            List[J] := Temp
          END  {  of IF...THEN  }
      END  {  of FOR J loop  }
  END;  {  of PROCEDURE Sort  }
```

PROCEDURE Sort can be called by the statement

```
Sort (List, Length);
```

After suitable procedures are written for getting the data, printing a header, and printing the data, the main body of the program could be

```
BEGIN  {  Main Program  }
  reset (Data);
  GetData (List, Length);
  Sort (List, Length);
  PrintHeader;
  PrintData (List, Length)
END.  {  of main program  }
```

Arrays and Variable Parameters

Now let's reconsider the issue of value parameters and variable parameters used with arrays. Because value parameters require separate memory of approximately the same size as that used by actual parameters in the main program, value parameters that are array types can require a great deal of memory. Thus, many programmers use only variable parameters when they work with arrays. This saves memory and speeds execution. Since most of your programs are relatively short and process small data files, this will not be a major problem. However, as data bases become larger and you use more elaborate structures, you may wish to consider using variable parameters for arrays even when changes are not made in the variables.

Software Engineering Implications

Passing arrays is a software engineering concern. Passing arrays by reference results in a significant saving of memory. The problem this creates when several modules (teams)

use the same array is that inadvertent changes made in an array within a specific module now become changes in the array used by other modules. These side effects do not occur if the array is passed as a value parameter.

How do designers solve this problem? There is no clear solution. If the arrays are fairly small and memory allocation is not a problem, arrays should be passed as value parameters when possible. When conditions require arrays to be passed by reference, it is extremely important to guarantee that no unwanted changes are made. This requirement increases the need for careful and thorough documentation.

Data Abstraction

Now that you are somewhat comfortable with the concept of an array as a data structure, it is time to take a broader look at how data relate to structures used to store and manipulate data. When designing the solution to a problem, it is not important to be initially concerned about the specifics of how data will be manipulated. These implementation details can (and should) be dealt with at a fairly low level in a modular development. The properties of a data structure will, however, be part of the design at a fairly high level.

The separation between the conceptual definition of a data structure and its eventual implementation is called *data abstraction.* This process of deferring details to the lowest possible level parallels the method of designing algorithms: design first, and do implementation details last.

Data abstraction is not a well-defined process, but we will attempt to illustrate it here. Suppose you are designing a program that will be required to work with a list of names and an associated list of numbers (student names and test scores). Reasonable tasks would be to

1. Get the data
2. Sort the lists by name or number
3. Print the lists

In your design, you might have procedures such as

```
GetNames (<procedure here>);
GetScores (<procedure here>);
SortByName (<procedure here>);
SortByScore (<procedure here>);
PrintNamesAndScores (<procedure here>);
```

Even though you have not yet worked with the implementation details required to write the procedures, you could use data structure properties in a design. For example, at this point, you probably could design a problem solution using some of the previously mentioned procedures that work with an array of names and/or an array of associated test scores.

Abstract Data Types

Two abstraction concepts have been previously discussed: procedural abstraction and data abstraction. A third form of abstraction arises from the use of defined types. Specifically, an *abstract data type* (*ADT*) consists of a class of objects, a defined set of properties of these objects, and a set of operations for processing the objects.

Our work thus far has been fairly limited in terms of what can be considered an abstract data type. However, it is possible to think of an array as a list. The class of objects is then lists. Some properties of these lists include identical element type, order, varying lengths, and direct access to individual components. Operations for processing the lists include searching for an element, sorting in ascending or descending order, inserting an element, and deleting an element.

As before, it is not necessary to be overly concerned about specific implementation details at this point. But your growth as a computer scientist will be enhanced if you develop a perspective of abstract data types and use this perspective in the design of problem solutions.

Much of the remainder of this book is devoted to developing properties of data structures and operations for processing these structures. As you progress through the material on higher-dimensional arrays, records, files, and sets, try to analyze each structure with related properties and operations as an abstract data type.

Abstraction and Sorting

Now that we have seen how a sort can be coded, let's consider how we can make the sort more reusable. First, consider the exchange of elements

```
Temp := A[Index];
A[Index] := A[J];
A[J] := Temp
```

We can now write a procedure to perform this task:

```
PROCEDURE Swap (VAR Element1, Element2 : ItemType);
  VAR
    Temp : ItemType;
  BEGIN
    Temp := Element1;
    Element1 := Element2;
    Element2 := Temp
  END;  {  of PROCEDURE Swap  }
```

This procedure can be called by

```
Swap (Element1, Element2);
```

whenever it is needed. Note that the defined type ItemType has been used as a data type.

We can further abstract the selection sort by placing greater emphasis on enumerated data types. To illustrate, consider the definition section

```
CONST
  MaxLength = 50;

TYPE
  ItemType = integer;
  ListType = ARRAY [1..MaxLength] OF ItemType;

VAR
  List : ListType;
  ListLength : integer;
```

Given these definitions, we can rewrite the selection sort as

```
PROCEDURE SelectionSort (VAR List : ListType;
                         Length : integer);
  VAR
    J, K, Index : integer;
  BEGIN
    FOR J := 1 TO Length - 1 DO
      BEGIN
        Index := J;
        FOR K := J + 1 TO Length DO
          IF List[K] > List[Index] THEN
            Index := K;
        IF Index <> J THEN
          Swap (List[Index], List[J])
      END  {  of FOR J loop  }
  END;  {  of PROCEDURE SelectionSort  }
```

This procedure can be called by

```
SelectionSort (List, Length)
```

PROCEDURE SelectionSort can now be used to sort arrays with different item types by redefining ItemType in the **TYPE** definition section.

EXERCISES 7.4

1. Assume the following declarations have been made in a program.

```
TYPE
  Row = ARRAY [1..10] OF integer;
  Column = ARRAY [1..30] OF real;
  String20 = ARRAY [1..20] OF char;
  Week = (Sun, Mon, Tues, Wed, Thur, Fri, Sat);
VAR
  List1, List2 : Row;
  Aray : Column;
  Name1, Name2 : String20;
  Day : Week;
  A, B : ARRAY [1..10] OF integer;
```

Indicate which of the following are valid **PROCEDURE** declarations. Write an appropriate line of code that will call each procedure that is valid. Include an explanation for declarations that are invalid.

a. `PROCEDURE NewList (X : Row; Y : Column);`
b. `PROCEDURE NewList (VAR X : Row : VAR Y : Column);`
c. `PROCEDURE NewList (X : ARRAY [1..10] OF integer);`
d. `PROCEDURE NewList (VAR X, Y : Row);`
e. `PROCEDURE NewList (VAR Column : Column);`
f. `PROCEDURE WorkWeek (Days : ARRAY [Mon..Fri] OF Week);`
g. `PROCEDURE Surname (X : Name);`
h. `PROCEDURE Surnames (X, Y : String20);`
i. `PROCEDURE GetData (X : Week; VAR Y : Name);`
j. `PROCEDURE Table (VAR X : Row; VAR Y : Row);`

2. Write a test program that illustrates what happens when you define an array structure in a procedure heading. For example

```
PROCEDURE Sort (List : ARRAY [1..20] OF real);
```

3. When possible, use the **TYPE** and **VAR** declaration sections in Exercise 1 to write **PROCEDURE** declarations so each of the following statements in the main program is an appropriate call to a procedure. Explain any inappropriate calls.

a. `OldList (List1, Aray);`

b. `ChangeList (List1, Name1, Day);`

c. `Scores (A, B);`

d. `Surname (String20);`

4. Write an appropriate **PROCEDURE** declaration and a line of code to call the procedure for each of the following.

a. A procedure to **read** 20 test scores into an array and save them for later use

b. A procedure to count the number of occurrences of the letter A in an array of 50 characters

c. A procedure to take two arrays of 10 integers each and produce a sorted array of 20 integers for later use

d. A procedure to **read** integer test scores from a data file, count the number of scores, count the number of scores ≥ 90, and save this information for later use

5. Assume the following definition and declarations have been made.

```
TYPE
  Column10 = ARRAY [1..10] OF integer;
VAR
  List1, List2 : Column10;
  K : integer;
```

Indicate the contents of each array after the call to the corresponding procedure has been made.

a.
```
PROCEDURE Sample (VAR List1 : Column10;
                      List2 : Column10);
  VAR
    J : integer;
  BEGIN
    FOR J := 1 TO 10 DO
      BEGIN
        List1[J] := J * J;
        List2[J] := List[J] MOD 2
      END
  END;  { of PROCEDURE Sample  }

BEGIN  { Main program  }
  .
  .
  .
  FOR K := 1 TO 10 DO
    BEGIN
      List1[K] := 0;
      List2[K] := 0
    END;
  Sample (List1, List2);
```

b. Replace the procedure call with

```
Sample (List2, List1);
```

c. Replace the procedure call with the consecutive calls

```
Sample (List1, List2);
Sample (List2, List1);
```

6. For each of the following, declare appropriate variables, write the indicated procedures, and call the procedures from the main program.
   a. Read a line of text from an input file that contains 30 characters.
   b. Count the number of blanks in the line of text.
   c. Print the line of text in reverse order, and print the number of blanks.
7. Write a procedure to examine an array of integers and then return the maximum value, minimum value, and number of negative values to the main program.
8. Write **PROCEDURE** BubbleSort for the bubble sort of Section 7.3. Show how it would be called from the main program.
9. Write **PROCEDURE** Exchange for the bubble sort that will exchange values of array components. Then rewrite the bubbles sort using **PROCEDURE** Exchange.
10. Discuss some details of how you would implement reading a list of names into an array.
11. Suppose you have an array of student names and an array of these students' test scores. How would the array of names be affected if you sorted the test scores from high to low?

7.5 Packed Arrays

OBJECTIVES

- to be able to use correct notation for packed arrays
- to understand the advantages and disadvantages of packed arrays
- to use string variables

One weakness of standard Pascal is the absence of a *string data type.* Since this text is written assuming standard Pascal is being used, this section shows how arrays can be used to simulate a string data type. Most nonstandard versions of Pascal do, however, have such a type. If your version of Pascal has the string data type available, you may wish to skip this section.

Basic Idea and Notation

Arrays are useful for handling large amounts of data. One of the disadvantages of using arrays, however, is that they require large amounts of memory. In particular, arrays of character data use much more memory than is necessary. To illustrate, let's take a closer look at an array declared by

```
VAR
  Examine : ARRAY [1..5] OF char;
```

When this structured variable is declared, the following variables are reserved.

Examine	
	Examine[1]
	Examine[2]
	Examine[3]
	Examine[4]
	Examine[5]

Each component of the array Examine is one *word* in memory, and each word consists of several *bytes.* Let's consider the array Examine, in which each word consists of four bytes. The array can be pictured as

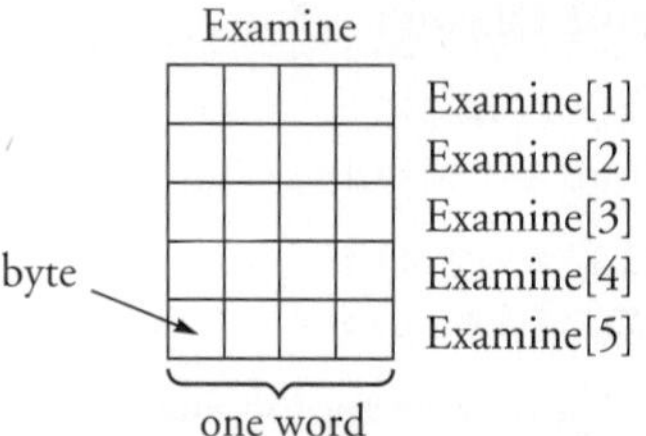

We can assign the word "HELLO" to the array Examine by either

```
Examine[1] := 'H';
Examine[2] := 'E';
Examine[3] := 'L';
Examine[4] := 'L';
Examine[5] := 'O';
```

or

```
Examine := 'HELLO'
```

depending upon which version of Pascal is being used. In either case, after the assignment, the array will look like

Examine

H				Examine[1]
E				Examine[2]
L				Examine[3]
L				Examine[4]
O				Examine[5]

because a byte is the unit of storage necessary for storing a character variable.

As you can see, 20 bytes of storage have been reserved but only five have been used. Pascal provides a more efficient way of defining arrays that does not use unnecessary amounts of storage space. Instead of declaring a variable as an array, we can  declare a variable as a *packed array.* Given this declaration, the computer then packs the data in consecutive bytes.

Packed arrays can be used with any data type. However, it is not always wise to do so because it takes longer to access individual components of a packed array than it does to access individual components of an array that has not been declared as packed. Storage space is saved, but time may be lost. For more information on using arrays that are packed and arrays that are not packed (*unpacked arrays*), see Appendix 8.

Now let's consider the declaration

```
TYPE
  String5 = PACKED ARRAY [1..5] OF char;
VAR
  Examine : String5;
```

and the assignment of the word "HELLO" as before. Using a packed array, we then have the following in memory.

Examine

H	E	L	L	O			

Notice that less than two words (five bytes) are used to store what previously required five words (20 bytes). We can still access the individual components as before. For example

```
writeln (Examine[2]);
```

produces

```
E
```

as a line of output.

Character Strings

Every programming language must be able to handle character data. Names, words, phrases, and sentences are frequently part of some information that must be analyzed. In standard Pascal, character strings are formed by declaring packed arrays of character variables. For example, if the first 20 spaces of an input line are reserved for a customer's name, an appropriate character string could be declared by

```
TYPE
  NameString = PACKED ARRAY [1..20] OF char;
VAR
  Name : NameString;
```

If the line of input is

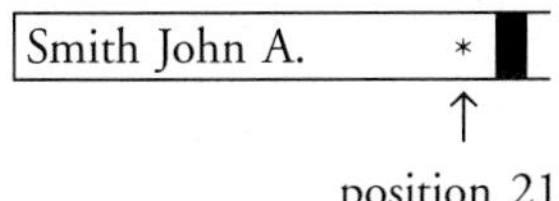

position 21

we can read the name into the packed array by the code

```
FOR J := 1 TO 20 DO
  read (DataFile, Name[J]);
```

Now when we refer to the array Name, we can envision the string

```
'Smith John A.'
```

But since we have declared a fixed length string, the actual string is

```
'Smith John A.       '
```

There are at least three important uses for string variables.

1. String variables of the same length can be compared (Boolean values); this permits alphabetizing.
2. String variables can be written using a single **write** or **writeln** statement; they cannot be read using a single **read** statement.
3. A single assignment statement can assign text to a string variable.

Let's examine each use individually.

Comparing String Variables

Strings of the same length can be compared using the standard relational operators: =, <, >, <>, <=, and >=. For example, if 'Smith' and 'Jones' are strings, then 'Smith' < 'Jones', 'Smith' <> 'Jones', and so on, are all valid Boolean expressions. The Boolean value is determined by the collating sequence. Using the collating sequence for the ASCII character set, the following comparisons yield the indicated values.

Comparison	Boolean Value
'Smith' < 'Jones'	**false**
'Jake' < 'John'	**true**
'ABC' = 'ABA'	**false**
'Smith Doug' < 'Smith John'	**true**

But what happens if we want to evaluate 'William Joe' < 'Williams Bo'? Since a character-by-character comparison is implemented by the computer, no decision is made until the blank following the "m" in William is compared to the "s" in Williams. Using the full ASCII character code, this Boolean expression is **true,** which is how these strings are alphabetized.

Writing String Variables

Recall the declaration

```
TYPE
  NameString = PACKED ARRAY [1..20] OF char;
VAR
  Name : NameString;
```

When data are read from an input file, a loop is used to get the data one character at a time.

```
FOR J := 1 TO 20 DO
  read (DataFile, Name[J]);
```

If we now want to write the string Name, we can use a single **write** or **writeln** statement, such as

```
writeln (Name);
```

It is not necessary to print a string that contains a separate reference to each character.

Assigning Text to a String

T

The third feature of string variables is that a single assignment statement can be used to assign text to a string. If Name is a string of length 20, then

```
Name := 'Smith John A.       ';
```

is a valid statement. Note that there must be exactly 20 characters in the text string in order for this assignment to be valid. The statements

```
Name := 'Smith John A.';
Name := 'Theodore Allen Washington';
```

are both invalid because the text strings are not exactly 20 characters long.

Some standard problems will be encountered when trying to read data into a packed array. First, assume we have to read a line of data that consists of a company name. Further, assume we do not know the length of the name. The input line could be

```
Prudent Investors Company
```

or

```
Com Mfg. Co.
```

If we know the company name will be no more than 30 characters long, we can declare a fixed length array in the following manner.

```
CONST
  MaxLength = 30;
TYPE
  String30 = PACKED ARRAY [1..MaxLength] OF char;
VAR
  CompanyName : String30;
```

The name can then be read by the segment of code

```
StringLength := 0;
WHILE NOT eoln(DataFile) AND (StringLength < 30) DO
  BEGIN
    StringLength := StringLength + 1;
    read (DataFile, CompanyName[StringLength])
  END;  {  of WHILE NOT eoln DO  }
readln (DataFile);
FOR J := (StringLength + 1) TO 30 DO
  CompanyName[J] := ' ' {  blank fills the rest of name  }
```

This will read the name and then fill the array with blanks to the desired length. Applied to the two data lines just mentioned, this segment of code would produce the following character strings.

```
'Prudent Investors Company     '
'Com Mfg. Co.                  '
```

Second, we may want to read data from an input file in which a field of fixed length is used for some character data. For example, suppose the first 30 spaces of an input line are reserved for the company name and that some other information is also to appear on the same line. We could have

```
Prudent Investors Company     1905 South Drive
                              ↑
                           column 31
```

This data can be accessed by the loop

```
FOR J := 1 TO 30 DO
  read (DataFile, CompanyName[J]);
```

Although the second format for an input file is easier to use, it is sometimes difficult to obtain data in such a precise manner. Hence, we must be able to read data both ways.

Strings in a Program

We are now ready to write a short program using packed arrays. Suppose we want to get two names from a data file, arrange them alphabetically, and then print the alphabetized list. Assume the names are in a field of fixed length 25 on two adjacent lines. A first-level pseudocode development is

1. Get the data (**PROCEDURE** GetData)
2. Arrange alphabetically (**PROCEDURE** Alphabetize)
3. Print the data (**PROCEDURE** PrintData)

A procedure to get one line of data is

```
PROCEDURE GetData (VAR Name : NameString);
  VAR
    J, StringLength : integer;
  BEGIN
    StringLength := 0;
    WHILE NOT eoln(DataFile) AND (StringLength < 25) DO
      BEGIN
        StringLength := StringLength + 1;
        read (DataFile, Name[StringLength])
      END;  {  of WHILE NOT eoln DO  }
    readln (DataFile);
    FOR J := (StringLength + 1) TO 25 DO
      Name[J] := ' ' {  blank fills the rest of name  }
  END;  {  of PROCEDURE GetData  }
```

After the two names have been read from the input file, they can be arranged alphabetically by

```
PROCEDURE Alphabetize (VAR Name1, Name2 : NameString);
  VAR
    Temp : NameString;
  BEGIN
    IF Name2 < Name1 THEN
      BEGIN  {  Exchange when necessary  }
        Temp := Name1;
        Name1 := Name2;
        Name2 := Temp
      END  {  of IF...THEN  }
  END;  {  of PROCEDURE Alphabetize  }
```

The procedure for printing the name should include some header and some formatting of the names. For example, suppose you want to say

```
The alphabetized list is below.
--- ------------ ---- -- -----
```

and then print the list indented 10 spaces after skipping two lines. A procedure to do this is

```
PROCEDURE PrintData (Name1, Name2 : NameString);
  BEGIN
    writeln;
    writeln (Skip:10, 'The alphabetized list is below.');
    writeln (Skip:10, '--- ------------ ---- -- -----');
    writeln;
    writeln (Skip:20, Name1);
    writeln (Skip:20, Name2)
  END;  {  of PROCEDURE PrintData  }
```

We can now write the complete program.

```
PROGRAM SampleNames (input, output, DataFile);

CONST
  Skip = ' ';
  MaxLength = 25;

TYPE
  NameString = PACKED ARRAY [1..MaxLength] OF char;

VAR
  Name1, Name2 : NameString;
  DataFile : text;

{*************************************************************}

PROCEDURE GetData (VAR Name : NameString);

  {  Given:   Nothing                                         }
  {  Task:    Read a name from the data file                  }
  {  Return:  One name (string of MaxLength characters)       }
```

```
PROCEDURE GetData (VAR Name : NameString);

  {  Given:   Nothing                                              }
  {  Task:    Read a name from the data file                       }
  {  Return:  One name (string of MaxLength characters)            }

  VAR
    J, StringLength : integer;
  BEGIN
    StringLength := 0;
    WHILE NOT eoln(DataFile) AND (StringLength < MaxLength) DO
      BEGIN
        StringLength := StringLength + 1;
        read (DataFile, Name[StringLength])
      END;
    readln (DataFile);
    FOR J := (StringLength + 1) TO MaxLength DO
      Name[J] := ' ' {  Blank fills the remainder of Name          }
  END;  {  of PROCEDURE GetData  }

{*************************************************************}

PROCEDURE Alphabetize (VAR Name1, Name2 : NameString);

  {  Given:   Two names                                            }
  {  Task:    Sort the names alphabetically                        }
  {  Return:  The names in sorted order                            }

  VAR
    Temp : NameString;
  BEGIN
    IF Name2 < Name1 THEN
      BEGIN                          {  Exchange when necessary  }
        Temp := Name1;
        Name1 := Name2;
        Name2 := Temp
      END  {  of IF...THEN  }
  END;  {  of PROCEDURE Alphabetize  }

{*************************************************************}

PROCEDURE PrintData (Name1, Name2 : NameString);

  {  Given:   Names in alphabetical order                          }
  {  Task:    Print the names                                      }
  {  Return:  Nothing                                              }

  BEGIN
    writeln;
    writeln (Skip:10, 'The alphabetized list is below.');
    writeln (Skip:10, '--- ------------ ---- -- -----');
    writeln;
    writeln (Skip:20, Name1);
    writeln (Skip:20, Name2)
  END;  {  of PROCEDURE PrintData  }
```

```
{*************************************************************}

BEGIN  {  Main program  }
  reset (DataFile);
  GetData (Name1);
  GetData (Name2);
  Alphabetize (Name1, Name2);
  PrintData (Name1, Name2)
END.  {  of main program  }
```

EXERCISES 7.5

1. Indicate which of the following string comparisons are valid. For those that are, indicate whether they are **true** or **false** using the full ASCII character set.
   a. `'Mathematics' <> 'CompScience'`
   b. `'Jefferson' < 'Jeffersonian'`
   c. `'Smith Karen' < 'Smithsonian'`
   d. `'#45' <= '$45'`
   e. `'Hoof in mouth' = 'Foot in door'`
   f. `'453012' > '200000'`
2. Write a test program that allows you to examine the Boolean expression

   `'William Joe' < 'Williams Bo'`
3. Suppose Message is declared as

   ```
   TYPE
     String50 = PACKED ARRAY [1..50] OF char;
   VAR
     Message : String50;
   ```

   and the input file consists of the line

   `To err is human. Computers do not forgive.`

   What output is produced by each of the following segments?

   a.
   ```
   FOR J := 1 TO 50 DO
       IF NOT eoln(Data) THEN
         read (Data, Message[J])
       ELSE
         Message[J] := ' ';
     writeln (Message);
   ```
   b.
   ```
   FOR J := 1 TO 50 DO
       IF NOT eoln(Data) THEN
         read (Data, Message[J])
       ELSE
         Message[J] := ' ';
     Count := 0;
     FOR J := 1 TO 50 DO
       IF Message[J] = ' ' THEN
         Count := Count + 1;
     writeln (Message);
     writeln ('There are', Count:3, ' blanks.':8);
   ```
   c.
   ```
   FOR J := 1 TO 20 DO
       read (Data, Message[2+J]);
     FOR J := 21 TO 40 DO
       Message[J] := ' ';
     FOR J := 41 TO 50 DO
       Message[J] := '*';
     writeln (Message);
   ```

d.
```
FOR J := 1 TO 50 DO
  IF NOT eoln(Data) THEN
    read (Data, Message[J])
  ELSE
    Message[J] := ' ';
writeln (Message);
FOR J := 50 DOWNTO 1 DO
  write (Message[J]);
```

4. Assume the following declarations.

```
TYPE
  String10 = PACKED ARRAY [1..10] OF char;
  String20 = PACKED ARRAY [1..20] OF char;
VAR
  A, B : String10;
  C : String20;
```

a. Indicate whether the following are valid or invalid. For those that are invalid, explain why.

i.
```
A := B;
```
ii.
```
C := A + B;
```
iii.
```
FOR J := 1 TO 20 DO
   C[J] := A[J] + B[J];
```
iv.
```
FOR J := 1 TO 20 DO
  IF J <= 10 THEN
    A[J] := C[J]
  ELSE
    B[J-10] := C[J];
```

b. Write a segment of code that will make the string C consist of the strings A and B, where the lesser (alphabetically) of A and B is the first half of C.

5. Assume a packed array Message of length 100 has been declared and data have been read into it from an input file. Write a segment of code to count the number of occurrences of the letter "M" in the string Message.

6. Write a test program to see what happens if you try to read in an entire packed array with one **read** or **readln** statement.

7.6 Searching Algorithms

OBJECTIVES

- to be able to use a sequential search to find the first occurrence of a value
- to be able to use a sequential search to find all occurrences of a value
- to be able to use a binary search to find a value
- to understand the relative efficiency of a binary search compared to a sequential search

The need to search an array for a value is a common problem. For example, we may wish to replace a test score for a student, delete a name from a directory or mailing list, or upgrade the pay scale for certain employees. These and other problems require us to be able to examine elements in some list until the desired value is located. When it is found, some action is taken. In this section, we assume all lists are nonempty.

Sequential Search

The first searching algorithm we will examine is the most common method, a *sequential (linear) search*. This process is accomplished by examining the first element in some list and then proceeding to examine the elements in the order in which they appear until a match is found. Variations of this basic process include searching a sorted list for the first occurrence of a value, searching a sorted list for all occurrences of a value, and searching an unsorted list for the first occurrence of a value.

To illustrate a sequential search, suppose we have an array A of integers and we want to find the first occurrence of some particular value (Num). If the desired value is located as we search the array, its position is printed. If the value is not in the array, an appropriate message should be printed. The code for such a search is

```
Index := 1;
WHILE (Num <> A[Index]) AND (Index < Length) DO
  Index := Index + 1;
```

This can be written as a procedure. For example, **PROCEDURE** Search, which searches for the desired number, follows.

```
PROCEDURE Search   (VAR A : NumList;
                    Num, Length : integer;
                    VAR Index : integer;
                    VAR Found : boolean);

  {  Given :   An array A; a number Num to search for  }
  {                 the array length Length; and a      }
  {                 boolean flag Found                  }
  {  Task:     Search the array for the first          }
  {                 occurrence of Num; Found should     }
  {                 indicate whether or not a match     }
  {                 is found                            }
  {  Return:   The index of the number being search     }
  {                 for; a boolean value indicating     }
  {                 whether or not the number has       }
  {                 been located                        }

  VAR
    Index : integer;
  BEGIN
    Found := false;
    Index := 1;
    WHILE (Num <> A[Index]) AND (Index < Length) DO
      Index := Index + 1;
    IF Num = A[Index] THEN
      Found := true
  END;  {  of PROCEDURE Search  }
```

This procedure can be called by

```
Search (List, Num, Length, Index, Found);
```

A reasonable message for output is

```
IF Found THEN
  writeln (Num, ' is in position', Index:5)
ELSE
  writeln (Num, ' is not in the list.')
```

Now let's consider some variations of this problem. Our code works for both a sorted list and an unsorted list. However, if we are searching a sorted list, the algorithm can be improved. For example, if the array components are sorted from low to high, we need to continue the search only until the value in an array component exceeds the value of Num. At that point, there is no need to examine the remaining components. The only change required in the loop for searching is to replace

```
Num <> A[Index]
```

with

```
Num > A[Index]
```

Thus, we have

```
Index := 1;
WHILE (Num > A[Index]) AND (Index < Length) DO
  Index := Index + 1;
```

A relatively easy modification of the sequential search is to examine a list for all occurrences of some value. In searching an array, we would generally print the positions and values when a match is found. To illustrate, if A is an array of integers and Num has an integer value, we can search A for the number of occurrences of Num by

```
Count := 0;
FOR Index := 1 TO Length DO
  IF Num = A[Index] THEN
    BEGIN
      Count := Count + 1;
      writeln (Num, ' is in position', Index:5)
    END;
```

This code works for an unsorted list. A modification of the code for working with a sorted list is included as an exercise at the end of this section.

Binary Search

Searching relatively small lists sequentially does not require much computer time. However, when the lists get longer (for example, telephone directories and lists of credit card customers), sequential searches are inefficient. In a sense, they correspond to looking up a word in the dictionary by starting at the first word and proceeding word-by-word until the desired word is found. Since extra computer time means considerably extra expense for most companies where large amounts of data must be frequently searched, a more efficient method of searching is needed.

If the list has been sorted, it can be searched for a particular value by a method referred to as a binary search. Essentially, a *binary search* consists of examining the middle value of an array to see which half contains the desired value. The middle value of this half is then examined to see which half of the half contains the value in question. This halving process is continued until the value is located or it is determined that the value is not in the list. (Remember, in order to use a binary search, the list must be sorted; the sorting process has its own costs, which should be evaluated, but this subject is outside the scope of this text.)

The code for this process is relatively short. If A is the array to be searched for Num and if First, Mid, and Last are integer variables such that First contains the index of the first possible position to be searched and Last contains the index of the last possible position, the code for searching a list in ascending order is

```
Found := false;
WHILE NOT Found AND (First <= Last) DO
  BEGIN
    Mid := (First + Last) DIV 2;
    IF Num < A[Mid] THEN
      Last := Mid - 1
```

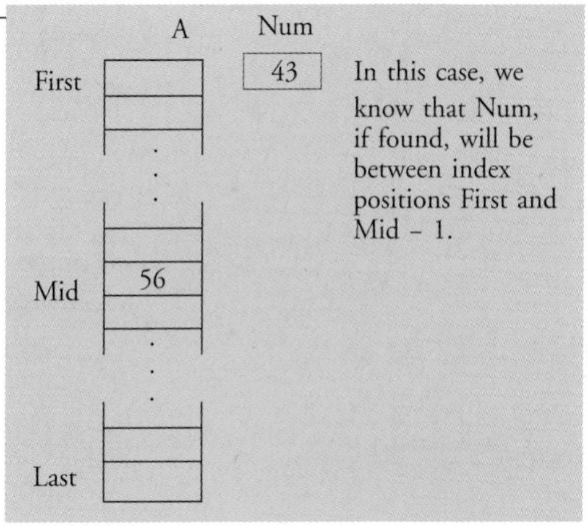

A Num
First 43
Mid 56
Last

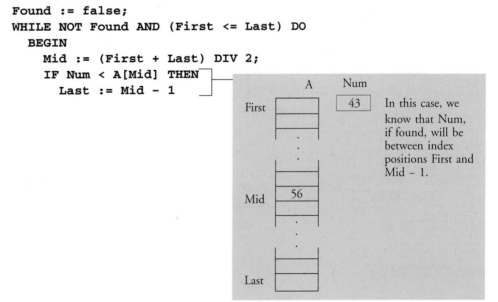

In this case, we know that Num, if found, will be between index positions First and Mid − 1.

```
    ELSE IF Num > A[Mid] THEN
      First := Mid + 1
    ELSE
      Found := true
  END;
```

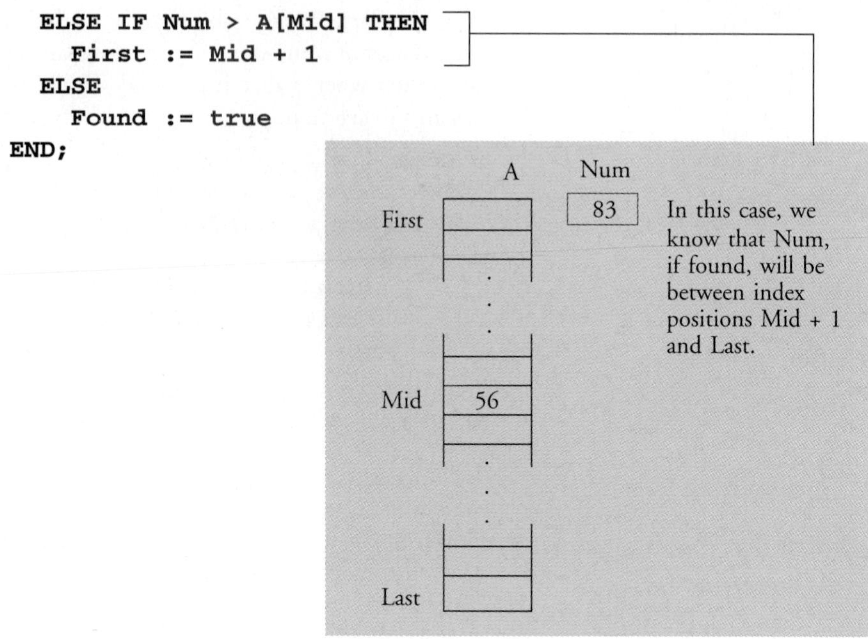
A
Num
83
First
Mid
56
Last
In this case, we know that Num, if found, will be between index positions Mid + 1 and Last.

When this loop is executed, it is exited when the value is located or it is determined that the value is not in the list. Depending upon what is to be done with the value being looked for, we can modify action at the bottom of the loop or use the values in Found and Mid outside the loop. For example, if we just want to know where the value is, we can change

```
Found := true
```

to

```
BEGIN
  Found := true;
  writeln (Num, ' is in position', Mid:5)
END;
```

Before continuing, let's walk through this search to better understand how it works. Assume A is the array

4	7	19	25	36	37	50	100	101	205	220	271	306	321
A[1]													A[14]

with values as indicated. Further assume Num contains the value 25. Then First, Last, and Num have the initial values

1	14	25
First	Last	Num

A listing of values by each pass through the loop produces

	First	Last	Mid	A[Mid]	Found
Before loop	1	14	Undefined	Undefined	**false**
After first pass	1	6	7	50	**false**
After second pass	4	6	3	19	**false**
After third pass	4	4	5	36	**false**
After fourth pass	4	4	4	25	**true**

To illustrate what happens when the value being looked for is not in the array, suppose Num contains 210. The listing of values then produces

	First	Last	Mid	A[Mid]	Found
Before loop	1	14	Undefined	Undefined	**false**
After first pass	8	14	7	50	**false**
After second pass	8	10	11	220	**false**
After third pass	10	10	9	101	**false**
After fourth pass	11	10	10	205	**false**

At this stage, First > Last and the loop is exited.

Inserting and Deleting in a Sorted Array

Arrays are typically searched because we want to either insert an element into the array or delete an element from the array. To illustrate, let's consider array A

2	5	8	10	10	12	15	18	21	30
A[1]	A[2]								A[10]

If we remove element 12 from the array, we end up with

2	5	8	10	10	15	18	21	30
A[1]	A[2]							A[9]

Note 12 has been deleted from the array and each element listed "after" 12 in the array has been "advanced" one position.

To illustrate what happens when an element is to be inserted into an array, again consider array A

2	5	8	10	10	12	15	18	21	30
A[1]	A[2]								A[10]

If we want to insert 17 into the sorted array, we first determine it belongs between 15 and 18. We then reassign elements 18, 21, and 30 to produce

2	5	8	10	10	12	15		18	21	30
A[1]	A[2]						↑ 17 goes here			A[11]

The number 17 is then assigned to the appropriate array component to produce the array

2	5	8	10	10	12	15	17	18	21	30
A[1]	A[2]									A[11]

Writing the code for inserting and deleting elements in a sorted array is deferred to the exercises at the end of this section.

Relative Efficiency of Searches

Now let's examine briefly the efficiency of a binary search compared to a sequential search. For purposes of this discussion, assume a sequential search on a list of 15 items requires at most 15 microseconds. The nature of a sequential search is such that every time the list length is doubled, the maximum searching time is also doubled. Figure 7.1 illustrates this increase.

◆ FIGURE 7.1
Sequential search

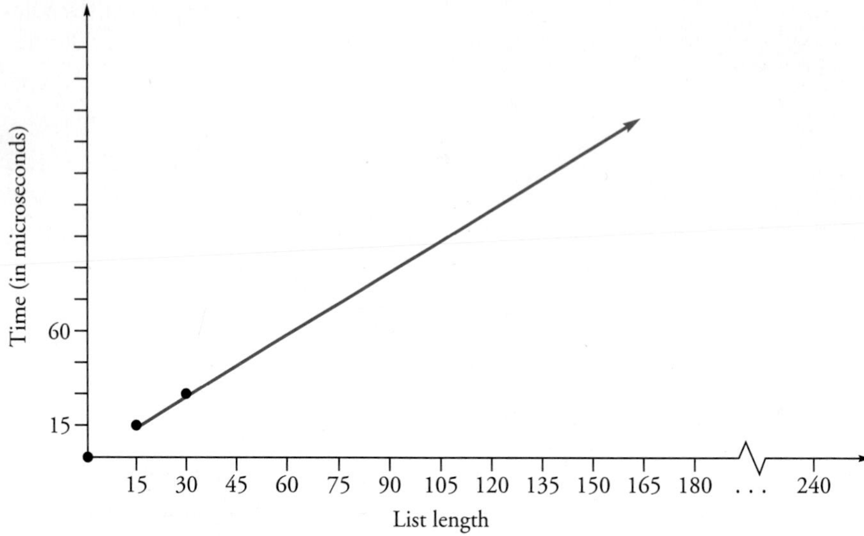

Next, assume a list of 15 items requires a maximum of 60 microseconds when searched by a binary search. Since this process consists of successively halving the list, at most four passes will be required to locate the value. This means each pass uses 15 microseconds. When the list length is doubled, it requires only one more pass. Thus, a list of 30 items requires 75 microseconds and a list of 60 items requires 90 microseconds. This is shown graphically in Figure 7.2.

◆ FIGURE 7.2
Binary search

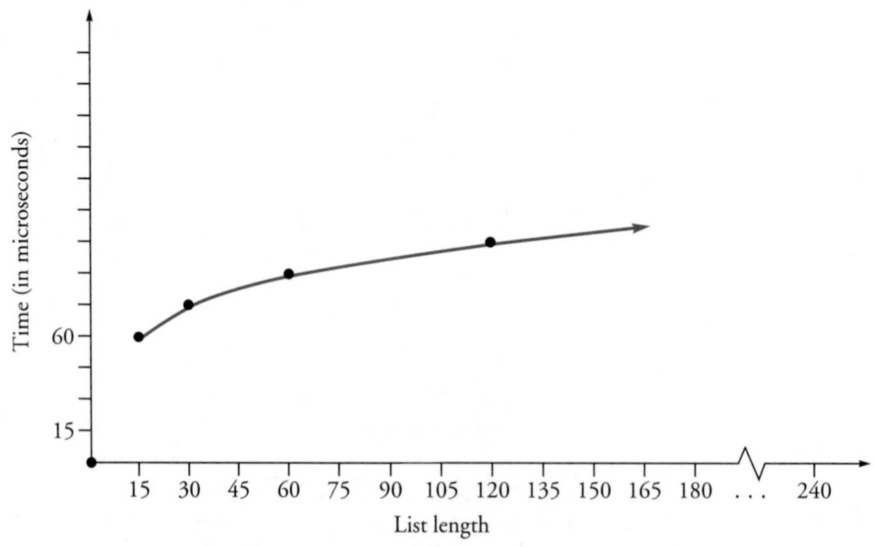

◆ **FIGURE 7.3**
Sequential search versus binary search

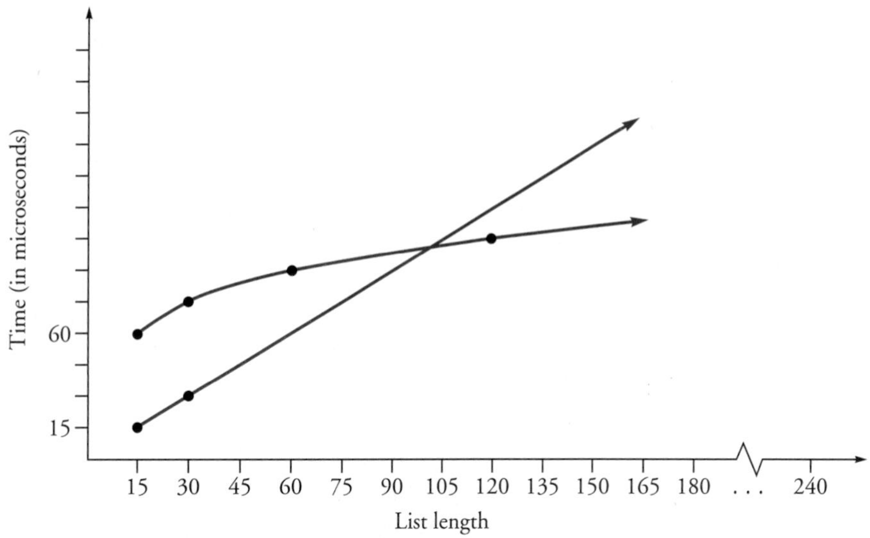

The comparison of these sequential and binary searches is shown in Figure 7.3.

EXERCISES 7.6

1. Write a sequential search using a **FOR** loop to locate and print all occurrences of the same value.
2. Discuss whether or not **PROCEDURE** Search can be rewritten as a function.
3. Modify the sequential search by putting a counter in the loop to count how many passes are made when searching a sorted array for a value. Write and run a program that uses this version on lists of length 15, 30, 60, 120, and 240. In each case, search for a value that is
   a. In the first half
   b. In the second half
   c. Not there

   Plot your results on a graph.
4. Repeat Exercise 3 for a binary search.
5. Suppose the array A is

18	25	37	92	104
A[1]				A[5]

   Trace the values using a binary search to look for
   a. 18
   b. 92
   c. 76
6. Write a procedure to search a sorted list and remove all duplicate elements.
7. Suppose a sorted list of social security numbers is in secondary storage in a file named StudentNum.
   a. Show how this file can be searched for a certain number using a sequential search.
   b. Show how this file can be searched for a certain number using a binary search.
   c. Show how a binary search can be used to indicate where a new number can be inserted in proper order.
   d. Show how a number can be deleted from the file.

8. Write a procedure to read text from a data file and determine the number of occurrences of each vowel.

9. Using a binary search on an array of length 35, what is the maximum number of passes through the loop that can be made when searching for a value?

10. Using worst-case possibilities of 3 microseconds for a sequential search of a list of 10 items and 25 microseconds for a binary search of the same list, construct a graph illustrating the relative efficiency for these two methods applied to lists of longer lengths.

11. Modify the sequential search that you developed in Exercise 1 to list all occurrences of a value so it can be used on a sorted list; that is, have the search stop after the desired value has been passed in the list.

12. Discuss methods that can be used to design programs to guard against searching empty lists.

13. Write a procedure to

  a. Insert an element into a sorted array.

  b. Delete an element from a sorted array.

14. The length of a string is the number of positions from the first nonblank character to the last nonblank character. Thus, the packed array

T	h	i	s		i	s		a		s	t	r	i	n	g	.													

would have a length of 17. Write a function that receives a packed array of type [1 . . 30] of **char** and returns the length of the string.

FOCUS ON PROGRAM DESIGN

The sample program for this chapter features the use of arrays and subprograms. Since sorting an array is a common practice, it has been included as part of the program. Specifically, suppose the Home Sales Realty Company, Inc., wants to print a list containing the amount of all sales for a month. Each sale amount is recorded on a separate line of input, and the number of homes sold is less than 20. Write a program to

1. Read the data from the input file.

2. Print the data in the order in which it is read with a suitable header and formatting.

3. Print a sorted list (high to low) of sales with a suitable header and formatting.

4. Print the total number of sales for the month, the total amount of sales, the average sale price, and the company commission (7 percent).

Sample input would be

```
 85000
 76234
115100
 98200
121750
 76700
```

where each line represents the sale price of a home. Typical output would include an unsorted list of sales, a sorted list of sales, and appropriate summary data. A first-level pseudocode development is

1. Get data (**PROCEDURE** GetData)
2. Print header (**PROCEDURE** PrintH1)
3. Print unsorted list (**PROCEDURE** PrintList)

4. Sort list (**PROCEDURE** Sort)
5. Print header (**PROCEDURE** PrintH2)
6. Print sorted list (**PROCEDURE** PrintList)
7. Compute data (**FUNCTION** Total and **PROCEDURE** Compute)
8. Print results (**PROCEDURE** PrintResults)

Notice **PROCEDURE** PrintList is called twice and **PROCEDURE** PrintResults includes output for total number of sales, total amount of sales, average sale price, and company commission, all printed with suitable headings.

A structure chart for the program is given in Figure 7.4.

◆ FIGURE 7.4
Structure chart for Home Sales Realty Company, Inc., program

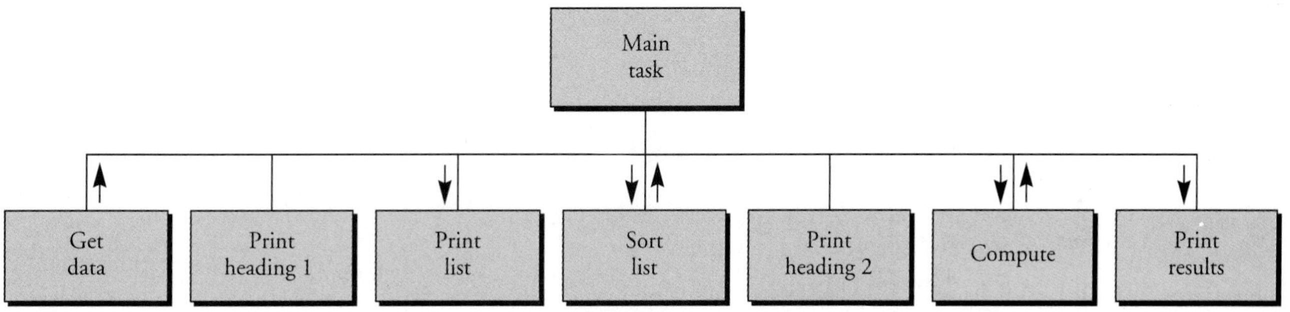

Module specifications for the main modules are

1. GetData Module
   Data received: None
   Information returned: Sales for a month
   Number of sales
   Logic: Use a **WHILE** loop to read entries into an array.
2. PrintHeading1 Module
   Data received: None
   Information returned: None
   Logic: Use **writeln** statements to print a suitable heading for unsorted list.
3. PrintList Module
   Data received: Array of sales with number of sales
   Information returned: None
   Logic: Use a **FOR** loop with the array length as a loop control variable to print the list of sales for a month.
4. Sort Module
   Data received: Unsorted array of sales
   Number of sales
   Information returned: Sorted array of sales
   Logic: Use a selection sort to sort the array.
5. PrintHeading2 Module
   Data received: None
   Information returned: None
   Logic: Use **writeln** statements to print a suitable heading for the sorted list.

6. Compute Module
   Data received: Array of sales with number of sales
   Information returned: Total sales
   Average sale
   Company commission
   Logic: Use a function to compute the total sales.
   Use a procedure to compute the average sale.
   Compute company commission by using the defined constant CommissionRate.

7. PrintResults Module
   Data received: Number of sales
   Total sales
   Average sales
   Company commission
   Information returned: None
   Logic: Use **writeln** statements to print a summary report.

The main program is

```
BEGIN  {  Main program  }
  GetData (JuneSales, Length);
  PrintHeading1;
  PrintList (JuneSales, Length);
  Sort (JuneSales, Length);
  PrintHeading2;
  PrintList (JuneSales, Length);
  Compute (TotalSales, AverageSale, CompanyCom, JuneSales, Length);
  PrintResults (TotalSales, AverageSale, CompanyCom, Length)
END.  {  of main program  }
```

The complete program for this problem follows.

```
PROGRAM MonthlyList (input, output, SalesList);

{  This program illustrates the use of arrays with procedures and   }
{  functions.  Note the use of both value and variable parameters.  }
{  Also note a procedure is used to sort the array.                 }

CONST
  Skip = ' ';
  CommissionRate = 0.07;
  MaxLength = 20;

TYPE
  List = ARRAY [1..MaxLength] OF real;

VAR
  JuneSales : List;                  {  Number of June sales        }
  TotalSales,                        {  Total of June sales         }
  AverageSale,                       {  Amount of average sale      }
  CompanyCom : real;                 {  Commission for the company  }
  Length : integer;                  {  Array length of values      }
  SalesList : text;                  {  Data file of sales          }
```

```
{****************************************************************** }

PROCEDURE GetData (VAR JuneSales : List;
                   VAR Length : integer);

  {  Given:   Nothing                                                }
  {  Task:    Read selling prices into array JuneSales               }
  {  Return:  Array of JuneSales and array length                    }

  BEGIN                                                                 1
    Length := 0;
    WHILE NOT eof(SalesList) AND (Length < MaxLength) DO
      BEGIN
        Length := Length + 1;
        readln (SalesList, JuneSales[Length])
      END  {  of WHILE NOT eof  }
  END;  {  of PROCEDURE GetData  }

{****************************************************************** }

PROCEDURE PrintHeading1;

  {  Given:   Nothing                                                }
  {  Task:    Print a heading for the unsorted list of sales         }
  {  Return:  Nothing                                                }

  BEGIN                                                                 2
    writeln ('An unsorted list of sales for the');
    writeln ('month of June is as follows:');
    writeln ('--------------------------------');
    writeln
  END;  {  of PROCEDURE PrintHeading1  }

{****************************************************************** }

PROCEDURE PrintList (JuneSales : List;
                     Length : integer);

  {  Given:   An unsorted array (with length) of sales for June      }
  {  Task:    Print the list                                         }
  {  Return:  Nothing                                                }
                                                                        3
  VAR
    J : integer;
  BEGIN
    FOR J := 1 TO Length DO
      writeln (Skip:4, '<', J:2, '>', '$':2, JuneSales[J]:11:2)
  END;  {  of PROCEDURE PrintList  }

{******************************************************************}
```

```
PROCEDURE Swap (VAR Num1, Num2 : real);

  {  Given:   Two reals in Num1 and Num2                                }
  {  Task:    Interchange their values                                  }
  {  Return:  Interchanged values                                       }
  VAR
    Temp : real;
  BEGIN
    Temp := Num1;
    Num1 := Num2;
    Num2 := Temp
  END;  {  of PROCEDURE Swap  }

{*************************************************************}

PROCEDURE Sort (VAR JuneSales : List;
                Length : integer);

  {  Given:   An unsorted array (with length) of sales for June     }      4
  {  Task:    Use a selection sort to sort the list                 }
  {  Return:  A sorted list of sales for June                       }

  VAR
    J, K, Index : integer;
    Temp : real;
  BEGIN
    FOR J := 1 TO Length - 1 DO
      BEGIN
        Index := J;
        FOR K := J + 1 TO Length DO
          IF JuneSales[K] > JuneSales[Index] THEN
            Index := K;
        IF Index <> J THEN
          Swap (JuneSales[Index], JuneSales[J])
      END  {  of FOR J loop  }
  END;  {  of PROCEDURE Sort  }

{*************************************************************}

PROCEDURE PrintHeading2;

  {  Given:   Nothing                                               }
  {  Task:    Print a heading for the sorted list of sales          }
  {  Return:  Nothing                                               }

  BEGIN                                                                    5
    writeln;
    writeln ('Sales for the month of June');
    writeln ('sorted from high to low are:');
    writeln ('---------------------------');
    writeln
  END;  {  of PROCEDURE PrintHeading2  }

{*************************************************************}
```

```
FUNCTION Total (JuneSales : List;
                Length : integer) : real;

  {  Given:   An array (with length) of sales for June           }
  {  Task:    Sum the array components                           }
  {  Return:  Total of sales for June                            }

  VAR
    J : integer;
    Sum : real;
  BEGIN
    Sum := 0;
    FOR J := 1 TO Length DO
      Sum := Sum + JuneSales[J];
    Total := Sum
  END;  {  of FUNCTION Total  }

{*******************************************************************}   6

PROCEDURE Compute (VAR TotalSales, AverageSale, CompanyCom : real;
                   VAR JuneSales : List;
                   Length : integer);

  {  Given:   An array (with length) of sales for June           }
  {  Task:    Compute TotalSales, AverageSale, and CompanyCom    }
  {               for the month of June                          }
  {  Return:  TotalSales, AverageSale, and CompanyCom            }

  BEGIN
    TotalSales := Total(JuneSales, Length);
    AverageSale := TotalSales / Length;
    CompanyCom := TotalSales * CommissionRate
  END;  {  of PROCEDURE Compute  }

{*******************************************************************}

PROCEDURE PrintResults (TotalSales, AverageSale, CompanyCom : real;
                        Length : integer);

  {  Given:   TotalSales, AverageSale, CompanyCom, and number    }
  {               of sales (Length) for June                     }
  {  Task:    Print summary information for the month            }
  {  Return:  Nothing                                            }

  BEGIN
    writeln;
    writeln ('There were', Length:2, ' sales during June.');   7
    writeln;
    writeln ('The total sales were', '$':2, TotalSales:12:2);
    writeln;
    writeln ('The average sale was', '$':2, AverageSale:12:2);
    writeln;
    writeln ('The company commission was', '$':2, CompanyCom:12:2);
    writeln
  END;  {  of PROCEDURE PrintResults  }
```

```
{*****************************************************************}

BEGIN  {  Main program  }
  reset (SalesList);
  GetData (JuneSales, Length);
  PrintHeading1;
  PrintList (JuneSales, Length);
  Sort (JuneSales, Length);
  PrintHeading2;
  PrintList (JuneSales, Length);
  Compute (TotalSales, AverageSale, CompanyCom, JuneSales, Length);
  PrintResults (TotalSales, AverageSale, CompanyCom, Length)
END.  {  of main program  }
```

The output for this program is

```
An unsorted list of sales for the
month of June is as follows:
---------------------------------

    < 1> $   85000.00
    < 2> $   76234.00
    < 3> $  115100.00
    < 4> $   98200.00
    < 5> $  121750.00
    < 6> $   76700.00

Sales for the month of June
sorted from high to low are:
----------------------------

    < 1> $  121750.00
    < 2> $  115100.00
    < 3> $   98200.00
    < 4> $   85000.00
    < 5> $   76700.00
    < 6> $   76234.00

There were 6 sales during June.

The total sales were $   572984.00

The average sale was $    95497.33

The company commission was $    40108.88
```

RUNNING AND DEBUGGING HINTS

1. Be careful not to misuse type identifiers. For example, in

```
TYPE
  String = PACKED ARRAY [1..10] OF char;
VAR
  Word : String;
```

String is a data type; hence, a reference such as String := 'First name' is incorrect.

2. Do not use a subscript that is out of range. Suppose we have

```
VAR
  List : ARRAY [1..6] OF integer;
```

An inadvertent reference such as

```
FOR J := 1 TO 10 DO
  writeln (List[J]);
```

may produce an error message indicating that the subscript is out of range.

3. Counters are frequently used with loops and arrays. Be sure the final value is the correct value. For example

```
Count := 1;
WHILE NOT eof(<file name>) DO
  BEGIN
    readln (<file name>, A[Count]);
    Count := Count + 1
  END;
```

used on the data file

| 18 ■ 21 ■ 33 ■ ■ |

will have a value of 4 in Count when this loop is exited. This could be corrected by rewriting the segment as

```
Count := 0;
WHILE NOT eof(<file name>) DO
  BEGIN
    Count := Count + 1;
    readln (<file name>, A[Count])
  END;
```

4. Comparing array components can lead to errors in using subscripts. Two common misuses are
   a. Attempting to compare A[J] to A[J+1]. If this does not stop at array length – 1, then J + 1 will be out of range.
   b. Attempting to compare A[J–1] to A[J]. This presents the same problem at the beginning of an array. Remember, J – 1 cannot have a value less than the initial index value.
5. Make sure the array index is correctly initialized. For example

```
J := 0;
WHILE NOT eof(<file name>) DO
  BEGIN
    J := J + 1;
    readln (<file name>, A[J])
  END;
```

Note the first value is then read into A[1].

(*continued*)

RUNNING AND DEBUGGING HINTS (CONTINUED)

6. After using a sequential search, make sure you check to see if the value has been found. For example, if Num contains the value 3 and A is the array

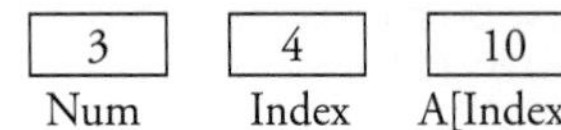

the search

```
Index := 1;
WHILE (Num <> A[Index]) AND (Index < Length) DO
  Index := Index + 1;
```

yields values

3	4	10
Num	Index	A[Index]

Depending upon program use, you should check for Num = A[Index] or use a Boolean flag to indicate if a match has been found.

SUMMARY

Key Terms

abstract data type (ADT)
array
binary search
byte
component (element) of an array
data abstraction
index (subscript)
index type
packed array
selection sort
sequential (linear) search
string data type
unpacked array
word

Keywords

ARRAY **PACKED** **string**

Key Concepts

- An array is a structured variable; a single declaration can reserve several variables.
- It is good practice to define array types in the **TYPE** definition section and then to declare a variable of that type; for example

```
CONST
  ListMax = 30;
TYPE
  NumList = ARRAY [1..ListMax] OF real;
VAR
  List : NumList
```

- Arrays can be visualized as lists; thus, the previous array could be envisioned as

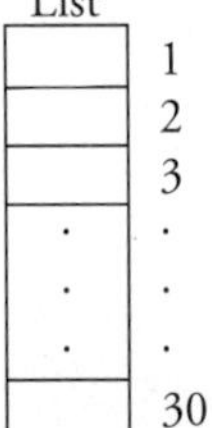

- Each component of an array is a variable of the declared type and can be used in the same way as any other variable of that type.
- Loops can be used to read data into arrays; for example

```
J := 0;
WHILE NOT eof(<file name>) AND (J < MaxLength) DO
  BEGIN
    J := J + 1;
    readln (<file name>, List[J])
  END;
```

- Loops can be used to print data from arrays; for example, if Score is an array of 20 test scores, they can be printed by

```
FOR J := 1 TO 20 DO
  writeln (Score[J]);
```

- Manipulating components of an array is generally accomplished by using the index as a loop variable; for example, assuming the previous Score, to find the smallest value in the array we can use

```
Small := Score[1];
FOR J := 2 TO 20 DO
  IF Score[J] < Small THEN
    Small := Score[J];
```

- A selection sort is one method of sorting elements in an array from high to low or low to high; for example, if A is an array of length *n*, a low-to-high sort is

```
FOR J := 1 TO N - 1 DO
  BEGIN
    Index := J;
    FOR K := J + 1 TO N DO
      IF A[K] < A[Index] THEN
        Index := K;
    IF Index <> J THEN
      BEGIN
        Temp := A[Index];
        A[Index]:= A[J];
        A[J]:= Temp
      END  {  of exchange  }
  END;  {  of selection sort  }
```

- A bubble sort sorts an array by comparing consecutive elements in the array and exchanging them if they are out of order; several passes through the array are made until the list is sorted.
- When arrays are to be passed to subprograms, the type should be defined in the **TYPE** section; thus, we could have

```
TYPE
  List200 = ARRAY [1..200] OF real;

PROCEDURE Practice (X : List200);
```

- If the array being passed is a variable parameter, it should be declared accordingly; for example

```
PROCEDURE GetData (VAR X : List200);
```

- Sorting arrays is conveniently done by using procedures; such procedures facilitate program design.

- Data abstraction is the process of separating a conceptual definition of a data structure from its implementation details.
- An abstract data type (ADT) consists of a class of objects, a defined set of properties for these objects, and a set of operations for processing the objects.
- Character strings can be formed by declaring packed arrays of character variables to reduce the memory required for string storage and manipulation; a typical packed array declaration is

```
TYPE
  String20 = PACKED ARRAY [1..20] OF char;
VAR
  Name : String20;
```

- Character strings (packed arrays of characters) can be compared; this facilitates alphabetizing a list of names.
- Character strings can be printed using a single **write** or **writeln** statement; thus, if Name is a packed array of characters, it can be printed by

```
writeln (Name:30);
```

- Packed arrays of characters must still be read one character at a time.
- A single assignment statement can be used to assign a string to a packed array of the same length; for example,

```
Name := 'Smith John';
```

- A sequential search of a list consists of examining the first item in a list and then proceeding through the list in sequence until the desired value is found or the end of the list is reached; code for this search is

```
Index := 1;
WHILE (Num <> A[Index]) AND (Index < Length) DO
  Index := Index + 1;
```

- A binary search of a list consists of deciding which half of the list contains the value in question and then which half of that half contains the value, and so on; code for this search is

```
Found := false;
WHILE NOT Found AND (First <= Last) DO
  BEGIN
    Mid := (First + Last) DIV 2;
    IF Num < A[Mid] THEN
      Last := Mid - 1
    ELSE IF Num > A[Mid] THEN
      First := Mid + 1
    ELSE
      Found := true
  END;
```

PROGRAMMING PROBLEMS AND PROJECTS

1. Write a program to read an unknown number of integer test scores from an input file (assume at most 150 scores). Print out the original list of scores, the scores sorted from low to high, the scores sorted from high to low, the highest score, the lowest score, and the average score.
2. Write a program to help you balance your checkbook. The input should consist of the beginning balance and then a sequence of transactions, each followed by

a transaction code. Deposits are followed by a D and withdrawals are followed by a W. The output should consist of a list of transactions, a running balance, an ending balance, the number of withdrawals, and the number of deposits. Include an appropriate message for overdrawn accounts.

3. Write a program to read a line of text as input. Print out the original line of text, the line of text in reverse order, and the number of vowels contained in the line.

4. Write a program that sorts data of type **real** as they are read from the input file. Do this by putting the first data item in the first component of an array and then inserting each subsequent number in the array in order from high to low. Print out the sorted array. Assume there are at most 25 numbers.

5. A palindrome is a word (or number) that is the same forward and backward. Write a program to read several lines of text as input. Inspect each word to see if it is a palindrome. The output should list all palindromes and a count of the number of palindromes in the message.

6. One of the problems faced by designers of word processors is to print text without separating a word at the end of a line. Write a program to read several lines of text as input. Then print the message with each line starting in column 10 and no line exceeding column 70. No word should be separated at the end of a line.

7. Your local state university has to raise funds for an art center. The first step is to contact 20 previously identified donors and ask for additional donations. Because the donors wish to remain anonymous, only the respective totals of their previous donations are listed in a data file. After they are contacted, the additional donations are listed at the end of the data file in the same order as the first 20 entries. Write a computer program to read the first 20 entries into one array and the second 20 entries into a second array. Compute the previous total donations and the new donations for the art center. Print the following.

   a. The list of previous donations
   b. The list of new donations
   c. An unsorted list of total donations
   d. A sorted list of total donations
   e. Total donations before the fund drive
   f. Total donations for the art center
   g. The maximum donation for the art center

8. Write a program that can be used as a text analyzer. Your program should be capable of reading an input file and keeping track of the frequency of occurrence of each letter of the alphabet. There should also be a count of all characters (including blanks) encountered that are not in the alphabet. Your output should be the data file (printed line-by-line) followed by a histogram reflecting the frequency of occurrence of each letter in the alphabet. For example, the following histogram indicates five occurrences of a, two of b, and three of c.

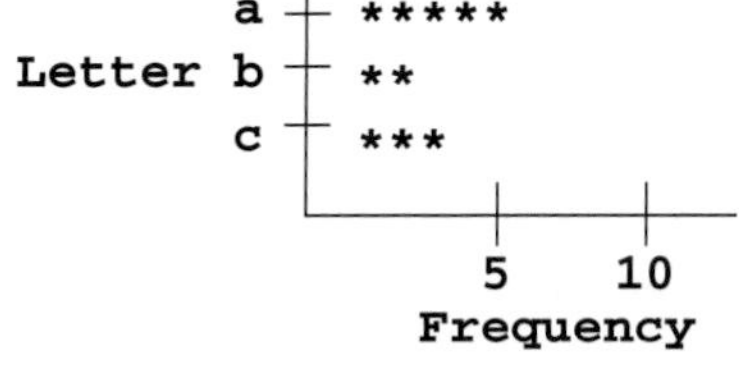

9. The Third Interdenominational Church has on file a list of all of its benefactors (a maximum of 20 names, each up to 30 characters) and an unknown number of amounts that each has donated to the church. You have been asked to write a program to do the following.
   a. Print the name of each donor and the amount (in descending order) of any donations given by that donor.
   b. Print the total amounts in ascending order.
   c. Print the grand total of all donations.
   d. Print the largest single amount donated and the name of the benefactor who made this donation.
10. Read in a list of 50 integers from the data file NumberList. Place the even numbers in an array called Even, the odd numbers in an array called Odd, and the negatives in an array called Negative. Print all three arrays after all numbers have been read.
11. Read in 300 real numbers. Print the average of the numbers followed by all the numbers that are greater than the average.
12. Read in the names of five candidates in a class election and the number of votes received by each. Print the list of candidates, the number of votes each received, and the percentage of the total vote each received sorted in order from the winner to the person with the fewest votes. Assume all names are 20 characters in length.
13. In many sports events, contestants are rated by judges, with an average score being determined by discarding the highest and lowest scores and averaging the remaining scores. Write a program in which eight scores are entered, and the average score for the contestant is computed.
14. Given a list of 20 test scores (integers), print the score that is nearest to the average.
15. The Game of Nim is played with three piles of stones. There are three stones in the first pile, five stones in the second, and eight stones in the third. Two players alternate taking as many stones as they like from any one pile. Play continues until someone is forced to take the last stone. The person taking the last stone loses. Write a program that permits two people to play the game of Nim; use an array to keep track of the number of stones in each pile.
16. There is an effective strategy that can virtually guarantee victory in the game of Nim. Devise a strategy, and modify the program in Problem 15 so the computer plays against a person. Your program should be virtually unbeatable if the proper strategy is developed.
17. The median of a set of numbers is the value in the middle of the set if the set is arranged in order. The mode is the number listed most often. Given a list of 21 numbers, print the median and mode of the list.
18. Rewrite Problem 17 to permit the use of any length list of numbers.
19. The standard deviation is a statistic frequently used in education measurement. Write a program that, given a list of test scores, will find and print the standard deviation of the numbers. If the N scores are represented by $X_1, X_2, \ldots, X_N$ and the average score is denoted by $\overline{X}$, then the standard deviation is

$$\sqrt{\frac{\sum_{i=1}^{N} (X_i - \overline{X})^2}{N - 1}}$$

20. Revise Problem 19 so that after the standard deviation is printed, you can print a list of test scores that are more than one standard deviation below the average and a list of the scores that are more than one standard deviation above the average.

21. The z-score is defined as the score earned on a test divided by the standard deviation. Given a data file containing an unknown number of test scores (at most 100), print a list showing each test score (from highest to lowest) and the corresponding z-score.

■ **22.** Salespeople for the Wellsville Wholesale Company earn a commission based upon their sales. The commission rates are shown in the following table.

Sales	Commission
$0–1000	3%
1001–5000	4.5%
5001–10,000	5.25%
over 10,000	6%

In addition, any salesperson who sells above the average of all salespeople receives a $50 bonus, and the top salesperson receives an additional $75 bonus. Given the names of 20 salespeople and the amounts sold by each, write a program that prints a table showing the salesperson's name, the amount sold, the commission rate, and the total amount earned. The average sale should also be printed.

23. Ms. Alicia Citizen, your school's Student Government advisor, has come to you for help. She wants you to write a program to total votes for the next Student Government election. There are 15 candidates running in the election and five positions to be filled. Each person can vote for up to five candidates. The five highest vote-getters will be the winners.

A data file called VoteList contains a list of candidates (by candidate number) voted for by each student. Any line of the file may contain up to five numbers; if it contains more than five numbers, it is discarded as a void ballot. Write a program to read the file and print a list of the total votes received by each candidate. Also print the five highest vote-getters in order from highest to lowest vote totals.

24. The data file InstructorList contains a list of the instructors in your school along with the room number to which each is assigned. Write a program that, given the name of the instructor, does a linear search to find and print the room to which the instructor is assigned.

25. Rewrite your program in Problem 24 so that, given a room number, the name of the instructor assigned to that room is found using a binary search. Assume the file is arranged in order of room numbers.

26. Write a language translation program that permits the entry of a word in English and prints the corresponding word in another language. The dictionary words can be stored in separate arrays. The English array should be sorted in alphabetical order prior to the first entry of a word to be translated.

27. Elementary- and middle-school students are often given the task of converting numbers from one base to another. For example, 19 in base 10 is 103 in base 4 $(1 \times 4^2 + 0 \times 4^1 + 3 \times 4^0)$. Conversely, 123 in base 4 is 27 in base 10. Write an interactive program that allows the user to choose from the following

```
     <1>  Convert from base 10 to base A.
     <2>  Convert from base A to base 10.
     <3>  Quit
```

If options 1 or 2 are chosen, the user should then enter the intended base and the number to be converted. A sample run of the program would produce the following output.

```
This program allows you to convert between bases.
Which of the following would you like?

     <1>  Convert from base 10 to base A
     <2>  Convert from base A to base 10
     <3>  Quit

Enter your choice and press <Enter>.
1

Enter the number in base 10 and press <Enter>.
237

Enter the new base and press <Enter>.
4

The number 237 in base 4 is:  3231

Press <Enter> to continue

This program allows you to convert between bases.
Which of the following would you like?

     <1>  Convert from base 10 to base A
     <2>  Convert from base A to base 10
     <3>  Quit

Enter your choice and press <Enter>.
2

What number would you like to have converted?
2332

Converting to base 10, we get:

     2 *    1 =         2
     3 *    4 =        12
     3 *   16 =        48
     2 *   64 =       128
                    -----
The base 10 value is   190

Press <Enter> to continue

This program allows you to convert between bases.
Which of the following would you like?
```

```
    <1>  Convert from base 10 to base A
    <2>  Convert from base A to base 10
    <3>  Quit

Enter your choice and press <Enter>.
3
```

28. A popular children's game is Hangman. The first player selects a word, and the second player guesses letters that may be in that word. Whenever a correct choice is made by the second player, he or she is shown the partially completed word. The game terminates when the correct word is guessed by the second player (the second player wins) or when a predetermined number of incorrect choices of letters have been made by the second player (the first player wins).

Write an interactive version of this game that can be played by two players. Output should include a display of all letters previously selected by the second player. Allow the players to choose from different levels of difficulty, using the following scale.

Number of Misses	*Level of Difficulty*
0–3	Expert
4–6	Very Good
7–10	Average
11–16	Beginner
17–25	Needs Practice

COMMUNICATION IN PRACTICE

1. Write a short paper describing the selection sort.
2. One of the principles underlying the concept of data abstraction is that the implementation details of data structures should be deferred to the lowest possible level. To illustrate, consider the high-level design to which we referred in our previous discussion of data abstraction. Our program required you to work with a list of names and an associated list of student test scores. The following procedures were suggested.

    GetNames (<procedure here>);
    GetScores (<procedure here>);
    SortByName (<procedure here>);
    SortByScore (<procedure here>);
    PrintNamesAndScores (<procedure here>);

    Write complete documentation for each of these modules, including a description of all parameters and data structures required. Present your documentation to the class. Ask if your classmates have questions about the number or type of parameters, the data structures required, and/or the main tasks to be performed by each module.
3. Contact programmers at your university and/or some businesses and discuss with them the use of lists as a data type. Ask what kinds of programming problems require the use of a list, how the programmers handle data entry (list length), and what operations they perform on the list (search, sort, and so on). Give an oral report of your findings to the class.
4. Select a programming problem from this chapter that you have not yet worked. Construct a structure chart and write all documentary information necessary for the problem you have chosen. Do not write code. When you are finished, have a classmate read your documentation to see if it makes clear precisely what is to be done.

CHAPTER

8 Arrays of More Than One Dimension

CHAPTER OUTLINE

Chapter 7 illustrated the significance and uses of one-dimensional arrays. There are, however, several kinds of problems that require arrays of more than one dimension. For example, if we want to work with a table that has both rows and columns, a one-dimensional array will not suffice. Such problems can be solved using arrays of more than one dimension.

8.1 Two-Dimensional Arrays

OBJECTIVES

- to be able to declare two-dimensional arrays
- to be able to use correct notation for two-dimensional arrays
- to be able to create tabular output using two-dimensional arrays
- to be able to **read** and **write** with two-dimensional arrays
- to be able to manipulate components of two-dimensional arrays
- to be able to use two-dimensional arrays with procedures

Basic Idea and Notation

One-dimensional arrays are very useful when working with a row or column of numbers. However, suppose we want to work with data that are best represented in tabular form. For example, box scores in baseball are reported with one player name listed for each row and one statistic listed for each column. Another example is an instructor's grade book, in which a student name is listed for each row and his or her test and/or quiz scores are listed for each column. In both cases, a multiple reference is needed for a single data item.

In Pascal, multiple reference is accomplished by the use of *two-dimensional arrays*. In these arrays, the row subrange always precedes the column subrange and the two subranges are separated by commas. To illustrate, suppose we want to print the table

```
1   2   3   4
2   4   6   8
3   6   9  12
```

where we need to access both the row and column for a single data entry. This table could be produced by either of the following declarations.

```
1. VAR
     Table : ARRAY [1..3, 1..4] OF integer;
2. TYPE
     Matrix = ARRAY [1..3, 1..4] OF integer;
   VAR
     Table : Matrix;
```

The index [1 . . 3, 1 . . 4] of each of these declarations differs from one-dimensional arrays. These declarations reserve memory that can be visualized as three rows, each of which holds four variables. Thus, 12 variable locations are reserved, as shown.

Table

As a second illustration of the use of two-dimensional arrays, suppose we want to print the batting statistics for a softball team of 15 players. If the statistics consist of at bats (AB), hits (H), runs (R), and runs batted in (RBI) for each player, we naturally choose to work with a 15 × 4 table. Hence, a reasonable variable declaration is

```
TYPE
  Table15X4 = ARRAY [1..15, 1..4] OF integer;
VAR
  Stats : Table15X4;
```

The reserved memory area can be visualized as

Stats

with 60 variable locations reserved.

Before we proceed further, let's examine another method of declaring two-dimensional arrays. Our 3 × 4 table can be thought of as three arrays, each of length four, as follows:

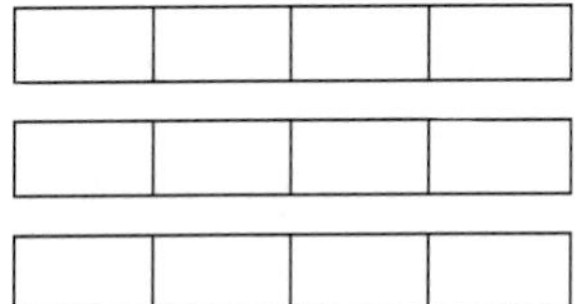

Hence, we have a list of arrays and we can declare the table by

```
TYPE
  Row = ARRAY [1..4] OF integer;
  Matrix = ARRAY [1..3] OF Row;
VAR
  Table : Matrix;
```

The softball statistics can be declared by

```
CONST
  NumberOfStats = 4;
  RosterSize = 15;
```

```
TYPE
  PlayerStats = ARRAY [1..NumberOfStats] OF integer;
  TeamTable = ARRAY [1..RosterSize] OF PlayerStats;
VAR
  Stats : TeamTable;
```

Semantic indices, such as enumerated types, can be utilized by

```
TYPE
  Stat = (AtBat, Hits, Runs, RBI);
  StatChart = ARRAY [1..RosterSize, Stat] OF integer;
VAR
  Player : StatChart;
```

In this case, a typical entry is

```
Player[5, Hits] := 2;
```

In general, a two-dimensional array can be defined by

> **ARRAY** [<row index>, <column index>] **OF** <element type>
>
> or
>
> TYPE
> RowType = **ARRAY** [<column index>] **OF** <element type>;
> Matrix = **ARRAY** [<row index>] **OF** RowType;

Whichever method of declaration is used, the problem now is to access individual components of the two-dimensional array. For example, in the table

1	2	3	4
2	4	6	8
3	6	9	12

the 8 is in row 2 and column 4. Note that both the row position and the column position of an element must be indicated. Therefore, in order to put 8 in this position, we can use assignment statements such as

```
Row := 2;
Column := 4;
Table[Row, Column] := 8;
```

This assignment statement could be used with either of the declaration forms mentioned earlier.

Next, let's assign the values just given to the appropriate variables in Table by using 12 assignment statements, as follows:

```
Table[1,1] := 1;
Table[1,2] := 2;
Table[1,3] := 3;
Table[1,4] := 4;
Table[2,1] := 2;
Table[2,2] := 4;
Table[2,3] := 6;
Table[2,4] := 8;
Table[3,1] := 3;
Table[3,2] := 6;
Table[3,3] := 9;
Table[3,4] := 12;
```

When working with charts or tables of a fixed grid size (say 15 × 4), descriptive identifiers could be

```
Chart15X4
```

or

```
Table15X4
```

If the numbers of rows and columns vary for different runs of the program (for example, the number of players on a team could vary from year to year), you could define a type by

```
CONST
  NumRows = 15;
  NumColumns = 4;
TYPE
  RowRange = 1..NumRows;
  ColumnRange = 1..NumColumns;
  Table = ARRAY [RowRange, ColumnRange] OF integer;
VAR
  Stats : Table;
```

As you can see, this process is extremely tedious. Instead, we can note the relationship between the indices and the assigned values and make the row index Row and the column index Column. The values to be assigned are then Row * Column, and we can use nested loops to perform these assignments, as follows:

```
FOR Row := 1 TO 3 DO
  FOR Column := 1 TO 4 DO
    Table[Row, Column] := Row * Column;
```

Since two-dimensional arrays frequently require us to work with nested loops, let's examine what this segment of code does more closely. When Row := 1, the loop

```
FOR Column := 1 TO 4 DO
  Table[1, Column] := 1 * Column;
```

is executed. This performs the four assignments

```
Table[1,1] := 1 * 1;
Table[1,2] := 1 * 2;
Table[1,3] := 1 * 3;
Table[1,4] := 1 * 4;
```

and we have the memory area

Table

1	2	3	4

Similar results hold for Row := 2 and Row := 3, and we produce a two-dimensional array that can be visualized as

Table

1	2	3	4
2	4	6	8
3	6	9	12

The following examples will help you learn to work with and understand the notation for two-dimensional arrays.

EXAMPLE 8.1

Let's assume the declaration

```
TYPE
  Table5X4 = ARRAY [1..5, 1..4] OF integer;
VAR
  Table : Table5X4;
```

has been made, and consider the segment of code

```
FOR Row := 1 TO 5 DO
  FOR Column := 1 TO 4 DO
    Table[Row, Column] := Row DIV Column;
```

When Row := 1, the loop

```
FOR Column := 1 TO 4 DO
  Table[1, Column] := 1 DIV Column;
```

is executed, resulting in the assignment statements

```
Table[1,1] := 1 DIV 1;
Table[1,2] := 1 DIV 2;
Table[1,3] := 1 DIV 3;
Table[1,4] := 1 DIV 4;
```

The contents of the memory area after that first pass through the loop are

Table

1	0	0	0

When Row := 2, the assignments are

```
Table[2,1] := 2 DIV 1;
Table[2,2] := 2 DIV 2;
Table[2,3] := 2 DIV 3;
Table[2,4] := 2 DIV 4;
```

Table now has the values

Table

1	0	0	0
2	1	0	0

The contents of Table after the entire outside loop has been executed are

Table

1	0	0	0
2	1	0	0
3	1	1	0
4	2	1	1
5	2	1	1

EXAMPLE 8.2

Let's declare a two-dimensional array and write a segment of code to produce the memory area and contents depicted here.

2	3	4	5	6	7	8
3	4	5	6	7	8	9
4	5	6	7	8	9	10
5	6	7	8	9	10	11

An appropriate definition is

```
TYPE
  Table4X7 = ARRAY [1..4, 1..7] OF integer;
```

or

```
TYPE
  Table4X7 = ARRAY [1..4] OF
                ARRAY [1..7] OF integer;
VAR
  Table : Table4X7;
```

A segment of code to produce the desired contents is

```
FOR Row := 1 TO 4 DO
  FOR Column := 1 TO 7 DO
    Table[Row, Column] := Row + Column;
```

Reading and Writing

Most problems that involve the use of two-dimensional arrays require data to be read from an input file into the array and values to be written from the array to create some tabular form of output. For example, consider the two-dimensional array for softball statistics

```
TYPE
  Table15X4 = ARRAY [1..15, 1..4] OF integer;
VAR
  Stats : Table15X4;
```

If the data file consists of 15 lines and each line contains statistics for one player as follows

```
AB  H  R  RBI
4   2  1  1   (player #1)
3   1  0  1   (player #2)
.             .
.             .
.             .
0   0  0  0   (player #15)
```

we can get the data from the file by reading it one line at a time for 15 lines. This is done using nested loops, as follows:

```
FOR Row := 1 TO 15 DO
  BEGIN
    FOR Column := 1 TO 4 DO
      read (Stats[Row, Column]);
    readln
  END;
```

When Row := 1, the loop

```
FOR Column := 1 TO 4 DO
  read (Stats[Row, Column]);
```

reads the first line of data. In a similar manner, as Row assumes the values 2 through 15, the lines 2 through 15 are read. After the data are read into an array, some operations and/or updating will be performed and we will display the data in tabular form. For example, suppose we want to print the softball statistics in the 15 × 4 table using only three spaces for each column. We note the following.

1. Three spaces per column can be controlled by formatting the output.
2. One line of output can be generated by a **FOR** loop containing a **write** statement; for example

```
FOR Column := 1 TO 4 DO
  write (Stats[Row, Column]:3);
```

3. The output buffer is dumped to the printer after each **write** loop by using **writeln**.
4. We do this for 15 lines by employing another loop:

```
FOR Row := 1 TO 15 DO
  BEGIN
    FOR Column := 1 TO 4 DO
      write (Stats[Row, Column]:3);
    writeln
  END;
```

This last segment of code produces the desired output.

In actual practice, we will also be concerned with headings for our tables and with how the data are positioned on the page. For example, suppose we want to identify the columns of softball statistics as AB, H, R, and RBI, underline the headings, and start the output (AB) in column 25. The following segment of code accomplishes our objectives.

```
writeln (Skip:24,'AB H  R RBI');
writeln (Skip:24,'-----------');
writeln;
FOR Row := 1 TO 15 DO
  BEGIN
    write (Skip:22);  {  Set the left margin  }
    FOR Column := 1 TO 4 DO
      write (Stats[Row, Column]:3);
    writeln  {  Advance to next line  }
  END;
```

The data file used earlier for our ballplayers produces an output of

```
AB H   R RBI
-----------

4  2  1  1
3  1  0  1
   .
   .
   .
0  0  0  0
```

Manipulating Two-Dimensional Array Components

Often we want to work with some but not all of the components of an array. For example, suppose we have a two-dimensional array of test scores for students in a class. If there are 20 students with five scores each, an appropriate two-dimensional array can be declared as

```
TYPE
  Table20X5 = ARRAY [1..20, 1..5] OF integer;
VAR
  Score : Table20X5;
```

After the scores have been read into the array Score, we can envision the memory area as follows:

Score

98	86	100	76	95	(student #1)
72	68	65	74	81	(student #2)
85	81	91	84	83	(student #3)
					.
					.
					.
76	81	72	87	80	(student #20)

When printing a table with test scores, we usually compute several items, including total points for each student, percentage grade for each student, and average score for each test. Thus, we need to declare three additional data structures:

1. An array of length 20 for the total points
2. An array of length 20 for the percentage grades
3. An array of length 5 for the test averages

Let's examine what is required for each of these computations. First, to get the total points for each student, we declare a one-dimensional array to store these values, so we can assume the declaration

```
TYPE
  List20 = ARRAY [1..20] OF integer;
VAR
  TotalPoints : List20;
```

Since the first student's test scores are in the first row, we can write

```
TotalPoints[1] := Score[1,1] + Score[1,2] +
                  Score[1,3] + Score[1,4] +
                  Score[1,5];
```

To compute this total for each student, we can use the loop

```
FOR Student := 1 TO 20 DO
  TotalPoints[Student] := Score[Student, 1] +
                          Score[Student, 2] +
                          Score[Student, 3] +
                          Score[Student, 4] +
                          Score[Student, 5];
```

which produces the array of totals

TotalPoints

455	TotalPoints[1]
360	TotalPoints[2]
424	TotalPoints[3]
.	.
.	.
.	.
396	TotalPoints[20]

If the two-dimensional array has several columns, we can use a loop to sum an array of numbers. We can, for instance, write a loop to sum the five test scores for the first student in our table:

```
TotalPoints[1] := 0;
FOR Test := 1 TO 5 DO
  TotalPoints[1] := TotalPoints[1] + Score[1, Test];
```

To do this for each student, we use a second loop:

```
FOR Student := 1 TO 20 DO
  BEGIN
    TotalPoints[Student] := 0;
    FOR Test := 1 TO 5 DO
      TotalPoints[Student] := TotalPoints[Student] +
                              Score[Student, Test]
  END;
```

The second task in our problem is to compute the percentage grade for each student. If we want to save these percentages, we can declare an array by

```
TYPE
  Column20 = ARRAY [1..20] OF real;
VAR
  Percent : Column20;
```

and include a segment of code

```
FOR Student := 1 TO 20 DO
  Percent[Student] := TotalPoints[Student] / 5;
```

The third task is to determine the average score for each of the five tests. To find each of these numbers, we need to add all 20 scores for each test and divide the respective total by 20. First, we need to find the sum of each column and to declare an array in which to store the averages. The declaration can be

```
TYPE
  List5 = Array [1..5] OF real;
VAR
  TestAv: List5;
```

We now need a loop to find the total of each column. Assuming that an integer variable Sum is declared, we can sum the first column by

```
Sum := 0;
FOR Student := 1 TO 20 DO
  Sum := Sum + Score[Student, 1];
```

We can now find the average score by

```
TestAv[1] := Sum / 20;
```

To do this for each column, we use a second loop:

```
FOR Test := 1 TO 5 DO           {  Test is the column subscript  }
  BEGIN
    Sum := 0;
    FOR Student := 1 TO 20 DO   {  Student is the row subscript  }
      Sum := Sum + Score[Student, Test];
    TestAv[Test] := Sum / 20
  END;
```

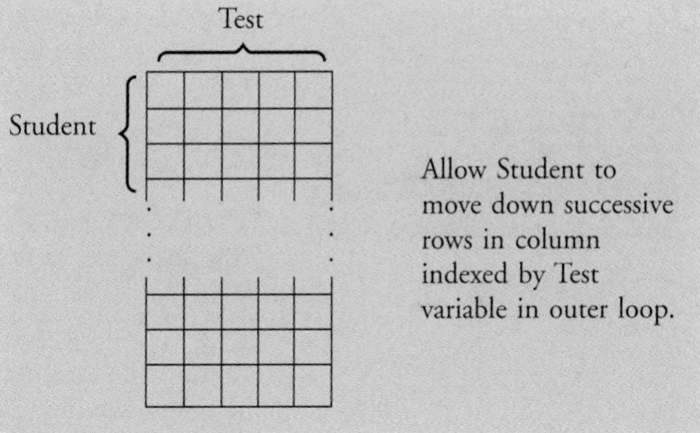
Test
Student
Allow Student to move down successive rows in column indexed by Test variable in outer loop.

A concluding example of manipulating elements of two-dimensional arrays follows.

EXAMPLE 8.3

Let's assume we have the declarations

```
CONST
  NumRows = 20;
  NumColumns = 50;
TYPE
  Table = ARRAY [1..NumRows,
                 1..NumColumns] OF integer;
  List = ARRAY [1..NumRows] OF integer;
VAR
  Chart : Table;
  Max : List;
```

and values have been read into the two-dimensional array from an input file. Let's write a segment of code to find the maximum value in each row and then store this value in the array Max. To find the maximum of the first row, we can write

```
Max[1] := Chart[1,1];
FOR Column := 2 TO NumColumns DO
  IF Chart[1, Column] > Max[1] THEN
    Max[1] := Chart[1, Column];
```

To do this for each of the rows, we use a second loop:

```
FOR Row := 1 TO NumRows DO
  BEGIN
    Max[Row] := Chart[Row, 1];
    FOR Column := 2 TO NumColumns DO
      IF Chart[Row, Column] > Max[Row] THEN
        Max[Row] := Chart[Row, Column]
  END;
```

Procedures and Two-Dimensional Arrays

When we start writing programs with two-dimensional arrays, we will use procedures as before to maintain the top-down design philosophy. As with one-dimensional arrays, there are three relatively standard uses of procedures in most problems involving two-dimensional arrays: to get the data, to manipulate the data, and to display the data.

When using procedures with data that require the use of an array as a data structure, the array type must be defined in the **TYPE** section. The actual parameters and formal parameters can then be of the defined array type. As with one-dimensional arrays, we pass two-dimensional arrays by reference to conserve memory allocation.

EXAMPLE 8.4

Western Jeans, Inc., wants to develop a program to keep track of its inventory of jeans. The jeans are coded by waist size and inseam. The waist sizes are the integer values from 24 to 46, and the inseams are the integer values from 26 to 40. Thus, there are 23 waist sizes and 15 inseams for each waist size. The first 23 lines of the data file contain the starting inventory. Each line corresponds to a waist size and contains 15 integers, one for each inseam. The next 23 lines of the data file contain the sales information for a day. Let's write a program to find and print the closing inventory. A first-level pseudocode development for this program is

1. Get starting inventory
2. Get new sales
3. Update inventory
4. Print heading
5. Print closing inventory

Each of these steps uses a procedure.

Since there are 23 waist sizes and 15 inseams, we use the definitions

```
CONST
  FirstWaist = 24;
  LastWaist = 46;
  FirstInseam = 26;
  LastInseam = 40;
```

```
TYPE
  WaistSizes = FirstWaist..LastWaist;
  InseamSizes = FirstInseam..LastInseam;
  Table = ARRAY [WaistSizes, InseamSizes] OF integer;
```

and declare the variables

```
VAR
  Inventory : Table;
  Sales : Table;
```

Assuming variables have been declared and constants have been defined as needed, we write the following procedure to get the starting inventory.

```
PROCEDURE GetData (VAR Matrix : Table);
  VAR
    Row, Column : integer;
  BEGIN
    FOR Row := FirstWaist TO LastWaist DO
      BEGIN
        FOR Column := FirstInseam TO LastInseam DO
          read (Data, Matrix[Row, Column]);
        readln (Data)
      END
  END;
```

This procedure can be called from the main program by

```
GetData (Inventory);
```

The next task is to get the sales for a day. Because this merely requires reading the next 23 lines from the data file, we do not need to write a new procedure. We can call GetData again by

```
GetData (Sales);
```

We now need a procedure to update the starting inventory. This updating can be accomplished by sending both two-dimensional arrays to a procedure and then finding the respective differences of components:

```
PROCEDURE Update (VAR Inventory : Table;
                  VAR Sales : Table);
  VAR
    Row, Column : integer;
  BEGIN
    FOR Row := FirstWaist TO LastWaist DO
      FOR Column := FirstInseam TO LastInseam DO
        Inventory[Row, Column] := Inventory[Row, Column] -
                                  Sales[Row, Column]
  END;
```

This procedure is called by the statement

```
Update (Inventory, Sales);
```

The procedure for the heading is the same as before, so we do not need to write it here. Let's assume the arrays have been assigned the necessary values. The output procedure then will be

```
PROCEDURE PrintData (VAR Inventory : Table);
  CONST
    Mark = ' !';
  VAR
    Row, Column : integer;
  BEGIN
    FOR Row := FirstWaist TO LastWaist DO
      BEGIN
        write (Row:6, Mark);
        FOR Column := FirstInseam TO LastInseam DO
          write (Inventory[Row, Column]:4);
        writeln;
        writeln (Mark:6)
      END  { of printing one row  }
  END;
```

This procedure can be called from the main program by

```
PrintData (Inventory);
```

Once these procedures are written, the main program becomes

```
BEGIN  {  Main program  }
  reset (Data);
  GetData (Inventory);
  GetData (Sales);
  Update (Inventory, Sales);
  PrintHeading;
  PrintData (Inventory)
END.  {  of main program  }
```

EXERCISES 8.1

1. Use both the **ARRAY** [. . , . .] and **ARRAY** [. .] **OF ARRAY** [. .]forms to define a two-dimensional array type for each of the following.
   a. A table with real number entries that shows the prices of four different drugs charged by five drug stores.
   b. A table with character entries that shows the grades earned by 20 students in six courses.
   c. A table with integer entries that shows the 12 quiz scores earned by 30 students in a class.
2. Write a test program to read integers into a 3 × 5 array and then print out the array components, together with each row sum and each column sum.
3. For each of the following declarations, sketch what is reserved in memory. In each case, state how many variables (memory locations) are available to the programmer.
   a.
   ```
   TYPE
     ShippingCostTable = ARRAY [1..10] OF
                         ARRAY [1..4] OF real;
     GradeBookTable = ARRAY [1..35, 1..6] OF integer;
   VAR
     ShippingCost : ShippingCostTable;
     GradeBook : GradeBookTable;
   ```
   b.
   ```
   TYPE
     Matrix = ARRAY [1..3, 2..6] OF integer;
   VAR
     A : Matrix;
   ```

c.
```
TYPE
  Weekdays = (Mon, Tues, Wed, Thur, Fri);
  Chores = (Wash, Iron, Clean, Mow, Sweep);
  ScheduleTable = ARRAY [Weekdays, Chores] OF boolean;
VAR
  Schedule : ScheduleTable;
```

d.
```
TYPE
  Questions = 1..50;
  Answers = 1..5;
  Table = ARRAY [Questions, Answers] OF char;
VAR
  AnswerSheet : Table;
```

4. Assume array A has been declared as

```
TYPE
  Table3X5 = ARRAY [1..3, 1..5] OF integer;
VAR
  A : Table3X5;
```

Indicate the array contents produced by each of the following.

a.
```
FOR J := 1 TO 3 DO
  FOR K := 1 TO 5 DO
    A[J,K] := J - K;
```

b.
```
FOR J := 1 TO 3 DO
  FOR K := 1 TO 5 DO
    A[J,K] := J;
```

c.
```
FOR K := 1 TO 5 DO
  FOR J := 1 TO 3 DO
    A[J,K] := J;
```

d.
```
FOR J := 3 DOWNTO 1 DO
  FOR K := 1 TO 5 DO
    A[J,K] := J MOD K;
```

5. Let the two-dimensional array A be declared by

```
TYPE
  Table3X6 = ARRAY [1..3, 1..6] OF integer;
VAR
  A : Table3X6;
```

Write nested loops that cause the following values to be stored in A.

a. A

3	4	5	6	7	8
5	6	7	8	9	10
7	8	9	10	11	12

b. A

0	0	0	0	0	0
0	0	0	0	0	0
0	0	0	0	0	0

c. A

2	2	2	2	2	2
4	4	4	4	4	4
6	6	6	6	6	6

6. Declare a two-dimensional array, and write a segment of code that reads the following input file into the array.

```
13.2 15.1 10.3 8.2 43.6
37.2 25.6 34.1 17.0 15.2
```

7. Suppose an input file contains 50 lines of data and the first 20 spaces of each line are reserved for a customer's name. The rest of the line contains other information. Declare a two-dimensional array to hold the names, and write a segment of code to read the names into the array. A sample line of input is

```
Smith John O        268-14-1801
                    ↑
               position 21
```

8. Assume the declaration

```
TYPE
  Table4X5 = ARRAY [1..4, 1..5] OF real;
VAR
  Table : Table4X5;
```

has been made and values have been read into Table as follows:

Table

-2.0	3.0	0.0	8.0	10.0
0.0	-4.0	3.0	1.0	2.0
1.0	2.0	3.0	8.0	-6.0
-4.0	1.0	4.0	6.0	82.0

Indicate what the components of Table will be after each of the following segments of code is executed.

a.
```
FOR J := 1 TO 4 DO
  FOR K := 1 TO 5 DO
    IF J MOD K = 0 THEN
      A[J,K] := 0.0
    ELSE
      A[J,K] := -1.0;
```

b.
```
FOR J := 1 TO 4 DO
  IF A[J,1] <> 0.0 THEN
    FOR K := 1 TO 5 DO
      A[J,K] := A[J,K] / A[J,1];
```

c.
```
FOR K := 1 TO 5 DO
  IF A[1,K] = 0.0 THEN
    FOR J := 2 TO 4 DO
      A[J,K] := 0.0;
```

9. Let the two-dimensional array Table be declared as in Exercise 8. Declare additional arrays as needed, and write segments of code for each of the following.
   a. Find and save the minimum of each row.
   b. Find and save the maximum of each column.
   c. Find the total of all the components.

10. Example 8.4 illustrates the use of procedures with two-dimensional arrays. For actual use, Western Jeans would also need a list indicating what to order to maintain

the inventory. Write a procedure (assuming all declarations have been made) to print a table indicating which sizes of jeans have a supply of less than 4. Do this by putting '*' in the cell if the supply is low or ' ' in the cell if the supply is adequate.

11. Suppose you want to work with a table that has three rows and eight columns of integers.
   a. Declare an appropriate two-dimensional array that can be used with procedures.
   b. Write a procedure to replace all negative numbers with zero.
   c. Show what is needed to call this procedure from the main program.

12. If A and B are matrices of size $m \times n$, then their sum $A + B$ is defined by $A + B = [a + b]_{ij}$, where a and b are corresponding components in A and B. Write a program to do the following.
   a. Read values into two matrices of size $m \times n$.
   b. Compute the sum.
   c. Print out the matrices and the sum.

13. If A and B are matrices of sizes $m \times n$ and $n \times p$, respectively, then their product is defined to be the $m \times p$ matrix AB, where

$$AB = [c_{ik}],\ c_{ik} = \sum_{j=1}^{n} a_{ij}b_{jk}$$

Write a program to do the following.
   a. Read values into two matrices that have a defined product.
   b. Compute their product.
   c. Print out the matrices and their product.

8.2 Arrays of String Variables

OBJECTIVES

- to understand that an array of string variables is a two-dimensional array
- to be able to declare an array of string variables
- to be able to read data into an array of string variables
- to be able to alphabetize a list of names

Basic Idea and Notation

Recall from Section 7.5 that we define string variables as packed arrays of characters. A typical declaration for a name 20 characters in length is

```
TYPE
  NameString = PACKED ARRAY [1..20] OF char;
VAR
  Name : NameString;
```

Thus, Name could be envisioned as

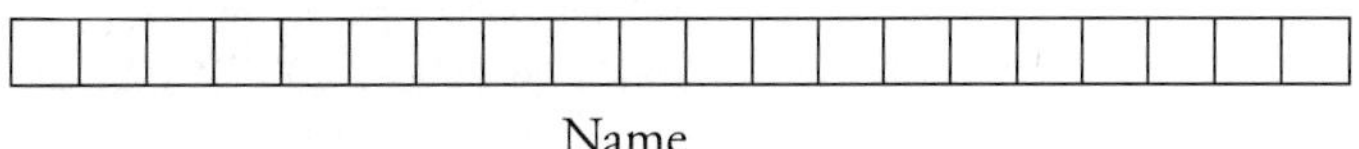

Name

It is a natural extension to consider the problem of working with an array of strings. For example, if we need a data structure for 50 names, this can be declared by

```
TYPE
  NameString = PACKED ARRAY [1..20] OF char;
  NameList = ARRAY [1..50] OF NameString;
VAR
  Name : NameList;
```

Name can then be envisioned as

Name

Name[1]
Name[2]
Name[3]
.
.
.
Name[50]

where each component of Name is a packed array of 20 characters. (Many compilers have a string type that behaves differently.)

Alphabetizing a List of Names

One standard problem that programmers face is alphabetizing a list of names. For example, programs that work with class lists, bank statements, magazine subscriptions, names in a telephone book, or credit card customers require alphabetizing. As indicated, Pascal provides the facility for using an array of packed arrays as a data structure for such lists.

Problems that require the user to alphabetize names contain at least three main tasks: get the data, alphabetize the list, and print the list. Before writing procedures for each of these tasks, let's consider some associated problems. When getting the data, the programmer will usually encounter one of three formats. First, data may be entered with a constant field width for each name. Each name is then typically followed by some additional data item. Thus, if each name uses 20 character positions and position 21 contains the start of numeric data, the data file might be

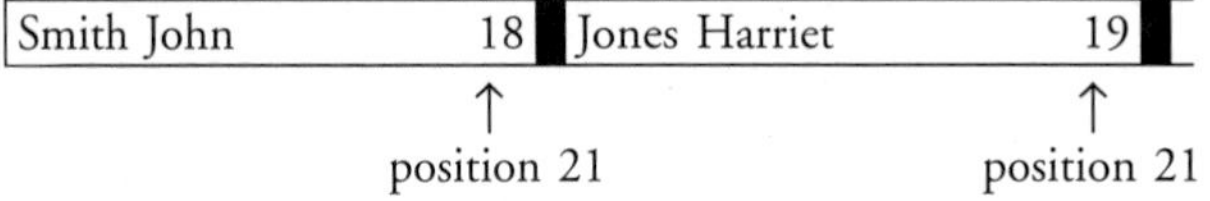

In this case, the name can be read into the appropriate component by a fixed loop. The first name can be accessed by

```
FOR K := 1 TO 20 DO
  read (Data, Name[1,K]);
```

and the second name can be accessed by

```
FOR K := 1 TO 20 DO
  read (Data, Name[2,K]);
```

A second form for entering data is to use some symbol to indicate the end of a name. When the data are in this form, the user must be able to recognize the symbol and fill the remaining positions with blanks. Thus, the data file can be

Smith John*18 ▮ Jones Harriet*19 ▮

In this case, the first name can be obtained by

```
K := 0;
read (Data, Ch);
WHILE (Ch <> '*') AND (K < 20) DO
  BEGIN
    K := K + 1;
    Name[1,K] := Ch;
    read (Data, Ch)
  END;
```

```
FOR J := K + 1 TO 20 DO
  Name[1,J] := ' ';
```

This process will fill the remaining name positions with blanks. Thus, Name[1] is

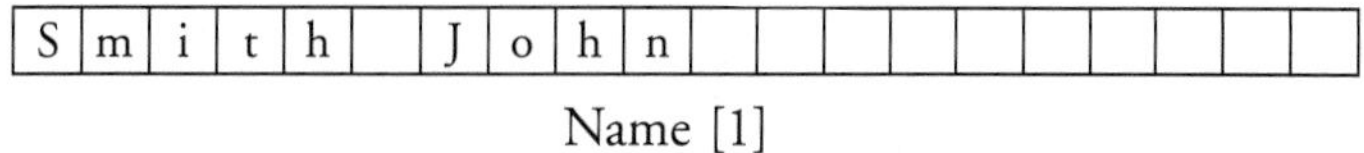

Name [1]

The second name in the data file would be similarly read. The only change is from Name[1,K] to Name[2,K].

A third possibility is that the name is entered on a separate line from other related data items. Thus, the data file could be

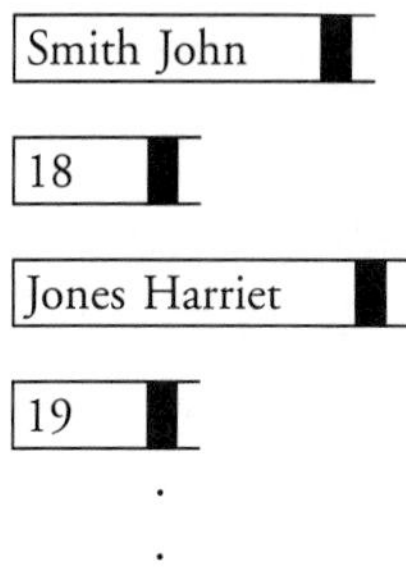

.
.
.

In this case, an end-of-file condition can be used to read the data. Typical code for input would be

```
Index := 1;
WHILE NOT eof(Data) DO
  BEGIN
    readln (Data, Name[Index]);
    readln (Data, Age[Index]);
    Index := Index + 1
  END;
```

The next problem in getting data is determining how many lines are available. If the number of lines is known, a **FOR** loop can be used. More realistically, however, there will be an unknown number of lines and the user will need the **eof** condition in a variable control loop and a counter to determine the number of names. To illustrate, assume there are an unknown number of data lines and each line contains a name in the first 20 positions. If the declaration section of a program is

```
TYPE
  NameString = PACKED ARRAY [1..20] OF char;
  NameList = ARRAY [1..50] OF NameString;
VAR
  Name: NameList;
  Length : integer;
```

then a procedure to get the data is

```
PROCEDURE GetData (VAR Name : NameList;
                   VAR Length : integer);
  VAR
    K : integer;
```

```
BEGIN
  reset (Data);
  Length := 0;
  WHILE NOT eof(Data) AND (Length < 50) DO
    BEGIN
      Length := Length + 1;             {  Increment counter    }
      FOR K := 1 TO 20 DO
        read (Data, Name[Length, K]);   {  Get a name           }
      readln (Data)                     {  Advance the pointer  }
    END;
  IF NOT eof(Data) THEN
    writeln ('There are more data.')
END;  {  of PROCEDURE GetData  }
```

This procedure is called from the main program by

```
GetData (Name, Length);
```

Now let's consider the problem of alphabetizing a list of names. If we assume the same data structure and let Length represent the number of names, a procedure to sort the list alphabetically (using the selection sort discussed in Section 7.3) is

```
PROCEDURE SelectionSort (VAR Name : NameList;
                         Length : integer);
  VAR
    J, K, Index : integer;
    Temp : NameString;
  BEGIN
    FOR J := 1 TO Length - 1 DO
      BEGIN
        Index := J;
        FOR K := J + 1 TO Length DO
          IF Name[K] < Name[Index] THEN
            Index := K;
        IF Index <> J THEN
          BEGIN
            Temp := Name[Index];
            Name[Index] := Name[J];
            Name[J] := Temp
          END  {  of exchange  }
      END  {  of sort  }
  END;  {  of PROCEDURE SelectionSort  }
```

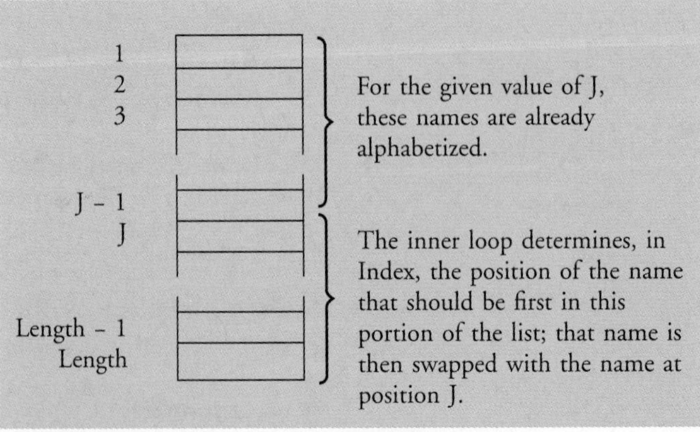
1
2
3
J - 1
J
Length - 1
Length
For the given value of J, these names are already alphabetized.
The inner loop determines, in Index, the position of the name that should be first in this portion of the list; that name is then swapped with the name at position J.

This procedure is called from the main program by

```
SelectionSort (Name, Length);
```

Once the list of names has been sorted, the user often wants to print the sorted list. A procedure to do this is

```
PROCEDURE PrintData (VAR Name : NameList;
                         Length : integer);
  VAR
    J : integer;
  BEGIN
    FOR J := 1 TO Length DO
      writeln (Name[J]:50)
  END;  {  of PROCEDURE PrintData  }
```

This procedure is called from the main program by

```
PrintData (Name, Length);
```

We can now use these procedures in a simple program that gets the names, sorts them, and prints them as follows:

```
BEGIN  {  Main program  }
  GetData (Name, Length);
  SelectionSort (Name, Length);
  PrintData (Name, Length)
END.  {  of main program  }
```

EXERCISES 8.2

1. Assume the declarations and definitions

```
TYPE
  String20 = PACKED ARRAY [1..20] OF char;
  StateList = ARRAY [1..50] OF String20;
VAR
  State : StateList;
```

have been made and an alphabetical listing of the 50 states of the United States of America is contained in the data structure State. Further, assume each state name begins in position one of each component. Indicate the output for each of the following.

a.
```
FOR J := 1 TO 50 DO
  IF State[J,1] = 'O' THEN
    writeln (State[J]:35);
```

b.
```
FOR J := 50 DOWNTO 1 DO
  IF J MOD 5 = 0 THEN
    writeln (State[J]:35);
```

c.
```
FOR J := 1 TO 50 DO
  writeln (State[J,1]:10, State[J,2]);
```

d.
```
CountA := 0;
FOR J := 1 TO 50 DO
  FOR K := 1 TO 20 DO
    IF State[J,K] = 'A' THEN
      CountA := CountA + 1;
writeln (CountA:20);
```

2. Assume you have a sorted list of names in the form last name, first name. Write a fragment of code to inspect the list of names and print the full name of each Smith on the list.

3. The procedure used in this section to get names from a data file assumes the names in the data file are of fixed length and there is an unknown number of data lines. Modify the procedure for each of the following situations.
   a. Variable length names followed by '*' and a known number of data lines
   b. Variable length names followed by '*' and an unknown number of data lines
   c. Fixed length names (20 characters) and a known number of data lines
   d. Names entered in the form first name, space, last name that are to be sorted by last name.
4. If each line of a data file contains a name followed by an age, such as

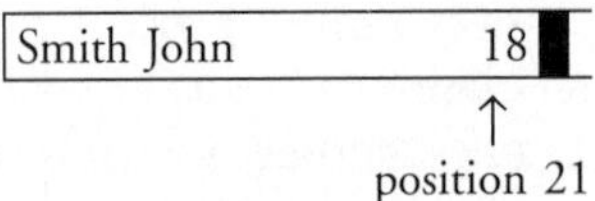

the data will be put in two arrays: one for the names, and one for the ages. Show how the sorting procedure can be modified so the array of ages will be in the same order as the array of names.
5. Write a complete program to read 10 names from an input file (where each line contains one name of 20 characters), sort the names in reverse alphabetical order, and print the sorted list.

8.3 Parallel Arrays

OBJECTIVES

- to understand when parallel arrays should be used to solve a problem
- to be able to use parallel arrays to solve a problem

In many practical situations, more than one type of array is required to handle the data. For example, we may wish to keep a record of names of people and their donations to a charitable organization. We can accomplish this by using a packed array of names and an equally long array of donations. Programs for such situations can use *parallel arrays*—arrays of the same length with elements in the same relative positions in each array. These arrays have the same index type. However, most uses of parallel arrays have the added condition that there be different data types for the array components; otherwise, a two-dimensional array would suffice. Generally, in situations that call for two or more arrays of the same length but of different data types, parallel arrays can be used. Later, we will see that this situation can also be handled as a single array of records.

Using Parallel Arrays

Let's look at a typical problem that requires working with both a list of names and a list of numbers. Suppose the input file consists of 30 lines, of which each contains a name in the first 20 spaces and an integer starting in space 21 that is the amount of a donation. We are to read all data into appropriate arrays, alphabetize the names, print the alphabetized list with the amount of each donation, and find the total of all donations.

This problem can be solved by using parallel arrays for the list of names and the list of donations. Appropriate declarations are

```
CONST
  NumberOfDonors = 30;
TYPE
  NameString = PACKED ARRAY [1..20] OF char;
  IndexType = 1..NumberOfDonors;
  NameList = ARRAY [IndexType] OF NameString;
  AmountList = ARRAY [IndexType] OF integer;
VAR
  Donor : NameList;
  Amount : AmountList;
```

COMMUNICATION AND STYLE TIPS

Since parallel arrays use the same index type, definitions could have the form

```
CONST
  NumberOfDonors = 30;
TYPE
  String20 = PACKED ARRAY [1..20] OF char;
  IndexType = 1..NumberOfDonors;
  NameList = ARRAY [IndexType] OF String20;
  AmountList = ARRAY [IndexType] OF integer;
```

A procedure to read the data from an input file is

```
PROCEDURE GetData (VAR Donor : NameList;
                   VAR Amount : AmountList);
  VAR
    J, K : integer;
  BEGIN
    FOR J := 1 TO NumberOfDonors DO
      BEGIN
        FOR K := 1 TO 20 DO
          read (Data, Donor[J,K]);
        readln (Data, Amount[J])
      END  { of FOR J loop }
  END;  { of PROCEDURE GetData }
```

This procedure can be called by

```
GetData (Donor, Amount);
```

After this procedure is called from the main program, the parallel arrays can be envisioned as

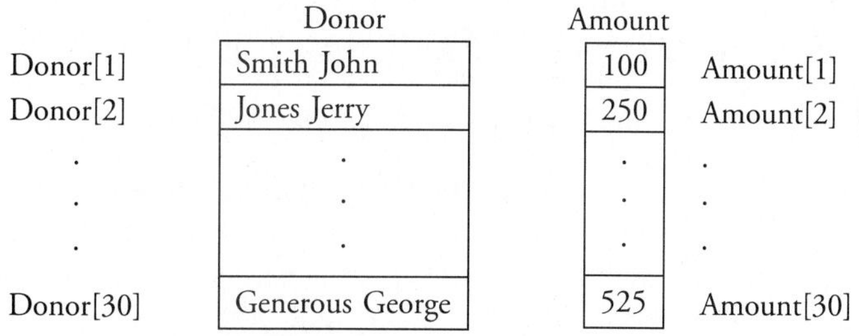

	Donor	Amount	
Donor[1]	Smith John	100	Amount[1]
Donor[2]	Jones Jerry	250	Amount[2]
.	.	.	.
.	.	.	.
.	.	.	.
Donor[30]	Generous George	525	Amount[30]

The next task is to alphabetize the names. However, we must be careful to keep the amount donated with the name of the donor. This can be accomplished by passing both the list of names and the list of donations to the sorting procedure and modifying the code to include exchanging donation amounts whenever the names are exchanged. Since NumberOfDonors is defined in the constant section, a Length argument is not needed. Using the procedure heading

```
PROCEDURE Sort (VAR Donor : NameList;
                VAR Amount : AmountList);
```

the code for sorting is changed in order to interchange both a name and an amount. Thus

```
TempDonor := Donor[Index];
Donor[Index] := Donor[J];
Donor[J] := TempDonor;
```

becomes

```
TempDonor := Donor[Index];
TempAmount := Amount[Index];
Donor[Index] := Donor[J];
Amount[Index] := Amount[J];
Donor[J] := TempDonor;
Amount[J] := TempAmount;
```

The procedure for sorting the list of names and rearranging the list of donations accordingly is called by

```
Sort (Donor, Amount);
```

The next task this program requires is to find the total of all donations. The following function can perform this task.

```
FUNCTION Total (Amount : AmountList) : integer;
  VAR
    Sum, J : integer;
  BEGIN
    Sum := 0;
    FOR J := 1 TO NumberOfDonors DO
      Sum := Sum + Amount[J];
    Total := Sum
  END;  {  of FUNCTION Total  }
```

This function is called by

```
TotalDonations := Total(Amount);
```

where TotalDonations has been declared as a variable of type **integer.**

Our last task is to print the alphabetized list together with the respective donations and the total of all donations. If Donor and Amount have been sorted appropriately, we can use the following procedure to produce the desired output.

```
PROCEDURE PrintData (VAR Donor : NameList;
                     VAR Amount : AmountList;
                     TotalDonations : integer);
  VAR
    J : integer;
  BEGIN
    FOR J := 1 TO NumberOfDonors DO
      BEGIN
        write (Donor[J]:40);
        writeln ('$':2, Amount[J]:5)
      END;  {  of FOR J loop  }
    writeln ('------':47);
    writeln ('Total':40, '$':2, TotalDonations:5);
    writeln
  END;  {  of PROCEDURE PrintData  }
```

A NOTE OF INTEREST

Computer Ethics: Worms

In *The Shockwave Rider* (1975), J. Brunner developed the notion of an omnipotent "tapeworm" program running loose through a network of computers—an idea that seemed rather disturbing but was then well beyond current capabilities. The basic model, however, was a very provocative one: a program or a computation that can move from machine to machine, harnessing resources as needed and replicating itself when necessary.

On November 2, 1988, Cornell computer science graduate student Robert Morris released a worm program into the ARPANET. Over an eight-hour period, it invaded between 2500 and 3000 VAX and Sun computers running the Berkeley UNIX operating system. The worm program disabled virtually all of the computers by replicating rampantly and clogging them with many copies. Many of the computers had to be disconnected from the network until all copies of the worm could be expurgated and until the security loopholes that the worm used to gain entry could be plugged. Most computers were fully operational within two or three days. No files were damaged on any of the computers invaded by the worm.

This incident gained much public attention and produced a widespread outcry in the computer community, perhaps because so many people saw that they had been within a hair's breadth of losing valuable files. After an investigation, Cornell suspended Morris and decried his action as irresponsible. In July 1989, a grand jury brought an indictment against Morris for violation of the Federal Computer Privacy Act of 1986. He was tried and convicted in January 1990.

This is called by

```
PrintData (Donor, Amount, TotalDonations);
```

A complete program for this problem follows.

```
PROGRAM Donations (input, output, Data);

{  This program reads data from an input file where each line   }
{  consists of a donor name followed by the amount donated.     }
{  Output consists of an alphabetically sorted list together    }
{  with the amount of each donation.  This is accomplished by   }
{  using parallel arrays.  The total amount donated is also     }
{  listed.                                                      }

CONST
  NumberOfDonors = 30;
  MaxLength = 20;

TYPE
  NameString = PACKED ARRAY [1..MaxLength] OF char;
  IndexType = 1..NumberOfDonors;
  NameList = ARRAY [IndexType] OF NameString;
  AmountList = ARRAY [IndexType] OF integer;

VAR
  Donor : NameList;               {  An array for donor names      }
  Amount : AmountList;            {  An array for amounts donated  }
  TotalDonations : integer;       {  Total amount donated          }
  Data : text;                    {  Names and amounts donated     }

{***************************************************************}
```

```
PROCEDURE GetData (VAR Donor : NameList;
                   VAR Amount : AmountList);

  {  Given:   Nothing                                          }
  {  Task:    Read names and donations into respective arrays  }
  {  Return:  Parallel arrays of names and donations           }

  VAR
    J, K : integer;
  BEGIN
    FOR J := 1 TO NumberOfDonors DO
      BEGIN
        FOR K := 1 TO MaxLength DO
          read (Data, Donor[J,K]);
        readln (Data, Amount[J])
      END  {  of FOR J loop  }
  END;  {  of PROCEDURE GetData  }

{*****************************************************************}

PROCEDURE SelectionSort (VAR Donor : NameList;
                         VAR Amount : AmountList);

  {  Given:   Unsorted parallel arrays of names and donations  }
  {  Task:    Sort alphabetically                              }
  {  Return:  An alphabetically sorted list of names with      }
  {                 respective donations                       }

  VAR
    TempDonor : NameString;
    TempAmount : integer;
    J, K, Index : integer;
  BEGIN
    FOR J := 1 TO NumberOfDonors - 1 DO
      BEGIN
        Index := J;
        FOR K := J + 1 TO NumberOfDonors DO
          IF Donor[K] < Donor[Index] THEN
            Index := K;
        IF Index <> J THEN            {  Exchange if necessary  }
          BEGIN
            TempDonor := Donor[Index];
            TempAmount := Amount[Index];
            Donor[Index] := Donor[J];
            Amount[Index] := Amount[J];
            Donor[J] := TempDonor;
            Amount[J] := TempAmount
          END  {  of exchange  }
      END  {  of one pass  }
  END;  {  of PROCEDURE SelectionSort  }

{*****************************************************************}
```

```
FUNCTION Total (Amount : AmountList) : integer;

  {  Given:    An array of amounts                                    }
  {  Task:     Sum the components of the array                        }
  {  Return:   The total of array components                          }

  VAR
    Sum, J : integer;
  BEGIN
    Sum := 0;
    FOR J := 1 TO NumberOfDonors DO
      Sum := Sum + Amount[J];
    Total := Sum
  END;  {  of FUNCTION Total  }

{*************************************************************}

PROCEDURE PrintHeading;

  {  Given:    Nothing                                                }
  {  Task:     Print a heading for the output                         }
  {  Return:   Nothing                                                }

  BEGIN
    writeln ('Donor Name':33, 'Donation':15);
    writeln ('----------':33, '--------':15);
    writeln
  END;  {  of PROCEDURE PrintHeading  }

{*************************************************************}

PROCEDURE PrintData (VAR Donor : NameList;
                     VAR Amount : AmountList;
                     TotalDonations : integer);

  {  Given:    Parallel arrays of names/donations and total           }
  {                 donations                                         }
  {  Task:     Print a list of names and amounts donated; end         }
  {                 with the total of all donations                   }
  {  Return:   Nothing                                                }

  VAR
    J : integer;
  BEGIN
    FOR J := 1 TO NumberOfDonors DO
      BEGIN
        write (Donor[J]:40);
        writeln ('$':2, Amount[J]:5)
      END;  {  of FOR J loop  }
    writeln ('------':47);
    writeln ('Total':40, '$':2, TotalDonations:5);
    writeln
  END;  {  of PROCEDURE PrintData  }

{*************************************************************}
```

```
BEGIN  {  Main program  }
  reset (Data);
  GetData (Donor, Amount);
  SelectionSort (Donor, Amount);
  TotalDonations := Total(Amount);
  PrintHeading;
  PrintData (Donor, Amount, TotalDonations)
END.  {  of main program  }
```

Output created from an input file of 30 lines is

```
          Donor Name          Donation
          ----------          --------

     Alexander Candy          $  300
     Anderson Tony            $  375
     Banks Marj               $  375
     Born Patty               $  100
     Brown Ron                $  200
     Darnell Linda            $  275
     Erickson Thomas          $  100
     Fox William              $  300
     Francis Denise           $  350
     Generous George          $  525
     Gillette Mike            $  350
     Hancock Kirk             $  500
     Higgins Sam              $  300
     Janson Kevin             $  200
     Johnson Ed               $  350
     Johnson Martha           $  400
     Jones Jerry              $  250
     Kelly Marvin             $  475
     Kneff Susan              $  300
     Lasher John              $  175
     Lyon Elizabeth           $  425
     Moore Robert             $  100
     Muller Marjorie          $  250
     Smith John               $  100
     Trost Frostie            $   50
     Trudo Rosemary           $  200
     Weber Sharon             $  150
     Williams Art             $  350
     Williams Jane            $  175
     Wilson Mary              $  275
                              ------
                        Total $ 8275
```

EXERCISES 8.3

1. Which of the following are appropriate declarations for parallel arrays? Explain.

a.
```
TYPE
    String15 = PACKED ARRAY [1..15] OF char;
    List15 = ARRAY [1..15] OF real;
  VAR
    Names : ARRAY [1..10] OF String15;
    Amounts : List15;
```

b.
```
TYPE
  Chart = ARRAY [1..12, 1..10] OF integer;
  String10 = PACKED ARRAY [1..10] OF char;
  List = ARRAY [1..12] OF String10;
VAR
  Table : Chart;
  Names : List;
```

2. Write a test program to read names and amounts from a data file. Your program should print both lists and the total of the amounts. Assume each line of data is similar to

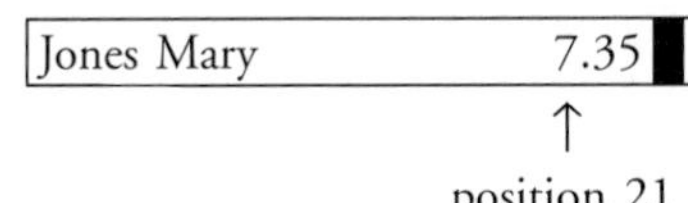

3. Parallel arrays can be used when working with a list of student names and the grades the students receive in a class.
   a. Define array types, and declare subsequent arrays that could be used in such a program.
   b. Write a function that counts the number of occurrences of each letter grade A, B, C, D, and E.
4. Declare appropriate arrays and write a procedure to read data from an input file with an unknown number of lines (but less than 100), where each line contains a name (20 spaces), an age (integer), a marital status (character), and an income (real). A typical data line is

Smith John 35M 28502.16

5. Modify the code in Exercise 4 to accommodate data entered in the data file in the following format:

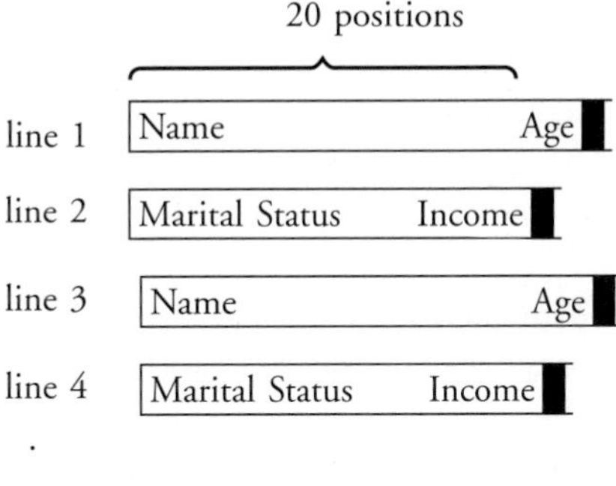

6. Write a procedure to sort the arrays you declared in Exercise 4 according to income.

8.4 Higher-Dimensional Arrays

Thus far, we have worked with arrays of one and two dimensions. Arrays of three, four, or more dimensions can also be declared and used. Pascal places no limitation upon the number of dimensions of an array.

Declarations of Higher-Dimensional Arrays

Declarations of *higher-dimensional arrays* usually assume one of two basic forms. First, a three-dimensional array type can be defined using the form

ARRAY [1 . . 3, 1 . . 4, 1 . . 5] **OF** <data type>

OBJECTIVES

- To understand when arrays of three or more dimensions are needed in a program
- to be able to define and declare data structures for higher-dimensional arrays
- to be able to use higher-dimensional arrays in a program

Each dimension can vary in any of the ways used for arrays of one or two dimensions, and the data type can be any standard or user-defined ordinal data type. Second, a three-dimensional array can be defined as an array of two-dimensional arrays using the form

ARRAY [1 . . 3] **OF ARRAY** [1 . . 4, 1 . . 5] **OF** <data type>

Each of these declarations will reserve 60 locations in memory. This can be visualized as shown in Figure 8.1.

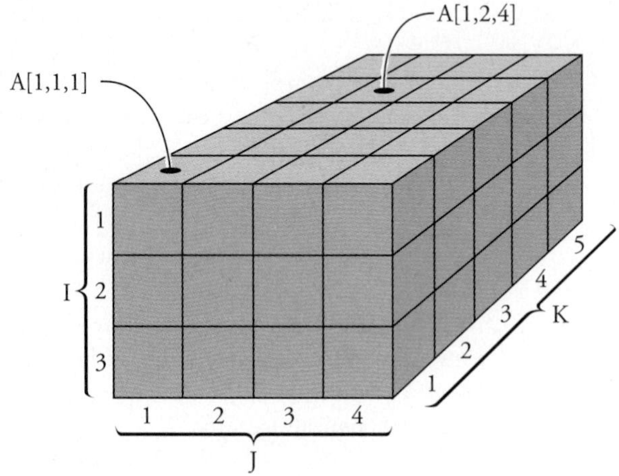

◆ **FIGURE 8.1**
Three-dimensional array with components A[I,J,K]

An array of dimension n can be defined by

ARRAY [1 . . a_1, 1 . . a_2, . . . , 1 . . a_n] **OF** <data type>

which would reserve $a_1 * a_2 * \cdots * a_n$ locations in memory. A general definition is

ARRAY [a_1 . . b_1, a_2 . . b_2, . . . , a_n . . b_n] **OF** <data type>

where $a_i \leq b_i$ for $1 \leq i \leq n$.

It is possible to visualize multidimensional arrays in an inductive manner. As examples, a four-dimensional array can be visualized as a one-dimensional array with each component being a three-dimensional array; a five-dimensional array can be visualized as a one-dimensional array with each component being a four-dimensional array; and so on.

Declarations and uses of higher-dimensional arrays are usually facilitated by descriptive names and user-defined data types. For example, suppose we want to declare a three-dimensional array to hold the contents of a book of tables. If there are 50 pages and each page contains a table composed of 15 rows and 10 columns, a reasonable declaration is

```
TYPE
  Page = 1..50;
  Row = 1..15;
  Column = 1..10;
  Book = ARRAY [Page, Row, Column] OF integer;
VAR
  Item : Book;
```

When this declaration is compared to

```
TYPE
  Book = ARRAY [1..50, 1..15, 1..10] OF integer;
VAR
  Item : Book;
```

we realize both arrays are identical in structure. However, in the first declaration, it is easier to see what the dimensions represent.

Accessing Components

Elements in higher-dimensional arrays are accessed and used in a manner similar to two-dimensional arrays. The difference is that in a three-dimensional array, each element needs three indices for reference. A similar result holds for other dimensions. To illustrate the use of this notation, recall the declaration

```
TYPE
  Page = 1..50;
  Row = 1..15;
  Column = 1..10;
  Book = ARRAY [Page, Row, Column] OF integer;
VAR
  Item : Book;
```

If we want to assign a 10 to the item on page three, row five, column seven, the statement

```
Item[3,5,7] := 10;
```

accomplishes this. Similarly, this item can be printed by

```
write (Item[3,5,7]);
```

Using this same declaration, we can do the following.

1. Print the fourth row of page 21 with the segment of code

```
FOR K := 1 TO 10 DO
  write (Item[21,4,K]:5);
writeln;
```

2. Print the top row of every page by using

```
FOR I := 1 TO 50 DO
  BEGIN
    FOR K := 1 TO 10 DO
      write (Item[I,1,K]:5);
    writeln
  END;
```

3. Print page 35 by using

```
FOR J := 1 TO 15 DO
  BEGIN
    FOR K := 1 TO 10 DO
      write (Item[35,J,K]:5);
    writeln
  END;
```

4. Print every page that does not have a zero in the first row and the first column by using

```
FOR I := 1 TO 50 DO
  IF Item[I,1,1] <> 0 THEN
    FOR J := 1 TO 15 DO
      BEGIN
        FOR K := 1 TO 10 DO
          write (Item[I,J,K]:5);
        writeln
      END;
```

As another illustration of the use of higher-dimensional arrays, consider the situation in which the manager of a high-rise office complex wants to develop a program that keeps track of the tenants in each office. Suppose there are 20 floors, each having the floor plan shown in Figure 8.2. Each wing contains five rooms.

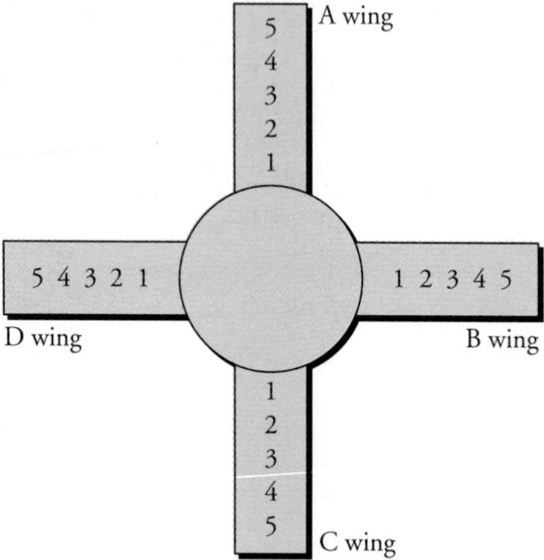

◆ FIGURE 8.2
High-rise floor plan

First, let's declare an appropriate array where the tenant's name can be stored. (Assume each name consists of 20 characters.) This can be accomplished by

```
TYPE
  Floors = 1..20;
  Wings = 'A'..'D';
  Offices = 1..5;
  Name = PACKED ARRAY [1..20] OF char;
  Occupant = ARRAY [Floors, Wings, Offices] OF Name;
VAR
  Tenant : Occupant;
  Floor : Floors;
  Wing : Wings;
  Office : Offices;
```

Note this is really a four-dimensional array, since the data type Name is **PACKED ARRAY.**

Now let's write a segment of code to print a list of names of all tenants on the top floor. To get the names of all tenants of the twentieth floor, we need to print the names for each office in each wing. Assuming a field width of 30 columns, the following code completes the desired task.

```
FOR Wing := 'A' TO 'D' DO
  FOR Office := 1 TO 5 DO
    writeln (Tenant[20, Wing, Office]:30);
```

How would we write a segment of code to read the name of the new tenant on the third floor (B wing, room 5) from the data file? Recall that character strings must be read one character at a time. Tenant [3,'B',5] is the variable name. Since this is a packed array, the code for reading is

```
FOR L := 1 TO 20 DO
  read (Tenant[3,'B',5,L]);
```

Assume the string 'Unoccupied   ' has been entered for each vacant office and we are to write a segment of code to list all vacant offices. This problem requires us to examine every name and print the location of the unoccupied offices. Hence, when we encounter the name 'Unoccupied   ', we want to print the respective indices. This is accomplished by

```
FOR Floor := 1 TO 20 DO
  FOR Wing := 'A' TO 'D' DO
    FOR Office := 1 TO 5 DO
      IF Tenant[Floor, Wing, Office] = 'Unoccupied          '
        THEN writeln (Floor:5, Wing:5, Office:5);
```

As you can see, working with higher-dimensional arrays requires very careful handling of the indices. Nested loops are frequently used to process array elements, and proper formatting of output is critical.

EXERCISES 8.4

1. How many memory locations are reserved in each of the following declarations?

   a.
   ```
   TYPE
     Block = ARRAY [1..2, 1..3, 1..10] OF char;
   VAR
     A : Block;
   ```
   b.
   ```
   TYPE
     Block = ARRAY [-2..3] OF ARRAY [2..4, 3..6] OF real;
   VAR
     A : Block;
   ```
   c.
   ```
   TYPE
     Color = (Red, Black, White);
     Size = (Small, Large);
     Year = 1950..1960;
     Specifications = ARRAY [Color, Size, Year];
   VAR
     A : Specifications;
   ```
   d.
   ```
   TYPE
     String15 = PACKED ARRAY [1..15] OF char;
     List10 = ARRAY [1..10] OF String15;
     NameTable = ARRAY [1..4] OF List10;
   VAR
     A : NameTable;
   ```

2. Write a test program to read values into an array of size 3 × 4 × 5. Assuming this represents three pages, each of which contains a 4 × 5 table, print out the table for each page together with a page number.

3. Declare a three-dimensional array that a hospital could use to keep track of the types of rooms available: private (P), semiprivate (S), and ward (W). The hospital has four floors, five wings, and 20 rooms in each wing.

4. Consider the declaration

```
TYPE
  Pages = 1..50;
  Rows = 1..15;
  Columns = 1..10;
  Book = ARRAY [Pages, Rows, Columns] OF integer;
VAR
  Page : Pages;
  Row : Rows;
  Column : Columns;
  Item : Book;
```

a. Write a segment of code to do each of the following.
   i. Print the fourth column of page 3.
   ii. Print the top seven rows of page 46.
   iii. Create a new page 30 by adding the corresponding elements of page 31 to page 30.

b. What is a general description of the output produced by the following segments of code?

i.
```
FOR Page := 1 TO 15 DO
  BEGIN
    FOR Column := 1 TO 10 DO
      write (Item[Page, Page, Column]:4);
    writeln
  END;
```

ii.
```
FOR Page := 1 TO 50 DO
  FOR Column := 1 TO 10 DO
    writeln (Item[Page, Column, Column]:(Column+4));
```

Use the following problem statement, definitions, and declarations for Exercises 5–8.

An athletic conference consisting of 10 universities wishes to have a program to keep track of the number of athletic grants-in-aid for each team at each institution. The conference programmer has defined the following structure.

```
CONST
  MaxGrants = 90;
TYPE
  Schools = 'A'..'J';
  Sports = (Baseball, Basketball, CrossCountry,
            FieldHockey, Football, Golf, Gymnastics,
            Swimming, Tennis, Track, Volleyball, Wrestling);
  Sex = (Male, Female);
  NumberOfGrants = 0..MaxGrants;
  GrantChart = ARRAY [Schools, Sports, Sex] OF NumberOfGrants;
VAR
  NumGrants : integer;
  Grants : GrantChart;
  School : Schools;
  Sport : Sports;
  Gender : Sex;
```

5. How many memory locations are reserved in the array Grants?
6. Explain what tasks are performed by each of the following segments of code.
   a.
```
NumGrants := 0;
FOR School := 'A' TO 'J' DO
  FOR Sport := Baseball TO Wrestling DO
    NumGrants := NumGrants +
                 Grants[School, Sport, Female];
```
   b.
```
Sum := 0;
FOR School := 'A' TO 'J' DO
  FOR Sport := Baseball TO Wrestling DO
    FOR Gender := Male TO Female DO
      IF Grants[School, Sport, Gender] = 0 THEN
        Sum := Sum + 1;
```
7. Write a segment of code for each of the following tasks.
   a. Find the total number of grants for each university.
   b. Find the total number of grants for each sport.
   c. List all schools that have 10 or more grants in field hockey.
8. Explain how a **CASE** statement can be used to help display all sports (indicate male or female) and the number of grants in each sport for school D.

FOCUS ON PROGRAM DESIGN

This program simulates the solution to a problem that could be posed by a small airline. Mountain-Air Commuters, Inc., is a small airline commuter service. Each of its planes is a 30-passenger plane with a floor plan as follows:

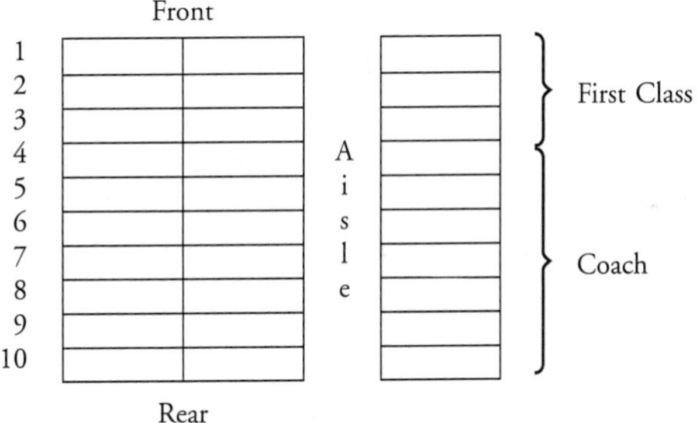

The first three rows are designated as first class because the seats are wider and there is more leg room. (In reality, most commuter planes do not have a first class section. However, rather than include the large data base needed for larger planes, we simulate the problem using a seating plan with only 10 rows.)

Write a program that assigns seats to passengers on a first-come, first-served basis according to the following rules.

1. First class and coach requests must be honored; if seats in the requested sections are full, the customer's name should go on a waiting list for the next flight.
2. Specific seat requests should be honored next; if a requested seat is occupied, the person should be placed in the same row, if possible.
3. If a requested row is filled, the passenger should be seated as far forward as possible.

4. If all seats are filled, the passenger's name should be put on a waiting list for the next flight.

Output should include a seating chart, with passenger names appropriately printed, and a waiting list for the next flight. Each data line (input) contains the passenger's name, first class (F) or coach (C) designation, and seat request indicating the row and column desired.

A typical line of data would be

```
Smith John                    C 5 2
```

where C represents a coach choice, 5 is a request for row five, and 2 is the preferred seat.

A first-level pseudocode development for this problem is

1. Initialize variables
2. **WHILE NOT eof DO** process a name
3. Print a seating chart
4. **IF** there is a waiting list **THEN** print the list

A complete structure chart for this problem is given in Figure 8.3.
Module specifications for the main modules are

1. Initialize Module
Data received: None
Information returned: Value for WaitCount
Value for EmptyWaitingList
Value for SeatPlan
Logic: Assign beginning values to the parameters.
Use nested loops to initialize the array SeatPlan.

2. ProcessAName Module
Data received: None
Information returned: A seating chart
A Boolean value for extra passengers
A waiting list for the next flight
Logic: Get a name, section choice, and seat preference.
Search to see if a seat can be found.
If yes, then ticket.
If no, then save relevant information.

3. PrintSeatingChart Module
Data received: A two-dimensional array of names of ticketed passengers.
Information returned: None
Logic: Print the seating plan, indicating row, section, and seat choice for each passenger.

4. PrintWaitingList Module
Data received: Parallel arrays for the passenger's name, section choice, and seat preference
Information returned: None
Logic: Use a loop to print an appropriately titled list of passengers for the next flight.

A further development of the pseudocode is

◆ FIGURE 8.3
Structure chart for Mountain-Air Commuters, Inc., problem

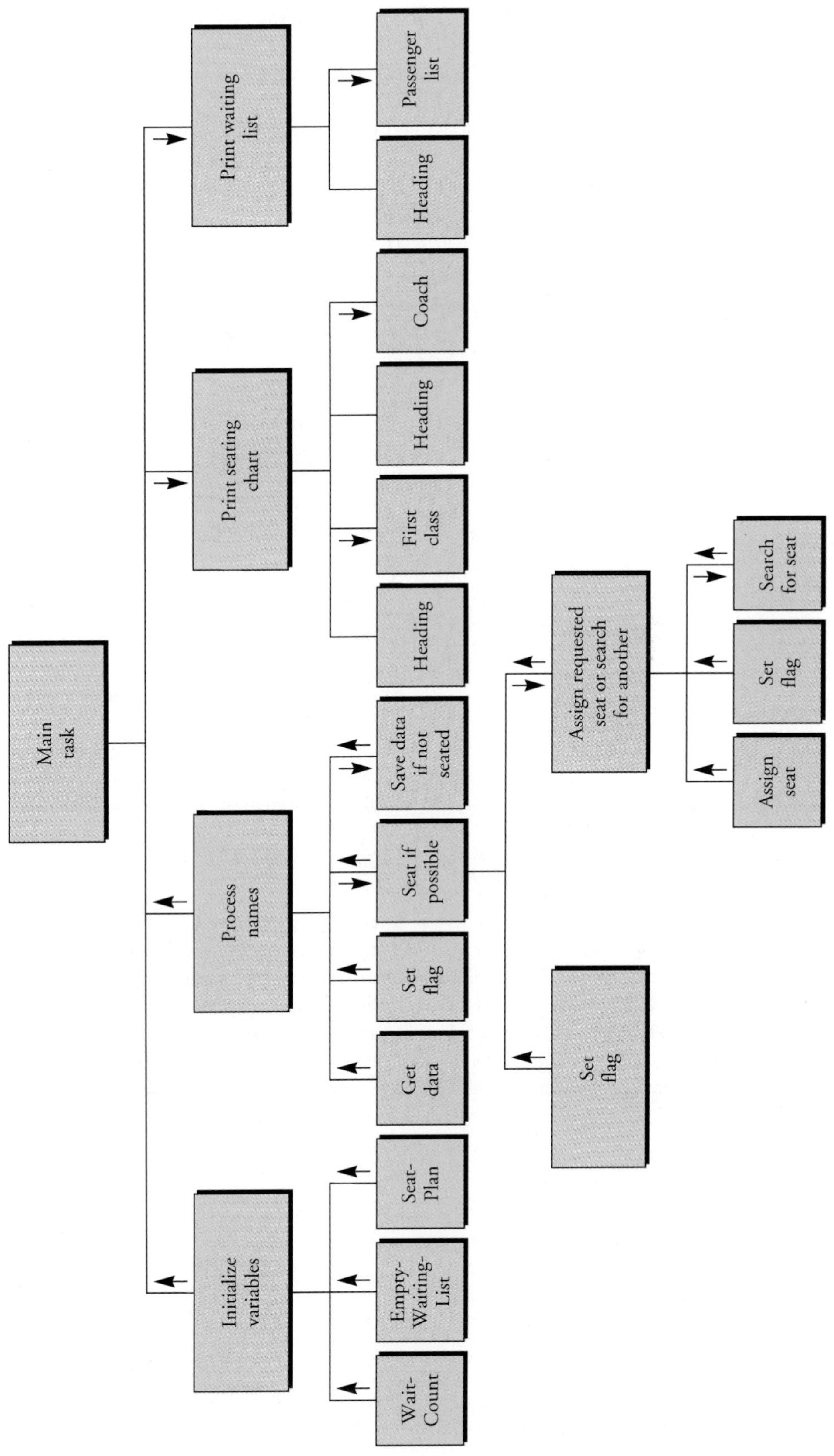

1. Initialize variables
   1.1 initialize WaitCount
   1.2 initialize EmptyWaitingList
   1.3 initialize SeatPlan
2. **WHILE NOT eof DO** process a name
   2.1 get passenger information
   2.2 set Boolean flag Seated for **false**
   2.3 seat if possible
   2.4 **IF NOT** seated **THEN** save relevant information
3. Print a seating chart
   3.1 print a heading
   3.2 print the first class section
   3.3 print a heading
   3.4 print the coach section
4. **IF** there is a waiting list **THEN** print the list
   4.1 print a heading
   4.2 print passenger list with four columns

Step 2.3 needs some additional refinement. Further development yields

2.3 seat if possible
    2.3.1 set Seated to **false**
    2.3.2 **IF** requested seat is available **THEN**
        2.3.2.1 assign seat
        2.3.2.2 set Seated to **true**
        ELSE
        2.3.2.3 search for another seat

A complete program for this problem follows.

```
PROGRAM AirlineSeating (input, output, Data);

{  This program prints a seating plan for an airline.  Passengers     }
{  are assigned seats on a first-come, first-served basis.  Requests  }
{  for first class or coach must be honored.  If all seats are        }
{  filled in a section, the passenger's name and seat preference are  }
{  placed on a waiting list for the next flight.  Features of this    }
{  program include:  defined constants, user-defined data types,      }
{  multidimensional arrays, and subprograms for modular development.  }

CONST
  NumRows = 10;
  NumColumns = 3;
  MaxLength = 25;
  FirstClassBegin = 1;
  FirstClassEnd = 3;
  CoachBegin = 4;
  CoachEnd = 10;
  EmptyString = '                         ';
  Skip = ' ';
  MaxNameLength = 20;
```

```
TYPE
  NameString = PACKED ARRAY [1..MaxNameLength] OF char;
  SeatingPlan = ARRAY [1..NumRows, 1..NumColumns] OF NameString;
  NotSeatedList = ARRAY [1..MaxLength] OF NameString;
  SectionOptionList = ARRAY [1..MaxLength] OF char;
  SeatChoiceList = ARRAY [1..MaxLength, 1..2] OF integer;

VAR
  Seated : boolean;                        {  Indicator for seat found     }
  WaitingList : NotSeatedList;             {  Name list for next flight    }
  WaitCount : integer;                     {  Counter for waiting list     }
  EmptyWaitingList : boolean;              {  Indicator for empty list     }
  Seat : SeatingPlan;                      {  2-dimensional seat array     }
  Name : NameString;                       {  String for names             }
  SectionChoice : char;                    {  First class or coach         }
  RowChoice, ColumnChoice : integer;       {  Seat preference              }
  SectionOption : SectionOptionList;       {  Array of section options     }
  SeatChoice : SeatChoiceList;             {  Array of seat choices        }
  Data : text;                             {  Names, section/seat choice   }

{*******************************************************************}

PROCEDURE Initialize (VAR Seat : SeatingPlan);

  {  Given:   A two-dimensional array of strings                       }
  {  Task:    Initialize all cells to an empty string                  }
  {  Return:  An initialized 2-dimensional array                       }

  VAR                                                                     1
    J, K : integer;
  BEGIN
    FOR J := 1 TO NumRows DO
      FOR K := 1 TO NumColumns DO
        Seat[J,K] := EmptyString
  END;  {  of PROCEDURE Initialize  }

{*******************************************************************}

PROCEDURE GetAName (VAR Name : NameString;
                    VAR SectionChoice : char;
                    VAR RowChoice, ColumnChoice : integer);

  {  Given:   Nothing                                                  }
  {  Task:    Read a name and section and seat preferences from the    }
  {                input file                                          }
  {  Return:  Passenger name and section and seat preferences          }

  VAR
    J : integer;
  BEGIN
    FOR J := 1 TO MaxNameLength DO
      read (Data, Name[J]);
    readln (Data, SectionChoice, RowChoice, ColumnChoice)
  END;  {  of PROCEDURE GetAName  }
```

```
{*********************************************************************}

PROCEDURE SeatIfPossible (Name : NameString;
                          VAR Seat : SeatingPlan;
                          RowChoice, ColumnChoice : integer;
                          SectionChoice : char;
                          VAR Seated : boolean);

  {  Given:   Passenger name and section and seat preferences        }
  {  Task:    If requested seat is available, assign to seat; if     }
  {                seat is not available, use Search to check for an }
  {                alternate seat                                    }
  {  Return:  Seat assignment if one has been made; Boolean flag to  }
  {                indicate if seat was found                        }

  PROCEDURE Search (Name : NameString;
                    VAR Seat : SeatingPlan;
                    VAR Seated : boolean;
                    FirstRow, LastRow : integer);

    {  Given:   Passenger name, current seating chart, row designa-  }
    {                tors for first class and coach sections         }
    {  Task:    Search indicated rows to see if an alternate seat is }
    {                available; if yes, assign passenger to it       }
    {  Return:  Updated seating plan and Boolean flag indicating     }
    {                whether or not a seat was found                 }

    VAR
      Row, Column : integer;
    BEGIN  {  PROCEDURE Search  }
      Seated := false;
      Row := FirstRow;
      REPEAT
        Column := 1;                          {  Start searching rows  }
        REPEAT                                      {  Search one row  }
          IF Seat[Row, Column] = EmptyString THEN
            BEGIN
              Seat[Row, Column] := Name;
              Seated := true
            END
          ELSE
            Column := Column + 1;
        UNTIL Seated OR (Column > NumColumns);
        Row := Row + 1                            {  Search next row  }
      UNTIL Seated OR (Row > LastRow)
    END;  {  of PROCEDURE Search  }

  BEGIN  {  PROCEDURE SeatIfPossible  }
    Seated := false;
    IF Seat[RowChoice, ColumnChoice] = EmptyString THEN
      BEGIN
        Seat[RowChoice, ColumnChoice] := Name;
        Seated := true
      END
```

2

```
    ELSE
      CASE SectionChoice OF
        'F' : Search (Name, Seat, Seated,
                      FirstClassBegin, FirstClassEnd);
        'C' : Search (Name, Seat, Seated,
                      CoachBegin, CoachEnd)
      END  {  of CASE SectionChoice  }
  END;  {  of PROCEDURE SeatIfPossible  }

{*******************************************************************}

PROCEDURE PrintSeatingChart (VAR Seat : SeatingPlan);

  {  Given:   The seating chart and a 2-dimensional array of names    }
  {  Task:    Print the passenger names in rows and columns accord-   }
  {               ing to their assigned seats                         }
  {  Return:  Nothing                                                 }

  VAR
    J, K : integer;
  BEGIN
    writeln;
    writeln (Skip:10, 'MOUNTAIN-AIR COMMUTERS');
    writeln (Skip:15, 'Seating Chart');
    writeln;
    writeln ('First class section');
    writeln ('-------------------');
    writeln;
    FOR J := 1 TO FirstClassEnd DO
      BEGIN
        FOR K := 1 TO NumColumns DO
          write (Seat[J,K]:22);
        writeln
      END;  {  of FOR J loop  }
    writeln;
    writeln ('Coach section');
    writeln ('-------------');
    writeln;
    FOR J := CoachBegin TO CoachEnd DO
      BEGIN
        FOR K := 1 TO NumColumns DO
          write (Seat[J,K]:22);
        writeln
      END;  {  of FOR J loop  }
    writeln
  END;  {  of PROCEDURE PrintSeatingChart  }

{*******************************************************************}

PROCEDURE PrintWaitingList (VAR WaitingList : NotSeatedList;
                            VAR SectionOption : SectionOptionList;
                            VAR SeatChoice : SeatChoiceList;
                            WaitCount : integer);
```

3

```
  {  Given:   An array of names of passengers not seated, and the      }
  {                section and seat preferences for each               }
  {  Task:    Print a waiting list for the next flight                 }
  {  Return:  Nothing                                                  }

  VAR
    J : integer;
  BEGIN                                                                    4
    writeln;
    writeln (Skip:10, 'Waiting list for next flight');
    writeln;
    writeln ('NAME':10, 'SECTION CHOICE':27,
             'ROW NUMBER':15, 'COLUMN NUMBER':15);
    write ('-----------------------------------');
    writeln ('-----------------------------------');
    writeln;
    FOR J := 1 TO WaitCount DO
      writeln ('<', J:2, '>', WaitingList[J]:22, SectionOption[J]:4,
               SeatChoice[J,1]:18, SeatChoice[J,2]:13)
  END;  {  of PROCEDURE PrintWaitingList  }

{*********************************************************************}

BEGIN  {  Main program  }
  reset Data;
  WaitCount := 0;
  EmptyWaitingList := true;
  Initialize (Seat);
  WHILE NOT eof(Data) DO
    BEGIN
      GetAName (Name, SectionChoice, RowChoice, ColumnChoice);
      Seated := false;
      SeatIfPossible (Name, Seat, RowChoice, ColumnChoice,
                      SectionChoice, Seated);
      IF NOT Seated THEN         {  Save information for waiting list  }
        BEGIN
          WaitCount := WaitCount + 1;
          WaitingList[WaitCount] := Name;
          SectionOption[WaitCount] := SectionChoice;
          SeatChoice[WaitCount, 1] := RowChoice;
          SeatChoice[WaitCount, 2] := ColumnChoice;
          EmptyWaitingList := false
        END  {  of IF NOT Seated  }
    END;  {  of WHILE NOT eof  }
  PrintSeatingChart (Seat);
  IF NOT EmptyWaitingList THEN
    PrintWaitingList (WaitingList, SectionOption, SeatChoice,
                      WaitCount)
END.  {  of main program  }
```

Using the data file

```
Smith John           F 3 2
Alexander Joe        C 9 3
Allen Darcy          F 3 2
Jones Mary           C 8 1
Humphrey H           C 8 2
Johnson M            F 3 1
Eastman Ken          F 1 1
Winston Sam          C 8 3
Smythe Susan         C 9 1
Hendricks J B        C 9 2
Hanson Cynthia       C 9 3
Zoranson Steve       C 10 1
Radamacher Joe       C 10 3
Borack Bill          C 10 2
Seracki Don          C 9 2
Henry John           F 1 2
Steveson Enghart     F 1 3
Johansen Mary        F 2 1
Smith Martha         F 2 2
Jones Martha         F 2 3
Rinehart Jim         F 3 3
Rinehart Jane        F 3 2
Swenson Cecil        C 4 1
Swenson Carol        C 4 2
Byes Nikoline        C 4 3
Byes Jennifer        C 5 3
Harris John          C 5 2
Harris Judy          C 5 1
Hartman F G          C 6 1
Hartman D T          C 6 2
Lakes William        C 6 3
Lampton George       C 7 1
Hayes Woodrow        C 7 2
Champion M G         C 7 3
Thomas Lynda         C 8 1
Sisler Susan         C 8 2
Stowers Steve        C 8 3
Banks M J            C 5 3
Banks H W            C 5 2
Brown Susan          C 3 1
Wince Ann            C 8 2
Wince Joanne         C 8 1
```

sample output is

```
              MOUNTAIN-AIR COMMUTERS
                   Seating Chart

First class section
-------------------

  Allen Darcy            Eastman Ken            Henry John
  Steveson Enghart       Johansen Mary          Smith Martha
  Johnson M              Smith John             Jones Martha

Coach section
-------------

  Hanson Cynthia         Seracki Don            Swenson Cecil
  Swenson Carol          Byes Nikoline          Byes Jennifer
  Harris John            Harris Judy            Hartman F G
  Hartman D T            Lakes William          Lampton George
  Jones Mary             Humphrey H             Winston Sam
  Smythe Susan           Hendricks J B          Alexander Joe
  Zoranson Steve         Borack Bill            Radamacher Joe

          Waiting list for next flight

      NAME             SECTION CHOICE     ROW NUMBER  COLUMN NUMBER
---------------------------------------------------------------------
< 1>  Rinehart Jim           F                3            3
< 2>  Rinehart Jane          F                3            2
< 3>  Hayes Woodrow          C                7            2
< 4>  Champion M G           C                7            3
< 5>  Thomas Lynda           C                8            1
< 6>  Sisler Susan           C                8            2
< 7>  Stowers Steve          C                8            3
< 8>  Banks M J              C                5            3
< 9>  Banks H W              C                5            2
<10>  Brown Susan            C                3            1
<11>  Wince Ann              C                8            2
<12>  Wince Joanne           C                8            1
```

RUNNING AND DEBUGGING HINTS

1. Use subrange types with descriptive identifiers to specify index ranges. For example

```
TYPE
  Page = 1..50;
  Row = 1..15;
  Column = 1..10;
  Book = ARRAY [Page, Row, Column] OF real;
```

2. Develop and maintain a systematic method of processing nested loops. For example, students with mathematical backgrounds will often use I, J, and K as index variables for three-dimensional arrays.
3. Be careful to properly subscript multidimensional array components.
4. When using an array of packed arrays as a list of strings, remember that in standard Pascal, strings must be read in one character at a time. However, strings can be written by a single **writeln** command.
5. When sorting one array in a program that uses parallel arrays, remember to make similar component exchanges in all arrays.
6. Define all data structures in the **TYPE** definition section.

SUMMARY

Key Terms

higher-dimensional array parallel array two-dimensional array

Key Concepts

- Two-dimensional arrays can be declared in several ways; one descriptive method is

```
TYPE
  Chart4X6 = ARRAY [1..4, 1..6] OF real;
VAR
  Table : Chart4X6;
```

- Nested loops are frequently used to **read** and **write** values in two-dimensional arrays; for example, data can be read by

```
FOR Row := 1 TO 4 DO
  FOR Column := 1 TO 6 DO
    read (Table[Row, Column]);
```

- When processing the components of a single row or single column, leave the appropriate row or column index fixed and let the other index vary as a loop index; for example, to sum row 3, use

```
Sum := 0;
FOR Column := 1 TO NumOfColumns DO
  Sum := Sum + A[3, Column];
```

  To sum column 3, use

```
Sum := 0;
FOR Row := 1 TO NumOfRows DO
  Sum := Sum + A[Row, 3];
```

- An array of strings in Pascal is a special case of a two-dimensional array; the data structure is an array of packed arrays and can be declared by

```
TYPE
  String20 = PACKED ARRAY [1..20] OF char;
  NameList = ARRAY [1..50] OF String20;
VAR
  Name : NameList;
```

- Arrays of strings (packed arrays of characters) can be alphabetized by using the selection sort.
- Three standard procedures used in programs that work with arrays of strings are (1) get the data, (2) alphabetize the array, and (3) print the alphabetized list.
- Parallel arrays may be used to solve problems that require arrays of the same index type but of different data types.
- A typical problem in which parallel arrays would be used involves working with a list of names and an associated list of numbers (for example, test scores). In Chapter 9, we will see that working with two such lists can also be done with a single array of records.
- A typical data structure declaration for using names and scores is

```
TYPE
  NameString = PACKED ARRAY [1..20] OF char;
  NameList = ARRAY [1..30] OF NameString;
  ScoreList = ARRAY [1..30] OF integer;
```

```
VAR
  Name : NameList;
  Score : ScoreList;
```

- Data structures for solving problems can require arrays of three or more dimensions.
- A typical declaration for an array of three dimensions is

```
TYPE
  Dim1 = 1..10;
  Dim2 = 1..20;
  Dim3 = 1..30;
  Block = ARRAY [Dim1, Dim2, Dim3] OF real;
VAR
  Item : Block;
```

  In this array, a typical component is accessed by

```
Item[I,J,K]
```

- Nested loops are frequently used when working with higher-dimensional arrays; for example, all values on the first level of array Item as just declared can be printed by

```
FOR J := 1 TO 20 DO
  BEGIN
    FOR K := 1 TO 30 DO
      BEGIN
        write (Item[1,J,K]:5:2);
        writeln
      END;  {  of 1 line  }
    writeln
  END;  {  of 20 lines  }
```

- When working with subprograms, array variables are usually passed by reference.

PROGRAMMING PROBLEMS AND PROJECTS

1. The local high school sports boosters are conducting a fund drive to help raise money for the athletic program. As each donation is received, the person's name and donation amount are entered on one line in a data file. Write a program to do the following.
   a. Print an alphabetized list of all donors and their corresponding donations.
   b. Print a list of donations from high to low together with the donors' names.
   c. Compute and print the average and total of all donations.
2. Because they did not meet their original goal, your local high school sports boosters (Problem 1) are at it again. For their second effort, each donor's name and donation are added on a separate line at the end of the previously sorted list. Write a program to produce the lists, average, and total in Problem 1. No donor's name should appear more than once in a list.
3. Dr. Lae Z. Programmer (Problems 5, 22, and 23, Chapter 4; Problem 13, Chapter 5; and Problem 5, Chapter 6) now expects you to write a program to do all record keeping for the class. For each student, consecutive lines of the data file contain the student's name, 10 quiz scores, six program scores, and three examination scores. Your output should include the following.
   a. An alphabetized list together with
      (1) quiz total
      (2) program total
      (3) examination total
      (4) total points
      (5) percentage grade
      (6) letter grade

   b. The overall class average
   c. A histogram depicting the grade distribution
4. The All Metro Basketball Conference consists of 10 teams. The conference commissioner has created a data file in which each line contains one school's name, location, and nickname for the school team. You are to write a program to read this data and then produce three lists, each of which contains all information about the school. All lists are to be sorted alphabetically: the first, by school name; the second, by school location; and the third, by nickname.
5. Upgrade the program for Mountain-Air Commuters, Inc., in the Focus on Program Design so it can be used for each of five daily flights. Passengers on a waiting list must be processed first. Print a seating chart for each flight.
6. Add yet another upgrade to the Mountain-Air Commuters, Inc., program. Write an interactive version to consider the possibility of seating passengers who wish to be seated together in the same row. If no such seating is possible, these passengers should be given a choice of alternate seating (if possible) or of taking a later flight.
7. Salespersons at the McHenry Tool Corporation are given a monthly commission check. The commission is computed by multiplying the salesperson's gross monthly sales by the person's commission rate.

   Write a program to compute a salesperson's monthly commission computed to the nearest cent. The program should prepare a list of all salespersons in descending order based upon monthly commission earned, with the person earning the highest commission on top. Each salesperson's commission should be printed next to his or her name. At the bottom of the list, indicate the total monthly commission (summed across all salespersons) and the average commission per salesperson. McHenry never employs more than 60 salespersons.

   Any names of persons who have invalid data should be printed out separately. Data are invalid if the commission rate is not between 0.01 and 0.50 or if the gross monthly sales figure is negative.
8. In order to reduce their costs, the McHenry Tool Corporation (Problem 7) is switching from monthly to biannual commission checks. The commission is now computed by multiplying a person's commission rate by the sum of his or her gross monthly sales for a six-month period. McHenry has asked you to develop the necessary computer program. The program should differ from Problem 7 in the following ways.
   a. Each name on the output should be followed by the six figures for gross monthly sales. The columns should be labeled "January" through "June." Total six-month gross sales should be given next, followed by rate of commission and the amount of the six-month commission check to the nearest cent.
   b. Commission rates are based upon gross six-month sales as follows.

Sales	Commission Rate (%)
0–$19,999	3.0
$20,000–$39,999	5.0
$40,000–59,999	5.5
$60,000–79,999	6.0
$80,000–89,999	6.5
$90,000 or more	8.0

c. At the bottom of each column, the program should provide the total and the mean for that column. (The column for commission rates does not require a total, only a mean.)

9. The dean of a small undergraduate college (with an enrollment of less than 2000) has asked you to write a program to figure grade point averages for an unknown number of students. The output should be an alphabetized roster showing the gender, identification number (social security number), grade point average (rounded to three decimal places), and class status (freshman, sophomore, junior, or senior) for each student.

   The data provide the name, gender (M or F), social security number (ID), and number of semesters completed. Also provided are the number of courses taken and the letter grade and number of credits for each course. The possible letter grades are A (4 points), B (3 points), C (2 points), D (1 point), and E (0 points). Class status is determined by the number of credits, as follows:

1–25 credits	freshman
26–55 credits	sophomore
56–85 credits	junior
86 or more credits	senior

10. You have just started to work for the Michigan Association of Automobile Manufacturers and have been asked to analyze sales data gathered on five subcompact cars for the last six months. Your analysis should be in table form and should include the name of each make and model, a model's sales volume for each month, a model's total and average sales volumes for six months, a model's total sales revenue for six months, and the total and average sales volumes for each month. In addition, your output should include the total and average sales volumes of all models for the entire six months and the make and model name of the car with the largest total sales revenue and the amount of that revenue.

11. You have been asked to write a program to assist with the inventory and ordering for Tite-Jeans, Inc. The company manufactures three styles: straight, flair, and peg. In each style, waist sizes vary by integer values from 24 to 46 and inseams vary by integer values from 26 to 40. Write a program to do the following.
    a. Read in the starting inventory.
    b. Read in daily sales.
    c. Print the ending inventory for each style.
    d. Print order charts for each style that is low in stock (fewer than 3).
    e. Print an emergency order list for each style that is out of stock.

12. You have been asked to write a program that will grade the results of a true-false quiz and display the results in tabular form. The quiz consists of 10 questions. The data file for this problem consists of (1) correct responses (answer key) on line one, and (2)a four-digit student identification number followed by that student's 10 responses on each successive line. Thus, the data file would be

```
TFFTFTTFTT
0461 TTFTTFTFTT
3218 TFFTTTTFTT
.
.
.
```

Your program should read the key and store it in an array. It should then read the remaining lines, storing the student identification numbers in one array and the number of correct responses in a parallel array. Output should consist of a table with three columns: one for the student identification number, one for the number of correct responses, and one for the quiz grade. Grade assignments are A (10 correct), B (9), C (8–7), D (6–5), E (4–0). Your output should also include the quiz average for the entire class.

13. A few members (total unknown, but no more than 25) at Oakland Mountain Country Club want to computerize their golf scores. Each member plays 20 games: some play 18 holes; and some, 9 holes. Each member's name (no more than 20 characters) is written on a data card, followed on a second card by the 20 scores. Each score is immediately followed by an E or an N, indicating 18 or nine holes, respectively.

Write a program to read all the names and scores into two parallel two-dimensional arrays. Calculate everyone's 18-hole average. (Double the nine-hole scores before you store them in the array, and treat them as 18-hole scores.) Calculate how much each average is over or under par. (Par is 72 and should be declared as a constant.) Output should be each name, average, difference from par, and scores.

14. Write a program to keep statistics for a basketball team consisting of 15 players. Statistics for each player should include shots attempted, shots made, and shooting percentage; free throws attempted, free throws made, and free throw percentage; offensive rebounds and defensive rebounds; assists; turnovers; and total points. Appropriate team totals should be listed as part of the output.

15. A magic square is a square array of positive integers such that the sum of each row, column, and diagonal is the same constant. For example

16	3	2	13
5	10	11	8
9	6	7	12
4	15	14	1

is a magic square with a constant of 34. Write a program to input four lines of four positive integers. The program should then determine whether or not the square is a magic square. Program efficiency should be such that computation ends as soon as two different sums have been computed.

16. Pascal's Triangle can be used to recognize coefficients of a quantity raised to a power. The rules for forming this triangle of integers are such that each row must start and end with a 1 and each entry in a row is the sum of the two values diagonally above the new entry. Thus, four rows of Pascal's Triangle are

```
      1
    1   1
  1   2   1
1   3   3   1
```

This triangle is a convenient way to determine the coefficients of a quantity of two terms raised to a power (binomial coefficients). For example

$$(a + b)^3 = 1a^3 + 3a^2b + 3ab^2 + 1b^3$$

where the coefficients 1, 3, 3, and 1 come from the fourth row of Pascal's Triangle.

Write a complete program to print out Pascal's Triangle for 10 rows.

17. Your former high school principal wants you to develop a program to maintain a list of the 20 students in the school with the highest scores on the SAT test. Input is from a text file containing the name (20 characters) and the total SAT score (verbal plus mathematical). Write a program that reads all the data and then prints out a list of the 20 highest scores from high to low and the students' names. Assume no two students have the same score.

18. The transpose of a matrix (table) is a new matrix with the row and column positions reversed. Thus, the transpose of matrix A, an $M \times N$ matrix is an $N \times M$ matrix with each element $A[m,n]$ stored in $B[n,m]$. Given a 3×5 matrix of integers, create a matrix that is its transpose. Print both the original matrix and the new matrix.

■ **19.** Mr. Laven, a mathematics instructor at your college, wants you to write a program to help him keep his students' grades. He wants to keep track of up to 30 grades each for up to 35 students. Your program should read grades and names from a text file, and then print the following.

a. A table showing the names in alphabetical order and the grades received by each student.

b. An alphabetical list of students with their corresponding total points and average score.

c. A list of averages from high to low with corresponding students' names.

20. Write a program in which a person can enter data into a 5×7 matrix. Print the original matrix along with the average of each row and column.

21. Matrix M is symmetric if it has the same number of rows as columns and if each element $M[x,y]$ is equal to $M[y,x]$. Write a program to check a matrix entered by the user to see if it is symmetric or not.

22. The determinant of a 2×2 matrix

$$A = \begin{bmatrix} a & b \\ c & d \end{bmatrix}$$

is $\det A = \begin{vmatrix} a & b \\ c & d \end{vmatrix} = ad - bc.$

The determinant of a 3×3 matrix

$$A = \begin{bmatrix} a & b & c \\ d & e & f \\ g & h & i \end{bmatrix}$$

is $\det A = a\begin{vmatrix} e & f \\ h & i \end{vmatrix} - b\begin{vmatrix} d & f \\ g & i \end{vmatrix} + c\begin{vmatrix} d & e \\ g & h \end{vmatrix}.$

Write an interactive program that computes the determinant of a 3×3 matrix. Input consists of reals forming the 3×3 matrix. Output should be a display that includes the input matrix, a developmental step using 2×2 submatrices, and the value of the determinant. The program should contain a function for computing the determinant of a 2×2 matrix.

■ **23.** The following table shows the total sales for salespeople of the Falcon Manufacturing Company.

Salesperson	Week 1	Week 2	Week 3	Week 4
Anna, Michael	30	25	45	18
Henderson, Marge	22	30	32	35
Johnson, Fred	12	17	19	15
Striker, Nancy	32	30	33	31
Ryan, Renee	22	17	28	16

The price of the product being sold is $1985.95. Write a program that permits the input of the previous data and prints both a replica of the original table and a table showing the dollar value of sales for each individual during each week along with his or her total sales. Also print the total sales for each week and the total sales for the company.

24. The computer science office wants you to develop a computerized system for finding telephone numbers of students. The program should read a list of up to 20 students and their telephone numbers from a text file. It should permit the entry of a student's name and then print the name and telephone number. (A binary search could be used for this.) If the name is not found, an appropriate message should be printed.

25. A graph in the field of graph theory consists of a collection of vertices and edges. For example, graph G

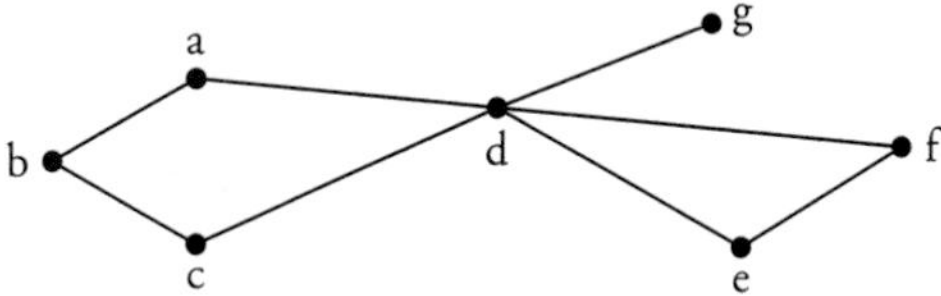

contains seven vertices and eight edges. Two vertices are adjacent if they are joined by an edge. In graph G, therefore, *a* is adjacent to *b* but *a* is not adjacent to *g*.

The adjacency matrix of a graph is a square matrix consisting of 1s and 0s, which indicate whether or not two vertices are adjacent. If the two vertices are adjacent, the corresponding entry is a 1; if they are not adjacent, the entry is a 0. For graph G, the adjacency matrix is as follows:

	a	*b*	*c*	*d*	*e*	*f*	*g*
a	0	1	0	1	0	0	0
b	1	0	1	0	0	0	0
c	0	1	0	1	0	0	0
d	1	0	1	0	1	1	1
e	0	0	0	1	0	1	0
f	0	0	0	1	1	0	0
g	0	0	0	1	0	0	0

Write a program that accepts as input the adjacency matrix of graph G. Each input line represents one row of the graph. Output should consist of the adjacency matrix with vertices indicated for the rows and columns and a list of all edges in the graph.

26. Write a program to permit two people to play the game of Battleship. Your program should record the ship positions, hits, misses, and ship sinkings for each player.
27. Rewrite the Battleship program (Problem 26) to have a person play against the computer.

COMMUNICATION IN PRACTICE

1. Select a problem from the Programming Problems and Projects in this chapter that you have not done. Write documentation for that problem that includes a complete description of the following.
   a. Required input
   b. Required output
   c. Required processing and computation
2. Assume you are directing the development of a spelling checker to be used in conjunction with a text editor. Work up a complete set of specifications that can be used by the team who will do the actual development. Your specifications should include a description of the main tasks to be performed by the team, a statement of the expected form of input and output for the finished product, and documentation standards to be included in the development of each component.
3. Arrange a visit with a travel agent or an airline reservation agent, and discuss the information the agent requests from prospective passengers. If possible, have the agent set up a mock booking using the computerized reservation system. Examine the screen displays.

   Prepare a report of your visit for the class. Be sure to discuss how the designers of the reservation system may have used multidimensional arrays.
4. Contact someone who uses a spreadsheet as part of his or her daily work. Have the person show you several routine operations with the spreadsheet. In particular, find out how to adjust the size of the spreadsheet, sum rows, sum columns, and use functions to define entries for specific locations.

   Give an oral report of your discussion to your class. Explain how the various spreadsheet operations relate to what you have studied about two-dimensional arrays.
5. Select a problem from the Programming Problems and Projects in this chapter that you have not done. Construct a structure chart and write all documentary information necessary for the problem you have chosen. Do not write code. When you are finished, have a classmate read your documentation to see if it is clear precisely what is to be done.
6. Delete all documentation from one of the programs you prepared for this chapter. Exchange your modified version with a student who has prepared a similar version. Write documentation for the exchanged program. Compare your results with your classmate's original version.

CHAPTER 9 Records

CHAPTER OUTLINE

Chapters 7 and 8 dealt extensively with the concept of the structured data type **ARRAY.** When we declare an array, we reserve a predetermined number of memory locations. The variables representing these memory locations are of the same base type and can be accessed by reference to the index of an array element.

All components of an array must be of the same data type—a serious limitation since in many situations this is not possible. For example, a bank may wish to keep a record of the name, address, telephone number, marital status, social security number, annual salary, total assets, and total liabilities of each customer. As we saw in Chapter 8, parallel arrays can be used to solve some of these problems. Fortunately, Pascal provides another structured data type, **RECORD,** which allows heterogeneous information to be stored, accessed, and manipulated. A record contains fields, which can be of different data types. In this chapter, we will learn how to declare records, how to access the various fields within a record, and how to work with arrays of records.

9.1 Record Definitions

OBJECTIVES

- to understand the basic idea of **RECORD** as a structured data type
- to be able to declare a **RECORD**
- to be able to use fields of a **RECORD**

RECORD as a Structured Data Type

A *record* is a collection of fields that may be treated as a whole or individually. To illustrate, a record that contains fields for a customer's name, age, and annual income could be visualized as shown in Figure 9.1.

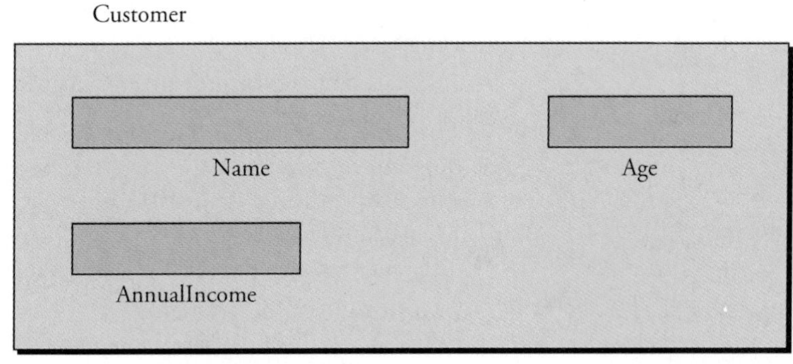

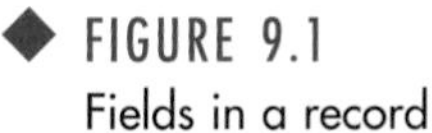
FIGURE 9.1
Fields in a record

This schematic representation may help you understand why a record is considered a structured data type and may help familiarize you with the idea of using fields in a record.

RECORD Definition and Declaration

Now let's consider our first example of a formally declared record. Assume we want a record to contain a customer's name, age, and annual income. The following definition and subsequent declaration can be made.

```
TYPE
  CustomerInfo = RECORD
                   Name : PACKED ARRAY [1..30] OF char;
                   Age : integer;
                   AnnualIncome : real
                 END;  {  of RECORD CustomerInfo  }
VAR
  Customer : CustomerInfo;
```

Components of a record are called *fields,* and each field has an associated data type. The general form for defining a record data type using the **TYPE** definition section is

```
TYPE
  <type identifier> = RECORD
                        <field identifier 1> : <data type 1>;
                        <field identifier 2> : <data type 2>;
                              .                    .
                              .                    .
                              .                    .
                        <field identifier n> : <data type n>
                      END  {  of RECORD definition  }
```

The syntax diagram for this is

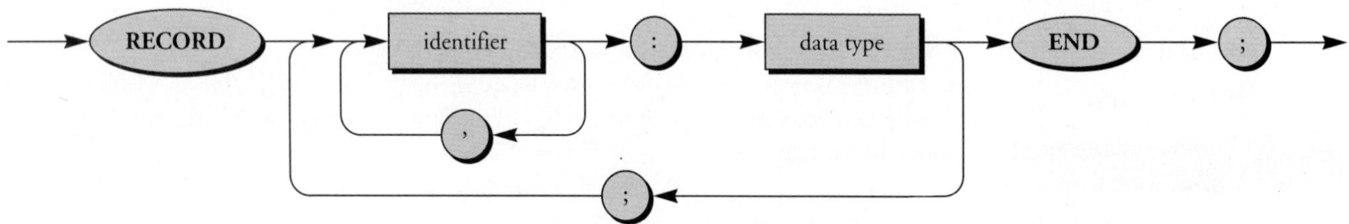

The following comments are in order concerning this form.

1. The type identifier can be any valid identifier. It should be descriptive to enhance program readability.
2. The reserved word **RECORD** must precede the field identifiers.
3. Each field identifier within a record must be unique. However, field identifiers in different records may use the same name. Thus

```
FirstRecord = RECORD
                Name : PACKED ARRAY [1..30] OF char;
                Age : integer
              END;  {  of RECORD FirstRecord  }
```

and

```
SecondRecord = RECORD
                 Name : PACKED ARRAY [1..30] OF char;
                 Age : integer;
                 IQ : integer
               END;  {  of RECORD SecondRecord  }
```

can both be defined in the same program.

4. Data types for fields can be user-defined. Thus, our earlier definitions could be

```
TYPE
  NameString = PACKED ARRAY [1..30] OF char;
  CustomerInfo = RECORD
                   Name : NameString;
                   Age : integer;
                   AnnualIncome : real
                 END;  {  of RECORD CustomerInfo  }
VAR
  Customer : CustomerInfo;
```

5. **END** is required to signify the end of a **RECORD** definition. This is the second instance (remember **CASE**?) in which **END** is used without a **BEGIN.**
6. Fields of the same base type can be declared together. Thus

```
Info = RECORD
         Name : NameString;
         Age, IQ : integer
       END;  {  of RECORD Info  }
```

is appropriate. However, it is good practice to list each field separately to enhance readability and to reinforce the concept of fields in a record.

The following example defines another record.

EXAMPLE 9.1

Let's define a record for a college student to contain a field for each of the following: student's name (Smith Jane), social security number (111-22-3333), class status (Fr, So, Jr, or Sr), previous credit hours earned (56), credit hours being taken (17), and grade point average (3.27). We can define a record and declare an appropriate variable as follows:

```
TYPE
  NameString = PACKED ARRAY [1..30] OF char;
  String11 = PACKED ARRAY [1..11] OF char;
  Class = (Fr, So, Jr, Sr);
  StudentInfo = RECORD
                  Name : NameString;
                  SSN : String11;
                  Status : Class;
                  HoursEarned : 0..999;
                  HoursTaking : 0..30;
                  GPA : real
                END;  {  of RECORD StudentInfo  }
VAR
  Student : StudentInfo;
```

Fields in a Record

Now that we know how to define a record, we need to examine how to access fields in a record. For the purposes of our discussion, let's consider a record defined by

```
TYPE
  NameString = PACKED ARRAY [1..30] OF char;
  Employee = RECORD
               Name : NameString;
               Age : integer;
               MaritalStatus : char;
               Wage : real
             END;  {  of RECORD Employee  }
VAR
  Programmer : Employee;
```

Programmer can be visualized as shown in Figure 9.2.

◆ FIGURE 9.2
Defined fields in Programmer

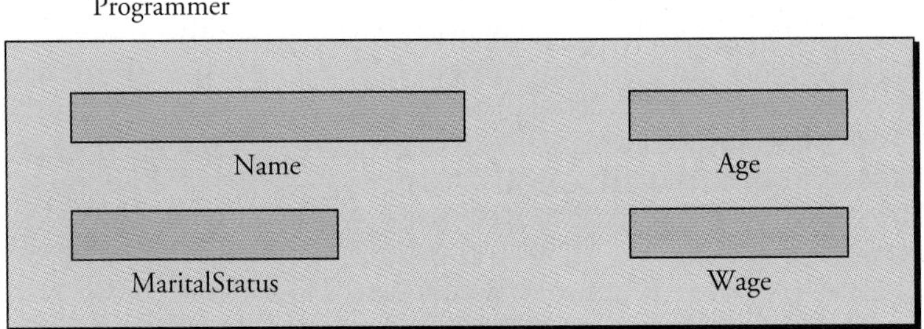

Each field within a record is a variable and can be uniquely identified by

<record name>.<field name>

The period is a *field selector* that separates the record name from the field name. Thus, the four field variables are

```
Programmer.Name
Programmer.Age
Programmer.MaritalStatus
Programmer.Wage
```

Each of these variables can be used in any manner consistent with the defined base type. To illustrate, if Programmer.Name and Programmer.Age have been assigned values and we wish to print the names of those employees under 30 years of age, we could have a fragment of code such as

```
IF Programmer.Age < 30 THEN
  writeln (Programmer.Name:40);
```

If we wish to compute gross salary, we might have

```
read (Hours);
GrossSalary := Hours * Programmer.Wage;
```

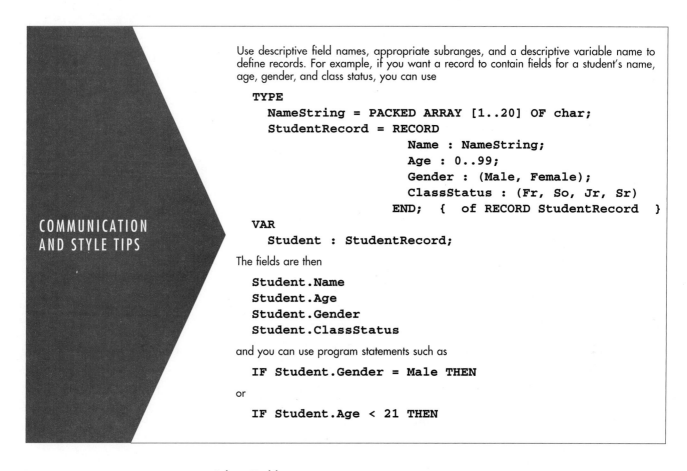

COMMUNICATION AND STYLE TIPS

Use descriptive field names, appropriate subranges, and a descriptive variable name to define records. For example, if you want a record to contain fields for a student's name, age, gender, and class status, you can use

```
TYPE
  NameString = PACKED ARRAY [1..20] OF char;
  StudentRecord = RECORD
                    Name : NameString;
                    Age : 0..99;
                    Gender : (Male, Female);
                    ClassStatus : (Fr, So, Jr, Sr)
                  END;  { of RECORD StudentRecord  }
VAR
  Student : StudentRecord;
```

The fields are then

```
Student.Name
Student.Age
Student.Gender
Student.ClassStatus
```

and you can use program statements such as

```
IF Student.Gender = Male THEN
```

or

```
IF Student.Age < 21 THEN
```

Other Fields

Thus far, our fields have been declared directly. Sometimes, when the structure of a record is being established, the data type of a field needs more development. For example, suppose we wish to declare a record for each student in a class and the record is to contain student name, class name, four test scores, 10 quiz scores, final average, and letter grade. This can be visualized as shown in Figure 9.3.

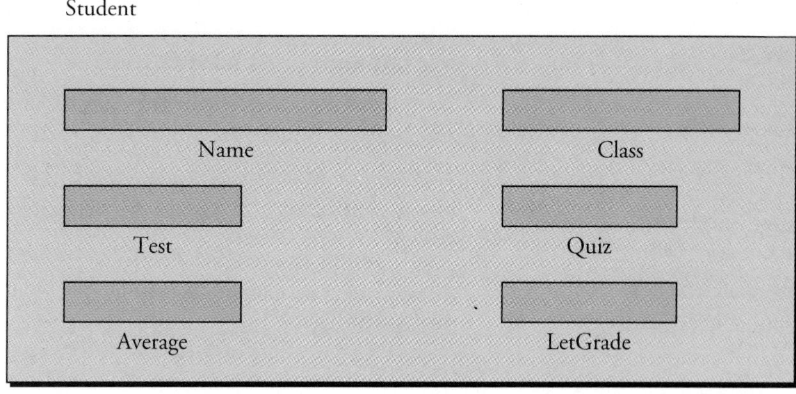

◆ FIGURE 9.3
Fields in Student

In this case, Test and Quiz are both arrays. Thus, a subsequent development is shown in Figure 9.4.

◆ FIGURE 9.4
Arrays as fields in a record

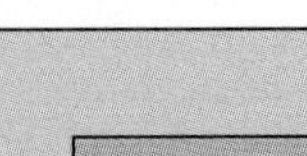

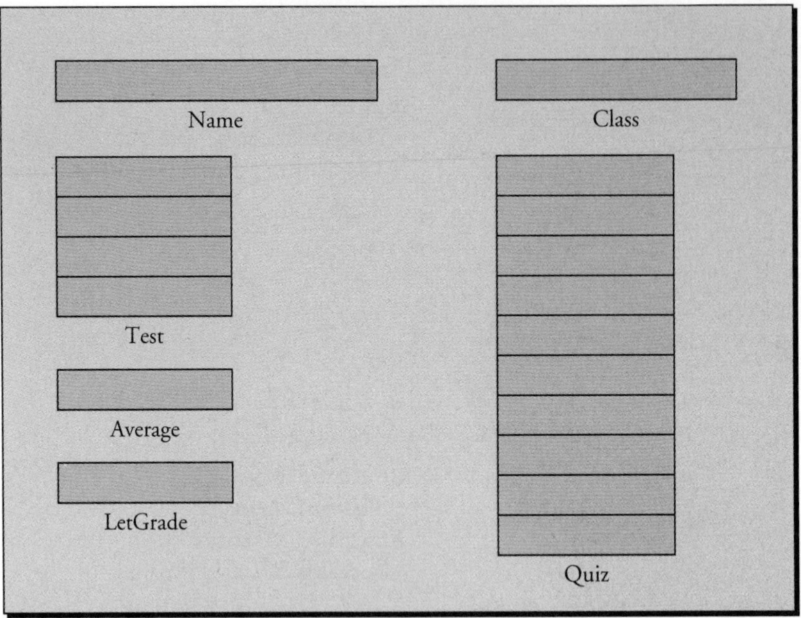

The record in Figure 9.4 can now be formally defined by

```
TYPE
  NameString = PACKED ARRAY [1..30] OF char;
  String10 = PACKED ARRAY [1..10] OF char;
  TestScores = ARRAY [1..4] OF integer;
  QuizScores = ARRAY [1..10] OF integer;
  StudentInfo = RECORD
                  Name : NameString;
                  Class : String10;
                  Test : TestScores;
                  Quiz : QuizScores;
                  Average : real;
                  LetGrade : char
                END;  {  of RECORD StudentInfo  }
VAR
  Student : StudentInfo;
```

If the student associated with this record earns an 89 on the first test and a 9 (out of 10) on the first quiz, this information can be entered by reading the values or by assigning them appropriately. Thus, either

```
read (Student.Test[1], Student.Quiz[1]);
```

or

```
Student.Test[1] := 89;
Student.Quiz[1] := 9;
```

will suffice.

EXERCISES 9.1

1. Explain why records are structured data types.
2. Write a test program to
   a. Define a **RECORD** type in which the record contains fields for your name and your age.

b. Declare a record variable to be of this type.
c. Read your name and age from a data file.
d. Print your name and age.

3. Discuss the similarities and differences between arrays and records as structured data types.
4. Use the **TYPE** definition section to define each of the three records illustrated in Figure 9.5. In each case, declare a record variable of the defined type.

◆ FIGURE 9.5
Records with fields illustrated

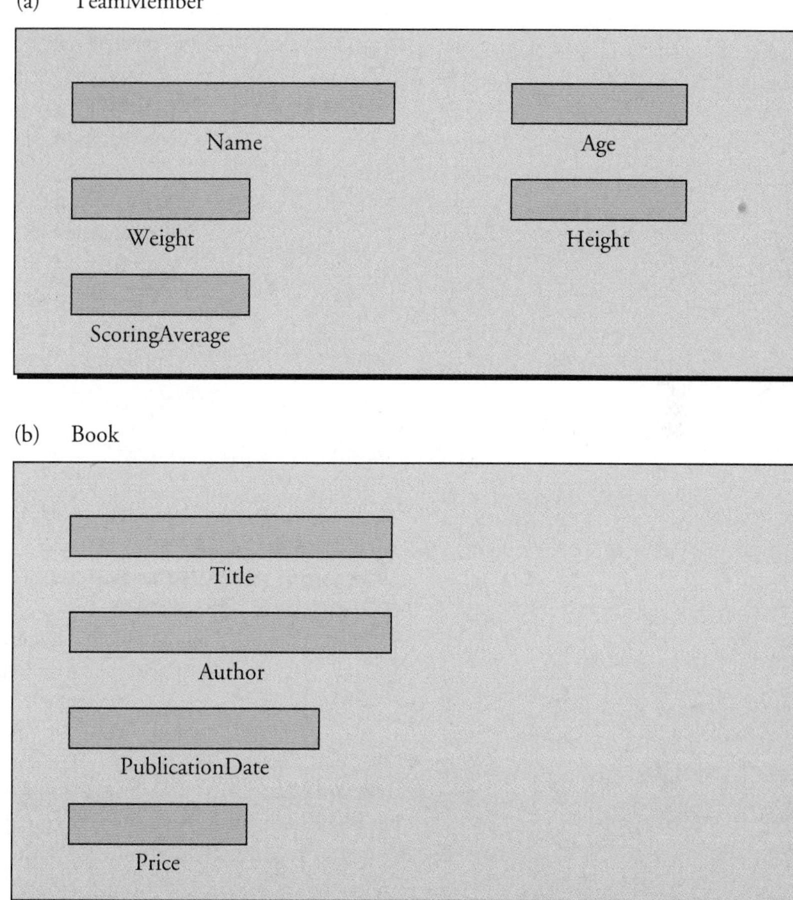

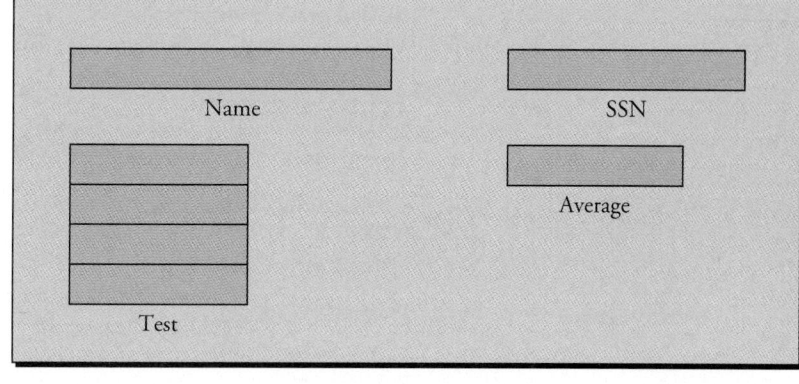

5. Draw a schematic representation of each of the following record definitions.

a.
```
TYPE
  NameString = PACKED ARRAY [1..30] OF char;
  String11 = PACKED ARRAY [1..11] OF char;
  EmployeeInfo = RECORD
                   Name : NameString;
                   SSN : String11;
                   NumOfDep : integer;
                   HourlyWage : real
                 END;
VAR
  Employee : EmployeeInfo;
```

b.
```
TYPE
  HouseInfo = RECORD
                Location : PACKED ARRAY [1..20]
                             OF char;
                Age : integer;
                NumRooms : integer;
                NumBaths : integer;
                BuildingType : (Brick, Frame);
                Taxes : real;
                Price : real
              END;
VAR
  House : HouseInfo;
```

c.
```
TYPE
  NameString = PACKED ARRAY [1..30] OF char;
  String20 = PACKED ARRAY [1..20] OF char;
  String8 = PACKED ARRAY [1..8] OF char;
  PhoneBook = RECORD
                Name : NameString;
                Address : ARRAY [1..4] OF String20;
                PhoneNum : String8
              END;
VAR
  PhoneListing : PhoneBook;
```

6. Use the **TYPE** definition section to define an appropriate **RECORD** type for each of the following. In each case, also declare an appropriate record variable.

   a. Families in your former school district: each record should contain the last name, parents' first and last names, address, number of children, and ages of children.

   b. Students in a school system: each record should contain the student's name, identification number, classification (Fr, So, Jr, or Sr), courses being taken (at most, six), and grade point average.

7. Find all errors in each of the following definitions or declarations.

a.
```
TYPE
  Info : RECORD
           Name = PACKED ARRAY [1..30] OF char;
           Age : 0..100
         END;
```

b.
```
TYPE
  Member = RECORD
             Age : integer;
             IQ : integer
           END;
```

```
   VAR
     Member : Member;
c. VAR
     Member = RECORD
                Name : PACKED ARRAY [1..30] OF char;
                Age : 0..100;
                IQ = 50..200
              END;
```

8. Given the record defined by

```
TYPE
  NameString = PACKED ARRAY [1..30] OF char;
  Weekdays = (Mon, Tues, Wed, Thur, Fri);
  ListOfScores = ARRAY [1..5] OF integer;
  Info = RECORD
           Name : NameString;
           Day : Weekdays;
           Score : ListOfScores;
           Average : real
         END;
VAR
  Contestant : Info;
  Sum : integer;
```

assume values have been assigned as shown in Figure 9.6.

◆ FIGURE 9.6

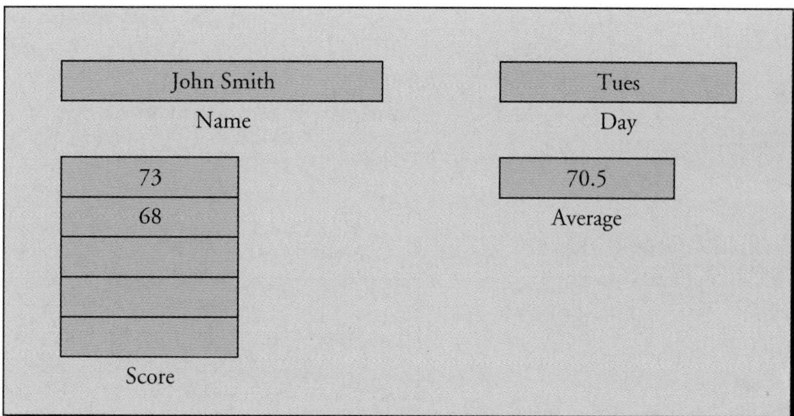

Indicate which of the following are valid; explain any invalid statements.

a. `Day := Wed;`

b. `Contestant.Day := Wed;`

c. `Score := 70;`

d. `Score[3] := 70;`

e. `Contestant.Score[3] := 70;`

f. `Contestant[3].Score := 70;`

g.
```
FOR J := 1 TO 5 DO
  Sum := Sum + Contestant.Score[J];
```

```
h. Contestant.Score[3] := Score[2];
i. Contestant.Score[3] := Contestant.Score[2] + 3;
j. Average := (Score[1] + Score[2] + Score[3]) / 3;
k. IF Contestant.Day < Wed THEN
     Contestant.Average := Contestant.Score[1] +
                           Contestant.Score[2];
l. writeln (Contestant.Name:40, Contestant.Average:10:2);
```

9.2 Using Records

OBJECTIVES

- to be able to use **WITH . . . DO** when using records in a program
- to be able to copy complete records
- to be able to use a procedure to read data into a record
- to be able to use a procedure to print data from a record

The previous section introduced the concept of **RECORD** as a structured data type. At this stage, you should be comfortable with this concept and be able to use the **TYPE** definition section to define such a data type. In this section, we will examine methods of working with records.

WITH . . . DO Using Records

Let's consider a record that contains fields for a student's name, three test scores, and test average. This field can be defined by

```
CONST
  NameLength = 20;
  NumTests = 3;
TYPE
  NameString = PACKED ARRAY [1..NameLength] OF char;
  TestList = ARRAY [1..NumTests] OF integer;
  StudentRecord = RECORD
                    Name : NameString;
                    Score : TestList;
                    Average : real
                  END;  { of RECORD StudentRecord }
VAR
  Student : StudentRecord;
```

and envisioned as shown in Figure 9.7.

◆ FIGURE 9.7
Fields in Student

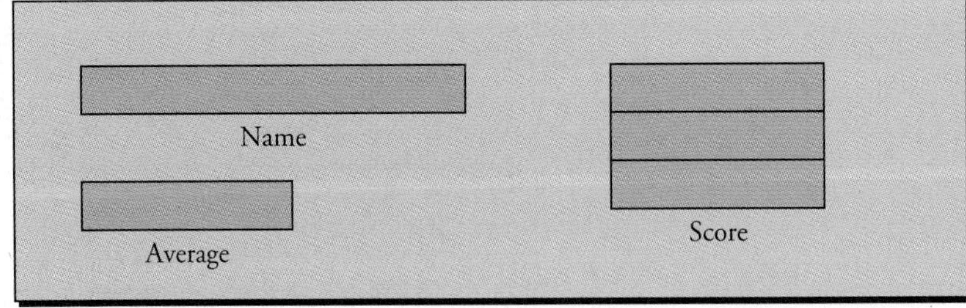

To use this record, we need to assign or read data into appropriate fields. Therefore, assume a line of data is

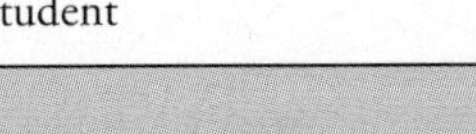

T This data can be read by the fragment of code

```
FOR J := 1 TO NameLength DO
  read (DataFile, Student.Name[J]);
FOR J := 1 TO NumTests DO
  read (DataFile, Student.Score[J]);
readln (DataFile);
```

The average can be computed by

```
Student.Average := (Student.Score[1] +
                    Student.Score[2] +
                    Student.Score[3]) / NumTests;
```

Notice each field identifier includes the record name. Fortunately, when working with fields of a record, Pascal provides a more convenient method of referring to these fields: a **WITH . . . DO** statement. Using this option, the previous fragment can be rewritten as

```
WITH Student DO
  BEGIN
    FOR J := 1 TO NameLength DO
      read (DataFile, Name[J]);
    FOR J := 1 TO NumTests DO
      read (DataFile, Score[J]);
    readln (DataFile);
    Average := (Score[1] + Score[2] + Score[3]) / NumTests
  END;  {  of WITH...DO  }
```

Formally, a **WITH . . . DO** statement has the form

> **WITH** <record name> **DO**
> **BEGIN**
> <statement 1>;
> <statement 2>;
> .
> .
> .
> <statement *n*>
> **END**

where the statements used can refer to the field identifiers but do not include the record name as part of the field identifier. This eliminates the use of the period following the record name. Thus, instead of Student.Score[J], we can use Score[J].

As a second illustration, suppose we have a record defined as

```
TYPE
  NameString = PACKED ARRAY [1..20] OF char;
  PatientInfo = RECORD
                  Name : NameString;
                  Age : integer;
                  Height : integer;
                  Weight : integer;
                  Gender : char
                END;  {  of RECORD PatientInfo  }
VAR
  Patient : PatientInfo;
```

Values can be assigned to the various fields specifically by

```
Patient.Name := 'Jones Connie       ';
Patient.Age := 19;
Patient.Height := 67;
Patient.Weight := 125;
Patient.Gender := 'F';
```

or by

```
WITH Patient DO
  BEGIN
    Name := 'Jones Connie       ';
    Age := 19;
    Height := 67;
    Weight := 125;
    Gender := 'F'
  END;  {  of WITH...DO  }
```

A single **WITH . . . DO** statement can be used with more than one record. For example, given the previous two record definitions, it is possible to write

```
WITH Student, Patient DO
  BEGIN
    Average := (Score[1] + Score[2] + Score[3]) / 3;
    Age := 19
  END;  {  of WITH...DO  }
```

This is equivalent to the nested use of **WITH . . . DO**, as follows:

```
WITH Student DO
  WITH Patient DO
    BEGIN
      Average := (Score[1] + Score[2] + Score[3]) / 3;
      Age := 19
    END;
```

In this nesting, the record identifier is associated with each field defined in that record. Thus

```
Age := 19
```

can be thought of as

```
Patient.Age := 19
```

Since Average is not a field in Patient, it will not be associated with the record identifier Patient. It will, however, be associated with the record identifier Student.

Unique field identifiers are not required when more than one record is used in a single **WITH . . . DO** statement. Instead, field identifiers are associated with the innermost record containing a field with that identifier. Innermost, in this sense, means the last listed record in the **WITH . . . DO** statement that contains the field in question. Thus

```
WITH Student, Patient DO
  writeln (Name);
```

causes Patient.Name to be printed.

In general, the use of multiple records in a single **WITH . . . DO** statement should be avoided when making a reference to a field identifier that is contained in more than one record. This reduces the possibility of misreading code and getting unexpected results.

Copying Records

How can information contained in one record be transferred to another record? This must be done, for example, when we want to sort an array of records. To illustrate how records can be copied, consider the definitions and declarations

```
TYPE
  InfoA = RECORD
            Field1 : integer;
            Field2 : real;
            Field3 : char
          END;  {  of RECORD InfoA  }
  InfoB = RECORD
            Field1 : integer;
            Field2 : real;
            Field3 : char
          END;  {  of RECORD InfoB  }
VAR
  Rec1, Rec2 : InfoA;
  Rec3 : InfoB;
```

The three records declared can be envisioned as shown in Figure 9.8.

◆ FIGURE 9.8
Copying records

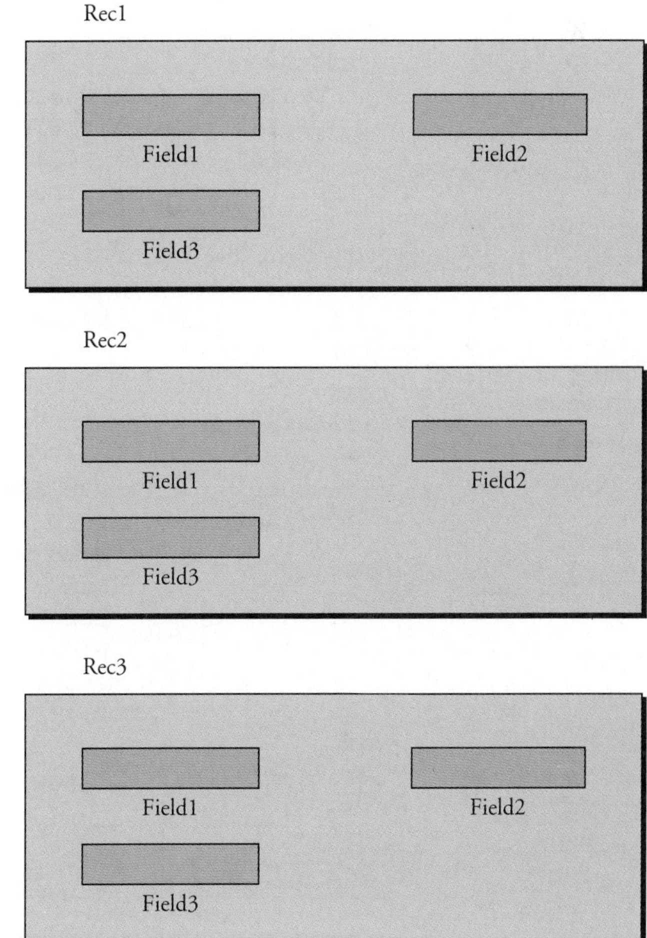

Now, suppose data have been assigned to Rec1 by

```
WITH Rec1 DO
  BEGIN
    Field1 := 25;
    Field2 := 89.5;
    Field3 := 'M'
  END;  {  of WITH...DO  }
```

These data can be copied to the corresponding fields of Rec2 by

```
Rec2 := Rec1;
```

This single assignment statement accomplishes

```
Rec2.Field1 := Rec1.Field1;
Rec2.Field2 := Rec1.Field2;
Rec2.Field3 := Rec1.Field3;
```

Such an assignment can only be made when the records are of identical type. For example, notice InfoA and InfoB have the same structure but have been defined as different types. In this case, if we wish to assign the values in the fields of Rec1 to the corresponding fields of Rec3, the statement

```
Rec3 := Rec1;
```

produces a compilation error. Although Rec1 and Rec3 have the same structure, they are not of identical type. In this case, the information can be transferred by

```
WITH Rec3 DO
  BEGIN
    Field1 := Rec1.Field1;
    Field2 := Rec1.Field2;
    Field3 := Rec1.Field3
  END;  {  of WITH...DO  }
```

Reading Data into a Record

Once a record has been defined for a program, one task is to get data into the record. This is usually accomplished by reading from a data file. To illustrate, assume we have a record defined by

```
CONST
  NameLength = 20;
TYPE
  NameString = PACKED ARRAY [1..NameLength] OF char;
  PatientInfo = RECORD
                  Name : NameString;
                  Age : integer;
                  Height : integer;
                  Weight : integer;
                  Gender : char
                END;  {  of RECORD PatientInfo  }
VAR
  Patient : PatientInfo;
```

and a line of data is

```
Smith Mary                    21 67 125F■
```

This data could be read from the main program, but good program design would have us use a procedure for this task. The user-defined data type PatientInfo and a variable parameter must be used in the procedure heading. Thus, an appropriate procedure is

```
PROCEDURE GetData (VAR Patient : PatientInfo);
  VAR
    J : integer;
  BEGIN
    WITH Patient DO
      BEGIN
        FOR J := 1 TO NameLength DO
          read (DataFile, Name[J]);
        readln (DataFile, Age, Height, Weight, Gender)
      END  {  of WITH...DO  }
  END;  {  of PROCEDURE GetData  }
```

This procedure is called from the main program by

```
GetData (Patient);
```

As a second example of getting data for a record, let's write a program to be used to compute the grades of students in a class. As part of the program, a record type can be declared as

```
CONST
  NumQuizzes = 10;
  NumTests = 4;
  NameLength = 20;
TYPE
  NameString = PACKED ARRAY [1..NameLength] OF char;
  QuizList = ARRAY [1..NumQuizzes] OF integer;
  TestList = ARRAY [1..NumTests] OF integer;
  StudentRecord = RECORD
                    Name : NameString;
                    Quiz : QuizList;
                    Test : TestList;
                    QuizTotal : integer;
                    TestAverage : real;
                    LetterGrade : 'A'..'E'
                  END;  {  of RECORD StudentRecord  }
VAR
  Student : StudentRecord;
```

If each line of data contains a student's name, 10 quiz scores, and four test scores and looks like

```
Smith Mary J.           9 8 10 7 10 9 8 10 9 10 89 92 85 97
\_____________________/ \_____________________/ \_________/
         Name                 Quiz scores       Test scores
```

a procedure to get these data is

```
PROCEDURE GetData (VAR Student : StudentRecord);
  VAR
    J : integer;
  BEGIN
    WITH Student DO
      BEGIN
        FOR J := 1 TO NameLength DO
          read (DataFile, Name[J]);
        FOR J := 1 TO NumQuizzes DO
          read (DataFile, Quiz[J]);
```

```
        FOR J := 1 TO NumTests DO
          read (DataFile, Test[J])
      END;  { of WITH...DO  }
    readln (DataFile)
  END;  { of PROCEDURE GetData  }
```

This procedure is called from the main program by

```
GetData (Student);
```

Now let's continue this example by writing a function to compute the test average for a student. Since this average is found by using the four test scores in the record, such a function could be

```
FUNCTION TestAv (Test : TestList) : real;
  VAR
    J : integer;
    Sum : integer;
  BEGIN
    Sum := 0;
    FOR J := 1 TO NumTests DO
      Sum := Sum + Test[J];
    TestAv := Sum / NumTests
  END;  { of FUNCTION TestAv  }
```

Since the array of test scores is the only parameter sent to the function and the average is normally stored in the field TestAverage, this function can be called by

```
Student.TestAverage := TestAv(Student.Test);
```

Printing Data from a Record

After information has been entered in fields of a record and appropriate calculations have been made, the next step is to print information from the record. Since this is frequently done in a procedure, let's assume the previous record for a student has the values illustrated in Figure 9.9.

◆ FIGURE 9.9
Fields with values

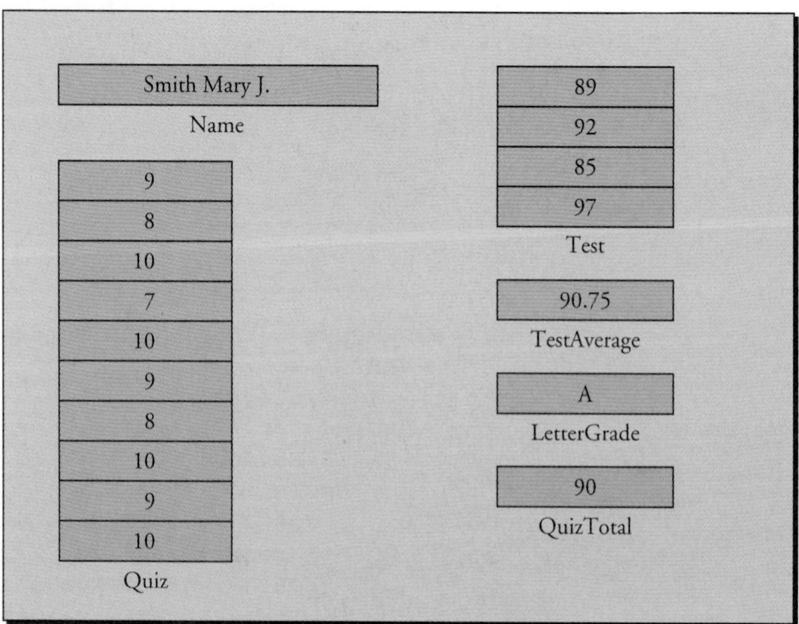

A NOTE OF INTEREST

Using Key Fields in Records

The need to search records by certain key fields is a basic and very important process. To illustrate, consider how Ted Celentino, a former director of PARS applications for the on-line reservation system of TWA, responded to the question, "How are reservations indexed?" He said:

By the passenger's name, flight number, and departure date. All three are needed. If a passenger forgets his or her flight number, the agent can try to find a record of it by looking through all flights to the appropriate destination at that particular travel time. It's rare that a passenger doesn't know at least a couple of pieces of information that lead to his or her record.

If we want the output for a student to be

```
Name:          Smith Mary J.
Quiz Scores:   9 8 10 7 10 9 8 10 9 10
Quiz Total:    90
Test Scores:   89 92 85 97
Test Average:  90.75
Letter Grade:  A
```

a procedure that produces this is

```
PROCEDURE PrintData (Student : StudentRecord);
  CONST
    Skip = ' ';
  VAR
    J : integer;
  BEGIN
    writeln;
    WITH Student DO
      BEGIN
        writeln ('Name:', Skip:9, Name);
        write ('Quiz Scores:');
        FOR J := 1 TO NumQuizzes DO
          write (Quiz[J]:3);
        writeln;
        writeln ('Quiz Total:', QuizTotal:5);
        write ('Test Scores:');
        FOR J := 1 TO NumTests DO
          write (Test[J]:4);
        writeln;
        writeln ('Test Average:', TestAverage:6:2);
        writeln, ('Letter Grade:', LetterGrade:2)
      END  {  of WITH...DO  }
  END;  {  of PROCEDURE PrintData  }
```

This procedure is called from the main program by

```
PrintData (Student);
```

EXAMPLE 9.2

As a concluding example, let's consider a short, interactive program that uses records and procedures to perform the arithmetic operation of multiplying two fractions. The program declares a record for each fraction and uses procedures to get the data, multiply the fractions, and print the results. Before writing this program, let's examine appropriate record definitions and a procedure for computing the product. A definition is

```
TYPE
  RationalNumber = RECORD
                     Numerator : integer;
                     Denominator : integer
                   END;  {  of RECORD RationalNumber  }
VAR
  X, Y, Product : RationalNumber;
```

A procedure for computing the product is

```
PROCEDURE ComputeProduct (X, Y : RationalNumber;
                          VAR Product : RationalNumber);
  BEGIN
    WITH Product DO
      BEGIN
        Numerator := X.Numerator * Y.Numerator;
        Denominator := X.Denominator * Y.Denominator
      END  {  of WITH...DO  }
  END;  {  of PROCEDURE ComputeProduct  }
```

Product: 15 Numerator, 35 Denominator := X: 5 Numerator, 7 Denominator * Y: 3 Numerator, 5 Denominator

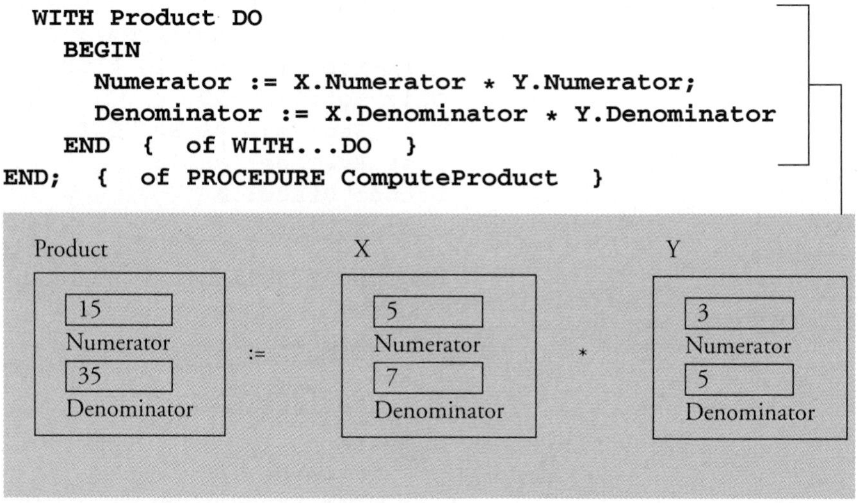

This procedure is called from the main program by

```
ComputeProduct (X, Y, Product);
```

A complete program for this problem follows.

```
PROGRAM Fractions (input, output);

{  This program illustrates the use of records with procedures.  }
{  In particular, procedures are used to get the data, perform   }
{  computations, and print the results.  The specific task is    }
{  to compute the product of two rational numbers.               }

TYPE
  RationalNumber = RECORD
                     Numerator : integer;
                     Denominator : integer
                   END;  {  of RECORD RationalNumber  }

VAR
  X, Y, Product : RationalNumber;
  MoreData : boolean;
  Response : char;
```

```
{*************************************************************}

PROCEDURE GetData (VAR X, Y : RationalNumber);

  {  Given:   Nothing                                           }
  {  Task:    Have entered from the keyboard the numerators and }
  {               denominators of two fractions                 }
  {  Return:  Two records, each containing a field for the      }
  {               numerator and denominator of a fraction       }

  BEGIN
    WITH X DO
      BEGIN
        write ('Enter the numerator a of a/b.  ');
        readln (Numerator);
        write ('Enter the denominator b of a/b.  ');
        readln (Denominator)
      END;  {  of WITH X DO  }
    WITH Y DO
      BEGIN
        write ('Enter the numerator a of a/b.  ');
        readln (Numerator);
        write ('Enter the denominator b of a/b.  ');
        readln (Denominator)
      END  {  of WITH Y DO  }
  END;  {  of PROCEDURE GetData  }

{*************************************************************}

PROCEDURE ComputeProduct (X, Y : RationalNumber;
                          VAR Product : RationalNumber);

  {  Given:   Records for two fractions                         }
  {  Task:    Compute the product and store result              }
  {  Return:  Product of the fraction                           }

  BEGIN
    WITH Product DO
      BEGIN
        Numerator := X.Numerator * Y.Numerator;
        Denominator := X.Denominator * Y.Denominator
      END  {  of WITH...DO  }
  END;  {  of PROCEDURE ComputeProduct  }

{*************************************************************}

PROCEDURE PrintResults (X, Y, Product : RationalNumber);

  {  Given:   Records for each of two given fractions and their }
  {                product                                      }
  {  Task:    Print an equation stating the problem and answer; }
  {                standard fraction form should be used as     }
  {                output                                       }
  {  Return:  Nothing                                           }
```

```
  BEGIN
    writeln;
    writeln (X.Numerator:13, Y.Numerator:6, Product.Numerator:6);
    writeln ('--- * --- = ---':26);
    writeln (X.Denominator:13, Y.Denominator:6,
             Product.Denominator:6);
    writeln
  END;  {  of PROCEDURE PrintResults  }

{*****************************************************************}

BEGIN  {  Main program  }
  MoreData := true;
  WHILE MoreData DO
    BEGIN
      GetData (X, Y);
      ComputeProduct (X, Y, Product);
      PrintResults (X, Y, Product);
      write ('Do you wish to see another problem?  <Y> or <N>  ');
      readln (Response);
      MoreData := (Response = 'Y') OR (Response = 'y');
      writeln
    END  {  of WHILE...DO  }
END.  {  of main program  }
```

A sample run of this program produces

```
Enter the numerator a of a/b.  3
Enter the denominator b of a/b.  4
Enter the numerator a of a/b.  1
Enter the denominator b of a/b.  2

            3     1     3
           --- * --- = ---
            4     2     8

Do you wish to see another problem?  <Y> or <N>  Y

Enter the numerator a of a/b.  3
Enter the denominator b of a/b.  2
Enter the numerator a of a/b.  7
Enter the denominator b of a/b.  10

            3     7    21
           --- * --- = ---
            2    10    20

Do you wish to see another problem?  <Y> or <N>  Y

Enter the numerator a of a/b.  2
Enter the denominator b of a/b.  3
Enter the numerator a of a/b.  4
Enter the denominator b of a/b.  5
```

```
        2     4     8
       --- * --- = ---
        3     5    15

Do you wish to see another problem?  <Y> or <N>  N
```

EXERCISES 9.2

1. Assume a program contains the **TYPE** definition and **VAR** declaration sections

```
TYPE
  Info1 = RECORD
             Initial : char;
             Age : integer
           END;
  Info2 = RECORD
             Initial : char;
             Age : integer
           END;
VAR
  Cust1, Cust2 : Info1;
  Cust3, Cust4 : Info2;
```

Indicate which of the following statements are valid. Give an explanation for each one that is invalid.

a. `Cust1 := Cust2;`

b. `Cust2 := Cust3;`

c. `Cust3 := Cust4;`

d.
```
WITH Cust1 DO
  BEGIN
    Initial := 'W';
    Age := 21
  END;
```

e.
```
WITH Cust1, Cust2 DO
  BEGIN
    Initial := 'W';
    Age := 21
  END;
```

2. Write a test program to see what happens when two different records with the same field name are used in a single **WITH . . . DO** statement. Use the declarations and **TYPE** definitions in Exercise 1. For example

```
WITH Student1, Student2 DO
  Age := 21;
writeln (Student1.Age);
writeln (Student2.Age);
```

3. Assume the **TYPE** and **VAR** sections of a program include

```
TYPE
  NameString = PACKED ARRAY [1..20] OF char;
  String11 = PACKED ARRAY [1..11] OF char;
  Info = RECORD
           Name : NameString;
           SSN : String11;
```

```
            Age : integer;
            HourlyWage : real;
            HoursWorked : real;
            Volunteer : boolean
          END;
VAR
  Employee1, Employee2 : Info;
```

a. Show three different methods of transferring all information from the record for Employee1 to the record for Employee2.

b. Suppose you wish to transfer all information from the record for Employee1 to the record for Employee2 except HoursWorked. Discuss different methods for doing this. Which do you feel is the most efficient?

4. Assume the **TYPE** and **VAR** sections of a program are the same as in Exercise 3. Write a procedure to be used to read information into such a record from a data file. A typical line of data is

```
Smith Jane M.           111-22-3333 25 10.50 41.5Y
```

where Y indicates the worker is a volunteer (**true**) and N indicates the worker is not a volunteer (**false**).

5. Assume a record has been declared by

```
TYPE
  NameString = PACKED ARRAY [1..20] OF char;
  StudentInfo = RECORD
                  Name : NameString;
                  TotalPts : 0..500;
                  LetterGrade : char
                END;
VAR
  Student : StudentInfo;
```

Write a function to compute a student's letter grade based upon cutoff levels of 90 percent, 80 percent, 70 percent, and 60 percent. Show how this function is used in a program to assign the appropriate letter grade to the appropriate field of a student's record.

6. Review Example 9.2, in which two fractions are multiplied. In a similar fashion, write procedures for

a. Dividing two fractions (watch out for zero).

b. Adding two fractions.

c. Subtracting two fractions.

7. Some instructors throw out the lowest test score for each student when computing the student's test average. Assume a record Student of type StudentRecord has been declared and data have been read into the appropriate fields.

a. Write a function to compute the test average using the best three scores.

b. Show how a constant in the **CONST** section can be used to generalize this function to find the best $n - 1$ of n scores.

c. Rewrite the function using a sort to sort the array of scores from high to low, and then add the first three scores from the array.

d. Must the entire array be sorted in order to find the three highest scores? Explain.

8. Show how the program Fractions in Example 9.2 can be modified to check for nonzero denominators.

9.3 Data Structures with Records

OBJECTIVES

- to be able to declare a nested record
- to be able to use nested records in a program
- to be able to declare an array of records
- to be able to use an array of records in a program
- to be able to sort an array of records by a field
- to be able to use procedures for working with an array of records

Nested Records

The first concept to be examined in this section is that of a *nested record,* or a record that is a field in another record. For example, suppose you are working on a program to be used by a biology department and part of your work is to declare a record for a faculty member. This record is to contain fields for the person's name, office number, telephone number, and supply order. Let's assume the supply order information is to contain the company name, a description of the item ordered, its price, and the quantity ordered. The record for each faculty member, with SupplyOrder as a record within a record, can be visualized as shown in Figure 9.10.

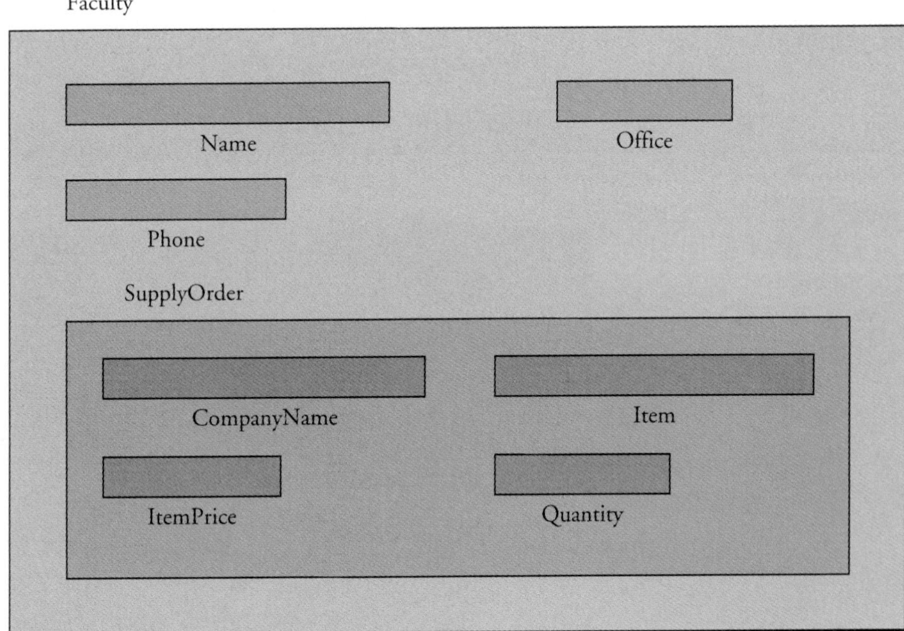

◆ FIGURE 9.10
Illustration of a nested record

Now let's look at how such a record can be declared. One possible method is

```
TYPE
  String20 = PACKED ARRAY [1..20] OF char;
  String12 = PACKED ARRAY [1..12] OF char;
  OrderInfo = RECORD
                 CompanyName : String20;
                 Item : String20;
                 ItemPrice : real;
                 Quantity : integer
              END;  {  of RECORD OrderInfo  }
  FacultyInfo = RECORD
                   Name : String20;
                   Office : integer;
                   Phone : String12;
                   SupplyOrder : OrderInfo
                 END;  {  of RECORD FacultyInfo  }
VAR
  Faculty : FacultyInfo;
```

We must now consider how to access fields in the nested record. We do this by using successive field selectors. Thus

```
Faculty.Name
Faculty.Office
Faculty.Phone
```

refer to the first three fields of Faculty, and

```
Faculty.SupplyOrder.CompanyName
Faculty.SupplyOrder.Item
Faculty.SupplyOrder.ItemPrice
Faculty.SupplyOrder.Quantity
```

are used to access fields of the nested record

```
Faculty.SupplyOrder
```

Using WITH . . . DO

As expected, **WITH . . . DO** can be used with nested records. Let's consider the problem of assigning data to the various fields of Faculty as previously declared. Assume we wish to have values assigned as shown in Figure 9.11.

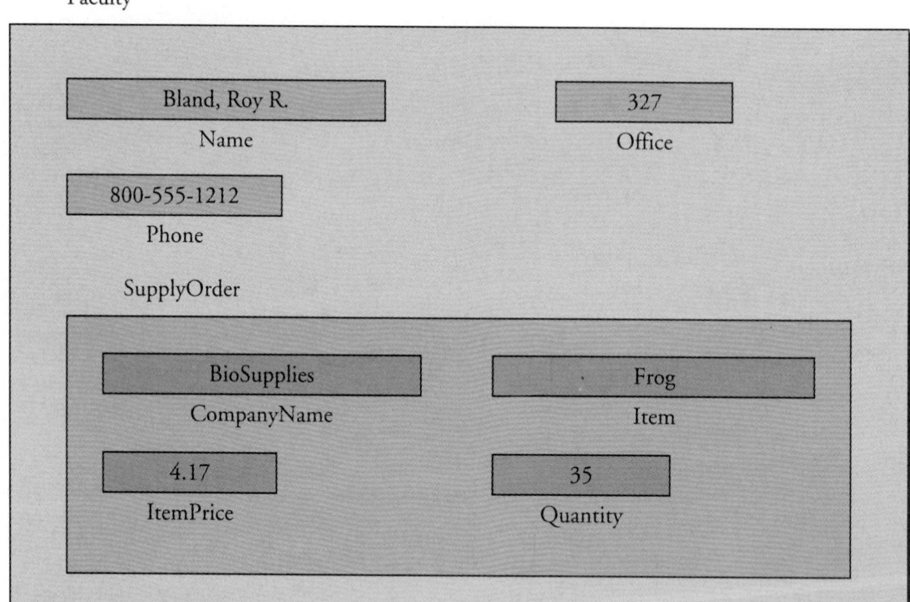

◆ FIGURE 9.11
Values in fields of a nested record

We can then use the assignment statements

```
WITH Faculty DO
  BEGIN
    Name := 'Bland, Roy R.          ';
    Office := 327;
    Phone := '800-555-1212';
    SupplyOrder.CompanyName := 'BioSupplies          ';
    SupplyOrder.Item := 'Frog                ';
    SupplyOrder.ItemPrice := 4.17;
    SupplyOrder.Quantity := 35
  END;
```

Note the last four assignment statements all use fields in the record SupplyOrder. Thus, a **WITH . . . DO** statement can be used there in the following manner.

```
WITH Faculty DO
  BEGIN
    Name := 'Bland, Roy R.        ';
    Office := 327;
    Phone := '800-555-1212';
    WITH SupplyOrder DO
      BEGIN
        CompanyName := 'BioSupplies          ';
        Item := 'Frog                ';
        ItemPrice := 4.17;
        Quantity := 35
      END  {  of WITH SupplyOrder DO  }
  END;  {  of WITH Faculty DO  }
```

A third way to accomplish our task is to use **WITH . . . DO** with both the main record name and the nested record name, as follows:

```
WITH Faculty, SupplyOrder DO
  BEGIN
    Name := 'Bland, Roy R.        ';
    Office := 327;
    Phone := '800-555-1212';
    CompanyName := 'BioSupplies          ';
    Item := 'Frog                ';
    ItemPrice := 4.17;
    Quantity := 35
  END;  {  of WITH...DO  }
```

Since SupplyOrder is nested within Faculty, each reference is distinctly identified and the fragment accomplishes our objective. When using nested records, it is important to identify fields distinctly. To illustrate, suppose Faculty1 and Faculty2 are also of type FacultyInfo. Then each of the following statements is valid.

```
Faculty1.Name := Faculty2.Name;
Faculty1.SupplyOrder.Item := Faculty2.SupplyOrder.Item;
Faculty1.SupplyOrder := Faculty2.SupplyOrder;
```

Note in the third statement, the contents of an entire record are being transferred. This statement is valid because both records are of type OrderInfo.

To illustrate some attempts to use inappropriate designators, let's assume Faculty, Faculty1, and Faculty2 are of type FacultyInfo and consider the following inappropriate references. In the designator

```
Faculty.Item := 'Frog                '; { Incorrect }
```

the intermediate descriptor is missing. Thus, something like

```
Faculty.SupplyOrder.Item
```

is needed. In

```
SupplyOrder.Quantity := 35; { Incorrect }
```

no reference is made to which record is being accessed. A record name must be stated, such as

```
Faculty1.SupplyOrder.Quantity
```

As our final example of working with nested records, let's write a procedure to get data from a data file for a record of type FacultyInfo with the definitions and declarations

```
TYPE
  String20 = PACKED ARRAY [1..20] OF char;
  String12 = PACKED ARRAY [1..12] OF char;
  OrderInfo = RECORD
                CompanyName : String20;
                Item: String20;
                ItemPrice : real;
                Quantity : integer
              END;  {  of RECORD OrderInfo  }
  FacultyInfo = RECORD
                  Name : String20;
                  Office : 100..399;
                  Phone : String12;
                  SupplyOrder : OrderInfo
                END;  {  of RECORD FacultyInfo  }
VAR
  Faculty : FacultyInfo;
```

If we assume the data for a faculty member are on two lines of the data file and are of the form

(line 1) `Bland, Roy R.          327 800-555-1212▌`

(line 2) `BioSupplies            Frog                4.17 35▌`

a procedure to obtain these data is

```
PROCEDURE GetData (VAR Faculty : FacultyInfo);
  VAR
    J : integer;
    Blank : char;
  BEGIN
    WITH Faculty, SupplyOrder DO
      BEGIN
        FOR J := 1 TO 20 DO
          read (Data, Name[J]);
        read (Data, Office);
        read (Data, Blank);  {  Move the pointer  }
        FOR J := 1 TO 12 DO
          read (Data, Phone[J]);
        readln (Data);  {  Go to beginning of the next line  }

        {  Now read the second line  }
        FOR J := 1 TO 20 DO
          read (Data, CompanyName[J]);
        FOR J := 1 TO 20 DO
          read (Data, Item[J]);
        readln (Data, ItemPrice, Quantity)
      END  {  of WITH Faculty, SupplyOrder DO  }
  END;  {  of PROCEDURE GetData  }
```

This procedure is called from the main program by

```
GetData (Faculty);
```

A NOTE OF INTEREST

Computer Insecurity

In February of 1994, college administrators across the country appealed to students and faculty members to change the way they log on to their computers after security experts announced that tens of thousands of passwords had been stolen by hackers on the Internet. The Computer Emergency Response Team Coordination Center—a federally financed unit responsible for security on the Internet—issued the alert after a rash of break-ins. The Internet, a worldwide web of computer networks, is used by an estimated 20 million people at the date of this writing.

Security experts said hundreds of Internet computers had been affected, including those at dozens of colleges, but declined to identify them. Institutions that fall victim to attacks often shun publicity because they want to avoid embarrassment and because they are afraid they may become targets for other hackers.

FBI Seeks Culprits

Some administrators, still unsure about whether their computers had been attacked, looked through their systems for evidence of intruders. The Federal Bureau of Investigation maintains on-going searches for the culprits.

Computer administrators in higher education had varying opinions about what the event would mean to the future of the Internet. Although none of them suggested that their institutions would permanently disconnect from the Internet, several said universities might need to rethink what kinds of data should be stored in computers connected to the network. Others, puzzled by all the hullabaloo, said that battles with "crackers"—a name given to mean-spirited hackers—were part of business as usual on the Internet. Computer-system administrators at some colleges and universities said they were forcing users to change passwords on systems under their control and encouraging users of other systems on their campuses to do likewise.

The following guidelines are helpful to anyone who uses on-line services.

Tips from Campus Computer Experts to Protect Passwords

- Change passwords as frequently as possible.
- Avoid writing down a password.
- Do not cooperate with anyone who orders you to use a specific password. Crackers occasionally call users at random and impersonate administrators of their local computer systems. Report such incidents in person to local system administrators.
- Never include your password in electronic mail unless you are using an encryption program to scramble your messages. Electronic mail can be read by others as it travels through the network.
- Passwords should never be actual words. Crackers can run dictionary programs that try every word in the language until the password is found. (Until recently, some security experts advised that selecting memorable foreign words was relatively safe, but the sophisticated cracker is now armed with dictionaries that cover a multitude of languages.)
- Do not choose passwords that consist of nicknames, birth dates, names of spouses or children, or other information that might be known to a cracker.
- The passwords that are hardest to crack consist of jumbles of letters, numbers, and punctuation marks. However, some punctuation marks should not be used on some systems. One useful strategy for creating memorable passwords involves using the first few letters of each word of a phrase or book title, much like military abbreviations. The password "AMHERDIC" could be made from *The American Heritage Dictionary*, for example. But don't build a password out of a phrase that you use to sign your electronic mail.
- Whenever possible, use a telephone and a modem to dial directly into a remote computer and avoid using the telnet command through the Internet. The telephone system is much more secure than the Internet.

Array of Records

Next, we will use structured data types to look at an array of records. It is easy to imagine needing to make a list of information about several people, events, or items. Furthermore, it is not unusual for the information about a particular person, event, or item to consist of several different data items. When this situation occurs, a record can be defined for each person, event, or item and an array of these records can be used to achieve the desired result. In such situations, an *array of records* is frequently used instead of a parallel array.

For example, suppose the local high school sports boosters want a program to enable them to keep track of the names and donations of its members. Let's assume a maximum of 50 members are making a donation. This problem was solved in Chapter 8 by using parallel arrays; it can now be solved by using an array of records. Each record will have two fields: the donor's name, and the amount donated. The record can be visualized as shown in Figure 9.12.

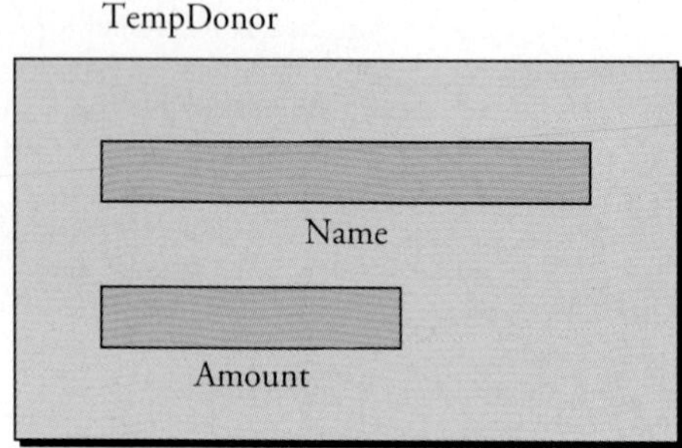

◆ FIGURE 9.12
Fields in TempDonor

We will now declare an array of these records to produce the arrangement shown in Figure 9.13.

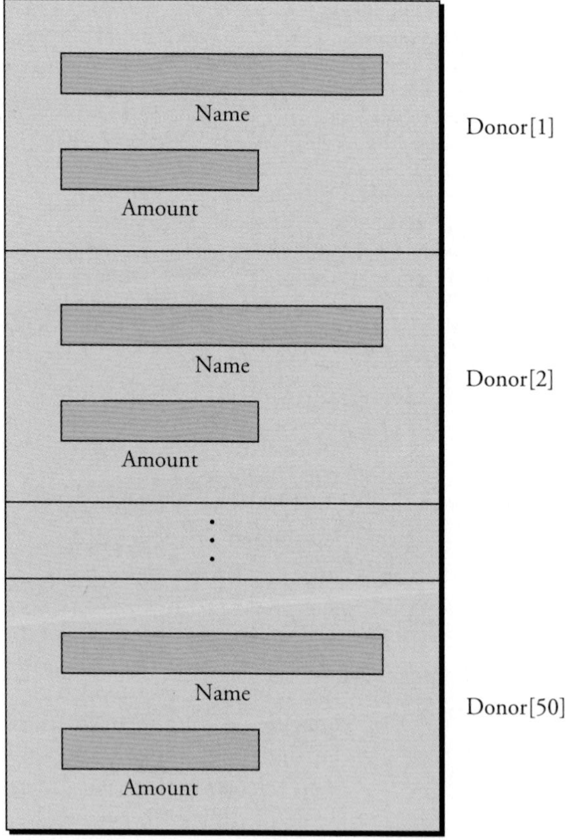

◆ FIGURE 9.13
Illustration of an array of records

The necessary definitions and declarations are

```
CONST
  ClubSize = 50;
TYPE
  NameString = PACKED ARRAY [1..20] OF char;
  MemberInfo = RECORD
                 Name : NameString;
                 Amount : real
               END;  {  of RECORD MemberInfo  }
  DonorList = ARRAY [1..ClubSize] OF MemberInfo;
VAR
  Donor : DonorList;
  TempDonor : MemberInfo;
  Count : integer;
```

Before we proceed, the following should be noted.

1. Structures are built in the **TYPE** definition section to facilitate later work with procedures and functions.
2. Each record is now an array element and can be accessed by a reference to the index. Thus, if the third member's name is Tom Jones and he donates $100.00, we can write

```
Donor[3].Name := 'Jones Tom           ';
Donor[3].Amount := 100.0;
```

   Better still, we can use **WITH . . . DO** to get

```
WITH Donor[3] DO
  BEGIN
    Name := 'Jones Tom           ';
    Amount := 100.0
  END;  {  of WITH...DO  }
```

3. Since all records in an array are of identical type, the contents of two records can be interchanged by

```
TempDonor := Donor[J];
Donor[J] := Donor[K];
Donor[K] := TempDonor;
```

   This is needed if records are to be sorted by one of their fields.
4. The distinction in syntax should be noted when using an array of records versus an array as a field within a record. For example, if an array of five scores has been defined as a field in an array of records, as shown in Figure 9.14, the following distinctions should be noted.
   a. `Student[2].Average` (Average for student 2)
   b. `Student[2].Score[4]` (Score on test 4 for student 2)
   c. `Student.Score[2]` (Not defined; Student is an array)

◆ FIGURE 9.14
Array of records

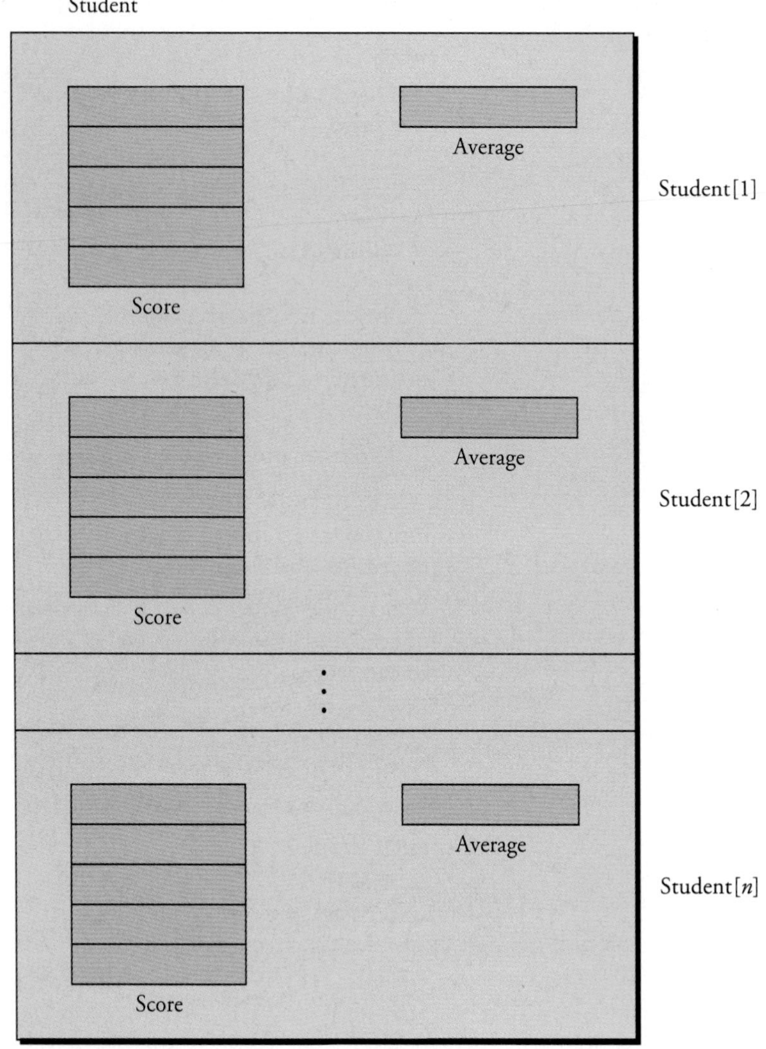

Now let's return to the problem posed by the sports boosters. A first-level pseudocode design is

1. Get the data
2. Sort alphabetically by name
3. Print the sorted list

If we assume each line of the data file is of the form

a procedure to get the data is not difficult. We have to remember, however, to count the actual number of donors read. Such a procedure is

```
PROCEDURE GetData (VAR Donor : DonorList;
                   VAR Count : integer);
  VAR
    J : integer;
  BEGIN
    Count := 0;
    WHILE NOT eof(DataFile) AND (Count < ClubSize) DO
      BEGIN
        Count := Count + 1;
        WITH Donor[Count] DO
          BEGIN
            FOR J := 1 TO 20 DO
              read (DataFile, Name[J]);
            readln (DataFile, Amount)
          END  {  of WITH Donor[Count] DO  }
      END  {  of WHILE NOT eof  }
  END;  {  of PROCEDURE GetData  }
```

This procedure is called from the main program by

```
GetData (Donor, Count);
```

and Count will contain the actual number of donors after the procedure is called.

The next procedure in this problem will require a sort. A sort that actually exchanges entire records is not very efficient. When working with an array of records, it is more efficient to use an *index sort*, which essentially uses a separate array to reorder the indices in the desired order. However, the formal development of this sorting technique is deferred to a subsequent course. For now, recall the selection sort developed in Chapter 7, as follows:

```
FOR J := 1 TO N - 1 DO {  Find the minimum N - 1 times  }
  BEGIN
    Index := J;
    FOR K := J + 1 TO N DO
      IF A[K] < A[Index] THEN  {  Find smallest number  }
        Index := K;
    IF Index <> J THEN
      Swap (A[Index], A[J])
  END;  {  of one pass  }
```

With suitable changes, the array of records can be sorted alphabetically by

```
PROCEDURE Sort (VAR Donor : DonorList;
                Count : integer);
  VAR
    J, K, Index : integer;
    Temp : MemberInfo;
```

```
BEGIN
  FOR J := 1 TO Count - 1 DO
    BEGIN
      Index := J;
      FOR K := J + 1 TO Count DO
        IF Donor[K].Name < Donor[Index].Name THEN
          Index := K;
      IF Index <> J THEN
        Swap (Donor[Index], Donor[J])
    END  {  of FOR loop  }
END;  {  of PROCEDURE Sort  }
```

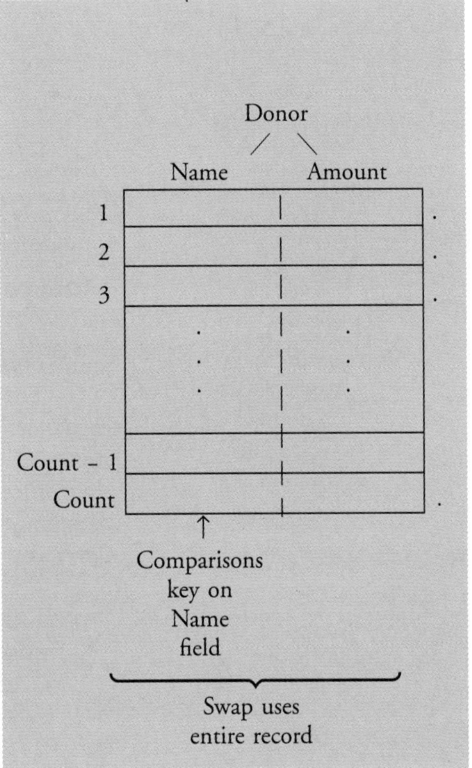

This procedure is called from the main program by

```
Sort (Donor, Count);
```

In this procedure, note the sort is by only one field in the record—specifically, the donor's name:

```
IF Donor[K].Name < Donor[Index].Name THEN
```

However, when the names are to be exchanged, contents of the entire record are exchanged by

```
Temp := Donor[Index];
```

We conclude this program by writing a procedure to print the results. If we want the output to be

```
                    Local Sports Boosters
                        Donation List
          ----------------------------------------

             Name                           Amount
             ----                           ------

          Alexander Candy                   300.00
          Born Patty                        100.00
          Generous George                   525.00
          Lasher John                       175.00
          Smith John                        100.00
              .                                .
              .                                .
              .                                .
```

a procedure to produce this is

```
PROCEDURE PrintList (VAR Donor : DonorList;
                     Count : integer);
  CONST
    Skip = ' ' ;
  VAR
    J : integer;
  BEGIN
    writeln;
    writeln (Skip:21, 'Local Sports Boosters');
    writeln (Skip:25, 'Donation List');
    writeln (Skip:10, '----------------------------------------');
    writeln;
    writeln (Skip:13, 'Name', Skip:27, 'Amount');
    writeln (Skip:13, '----', Skip:27, '------');
    writeln;

    {  Now print the list  }
    FOR J := 1 TO Count DO
      WITH Donor[J] DO
        writeln (Skip:10, Name, Amount:20:2);
    writeln
  END;  {  of PROCEDURE PrintList  }
```

With these three procedures available, the main program is then

```
BEGIN  {  Main program  }
  reset (DataFile);
  GetData (Donor, Count);
  Sort (Donor, Count);
  PrintList (Donor, Count)
END.  {  of main program  }
```

This example is less involved than many of your problems will be, but it does illustrate an array of records, appropriate notation for fields in an array of records, how to sort an array of records by using one field of the records, and the use of procedures with an array of records.

EXERCISES 9.3

1. Consider the declaration

```
TYPE
  B = RECORD
        C : real;
        D : integer
      END;
  A = RECORD
        E : boolean;
        F : B
      END;
VAR
  G : A;
```

a. Give a schematic representation of the record G.

b. Indicate which of the following are valid references.

i. `G.E`	vi. `A.F.C`
ii. `G.C`	vii. `A.E`
iii. `G.F. D`	viii. `WITH G DO`
iv. `F.D`	ix. `WITH G, F DO`
v. `G.A`	x. `G.F.C`

c. Why would it be incorrect to define record A before record B?

2. Write a test program that illustrates the difference between an array of records and a record with an array component.

3. Give an appropriate definition and declaration for a record that is to contain fields for a person's name, address, social security number, annual income, and family information. Address is a record with fields for street address, city, state abbreviation, and zip code. Family information is a record with fields for marital status (S, M, W, or D) and number of children.

4. Consider the definitions and subsequent declarations

```
TYPE
  NameString = PACKED ARRAY [1..20] OF char;
  Mood = (Quiet, Bright, Surly);
  CurrentHealth = (Poor, Average, Good);
  PatientStatus = RECORD
                    Mental : Mood;
                    Physical : CurrentHealth
                  END;  { of RECORD PatientStatus  }
  PatientInfo = RECORD
                  Name : NameString;
                  Status : PatientStatus;
                  PastDue : boolean
                END;  { of RECORD PatientInfo  }
VAR
  Patient1, Patient2 : PatientInfo;
```

a. Give a schematic representation for Patient1.

b. Show how a single letter (Q, B, or S) can be read from a data file, and then have the appropriate value assigned to Patient1.Status.Mental.

c. Write a procedure to read a line of data and assign (if necessary) appropriate values to the various fields. A typical data line is

Smith Sue	BAF

and indicates that Sue Smith's mood is bright, her health is average, and her account is not past due.

5. Declare an array of records to be used for 15 players on a basketball team. The following information is needed for each player: name, age, height, weight, scoring average, and rebounding average.

6. Declare an array of records to be used for students (at most, 40) in a classroom. Each record should contain fields for a student's name, social security number, 10 quiz scores, three test scores, overall average, and letter grade.

7. Consider the following declaration of an array of records.

```
CONST
  ClassSize = 35;
TYPE
  NameString = PACKED ARRAY [1..20] OF char;
  Attendance = (Excellent, Average, Poor);
  TestList = ARRAY [1..4] OF integer;
  StudentInfo = RECORD
                  Name : NameString;
                  Atten : Attendance;
                  Test : TestList;
                  Aver : real
                END;
  StudentList = ARRAY [1..ClassSize] OF StudentInfo;
VAR
  Student : StudentList;
```

a. Give a schematic representation for Student.

b. Explain what the following function accomplishes.

```
FUNCTION GuessWhat (Test : TestList) : real;
  VAR
    K, Sum : integer;
  BEGIN
    Sum := 0;
    FOR K := 1 TO 4 DO
      Sum := Sum + Test[K];
    GuessWhat := Sum / 4
  END;
```

c. Write a procedure to print out the information for one student. In this procedure, the entire word describing attendance is to be printed.

8. Reconsider the problem in this section that kept a record of the name and amount donated for each member of the local high school boosters club. Expanding on that problem, write a procedure or function for each of the following.

a. Find the maximum donation, and print out the amount together with the donor's name.

b. Find the sum of all donations.

c. Find the average of all donations.

d. Sort the array according to size of donation (largest first).

9.4 Record Variants

OBJECTIVES

- to be able to define a record with a variant part
- to be able to use a record that contains a variant part

You should have noticed by now that when records are defined, each record has certain fixed fields. Since it is sometimes desirable to use a record structure in which the number and type of fields vary, Pascal allows records to be defined with a *variant part.* For example, a real estate company might want the records for their customers to contain different information depending upon whether the property for sale is a house or a business. For houses, the number of bedrooms and bathrooms and the presence or absence of a fireplace could be indicated; for businesses, the number of offices and possible rental income could be listed.

Defining a Variant Part

In order to define the variant part of a record, we use a form of the **CASE** statement to specify which fields should be included. Then, depending upon the value of the identifier in the **CASE** part of the definition, the desired fields are listed. In the real estate example, we could have

```
TYPE
  PropertyType = (House, Business);
  Listing = RECORD
              CASE Kind : PropertyType OF
                House    : (NumBedrms : integer;
                            NumBaths : integer;
                            Fireplace : boolean);
                Business : (NumOffices : integer;
                            RentalIncome : integer)
            END;  {  of RECORD Listing  }
VAR
  Property : Listing;
```

Now Property is a record with a variant part. Kind is not a reserved word; it is called the *tag field.* Depending upon the value assigned to Kind, the appropriate fields are available. If the assignment

```
Property.Kind := House;
```

is made, the record can be envisioned as shown in Figure 9.15(a). If the assignment

◆ FIGURE 9.15
Fields in a variant record

(a) Property

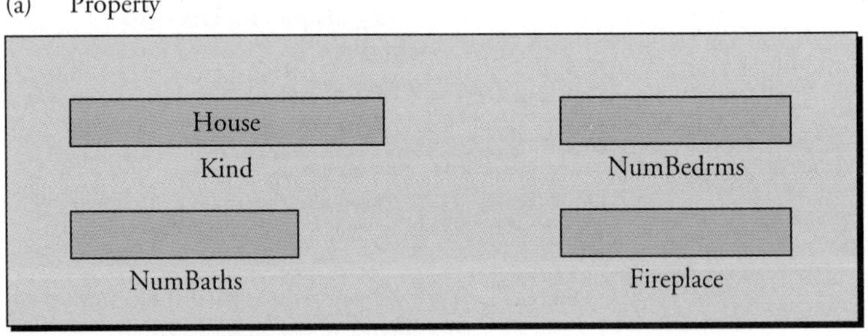

(b) Property

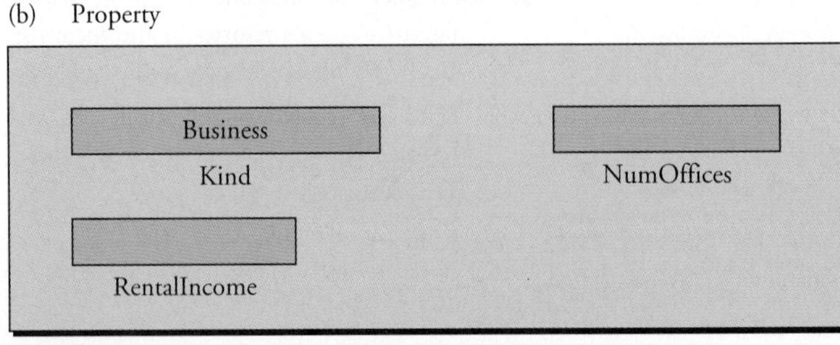

```
Property.Kind := Business;
```

is made, the record can be envisioned as illustrated in Figure 9.15(b).

In actual practice, records with variant parts usually have fixed parts also. Suppose the address and price of each property listed for sale is to be included. Since fields for these data must be defined for every record, those fields are referred to as the *fixed part.* A complete definition is

```
TYPE
  PropertyType = (House, Business);
  String30 = PACKED ARRAY [1..30] OF char;
  Listing = RECORD
              Address : String30;            } fixed
              Price : integer;               } part
              CASE Kind : PropertyType OF
                House    : (NumBedrms : integer;      }
                            NumBaths : integer;       } variant
                            Fireplace : boolean);     } part
                Business : (NumOffices : integer;     }
                            RentalIncome : integer)   }
            END;  { of RECORD Listing }
VAR
  Property : Listing;
```

The following points concerning variant parts should now be made.

1. The variant part of a record must be listed after the fixed part.
2. Only one variant part can be defined in a record.
3. The data type for the tag field must be ordinal.
4. Only one **END** statement is used to terminate the definition. It terminates both **CASE** and **RECORD**.

Records with variant parts are defined by the following form.

```
<record name> = RECORD
                  <field 1> : <type>;          }
                  <field 2> : <type>;          }
                      .                        } fixed
                      .                        } part
                      .                        }
                  <field n> : <type>;          }
                  CASE <tag field> : <tag type> OF
                    <value 1> : (<field list>);  }
                    <value 2> : (<field list>);  }
                      .                          } variant
                      .                          } part
                      .                          }
                    <value m> : (<field list>)   }
                END
```

It is possible to completely avoid the use of variant parts of a record by listing all possible fields in the fixed part and then using them appropriately. However, this usually means that more storage is required. To illustrate, let's consider how memory is allocated. For each field in the fixed part of the previous example, an area in memory is reserved as follows:

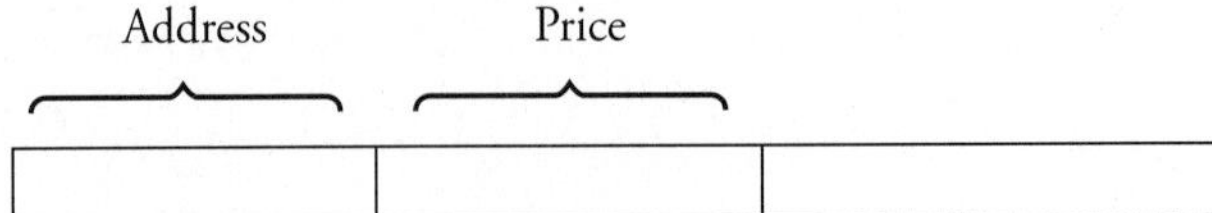

For the variant part of the record, a single area is reserved that will subsequently be utilized by the fields that are determined by the value of the tag field. In this sense, the fields overlap as indicated.

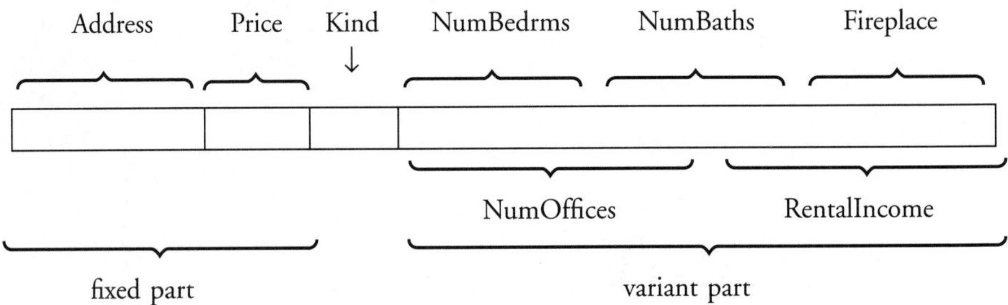

A note of caution is in order when variant records are included as part of programs. Careful programming is needed to properly initialize the variant part or unexpected results can be obtained. For example, using the previous illustration, suppose the initial value of Kind is House with values for NumBedrms, NumBaths, and Fireplace. If a subsequent value of Kind is Business and no new data are read or assigned, the value of NumOffices can in fact be NumBedrms.

We close this section with an example that illustrates a definition and subsequent use of a record with a variant part.

EXAMPLE 9.3

Let's define a record to be used when working with plane geometric figures. The record should have fixed fields for the type of figure (a single character designator) and area. The variant part should have fields for the information needed to compute the area. After the record is defined, we will write a procedure to get data from a line of the data file. We will then write a function that can be used to compute the area of the plane figure. To complete the definition of the record, let's assume we are working with at most the geometric figures circle, square, and triangle (C, S, and T, respectively). An appropriate definition is

```
TYPE
  FigureShape = (Circle, Square, Triangle);
  FigureInfo = RECORD
                 Object : char;
                 Area : real;
```

```
                    CASE Shape : FigureShape OF
                      Circle   : (Radius : real);
                      Square   : (Side : real);
                      Triangle : (Base, Height : real)
                  END;  {  of RECORD FigureInfo  }
VAR
  Figure : FigureInfo;
```

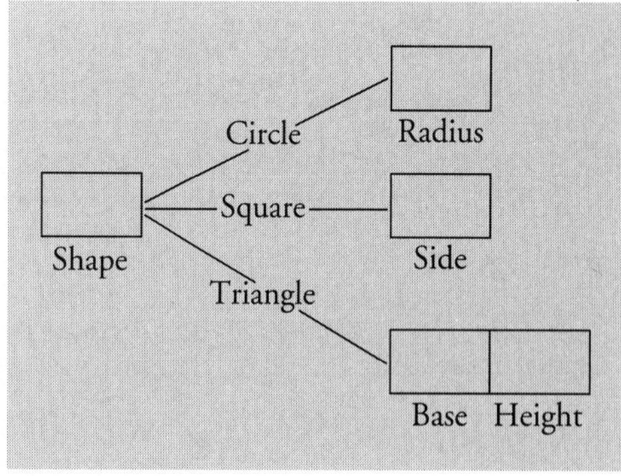

Each data line consists of a single character designating the kind of figure followed by appropriate information needed to compute the area. For example

```
T 6.0 8.0■
```

represents a triangle with base 6.0 and height 8.0. A procedure to get a line of data is

```
PROCEDURE GetData (VAR Figure : FigureInfo);
  BEGIN
    WITH Figure DO
      BEGIN
        read (Data, Object);
        CASE Object OF
          'C' : BEGIN
                  Shape := Circle;
                  readln (Data, Radius)
                END;
          'S' : BEGIN
                  Shape := Square;
                  readln (Data, Side)
                END;
          'T' : BEGIN
                  Shape := Triangle;
                  readln (Data, Base, Height)
                END
        END  {  of CASE Object  }
      END  {  of WITH...DO  }
  END;  {  of PROCEDURE GetData  }
```

A NOTE OF INTEREST

Artist of Interface

Millions of people encounter the graphic art of Susan Kare every day, and many more will experience her unusual work in the months ahead. Her carefully crafted images have won a place among the cultural symbols of our age, yet few people have any idea who she is or where her work can be seen.

Only a handful of industry insiders know that Kare is the artist responsible for the graphic appearance of some of the country's best-known computer software. Based in San Francisco, she designed most of the distinctive icons, typefaces and other graphic elements that gave the original Macintosh computer its characteristic—and widely emulated—appearance. Many consider her to be the mother of the famous Macintosh trash can.

Since then, Kare has parlayed her initial work for Apple Computer, Inc., into a full-time business, designing graphical user interfaces, or GUIs, for computer companies and software developers. The user interface is the software that allows an operator to control a personal computer and direct its functions. A decade ago, most interfaces forced the user to type cryptic commands in a blank space on the display.

With the introduction of the Macintosh in 1984, Apple pushed the world toward the graphic interface, which provides greater ease of use. A graphic interface allows an operator to control the computer by manipulating symbols displayed on its monitor, usually with a mouse or trackball.

The growing demand for graphical user interfaces has forced Kare to turn down work. She has rejected potential clients in part because she refuses to hire people to share the work load. "I do every job myself because I think of it as an art," she said. She works almost entirely on a computer, shunning traditional artist's tools for their electronic successors. "Anything that's bound for the screen, I do on the screen," she said. If there is a secret to her work, it is its simplicity, restraint, and common sense.

This is called from the main program by

```
GetData (Figure);
```

Finally, a function to compute the area is

```
FUNCTION ComputeArea (Figure : FigureInfo) : real;
  CONST
    Pi = 3.14159;
  BEGIN
    WITH Figure DO
      BEGIN
        CASE Shape OF
          Circle   : ComputeArea := Pi * sqr(Radius);
          Square   : ComputeArea := sqr(Side);
          Triangle : ComputeArea := 0.5 * Base * Height
        END  {  of CASE Shape  }
      END  {  of WITH...DO  }
  END;  {  of FUNCTION ComputeArea  }
```

This function is called by

```
Figure.Area := ComputeArea(Figure);
```

EXERCISES 9.4

1. Explain how memory can be saved when records with variant parts are declared.
2. Assume a record is defined by

```
TYPE
  TagType = (One, Two);
  Info = RECORD
           Fixed : integer;
```

```
        CASE Tag : TagType OF
          One : (A, B : integer);
          Two : (X : real; Ch : char)
      END;  {  of RECORD Info  }
```

and the variable declaration section of a program includes

```
VAR
  RecordCheck : Info;
```

What output is produced by the following fragment of code?

```
WITH RecordCheck DO
  BEGIN
    Fixed := 1000;
    Tag := One;
    A := 100;
    B := 500;
    writeln (Fixed:15, A:15, B:15);
    Tag := Two;
    X := 10.5;
    Ch := 'Y';
    writeln (Fixed:15, X:15:2, Ch:15);
    writeln (A:15, B:15, X:15:2, Ch:15)
  END;
```

3. Find all errors in the following definitions.

a.
```
TYPE
  Info = RECORD
           A : real;
           CASE Tag : TagType OF
             B : (X, Y : real);
             C : (Z : boolean)
         END;
```

b.
```
TYPE
  TagType = (A, B, C);
  Info = RECORD
           D : integer;
           Flag : boolean;
           CASE Tag : TagType OF
             A : (X, Y : real);
             B : (Z : real)
         END;
```

c.
```
TYPE
  TagType = (A, B, C);
  Info = RECORD
           D : integer;
           Flag : boolean
           CASE Tag OF
             A : (X : real);
             B : (Y : real);
             C : (Z : real)
         END;
```

d.
```
TYPE
  TagType = (A, B, C);
  Info = RECORD
           D : integer;
           CASE Tag1 : TagType OF
             A : (X : real);
             B : (Y : real);
             C : (Z : real)
           END;  {  of CASE  }
           CASE Tag2 : TagType OF
             A : (X1 : real);
             B : (Y1 : real);
             C : (Z1 : real)
         END;  {  of RECORD Info  }
```

4. Redefine the following record without using a variant part.

```
TYPE
  WhichShape = (Circle, Square, Triangle);
  FigureInfo = RECORD
                 Object : char;
                 Area : real;
                 CASE Shape : WhichShape OF
                   Circle   : (Radius : real);
                   Square   : (Side : real);
                   Triangle : (Base, Height : real)
               END;
VAR
  Figure : FigureInfo;
```

5. Using the record defined in Exercise 4, indicate the names of the fields available and provide an illustration of these fields after each of the following assignments is made.
   a. `Shape := Circle;`
   b. `Shape := Square;`
   c. `Shape := Triangle;`
6. Redefine the record defined in Exercise 4 to include rectangles and parallelograms.
7. Define a record with a variant part to be used for working with various publications. For each record, there should be fields for the author, title, and date. If the publication is a book, there should be fields for the publisher and city. If the publication is an article, there should be fields for the journal name and volume number.

FOCUS ON PROGRAM DESIGN

The sample program for this chapter features working with an array of records. The array is first sorted using the field containing a name and then sorted using the field containing a real number.

Let's write a program to help your local high school sports boosters keep records of donors and amounts donated. The data file consists of a name (first 20 positions) and an amount donated (starting in position 21) on each line. For example

```
Jones Jerry         250■
```

Your program should get the data from the data file and read it into a record for each donor. Output should consist of two lists:

1. An alphabetical listing together with the amount donated.
2. A listing sorted according to the amount donated.

A first-level pseudocode development for this problem is

1. Get the data
2. Sort by name
3. Print the first list
4. Sort by amount
5. Print the second list

Module specifications for the main modules are

1. GetData Module
Data received: None
Information returned: Array of records containing names, amounts, and array length
Logic: Use a **WHILE NOT eof** loop with a counter to read the data file.

2. SortByName Module
Data received: Unsorted array of records containing names and amounts with the list length
Information returned: An alphabetized list of names with associated amounts
Logic: Use a selection sort to sort the array of records.

3. PrintList Module
Data received: Array of records
Array length
Information returned: None
Logic: Call procedure PrintHeading.
Use a loop to print the names and amounts.

4. SortByAmount Module
Data received: Array of records sorted alphabetically
List length
Information returned: Array of records sorted by size of donation
Logic: Use a selection sort to sort the list of donations.

A refinement of the pseudocode yields

1. Get the data
   WHILE NOT eof DO
   1.1 get a name
   1.2 get the amount
2. Sort by name (use selection sort)
3. Print the first list
   3.1 print a heading
   3.2 print the names and amounts
4. Sort by amount (use selection sort)
5. Print the second list
   5.1 print a heading
   5.2 print the names and amounts

A complete structure chart for this problem is given in Figure 9.16.

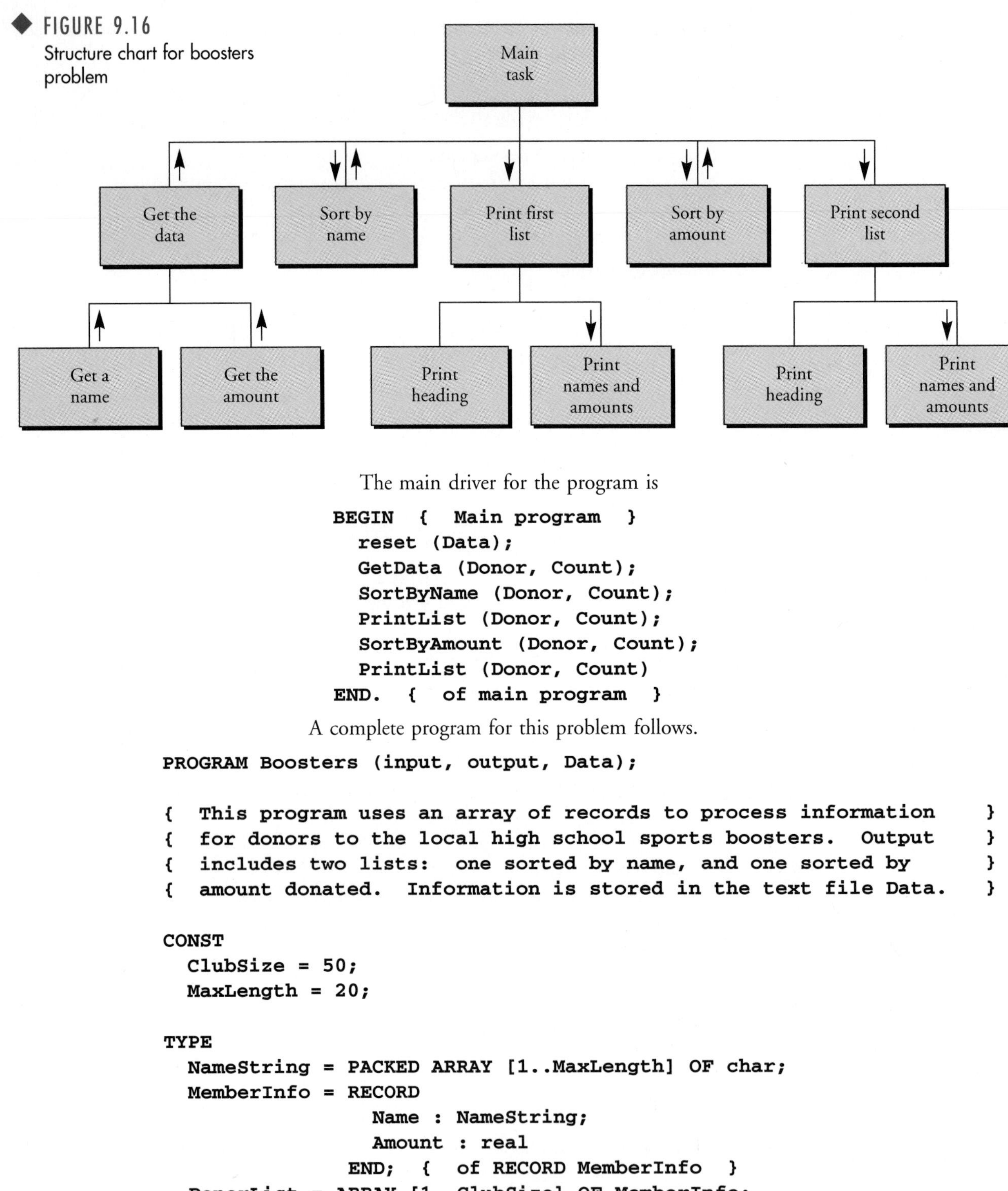

◆ FIGURE 9.16
Structure chart for boosters problem

The main driver for the program is

```
BEGIN  {  Main program  }
  reset (Data);
  GetData (Donor, Count);
  SortByName (Donor, Count);
  PrintList (Donor, Count);
  SortByAmount (Donor, Count);
  PrintList (Donor, Count)
END.  {  of main program  }
```

A complete program for this problem follows.

```
PROGRAM Boosters (input, output, Data);

{  This program uses an array of records to process information     }
{  for donors to the local high school sports boosters.  Output     }
{  includes two lists:  one sorted by name, and one sorted by       }
{  amount donated.  Information is stored in the text file Data.    }

CONST
  ClubSize = 50;
  MaxLength = 20;

TYPE
  NameString = PACKED ARRAY [1..MaxLength] OF char;
  MemberInfo = RECORD
                 Name : NameString;
                 Amount : real
               END;  {  of RECORD MemberInfo  }
  DonorList = ARRAY [1..ClubSize] OF MemberInfo;

VAR
  Count : integer;          {  Counter for number of donors          }
  Donor : DonorList;        {  Array of records, one for each donor  }
  Data : text;              {  Data file of names and amounts        }
```

```
{*****************************************************************}

PROCEDURE GetData (VAR Donor : DonorList;
                   VAR Count : integer);

  {  Given:   Nothing                                              }
  {  Task:    Read donor names and amounts from the text file      }
  {                Data into an array of records                   }
  {  Return:  An array of records and number of donors             }

  VAR
    J : integer;
  BEGIN
    Count := 0;
    WHILE NOT eof(Data) AND (Count < ClubSize) DO                   1
      BEGIN
        Count := Count + 1;
        WITH Donor[Count] DO
          BEGIN
            FOR J := 1 TO MaxLength DO
              read (Data, Name[J]);
            readln (Data, Amount)
          END  {  of WITH...DO  }
      END;  {  of WHILE NOT eof  }
    IF NOT eof(Data) THEN
      writeln ('Not all data read.')
  END;  {  of PROCEDURE GetData  }

{*****************************************************************}

PROCEDURE Swap (VAR Record1, Record2 : MemberInfo);

  {  Given:   Two records                                          }
  {  Task:    Interchange contents of records                      }
  {  Return:  Records with contents interchanged                   }

  VAR
    Temp : MemberInfo;
  BEGIN
    Temp := Record1;
    Record1 := Record2;
    Record2 := Temp
  END;  {  of PROCEDURE Swap  }

{*****************************************************************}

PROCEDURE SortByName (VAR Donor : DonorList;
                      Count : integer);

  {  Given:   An array of records and number of records            }
  {  Task:    Sort alphabetically by the field Donor[J].Name       }  2
  {  Return:  An alphabetized array of records                     }
```

```
  VAR
    J, K, Index : integer;
    Temp : MemberInfo;
  BEGIN
    FOR J := 1 TO Count - 1 DO
      BEGIN
        Index := J;
        FOR K := J + 1 TO Count DO
          IF Donor[K].Name < Donor[Index].Name THEN
            Index := K;
        IF Index <> J THEN
          Swap (Donor[Index], Donor[J])
      END  {  of FOR J loop  }
  END;  {  of PROCEDURE SortByName  }

{*****************************************************************}

PROCEDURE SortByAmount (VAR Donor : DonorList;
                        Count : integer);

  {  Given:   An array of records and number of records        }
  {  Task:    Sort by amount donated, Donor[J].Amount          }
  {  Return:  An array of records sorted by amount donated     }

  VAR
    J, K, Index : integer;
    Temp : MemberInfo;
  BEGIN
    FOR J := 1 TO Count - 1 DO                                   4
      BEGIN
        Index := J;
        FOR K := J + 1 TO Count DO
          IF Donor[K].Amount > Donor[Index].Amount THEN
            Index := K;
        IF Index <> J THEN
          Swap (Donor[Index], Donor[J])
      END  {  of FOR J loop  }
  END;  {  of PROCEDURE SortByAmount  }

{*****************************************************************}

PROCEDURE PrintHeading;

  {  Given:   Nothing                                          }
  {  Task:    Print a heading for the output                   }
  {  Return:  Nothing                                          }

  CONST
    Skip = ' ';                                                  3
  BEGIN
    writeln (Skip:7, 'Local Sports Boosters');
    writeln (Skip:11, 'Donation List');
    writeln ('-----------------------------------');
```

```
    writeln;
    writeln (Skip:5, 'Name', Skip:20, 'Amount');
    writeln (Skip:5, '----', Skip:20, '------');
    writeln
  END;  {  of PROCEDURE PrintHeading  }

{*****************************************************************}

PROCEDURE PrintList (VAR Donor : DonorList;
                         Count : integer);

  {  Given:   An array of records and number of records          }
  {  Task:    Print a list containing one column for the name and  }
  {                one column for the amount donated; output       }
  {                directed to the printer                         }
  {  Return:  Nothing                                              }

  CONST
    Skip = ' ';
  VAR
    J : integer;
  BEGIN
    PrintHeading;
    FOR J := 1 TO Count DO
      WITH Donor[J] DO
        writeln (Name, '$':8, Amount:7:2);
    writeln;
    writeln;
    writeln
  END;  {  of PROCEDURE PrintList  }

{*****************************************************************}

BEGIN  {  Main program  }
  reset (Data);
  GetData (Donor, Count);
  SortByName (Donor, Count);
  PrintList (Donor, Count);
  SortByAmount (Donor, Count);
  PrintList (Donor, Count)
END.  {  of main program  }
```

The output from this program is

```
            Local Sports Boosters
                Donation List
      ----------------------------------

          Name                     Amount
          ----                     ------

      Alexander Candy            $ 300.00
      Anderson Tony              $ 375.00
      Banks Marj                 $ 375.00
```

```
Born Patty                    $ 100.00
Brown Ron                     $ 200.00
Darnell Linda                 $ 275.00
Erickson Thomas               $ 100.00
Fox William                   $ 300.00
Francis Denise                $ 350.00
Generous George               $ 525.00
Gillette Mike                 $ 350.00
Hancock Kirk                  $ 500.00
Higgins Sam                   $ 300.00
Janson Kevin                  $ 200.00
Johnson Ed                    $ 350.00
Johnson Martha                $ 400.00
Jones Jerry                   $ 250.00
Kelly Marvin                  $ 475.00
Kneff Susan                   $ 300.00
Lasher John                   $ 175.00
Lyon Elizabeth                $ 425.00
Moore Robert                  $ 100.00
Muller Marjorie               $ 250.00
Smith John                    $ 100.00
Trost Frostie                 $  50.00
Trudo Rosemary                $ 200.00
Weber Sharon                  $ 150.00
Williams Art                  $ 350.00
Williams Jane                 $ 175.00
Wilson Mary                   $ 275.00


       Local Sports Boosters
           Donation List
----------------------------------

     Name                   Amount
     ----                   ------

Generous George               $ 525.00
Hancock Kirk                  $ 500.00
Kelly Marvin                  $ 475.00
Lyon Elizabeth                $ 425.00
Johnson Martha                $ 400.00
Anderson Tony                 $ 375.00
Banks Marj                    $ 375.00
Francis Denise                $ 350.00
Gillette Mike                 $ 350.00
Johnson Ed                    $ 350.00
Williams Art                  $ 350.00
Higgins Sam                   $ 300.00
Alexander Candy               $ 300.00
Kneff Susan                   $ 300.00
Fox William                   $ 300.00
Darnell Linda                 $ 275.00
Wilson Mary                   $ 275.00
```

```
Muller Marjorie          $ 250.00
Jones Jerry              $ 250.00
Trudo Rosemary           $ 200.00
Brown Ron                $ 200.00
Janson Kevin             $ 200.00
Lasher John              $ 175.00
Williams Jane            $ 175.00
Weber Sharon             $ 150.00
Erickson Thomas          $ 100.00
Born Patty               $ 100.00
Smith John               $ 100.00
Moore Robert             $ 100.00
Trost Frostie             $ 50.00
```

RUNNING AND DEBUGGING HINTS

1. Be sure to use the full field name when working with fields in a record. You should leave off the record name only when using **WITH . . . DO**.
2. Terminate each record definition with an **END** statement. This is an instance when **END** is used without a **BEGIN**.
3. Although field names in different record types can be the same, you are encouraged to use distinct names. This enhances readability and reduces the chances of making errors.
4. Be careful to note the distinction in syntax when using an array of records versus an array as a field within a record. For example, be able to distinguish between Student[K].Average, Student.Score[J], and Student[K].Score[J].

SUMMARY

Key Terms

array of records
field
field selector
fixed part
index sort
nested records
record
tag field
variant part

Keywords

RECORD **WITH**

Key Concepts

- A **RECORD** is a structured data type that is a collection of fields; the fields may be treated as a whole or individually.
- Fields in a record can be of different data types.
- Records can be declared or defined by

```
<record name> = RECORD
                  <field identifier 1> : <data type 1>;
                  <field identifier 2> : <data type 2>;
                            .                  .
                            .                  .
                            .                  .
                  <field identifier n> : <data type n>
                END;  {  of RECORD definition  }
```

- Fields can be accessed as variables by
  <record name>.<field identifier>
- Records can be schematically represented as shown in Figure 9.17.

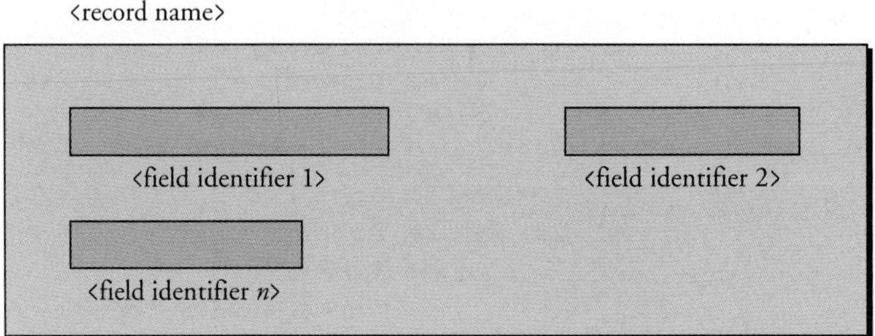

◆ FIGURE 9.17
Fields in a record

- You can use **WITH** <record name> **DO** rather than make a specific reference to the record name with each field of a record; thus, you can use

```
WITH Student DO
  BEGIN
    Name := 'Smith John          ';
    Average := 93.4;
    Grade := 'A'
  END;
```

  instead of

```
Student.Name := 'Smith John          ';
Student.Average := 93.4;
Student.Grade := 'A';
```

- If two records, A and B, are of identical type, the contents of all fields of one record may be assigned to the corresponding fields of the other by a single assignment statement, such as

```
A := B;
```

- Either entire records or fields within a record can be passed to appropriate subprograms.
- A record can be used as a field in another record.
- A **WITH . . . DO** statement can be used to access fields of nested records.
- Records can be used as components of an array.
- An array of records can be sorted by one of the fields in each record.
- Records with variant parts list all fixed fields (if any) first and then use a **CASE** statement to list the variant fields; for example

```
TYPE
  MaritalStatus = (Married, Single, Divorced);
  NameString = PACKED ARRAY [1..20] OF char;
  Info = RECORD
           Name : NameString;
           CASE Status : MaritalStatus OF
             Married  : (SpouseName : NameString;
                         NumKids : integer);
             Single   : (Gender : char;
                         Age : integer);
```

```
                    Divorced : (NumKids : integer;
                                Age : integer;
                                Gender : char;
                                LivesAlone : boolean)
                END;  {  of RECORD Info  }
VAR
  Customer : Info;
```

◆ After a value has been assigned to a tag field, the remaining record fields are the ones listed in the **CASE** part of the definition; for example, using the previous definition and assuming

```
Customer.Status := Divorced;
```

the record fields can be envisioned as shown in Figure 9.18.

◆ FIGURE 9.18
Value of a tag field

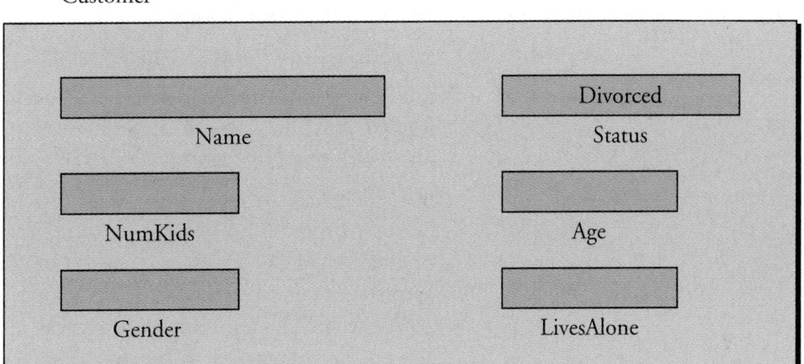

PROGRAMMING PROBLEMS AND PROJECTS

1. Write a program to be used by the registrar of a university. The program should get information from a data file and the data for each student should include student name, student number, classification (1 - freshman, 2 - sophomore, 3 - junior, 4 - senior, or 7 - special student), hours taking, hours completed, and grade point average. Output should include an alphabetical list of all students, an alphabetical list of students in each class, and a list of all students in order by grade point average.
2. Robert Day, basketball coach at Indiana College, wants you to write a program to help him analyze information about his basketball team. He wants a record for each player to contain the player's name, position played, high school from which the player graduated, height, scoring average, rebounding average, grade point average, and seasons of eligibility remaining.

   The program should read the information for each player from a data file. The output should include an alphabetized list of names together with other pertinent information, a list sorted according to scoring average, an alphabetized list of all players with a grade point average above 3.0, and an alphabetized list of high schools together with an alphabetized list of players who graduated from each school.
3. ■ Final grades in Dr. Lae Z. Programmer's (Problems 5, 22, and 23, Chapter 4; Problem 13, Chapter 5; Problem 5, Chapter 6; and Problem 3, Chapter 8) computer science class are to be computed using the following course requirements.

Requirement	Possible Points
1. Quiz scores (10 points each; count the best 10 out of 12)	100
2. Two hourly tests (100 points each)	200
3. Eight programming assignments (25 points each)	200
4. Two test program assignments (50 points each)	100
5. Final examination	100
Total	700

Cutoff percentages for the grades of A, B, C, D, and E are 90 percent, 80 percent, 70 percent, and 55 percent, respectively; grade E is less than 55 percent.

Write a program to keep a record of each student's name, social security number, quiz scores (all 12), hourly test scores, programming assignment scores, test program scores, and final examination score. Your program should read data from a data file, compute total points for each student, calculate the letter grade, and output the results. The output should be sorted by total points from high to low and should include all raw data, the 10 best quiz scores, total points, percentage score, and letter grade. Use procedures and functions where appropriate.

4. Write a program to input an unknown number of pairs of fractions with an operation sign (+, –, *, or /) between the fractions. The program should perform the operation on the fractions or indicate that the operation is impossible. Answers should be reduced to lowest terms.

```
Sample Input        Sample Output

                     3      5      19
3/4 + 5/6           --- + --- = ---
                     4      6      12

                     4      1       5
4/9 - 1/6           --- - --- = ---
                     9      6      18

                     4      0
4/5 / 0/2           --- / --- = Impossible
                     5      2

                     4      7
4/3 + 7/0           --- + --- = Impossible
                     3      0

                     6     20       8
6/5 * 20/3          --- * --- = ---
                     5      3       1
```

5. Complex numbers are numbers of the form $a + bi$ where a and b are real and i represents $\sqrt{-1}$. Complex number arithmetic is defined by

Sum	$(a + bi) + (c + di) = (a + c) + (b + d)i$
Difference	$(a + bi) - (c + di) = (a - c) + (b - d)i$
Product	$(a + bi)(c + di) = (ac - bd) + (ad + bc)i$
Quotient	$\dfrac{(a + bi)}{(c + di)} = \dfrac{ac + bd}{c^2 + d^2} + \dfrac{bc - ad}{c^2 + d^2}i$

Write a program to be used to perform these calculations on two complex numbers. Each line of data consists of a single character designator (S, D, P, or Q) followed by four reals representing two complex numbers. For example, $(2 + 3i) + (5 - 2i)$ is represented by

```
S2 3 5 -2
```

A record should be used for each complex number. The output should be in the form $a + bi$.

6. The ReadMore Public Library wants you to develop a program to keep track of the books checked out. Information for each book should be kept in a record, and the fields should include the author's name, a nonfiction designator (**boolean**), the title, the library catalog number, and the copyright date. Each customer can check out at most 10 books.

   Your program should read information from a data file and print two lists alphabetized by author name: one for nonfiction and the other for fiction. A typical data line is

```
Kidder Tracy        T Soul of New Machine        81.6044 1982
                    ↑                            ↑
               position 21                  position 52
```

7. Modify Problem 6 so a daily printout is available that contains a summary of the day's transactions at the ReadMore Public Library. A record for each customer should contain the customer's name and library card number. Be sure to make provision for books that are returned.
8. Write a program to be used to keep track of bank accounts. Define a record that includes each customer's name, account number, starting balance, transaction record, and ending balance. The transaction record should list all deposits and withdrawals. A special message should be printed whenever there are insufficient funds for a withdrawal. When a name is read from the data file, all previous records should be searched to see if the user is processing a new account. The final output for each customer should look like a typical bank statement.
9. Write a program that uses records to analyze poker hands. Each hand consists of five records (cards). Each record should have one field for the suit and one field for the value. Rankings for the hands from high to low are

straight flush	three of a kind
four of a kind	two pair
full house	one pair
flush	none of the above
straight	

   Your program should read data for five cards from a data file, evaluate the hand, and print the hand together with a message indicating its value.

10. Problem 9 can be modified in several ways. One modification is to compare two different hands using only the rank indicated. A second (more difficult) modification is to also compare hands that have the same ranks; for example, a pair of 8s is better than a pair of 7s. Extend Problem 9 to incorporate some of these modifications.

11. Divers at the Olympics are judged by seven judges. Points for each dive are awarded according to the following procedure.

(1) Each judge assigns a score between 0.0 and 10.0, inclusive.

(2) The high score and low score are eliminated.

(3) The five remaining scores are summed, and this total is multiplied by 0.6. This result is then multiplied by the degree of difficulty of the dive (0.0 to 3.0).

The first level of competition consists of 24 divers, each of whom makes 10 dives. Divers with the 12 highest totals advance to the finals.

Write a program to keep a record for each diver. Each record should contain information for all 10 dives, the diver's name, and the total score. One round of competition consists of each diver making one dive. A typical line of data consists of the diver's name, degree of difficulty for the dive, and seven judges' scores. Part of your output should include a list of divers who advance to the finals.

12. The University Biology Department has a Conservation Club that works with the state Department of Natural Resources. Its project for the semester is to help capture and tag migratory birds. You have been asked to write a computer program to help the club store information. In general, the program must enable the user to enter information for each bird tagged interactively into an array of records and then store these data in a text file for subsequent use. For each bird tagged, you need a field for the tag number, tagging site, sex, bird type, date, and name of the DNR officer doing the tagging. After all data have been entered, the program should print one list sorted by tag number and one list sorted by bird type.

■ **13.** Ada Crown, your computer science instructor, wishes to monitor the maintenance record of her computers and has turned to you for help. She wants to keep track of the type of machine, its serial number (up to 10 characters), the year of purchase, and whether or not the machine is under service contract (use a **boolean** variable) .

Write a program that permits the entry of records, and then prints a list of the machines that are under warranty and a list of those that are not under warranty. Both lists should be arranged in order of serial number.

14. Most microcomputer owners soon develop a large, often unorganized library of software on several floppy disks. This is your chance to help them. Define a record that contains the disk number of each disk and a list of up to 30 program titles on each disk. Write a program to read a text file containing the information for a disk and then print an alphabetized list of the program titles on that disk.

15. Revise the program in Problem 14 to permit the user of the program to enter the desired program name and have the program print the number of disk(s) that contain the program.

16. Write a program to read records that contain the names, addresses, telephone numbers, and classes of some of your friends. Print a list of the names of the students in the file who are in your class.

■ **17.** The Falcon Manufacturing Company (Problem 23, Chapter 8) wishes to keep computerized records of its telephone-order customers. The records are to contain the name, street address, city, state, and zip code for each customer and include either a T if the customer is a business or an F if the customer is an individual. A 30-character description of each business and an individual's credit limit are also to be included in the record.

Write a program to read the information for the customer from a text file and print a list of the information for businesses and a separate list of the information for individuals. There are no more than 50 records in the file.

18. Write a program that can be used to analyze quadrilaterals. Input consists of four pairs of integers, each of which represents a point in the plane. It is assumed the points represent the vertices of a quadrilateral given in counterclockwise order. Your program should indicate whether the quadrilateral is a square, a rectangle, a rhombus, or none of the above. All names that apply to the quadrilateral should be listed.

19. Standard Pascal does not support a string data type. However, strings may be simulated by using a record with two fields: one for the length, and one for the characters in the string. The field for length should be of type **integer,** and the field for the string should be a packed array of characters with 256 positions. Write a program that receives strings as input and creates an appropriate record for each string. Your program should then be able to simulate the following string operations.

a. Determine the length of a string (the null string is of length zero). Do not count trailing blanks.

b. Make the string comparisons <, =, and >. The user should be able to compare strings of different lengths.

c. Concatenate strings. If String1 is "This is" and String2 is " one sentence.", the concatenation of String1 and String2 is "This is one sentence.".

Output from your program should be any input string and sufficient displays to demonstrate your string operations.

COMMUNICATION IN PRACTICE

1. Write a short paper that explains why the existence of the structured data type **RECORD** eliminates the need for working with parallel arrays. As part of your paper, show specifically how **PROGRAM** Donations in Section 8.3 can be rewritten using records.

2. Suppose you are part of a team that has been asked to develop a spreadsheet. Your specific task is to write all documentation for the sorting feature of the spreadsheet. The documentation is to include complete descriptions of forms of input and output, a logical development of the sorting process, and a description of the user interface message. Prepare a report that includes this documentation.

3. Visit your local registrar, and discuss how records of students are processed. Discover what data are kept in each record, how the data are entered, and what the fields of each record are. Have the registrar explain what operations are used with a student's record. Specifically, how is information added to or deleted from a record? Discuss the issue of sorting records. What kinds of lists must the registrar produce for those within the system who need information about students? Prepare a written report of your visit for the class. Be sure to include a graphic that shows how a student's record can be envisioned.

4. Select an unworked problem from the Programming Problems and Projects in this chapter. Construct a structure chart and write all documentary information necessary for this problem. Do not write code. When finished, have a classmate read your documentation to see if it is clear precisely what is to be done.
5. Modify one of the programs you developed in this chapter by deleting all documentation. Exchange your modified version with another student who has prepared a similar version. Write documentation for the exchanged program. Compare your results with the other student's original version.
6. Select a problem from the Programming Problems and Projects in this chapter that you have not done. For that problem, write documentation that includes a complete description of
   a. Required input
   b. Required output
   c. Required processing and computation

   Exchange your documentation with another student who has the same assignment. Compare your results.

CHAPTER 10 More about Files

CHAPTER OUTLINE

Chapter 6 introduced the concept of text files, which are used to provide data for a program and to store data between runs of a program. All data in a text file are stored as a sequence of characters of type **char.** We are now ready to examine files in more detail, beginning with the definition and use of binary files.

T

A note of caution is in order first, however. File manipulation is extremely system dependent. This is especially true in microcomputers. Since it is likely that your system differs from standard Pascal in some ways, you are encouraged to consult your system manual.

Files that cannot be defined as text files are *binary files.* Information is stored in binary files by using the internal binary representation of each component. This method differs from data storage in a text file, where components are stored as lines of characters.

The advantage of using binary files is that they can be much more efficiently processed. Because the binary representation of data is already available, conversion between character representation and appropriate binary representation is not needed. A disadvantage of using binary files is that they cannot be created, examined, or modified by using a text editor. Binary files must be created by a program. Furthermore, all operations with binary files must be done within programs. In the following sections, we see how these operations are performed.

10.1 Binary Files

OBJECTIVES

- to understand the basic idea of a file in Pascal
- to be able to define a file type
- to understand the concept of a buffer
- to understand the differences between files and arrays as structured data types

Basic Idea and Notation

Information can be saved between runs of a program by using secondary storage devices such as tapes or disks. (Personal computers use floppy or hard disks.) As a beginning programmer, you normally do not need to be concerned with the actual physical construct of these storage devices, but you do need to know how to work with them. To oversimplify, you need to be able to get data into a program, manipulate these data, and save the data (and results) for later use. If we write a program that computes grades for students in a class, for example, we need to enter data periodically for processing. Pascal solves this problem with the structured data type **FILE.** A *file* is a data structure that consists of a sequence of components that are all of the same type. A **FILE** data type is defined by

```
TYPE
   <file identifier> = FILE OF <data type>;
VAR
   <file name> : <file identifier>
```

Thus, if we wish to work with a file of integers, we define

```
TYPE
  FileOfInt = FILE OF integer;
VAR
  File1 : FileOfInt;
```

In this case, File1 is the desired file. Several comments are now in order.

1. Data entries in a file are called *components of the file.*
2. All components of a file must be of the same data type.
3. The only data type not permitted as a component of a file is another file type. This differs from arrays in that

   ARRAY [ ] **OF ARRAY** [ ] **OF** <data type>;

   is permitted, but

   FILE OF FILE OF <data type>;

   is not permitted.

Each of the following is a valid definition of a binary file type.

```
TYPE
  Identifier1 = FILE OF real;
  Identifier2 = FILE OF ARRAY [1..20] OF integer;
  Identifier3 = FILE OF boolean;
```

Files of records are frequently used in programs. Thus, to keep a record for each student in a class, we could have the definition

```
TYPE
  NameString = PACKED ARRAY [1..20] OF char;
  ExamScores = ARRAY [1..4] OF integer;
  QuizScores = ARRAY [1..10] OF integer;
  StudentInfo = RECORD
                  Name : NameString;
                  IDNumber : 0..999;
                  Exam : ExamScores;
                  Quiz : QuizScores;
                  Average : real;
                  Grade : char
                END;  {  of RECORD StudentInfo  }
  StudentFile = FILE OF StudentInfo;
VAR
  Student : StudentFile;
```

There is a difference between a text file and a file of characters. Although a text file consists of a sequence of characters, it also has "lines" separated by end-of-line markers. A file of characters, which is of the type **FILE OF char,** does not have line separators.

Comparison to Arrays

Binary files and one-dimensional arrays have some similarities. Both are structured data types, and components must be of the same type. There are, however, some important differences.

1. Files permit the user to store and retrieve information between runs of a program.
2. Only one component of a file is available at a time.
3. Files must be sequentially accessed; that is, when working with files, the user starts at the beginning and processes the components in sequence. It is not possible (as it is with arrays) to access some component directly without first having somehow moved through the previous components.
4. Files do not have a defined length. Once a file has been defined, the number of its components is limited only by the amount of storage available. However, this number is usually so large it can be considered unbounded.
5. Files are stored in secondary storage; arrays are stored only in memory.

File Window and Buffer Variables

Before we begin our specific work with files, we need to examine the concepts of a file window and a buffer variable. A file can be visualized as a sequence of components:

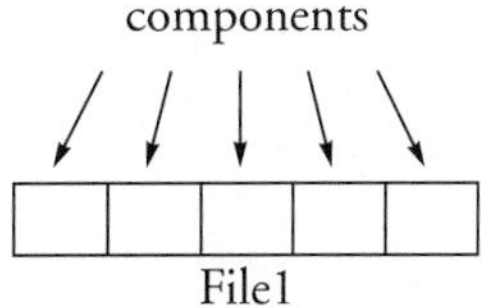

Only one of these components can be "seen" at a time. An imaginary window is associated with a file, and values can be transferred to (or from) a component of the file only through this *file window.* Thus, the window must be properly positioned before the user attempts to transmit data to or from a component.

This imaginary window has no name in Pascal. However, a related concept, called a *buffer variable,* is the actual vehicle through which values are passed to or from the file component. When a file is declared in a program, a buffer variable is automatically declared and therefore available to the programmer. To illustrate, given the declaration of FileA

```
TYPE
  FileInfo = FILE OF integer;
VAR
  FileA : FileInfo;
```

the buffer variable (FileA^ or FileA↑) can be used in the program. The buffer variable is always the file name followed by a caret (^) or an up arrow (↑). Historically, the phrase "up arrow" has been used when referring to buffer variables. However, we will use the caret symbol when designating buffer variables because it is available on computer keyboards (above the 6).

The buffer variable is not declared in the variable declaration section. In general, we have:

Declaration	Buffer Variable
VAR	
<file name> : **FILE OF** <data type>	<file name>^

The buffer variable is of the same data type as one component of the file. It allows the user to access data at the position of the file marker or pointer that is used when illustrating text files. Although it is intended to pass values to and from a file, a buffer variable can be used very much like a regularly declared variable of that type. From FileA, specifically, FileA^ is a variable of type **integer** and statements such as

A NOTE OF INTEREST

Relational Data Bases

One advance in data management that has gained tremendously in popularity and, in fact, is revolutionizing system development practices is the increased use of the data base management system, known as DBMS. An especially important development in data base technology is the relational data base.

The relational DBMS is based upon the concept of multiple "flat files" that are "related" via common fields. A flat file is essentially a two-dimensional matrix of columns and rows, where columns represent the fields contained in a record and rows contain different records. A simple example of the flat file concept is a spreadsheet, such as Lotus 1-2-3, although the analogy is somewhat misleading since spreadsheets are most commonly used for purposes other than data base management.

In a relational data base there are usually several flat files, each of which is used to store information about a different "entity" in the world. The objectives of relational technology are to insure that each file in the data base contains information about only the entity with which it is associated and to provide linkages between files that represent the relationships between those entities that exist in the real world.

Let's look at a simple example of a relational data base that is used to process customer orders. Such a relational data base would contain at least two files: one for customer data, and one for order data. The customer file would contain information (that is, fields) such as the customer's account number, name, address, and phone number; the order file would contain fields such as product number, product name, order quantity, unit cost, and total order cost. To enable the system to match an order to the customer who placed it, the customer's account number would also be contained in the order file. Thus, when the user needs to acquire combined order and customer information (for example, to prepare and mail an invoice), the two files can be temporarily "joined" together based upon common values in the respective customer account number fields in each file.

At the mainframe level of computing, the relational DBMS is one of several types of data base management systems; other types are hierarchical and network systems. At the microcomputer level, however, DBMS software is almost exclusively relational. Such common packages as dBASE III, RBase System V, and SQLBase are all relational and provide essentially the same basic structures and capabilities, even though they require different syntax to accomplish similar activities.

```
FileA^ := 21;
Age := FileA^;
GetData (FileA^);
```

where GetData is a procedure, are appropriate.

EXERCISES 10.1

1. Discuss the similarities between arrays and files.
2. Discuss the differences between arrays and files.
3. Which of the following are valid declarations of files? Explain those that are invalid. State the component type for those that are valid.

a.
```
TYPE
  FileOfAges = FILE OF 0..120;
VAR
  AgeFile : FileOfAges;
```
b.
```
TYPE
  NameString = PACKED ARRAY [1..20] OF char;
  FileOfNames = ARRAY [1..100] OF NameString;
VAR
  NameFile : FileOfNames;
```
c.
```
TYPE
  FileA = FILE OF real;
  FileB = FILE OF FileA;
VAR
  RealFile : FileB;
```

d.
```
TYPE
  FileOfInt = FILE [1..100] OF integer;
VAR
  File1 : FileOfInt;
```
e.
```
TYPE
  IntFile = FILE OF integer;
VAR
  OldFile, NewFile, TempFile : IntFile;
```
4. Assume a program contains the following definition and declaration sections. Which buffer variables are available? State the data type of each buffer variable.

```
TYPE
  FileOfAges = FILE OF 0..120;
  IntFile = FILE OF integer;
  RealFile = FILE OF real;
  TruthFile = FILE OF boolean;
  List20 = ARRAY [1..20] OF real;
  ListFile = FILE OF List20;
  StudentInfo = RECORD
                  Name : PACKED ARRAY [1..20] OF char;
                  Age : 0..120
                END;
  StudentFile = FILE OF StudentInfo;
VAR
  File1, File2 : FileOfAges;
  OldFile : StudentFile;
  NewFile : ListFile;
  TempFile : RealFile;
  TransFile : TruthFile;
  A, B, C : IntFile;
```

5. Define a file type and then declare a file to be used with records of patients for a physician. Information should include the name, address, height, weight, age, gender, and insurance company of each patient.

10.2 Working with Binary Files

OBJECTIVES

- to understand the concept of opening a file
- to be able to put data into a file using **write** or **put**
- to be able to retrieve data from a file using **read** or **get**
- to understand the difference between internal and external files
- to be able to use procedures when working with files

Now that we have examined the concepts of files, file windows, and buffer variables, we need to see how values are transmitted to and from file components. First, let's examine the process of putting data into a file.

Creating a File

Once a file has been declared in a program, entering data to the file is referred to as *writing to the file.* Before writing to a file, the file window must be positioned at the beginning of the file by using the standard procedure **rewrite.** This is referred to as *opening a file.* Thus, if FileA is declared by

```
TYPE
  IntFile = FILE OF integer;
VAR
  FileA : IntFile;
```

then

```
rewrite (FileA);
```

opens FileA to receive values of type **integer.** At this stage, the window is positioned at the beginning of FileA and FileA is ready to receive the first component. Any components previously stored in FileA are no longer available. Successive components may be stored in FileA, and each new component is appended to the previous list of components.

Most versions of Pascal allow the user to transfer (write) values to a file by assigning the desired value to the buffer variable and using the standard procedure **put** with the buffer variable as an argument. We can, for instance, store the values 10, 20, and 30 in FileA by

```
rewrite (FileA);   {  Open for writing  }
FileA^ := 10;
put (FileA);
FileA^ := 20;
put (FileA);
FileA^ := 30;
put (FileA);
```

The **put** procedure has the effect of transferring the value of the buffer variable to the component in the window and then advancing the window to the next component. After **put** is called, the buffer variable becomes unassigned; this sequence is illustrated in Table 10.1.

◇ TABLE 10.1
Using **put** to write to a file

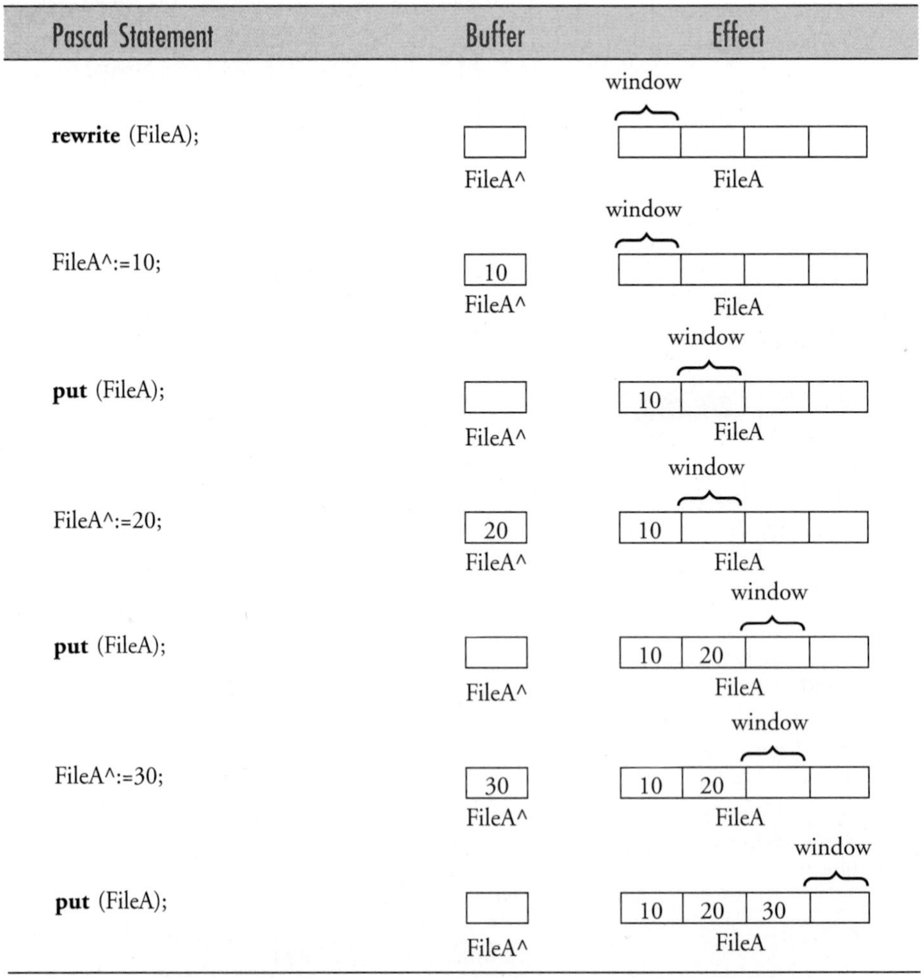

Pascal Statement	Buffer (FileA^)	Effect (FileA)
rewrite (FileA);	[ ]	window over 1st component: [ ] [ ] [ ] [ ]
FileA^:=10;	[10]	window over 1st component: [ ] [ ] [ ] [ ]
put (FileA);	[ ]	window over 2nd component: [10] [ ] [ ] [ ]
FileA^:=20;	[20]	window over 2nd component: [10] [ ] [ ] [ ]
put (FileA);	[ ]	window over 3rd component: [10] [20] [ ] [ ]
FileA^:=30;	[30]	window over 3rd component: [10] [20] [ ] [ ]
put (FileA);	[ ]	window over 4th component: [10] [20] [30] [ ]

Standard Pascal also allows values to be written to a file using the procedure **write.** When this procedure is used, the argument for **write** is preceded by the file name. Thus, the previous fragment could be

```
rewrite (FileA);   {  Open for writing  }
write (FileA, 10);
write (FileA, 20);
write (FileA, 30);
```

The procedure **writeln** can only be used with files of type **text.**

The Standard Function eof

The Boolean function **eof** can be used with binary files in much the same way as it is used with text files. When a file is opened for writing, an end-of-file marker is placed at the beginning of the file. This can be thought of as the window being positioned at the end-of-file marker. When a value is transferred into the file by **put** or **write,** the end-of-file marker is advanced to the same component position to which the window moves. The reason for this is relatively obvious. When retrieving data from a file, we need to know when we have reached the end of the file. The function **eof** is used with the file name for an argument. As expected, **eof** (<file name>) is **true** when the window is positioned at the end-of-file marker. When writing to a file, **eof** (<file name>) is always **true.**

Retrieving File Data

The process of retrieving data from a file is referred to as *reading from a file.* To retrieve data from a file, we open the file by using the standard procedure **reset.** Correct syntax is

reset (<file name>);

This has the effect of repositioning the window at the beginning of the file. Furthermore, when a file is open for reading, the value of the file component in the window is automatically assigned to the buffer variable. The window can be advanced to the next file component by a call to the standard procedure

get (<file name>);

Using the previous example of FileA with the values

10	20	30	■

FileA

we could transfer values to the main program by

```
reset (FileA);
N1 := FileA^;
get (FileA);
N2 := FileA^;
get (FileA);
N3 := FileA^;
```

The position of the window and the transfer of values for this segment of code are illustrated in Table 10.2.

◇ **TABLE 10.2**
Using **get** to read from a file

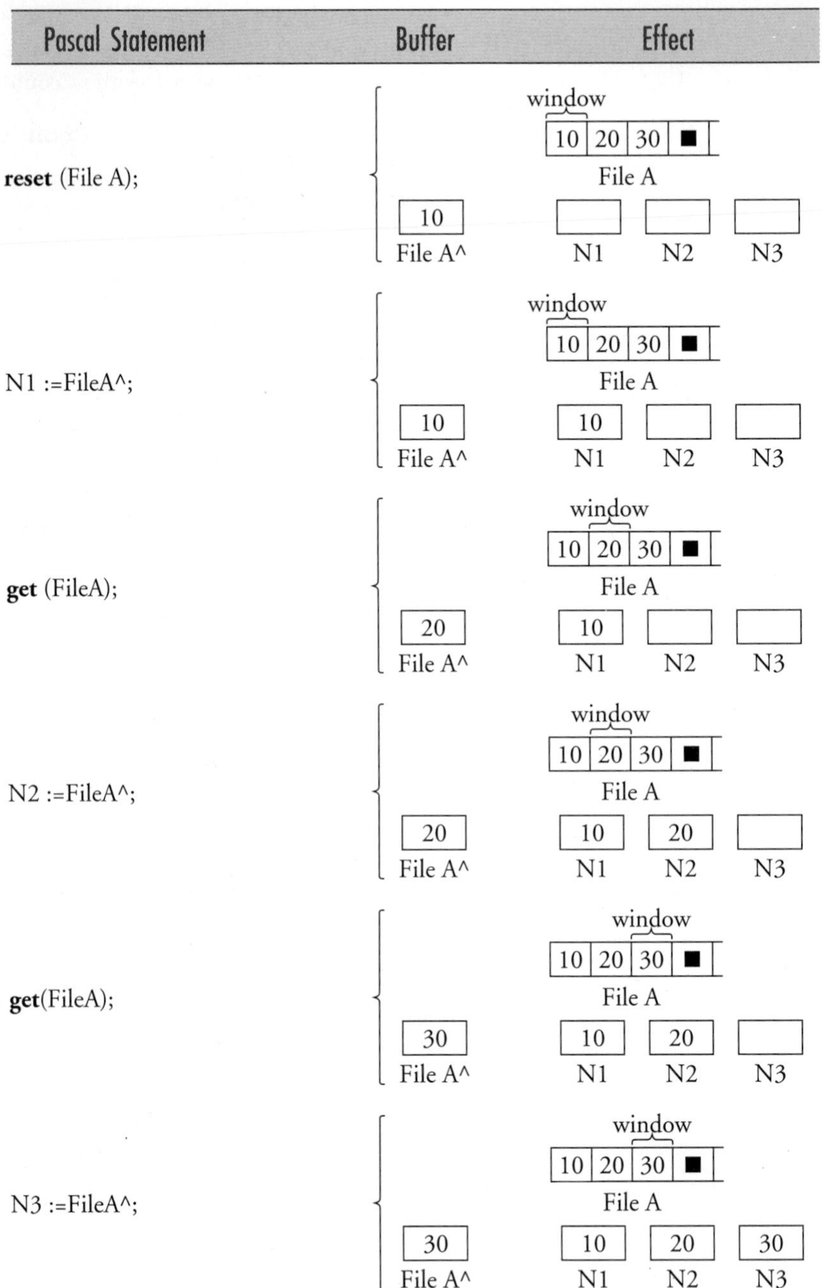

This example of retrieving data is a bit contrived since we know there are exactly three components before the end-of-file marker. A more realistic retrieval would use the **eof** function; for example

```
reset (FileA);
WHILE NOT eof(FileA) DO
  BEGIN
    .
    .    (process FileA^)
    .
    get (FileA)
  END;  {  of WHILE loop  }
```

The standard procedure **read** can also be used to transfer data from a file. After the file has been opened for reading, **read** can be used with the file name and variable names as arguments. Thus, the following can replace the previous code fragment.

```
reset (FileA);
read (FileA, N1);
read (FileA, N2);
read (FileA, N3);
```

The previous code using **get** helps to make the function of a buffer understandable. However, many students find **read** easier to use.

Opening Files

Files cannot be opened for writing and reading at the same time. When a file is opened for writing, it remains open to receive values that are appended to the file until the window is repositioned by either the **rewrite** or **reset** statement, or until the program is terminated. Thus, we may create a file and then add to it later in the program without reopening it. Similarly, before we first read from a file, it must be opened by **reset** (<file name>). Values can then be transferred from the file using either **read** or **get.**

Now let's consider a short example in which we do something with each component of a file.

EXAMPLE 10.1

Suppose we have a file of reals and we want to create another file by subtracting 5.0 from each component. Assume the following definitions and declarations.

```
TYPE
  RealFile = FILE OF real;
VAR
  OldFile : RealFile;
  NewFile : RealFile;
```

We can accomplish our objective by

```
reset (OldFile);  {  Open OldFile  }
rewrite (NewFile);  {  Open NewFile  }
WHILE NOT eof(OldFile) DO
  BEGIN
    NewFile^ := OldFile^ - 5.0;
    put (NewFile);
    get (OldFile)
  END;  {  of WHILE NOT eof  }
```

Procedures and Files

Much of the work of processing files is accomplished by using procedures. Thus, we should continue to use the **TYPE** definition section to define file types. Files can be used as arguments in a procedure call; however, in the procedure heading, files must be listed as variable parameters. This requirement is implicit in the fact that a file variable cannot be assigned all at once (as a value parameter can be).

EXAMPLE 10.2

Let's write a procedure to accomplish the task outlined in Example 10.1.

```
PROCEDURE Subtract5 (VAR OldFile, NewFile : RealFile);
  BEGIN
    reset (OldFile);
    rewrite (NewFile);
    WHILE NOT eof(OldFile) DO
      BEGIN
        NewFile^ := OldFile^ - 5.0;
        put (NewFile);
        get (OldFile)
      END  {  of WHILE loop  }
  END;  {  of PROCEDURE Subtract5  }
```

This procedure is called from the main program by

```
Subtract5 (OldFile, NewFile);
```

Even though no changes are made in OldFile, it is passed as a variable parameter.

Internal and External Files

T

Recall from Chapter 8 files that are used to store data in secondary storage between runs of a program are called external files; files that are used for processing only and are not saved in secondary storage are called internal files. External files must be listed in the program heading in the form

PROGRAM <name> (**input, output,** <external file name>)

They are declared in the variable declaration section. Internal files are not listed in the program heading but are also declared in the variable declaration section.

In a typical programming problem, an external file in secondary storage is to be updated in some form. This requires temporary internal files to be declared for use in the program. When the program is exited, all external files are saved in secondary storage while the internal files are no longer available.

Processing Files

Before looking at a specific problem about processing files, let's consider the general problem of updating an external file. Since we eventually will **rewrite** the external file, we must be careful not to erase the original contents before they have been saved and/or processed in some temporary internal file. We accomplish this by copying external files to temporary files and then working with the temporary files until the desired tasks are completed. At this point, we then copy the appropriate temporary file to the external file. In reality, this method may prove to be inefficient, but until you become more experienced in file manipulation, it is good practice to avoid working directly with external files.

Now let's consider a relatively short example of updating a file of test scores for students in a class. A detailed treatment of processing files is given in Section 10.3.

EXAMPLE 10.3

Let's assume the external file TotalPts consists of total points for each student in a class. Further, let's assume the data file contains test scores that are to be added (in the same order) to the previous totals to obtain new totals. A first-level pseudocode solution to this problem is

1. Copy the totals to a temporary file from the external file
2. Process the temporary file
3. Copy the temporary file to the external file

Assume the program heading is

```
PROGRAM Grades (input, output, TotalPts);
```

and the definitions and declarations are

```
TYPE
  IntFile = FILE OF integer;
VAR
  TotalPts : IntFile;
  Temp1File : IntFile;
  Temp2File : IntFile;
```

A procedure to copy the contents from one file to another is

```
PROCEDURE Copy (VAR OldFile, NewFile : IntFile);
  BEGIN
    reset (OldFile);
    rewrite (NewFile);
    WHILE NOT eof(OldFile) DO
      BEGIN
        NewFile^ := OldFile^;
        put (NewFile);
        get (OldFile)
      END  {  of WHILE loop  }
  END;  {  of PROCEDURE Copy  }
```

This procedure is called from the main program by

```
Copy (TotalPts, Temp1File);
```

We can now process Temp1File by adding corresponding scores from the data file. A procedure for this is

```
PROCEDURE AddScores (VAR OldFile, NewFile : IntFile);
  VAR
    NewScore : integer;
  BEGIN
    reset (OldFile);
    rewrite (NewFile);
    WHILE NOT eof(OldFile) DO
      BEGIN
        read (NewScore);  {  Get scores from data file  }
        NewFile^ := NewScore + OldFile^;
        put (NewFile);
        get (OldFile)
      END  {  of WHILE loop  }
  END;  {  of PROCEDURE AddScores  }
```

This procedure is called from the main program by

```
AddScores (Temp1File, Temp2File);
```

A NOTE OF INTEREST

Backup and Recovery of Data

The need for organizational backup and recovery procedures to prevent loss of data is due to two types of events: in particular, natural disasters and simple human errors. Natural disasters, although infrequent, are typically large-scale emergencies that can completely shut down, if not ruin, an organization's computer facilities. Examples are such potentially catastrophic events as fires, floods, and earthquakes. Human errors, on the other hand, are the most frequent cause of computer problems (has anyone NEVER erased the wrong file by mistake?) but may not be as crippling as natural disasters. Although they may not result in catastrophic loss, human errors are, at the least, a nuisance to affected individuals.

Organizations have developed a variety of backup and recovery procedures to cope with system failures and to reduce resultant losses. To reduce losses from natural disasters, some organizations have prepared contingency plans to cover backup computer locations, off-site program and data storage, and emergency staffing requirements. These contingency plans can usually be put into effect quickly and with minimal disruption of computer services. To minimize human errors (accidents can never be eliminated), organizations typically try to provide sound user-training programs and user-based physical backup measures.

A more recent problem regarding backup and recovery of data has emerged. Specifically, as storage and retrieval technology changes, old data storage can become difficult to access. As an illustration, see the *Note of Interest* on page 624.

At this stage, the updated scores are in Temp2File and they need to be stored in the external file TotalPts before the program is exited. This is done by another call to Copy in the main program. Thus

```
Copy (Temp2File, TotalPts);
```

achieves the desired results. The main program is then

```
BEGIN  {  Main program  }
  Copy (TotalPts, Temp1File);
  AddScores (Temp1File, Temp2File);
  Copy (Temp2File, TotalPts)
END.  {  of main program  }
```

Example 10.3 obviously overlooks some significant points. For example, how do we know that the scores match up or that each student's new score is added to that student's previous total? We will address these issues later in the chapter. Now let's see how one file can be appended to an existing file.

EXAMPLE 10.4

Let's assume files are named OldFile and NewFile and our task is to append NewFile to OldFile. We will use the temporary file TempFile to complete this task. A first-level pseudocode development for this problem is

1. Reset OldFile and NewFile
2. Open TempFile for writing
3. **WHILE NOT eof** (OldFile) **DO**
   3.1 write elements to TempFile
4. **WHILE NOT eof** (NewFile) **DO**
   4.1 write elements to TempFile
5. Copy TempFile to OldFile

Step 3 can be refined to

3. **WHILE NOT eof** (OldFile) **DO**
   3.1 write elements to TempFile
      3.1.1 assign OldFile buffer value to TempFile buffer
      3.1.2 write value to TempFile
      3.1.3 advance window of OldFile

The code for this step is

```
WHILE NOT eof(OldFile) DO
  BEGIN
    TempFile^ := OldFile^;
    put (TempFile);
    get (OldFile)
  END;  {  of WHILE NOT eof  }
```

The complete code for this example is left as an exercise at the end of this section.

EXERCISES 10.2

1. Review the difference between internal files and external files.
2. Write test programs that illustrate:
   a. What happens when you try to write to a file that has not been opened for writing.
   b. What happens when you try to get data from a file that has not been reset.
   c. What happens when a procedure uses a file as a value parameter.
3. Declare an appropriate file, and store the positive multiples of 7 that are less than 100.
4. Explain how the file in Exercise 3 can be saved for use in another program.
5. Consider the file with integer components.

   FivesFile

   Write a segment of code that would assign the values to variables A, B, C, and D, respectively, by using both **get** and **read** statements.
6. Consider the file declared by

   ```
   TYPE
     RealFile = FILE OF real;
   VAR
     Prices : RealFile;
   ```

   which has the component values

15.95	17.99	21.95	19.99	■	

   Prices

   a. Declare a new file, and put values in the components that are 15 percent less than the values in the components of Prices.
   b. Update the values in Prices so each value is increased by 10 percent.
7. Discuss the difference between **reset** and **rewrite.**
8. You have been asked to write a program to examine a file of integers and replace every negative number with zero. Assume IntFile has been appropriately declared and contains five integer values. Why will the following segment of code not work?

   ```
   rewrite (IntFile);
   FOR J := 1 TO 5 DO
     BEGIN
       get (IntFile);
       IF IntFile^ < 0 THEN
         IntFile^ := 0;
       put (IntFile)
     END;
   ```

9. Consider the files declared by

```
TYPE
  FileOfInt = FILE OF integer;
VAR
  File1, File2 : FileOfInt;
```

Find all errors in the following.

a.
```
reset (File1);
FOR J := 1 TO 5 DO
  BEGIN
    File1^ := 10 * J;
    put (File1)
  END;
```

b.
```
rewrite (File1);
FOR J := 1 TO 5 DO
  BEGIN
    File1^ := 10 * J;
    put (File1)
  END;
```

c.
```
rewrite (File1);
FOR J := 1 TO 5 DO
  BEGIN
    File1 := 10 * J;
    put (File1)
  END;
```

d.
```
rewrite (File1);
FOR J := 1 TO 5 DO
  File1^ := J * 10;
```

e.
```
reset (File2);
WHILE NOT eof(File1) DO
  BEGIN
    File2^ := File1^;
    put (File2);
    get (File1)
  END;
```

f.
```
reset (File2);
rewrite (File1);
WHILE NOT eof(File2) DO
  BEGIN
    File1^ := File2^;
    put (File1);
    get (File2)
  END;
```

10. Assume the files OldFile and NewFile are declared as

```
TYPE
  IntFile = FILE OF integer;
VAR
  OldFile, NewFile : IntFile;
```

For each of the following, further assume OldFile has the component values

-2	-1	0	1	2	■

OldFile

Indicate the values in the components of both OldFile and NewFile after each of the following segments of code is processed.

a.
```
reset (OldFile);
rewrite (NewFile);
WHILE NOT eof(OldFile) DO
  BEGIN
    IF OldFile^ > 0 THEN
      BEGIN
        NewFile^ := OldFile^;
        put (NewFile)
      END;
    get (OldFile)
  END;
```

b.
```
rewrite (OldFile);
rewrite (NewFile);
WHILE NOT eof(OldFile) DO
  BEGIN
    IF OldFile^ > 0 THEN
      BEGIN
        NewFile^ := OldFile^;
        put (NewFile)
      END
  END;
```

c.
```
reset (OldFile);
rewrite (NewFile);
WHILE NOT eof(OldFile) DO
  BEGIN
    NewFile^ := abs(OldFile^);
    put (NewFile);
    get (OldFile)
  END;
rewrite (OldFile);
reset (NewFile);
WHILE NOT eof(NewFile) DO
  BEGIN
    OldFile^ := NewFile^;
    put (OldFile);
    get (NewFile)
  END;
```

11. Assume OldFile and NewFile are as declared in Exercise 10. Furthermore, assume OldFile contains the values

8	−17	0	−4	21	■

OldFile

Indicate the output from the following segment of code and the values of the components in OldFile and NewFile.

```
reset (OldFile);
rewrite (NewFile);
```

```
WHILE NOT eof(OldFile) DO
  BEGIN
    NewFile^ := OldFile^;
    IF NewFile^ < 0 THEN
      writeln (NewFile^)
    ELSE
      put (NewFile);
    get (OldFile)
  END;
```

12. Assume you have declared three files (File1, File2, and File3) in a program such that the component type for each file is **real.** Further assume both File1 and File2 contain an unknown number of values. Write a segment of code to transfer the corresponding sum of the components from File1 and File2 to File3. Since File1 and File2 may have a different number of components, after one end-of-file marker is reached, you should add zeros until the next end-of-file marker is reached. Thus, your segment will produce

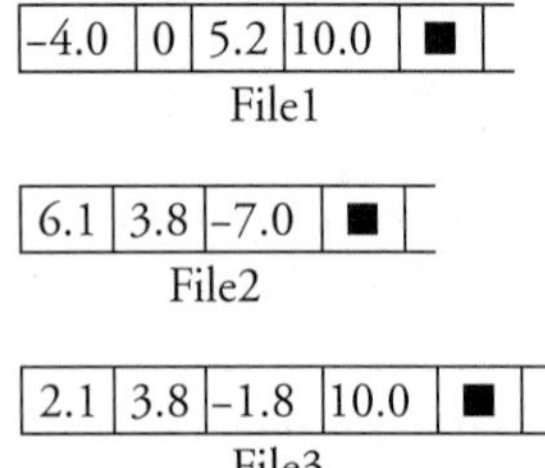

13. Write a complete program that finishes the work started in Example 10.4. Your program should print out the contents of each file used and of the final file.

10.3 Files with Structured Components

OBJECTIVES

- to be able to declare files that have records or arrays as components
- to understand why files with structured components are used
- to be able to create a file of records from a text file
- to be able to manipulate files with structured components

In actual practice, components of files are frequently some structured data type. A program might use a file of arrays or a file of records. When such a file is desired, the user declares it as an external file and then creates components from a text file. Once the data have been converted, the user can access an entire array or record rather than individual fields or components. The data are also saved in structured form between runs of a program. When data have been stored in structured components, it is relatively easy to update and work with these files. For example, a doctor might have a file of records for patients and wish to insert or delete records, choose to examine the individual fields of each record, print an alphabetical list of patients, or print a list of patients with unpaid bills.

Now let's examine a typical declaration. Suppose we are writing a program to use a file of records. Each record contains information about a student in a computer science class: the student's name, three test scores (in an array), identification number, and test average. A declaration for such a file could be

```
TYPE
  NameString = PACKED ARRAY [1..20] OF char;
  Scores = ARRAY [1..3] OF 0..100;
  StudentInfo = RECORD
                  Name : NameString;
                  Score : Scores;
                  IDNumber : 0..999;
                  Average : real
                END;  { of RECORD StudentInfo  }
```

```
    StudentFile = FILE OF StudentInfo;
  VAR
    Student : StudentFile;
```

Student is a file of records and can be illustrated as shown in Figure 10.1.

◆ FIGURE 10.1
File Student

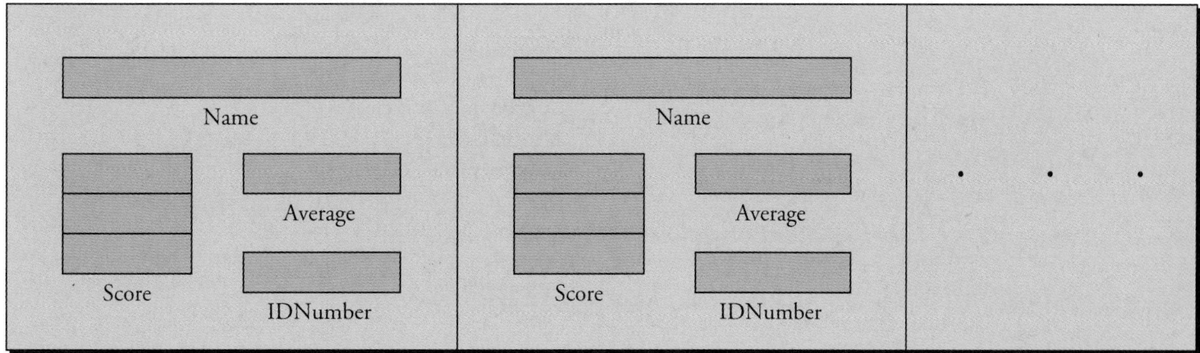

After Student has been properly opened for reading by **reset** (Student), the statement

```
  get (Student);
```

causes the contents of a record to be transferred to Student^. The field identifiers are

```
  Student^.Name
  Student^.IDNumber
  Student^.Score
  Student^.Average
```

Student^.Score is an array. Components of this array are

```
  Student^.Score[1]
  Student^.Score[2]
  Student^.Score[3]
```

If we wish to compute the average for a student whose record is in the buffer variable, we can write

```
  Sum := 0;
  WITH Student^ DO
    BEGIN
      FOR J := 1 TO 3 DO
        Sum := Sum + Score[J];
      Average := Sum / 3
    END;
```

At this stage, we may want to save this computed average for later use. Unfortunately, using **put** (Student) will not work because the file is open for reading rather than writing. We will solve this and other problems in the remainder of this section as we investigate methods of manipulating files.

Creating a File of Records

One of the first problems to be solved when working with files that contain structured variables is how to transfer data from some text file (usually **input**) to the appropriate file of structured components. Once the new file with structured components is created, it can be saved in secondary storage by declaring it as an external file. To illustrate the process of creating a file of records, let's continue the example of the file of records for students in a computer science class. Recall the definitions and subsequent declaration

```
TYPE
  NameString = PACKED ARRAY [1..20] OF char;
  Scores = ARRAY [1..3] OF 0..100;
  StudentInfo = RECORD
                  Name : NameString;
                  Score : Scores;
                  IDNumber : 0..999;
                  Average : real
                END;  {  of RECORD StudentInfo  }
  StudentFile = FILE OF StudentInfo;
VAR
  Student : StudentFile;
```

Before we can create the file of records, we need to know how data were entered in the text file (assume **input**). For purposes of this example, assume data for each student are contained on a single line, 20 positions are used for the name, and an identification number is followed by three test scores. Thus, the data file could be

Smith John 065 89 92 76	▮	Jones Mary 021 93 97 85	▮	■

T A procedure to create the file of records is

```
PROCEDURE CreateFile (VAR Student : StudentFile);
  VAR
    J : integer;
  BEGIN
    rewrite (Student);  {  Open for writing  }
    WHILE NOT eof(input) DO
      BEGIN  {  Get data for one record  }
        WITH Student^ DO
          BEGIN
            FOR J := 1 TO 20 DO
              read (Name[J]);
            read (IDNumber);
            readln (Score[1], Score[2], Score[3])
          END;  {  of WITH...DO  }
        put (Student)  {  Put buffer contents in file  }
      END  {  of WHILE NOT eof  }
  END;  {  of PROCEDURE CreateFile  }
```

This procedure is called from the main program by

```
CreateFile (Student);
```

After it is executed, we have the records shown in Figure 10.2.

◆ FIGURE 10.2
File Student with values

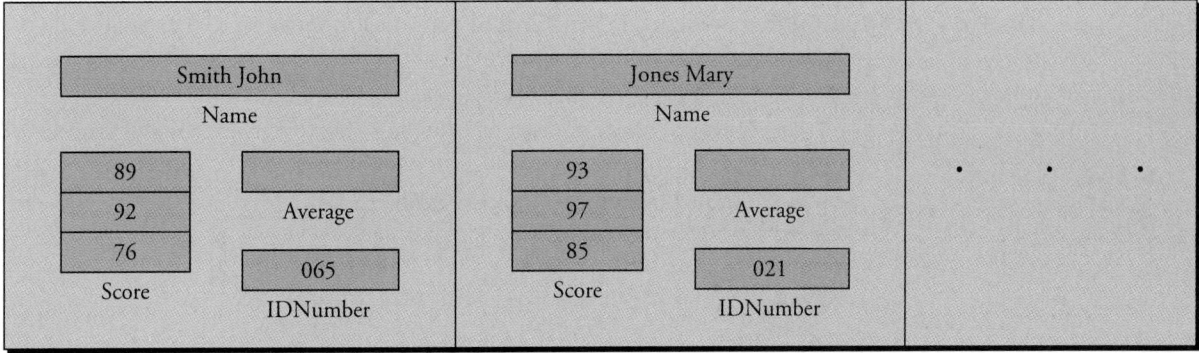

Storing Structured Files

Structured files may be stored in secondary memory for subsequent use. Files other than those of type **text** are stored as binary files. In this form, the data may be accessed by a program. However, an attempt to "look at" such a file by using a text editor or some other system command usually results in a display of gibberish characters.

Programmers need not worry about the form of data being stored. The change in representation is performed by the operating system. Even though you cannot "see" components of a file that has been saved in secondary memory, you should use files of structured components for the following reasons.

1. Values of structured file types can be read from or written to nontext files. For example, you can read or write an entire record.
2. The information in structured file types can be transferred more rapidly than it can in files of type **text** since the operating system does not do as much encoding and decoding.
3. Data are usually stored more compactly when saved as part of a structured file type.

A common error for beginning programmers is to create a text file that "looks like" a structured file and then attempt to use it as a structured file. For example, a text file of data may be arranged to look like a file of records by using a text editor. However, an attempt to read a record from this file results in an error. You must first create a file of records, as discussed previously.

File Manipulation

Several problems are typically involved with manipulating files and file components. Generally, a program starts with an existing file, revises it in some fashion, and then saves the revised file. Because files in standard Pascal must be accessed sequentially, this usually necessitates copying the existing external file to a temporary internal file, revising the temporary file, and copying the revised file to the external file. The existing external file is often referred to as the *master file.* The file containing changes to be made in the master file is called the *transaction file.*

To illustrate a simple update problem, let's again consider the problem using the file containing records for students in a computer science class. Assume the external file is named Student. Now suppose we wish to delete a record from Student (master file) because some student moved to Australia. This problem can be solved by searching Student sequentially for the record in question. The name in each record is examined; if the record is to be kept, it is put in a temporary file. The desired record is not transferred, thereby accomplishing the update. Finally, Student is rewritten by copying the contents of the temporary file to Student.

A first-level pseudocode development for this problem is

1. Get the name to be deleted
2. Search Student for a match and copy each nonmatch to TempFile
3. Copy the remainder of Student to TempFile
4. Copy TempFile to Student

Using the previous declarations and assuming that the name of the student whose record is to be deleted has been read into MovedAway, step 2 can be solved by

```
reset (Student);  {  Open the files  }
rewrite (TempFile);
Found := false;
WHILE NOT eof(Student) AND NOT Found DO
  BEGIN
    IF Student^.Name = MovedAway THEN
      Found := true
    ELSE
      BEGIN
        TempFile^ := Student^;
        put (TempFile)
      END;
    get (Student)
  END;  {  of search for a student name  }

{  Now copy the rest of student file  }
WHILE NOT eof(Student) DO
  BEGIN
    TempFile^ := Student^;
    put (TempFile);
    get (Student)
  END;  {  of WHILE NOT eof  }
```

We now need to copy TempFile to Student so the revised master file is saved as an external file. A procedure for this was developed in Section 10.2; it is called from the main program by

```
Copy (TempFile, Student);
```

As a second illustration of file manipulation, let's consider the standard problem of merging two sorted files. For example, suppose the master file is a file of records and each record contains a field for the name of a customer. Further assume this file has been sorted alphabetically by name. Now suppose an alphabetical listing of new customers is to be merged with the old file to produce a current file containing records for all customers sorted alphabetically by name.

As before, we use a temporary file to hold the full sorted list and then copy the temporary file to the master file. This can be envisioned as illustrated in Figure 10.3.

FIGURE 10.3
Merging files

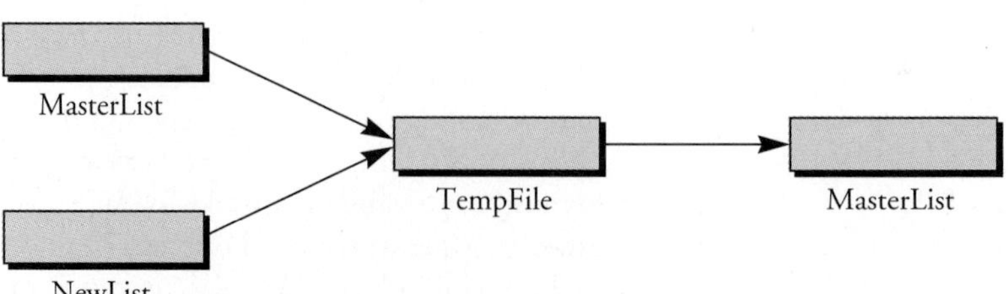

An algorithm for the merge is not too difficult. First, all files are opened. Then the initial records from MasterList and NewList are compared. The record containing the name that comes first alphabetically is transferred to TempFile. Then, as shown in the graphic documentation for the following program segment, the next record is obtained from the file containing the record that was transferred. This process continues until the end of one file is reached. At that time, the remainder of the other file is copied into TempFile.

Assuming each record has a field identified by Name, which is of type NameString, and FileType has been defined as the type for files being used, a procedure for merging follows.

```
PROCEDURE Merge (VAR Master, NewFile : FileType);
  VAR
    TempFile : FileType;
  BEGIN
    reset (Master);
    reset (NewFile);
    rewrite (TempFile);

    {  Compare top records until an eof of one of the
       input files is reached  }
    WHILE NOT eof(Master) AND NOT eof(NewFile) DO
      BEGIN
        IF Master^.Name < NewFile^.Name THEN
          BEGIN
            TempFile^ := Master^;
            get (Master)
          END
        ELSE
          BEGIN
            TempFile^ := NewFile^;
            get (NewFile)
          END;
        put (TempFile)
      END;
```

Current last record
Current record
Master
Current record
NewFile
TempFile
Transfer the smaller of these two records to the end of TempFile. Then advance within the file from which that record was taken.

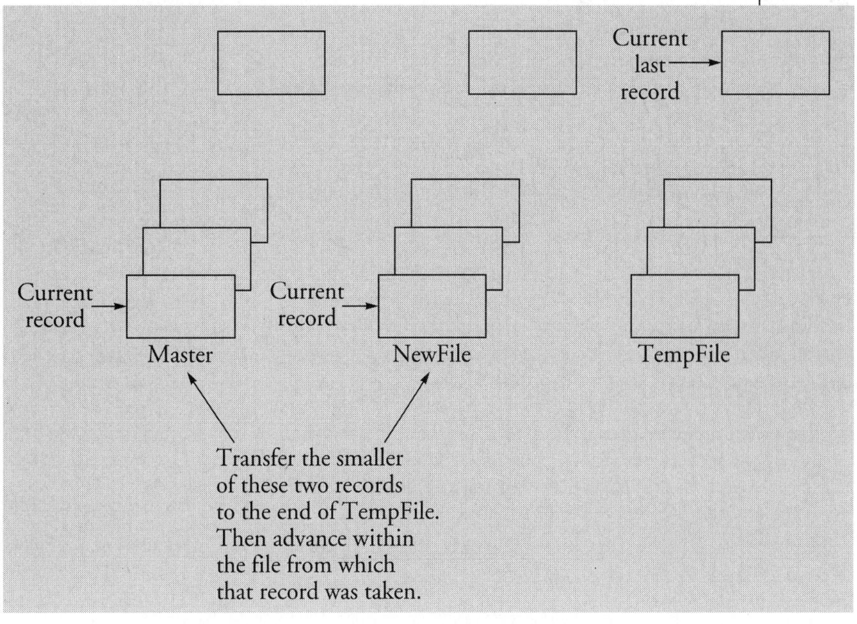

```
        {  Now copy the remaining names  }
        WHILE NOT eof(Master) DO
          BEGIN
            TempFile^ := Master^;
            put (TempFile);
            get (Master)
          END;
        WHILE NOT eof(NewFile) DO
          BEGIN
            TempFile^ := NewFile^;
            put (TempFile);
            get (NewFile)
          END;

        {  Now copy back to Master  }
        rewrite (Master);
        reset (TempFile);
        WHILE NOT eof(TempFile) DO
          BEGIN
            Master^ := TempFile^;
            put (Master);
            get (TempFile)
          END
      END;  {  of PROCEDURE Merge  }
```

This procedure can be called from the main program by

```
Merge (Master, NewFile);
```

A NOTE OF INTEREST

History Stuck on Old Computer Tapes

A slice of recent U.S. history has become as unreadable as Egyptian hieroglyphics before the discovery of the Rosetta stone. And more historic, scientific, and business data is in danger of dissolving into a meaningless jumble of letters, numbers, and computer symbols.

Paying millions to preserve the information is part of the price for the country's embrace of more and more powerful computers. Much information from the past 30 years is stranded on computer tape from primitive or discarded systems—it's unintelligible, or soon to be so.

Hundreds of thousands of Americans researching family history (the largest use of the National Archives) will find records of their relatives beyond reach. Detection of diseases, environmental threats, or shifts in social class could be delayed because data was lost before researchers even knew which questions to ask.

"The ability to read our nation's historical records is threatened by the complexity of modern computers," said Representative Bob Wise, chairman of a House information subcommittee that wants the government to start buying computers to preserve data for future researchers. A number of records already are lost or out of reach:

- A total of 200 reels of 17-year-old Public Health Service computer tapes were destroyed because no one could find out what the names and numbers on them meant.
- The government's Agent Orange Task Force, asked to determine whether Vietnam soldiers were sickened by exposure to the herbicide, was unable to decode Pentagon computer tapes containing the date, site, and size of every U.S. herbicide bombing during the war.
- The most extensive record of Americans who served in World War II exists only on 1600 reels of microfilm of computer punch cards. No staff, money, or machine is available to return the data to a computer so citizens can trace the war history of their relatives.
- Census data from the 1960s and NASA's early scientific observations of the earth and planets exist on thousands of reels of old tape. Some may have decomposed; others may fall apart if run through the balky equipment that survives from that era.

A final comment is in order. It is frequently necessary to work with files of records that have been sorted according to a field of the record. Since we might want to work with the records sorted according to some other field, we must first be able to sort an unsorted file. In general, this is done by transferring the file components to array components, sorting the array, and transferring the sorted array components back to the file. This means that we must have some idea of how many components are in the file and must declare the array length accordingly. The physical setting of a problem usually provides this information. For example, physicians will have some idea of how many patients (100, 200, or 1000) they see.

EXERCISES 10.3

1. Declare appropriate files for each of the following. Fields for each record are indicated.
   a. Flight information for an airplane, including flight number, airline, arrival time, origin, departure time, and destination.
   b. Bookstore inventory, including author, title, stock number, price, and quantity.
   c. Records for a magazine subscription agency, including name and address (indicating street number, street name, city, state, and zip code).
2. Write a test program that allows you to declare a file of records, read data into the file, and print information from selected records according to the value in some key field.
3. Suppose data in a text file contains information for students in a class. Information for each student will use three data lines, as illustrated.

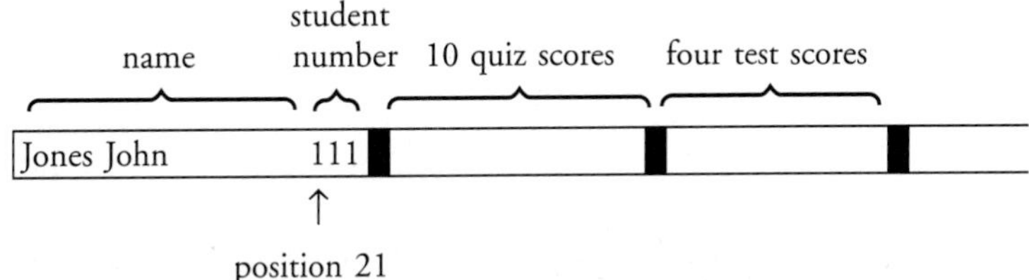

   a. Declare a file of records to be used to store these data.
   b. Write a procedure to create a file of records containing appropriate information from the text file.
   c. Write a procedure to sort the file alphabetically.
4. Illustrate the values of the components and fields in Student and Student^ during the first pass through the loop in **PROCEDURE** CreateFile on page 496.
5. Consider the file Student declared by

```
TYPE
  NameString = PACKED ARRAY [1..20] OF char;
  Scores = ARRAY [1..3] OF 0..100;
  StudentInfo = RECORD
                  Name : NameString;
                  Score : Scores;
                  IDNumber : 0..999;
                  Average : real
                END;
  StudentFile = FILE OF StudentInfo;
VAR
  Student : StudentFile;
```

Write a procedure for each of the following tasks. In each case, show how the procedure is called from the main program. (Assume the file has been alphabetized.)

a. Add one record in alphabetical order.

b. Add one record to the bottom of the file.

c. Update the record of 'Smith Jane ' by changing her score on the second test from an 82 to an 89.

d. The scores from the third test have just been entered into a data file. Each line contains an identification number followed by three integer scores. Update Student to include these scores. (The first two scores have already been transferred to the appropriate student records.)

e. Assume all test scores have been entered. Update Student by computing the test average for each student.

f. Print a list containing each student's name and test average; the list should be sorted by test average from high to low.

6. Extend the procedure that merges two files to a procedure that merges three files into a fourth file. The merge is to be accomplished by working with all three files simultaneously. Discuss the advantages and disadvantages of this method compared to the method of making repeated calls to **PROCEDURE** Merge that is developed in this section.

FOCUS ON PROGRAM DESIGN

The summary program for this chapter is an elementary version that could be expanded to a comprehensive programming project. Suppose the registrar at your institution wants you to develop a program for updating a file of student records. A master file of student records currently exists; it is sorted alphabetically. Each record contains a field for the student's name, ID number, grade point average, and total hours completed. This file is to be updated by information contained in a transaction file. Each line in the transaction file contains a student number, letter grade for a course taken, and number of credit hours for the course. A typical data line is

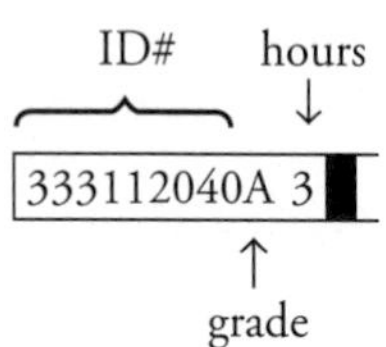

For each data line in the transaction file, your program should search the contents of the master file for a match. If a match is found, appropriate changes should be made in grade point average and total hours completed. If no match is found, the information should be printed in an Exception Report. After all transactions are completed, an alphabetized list should be printed and the master file should be updated.

A first-level pseudocode development for this program is

1. Open the files
2. Copy contents of MasterFile to an array
3. Update the records
4. Print the list
5. Update MasterFile

A complete structure diagram for this program is given in Figure 10.4.

◆ FIGURE 10.4
Structure chart for the file update program

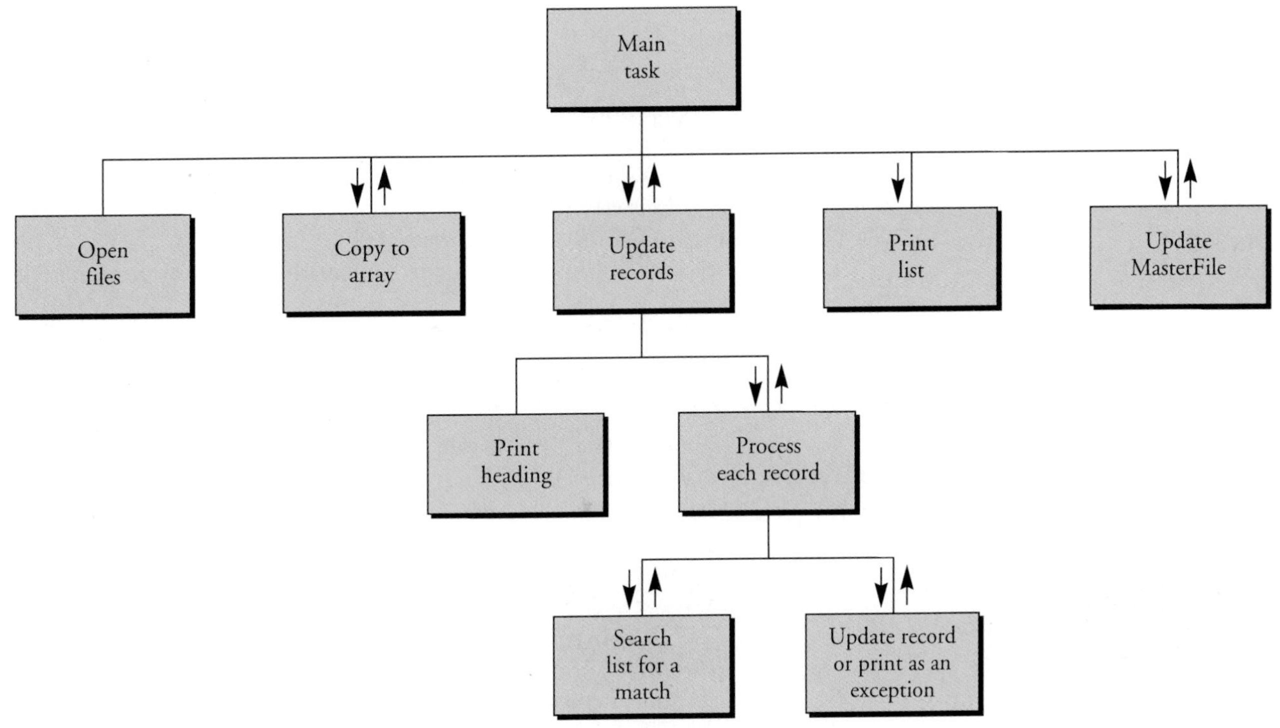

Module specifications for the main modules are

1. OpenFiles Module
   Data received: None
   Information returned: None
   Logic: Use **reset** to prepare files for reading.

2. LoadArray Module
   Data received: File of records
   Information returned: An array of records
   Number of records
   Logic: Copy contents of each record in MasterFile to a record in Student.
   Count the number of records in the array.

3. UpdateRecords Module
   Data received: An array of records
   Length of the array
   A transaction file
   Information returned: An updated array of records
   Logic: For each data line in TransactionFile, search for a match in the array.
   IF a match is found **THEN**
   update the record
   ELSE
   print out an Exception Report

4. PrintList Module
   Data received: A sorted array of records
   Length of the array
   Information returned: None
   Logic: Print a heading.
   Print contents of each record.
5. UpdateMasterFile Module
   Data received: An array of records
   Length of the array
   MasterFile of records
   Information returned: An updated MasterFile
   Logic: For each record in Student, copy contents into a record in MasterFile.

Further pseudocode development is

1. Open the files
   1.1 **reset** MasterFile
   1.2 **reset** TransactionFile
2. Copy contents of MasterFile to an array
   2.1 set counter to zero
   2.2 **REPEAT**
      2.2.1 increment counter
      2.2.2 copy contents of one record
      UNTIL eof (MasterFile)
3. Update the records
   3.1 print Exception Report heading
   3.2 **WHILE NOT eof** (TransactionFile) **DO**
      3.2.1 search for a match
      3.2.2 **IF NOT** Found **THEN**
      print as part of Exception Report
      ELSE
      update the record
4. Print the list
   4.1 print a heading
   4.2 print an alphabetized list
5. Update MasterFile
   5.1 **rewrite** MasterFile
   5.2 **FOR** each record in the array **DO**
   copy contents to a record in MasterFile

Step 3.2.1 is a sequential search of the array. If a match is found, the array position is returned; if not, a zero is returned. The portion of step 3.2.2 designed to update the record consists of incrementing the grade point average. A **CASE** statement is used to direct action for grades of A, B, C, D, E, W, and I. This program assumes valid data are contained in TransactionFile. A complete program for this problem follows.

```
PROGRAM FileUpdate (input, output, MasterFile, TransactionFile);

 {  This program updates a file of student records.  Transactions     }
 {  are stored in the text file TransactionFile.  Each line consists  }
 {  of a student number, grade for a course taken, and credit hours   }
 {  for the course.  The file of records is copied to an array of     }
 {  records for processing.  This facilitates searching for matches   }
 {  of student numbers.  It is assumed the master file is alphabe-    }
```

```
 {  tized.  If it is not, one could add a procedure to sort the        }
 {  array before rewriting the master file.                             }

CONST
  MaxLength = 200;
  NameLength = 20;
  IDLength = 9;

TYPE
  NameString = PACKED ARRAY [1..NameLength] OF char;
  IDString = PACKED ARRAY [1..IDLength] OF char;
  StudentRecord = RECORD
                    Name : NameString;
                    IDNumber : IDString;
                    GPA : real;
                    Hours : integer
                  END;  {  of RECORD StudentRecord  }
  StudentList = ARRAY [1..MaxLength] OF StudentRecord;
  RecordsFile = FILE OF StudentRecord;

VAR
  NumberOfRecords : integer;       {  Number of records read           }
  Student : StudentList;           {  Array of student records         }
  MasterFile : RecordsFile;        {  Master file of student records   }
  TransactionFile : text;          {  Transaction file for updating    }

{*******************************************************************}

PROCEDURE PrepareFiles (VAR MasterFile : RecordsFile;
                        VAR TransactionFile : text);

  {  Given:   Nothing                                                   }
  {  Task:    Open the files for reading                                }
  {  Return:  MasterFile and TransactionFile ready to be read           }   1

  BEGIN
    reset (MasterFile);
    reset (TransactionFile)
  END;  {  of PROCEDURE PrepareFiles  }

{*******************************************************************}

PROCEDURE LoadArray (VAR MasterFile : RecordsFile;
                     VAR Student : StudentList;
                     VAR NumberOfRecords : integer);

  {  Given:   Master file containing data for each student              }
  {  Task:    Create an array of student records from MasterFile        }
  {  Return:  Array of student records and number of records            }

  BEGIN
    NumberOfRecords := 0;                                                  2
    get (MasterFile);
```

```
    WHILE NOT eof(MasterFile) AND (NumberOfRecords < MaxLength) DO
      BEGIN
        NumberOfRecords := NumberOfRecords + 1;
        Student[NumberOfRecords] := MasterFile^;
        get (MasterFile)
      END;  {  of WHILE NOT eof  }
    IF NOT eof(MasterFile) THEN
      writeln ('There are more data.')
  END;  {  of PROCEDURE LoadArray  }

{*******************************************************************}

FUNCTION NewGPA (Hours, CourseHours : integer;
                 GPA, HonorPoints : real) : real;

  {  Given:   Total hours accumulated, credit hours for the course    }
  {               completed, current GPA, HonorPoints corresponding   }
  {               to the letter grade received                        }
  {  Task:    Compute the new grade point average                     }
  {  Return:  New grade point average                                 }

  VAR
    OldHours : integer;
  BEGIN
    OldHours := Hours;
    Hours := Hours + CourseHours;
    NewGPA := (OldHours * GPA + CourseHours * HonorPoints) / Hours
  END;  {  of FUNCTION NewGPA  }

{*******************************************************************}

FUNCTION SeqSearch (Student : StudentList;
                    IDNumber : IDString;
                    NumberOfRecords : integer) : integer;

  {  Given:   An array of student records, a student ID number, and   }
  {               the number of records                               }
  {  Task:    Sequentially search the array to find a match for the   }
  {               ID number                                           }
  {  Return:  The index of the record where a match is found;         }
  {               return 0 if no match is found                       }

  VAR
    Found : boolean;
    LCV : integer;
  BEGIN
    SeqSearch := 0;
    Found := false;
    LCV := 0;
    WHILE (LCV < NumberOfRecords) AND (NOT Found) DO
      BEGIN
        LCV := LCV + 1;
```

```
        IF Student[LCV].IDNumber = IDNumber THEN
          BEGIN
            SeqSearch := LCV;
            Found := true
          END  {  of IF...THEN  }
      END  {  of WHILE loop  }
  END;  {  of FUNCTION SeqSearch  }

{********************************************************************}

PROCEDURE UpdateRecords (VAR TransactionFile : text;
                         VAR Student : StudentList;
                         NumberOfRecords : integer);

  {  Given:   A transaction file for updating records, an array of     }
  {                student records, and number of student records      }
  {  Task:    Read a line from the transaction file; search array      }
  {                Student for a match of IDNumber; if a match,        }
  {                update hours and GPA; if not, print as part of      }
  {                Exception Report                                    }
  {  Return:  An updated array of student records                      }

  CONST
    Skip = ' ';
  VAR
    J, Index, CourseHours : integer;                                      3
    IDNumber : IDString;
    Grade : char;
    MatchFound : boolean;
  BEGIN

    {  Print heading for the Exception Report  }
    writeln ('EXCEPTION REPORT':35);
    writeln ('ID NUMBER':20, 'GRADE':12, 'HOURS':10);
    writeln (Skip:10, '--------------------------------');
    writeln;

    {  Now read the transaction file  }
    WHILE NOT eof(TransactionFile) DO
      BEGIN
        FOR J := 1 TO IDLength DO
          read (TransactionFile, IDNumber[J]);
        readln (TransactionFile, Grade, CourseHours);
        Index := SeqSearch(Student, IDNumber, NumberOfRecords);
        MatchFound := Index <> 0;
        IF MatchFound THEN                      {  Update student record  }
          WITH Student[Index] DO
            CASE Grade OF
              'A' : BEGIN
                      GPA := NewGPA(Hours, CourseHours, GPA, 4.0);
                      Hours := Hours + CourseHours
                    END;
```

```
               'B' : BEGIN
                       GPA := NewGPA(Hours, CourseHours, GPA, 3.0);
                       Hours := Hours + CourseHours
                     END;
               'C' : BEGIN
                       GPA := NewGPA(Hours, CourseHours, GPA, 2.0);
                       Hours := Hours + CourseHours
                     END;
               'D' : BEGIN
                       GPA := NewGPA(Hours, CourseHours, GPA, 1.0);
                       Hours := Hours + CourseHours
                     END;
               'E' : BEGIN
                       GPA := NewGPA(Hours, CourseHours, GPA, 0.0);
                       Hours := Hours + CourseHours
                     END;
               'W', 'I' : {  Do nothing  }
             END  {  of CASE Grade  }
         ELSE
           writeln (IDNumber:20, Grade:10, CourseHours:10)
       END  {  of WHILE NOT eof  }
   END;  {  of PROCEDURE UpdateRecords  }

{*********************************************************************}

PROCEDURE PrintList (VAR Student : StudentList;
                     NumberOfRecords : integer);

  {  Given:   An array of student records and number of records       }
  {  Task:    Print a list of records with appropriate heading        }
  {  Return:  Nothing                                                 }

  VAR
    J : integer;
  BEGIN

    {  Print a heading for the revised list  }
    writeln;
    writeln ('UPDATED REPORT':30);                                          4
    writeln ('STUDENT FILE LISTING':34);
    writeln;
    writeln ('NAME':10, 'ID NUMBER':25, 'GPA':8, 'CREDITS':10);
    write ('-----------------------------');
    writeln ('------------------------');
    writeln;

    {  Now print the list  }
    FOR J := 1 TO NumberOfRecords DO
      WITH Student[J] DO
        writeln (Name:20, IDNumber:15, GPA:8:2, Hours:8)
  END;  {  of PROCEDURE PrintList  }

{*********************************************************************}
```

```
PROCEDURE UpdateMasterFile (VAR MasterFile : RecordsFile;
                            VAR Student : StudentList;
                            NumberOfRecords : integer);

  {  Given:   An array of student records and the array length      }
  {  Task:    Copy the records into MasterFile for storage          }
  {  Return:  A file of student records                             }

  VAR                                                                 5
    J : integer;
  BEGIN
    rewrite (MasterFile);
    FOR J := 1 TO NumberOfRecords DO
      BEGIN
        MasterFile^ := Student[J];
        put (MasterFile)
      END  {  of FOR loop  }
  END;  {  of PROCEDURE UpdateMasterFile  }

{*******************************************************************}

BEGIN
  PrepareFiles (MasterFile, TransactionFile);
  LoadArray (MasterFile, Student, NumberOfRecords);
  UpdateRecords (TransactionFile, Student, NumberOfRecords);
  PrintList (Student, NumberOfRecords);
  UpdateMasterFile (MasterFile, Student, NumberOfRecords)
END.  {  of main program  }
```

If you use data in MasterFile as

```
BARRETT RODA         345678901 3.67 23
BORGNINE ERNIST      369325263 4.12 14
CADABRA ABRA         123450987 3.33 23
DJIKSTRA EDGAR       345998765 3.90 33
GARZELONI RANDY      444226666 2.20 18
GLUTZ AGATHA         320678230 3.00 22
HOLBRUCK HALL        321908765 3.50 29
HUNTER MICHAEL       234098112 2.50 22
JOHNSON ROSALYN      345123690 3.25 20
LOCKLEAR HEATHER     369426163 4.00 30
MCMANN ABAGAIL       333112040 3.97 41
MILDEW MORRIS        234812057 3.67 34
MORSE SAMUEL         334558778 3.00 28
NOVAK JAMES          348524598 1.50 13
OHERLAHE TERRY       333662222 2.75 21
RACKHAM HORACE       345878643 4.00 30
SNYDER JUDITH        356913580 2.75 24
VANDERSYS RALPH      367120987 3.23 22
VAUGHN SARAH         238498765 3.00 24
WIDGET WENDELL       444113333 1.25 10
WILSON PHILIP        345719642 3.00 25
WITWERTH JANUARY     367138302 2.10 20
WORDEN JACK          359241234 3.33 25
WOURTHY CONSTANCE    342092834 3.50 32
```

and data in TransactionFile as

```
333112040A 3
333112040A 4
333112040A 4
444113333A 3
444113333A 4
444113333A 3
444113333A 2
238498765A 3
238498765A 3
238498765A 4
238498766A 4
369325263A 3
369325263A 3
369325263A 4
369325263C 4
320678230A 5
320678230A 3
320678230A 3
320678230A 4
444226666A 3
444226666A 4
444226666A 3
444226667A 4
367138302A 3
367138302A 3
367138302A 3
367138302B 3
367120987A 4
367120987A 4
367120987A 3
367120987I 3
367120987A 3
369426163A 4
369426163A 3
345678901A 3
345678901A 4
345678901A 3
345678900A 4
123450987A 3
123450987A 3
123450987A 4
123450987E 3
234098112A 3
234098112A 3
444226666D 3
367138302D 3
123450987C 4
123450987D 3
123450987A 2
333112040D 4
```

```
333112040A 3
444113333D 4
444113333A 3
369235263D 4
369235263A 3
320678230D 3
320678230D 4
320678230W 3
334229023D 4
```

output for this program is

```
                EXCEPTION REPORT
           ID NUMBER        GRADE     HOURS
          --------------------------------

           238498766          A         4
           444226667          A         4
           345678900          A         4
           369235263          D         4
           369235263          A         3
           334229023          D         4

                 UPDATED REPORT
               STUDENT FILE LISTING

        NAME                  ID NUMBER     GPA   CREDITS
---------------------------------------------------------

BARRETT RODA                  345678901    3.77       33
BORGNINE ERNIST               369325263    3.77       28
CADABRA ABRA                  123450987    3.01       45
DJIKSTRA EDGAR                345998765    3.90       33
GARZELONI RANDY               444226666    2.66       31
GLUTZ AGATHA                  320678230    3.02       44
HOLBRUCK HALL                 321908765    3.50       29
HUNTER MICHAEL                234098112    2.82       28
JOHNSON ROSALYN               345123690    3.25       20
LOCKLEAR HEATHER              369426163    4.00       37
MCMANN ABAGAIL                333112040    3.78       59
MILDEW MORRIS                 234812057    3.67       34
MORSE SAMUEL                  334558778    3.00       28
NOVAK JAMES                   348524598    1.50       13
OHERLAHE TERRY                333662222    2.75       21
RACKHAM HORACE                345878643    4.00       30
SNYDER JUDITH                 356913580    2.75       24
VANDERSYS RALPH               367120987    3.53       36
VAUGHN SARAH                  238498765    3.29       34
WIDGET WENDELL                444113333    2.64       29
WILSON PHILIP                 345719642    3.00       25
WITWERTH JANUARY              367138302    2.53       32
WORDEN JACK                   359241234    3.33       25
WOURTHY CONSTANCE             342092834    3.50       32
```

RUNNING AND DEBUGGING HINTS

1. Be sure all files (except **input** and **output**) are properly opened for reading and writing. Remember you must **reset** before reading from a file and **rewrite** before writing to a file.
2. Don't try to read past the end-of-file marker. This is a common error that occurs when trying to **read** without a sufficient check for **eof.**
3. Be careful to use file names correctly in **read, readln, write, writeln,** and **eof** statements.
4. List all external files in the program heading, and be sure to declare them in the variable declaration section.
5. Be sure all files listed in a procedure heading are variable parameters.
6. Protect against working with empty files or empty lines of a text file.
7. Remember the file buffer is undefined when **eof** (<file name>) is **true.**

SUMMARY

Key Terms

binary file
buffer variable
component of a file
file
file window
master file
opening a file
reading from a file
transaction file
writing to a file

Keywords

FILE
get
put

Key Concepts

- A file is a sequence of components that are all of the same data type; a typical declaration is

```
TYPE
  RealFile = FILE OF real;
VAR
  FileA : RealFile;
```

- In standard implementations of Pascal, files must be accessed sequentially.
- File window is commonly used to describe the component of the file that is available for data to be passed to or from it.
- A buffer variable is an undeclared variable that is used to transfer data to or from a file component; if the file name is FileA, then the identifier for the buffer variable is FileA^.
- Before transferring values to a file (writing to a file), the file must be opened for writing by **rewrite** (<file name>). Values can then be transferred from the file buffer using **put** or **write** (<file name>, <value>); for example

```
rewrite (NewFile);
NewFile^ := 10;
put (NewFile);
```

or

```
rewrite (NewFile);
write (NewFile, 10);
```

- Before transferring values from a file (reading from a file), the file must be opened for reading by **reset** (<file name>). Values can then be transferred from the file by assignments from the file buffer and by using **get** (<file name>) or **read** (<file name>, <variable name>); for example

```
reset (NewFile);
A := NewFile^^;
get (NewFile);
```

or

```
reset (NewFile);
read (NewFile, A);
```

- An end-of-file marker is automatically placed at the end of the file as **eof** (<file name>) when a file is created.
- A file cannot be opened for reading and writing at the same time.
- When a file is declared as a parameter in a procedure heading, it must be listed as a variable parameter; for example

```
PROCEDURE Update (VAR OldFile, NewFile : <file type>);
```

- Components of a file can be arrays; the declaration

```
VAR
  F : FILE OF ARRAY [1..10] OF real;
```

can be depicted as shown in Figure 10.5, where F^ is an array and array components are denoted by F^[J].

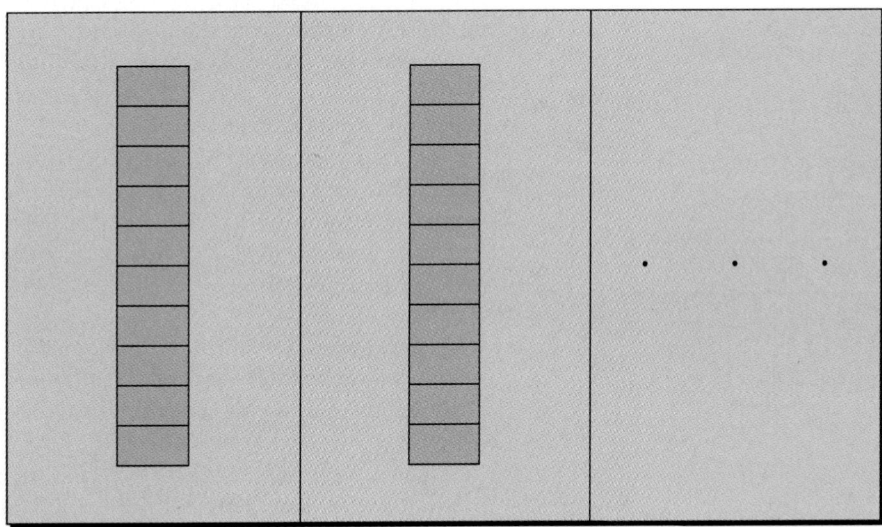

FIGURE 10.5
File of arrays

- File components can be records and can be declared by

```
TYPE
  RecType = RECORD
              Name : PACKED ARRAY [1..20] OF char;
              Age : 0..120;
              Gender : char
            END;  {  of RECORD RecType  }
VAR
  F : FILE OF RecType;
```

and depicted as shown in Figure 10.6. In this case, the buffer variable F^ is a record, and fields can be denoted by

```
F^.Name
F^.Age
F^.Gender
```

◆ FIGURE 10.6
File of records

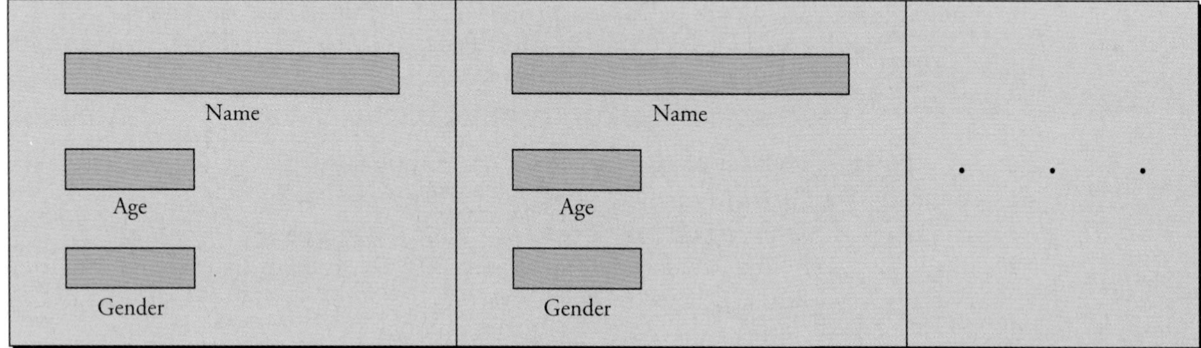

- Files with structured components frequently have to be processed and/or updated; for a file of records, you might insert or delete a record, sort the file by a field, merge two files, update each record, or produce a printed list according to some field.
- When updating or otherwise processing a file, changes are normally made in an internal (temporary) file and then copied back to the master (permanent) file.
- Since input data are generally in a text file, you need to create a file of structured components from the text file; you can then use **get** and **put** to transfer entire structures at one time.

PROGRAMMING PROBLEMS AND PROJECTS

1. *The Pentagon* is a mathematics magazine published by Kappa Mu Epsilon, a mathematics honorary society. Write a program to be used by the business manager for the purpose of generating mailing labels. The subscribers' information should be read into a file of records. Each record should contain one subscriber's name; address, including street and street number, apartment number (if any), city, two-letter abbreviation for the state, and zip code; and expiration information, including month and year.

   Your program should create an alphabetically sorted master file, print an alphabetical list for the office, print a mailing list sorted by zip code for bulk mailing, and denote all last issues by a special symbol.
2. The relentless Dr. Lae Z. Programmer (Problems 5, 22, and 23, Chapter 4; Problem 13, Chapter 5; Problem 5, Chapter 6; Problem 3, Chapter 8; and Problem 3, Chapter 9) now wants you to create a file of records for students in his computer science course. You should provide fields for the student's name, 10 quiz scores, six program scores, and three examination scores. Your program should do the following.
   a. Read in the names from a text file.
   b. Include procedures for updating quiz, program, and examination scores.

   c. Be able to update the file by adding or deleting a record.
   d. Print an alphabetized list of the data base at any given time.

3. Write a program to do part of the work of a word processor. Your program should read a text file and print it in paragraph form. The left margin should be in column 10; the right margin, in column 72. In the input file, a period will designate the end of each sentence and an asterisk (*) will denote a new paragraph. No word should be split between lines. Your program should save the edited file in a file of type **text.**

4. Slow-pitch softball is rapidly becoming a popular summer pastime. Assume your local community is to have a new women's league this year consisting of eight teams, with 15 players on each team. This league gets the field one night per week for four games. They will play a double round-robin so each team will play every other team twice, resulting in 14 games. Write a program to do the following.
   a. Create a file of records (one record for each team) in which the team name is included.
   b. Print a schedule.
   c. List the teams alphabetically by team name.
   d. Print a list of players for each team.

5. The registrar at State University (Problem 15, Chapter 4; Problem 3, Chapter 6) wants you to write an interactive program to assist with record keeping. Your program should create a file of records. The record for each student should contain the student's name, identification number, credit hours completed, number of credit hours in which currently enrolled, and grade point average. Your program should also contain a procedure for each of the following updates.
   a. List semester-end data of hours completed and grade point average for the semester.
   b. Insert a record.
   c. Delete a record.
   d. Print a list sorted alphabetically.
   e. Print a list sorted by grade point average.

6. The local high school sports boosters (Problems 1 and 2, Chapter 8) need more help. They want you to write a program to create a file of records in which each record contains the parents' names, the children's first names (at most 10 children), and the names of the sports in which the children have participated.

   A typical record is shown in Figure 10.7. Your program should create a file from a text file and save it for later use, print an alphabetical list of parents' names, and print a list of the names of parents of football players.

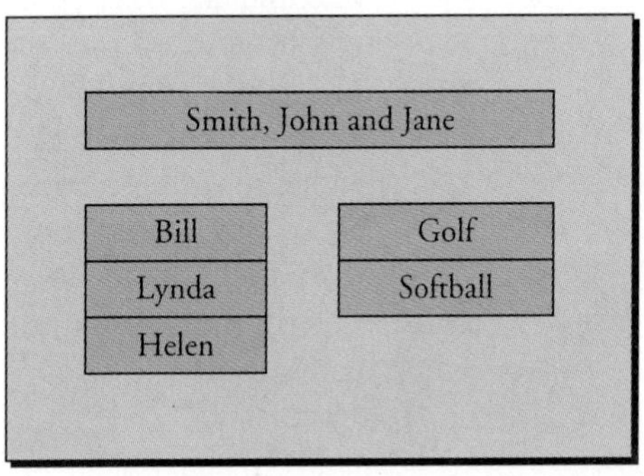

◆ FIGURE 10.7
Typical values for fields in a record

7. A popular use of text files is to help teachers create a bank of test items from which they can generate quizzes using some form of random selection. Write a program that allows you to create files of type **text** that contain questions for each of three chapters. Then generate two quizzes composed of three questions for each of the three chapters.

8. Public service departments must always be on the lookout for people who try to abuse the system by accepting assistance from similar agencies in different geographic areas. Write a program that compares the names from one county with those from another county and prints all of the names on both lists.

9. Write a program to be used by flight agents at an airport (see Exercise 1a, Section 10.3). Your program should use a file of records. The record for each flight should contain flight number, airline, arrival time, origin, departure time, and destination. Your program should list incoming flights sorted by time, list departing flights sorted by time, add flights, and delete flights.

10. Congratulations! You have just been asked to write a program that will assign dates for the Valentine's Day dance. Each student record should contain the student's name, age, gender (M or F), and the names of three date preferences (ranked). Your program should do the following.

    a. Create a master file from the input file.

    b. Create and save alphabetically sorted files of males and females.

    c. Print a list of couples for the dance. The genders must be opposite, and the age difference may be no more than three years. Dating preferences should be in the following form.

	CAN'T MISS!	
First request	Matches	First request
	GOOD BET!	
First request	Matches	Second request
Second request	Matches	First request
	GOOD LUCK!	
	Any other matches	
	OUT OF LUCK!	
	You are not on any list	

It's obvious (isn't it?) that a person can have at most one date for the dance.

11. A data file consists of an unknown number of real numbers. Write a program to read the file and print the highest value, lowest value, and average of the numbers in the file.

■ 12. The Falcon Manufacturing Company (Problem 23, Chapter 8; Problem 17, Chapter 9) wants you to write an inventory file program. The file should contain a 30-character part name, an integer part number, the quantity on hand, and the price of an item. The program should permit the entry of new items into and the deletion of existing items from the file. The items to be changed will be entered from the keyboard.

■ 13. Write a program for the Falcon Manufacturing Company (Problem 12) to allow a secretary to enter an item number, a quantity, and whether an item is to be added to or deleted from the stock. The program should prepare a new data file containing the updated information. If the user requests to remove more items than are on hand, an appropriate warning message should be issued.

■ 14. Write a program to read the inventory file of the Falcon Manufacturing Company (Problems 12 and 13) and then print a listing of the inventory. The program should print an asterisk (*) next to any quantity that is less than 50.

■ **15.** Revise the program that you wrote in answer to Problem 23 in Chapter 8 to permit the sales figures of the Falcon Manufacturing Company to be read from a file. Also revise the program so the information on the total dollar amount of sales for each product by each salesperson is written to a file for later use.

■ **16.** Write a program to read the total dollar sales file from Problem 15 for last month and the corresponding file for this month and print out a table showing the total sales by each salesperson for each product during the two-month period.

17. A data file contains an alphabetized list of the secondary students in your former high school; another data file contains an alphabetized list of the elementary students. Write a program to merge these two files and print an alphabetized list of all students in your former school.

18. The Andover Telephone Company (its motto is "We send your messages of Andover.") wants you to develop a computerized directory information system. The data file should contain the customer names and telephone numbers. Your program should permit the following.

a. The entry of new customers' names and telephone numbers.

b. The deletion of existing customers' names and telephone numbers.

c. The printing of all customers' names and their telephone numbers.

d. The entry from the keyboard of a customer's name with the program printing the telephone number (if found).

Whenever customers' names and numbers are to be added or deleted, the file should be updated accordingly. You may assume there are no more than 50 customers.

19. Revise the program you wrote to keep the grades of Mr. Laven's students (Problem 19, Chapter 8) so it reads the grades entered previously from a file and, when the program is complete, prints the updated list of grades.

20. Recognizing your talents as a programmer, the principal of the local high school wants you to write a program to work with a data file that contains the names of the students who are absent at the start of the school day. These names are kept as 30-character packed arrays. The program should permit the principal to enter the name of a student later in the day to check to see if that student was absent at the start of the day.

21. Revise Problem 13 in Chapter 9 to permit Ada Crown's computer maintenance records to be kept in a file. Your program should allow the data on a machine to be changed and new machines to be added.

COMMUNICATION IN PRACTICE

1. Select a program from the Programming Problems and Projects section in this chapter that you have not yet worked. Construct a structure chart and write all documentary information for this program. Include variable definitions, subprogram definitions, required input, and required output. When you are finished, have a classmate read your documentation to see if precisely what is to be done is clear.

2. Remove all documentation from a program you have written for this chapter. Exchange this modified version with another student who has done the same thing. Write documentation for the exchanged program. Compare your documentation with that originally written for the program. Discuss the differences and similarities with the other students in the class.

3. Contact a programmer at your university or some company or corporation to discuss data structures. Find out how much (if any) he or she uses arrays, records, and files. If the programmer does use arrays, records, or files, what kinds of programming problems require their use? Find out what kinds of operations are used with these data structures. What limitations do these structures possess for the problems that need to be solved? Write a complete report summarizing your discussion.
4. Problems involving data management are routinely addressed in nonprogramming courses taught in schools of business. These courses may be taught in departments such as Management Information Systems (MIS) or Business Information Systems (BIS). Contact an instructor of such a course and discuss the issue of using data structures to manage information. How are data structures presented to the classes? What are some typical real-world problems?

   Give an oral report of your discussion to your class. Compare and contrast the instructor's presentations with those provided in your own class. Use charts with transparencies as part of your presentation.
5. Select an unworked problem from the programming problems in this chapter. Construct a structure chart and write all necessary documentary information for this problem. Do not write code. Then have a classmate read your documentation to see if precisely what is to be done is clear.

CHAPTER 11 Recursion and Sorting

CHAPTER OUTLINE

The previous chapters have presented techniques for working with structured variables. In particular, we have seen how to sort lists in either ascending or descending order, search lists for some specific value, and merge lists that may or may not be sorted. In this chapter, we will examine additional techniques for working with structured variables. First, however, we will look at recursion—a powerful process available in Pascal. In subsequent chapters, we will use recursion to implement more sophisticated algorithms. These algorithms should make you aware of the problems associated with recursion and sorting.

Unfortunately, this chapter cannot answer all of the questions associated with recursion and sorting. This text and most beginning courses defer more extensive treatment and examination of other methods and their relative efficiency to later programming courses. A list of suggestions for further reading is included at the end of this chapter.

11.1 Recursion

OBJECTIVES

- to understand how recursion can be used to solve a problem
- to be able to use recursion to solve a problem
- to understand what happens in memory when recursion is used

In our previous work with subprograms, we have seen instances in which one subprogram calls another. In Chapter 4 on repetition, we saw how to use the **FOR**, **WHILE**, and **REPEAT** statements to control iterative processes. Now let's consider how we can use a subprogram that calls itself to control an iterative process.

Recursive Processes

Many problems can be solved by having a subtask call itself as part of the solution. This process is called *recursion;* subprograms that call themselves are *recursive subprograms.* Recursion is frequently used in mathematics. Consider, for example, the definition of $n!$ (n factorial) for a nonnegative integer n, which is defined by

$$0! = 1$$
$$1! = 1$$
$$n! = n * (n - 1)! \qquad \text{for } n > 1$$

Thus

$$\begin{aligned} 6! &= 6 * 5! \\ &= 6 * 5 * 4! \\ &= 6 * 5 * 4 * 3! \\ &= 6 * 5 * 4 * 3 * 2! \\ &= 6 * 5 * 4 * 3 * 2 * 1 \end{aligned}$$

Another well-known mathematical example is the Fibonacci sequence, in which the first term is 1, the second term is 1, and each successive term is defined to be the sum of the previous two terms. More precisely, the Fibonacci sequence

$$a_1, a_2, a_3, \ldots, a_n$$

is defined by

$$a_1 = 1$$
$$a_2 = 1$$
$$a_n = a_{n-1} + a_{n-2} \qquad \text{for } n > 2$$

This generates the sequence

1, 1, 2, 3, 5, 8, 13, 21, . . .

In both examples, note the general term is defined by using the previous term or terms.

What applications does recursion have for computing? In many instances, a procedure or function can be written to accomplish a recursive task. If the language allows a subprogram to call itself (Pascal does; FORTRAN does not), it is sometimes easier to solve a problem by applying this process.

EXAMPLE 11.1

As an example of a recursive function, consider the sigma function denoted by $\sum_{i=1}^{n} i$, which is used to compute the sum of integers from 1 to n.

```
FUNCTION Sigma (N : integer) : integer:
  BEGIN
    IF N <= 1 THEN
      Sigma := N
    ELSE
      Sigma := N + Sigma(N - 1)
  END;  { of FUNCTION Sigma  }
```

To illustrate how this recursive function works, suppose it is called from the main program by a statement such as

```
Sum := Sigma(5);
```

In the **ELSE** portion of the function, we first have

```
Sigma := 5 + Sigma(4)
```

At this stage, note Sigma(4) must be computed. This call produces

```
Sigma := 4 + Sigma(3)
```

If we envision these recursive calls as occurring on levels, we have

```
1. Sigma := 5 + Sigma(4)
   2. Sigma := 4 + Sigma(3)
      3. Sigma := 3 + Sigma(2)
         4. Sigma := 2 + Sigma(1)
            5. Sigma := 1
```

The end of the recursion has been reached. Now the steps for assigning values are reversed. Thus, we have

```
            5. Sigma :=1
         4. Sigma := 2 + 1  (= 3)
      3. Sigma := 3 + 3  (= 6)
   2. Sigma := 4 + 6  (= 10)
1. Sigma := 5 + 10  (= 15)
```

Thus, Sigma is assigned the value 15.

Before we analyze what happens in memory when recursive subprograms are used, some comments about recursion are in order.

1. The recursive process must have a well-defined termination. This termination is referred to as a *stopping state.* In Example 11.1, the stopping state is

```
IF N <= 1 THEN
  Sigma := N
```

2. The recursive process must have well-defined steps that lead to the stopping state. These steps are usually called *recursive steps.* In Example 11.1, these steps are

```
Sigma := N + Sigma(N - 1)
```

In the recursive call, note the parameter is simplified toward the stopping state.

What Really Happens?

What really happens when a subprogram calls itself? To understand this process, we need to examine the idea of a *stack.* Imagine a stack as a pile of cafeteria trays: the last tray put on the stack is the first one taken off the stack. This is what occurs in memory when a recursive subprogram is used. Each call to the subprogram can be thought of as the addition of a tray to the stack. In the sigma function in Example 11.1, the first call creates a level of recursion that contains the partially complete assignment statement

```
Sigma := 5 + Sigma(4)
```

This corresponds to the first tray in the stack. In reality, this is an area in memory waiting to receive a value for 5 + Sigma(4). At this level, operation is temporarily suspended until a value is returned for Sigma(4). However, the call Sigma(4) produces

```
Sigma := 4 + Sigma(3)
```

This corresponds to the second tray on the stack. As before, operation is temporarily suspended until Sigma(3) is computed. This process is repeated until finally the last call, Sigma(1), returns a value.

At this stage, the stack may be envisioned as illustrated in Figure 11.1. Since different areas of memory are used for each successive call to Sigma, each variable Sigma represents a different memory location.

The levels of recursion that have been temporarily suspended can now be completed in reverse order. Thus, since the assignment

```
Sigma(1) := 1
```

has been made

```
Sigma(2) := 2 + Sigma(1)
```

becomes

```
Sigma(2) := 2 + 1
```

This then permits

```
Sigma(3) := 3 + Sigma(2)
```

to become

```
Sigma(3) := 3 + 3
```

If we continue until the first level of recursion is reached, we obtain

```
Sigma := 5 + 10
```

This "unstacking" is illustrated in Figure 11.2.

◆ FIGURE 11.1
Stack for **FUNCTION** Sigma

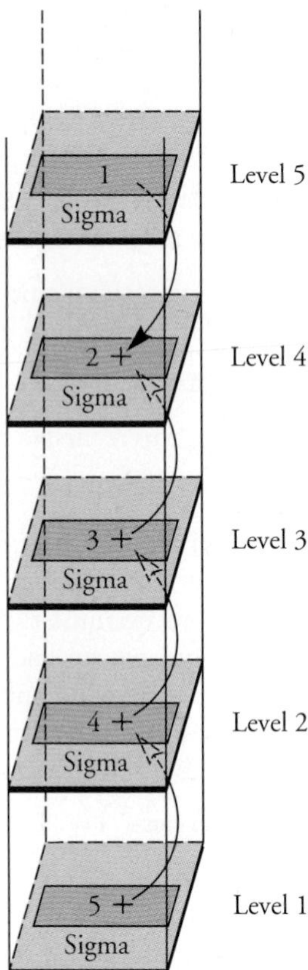

◆ FIGURE 11.2
"Unstacking" **FUNCTION** Sigma

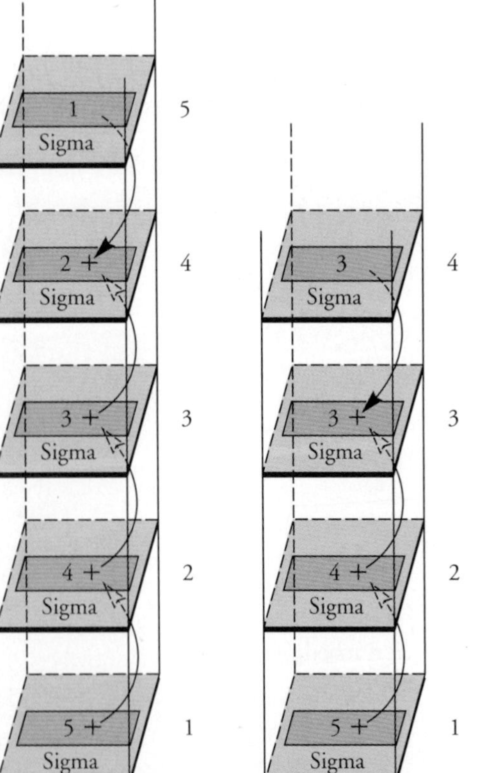

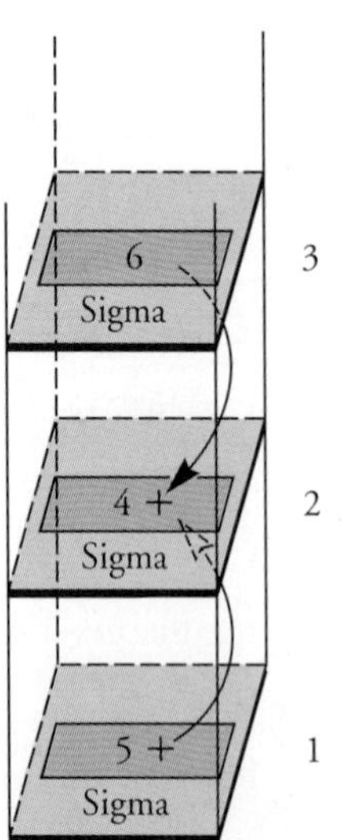

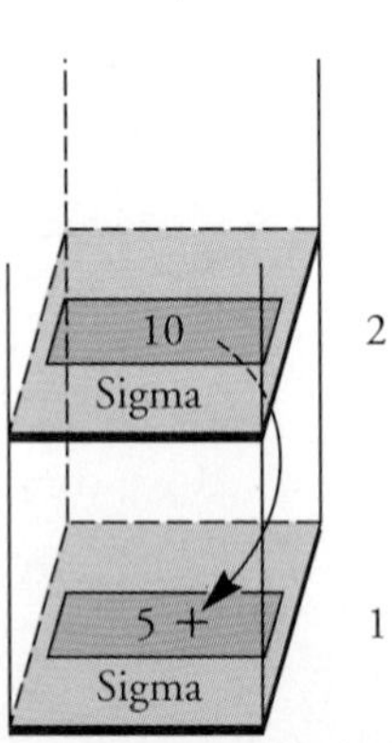

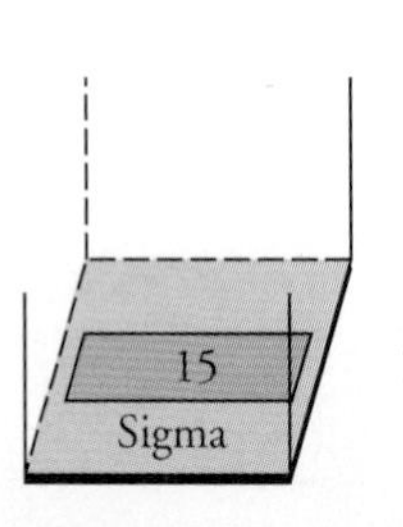

Note the recursive function illustrated in Example 11.1 uses a value parameter. In general, any formal parameter that relates to the size of the problem must be a value parameter. If the formal parameter (*N*, for example) were variable, it would not be possible to use the expression $N - 1$ as an actual parameter in a recursive call.

EXAMPLE 11.2

Now let's consider a second example of recursion in which a procedure is used recursively to print a line of text in reverse order. Assume the line of text has only one period and it is at the end of the line. The stopping state occurs when the character read is a period. Using the data line

This is a short sentence.■

a complete program follows.

```
PROGRAM LineInReverse (input, output, Data);

{  This program uses a procedure recursively to print a    }
{  line of text in reverse.                                }

VAR
  Data : text;

{**********************************************************}

PROCEDURE StackItUp;

  {  Given:   Nothing                                       }
  {  Task:    Read one character;  print if a period;       }
  {                if not, call this same procedure         }
  {  Return:  Nothing                                       }

  VAR
    OneChar : char;
  BEGIN
    read (Data, OneChar);
    IF OneChar <> '.' THEN
      StackItUp;
    write (OneChar)
  END;  {  of PROCEDURE StackItUp  }

{**********************************************************}

BEGIN  {  Main program  }
  reset (Data);
  StackItUp;
  writeln
END.  {  of main program  }
```

Output from this program is

```
  .ecnetnes trohs a si sihT
```

In this program, as each character is read, it is placed on a stack until the period is encountered. At that time, the period is printed. Then, as each level in the stack is passed through in reverse order, the character on that level is printed. The stack created while this program is running is illustrated in Figure 11.3.

◆ FIGURE 11.3
Stack created by **PROCEDURE** StackItUp

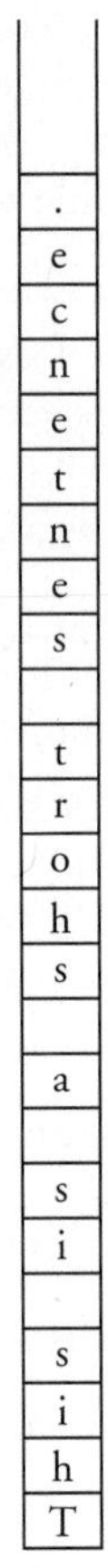

EXAMPLE 11.3

Now let's consider another example of a recursive function. Recall the factorial of a nonnegative integer n is defined to be

$$1 * 2 * 3 * \cdots * (n - 1) * n$$

and is denoted by $n!$. Thus

$$4! = 1 * 2 * 3 * 4$$

For the sake of completing this definition, $1! = 1$ and $0! = 1$. A recursive function to compute $n!$ is

```
FUNCTION Factorial (N : integer) : integer;
  BEGIN
    IF N = 0 THEN
      Factorial := 1
    ELSE
      Factorial := N * Factorial(N - 1)
  END;  {  of FUNCTION Factorial  }
```

If this function is called from the main program by a statement such as

```
Product := Factorial(4);
```

we envision the levels of recursion as

```
1. Factorial := 4 * Factorial(3)
  2. Factorial := 3 * Factorial(2)
    3. Factorial := 2 * Factorial(1)
      4. Factorial := 1 * Factorial(0)
        5. Factorial(0) := 1
```

Successive values would then be assigned in reverse order to produce

```
        5. Factorial(0) := 1
      4. Factorial := 1 * 1
    3. Factorial := 2 * 1
  2. Factorial := 3 * 2
1. Factorial := 4 * 6
```

Why Use Recursion?

You may have noticed the previous recursive functions Sigma and Factorial could have been written using other iterative control structures. For example, we could write

```
FUNCTION NonRecursiveSigma (N : integer) : integer;
  VAR
    J, Sum : integer;
  BEGIN
    Sum := 0;
    FOR J := 1 TO N DO
      Sum := Sum + J;
    NonRecursiveSigma := Sum
  END;  {  of FUNCTION NonRecursiveSigma  }
```

It is not coincidental that the recursive function Sigma can be rewritten using the function NonRecursiveSigma. In principle, any recursive subprogram can be rewritten in a nonrecursive manner. Furthermore, recursion generally requires more memory than equivalent nonrecursive iteration and is usually difficult for beginning programmers to comprehend. Why then do we use recursion? There are several reasons. First, a recursive thought process may be the best way to approach solving the problem. If so, the natural choice is to use recursion in a program. A classical example of this is the Towers of Hanoi problem, which involves a sequence of moving disks on pegs. This problem is fully developed as our next example.

Second, some recursive solutions can be very short compared to other iterative solutions. Nonrecursive solutions may require an explicit stack and unusual coding. In some instances, use of a recursive algorithm can be very simple, and some programmers consider recursive solutions elegant because of this simplicity. Again, the Towers of Hanoi problem in Example 11.4 provides an example of such elegance.

Third and finally, subsequent work in Pascal can be aided by recursion. For example, one of the fastest sorting algorithms available, the quick sort, uses recursion (see Section 11.2). Also, recursion is a valuable tool when working with dynamic data structures (Chapter 13).

Now that we know several reasons why recursion should be used, let's consider when recursion should not be used. If a solution to a problem is easier to obtain using nonrecursive methods, it is usually preferable to use them. A nonrecursive solution may require less execution time and use memory more efficiently. Referring to the previous examples, the recursive function Factorial should probably be written using iteration, but recursion would typically be used to reverse a line of text because a nonrecursive solution is difficult to write.

In summary, recursion is a powerful and necessary programming technique. You should become familiar with the use of recursive subprograms, learn to recognize when a recursive algorithm is appropriate, and be able to implement a recursive subprogram.

EXAMPLE 11.4

A classic problem called the Towers of Hanoi problem involves three pegs and disks, as depicted in Figure 11.4.

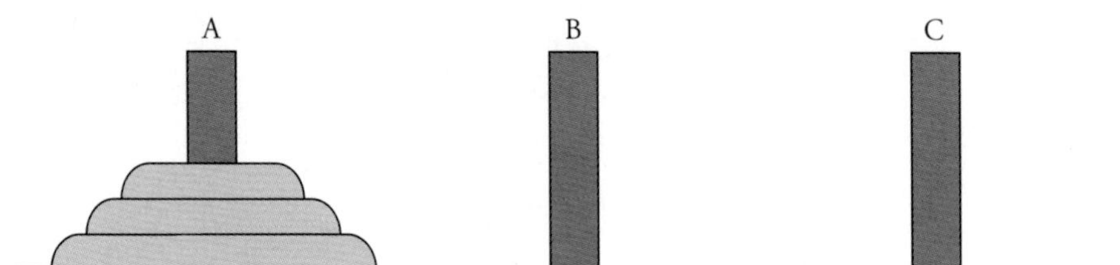

◆ FIGURE 11.4
Towers of Hanoi problem

The object is to move the disks from peg A to peg C. The rules are that only one disk may be moved at a time and a larger disk can never be placed on a smaller disk. (Legend has it that this problem—but with 64 disks—was given to monks in an ancient monastery. The world was to come to an end when all 64 disks were in order on peg C.)

To see how this problem can be solved, let's start with a one-disk problem. In this case, merely move the disk from peg A to peg C. The two-disk problem is almost as easy. Move disk 1 to peg B, then move disk 2 to peg C, and use the solution to the one-disk problem to move disk 1 to peg C. (Note the reference to the previous solution.)

Things get a little more interesting with a three-disk problem. First, use the two-disk solution to get the top two disks in order on peg B. Then move disk 3 to peg C. Finally, use the two-disk solution to move the two disks from peg B to peg C. Again, note the reference to the previous solution. By now, you should begin to see the pattern for solving the problem. However, before generalizing, let's look at the four-disk problem. As expected, the solution is to do the following.

1. Use the three-disk solution to move three disks to peg B.
2. Move disk four to peg C.
3. Use the three-disk solution to move the three disks from peg B to peg C.

This process can be generalized to the following solution to the problem for n disks.

1. Use the $n - 1$ disk solution to move $n - 1$ disks to peg B.
2. Move disk n to peg C.
3. Use the $n - 1$ disk solution to move $n - 1$ disks from peg B to peg C.

This general solution is recursive in nature because each particular solution depends upon a solution for the previous number of disks. The process continues until there is only one disk to move. This point corresponds to the stopping state when a recursive program is written to solve the problem. A complete interactive program that prints out each step in the solution to this problem follows.

```
PROGRAM TowersOfHanoi (input, output);

{  This program uses recursion to solve the classic Towers of   }
{  Hanoi problem.                                                }

VAR
  NumDisks : integer;

{****************************************************************}

PROCEDURE ListTheMoves (NumDisks : integer;
                        StartPeg, LastPeg, SparePeg : char);

  {  Given:   The number of disks to move, the initial peg       }
  {               StartPeg, the working peg SparePeg, and the    }
  {               destination peg LastPeg                        }
  {  Task:    Move NumDisks from StartPeg to LastPeg using       }
  {               SparePeg (involves recursive calls)            }
  {  Return:  Nothing                                            }

  BEGIN
    IF NumDisks = 1 THEN
      writeln ('Move a disk from ', StartPeg, ' to ', LastPeg)
    ELSE
      BEGIN
        ListTheMoves (NumDisks - 1, StartPeg, SparePeg, LastPeg);
        writeln ('Move a disk from ', StartPeg, ' to ', LastPeg);
        ListTheMoves (NumDisks - 1, SparePeg, LastPeg, StartPeg)
      END  {  of ELSE option  }
  END;  {  of PROCEDURE ListTheMoves  }

{****************************************************************}

BEGIN  {  Main program  }
  write ('How many disks in this game?  ');
  readln (NumDisks);
  writeln;
  writeln ('Start with ', NumDisks, ' disks on Peg A');
  writeln;
  writeln ('Then proceed as follows:');
  writeln;
  ListTheMoves (NumDisks, 'A', 'C', 'B')
END.  {  of main program  }
```

Sample runs for three-disk and four-disk problems produce the following output.

```
How many disks in this game?  3

Start with 3 disks on Peg A

Then proceed as follows:

Move a disk from A to C
Move a disk from A to B
Move a disk from C to B
```

```
Move a disk from A to C
Move a disk from B to A
Move a disk from B to C
Move a disk from A to C

How many disks in this game?  4

Start with 4 disks on Peg A

Then proceed as follows:

Move a disk from A to B
Move a disk from A to C
Move a disk from B to C
Move a disk from A to B
Move a disk from C to A
Move a disk from C to B
Move a disk from A to B
Move a disk from A to C
Move a disk from B to C
Move a disk from B to A
Move a disk from C to A
Move a disk from B to C
Move a disk from A to B
Move a disk from A to C
Move a disk from B to C
```

EXERCISES 11.1

1. Explain what is wrong with the following recursive function.

```
FUNCTION Recur (X : real) : real;
  BEGIN
    Recur := Recur(X / 2)
  END;
```

2. Write a recursive function that reverses the digits of a positive integer. If the integer used as input is 1234, output should be 4321.
3. Consider the following recursive function.

```
FUNCTION A (X : real;
            N : integer) : real;
  BEGIN
    IF N = 0 THEN
      A := 1.0
    ELSE
      A := X * A(X, N - 1)
  END;  { of FUNCTION A }
```

   a. What is the value of Y for each of the following?
      i. `Y := A(3.0, 2);`
      ii. `Y := A(2.0, 3);`
      iii. `Y := A(4.0, 4);`
      iv. `Y := A(1.0, 6);`
   b. Explain what standard computation is performed by **FUNCTION** A.
   c. Rewrite **FUNCTION** A using iteration rather than recursion.

4. Recall the Fibonacci sequence

   1, 1, 2, 3, 5, 8, 13, 21, . . .

   where for $n > 2$, the nth term is the sum of the previous two terms. Write a recursive function to compute the nth term in the Fibonacci sequence.
5. Write a function that uses iteration to compute $n!$.

11.2 Sorting Algorithms

OBJECTIVES

- to understand the algorithm for an insertion sort
- to be able to use an insertion sort in a program
- to understand the algorithm for a quick sort
- to be able to use a quick sort in a program

Several algorithms are available for sorting elements in arrays and files. We have worked with the selection sort since Chapter 7, where we also discussed the bubble sort. Two other commonly used sorting methods are the insertion sort and the quick sort. All of these sorts work relatively well for sorting small lists of elements.

However, when large data bases need to be sorted, a direct application of an elementary sorting process usually requires a great deal of computer time. Thus, some other sorting method is needed—one that might involve the use of a different algorithm or the division of the lists into smaller parts, sorting these parts, and then merging the lists back together. In more advanced courses, you will examine the relative efficiency of sorts and methods for handling large data bases. For now, let's consider these two sorting methods.

Insertion Sort

The purpose of a sort is to produce an array of elements sorted in either ascending or descending order. These elements are normally read from an input file into an array. Now let's see how an insertion sort arranges numbers in ascending order in an unsorted array.

The main principles of an *insertion sort* are

1. Put the first K elements of an array in order.
2. Move the K + 1 element into Temp.
3. Move the sorted elements (1 to K) down, one at a time, until the value in Temp can be placed in order in the previously sorted portion of the array.

To illustrate how this works, consider the array of integers

A
4
2
0
15
8

The first step is to put the value from A[2] into Temp by using

```
Temp := A[2];
```

This produces

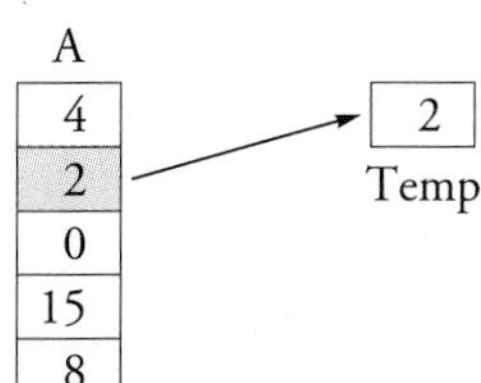

where the shaded cell can be thought of as waiting to receive a value. The value in Temp is then compared to values in the array before A[2]. Since A[1] > A[2], the value in A[1] is "moved down" to produce

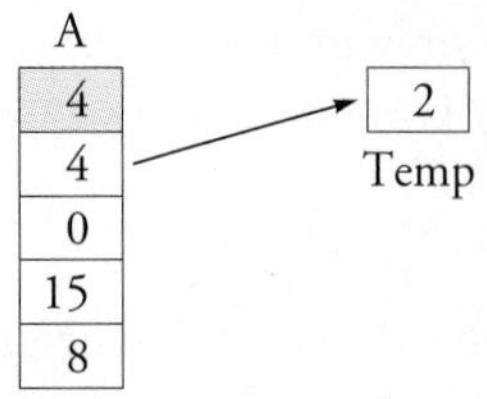

Since we are at the top of the array, the value in Temp is placed in A[1] to yield

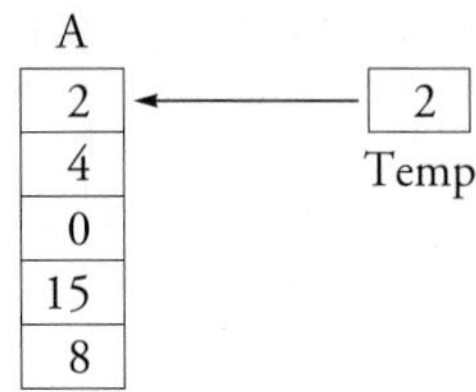

During the next pass, the value of A[3] is put into Temp and we have

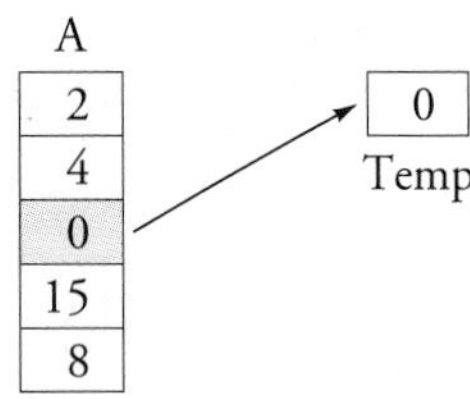

This value is compared to those above it. As long as Temp is less than an array element, the array element is shifted down. This process produces

A		
2		0
2		Temp
4		
15		
8		

At this stage, the value in Temp is inserted into the array to produce the partially sorted array

A
0
2
4
15
8

At the start of the next pass, Temp receives the value in A[4] to yield

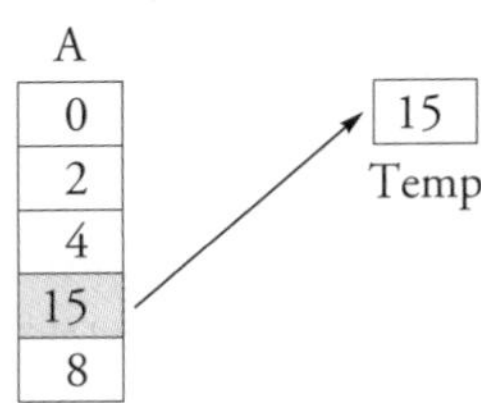

When the value in Temp is compared to the value in A[3], the process terminates because Temp > A[3]. Thus, using the partially sorted array improves the efficiency of the sort.

On the last pass, Temp receives the value from A[5] and we have

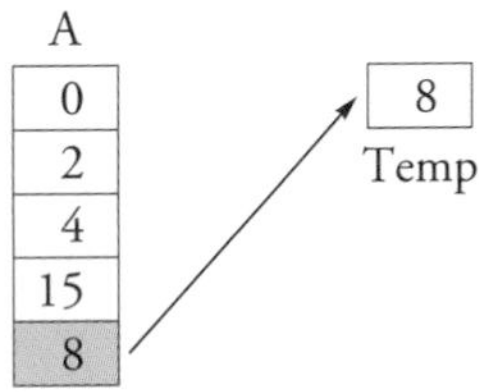

Since Temp < A[4], we next get

A		
0		8
2		Temp
4		
15		
15		

At this stage, Temp > A[3], so we insert the value of Temp into A[4] to produce the sorted array

A
0
2
4
8
15

In summary, the idea of an insertion sort is to do the following.

1. Remove an element from position K + 1 in the array.
2. Slide the previously sorted elements down the array until a position is found for the new element.
3. Insert the element in its proper position.
4. Continue this process until the array is sorted.

A procedure for the insertion sort follows.

```
PROCEDURE InsertionSort (VAR List : SortArray;
                         ListLength : integer);

  {  Given:   An array List with entries in locations 1          }
  {                through ListLength                             }
  {  Task:    Apply insertion sort logic to List                  }
  {  Return:  The array List with entries sorted in               }
  {                ascending order                                }

  VAR
    Index, K : integer;
    Temp : ElementType;
    Done : boolean;

  BEGIN
    FOR Index := 2 TO ListLength DO
      BEGIN
        Temp := List[Index];
        K := Index;
        Done := false;
        WHILE (K >= 2) AND (NOT Done) DO
          IF Temp < List[K-1] THEN
            BEGIN                             {  Move elements down    }
              List[K] := List[K-1];
              K := K - 1
            END  {  of IF...THEN option  }
          ELSE
            Done := true;  {  Found position for insertion  }
        List[K] := Temp                        {  Insert into array   }
      END  {  of FOR loop  }
  END;  {  of PROCEDURE InsertionSort  }
```

This procedure is called from the main program by

```
InsertionSort (UnsortedList, Length);
```

As expected, records can be sorted by examining some key field and then assigning the entire record accordingly. Thus, if an array type is

```
TYPE
  .
  .
  .
  StudentInfo = RECORD
                  Name : NameString;
                  Score : integer
                END;  {  of RECORD StudentInfo  }
  StudentList = ARRAY [1..ListLength] OF StudentInfo;
```

and the array is to be sorted according to student scores, the field comparison in **PROCEDURE** InsertionSort could be

```
IF Temp.Score < Student[K-1].Score
```

A NOTE OF INTEREST

Gene Mapping: Computer Scientists Examine Problems of Genome Project

Deciphering the human genome is much like trying to read the instructions on a computer disk filled with programs written in the zeros and ones of electronic code—without knowing the programming language.

That was the message from molecular biologists to computer scientists at a meeting sponsored by the National Research Council. The biologists hope to involve the computer scientists in the U.S. Human Genome Project, a 15-year, $3-billion effort to identify and locate the information contained in human chromosomes.

Computer scientists, with their experience in managing information and using arcane programming languages to store data and convey instructions, could be particularly valuable in helping to read and organize the 3 billion "letters" that make up the human genetic code, the biologists said.

"The entire program for making *me* is about 10 to the 10 bits" (about 10 trillion pieces of information), said Gerald J. Sussman, a professor of electrical engineering and computer science at the Massachusetts Institute of Technology. "It is no bigger than the U.S. Tax Code or the design documents for the U.S. space shuttle." Figuring out what that program is, he said, is a computer science problem.

Biologists said they needed computer scientists to

- Design easy-to-use data bases that can handle the millions of pieces of information that need to be correlated to fully understand genetics—and life.
- Design computer networks that will allow biologists to share information conveniently.
- Create procedures that will allow biologists to analyze information pulled from laboratory experiments.
- Write programs that will let biologists simulate the formation and development of proteins.

Quick Sort

One of the fastest sorting techniques available is the *quick sort,* which uses recursion and is based upon the idea of separating a list of numbers into two parts. One part contains numbers smaller than some number in the list; the other part contains numbers larger than the number. Thus, if an unsorted array originally contains

14	3	2	11	5	8	0	2	9	4	20
A[1]	A[2]				A[6]					A[11]

we select the element in the middle position, A[6], and then pivot on the value in A[6], which is 8 in our illustration. Our process then puts all values smaller than 8 on the left side and all values larger than 8 on the right side. This first subdividing produces

						Pivot ↓				
4	3	2	2	5	0	8	11	9	14	20
A[1]										A[11]

Each sublist is subdivided in the same manner until all sublists are in order. The array is then sorted. This is a recursive process.

Before we write a procedure for this sort, let's examine how it works. First, why do we choose the value in the middle position? Ideally, we would like to pivot on the median of the list. However, it is not efficient to find this value first, so we choose the value in the middle as a compromise. The index of this value is found by (First + Last) **DIV** 2, where First and Last are the indices of the initial and final array elements. We then identify a LeftArrow and RightArrow on the far left and far right, respectively. This can be envisioned as

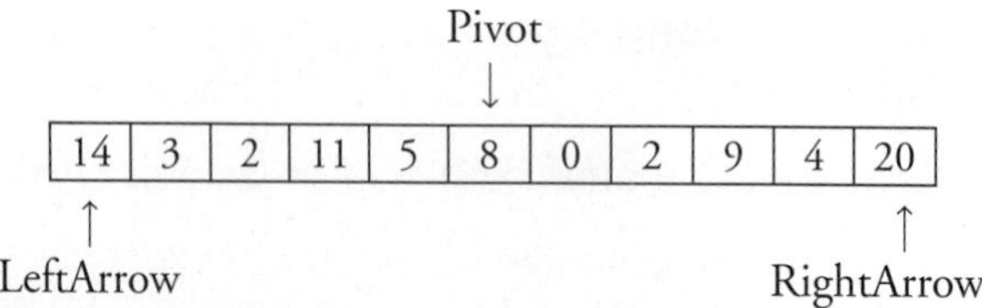

where LeftArrow and RightArrow represent the respective indices of the array components. Starting on the right, the RightArrow is moved left until a value less than or equal to the pivot is encountered. Similarly, LeftArrow is moved right until a value greater than or equal to the pivot is encountered. This produces

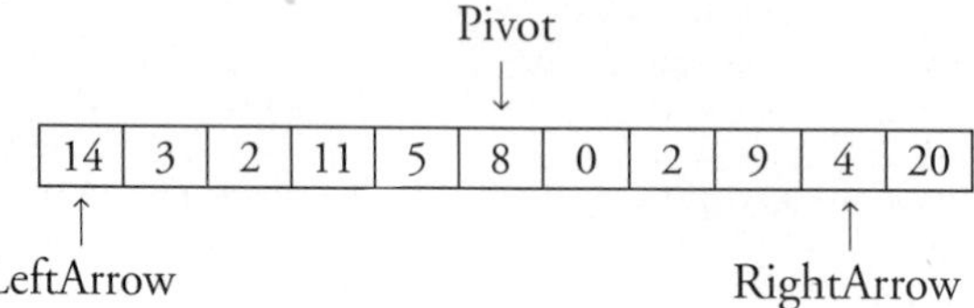

Since LeftArrow is already at a value greater than or equal to the pivot, it does not move. The contents of the two array components are now switched to produce

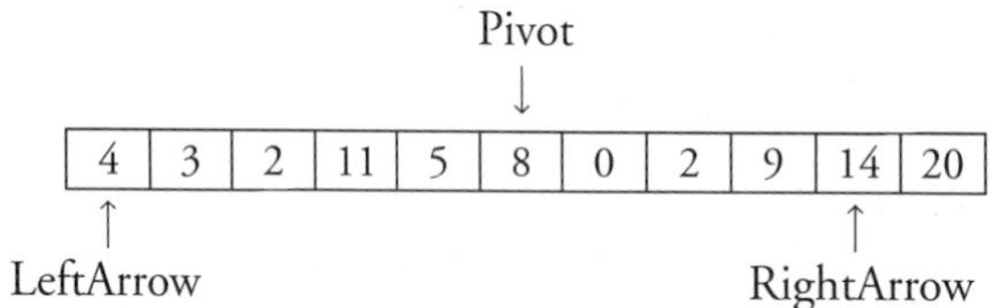

We continue by moving RightArrow left to produce

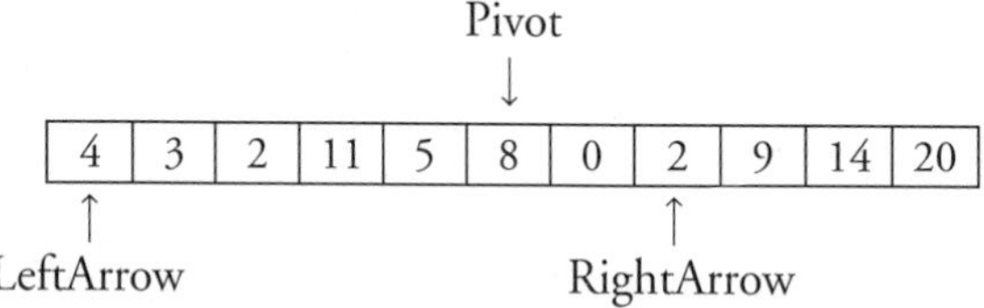

and by moving LeftArrow right to obtain

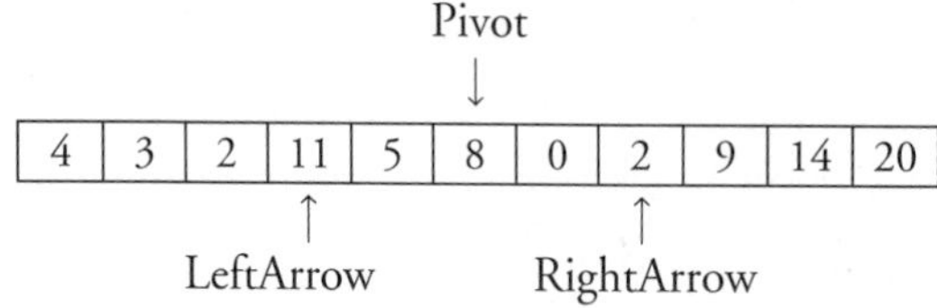

These values are exchanged to produce

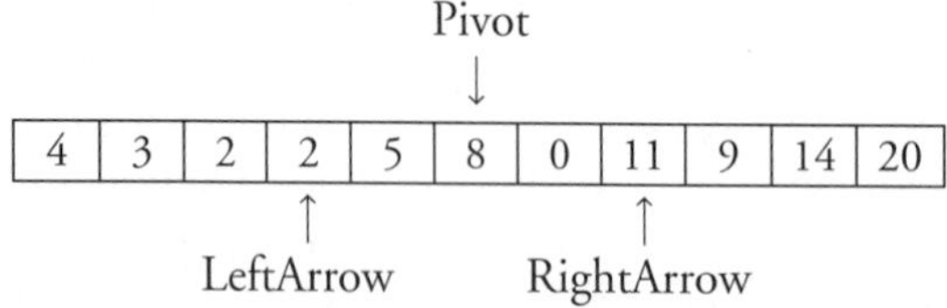

This process stops when LeftArrow > RightArrow is **true**. Since this is still **false** at this point, the next RightArrow move to the left produces

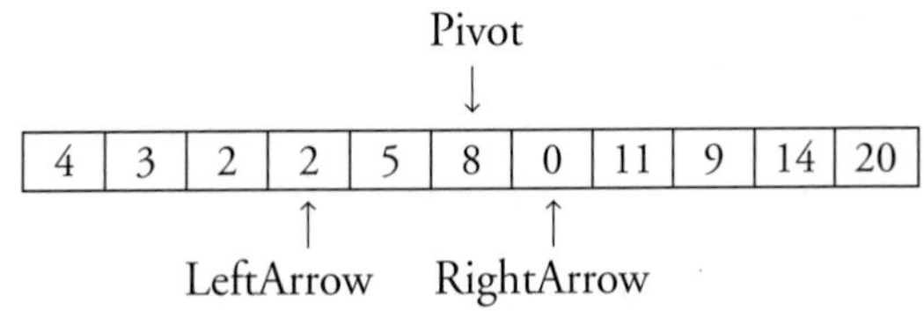

and the next LeftArrow move to the right yields

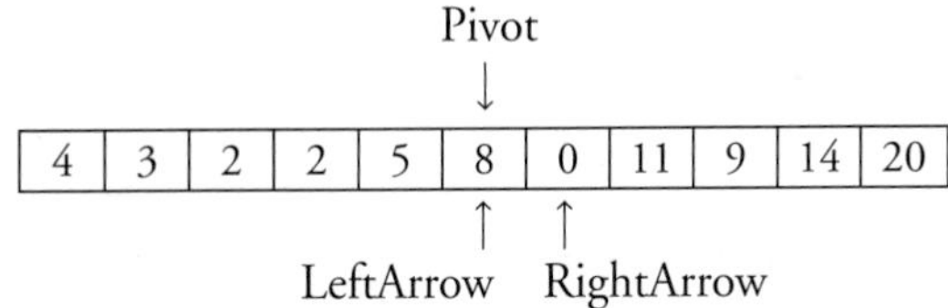

Since LeftArrow < Pivot is **false,** LeftArrow stops moving and an exchange is made to produce

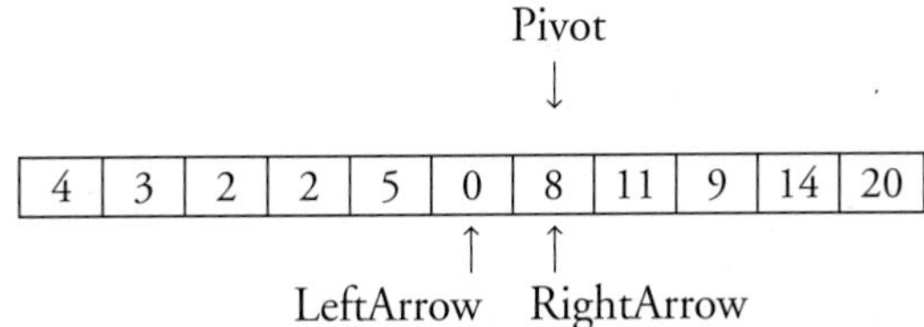

Notice the pivot, 8, has been exchanged and now occupies a new position. This is acceptable because Pivot is the value of the component, not the index. As before, RightArrow is moved left and Left Arrow is moved right to produce

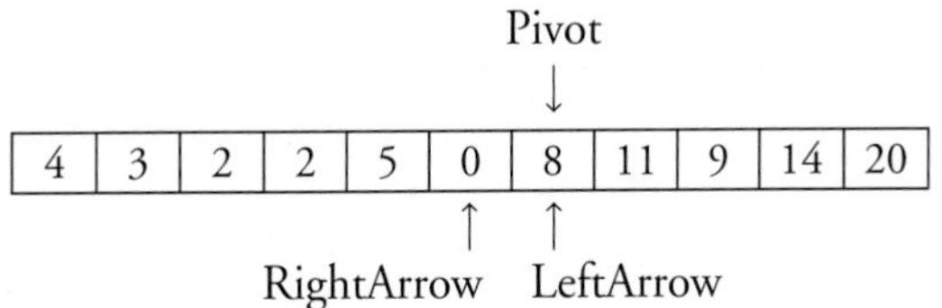

Since RightArrow < LeftArrow is **true,** the first subdividing is complete. At this stage, numbers smaller than Pivot are on the left side and numbers larger than Pivot are on the right side. This produces two sublists that can be envisioned as

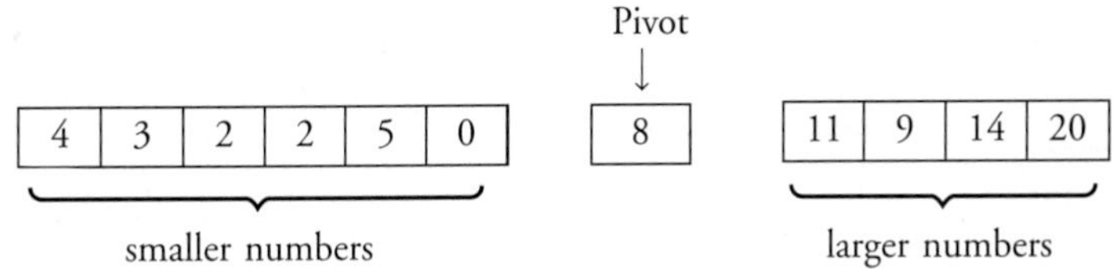

Each sublist can now be sorted by using the same procedure. This requires a recursive call to the sorting procedure. In each case, the array is passed as a variable parameter together with the right and left indices for the appropriate sublist. A procedure for this sort follows.

```
  PROCEDURE QuickSort (VAR Num : List;
                       Left, Right : integer);
    VAR
      Pivot, Temp, LeftArrow, RightArrow : integer;
    BEGIN
      LeftArrow := Left;
      RightArrow := Right;
      Pivot := Num[(Left + Right) DIV 2];
      REPEAT
        WHILE Num[RightArrow] > Pivot DO
          RightArrow := RightArrow - 1;
        WHILE Num[LeftArrow] < Pivot DO
          LeftArrow := LeftArrow + 1;
        IF LeftArrow <= RightArrow THEN
          BEGIN
            Temp := Num[LeftArrow];
            Num[LeftArrow] := Num[RightArrow];
            Num[RightArrow] := Temp;
            LeftArrow := LeftArrow + 1;
            RightArrow := RightArrow - 1
          END  {  of switching elements and then moving arrows  }
      UNTIL RightArrow < LeftArrow;
      IF Left < RightArrow THEN
        QuickSort (Num, Left, RightArrow);
      IF LeftArrow < Right THEN
        QuickSort (Num, LeftArrow, Right)
    END;  {  of PROCEDURE QuickSort  }
```

The design for a complete interactive program to illustrate the use of quick sort is

1. Fill the array
2. Sort the numbers
3. Print the list

The complete program follows.

```
PROGRAM UseQuickSort (input, output);

{  This program illustrates the quick sort as a sorting         }
{  algorithm.  The array elements are successively subdivided   }
{  into "smaller" and "larger" elements in parts of the array.  }
{  Recursive calls are made to PROCEDURE QuickSort.             }

CONST
  MaxLength = 30;

TYPE
  List = ARRAY [1..MaxLength] OF integer;

VAR
  Num : List;
  First, Last, Length : integer;

{****************************************************************}
```

```
PROCEDURE FillArray (VAR Num : List;
                     VAR Length : integer);

  {  Given:   Nothing                                            }
  {  Task:    Read numbers entered from the keyboard into the    }
  {               array Num                                      }
  {  Return:  An array of numbers, Num, and number of elements   }
  {               in the array                                   }

  VAR
    Index : integer;
  BEGIN
    Index := 0;
    REPEAT
      Index := Index + 1;
      write ('Enter an integer, -999 to quit.  ');
      readln (Num[Index])
    UNTIL Num[Index]= -999;
    Length := Index - 1
  END;  {  of PROCEDURE FillArray  }

{***************************************************************}

PROCEDURE QuickSort (VAR Num : List;
                     Left, Right : integer);

  {  Given:   An unsorted array of integers and array length    }
  {  Task:    Sort the array                                     }
  {  Return:  A sorted array of integers                         }

  VAR
    Pivot, Temp, LeftArrow, RightArrow : integer;
  BEGIN
    LeftArrow := Left;
    RightArrow := Right;
    Pivot := Num [(Left + Right) DIV 2];
    REPEAT
      WHILE Num [RightArrow] > Pivot DO
        RightArrow := RightArrow - 1;
      WHILE Num [LeftArrow] < Pivot DO
        LeftArrow := LeftArrow + 1;
      IF LeftArrow <= RightArrow THEN
        BEGIN
          Temp := Num[LeftArrow];
          Num[LeftArrow] := Num[RightArrow];
          Num[RightArrow]:= Temp;
          LeftArrow := LeftArrow + 1;
          RightArrow := RightArrow - 1
        END  {  of IF...THEN  }
    UNTIL RightArrow < LeftArrow;
    IF Left < RightArrow THEN
      QuickSort (Num, Left, RightArrow);
    IF LeftArrow < Right THEN
      QuickSort (Num, LeftArrow, Right)
  END;  {  of PROCEDURE QuickSort  }
```

```
{***************************************************************}

PROCEDURE PrintList (VAR Num : List;
                     Length : integer);

  {  Given:    A sorted array of numbers and array length         }
  {  Task:     Print the numbers                                  }
  {  Return:   Nothing                                            }

  VAR
    Index : integer;
  BEGIN
    writeln;
    writeln ('The sorted list is:');
    writeln;
    FOR Index := 1 TO Length DO
      writeln (Num[Index])
  END;  {  of PROCEDURE PrintList  }

{***************************************************************}

BEGIN  {  Main program  }
  FillArray (Num, Length);
  QuickSort (Num, 1, Length);
  PrintList (Num, Length)
END.  {  of main program  }
```

A sample run of this program using the previous data produces

```
Enter an integer, -999 to quit.  14
Enter an integer, -999 to quit.  3
Enter an integer, -999 to quit.  2
Enter an integer, -999 to quit.  11
Enter an integer, -999 to quit.  5
Enter an integer, -999 to quit.  8
Enter an integer, -999 to quit.  0
Enter an integer, -999 to quit.  2
Enter an integer, -999 to quit.  9
Enter an integer, -999 to quit.  4
Enter an integer, -999 to quit.  20
Enter an integer, -999 to quit.  -999

The sorted list is:

0
2
2
3
4
5
8
9
11
14
20
```

EXERCISES 11.2

1. Modify the insertion sort so it sorts numbers from an input file rather than from an array. Explain why **PROCEDURE** InsertionSort inserts the first element of the unsorted list into the first position of the sorted list.
2. Using the bubble sort discussed in Chapter 7, the array

17
0
3
2
8

requires five exchanges of elements. Since each exchange requires three assignment statements, there are 15 assignments for elements in the array. Sort the same array using the insertion sort, and determine the number of assignments made.

3. Modify the insertion sort by including a counter that counts the number of assignments of array elements made during a sort.
4. Using the modification in Exercise 3, sort lists of differing lengths that contain randomly generated numbers. Display the number of assignments made for each sort on a graph similar to the one shown in Figure 11.5. (Use lists with lengths of multiples of 10.)

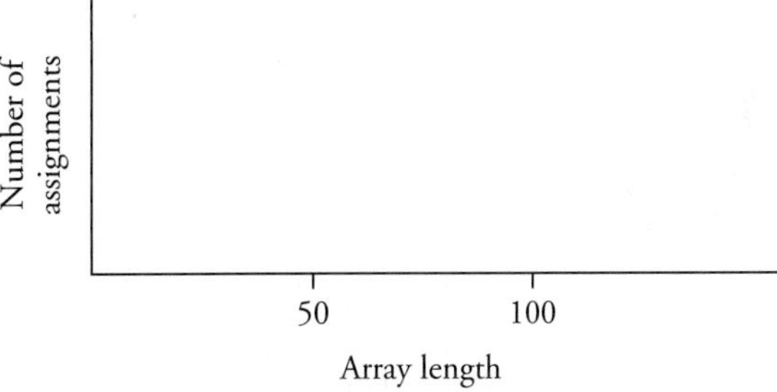

◆ FIGURE 11.5
Array length

5. Modify both the bubble sort and the selection sort discussed in Chapter 7 to include counters for the number of assignments made during a sort.
6. Use the modified version of all sorts to examine their relative efficiency; that is, run them on arrays of varying lengths and plot the results on a graph. What are your conclusions?
7. Write a short program to read numbers into an array, sort the array, print the sorted numbers, and save the sorted list for later use by some other program.
8. Modify all sorts to sort from high to low rather than low to high.
9. Sorting parallel arrays is a common practice. An example of parallel arrays is an array of names and a corresponding array of scores on a test. Modify the insertion sort and quick sort so you can sort a list of names and test scores.
10. Explain how an array of records with a key field, Name, can be sorted using a quick sort.
11. Suppose you are using a program that contains an array of records in which each record is defined by

```
TYPE
  .
  .
  .
  CustomerInfo = RECORD
                   Name : NameString;
                   AmountDue : real
                 END;  {  of RECORD CustomerInfo  }
```

a. Use the quick sort to sort and then print the records alphabetically.

b. Resort the array by the field AmountDue. Print a list ordered by AmountDue in which anyone with an amount due of more than $100 is designated with a triple asterisk (***).

12. Modify **PROCEDURE** QuickSort to use the first element (not the middle element) as the pivot in an array.

RUNNING AND DEBUGGING HINTS

1. Make sure recursive subprograms reach the stopping state.
2. Make sure recursive subprograms have well-defined recursive steps.
3. Use value parameters for any formal parameters that relate to the size of the problems in a recursive subprogram.
4. Sorting large files or long arrays can be very time consuming. Depending upon the number of elements to be processed, use some form of "divide and conquer"; that is, divide the list, sort the elements, and then merge them. Very large data bases may require several subdivisions and subsequent merges.
5. When you use a key field to sort records, be careful to compare only the key field and then exchange the entire record accordingly.

SUMMARY

Key Terms

insertion sort
quick sort
recursion
recursive step
recursive subprogram
stack
stopping state

Key Concepts

- Recursion is a process whereby a subprogram calls itself.
- A recursive subprogram must have a well-defined stopping state.
- Recursive solutions are usually elegant and short, but they generally require more memory than iterative solutions.
- An insertion sort creates a sorted array from an unsorted array by inserting elements one at a time in their respective order.
- A quick sort is one of the fastest sorting techniques available. It uses recursion and is based upon the idea of separating a list into two parts.

SUGGESTIONS FOR FURTHER READING

Recursion and sorting are subjects of numerous articles and books. This chapter provided some samples of each process. For variations and improvements on what is included here as well as on other techniques, the interested reader is referred to the following books, which many consider to be classics in the field.

Baase, Sara. "Sorting." Chapter 2 in *Computer Algorithms: Introduction to Design and Analysis.* Reading, MA: Addison-Wesley Publishing Co., 1978.

Cormen, T.H., Leiserson, C.G., and Rivest, R.L. Introduction to Algorithms. New York, NY: McGraw-Hill, 1990.

Gear, William. *Applications and Algorithms in Engineering and Science.* Chicago: Science Research Associates, 1978.

Horowitz, Ellis, and Sahni, Sartaz. "Divide and Conquer." Chapter 3 in *Fundamentals of Computer Algorithms.* Potomac, MD: Computer Science Press, 1978.

Knuth, Donald. *The Art of Computer Programming.* Vol. 3, *Sorting and Searching.* Reading, MA: Addison-Wesley Publishing Co., 1975.

PROGRAMMING PROBLEMS AND PROJECTS

■ **1.** Write a program to update a mailing list. Assume you have a sorted master file of records and each record contains a customer's name, address, and expiration code. Your program should input a file of new customers, sort the file, and merge the file with the master file to produce a new master.

■ **2.** Assume that the ReadMore Public Library (Problems 6 and 7, Chapter 9) stores information about books on its shelves in a file of records named OldFile. Information about a new shipment of books is contained in the data file. Both files are sorted alphabetically by book title. Write a program to be used to update OldFile. For each book in the input file, your program should search the existing file to see if the additional book is a duplicate. If it is, change a field in the record to indicate that an additional copy has been obtained. If it is not a duplicate, insert the record in sequence in the file.

3. The Bakerville Manufacturing Company has to lay off all employees who started working after a certain date. Write a program to do the following.

- **a.** Input a termination date.
- **b.** Search an alphabetical file of employee records to determine who will get a layoff notice.
- **c.** Create a file of employee records for those who are being laid off.
- **d.** Update the master file to contain only records of current employees.
- **e.** Produce two lists of those being laid off: one ordered alphabetically, and one ordered by hiring date.

4. The Bakerville Manufacturing Company (Problem 3) has achieved new prosperity and can rehire 10 employees who were recently laid off. Write a program to do the following.

- **a.** Search the file of previously terminated employees to find the 10 with the most seniority.
- **b.** Delete those 10 records from the file of employees who were laid off.
- **c.** Insert the 10 records alphabetically into the file of current employees.
- **d.** Print four lists as follows:
  - **i.** An alphabetical list of current employees
  - **ii.** A seniority list of current employees
  - **iii.** An alphabetical list of employees who were laid off
  - **iv.** A seniority list of employees who were laid off

5. The Shepherd Lions Club sponsors an annual cross-country race for area schools. Write a program to do the following.

- **a.** Create an array of records for the runners; each record should contain the runner's name, school, identification number, and time (in a seven-character string, such as 15:17:3).
- **b.** Print an alphabetical list of all runners.
- **c.** Print a list of schools entered in the race.
- **d.** Print a list of runners entered in the race; order the list by school name.
- **e.** Print the final finish order by sorting the records according to the order of finish and printing a numbered list according to the order of finish.

6. The greatest common divisor of two positive integers a and b, GCD(a,b), is the largest positive integer that divides both a and b. Thus, GCD(102, 30) = 6, which can be found by using the division algorithm as follows:

$$\begin{aligned} 102 &= 30 * 3 + 12 \\ 30 &= 12 * 2 + 6 \\ 12 &= 6 * 2 + 0 \end{aligned}$$

Note

$$\begin{aligned} \text{GCD}(102, 30) &= \text{GCD}(30, 12) \\ &= \text{GCD}(12, 6) \\ &= 6 \end{aligned}$$

In each case, the remainder is used for the next step. The process terminates when a remainder of zero is obtained. Write a recursive function that returns the GCD of two positive integers.

7. A palindrome is a number or word that is the same when read either forward or backward. As examples, 12321 and mom are palindromes. Write a recursive function that can be used to determine whether or not an integer is a palindrome. Use this function in a complete program that reads a list of integers and then displays the list with an asterisk following each palindrome.

8. Recall the Fibonacci sequence discussed at the beginning of this chapter. Write a recursive function that returns the nth Fibonacci number. Input for a call to the function will be a positive integer.

9. Probability courses often contain problems that require students to compute the number of ways r items can be chosen from a set of n objects. It is shown that there are

$$C(n, r) = \frac{n!}{r!(n-r)!}$$

such choices. This is sometimes referred to as "n choose r." To illustrate, if you wish to select three items from a total of five possible objects, there are

$$C(5, 3) = \frac{5!}{3!(5-3)!} = \frac{5 * 4 * 3 * 2 * 1}{(3 * 2 * 1)\,(2 * 1)} = 10$$

such possibilities.

In mathematics, the number $C(n,r)$ is a binomial coefficient because, for appropriate values of n and r, it produces coefficients in the expansion of $(x + y)^n$. Thus

$$(x + y)^4 = C(4, 0)x^4 + C(4, 1)x^3y + C(4, 2)x^2y^2 + C(4, 3)xy^3 + C(4, 4)y^4$$

a. Write a function that returns the value $C(n, r)$. Arguments for a function call will be integers n, r such that $n > r \geq 0$. (*Hint:* Simplify the expression

$$\frac{n!}{r!(n-r)!}$$

before computing.)

b. Write an interactive program that receives as input the power to which a binomial is to be raised. Output should be the expanded binomial.

COMMUNICATION IN PRACTICE

1. Select a programming problem that you have not worked from the Programming Problems and Projects section of this chapter. Construct a structure chart and write all documentary information for this program. Include variable definition, subprogram definition, required input, and required output. When you are finished, have a classmate read your documentation to see if it is clear precisely what is to be done.
2. Remove all documentation from a program you have written for this chapter. Exchange this modified version with another student who has done the same thing. Write documentation for the exchanged program. Compare your documentation with that of the original program. Discuss the differences and similarities with the other students in your class.
3. Form a team of three or four students, and identify some local business that has not yet computerized its customer records. The team should talk to the owner or manager to determine how the customer records are used, and then design an information processing system for the business. The system should include complete design specifications. Particular attention should be paid to searching and sorting. The team should then give an oral presentation to the class and use appropriate charts and diagrams to illustrate the design.
4. Write a short paper that describes how the quick sort works. Prepare a model that can be used to demonstrate this sorting technique to your class.

CHAPTER 12 Sets

CHAPTER OUTLINE

Thus far, we have investigated structured data types: arrays, records, and files. These data types are structured because when each one is declared, a certain structure is reserved to subsequently hold values. In an array, a predetermined number of elements that are all of the same type can be held. A record contains a predetermined number of fields that can hold elements of different types. A file is somewhat like an array but the length is not predetermined.

Another structured data type available in Pascal is a set. Since the implementation of sets varies greatly from system to system, you should check all of the statements and examples in this chapter on your system.

The goal of this chapter is to enable you to use sets when writing programs to solve problems. One fairly common use of sets is to guard against inadvertent keystrokes when users are working with interactive programs. But before you can use sets in a program, you must understand certain fundamentals. In particular, you must be able to properly define sets and use set operations.

12.1 Declarations and Terms

OBJECTIVES

- to be able to define a set as a data type
- to understand and be able to use the terms associated with sets: element of a set, universal set, subset, and empty set
- to be able to make an assignment to a set variable
- to understand what is meant by a set constant

Basic Idea and Notation

A *set* in Pascal is a structured data type that consists of a collection of distinct elements from an indicated base type (which must be an ordinal data type). Sets in Pascal are defined and used in a manner consistent with the use of sets in mathematics. A set type is defined by

> **TYPE**
> <type name> = **SET OF** <base type>

A set variable is then declared by

> **VAR**
> <variable name> : <type name>

In a program working with characters of the alphabet, we might have

```
TYPE
  Alphabet = SET OF 'A'..'Z';
VAR
  Vowels, Consonants : Alphabet;
```

In a similar fashion, if our program analyzes digits and arithmetic symbols, we might have

```
TYPE
  Units = SET OF 0..9;
  Symbols = SET OF '*'..'/';   {  Arithmetic symbols  }
VAR
  Digits : Units;
  ArithSym : Symbols;
```

In these examples, Alphabet, Units, and Symbols are set types. Vowels, Consonants, Digits, and ArithSym are set variables.

T A set can contain elements. These elements must be of the defined base type, which must be an ordinal data type. Most implementations of Pascal limit the maximum size of the base type of a set. This limit is such that a base type of **integer** is not allowed. Often the limit is at least 128, so base types of **char** and subranges of **integer** within 0..127 can usually be used.

Assignments to Sets

Once a set variable has been declared, it is undefined until an assignment of values is made. The syntax for making such an assignment is

<set name> := [<values>]

For example, we can have

```
Vowels := ['A', 'E', 'I', 'O', 'U'];
Consonants := ['B'..'D', 'F'..'H', 'J'..'N', 'P'..'T',
               'V'..'Z'];
Digits := [0..9];
ArithSym := ['+', '-', '*', '/'];
```

Notice the assigned values must be included in brackets and must be of the defined base type. Appropriate values depend upon the character set being used. Also, subranges of the base type can be used; thus

```
Consonants := ['B'..'D'];
```

is the same as

```
Consonants := ['B', 'C', 'D'];
```

It is also possible to have set constants. Just as 4, 'H', and -56.20 are constants, [2,4,6] is a constant. In the previous example, this could be caused by

```
Digits := [2,4,6];
```

As mentioned, sets are structured data types because, in a sense, they can be thought of as containing a list of elements. However, in listing the elements, notice each element can be listed only once and order makes no difference; thus, [2,4,6] is the same as [4,2,6].

Other Terminology

Once a value of the base type has been assigned to a set, it is an *element of the set*. Thus, if we have

```
Digits := [2,4,6];
```

2, 4, and 6 are elements of Digits. Testing membership in a set is discussed in the next section.

A NOTE OF INTEREST

Fractal Geometry and Benoit Mandelbrot

Fractal geometry as a serious mathematical endeavor began with the pioneering work of Benoit B. Mandelbrot, a Fellow of the Thomas J. Watson Research Center, IBM Corporation. Fractal geometry is a theory of geometric forms so complex they defy analysis and classification by traditional Euclidean means. Yet fractal shapes occur universally in the natural world. Mandelbrot has recognized them not only in coastlines, landscapes, lungs, and turbulent water flow but also in the chaotic fluctuation of prices on the Chicago commodity exchange.

Although Mandelbrot's first comprehensive publication of fractal theory took place in 1975, mathematicians were aware of some of its basic elements during the period from 1875 to 1925. However, because mathematicians at that time thought such knowledge of "fractal dimension" deserved little attention, their discoveries were left as unrelated odds and ends. Also, the creation of fractal illustrations—a laborious and nearly impossible task at the turn of the twentieth century—can now be done quickly and precisely using computer graphics. (Even personal computers can now be used to generate fractal patterns with relative ease.)

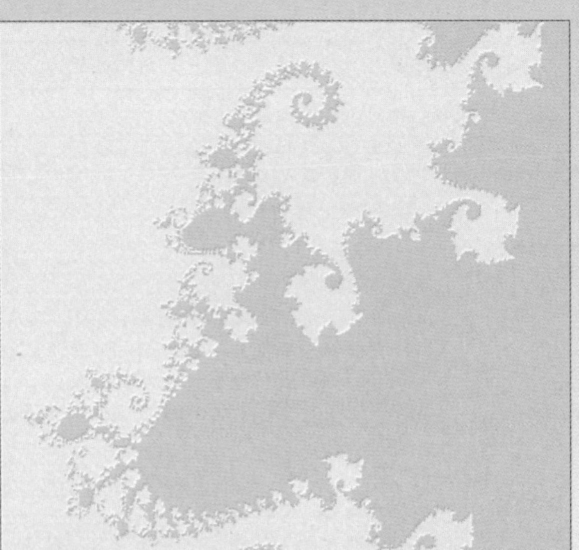

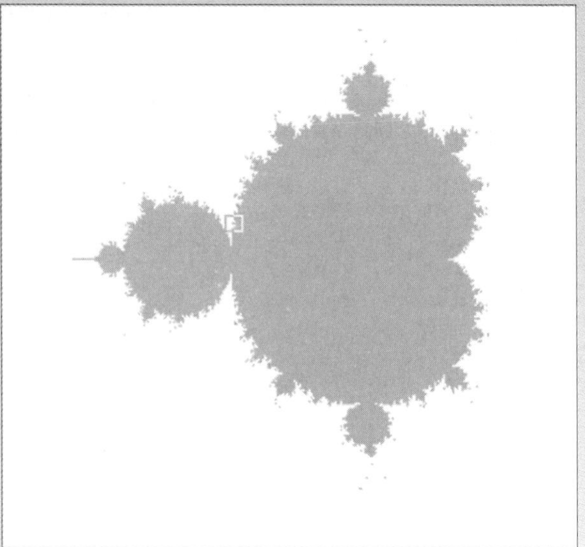

The figure on the left is an enlargement of the area of the Mandelbrot set defined by the square in the figure on the right.
Source: From *For All Practical Purposes: Introduction to Contemporary Mathematics.* By Consortium for Mathematics and Its Applications.

As in mathematics, any set that contains all possible values of the base type is called the *universal set.* In

```
Digits := [0..9];
```

Digits is a universal set. It is also possible to consider a set constant as a universal set. Thus, ['A' . . 'Z'] is a universal set if the **TYPE** definition section contains

```
<type name> = SET OF 'A'..'Z';
```

If A and B have been declared as sets of the same type and all of the elements of set A are also contained in set B, A is a *subset* of B. If we have

```
VAR
  A, B : Units;
```

and the assignments

```
A := [1,2,3,4,5];
B := [0..6];
```

have been made, A is a subset of B. However, B is not a subset of A because B contains two elements (0 and 6) that are not contained in A.

The *empty set,* or *null set,* is a set that contains no elements. It is denoted by [ ].

These definitions permit set theory results of mathematics to hold in Pascal. Some of these results follow.

1. The empty set is a subset of every set.
2. If A is a subset of B and B is a subset of C, then A is a subset of C.
3. Every set (of the base type) is a subset of the universal set.

EXERCISES 12.1

1. Find all errors in the following definitions and declarations. Explain your answers.

   a.
   ```
   TYPE
     Numbers = SET OF real;
   ```
   b.
   ```
   TYPE
     Numbers = SET OF integer;
   ```
   c.
   ```
   TYPE
     Alphabet : SET OF 'A'..'Z';
   ```
   d.
   ```
   TYPE
     Alphabet = SET OF ['A'..'Z'];
   ```
   e.
   ```
   TYPE
     Conditions = (Sunny, Mild, Rainy, Windy);
     Weather = SET OF Conditions;
   VAR
     TodaysWeather : Weather;
   ```
2. Write a test program to do the following.
   a. Discover if **char** is a permissible base type for a set.
   b. Determine the limitation on the size of the base type for a set.
3. Suppose set A is declared by
   ```
   TYPE
     Letters = SET OF 'A'..'Z';
   VAR
     A : Letters;
   ```
   a. Show how A can be made to contain the letters in your name.
   b. Assign the letters in the word PASCAL to set A.
   c. Assuming the assignment
   ```
   A := ['T', 'O', 'Y'];
   ```
   has been made, list all elements and subsets of set A.
4. Let the sets A, B, and U be declared by
   ```
   TYPE
     Alphabet = SET OF 'A'..'Z';
   VAR
     A, B, U : Alphabet;
   ```
   and the assignments
   ```
   A := ['B', 'F', 'J'..'T'];
   B := ['O'..'S'];
   U := ['A'..'Z'];
   ```
   be made. Indicate whether each of the following is **true** or **false**.
   a. [ ] is a subset of B
   b. B is an element of A
   c. B is a subset of A
   d. 'B' is an element of A
   e. 'B' is a subset of A
   f. A is a subset of U
   g. 'O' is an element of A

5. Assume the sets A, B, and U are declared as in Exercise 4. Find and explain all errors in the following assignment statements.

   a. `A := 'J'..'O';`
   b. `U := [];`
   c. `B := [A..Z];`
   d. `A := ['E', 'I', 'E', 'I', 'O'];`
   e. `[] := ['D'];`
   f. `B := ['A'..'T', 'S'];`

6. Let A be a set declared by

```
TYPE
  NumRange = 0..100;
VAR
  A : SET OF NumRange;
  M, N : integer;
```

   Indicate if the following assignment statements are valid or invalid. For those that are valid, list the elements of set A. For those that are invalid, explain why.

   a. `A := [19];`
   b. `A := 19;`
   c.
```
M := 80;
N := 40;
A := [M + N, M MOD N, M DIV N];
```
   d.
```
M := 10;
N := 2;
A := [M, M * N, M / N];
```

7. Define a set type and declare a set variable to be used for each of the following set values.

   a. Colors of the rainbow
   b. Class in school (Freshman, Sophomore, Junior, or Senior)
   c. Fruits
   d. Grades for a class

8. Explain why **SET** is not an enumerated data type.

12.2 Set Operations and Relational Operators

OBJECTIVES

- to understand the set operations union, intersection, and difference
- to be able to use sets with relational operators

Set Operations

Pascal provides for the set operations union, intersection, and difference where, in each case, two sets are combined to produce a single set. If A and B are sets of the same type, these operations are defined as follows:

- The *union* of A and B is A + B, where A + B contains any element that is in A or that is in B.
- The *intersection* of A and B is A * B, where A * B contains the elements that are in both A and B.
- The *difference* of A and B is A – B, where A – B contains the elements that are in A but that are not in B.

To illustrate, suppose A and B are sets that contain integer values and the assignment statements

```
A := [1..5];
B := [3..9];
```

are made. The values produced by set operations follow.

Set Operation	Values
A + B	`[1..9]`
A * B	`[3,4,5]`
A - B	`[1,2]`
B - A	`[6..9]`

Multiple operations can be performed with sets. When such an expression is encountered, the same operator priority prevails that exists when arithmetic expressions are evaluated. Thus, if A and B contain the values previously indicated, then

```
A + B - A * B
```

produces

```
[1..5] + [3..9]  -  [1..5] * [3..9]
                            ↓
[1..5] + [3..9]  -      [3,4,5]
       ↓
    [1..9]       -      [3,4,5]
                 ↓
          [1,2,6..9]
```

Relational Operators

Relational operators can also be used with sets in Pascal. These operators correspond to the normal set operators equal, not equal, subset, and superset. In each case, a Boolean value is produced. If A and B are sets, these operators are defined as shown in Table 12.1.

◇ TABLE 12.1
Set operations

Operator	Relational Expression	Definition
= (equal)	`A = B`	A is equal to B; that is, every element in A is contained in B and every element in B is contained in A.
<> (not equal)	`A <> B`	A does not equal B; that is, either A or B contains an element that is not contained in the other set.
<= (subset)	`A <= B`	A is a subset of B; that is, every element of A is also contained in B.
>= (superset)	`A >= B`	A is a superset of B (B is a subset of A); that is, every element of B is contained in A.

Boolean values associated with some set expressions follow.

Set Expression	Boolean Value
`[1,2,3] <= [0..10]`	**true**
`[0..10] <= [1,2,3]`	**false**
`[0..10] = [0..5, 6..10]`	**true**
`[] = ([1,2] - [0..10])`	**true**
`[1..5] <> [1..3, 4, 5]`	**false**
`[] <= [1,2,3]`	**true**

Set Membership

Membership in a set is indicated in Pascal by the reserved word **IN**. The general form is

<element> **IN** <set>

where <element> and <set> are type compatible. This returns a value of **true** if the element is in the set and a value of **false** if it is not. To illustrate, suppose A and B are sets and the assignments

```
A := [0..20];
B := [5..10];
```

are made. The values of expressions using **IN** follow.

Expression	Boolean Value
`10 IN A`	**true**
`5 IN (A - B)`	**false**
`20 IN B`	**false**
`7 IN (A * B)`	**true**
`80 DIV 20 IN A * B`	**?**

Note that the last expression cannot be evaluated until priorities are assigned to the operators. Fortunately, these priorities are identical to those for arithmetic expressions; **IN** is on the same level as relational operators, as shown in Table 12.2.

◇ TABLE 12.2
Operator priorities (including set operations)

Priority Level	Operators
1	( )
2	**NOT**
3	*, /, **MOD, DIV, AND**
4	+, −, **OR**
5	<, >, <=, >=, =, <>, **IN**

Operations at each level are performed in order from left to right as they appear in an expression. Thus, the expression

```
80 DIV 20 IN A * B
```

produces

```
80 DIV 20 IN A * B
    ↓
    4     IN A * B
               ↓
    4     IN [5..10]
          ↓
        false
```

EXERCISES 12.2

1. When using sets in Pascal, is >= the logical complement of <=? Give an example to illustrate your answer.
2. Let A and B be sets defined such that A := [0 . . 10] and B := [2,4,6,8,10] are valid. Write a test program to show each of the following.
   a. `A + B = A`
   b. `A * B = B`
   c. `A - B = [0,1,3,5,7,9]`

3. For each of the following sets A and B, find A + B, A * B, A – B, and B – A.
   a. `A := [-3..2,8,10], B := [0..4,7..10]`
   b. `A := [0,1,5..10,20], B := [2,4,6,7..11]`
   c. `A := [], B := [1..15]`
   d. `A := [0..5, 10, 14..20], B := [3,10,15]`
4. Given the following sets

```
A := [0,2,4,6,8,10];
B := [1,3,5,7,9];
C := [0..5];
```

   indicate the values in each of the following sets.
   a. `A * B - C`
   b. `A * (B - C)`
   c. `A * (B + C)`
   d. `A * B + A * C`
   e. `A - B * C`
   f. `A - (B - (A - B))`
   g. `A * (B * C)`
   h. `(A * B) * C`
5. Using sets A, B, and C with values assigned as in Exercise 4, indicate whether each of the following is **true** or **false**.
   a. `A * B = []`
   b. `C <= A + B`
   c. `[5] <= B`
   d. `A + B <> C`
   e. `A - B >= []`
   f. `(A + B = C) OR ([] <= B - C)`
6. In mathematics, when x is an element of set A, this is denoted by $x \in A$. If x is not in set A, we write $x \notin A$. Let B be a set declared by

```
VAR
  B : SET OF 0..10;
```

   Examine the following for validity, and decide how Pascal handles the "not an element of" concept.
   a. `4 NOT IN B`
   b. `4 NOT (IN B)`
   c. `NOT 4 IN B`
   d. `NOT (4 IN B)`
   e. `4 IN NOT B`
   f. `4 IN (NOT B)`
7. Write a short program to count the number of uppercase vowels in a text file. Your program should include the set type

```
TYPE
  AlphaUppercase = SET OF 'A'..'Z';
```

   and the set variable VowelsUppercase declared by

```
VAR
  VowelsUppercase : AlphaUppercase;
```

12.3 Using Sets

Uses of Sets

Now that we know how to declare sets, assign values to sets, and operate with sets, we need to examine some uses of sets in programs. First, however, we should note an important limitation of sets: as with other structured data types, sets cannot be read or written directly. However, the two processes—generating a set and printing the elements of a set—are not difficult to code. To illustrate generating a set, suppose we wish to create a set and have it contain all the characters in the alphabet in a line of

OBJECTIVES

- to understand how sets can be used in a program
- to be able to use sets in a program
- to understand the limitations of using sets with functions
- to be able to use sets with procedures

text. (For this example we assume the text file does not contain lowercase letters.) We can declare this set with

```
TYPE
  AlphaSymbols = 'A'..'Z';
  Symbols = SET OF AlphaSymbols;
VAR
  Alphabet : Symbols;
  SentenceChar : Symbols;
  Ch : char;
```

Code to generate the set SentenceChar is

```
Alphabet := ['A'..'Z'];
SentenceChar := [];
WHILE NOT eoln(Data) DO
  BEGIN
    read (Data, Ch);
    IF Ch IN Alphabet THEN
      SentenceChar := SentenceChar + [Ch]
  END;
```

In many examples, we assume the text file does not contain lowercase letters. As you will see in the Focus on Program Design section at the end of this chapter, a slight modification can be made to accommodate both uppercase and lowercase letters. For example, we can use both uppercase and lowercase letters by changing the set definitions to

```
TYPE
  Symbols = SET OF char;
VAR
  UppercaseAlphabet : Symbols;
  LowercaseAlphabet : Symbols;
  Alphabet: Symbols;
```

Alphabet can then be formed in the program by

```
UppercaseAlphabet := ['A'..'Z'];
LowercaseAlphabet := ['a'..'z'];
Alphabet := UppercaseAlphabet + LowercaseAlphabet;
```

or

```
Alphabet := ['A'..'Z', 'a'..'z']
```

The general procedure for placing values into a set is to initialize the set by assigning the empty set and then to use set union to add elements to the set.

The process of printing values of elements in a set is equally short. Assuming we know the data type of the elements in the set, a loop can be used where the loop control variable ranges over values of this data type. Whenever a value is in the set, it is printed. To illustrate, assume the set SentenceChar contains some alphabetical characters we wish to print. Since we know the data type of the elements in SentenceChar is characters in 'A' . . 'Z', we can print the contained values by

```
FOR Ch := 'A' TO 'Z' DO
  IF Ch IN SentenceChar THEN
    write (Ch:2);
writeln;
```

This fragment of code produces the output

```
A B C D E H I K L M N O P S T U V Y
```

when the set SentenceChar is formed from the line of text

```
THIS LINE (OBVIOUSLY MADE UP!) DOESN'T MAKE MUCH SENSE.
```

Now that you are familiar with how to generate elements in a set and subsequently print the contents of a set, let's examine some uses for sets in programs. Specifically, let's look at using sets to replace complex Boolean expressions, to protect a program against bad data, to protect against the use of invalid **CASE** statements, and to aid in interactive programming.

Suppose we are writing a program to analyze responses to questions on a standard machine-scored form. If we want a certain action to take place for every response of A, B, or C, instead of

```
IF (Response='A') OR (Response='B') OR (Response='C') THEN
```

we can use

```
IF Response IN ['A', 'B', 'C'] THEN
      .
      .
      .
```

To demonstrate protecting a program against bad data, suppose we are writing a program to use a relatively large data file. Further, suppose the data are entered by operators in such a fashion that the first entry on the first line for each customer is a single-digit followed by appropriate data for the customer. To make sure the code is entered properly, we can define a set ValidSym and assign it all of the appropriate symbols. Our program design can be

COMMUNICATION AND STYLE TIPS

Sets with appropriate names are particularly useful when checking data. For example, a typical problem when working with dynamic variables (to be discussed in Chapter 13) is to examine an arithmetic expression for correct form. Thus, 3 + 4 is a valid expression but 3 + * 4 is not. As part of a program that analyzes such expressions, you might choose to define the following sets.

```
TYPE
  ValidDigits = SET OF '0'..'9';
  Symbols = SET OF char;
VAR
  Digits : ValidDigits;
  ValidOperator : Symbols;
  LeftSymbol, RightSymbol : Symbols;
```

These sets can now be assigned values such as

```
Digits := ['0'..'9'];
ValidOperator := ['+', '*', '-', '/'];
LeftSymbol := ['(', '[', '{'];
RightSymbol := [')', ']', '}'];
```

```
read (Data, Sym);
IF Sym IN ValidSym THEN
  BEGIN
    .
    .  (action here)
    .
  END
ELSE
  (error message here)
```

Specifically, a program for printing mailing labels might require a 3, 4, or 5 to indicate the number of lines for the name and address that follow. If we are writing a program that also partially edits the data file, we can have

```
read (Data, NumLines);
IF NumLines IN [3,4,5] THEN
  BEGIN
    .
    .  (process number of lines)
    .
  END
ELSE
  (error message here)
```

The third use of sets is to protect against the use of invalid **CASE** statements. To illustrate, suppose we are working with a program that uses a **CASE** statement and the selector is a letter grade assigned to students. Without sets, the statement is

```
CASE LetGrade OF
  'A' : ...
  'B' : ...
  'C' : ...
  'D' : ...
  'E' : ...
END;  {  of CASE LetGrade  }
```

To protect against the possibility of assigning a value to LetGrade that is not in the **CASE** selector list, sets can be used as follows:

```
IF LetGrade IN ['A'..'E'] THEN
  CASE LetGrade OF
    'A' : ...
    'B' : ...
    'C' : ...
    'D' : ...
    'E' : ...
  END  {  of CASE LetGrade  }
ELSE
  (error message here)
```

A fourth use of sets is as an aid in writing interactive programs. Frequently a user will be asked to respond by pressing a certain key or keys. For example, the following message may be given.

```
Do you wish to continue?
<Y> or <N> and press <Enter>.
```

In such cases, two problems can occur. First, the user may use uppercase or lowercase letters for a correct response. Second, the user may inadvertently strike the wrong key.

A NOTE OF INTEREST

Object-Oriented Programming—Part 2

Object-oriented development is becoming increasingly important as a method to manage large and complex software systems. Object-oriented concepts are natural extensions of proper structured programming. If structured programming principles have been emphasized, the basic object-oriented idea of encapsulation logically follows.

Components of object-oriented programs are

Object. The object in object-oriented programming includes the basic data or data structure and the related procedures and functions required to keep the object complete. This makes the object like an abstract data type.

Method. A method is a procedure or function that becomes part of the object. It provides the abstraction to the object's data.

Encapsulation. The combining of data structure and methods is called encapsulation. If encapsulation is performed correctly, the user of the object should never need to access the data of the object directly. Procedure and function headers are added to type definitions to describe encapsulation of the methods. The type definitions become the interface to the unit.

The idea of a data structure being linked to its procedures has been standard practice in creating abstract data types for years and is not a new concept created by object-oriented languages. What *is* new and exciting is what can now be done with the object. Other objects can inherit those same procedures and functions, and those same procedures and functions can easily be altered, if the need arises, without having to rewrite the whole unit. In fact, in order to create new objects, the programmer only needs to use the unit to create new methods and data items or to rename the existing methods.

To make this part of the program correct and guard against bad data, we can have a set declared and initialized as

```
GoodResponse := ['Y', 'y', 'N', 'n'];
```

and then use a **REPEAT . . . UNTIL** loop as follows:

```
REPEAT
  writeln ('Do you wish to continue?');
  writeln ('<Y> or <N> and press <Enter>.');
  readln (Response)
UNTIL Response IN GoodResponse;
```

We can then use a **boolean** variable Continue by first assigning it the value **false** and then following the **REPEAT . . . UNTIL** loop with

```
Continue := Response IN ['Y', 'y'];
```

Sets with Functions

Sets can be used with subprograms. In general, set types can be used as parameters in much the same way arrays, records, and files are used. However, when working with functions, sets cannot be returned as values of a function because functions cannot return structured data types.

To illustrate using sets with functions, let's consider two examples.

EXAMPLE 12.1

Let's write a function to determine the cardinality (size or number of elements) of a set. Assuming appropriate **TYPE** definitions, such a function can be

```
FUNCTION Cardinality (S : <set type>) : integer;
  VAR
    Count : integer;
    X : <base type for set>;
  BEGIN
    Count := 0;
```

```
    FOR X := <initial value> TO <final value> DO
      IF X IN S THEN
        Count := Count + 1;
    Cardinality := Count
  END;
```

initial value . . . final value

If given X in set S, increase cardinality counter

Ⓢ

This function is called from the main program by

```
SetSize := Cardinality(<set name>);
```

EXAMPLE 12.2

In our second example, let's consider a function to find the maximum (largest ordinal) element of a set. This function is typically applied to a set that contains elements in some subrange of the integers, but you can easily modify the function by considering the ordinals of set elements.

```
FUNCTION MaxElement (S : <set type>) : <base type>;
  VAR
    Temp : <base type>;
    X : <base type>;
  BEGIN
    IF S = [] THEN
      BEGIN
        writeln ('You are working with an empty set!':40);
        MaxElement := <initial value>
      END  {  of IF...THEN option  }
    ELSE
      BEGIN
        Temp := <initial value>;
        FOR X := <initial value> TO <final value> DO
          IF (X IN S) AND (X > Temp) THEN
            Temp := X;
        MaxElement := Temp
      END  {  of ELSE option  }
  END;  {  of FUNCTION MaxElement  }
```

initial value . . . final value

Any new value of X which is also in S causes Temp to be adjusted

Ⓢ

This function is called from the main program by

```
Largest := MaxElement(<set name>);
```

Sets with Procedures

Recall sets cannot be returned as values of a function. However, when a program requires a set to be returned from a subprogram, the set can be used as a variable parameter with a procedure. In this manner, sets can be either generated or modified with subprograms. The Focus on Program Design section at the end of this chapter illustrates such a use.

EXERCISES 12.3

1. Modify the function MaxElement used in Example 12.2 to find the character in a line of text that is latest in the alphabet. Use this function with the Focus on Program Design code presented at the end of this chapter.
2. Write a test program to create a set that contains all the consonants from a line of text. Your program should also print all elements in the set.
3. Write a short program to reproduce a text file in which every vowel is replaced by an asterisk.
4. Modify the code used to find all the alphabet characters in a line of text so a complete text file rather than just one line can be analyzed.
5. Write a program to simulate the arithmetic operations indicated in a text file. Arithmetic expressions should always be of the form digit-symbol-digit (9 + 8), where all digits and symbols are given as data of type **char**. Your program should protect against bad operation symbols, bad digits (actually, nondigits), and division by zero.
6. To illustrate how sets can be used to protect against invalid values for **CASE** selectors, write a short program that uses a **CASE** statement. Run it with an invalid **CASE** selector value. Change the program so the **CASE** statement is protected by using a set. Rerun the program with the same invalid selector.
7. Write a Boolean function to analyze an integer between -9999 and 9999 that returns the value **true** if the integer contains only odd digits (1731) and the value **false** otherwise.
8. Write a function that returns the length of a string passed to the function as a packed array. Punctuation marks and internal blanks should add to the string length. Blanks at the beginning or end should not add to the length of the string.

FOCUS ON PROGRAM DESIGN

This sample program illustrates the use of a set as a variable parameter in a procedure. The specific problem is to write a program to determine the alphabetical characters used in a line of text. Output from the program is an echo print of the text line, a list of letters in the text, and the number of distinct letters used in the line.

A first-level pseudocode development for this problem is

1. Get the characters
2. Print distinct characters
3. Determine the cardinality of the set
4. Print a closing message

A structure chart for this program is given in Figure 12.1.

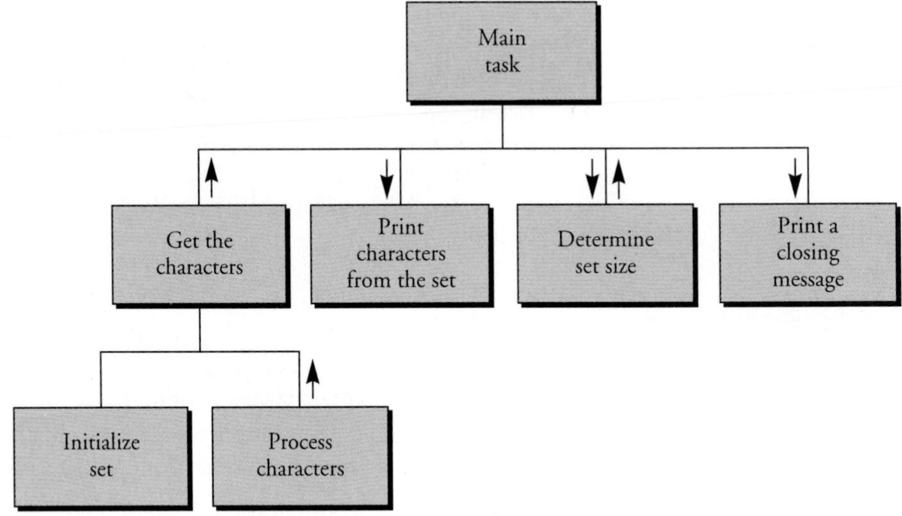

◆ FIGURE 12.1
Structure chart for **PROGRAM** SymbolCheck

Module specifications for the main modules are

1. GetLetters Module
   Data received: None
   Information returned: A set of letters from a sentence
   Logic: Initialize the set.
   Add (union) distinct letters from a line of text.
2. PrintSet Module
   Data received: A set of letters
   Information returned: None
   Logic: Use a **FOR** loop to scan the alphabet and print the distinct letters contained in the set.
3. Cardinality Module
   Data received: A set of letters
   Information returned: The cardinality of the set
   Logic: Use a function to count the number of distinct elements in a set.
4. PrintMessage Module
   Data received: Cardinality of the set
   Information returned: None
   Logic: Print a message indicating the set size.

A refinement of the pseudocode produces

```
1. Get the characters
   1.1 initialize set
   1.2 WHILE NOT eoln DO
       1.2.1 process a character
2. Print distinct characters
   2.1 FOR Ch := 'A' TO 'z' DO
         IF Ch is in the set THEN
           print Ch
```

3. Determine the cardinality of the set
   3.1 initialize counter to zero
   3.2 **FOR** Ch := 'A' **TO** 'z' **DO**
         IF Ch is in the set **THEN**
            increment counter
   3.3 assign count to function name
4. Print a closing message

Step 1.2.1 can be refined to

1.2.1 process a character
   1.2.1.1 read a character
   1.2.1.2 write a character (echo print)
   1.2.1.3 **IF** character is in the alphabet **THEN**
         add it to the set of characters

The main program is

```
BEGIN  {  Main program  }
  reset (Data);
  GetLetters (SentenceChar);
  PrintSet (SentenceChar);
  SetSize := Cardinality(SentenceChar);
  PrintMessage (SetSize)
END.  {  of main program  }
```

A complete program for this problem follows.

```
PROGRAM SymbolCheck (input, output, Data);

{  This program illustrates working with sets.  It reads a line  }
{  of text and determines the number of distinct letters in      }
{  that line.  Output includes the distinct letters and the set  }
{  cardinality.  Information for this program is stored in the  }
{  text file Data.                                               }

CONST
  Skip = ' ';

TYPE
  AlphaSymbols = SET OF char;

VAR
  SentenceChar : AlphaSymbols;       {  Set of possible letters  }
  SetSize : integer;                 {  Cardinality of the set   }
  Data : text;                       {  Data file                }

{*****************************************************************}

PROCEDURE GetLetters (VAR SentenceChar : AlphaSymbols);

  {  Given:    Nothing                                            }
  {  Task:     Read characters from the text file Data; echo      }
  {                print them; store the alphabetical characters  }
  {                in a set                                       }
  {  Return:   The set of letters contained in the line of text   }
```

```
  VAR
    Ch : char;
    Alphabet : AlphaSymbols;
  BEGIN
    SentenceChar := [];
    Alphabet := ['A'..'Z'] + ['a'..'z'];                            1
    writeln (Skip:10, 'The line of text is below:');
    writeln; write (Skip:10);
    WHILE NOT eoln(Data) DO
      BEGIN
        read (Data, Ch);
        write (Ch);                                  {  Echo print  }
        IF Ch IN Alphabet THEN
          SentenceChar := SentenceChar + [Ch]
      END;  {  of WHILE NOT eoln  }                 {  of one line  }
    writeln
  END;  {  of PROCEDURE GetLetters  }

{**************************************************************}

PROCEDURE PrintSet (SentenceChar : AlphaSymbols);

  {  Given:   A set of characters                                  }
  {  Task:    Print all characters in the set                      }
  {  Return:  Nothing                                              }

  VAR
    Ch : char;
  BEGIN                                                             2
    writeln;
    writeln (Skip:10, 'The letters in this line are:');
    writeln; write (Skip:10);
    FOR Ch := 'A' TO 'z' DO
      IF Ch IN SentenceChar THEN
        write (Ch:2);
    writeln
  END;  {  of PROCEDURE PrintSet  }

{**************************************************************}

FUNCTION Cardinality (SentenceChar : AlphaSymbols) : integer;

  {  Given:   A set of characters                                  }
  {  Task:    Determine the number of characters in the set        }
  {  Return:  The set size (cardinality)                           }

  VAR
    Count : integer
    X : char;                                                       3
```

```
  BEGIN
    Count := 0;
    FOR X := 'A' TO 'z' DO
      IF X IN SentenceChar THEN
        Count := Count + 1;
    Cardinality := Count
  END;  {  of FUNCTION Cardinality  }

{*****************************************************************}

PROCEDURE PrintMessage (SetSize : integer);

  {  Given:   The cardinality of the set                           }
  {  Task:    Print a closing message                              }
  {  Return:  Nothing                                              }    4

  BEGIN
    writeln; write (Skip:10);
    writeln ('There are', SetSize:5, ' letters in this sentence.')
  END;  {  of PROCEDURE PrintMessage  }

{*****************************************************************}

BEGIN  {  Main Program  }
  reset (Data);
  GetLetters (SentenceChar);
  PrintSet (SentenceChar);
  SetSize := Cardinality(SentenceChar);
  PrintMessage (SetSize)
END.  {  of main program  }
```

When this program is run on the line of text

```
The numbers -2, 5, 20 and symbols '?', ':' should be ignored.
```

the output is

```
The line of text is below:

The numbers -2, 5, 20 and symbols '?', ':' should be ignored.

The letters in this line are:

 T a b d e g h i l m n o r s u y

There are   16 letters in this sentence.
```

RUNNING AND DEBUGGING HINTS

1. When defining a set type, do not use brackets in the definition. Thus, the definition

```
TYPE
  Alphabet = SET OF ['A'..'Z'];
```

is incorrect. The correct form is

```
TYPE
  Alphabet = SET OF 'A'..'Z';
```

2. Remember to initialize a set before using it in a program. Declaring a set does not give it a value. If your declaration is

```
VAR
  Vowels : Alphabet;
```

the program should contain

```
Vowels := ['A', 'E', 'I', 'O', 'U'];
```

3. Attempting to add an element to a set rather than a set to a set is a common error. If you wish to add 'D' to the set ['A', 'B', 'C'], you should write

```
['A', 'B', 'C'] + ['D']
```

rather than

```
['A', 'B', 'C'] + 'D'
```

This is a particular problem when the value of a variable is to be added to a set. For example

```
['A', 'B', 'C'] + Ch;
```

should be

```
['A', 'B', 'C'] + [Ch];
```

4. Avoid confusing arrays and array notation with sets and set notation.
5. Remember certain operators (+, −, and *) have different meanings when used with sets.

SUMMARY

Key Terms

difference
element of a set
empty (null) set
intersection
set
subset
union
universal set

Keywords

IN
SET

Key Concepts

◆ In Pascal, a **SET** is a structured data type that consists of distinct elements from an indicated base type; sets can be declared by

```
TYPE
  Alphabet = SET OF char;
VAR
  Vowels : Alphabet;
  GoodResponse : Alphabet;
```

In this definition and declaration, Alphabet is a **SET** type and Vowels and GoodResponse are set variables.

- Values must be assigned to a set; for example

```
Vowels := ['A', 'E', 'I', 'O', 'U'];
GoodResponse := ['Y', 'y', 'N', 'n'];
```

- When listing elements in a set, order makes no difference and each element may be listed only once.
- Standard set operations in Pascal are defined to be consistent with set operations in mathematics; to illustrate, if

```
A := [1,2,3,4];
```

and

```
B := [3,4,5];
```

the union, intersection, and difference of these sets are as follows:

Term	Expression	Value
Union	`A + B`	`[1..5]`
Intersection	`A * B`	`[3,4]`
Difference	`A - B`	`[1,2]`
	`B - A`	`[5]`

- Set membership is denoted by using the reserved word **IN**. Such an expression returns a Boolean value, as shown for

```
A := [1,2,3,4];
```

Expression	Value
`2 IN A`	**true**
`6 IN A`	**false**

- The relational operators (<=, >=, <>, and =) can be used with sets to form Boolean expressions and return values consistent with expected subset and set equality relationships. This is illustrated for

```
A := [1,2,3];
B := [0..5];
C := [2,4];
```

Expression	Value
`A <= B`	**true**
`B <= C`	**false**
`B >= C`	**true**
`A = B`	**false**
`B <> C`	**true**

- Priority levels for set operations are consistent with priorities for arithmetic expressions; they are

Priority Level	Operation
1	( )
2	**NOT**
3	*, /, **MOD, DIV, AND**
4	+, −, **OR**
5	<, >, <=, >=, <>, =, **IN**

- Sets cannot be used with **read** or **write**; however, a set can be generated by initializing the set, assigning the empty set, and using set union to add elements to the set. For example, a set of characters in a text line can be generated by

```
S := [];
WHILE NOT eoln(Data) DO
  BEGIN
    read (Data, Ch);
    S := S + [Ch]
  END;
```

This set can be printed by using

```
FOR Ch := <initial value> TO <final value> DO
  IF Ch IN S THEN
    write (Ch:2);
```

- Four uses for sets in programs are to replace complex Boolean expressions, to protect a program (or segment) from bad data, to protect against the use of invalid **CASE** statements, and to aid in interactive programming.
- Sets can be used as parameters with subprograms.
- Sets cannot be returned as values of a function.
- Sets can be generated or modified through subprograms by using variable parameters with procedures.

PROGRAMMING PROBLEMS AND PROJECTS

Each of the following programming problems can be solved with a program using sets. Hints are provided to indicate some of the uses; you may, of course, find others.

1. Write a program to be used to simulate a medical diagnosis. Assume the symptoms are coded as follows:

Symptom	Code
Headache	1
Fever	2
Sore throat	3
Cough	4
Sneeze	5
Stomach pain	6
Heart pain	7
Muscle pain	8
Nausea	9
Back pain	10
Exhaustion	11
Jaundice	12
High blood pressure	13

Further assume each of the following diseases is characterized by the symptoms indicated here.

Disease	Symptoms
Cold	1,2,3,4,5
Flu	1,2,6,8,9
Migraine	1,9
Mononucleosis	2,3,11,12
Ulcer	6,9
Arteriosclerosis	7,10,11,13
Appendicitis	2,6

Your program should accept as input a person's name and symptoms (coded) and provide a preliminary diagnosis. Sets can be used for the following.

a. Bad data check

b. Symptoms = 1 . . 13;
Disease = **SET OF** Symptoms;

c. Cold, Flu, Migraine, Mononucleosis, Ulcer, Arteriosclerosis, Appendicitis : Disease;

2. Write a program to serve as a simple text analyzer. Input is any text file. Output should be three histograms: one each for vowel frequency, consonant frequency, and other symbol frequency. Your program should use a set for vowels, a set for consonants, and a set for other symbols.

3. Write an interactive program that allows the user to enter a date in numeric form (4 14 76) and then writes out the corresponding month, date, and year. For example, the input of 4 14 76 would produce output of

```
April fourteen, nineteen seventy-six
```

The program should work for any date during the twentieth century. Error messages should be printed for incorrect input. Thus, 4 31 76 should generate an error message because April has only 30 days. Also, 2 29 93 should produce an error because 1993 was not a leap year.

4. Write a program to serve as a simple compiler for a Pascal program. Your compiler should work on a program that uses only single-letter identifiers. Your compiler should create a set of identifiers and make sure identifiers are not declared twice, all identifiers on the left of an assignment are declared, and no type mismatch errors occur. For the purposes of your compiler program, assume the following.

(1) Variables are declared between **VAR** and **BEGIN**; for example

```
VAR
  X, Y : real;
  A, B, C : integer;
  M : char;
BEGIN
```

(2) Each program line is a complete Pascal statement.

(3) The only assignments are of the form X := Y.

Output should include the program line number and an appropriate error message for each error. Run your compiler with several short Pascal programs as text files. Compare your error list with the one given in Appendix 5.

5. A number in exponential notation preceded by a plus or minus sign may have the form

sign	positive integer	decimal	positive integer	E	sign	exponent (three digits)
⎿⏌	⎿___⏌	.	⎿___⏌		⎿⏌	⎿___⏌

For example, –45.302E+002 is the number –4530.2. If the number is in standard form, it will have exactly one digit on the left side of the decimal (–4.5302E+003).

Write a program to read numbers in exponential form from a text file, one number per line. Your program should check to see if each number is in proper form. For numbers that are in proper form, print out the number as given and the number in standard form.

6. Write a program to analyze a text file for words of differing lengths. Your program should keep a list of all words of lengths 1, 2, . . . , 10. It should also count the number of words with lengths exceeding 10.

A word ends when one alphabetical character is followed by a character not in the alphabet or when an end-of-line marker is reached. All words start with letters (7UP is not a word). Your output should be an alphabetized list for each word length. It should also include the number of words with lengths exceeding 10 characters. An apostrophe does not add to the length of a word.

7. The Falcon Manufacturing Company (Problem 23, Chapter 8; Problem 17, Chapter 9; Problems 12–16, Chapter 10) wants you to develop a computerized system that determines if customers are approved for credit. A customer number should be entered from the keyboard, and the program should print the credit limit for the customer if credit has been approved and "No credit" if it has not. Each line of a text file contains a customer number and credit limit. Valid customer numbers range from 100 to 999; credit limits are \$100, \$300, \$500, \$1000, and unlimited credit.

8. Write a program in which you read a text file and print out the number of times a character in the file matches a character in your name.

9. The Court Survey Corporation wishes to conduct a poll by sending questionnaires to men and women between 25 and 30 years of age who live in your state or any state adjacent to it. A text file containing names, street addresses, cities, states, zip codes, and ages is to be read. The program should print the names and addresses of those persons who match the criteria.

10. Write a program to test your ESP and that of a friend. Each of you should secretly enter 10 integers between 1 and 100. The program should check each list and print the values in both lists and the number of values in both lists.

11. Modify the Wellsville Wholesale Company commission problem (Problem 22, Chapter 7) to define the sales ranges as sets. Use these sets to verify input and determine the proper commission rate.

12. The Ohio Programmers' Association offices are in a large building with five wings lettered A through E. The office numbers in the wings are as follows:

Wing	Rooms
A	100–150 and 281–300
B	151–190 and 205–220
C	10–50 and 191–204
D	1–9 and 51–99
E	221–280 and 301–319

Write a program that enables the receptionist, Miss Lovelace, to enter an office number from the keyboard and then have the computer print the wing in which the office is located.

COMMUNICATION IN PRACTICE

1. Select a program from the Programming Problems and Projects section in this chapter that you have not yet worked. Construct a structure chart and write all documentary information for this program. Include variable definition, subprogram definition, required input, and required output. When you are finished, have a classmate read your documentation to see if it is clear precisely what is to be done.
2. Remove all documentation from a program you have written for this chapter. Exchange this modified version with another student who has done the same thing. Write documentation for the exchanged program. Compare your documentation with that originally written for the program. Discuss the differences and similarities with the other students in your class.
3. Not all programming languages include sets as a data structure. Examine several other languages to determine what data structures they include. Prepare a chart that compares and contrasts the data structures of Pascal (arrays, records, files, and sets) with the data structures of other languages. Give an oral presentation of your results to the class.

CHAPTER 13

Dynamic Variables and Data Structures

CHAPTER OUTLINE

Material in the previous chapters has focused almost exclusively on *static variables,* which have the following characteristics.

1. The size of a static variable (array length, for example) is fixed at compilation time.
2. A certain amount of memory is reserved for each static variable, and this memory is retained for the declared variables as long as the program or subprogram in which the variable is defined is active.
3. Static variables are declared in a variable declaration section.
4. The structure or existence of a static variable cannot be changed during a run of the program. (Two exceptions are the length of a file and records with variant parts.)

A disadvantage of using only static variables and data structures is that the number of variables needed in a program must be predetermined. Thus, if we are working with an array and we anticipate the need for 1000 locations, we would define

```
<name> = ARRAY [1..1000] OF <base type>
```

This creates two problems. We may overestimate the length of the array and use only part of it, thereby wasting memory. Or we may underestimate the necessary array length and be unable to process all the data until the program is modified.

Fortunately, Pascal solves these problems with the use of *dynamic variables.* Some of their characteristics follow.

1. Dynamic variable types are defined in the **TYPE** section.
2. Memory for dynamic variables is created as needed and returned when not needed during the execution of a program. Therefore, unneeded memory is not wasted and the programmer is limited only by the available memory.
3. A new (and significant) technique must be developed to form a list of dynamic variables; these lists are referred to as *dynamic structures.*

4. In some instances, working with dynamic structures can be a slower process than working with static structures; in particular, direct access of an array element has no analogue.
5. A significantly different method of accessing values stored in dynamic variables must be developed because memory locations are not predetermined.

Speed of execution also changes considerably when dynamic variables and data structures are used in a program. It takes much less time to manipulate dynamic variables than static variables. For long programs and large data bases, this savings of time becomes a significant issue.

A complete development of dynamic variables and data structures is left to other courses in computer science. However, when you have finished this chapter, you should have a reasonable understanding of dynamic variables and data structures and be able to use them in a program. Here, we will carefully develop one type of dynamic data structure (the linked list) and then introduce three others—the stack, queue, and binary tree.

You may find this material somewhat difficult. If so, do not get discouraged. Two reasons for the increased level of difficulty are that some of the work is not intuitive and that the level of abstraction is different from that of previous material. Therefore, as you work through this chapter, you are encouraged to draw several diagrams and write several short programs to help you understand concepts. You also may need to reread the chapter or particular sections to grasp the mechanics of working with dynamic variables.

13.1 Pointer Variables

OBJECTIVES

- to understand the difference between the address of a memory location and the value of a memory location
- to be able to define a pointer type
- to understand how a pointer variable is used to access a memory location
- to be able to use a pointer variable to manipulate data in a dynamic variable
- to be able to create and destroy dynamic variables during the execution of a program
- to understand the difference between a pointer variable and the dynamic variable to which it refers
- to be able to use **NIL** with pointer variables

Computer Memory

Computer memory can be envisioned as a sequence of memory locations, as shown in Figure 13.1(a). A memory location is an area where a value can be stored. When a variable is declared in the variable declaration section of a program, a memory location is reserved during execution of that program block. This memory location can be accessed by a reference to the variable name, and only data of the declared type can be stored there. Thus, if the declaration section is

```
VAR
  Sum : integer;
```

we can envision the memory location as shown in Figure 13.1(b). If the assignment

```
Sum := 56;
```

is made, we have the arrangement shown in Figure 13.1(c).

Each memory location has an *address.* This is an integer value that the computer must use as a reference to the memory location. When static variables such as Sum are used, the address of a memory location is used indirectly by the underlying machine instruction. However, when dynamic variables are used, the address is used directly as a reference or pointer to the memory location.

The *value* that is the address of a memory location must be stored somewhere in memory. In Pascal, the value is stored in a *pointer variable* (frequently denoted as Ptr), which is a variable of a predefined type that is used to contain the address of a memory location. To illustrate, assume Ptr is declared as a pointer variable. If 56 is stored in a memory location with the address 11640, we can envision it as shown in Figure 13.1(d).

◆ FIGURE 13.1(a)
Computer Memory

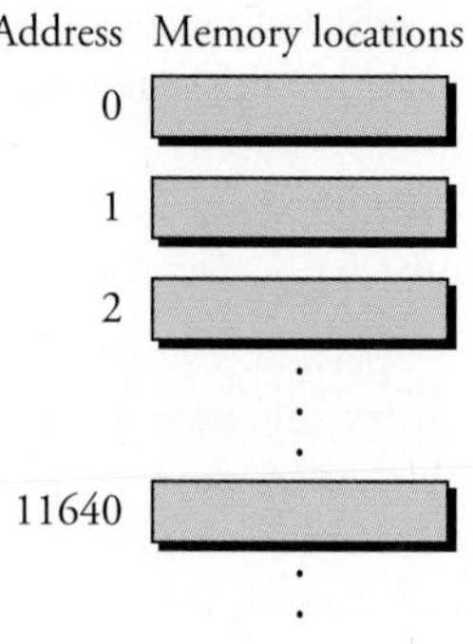

◆ FIGURE 13.1(b)
Variable location in memory

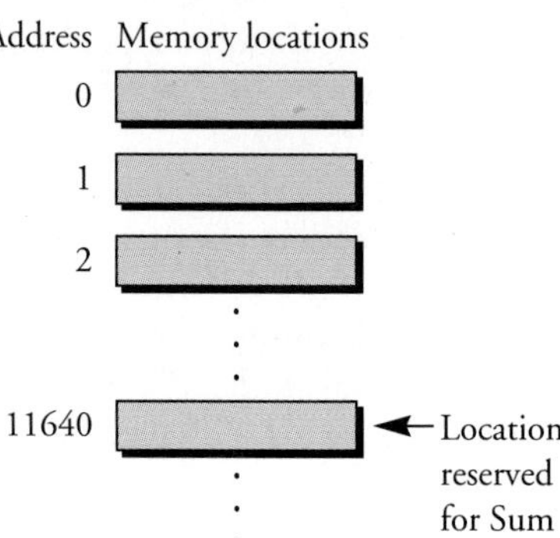

◆ FIGURE 13.1(c)
Value in variable Sum

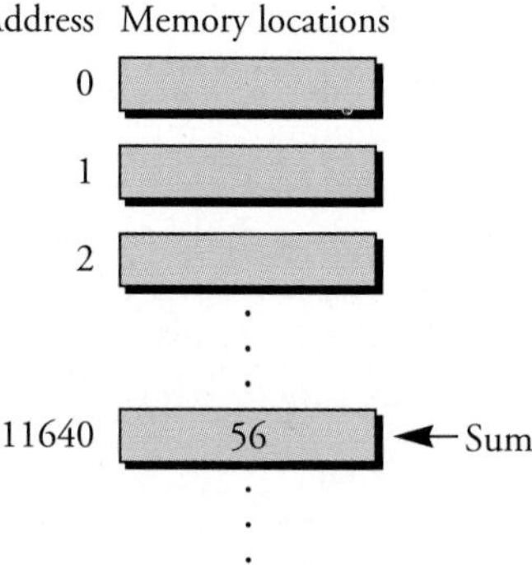

◆ FIGURE 13.1(d)
Relationship between a pointer variable and memory location

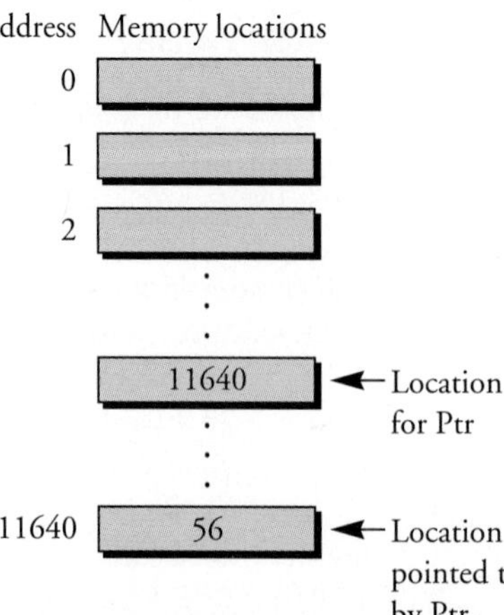

Working with Pointer Variables and Dynamic Variables

T Pointer variables are declared by using a caret (^) or an up arrow (↑) in front of the type name. Thus

```
TYPE
  Ages = 0..120;
  PointerToAges = ^Ages;
VAR
  Ptr : PointerToAges;
```

declares Ptr as a pointer variable. Ptr cannot be assigned values of type Ages; Ptr can only contain addresses of locations with values of type Ages.

Once this declaration has been made, a dynamic variable can be created. A dynamic variable, designated as Ptr^, is a variable accessed by a pointer variable. A dynamic variable is not declared in the declaration section of a program. Using the standard procedure **new** with a pointer variable

```
new (Ptr);  { This initializes a value for Ptr }
```

creates the dynamic variable Ptr^. This can be illustrated by

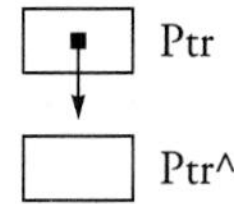

The pointer variable followed by a caret (or an up arrow) is always the identifier for a dynamic variable. We usually read Ptr^ as the object (variable) pointed to by Ptr.

To illustrate the relationship between pointer variables and dynamic variables, we have the previous declaration and the code

```
new (Ptr);
Ptr^ := 56;
```

This stage can be envisioned as

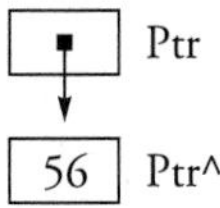

where Ptr contains the address of Ptr^.

Dynamic variables can be destroyed by using the standard procedure **dispose.** Thus, if we no longer need the value of a dynamic variable Ptr^

```
dispose (Ptr);
```

causes the pointer variable Ptr to no longer contain the address for Ptr^. In this sense, Ptr^ does not exist because nothing is pointing to it. This location has been returned to the computer for subsequent use.

Since pointer variables contain only addresses of memory locations, they have limited use in a program. Pointer variables of the same type can be used only for assignments and comparisons for equality. They cannot be used with **read, write,** or any arithmetic operation. To illustrate, assume we have the definition and declaration

```
TYPE
  Ages = 0..120;
VAR
  Ptr1, Ptr2 : ^Ages;
```

Then

```
new (Ptr1);
new (Ptr2);
```

create the dynamic variables Ptr1^ and Ptr2^, respectively. If the assignments

```
Ptr1^ := 50;
Ptr2^ := 21;
```

are made, we can envision this as

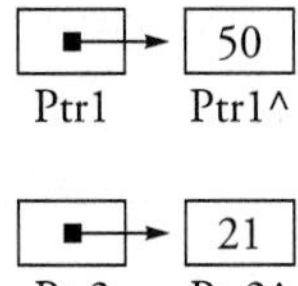

The expression Ptr1 = Ptr2 is then **false** and Ptr1 <> Ptr2 is **true.** If the assignment

```
Ptr1 := Ptr2;
```

is made, we can envision

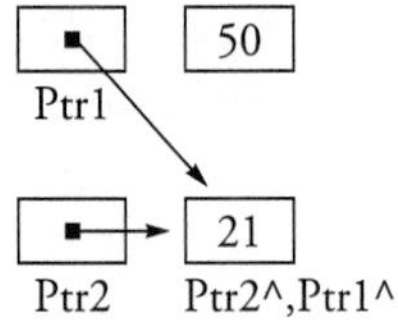

Then Ptr1 = Ptr2 is **true** and Ptr1 <> Ptr2 is **false.**

Note that in this last illustration, 50 no longer has anything pointing to it. Thus, there is now no way to access this value. Since we did not use **dispose,** the location has not been returned to the computer for subsequent reuse. Be careful to use **dispose** when necessary, or you could eventually run out of memory.

Dynamic variables can be used in any context used by static variables of the same type. To illustrate, assume the previous declarations for Ptr1 and Ptr2. If appropriate values (50 and 21) are in a data file, the segment

```
new (Ptr1);
new (Ptr2);
read (Ptr1^, Ptr2^);
writeln ('The average of', Ptr1^:5, ' and', Ptr2^:5,
         ' is', (Ptr1^ + Ptr2^) / 2:6:2);
```

produces

```
The average of   50 and   21 is 35.50
```

COMMUNICATION AND STYLE TIPS

Ptr or some identifier containing Ptr (for example, DataPtr) is frequently used when declaring pointer variables. This reinforces the difference between working with a pointer variable (Ptr) and working with a dynamic variable (Ptr^).

A NOTE OF INTEREST

When Will Object Technology Meet Its Potential?

Rebecca Wirfs-Brock, Director of Object Technology Services at Digitalk, addressed the issue of the potential of object technology in a guest editorial in a recent publication of the Journal of Object-Oriented Programming. *A summary of her comments follows.*

When will it be so easy to use objects that other competing technologies won't even be considered? Can we have a future in which objects nicely coexist with more traditional software? These questions are on the minds of industry watchers, application developers, and object technology suppliers alike. Sure, people really are starting to use objects. It isn't as controversial to start an object-oriented project as it used to be. Objects have come out of the research labs and are being used on management information systems (MIS) and engineering projects. For some, the rich development and prototyping environment alone is sufficient for them to switch. For others, touted benefits come with too high a risk factor and retraining cost. These people are waiting until enormous gains are well established and guaranteed.

I'm delighted that people are delivering software written in Smalltalk, C++, Eiffel, and CLOS. Proponents of object technology say it is easy to use. But developing applications with objects isn't a routine procedure just yet. It needs to get simpler.

Reusing software and constructing applications from standard components are great ideas. However, there are some fundamental hurdles that need to be cleared before we can efficiently build software this way.

Object-oriented application construction has many different dimensions that don't directly map to the ways engineers develop hardware. To achieve that next higher level of software productivity, we need to address the following needs.

- We need components that are easy to mix and match (for example, classes and subsystems of cooperating classes). These components should be supplied by different vendors and written in different languages with application-specific components.
- We must be able to use components in a variety of different contexts. Vendors need to supply us with components that work across different platforms.
- We need well-documented, standardized component libraries, subsystems, and architectural frameworks for building applications. We need to be able to construct simple applications largely by assembling them from components found in preexisting catalogs.
- For more complex applications, we need to construct applications out of subsystems, frameworks, and components organized and described in ways that are understandable without resorting to reading code. We need to be able to easily grasp accepted patterns for connecting these components.
- Finally, we need to enhance our ability to develop applications by refining existing components. Programming by refinement is an extremely powerful metaphor. It shouldn't be dropped when we adopt the mentality of construction from preexisting components. Refinement is what enables developers to add application-specific functionality while reusing most of an existing design.

Defining and Declaring Pointer Variables

The previous definition and declarations of pointer types and pointer variables are relatively uncomplicated. However, in actual practice, pointer types and variables are a bit more complex. In the next section, for example, we will work with a dynamic variable as a record type where one of the fields in the record type is a pointer of the same type. Thus, we can have

```
TYPE
  NameString = PACKED ARRAY [1..20] OF char;
  DataPtr = ^StudentInfo;
  StudentInfo = RECORD
                  Name: NameString;
                  Next : DataPtr
                END;  {  of RECORD StudentInfo  }
VAR
  Student : DataPtr;
```

Notice DataPtr makes a reference to StudentInfo before StudentInfo is defined. StudentInfo then contains a field of type DataPtr. This instance is an exception to the rule in Pascal that an identifier cannot be used before it is defined. Specifically, the following exception is permitted: pointer type definitions can precede definitions of their reference types. The reverse is not true; a structure cannot contain a field or component of a pointer type that has not yet been defined. We frequently want each record to point to another record. Using a record definition with one field for a pointer permits this.

Another note about working with pointers should be mentioned here. The reserved word **NIL,** which has the value of the null pointer that does not point to anything, can be assigned to a pointer variable. Thus, we can have

```
new (Student);
Student^.Next := NIL;
```

This allows pointer variables to be used in Boolean expressions and is needed in later work. For example, if we are forming a list of dynamic variables and each dynamic variable contains a pointer variable for pointing to the next dynamic variable, we can use **NIL** to know when we are at the end of a list. This idea and the concept of pointer type definitions are fully developed in the next section.

EXERCISES 13.1

1. Discuss the differences between static variables and dynamic variables.
2. Write a test program to declare a single pointer variable with an associated dynamic variable that can have values in the subrange 0 . . 50, and then do the following.
   a. Create a dynamic variable, assign the value 25 to it, and print the value.
   b. Create another dynamic variable, assign the value 40 to it, and print the value.

   At this stage of your program, where is the value 25 stored?
3. Illustrate the relationship between the pointer variables and dynamic variables produced by

```
TYPE
  Ptr = (Red, Yellow, Blue, Green);
VAR
  Ptr1, Ptr2 : ^Ptr;
BEGIN
  new (Ptr1);
  new (Ptr2);
  Ptr1^ := Blue;
  Ptr2^ := Red
END.
```

4. Assume the **TYPE** and **VAR** sections given in Exercise 3. Find all errors in the following.

   a.
   ```
   new (Ptr1^);
   ```
   b.
   ```
   new (Ptr2);
   Ptr2 := Yellow;
   ```
   c.
   ```
   new (Ptr1);
   new (Ptr2);
   Ptr1^ := Red;
   Ptr2^ := Ptr1^;
   ```
   d.
   ```
   new (Ptr1);
   new (Ptr2);
   Ptr1^ := Red;
   Ptr1^ := Ptr2^;
   ```
   e.
   ```
   new (Ptr1);
   new (Ptr2);
   Ptr1^ := Red;
   Ptr2^ := Ptr1;
   ```

5. Assume pointer variables are declared in the variable declaration section as

```
VAR
  RealPtr1, RealPtr2 : ^real;
  IntPtr1, IntPtr2 : ^integer;
  BoolPtr1, BoolPtr2 : ^boolean;
```

Indicate if the following are valid or invalid references. Give an explanation for each invalid reference.

a. `IntPtr1 := IntPtr1 + 1;`

b. `writeln (RealPtr2:30:2);`

c. `writeln (BoolPtr1^:15, IntPtr1^:15, RealPtr1^:15:2);`

d.
```
IF IntPtr1 < IntPtr2 THEN
  writeln ('All done');
```

e.
```
IF BoolPtr NOT NIL THEN
  new (BoolPtr2);
```

f.
```
IF RealPtr1 <> RealPtr2 THEN
  writeln (RealPtr1^:15:2, RealPtr2^:15:2);
```

g.
```
IF BoolPtr2 THEN
  new (BoolPtr1);
```

h.
```
IF BoolPtr2^ THEN
  new (BoolPtr1);
```

6. Assume the declarations given in Exercise 5. What output is produced by the following fragment of code?

```
new (IntPtr1);
new (IntPtr2);
new (RealPtr1);
new (BoolPtr1);
IntPtr1^ := 95;
IntPtr2^ := 55;
RealPtr1^ := (IntPtr1^ + IntPtr2^) / 2;
BoolPtr1^ := true;
WHILE BoolPtr1^ DO
  BEGIN
    writeln (RealPtr1^:20:2);
    RealPtr1^ := RealPtr1^ - 5;
    IF RealPtr1^ < 0 THEN
      BoolPtr1^ := false
  END;
```

13.2 Linked Lists

OBJECTIVES

- to understand why a linked list is a dynamic data structure
- to be able to create a linked list
- to understand how pointers are used to form a linked list
- to be able to print data from a linked list

A *linked list* can be implemented as a dynamic data structure and can be thought of as a list of data items where each item is linked to the next one by means of a pointer. Such a list can be envisioned as

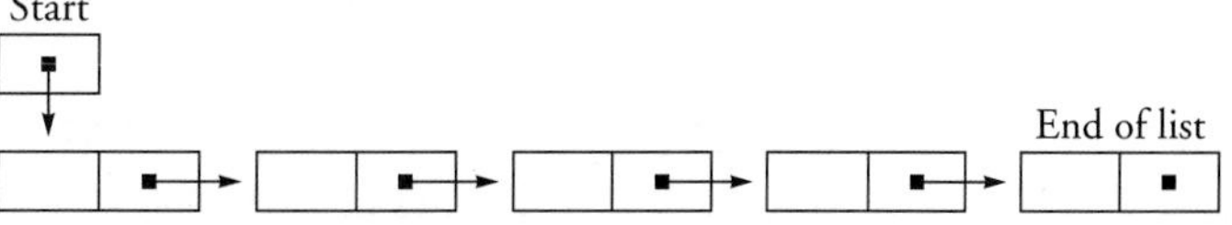

Items in a linked list are called *components* or *nodes.* These lists are similar to arrays; data of the same type can be stored in each node. As shown in the previous illustration, each node of a linked list can store certain data as well as point to the next node.

Consequently, a record is used for each node, and one field of the record is reserved for the pointer. If names of students are to be stored in a linked list, we can use the record definition from Section 13.1 as follows:

```
TYPE
  NameString = PACKED ARRAY [1..20] OF char;
  DataPtr = ^StudentInfo;
  StudentInfo = RECORD
                  Name : NameString;
                  Next : DataPtr
                END;  {  of RECORD StudentInfo  }
```

Thus, we can envision a list of names as

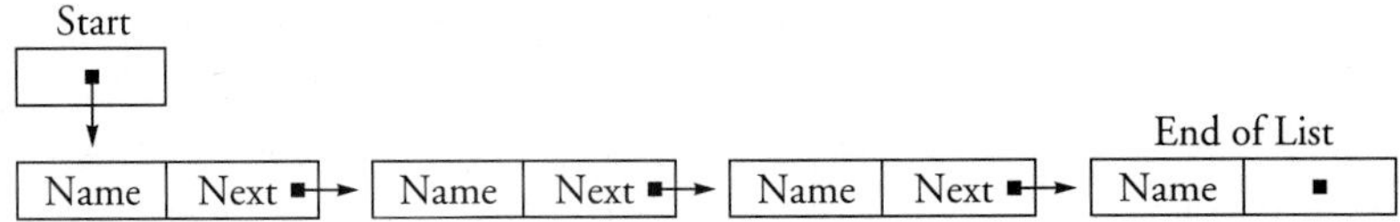

COMMUNICATION AND STYLE TIPS

When working with linked lists, the identifier Next is frequently used as the name of the field in the record that is the pointer variable. This is to remind you that you are pointing to the next record. It makes code such as

```
P := P^.Next;
```

more meaningful.

Creating a Linked List

To create a linked list, we need to be able to identify the first node, the relationship (pointer) between successive nodes, and the last node. Pointers are used to point to both the first and last node. An auxiliary pointer is also used to point to the newest node. The pointer to the first node (Start) is not changed unless a new node is added to the beginning of the list. The other pointers change as the linked list grows. Once a linked list is created, the last node is usually designated by assigning **NIL** to the pointer. To illustrate, let's see how a linked list that holds five names can be formed. Using the **TYPE** definition section

```
TYPE
  NameString = PACKED ARRAY [1..20] OF char;
  DataPtr = ^StudentInfo;
  StudentInfo = RECORD
                  Name : NameString;
                  Next : DataPtr
                END;  {  of RECORD StudentInfo  }
```

and the variable declaration section

```
VAR
  Start, Last, Ptr : DataPtr;
```

we can generate the desired list with the following segment of code.

```
BEGIN
  new (Start);
  Ptr := Start;  {  Pointer moves to first node  }
```

```
FOR J := 1 TO 4 DO
  BEGIN
    new (Last);
    Ptr^.Next := Last;
    Ptr := Last
  END;
Ptr^.Next := NIL;
```

When this code is executed

```
new (Start);
```

causes

Start

Start^

and

```
Ptr := Start;
```

produces

Start Ptr

Start^
Ptr^

Now that we have started our list, the first pass through the **FOR** loop produces the results shown in Table 13.1.

◇ TABLE 13.1
Adding a second node to a linked list

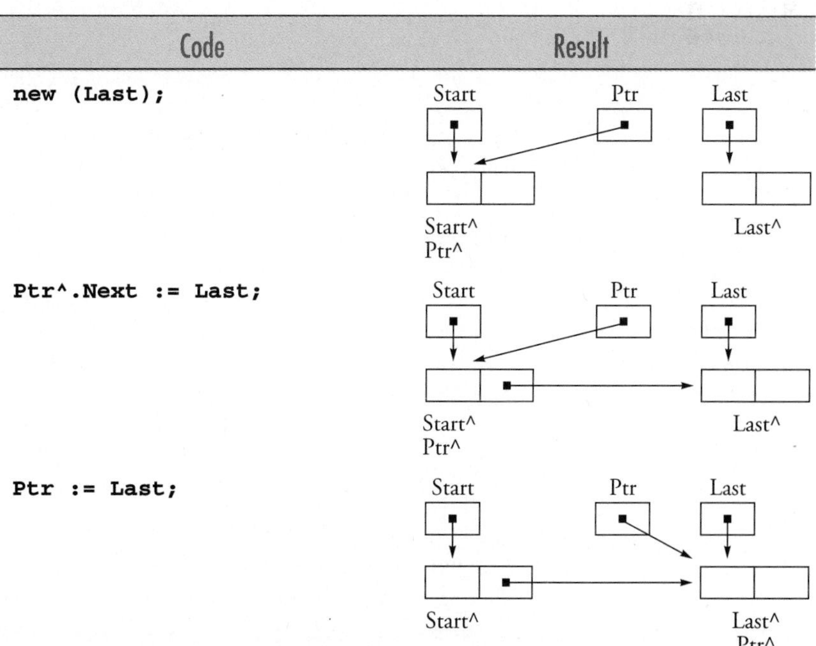

Code	Result
`new (Last);`	Start Ptr Last Start^ Ptr^ Last^
`Ptr^.Next := Last;`	Start Ptr Last Start^ Ptr^ Last^
`Ptr := Last;`	Start Ptr Last Start^ Last^ Ptr^

Similarly, the second pass through the **FOR** loop causes the list to grow as shown in Table 13.2.

◇ TABLE 13.2
Adding a third node to a linked list

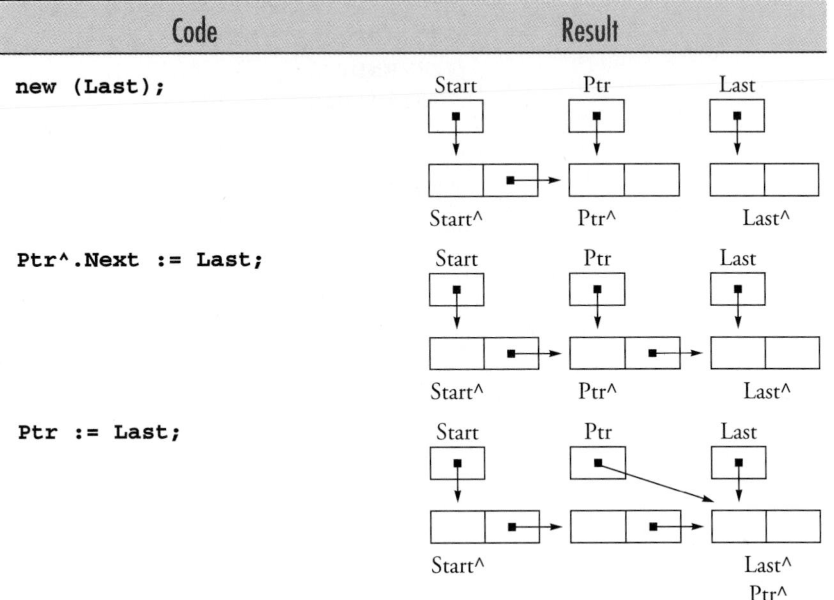

Code	Result
`new (Last);`	Start Ptr Last / Start^ Ptr^ Last^
`Ptr^.Next := Last;`	Start Ptr Last / Start^ Ptr^ Last^
`Ptr := Last;`	Start Ptr Last / Start^ Last^ Ptr^

Each pass through the body of the **FOR** loop adds one element to the linked list and causes both Ptr and Last to point to the last node of the list. After the loop has been executed four times, we have

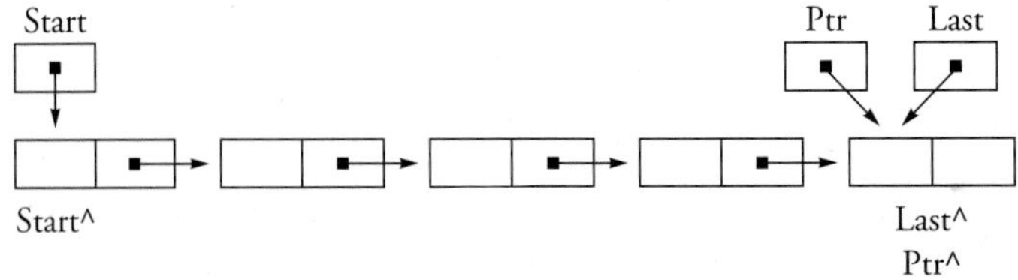

At this stage, the loop is exited and

```
Ptr^.Next := NIL;
```

produces

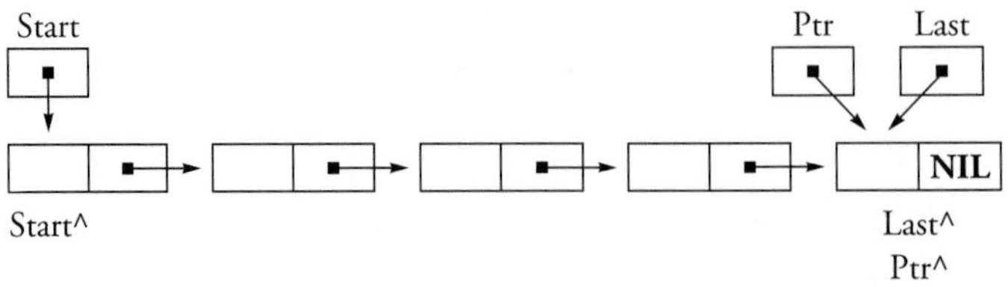

Now when we process the list, we can check the field name Next to determine when the end of the list has been reached. In this sense, the use of **NIL** here is similar to the use of **eof** with files.

EXAMPLE 13.1

Now let's create a linked list that can be used to simulate a deck of playing cards. We need 52 nodes, each of which is a record with a field for the suit (club, diamond, heart, or spade), a field for the number (1 to 13), and a field for the pointer. Such a record can be defined as

```
TYPE
  Pointer = ^Card;
  Suits = (Club, Diamond, Heart, Spade);
  Card = RECORD
           Suit : Suits;
           Num : 1..13;
           Next : Pointer
         END;  {  of RECORD Card  }
```

As before, we need three pointer variables; they can be declared as

```
VAR
  Start, Last, Ptr : Pointer;
```

If an ace is represented by the number 1, we can start our list with

```
BEGIN
  new (Start);
  Start^.Suit := Club;
  Start^.Num := 1;
  Ptr := Start;
  Last := Start;
```

This beginning can be envisioned as

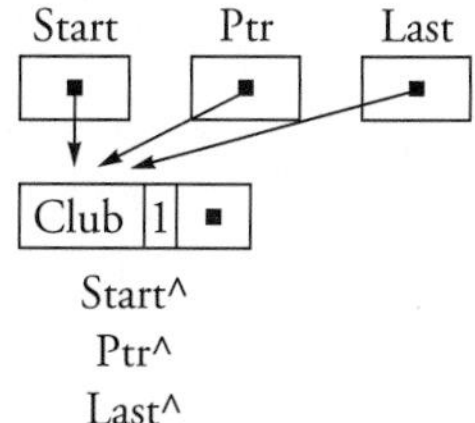

We can then generate the rest of the deck by

```
FOR J := 2 TO 52 DO
  BEGIN
    new (Last);
    IF Ptr^.Num = 13 THEN  {  Start a new suit  }
      BEGIN
        Last^.Suit := succ(Ptr^.Suit);
        Last^.Num := 1
      END  {  of IF...THEN option  }
    ELSE  {  Same suit, next number  }
      BEGIN
        Last^.Suit := Ptr^.Suit;
        Last^.Num := Ptr^.Num + 1
      END;  {  of ELSE option  }
    Ptr^.Next := Last;
    Ptr := Last
  END;  {  of FOR loop  }
Ptr^.Next := NIL;
```

The first time through this loop produces

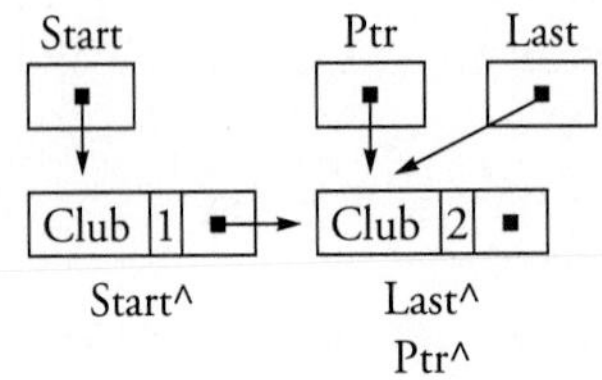

This loop is processed all 51 times and then exited, so when

```
Ptr^.Next := NIL;
```

is executed, we have the list shown in Figure 13.2.

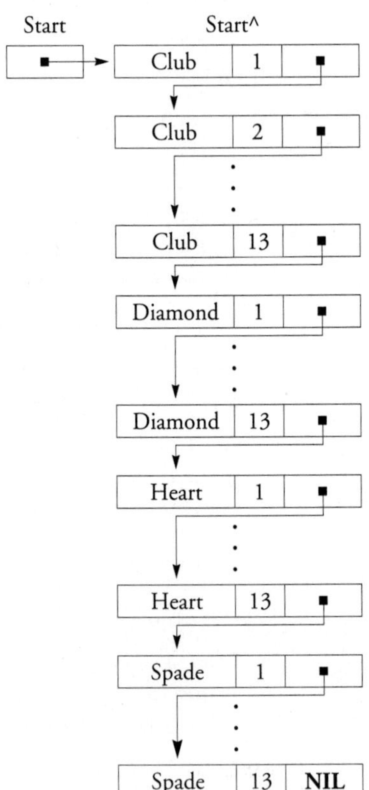

◆ FIGURE 13.2
A linked list simulating a deck of cards

Printing from a Linked List

Thus far, we have seen how to create a dynamic structure and assign data to components of such a structure. We conclude this section with a look at how to print data from a linked list.

The general idea is to start with the first component in the list, print the desired information, and then move sequentially through the list until the last component (**NIL**) is reached. Two aspects of this algorithm need to be examined. First, the loop control depends upon examining the current record for the value of **NIL** in the pointer field. If P is used to denote this field, we have

```
WHILE P <> NIL DO
  BEGIN
    .
    .
    .
  END;
```

Second, the loop increment is to assign the value of the Next field of the current record to the pointer (P) that is used as a loop control variable. To illustrate, assume the previous definitions and declarations are used to form a list of student names. If we declare the variable P by

```
VAR
  P : DataPtr;
```

we can then print the names with

```
BEGIN  {  Print names in list  }
  P := Start;
  WHILE P <> NIL DO
    BEGIN
      writeln (P^.Name);
      P := P^.Next
    END  {  of WHILE loop  }
END;  {  of printing names  }
```

In general, printing from a linked list is done with a procedure. In this case, only the external pointer (Start, in our examples) needs to be used as a parameter. To illustrate, a procedure to print the previous list of names is

```
PROCEDURE PrintNames (Start : DataPtr);
  VAR
    P : DataPtr;
  BEGIN
    P := Start;
    WHILE P <> NIL DO
      BEGIN
        writeln (P^.Name);
        P := P^.Next
      END  {  of WHILE loop  }
  END;  {  of PROCEDURE PrintNames  }
```

This procedure is called from the main program by

```
PrintNames (Start);
```

EXERCISES 13.2

1. Discuss the differences and similarities between arrays and linked lists.
2. Write a test program to transfer an unknown number of integers from a data file to a linked list and then print the integers from the linked list.
3. Write a procedure to be used with the test program you wrote in Exercise 2 to print the integers.
4. Explain why it is preferable to use a linked list when getting an unknown number of data items from a data file.

5. Suppose you are going to create a linked list of records, each of which contains the following information about a student: name, four test scores, 10 quiz scores, average, and letter grade.
   a. Define a record to be used for this purpose.
   b. What pointer type(s) and pointer variable(s) are needed?
   c. Assume the data for each student appear on one line in the data file in the following form.

```
Smith Mary              97 98 85 90 9 8 7 10 6 9 10 8 9 7
```

   i. Show how to get the data for the first student into the first component of a linked list.
   ii. Show how to get the data for the second student into the second component.
6. Why are three pointers (Start, Last, Ptr) used when creating a linked list?
7. Consider the following definitions and declarations.

```
TYPE
  P = ^Node;
  Node = RECORD
           Num : integer;
           Next : P
         END;
VAR
  A, B, C : P;
```

   a. Show how the schematic

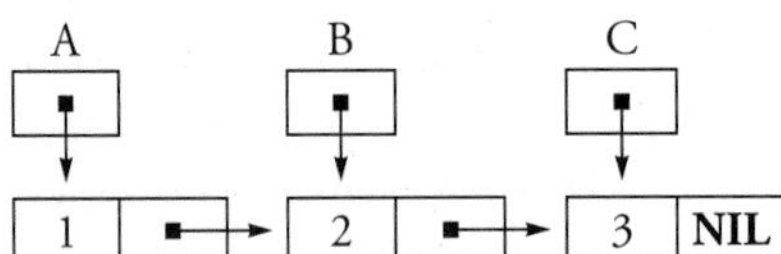

   would be changed by each of the following.
   i. `A := A^.Next;`
   ii. `B := A;`
   iii. `C := A^.Next;`
   iv. `B^.Num := C^.Num;`
   v. `A^.Num := B^.Next^.Num;`
   vi. `C^.Next := A;`
   b. Write one statement to change

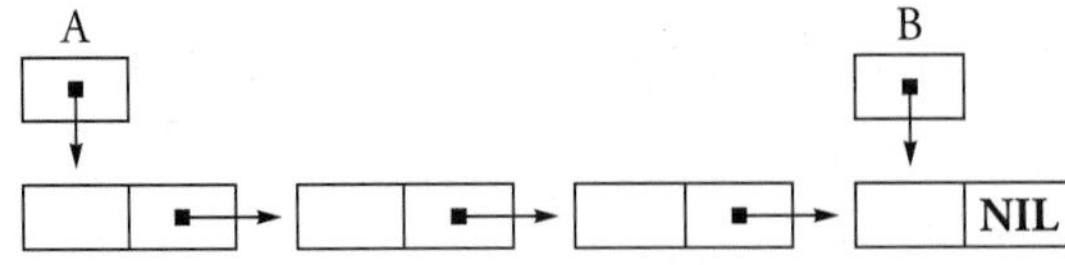

to

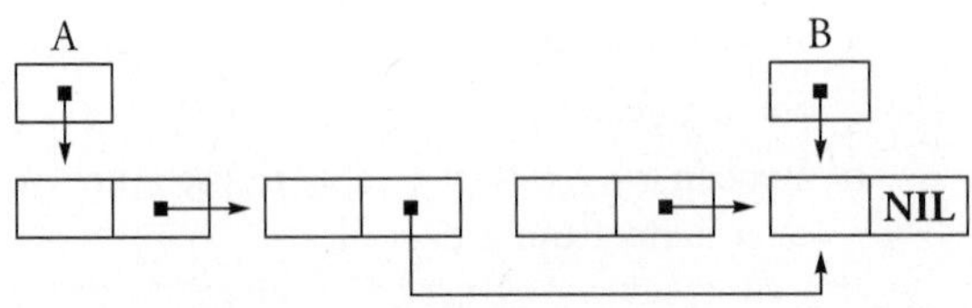

8. Assume the definitions and declarations in Exercise 7. Indicate the output for each of the following.

a.
```
new (A);
new (B);
A^.Num := 10;
B^.Num := 20;
B := A;
A^.Num := 5;
writeln (A^.Num, B^.Num);
```

b.
```
new (C);
C^.Num := 100;
new (B);
B^.Num := C^.Num MOD 8;
new (A);
A^.Num := B^.Num + C^.Num;
writeln (A^.Num, B^.Num, C^.Num);
```

c.
```
new (A);
new (B);
A^.Num := 10;
A^.Next := B;
A^.Next^.Num := 100;
writeln (A^.Num, B^.Num);
```

9. Write a function Sum to sum the integers in a linked list of integers. Show how the function is called from the main program.

13.3 Working with Linked Lists

OBJECTIVES

- to be able to insert an element into a linked list
- to be able to delete an element from a linked list
- to be able to update an ordered linked list
- to be able to search a linked list for an element

In this section, we will examine some of the basic operations required when working with linked lists. Working with a list of integers, we will learn how to create a sorted list by inserting elements. We will then update a linked list by searching it for a certain value and deleting that element from the list.

The following **TYPE** definition is used in most of this section.

```
TYPE
  DataPtr = ^Node;
  Node = RECORD
           Num : integer;
           Next : DataPtr
         END;
```

Since most of the operations examined here will be used later in this section, procedures are written for them.

Inserting an Element

Due to the dynamic nature of a linked list, we are able to insert an element into it. The three cases we will consider are inserting an element at the beginning, in the middle, and at the end of a list.

COMMUNICATION AND STYLE TIPS

When working with linked lists of records, Node is frequently used as the record identifier. This facilitates readability of program comments. Thus, comments such as "Get new node," "Insert a node," and "Delete a node" are meaningful.

The procedure for inserting an element at the beginning of a list is commonly called Push. Before we write code for this procedure, let's examine what should be done with the nodes and pointers. If the list is illustrated by

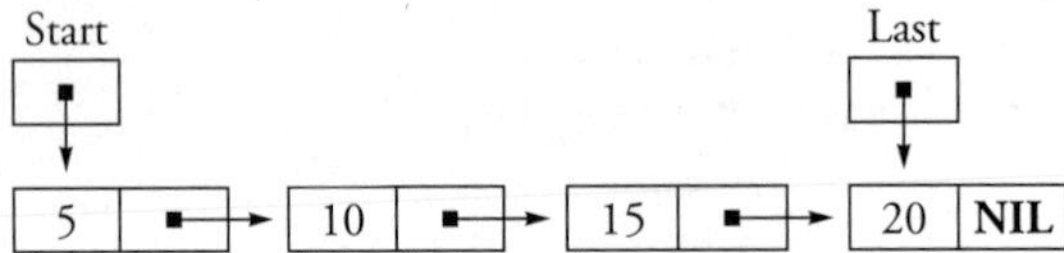

and we wish to insert

3 | ■

at the beginning of it, we need to get a new node with

```
new (P);
```

assign the appropriate value to Num, using

```
P^.Num := 3;
```

and reassign the pointers to produce the desired result. After the first two steps, we have the list

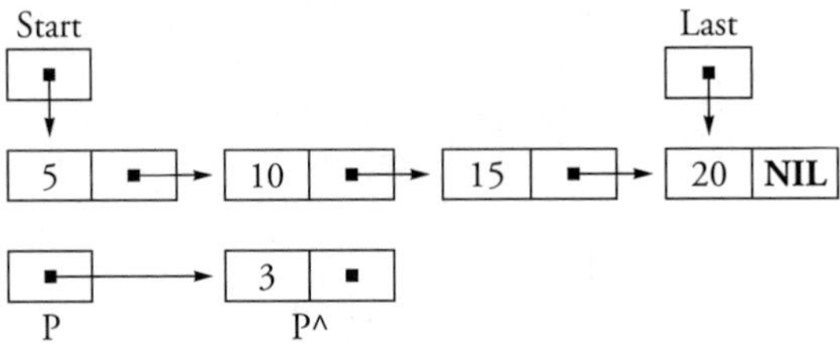

At this point

```
P^.Next := Start;
```

yields the list

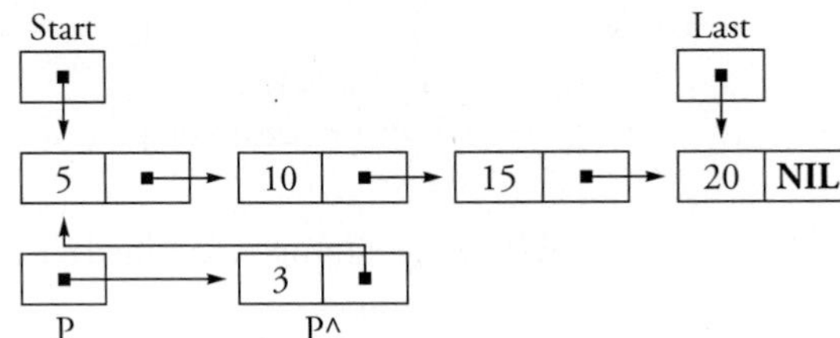

Then

```
Start := P;
```

yields the following list, in which **PROCEDURE** Push is now complete.

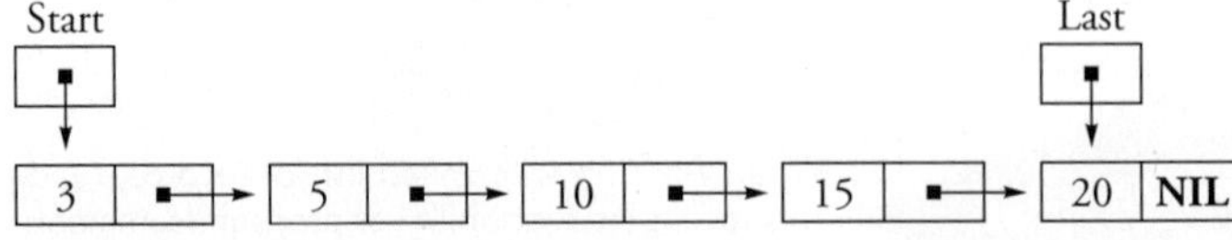

A procedure for this follows.

```
PROCEDURE Push (VAR Start : DataPtr;
                NewNum : integer);
  VAR
    P : DataPtr;
  BEGIN
    new (P);                { Get another node          }
    P^.Num := NewNum;       { Assign the data value     }
    P^.Next := Start;       { Point to the first node   }
    Start := P;             { Point to new first node   }
    IF Start^.Next = NIL THEN
      Last := Start   { For a list with only one node   }
  END;  { of PROCEDURE Push }
```

This procedure is called from the main program by

```
Push (Start, 3);
```

A note of caution is in order. This procedure is written assuming there is an existing list with **NIL** assigned to the pointer in the final node. If this procedure is implemented as the first step in creating a new list, the assignment

```
Start := NIL;
```

must have been made previously.

The basic process for inserting a node somewhere in a linked list other than at the beginning or end is to get a new node, find where it belongs, and put it in the list. In order to do this, we must start at the beginning of a list and search it sequentially until we find where the new node belongs. When we next change pointers to include the new node, we must know between which pair of elements in the linked list the new node is to be inserted. Thus, if

12	■

is to be inserted in an ordered linked list such as

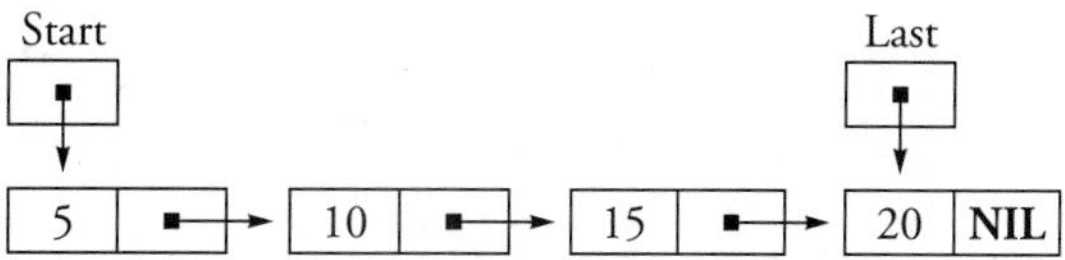

we need to know the link

10	■→	15	■→

is in the list. Once this pair of nodes is identified, the pointers will be changed to produce

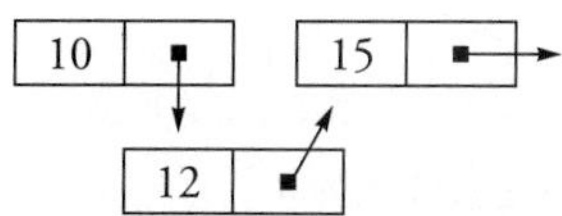

so the new list with the new node inserted is

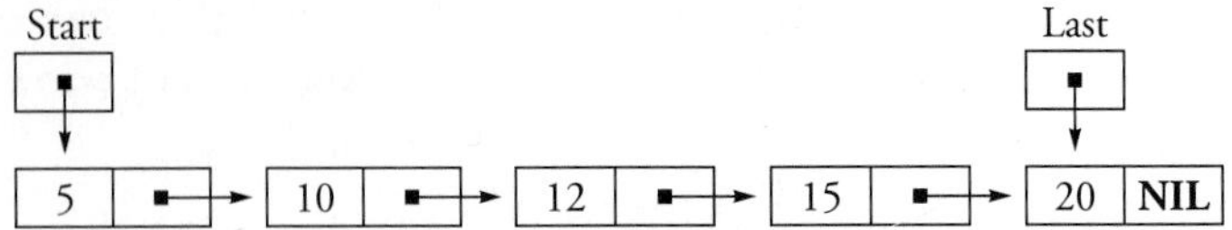

Now let's see how this can be done. We can get a new node with

```
new (P);
P^.Num := NewNum;   {  Where NewNum has the value 12  }
```

To find where the new node belongs, we need two pointer variables to keep track of successive pairs of elements as we traverse the list. Assume Before and Ptr have been appropriately declared. Then

```
Ptr := Start;
WHILE (Ptr <> NIL) AND (Ptr^.Num < NewNum) DO
  BEGIN
    Before := Ptr;
    Ptr := Ptr^.Next
  END;
```

will search the list for the desired pair. (We assume the node to be inserted is not at the beginning of the list.) Using the previous numbers, when this loop is completed, we have the arrangement

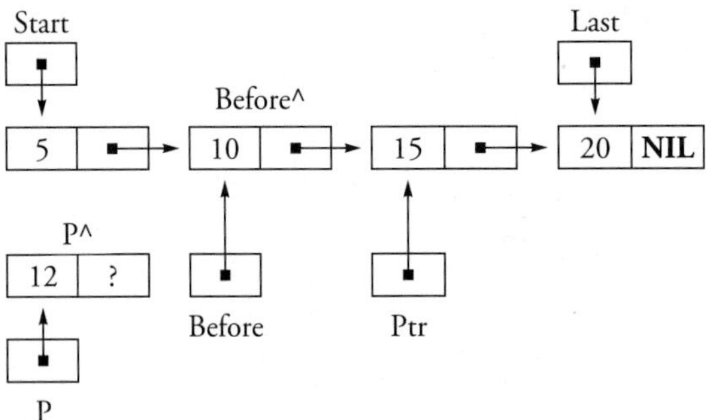

We can put the new node in the list by reassigning the pointers, using

```
P^.Next := Ptr;
Before^.Next := P;
```

The list can then be envisioned as

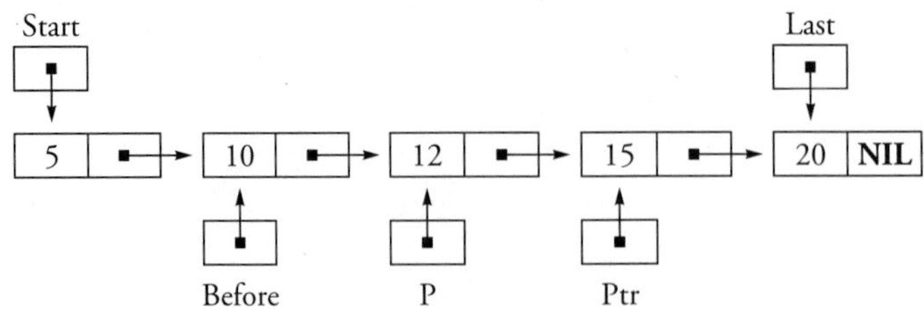

When this code is written together, we have

```
PROCEDURE InsertMiddle (Start : DataPtr;
                        NewNum : integer);
  VAR
    P, Ptr, Before : DataPtr;
```

```
BEGIN

  {  Get a new node  }
  New (P);
  P^.Num := NewNum;

  {  Find where it belongs  }
  Ptr := Start;
  WHILE (Ptr <> NIL) AND (Ptr^.Num < NewNum) DO
    BEGIN
      Before := Ptr;
      Ptr := Ptr^.Next
    END;

  {  Insert the new node  }
  P^.Next := Ptr;
  Before^.Next := P
END;  {  of PROCEDURE InsertMiddle  }
```

This procedure is called from the main program by

```
InsertMiddle (Start, 12);
```

The next problem to consider is how to insert a node at the end of a linked list. In the previous code, when Ptr is **NIL,** a reference to Ptr^ causes an error, so this cannot be used for inserting an element at the end of a list. This problem can be solved by using the Boolean variable Looking, initializing it to **true,** and changing the loop control to

```
WHILE (Ptr <> NIL) AND Looking DO
```

The body of the loop then becomes the **IF . . . THEN . . . ELSE** statement

```
IF Ptr^.Num > NewNum THEN
  Looking := false
ELSE
  BEGIN
    Before := Ptr;
    Ptr := Ptr^.Next
  END;  {  of ELSE option  }
```

The loop is followed by the statement

```
P^.Next := Ptr;
```

Thus, we have

```
new (P);
P^.Num := NewNum;
Ptr := Start;
Looking := true;
WHILE (Ptr <> NIL) AND Looking DO
  IF Ptr^.Num > NewNum THEN
    Looking := false
  ELSE
    BEGIN
      Before := Ptr;
      Ptr := Ptr^.Next
    END;  {  of ELSE option  }
```

```
P^.Next := Ptr;
Before^.Next := P;
Last := P;
```

To see how this segment of code permits an element to be inserted at the end of a list, suppose NewNum is 30 and the list is

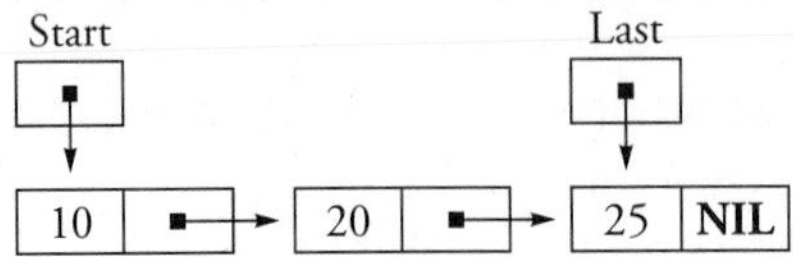

The initialization produces the list shown in Figure 13.3(a). Since Ptr <> **NIL** and Looking is **true,** the loop is entered. Ptr^.Num > NewNum (10 > 30) is **false,** so the **ELSE** option is exercised to produce the list shown in Figure 13.3(b). At this stage, Ptr <> **NIL** and Looking is still **true,** so the loop is entered again. Ptr^.Num > NewNum (20 > 30) is **false,** so the **ELSE** option produces the list shown in Figure 13.3(c). Since Ptr is not yet **NIL,** Ptr <> **NIL,** and Looking is **true,** the loop is entered. Ptr^.Num > NewNum is **false,** so the **ELSE** option produces the list shown in Figure 13.3(d).

◆ FIGURE 13.3(a)
Getting a new node for a linked list

◆ FIGURE 13.3(b)
Positioning Before and Ptr

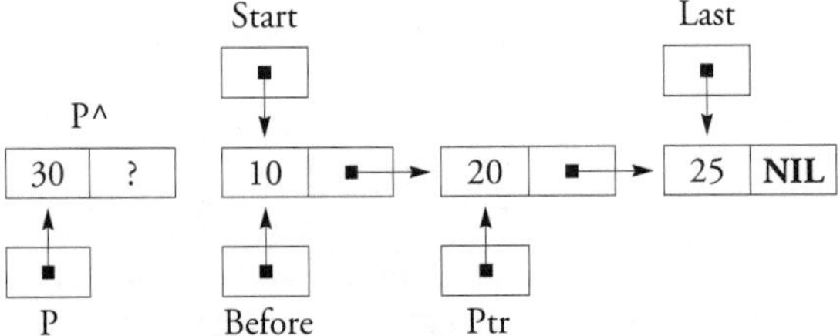

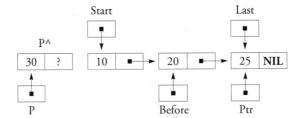

◆ FIGURE 13.3(c)
Moving Before and Ptr

◆ FIGURE 13.3(d)
Before and Ptr ready for insertion

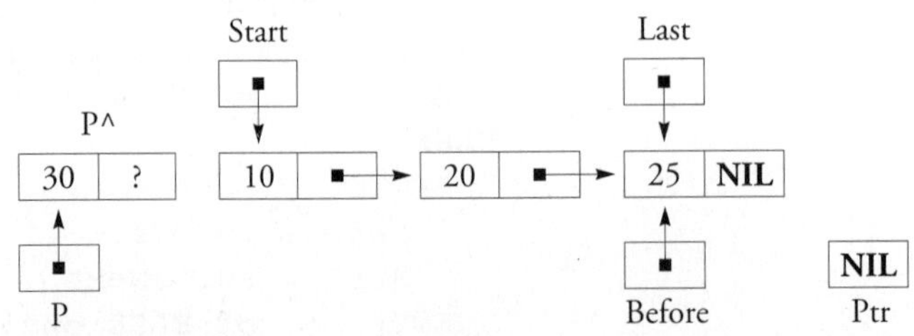

Now the condition Ptr <> **NIL** is **false,** so control is transferred to

```
P^.Next := Ptr;
```

When this line of code and the two lines following it are executed, we get the arrangement shown in Figure 13.3(e).

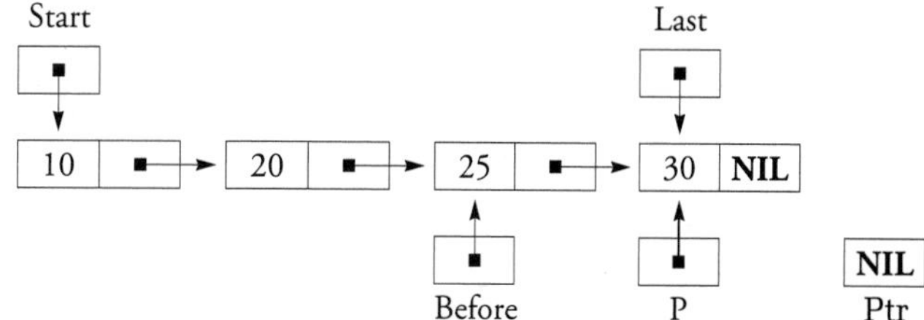

◆ FIGURE 13.3(e)
Insertion at end of linked list is complete

One final comment is in order. A slight modification of this procedure accommodates an insertion at the beginning of a list. You may choose to reserve Push for this purpose. However, a single procedure that can insert an element anywhere in a linked list follows.

```
PROCEDURE Insert (VAR Start, Last : DataPtr;
                  NewNum : integer);
  VAR
    P, Ptr, Before : DataPtr;
    Looking : boolean;
  BEGIN

    {  Initialize  }
    new (P);
    P^.Num := NewNum;
    Before := NIL;
    Ptr := Start;
    Looking := true;

    {  Check for empty list  }
    IF Start = NIL THEN
      BEGIN
        P^.Next := Start;
        Start := P
      END  {  of IF...THEN option  }
    ELSE
      BEGIN  {  Now start the loop  }
        WHILE (Ptr <> NIL) and Looking DO
          IF Ptr^.Num > NewNum THEN
            Looking := false
          ELSE
            BEGIN
              Before := Ptr;
              Ptr := Ptr^.Next
            END;  {  of ELSE option  }
```

```
            {  Now move the pointers  }
            IF Looking THEN
              Finish := Ptr;
            P^.Next := Ptr;

            {  Check for insert at beginning  }
            IF Before = NIL THEN
              Start := P
            ELSE
              Before^.Next := P
          END  {  of WHILE loop  }
      END;  {  of PROCEDURE Insert  }
```

EXAMPLE 13.2

To illustrate how **PROCEDURE** Insert can be used to create a linked list of integers sorted from high to low, let's develop a short program to read integers from a data file, create a linked list sorted from high to low, and print the contents of components in the linked list. A first-level pseudocode development for this problem is

1. Create the list
2. Print the list

Step 1 can be refined to

1. Create the list
   1.1 create the first node
   1.2 **WHILE NOT eof DO**
          insert in the list

A program that uses procedures for inserting an element and printing the list follows.

```
PROGRAM LinkListPrac (input, output);

{  This program is an illustration of using linked lists.  It     }
{  creates a sorted linked list from an unsorted data file and    }
{  then prints the contents of the list.  Procedures are used     }
{  to (1) insert into the list and (2) print the list.            }

TYPE
  DataPtr = ^Node;
  Node = RECORD
           Num : integer;
           Next : DataPtr
         END;  {  of RECORD Node  }

VAR
  Number : integer;     {  Number to be inserted                }
  Start,                {  Pointer for the beginning of the list  }
  Finish : DataPtr;     {  Pointer for the end of the list        }

{****************************************************************}
```

```
PROCEDURE Insert (VAR Start, Finish : DataPtr;
                  Number : integer);

  {  Given:   A linked list and number to be inserted in order  }
  {  Task:    Insert the number in numeric order in the         }
  {                linked list                                  }
  {  Return:  Nothing                                           }

  VAR
    P, Ptr, Before : DataPtr;
    Looking : boolean;
  BEGIN

    {  Initialize  }
    new (P);
    P^.Num := Number;
    Before := NIL;
    Ptr := Start;
    Looking := true;

    {  Now start the loop  }
    WHILE (Ptr <> NIL) AND Looking DO
      IF Ptr^.Num > Number THEN
        Looking := false
      ELSE
        BEGIN
          Before := Ptr;
          Ptr := Ptr^.Next
        END;  {  of ELSE option  }

    {  Now move the pointers  }
    IF Looking THEN
      Finish := Ptr;
    P^.Next := Ptr;

    {  Check for insert at beginning  }
    IF Before = NIL THEN
      Start := P
    ELSE
      Before^.Next := P
  END;  {  of PROCEDURE Insert  }

{*************************************************************}

PROCEDURE PrintList (Start : DataPtr);

  {  Given:   A pointer to the start of a linked list          }
  {  Task:    Print numbers from nodes of the linked list      }
  {  Return:  Nothing                                          }

  VAR
    P : DataPtr;
```

```
  BEGIN
    P := Start;
    WHILE P <> NIL DO
      BEGIN
        writeln (P^.Num);
        P := P^.Next
      END  {  of WHILE loop  }
  END;  {  of PROCEDURE PrintList  }

{*************************************************************}

BEGIN  {  Main program  }

  {  Start the list  }
  new (Start);
  readln (Number);
  Start^.Num := Number;
  Start^.Next := NIL;
  new (Finish);
  Finish := Start;                      {  List has only one node  }

  {  Now create the remainder of the list  }
  WHILE NOT eof DO
    BEGIN
      readln (Number);
      Insert (Start, Finish, Number)
    END;  {  of WHILE NOT eof  }
  PrintList (Start)
END.  {  of main program  }
```

When this program is run on the data file

42 ■	2 ■	-10 ■	0 ■	45 ■	100 ■	52 ■	78 ■	91 ■	99 ■	86 ■	■

the output is

```
-10
0
2
42
45
52
78
86
91
99
100
```

Deleting a Node

A second standard operation when working with linked lists is deleting a node. First let's consider the problem of deleting the first node in a list. This process is commonly called Pop. Before we write code for this procedure, however, let's examine what should be done with the pointers.

Deleting the first node essentially requires a reversal of the steps we follow when inserting a node at the beginning of a list. If the list is

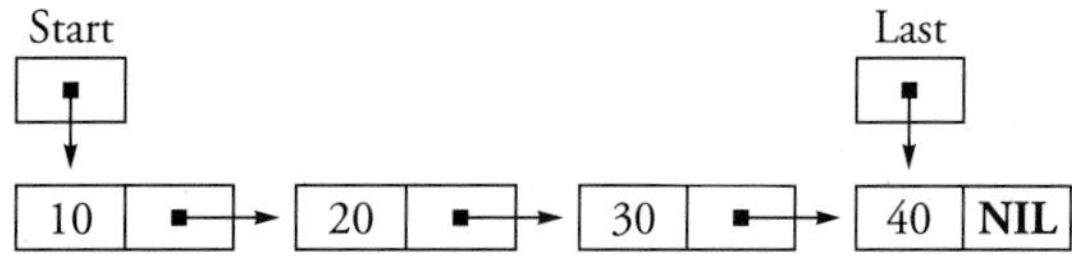

and we wish to produce the list

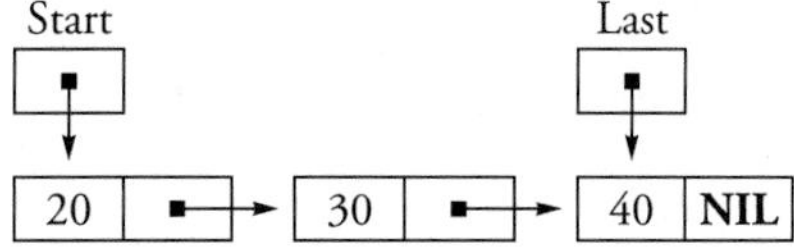

it might seem that

```
Start := Start^.Next;
```

can accomplish this. Not true. The use of this method poses two problems. First, you may (and probably will) want the values of some data fields returned to the main program. Thus, the values of the appropriate fields must be assigned to variable parameters. A second problem is the first node has not been returned to the computer for subsequent reuse. Since one advantage of using dynamic variables is that unused storage is not wasted, the procedure **dispose** should be used with this node.

We can now write a procedure to delete the first node. Assuming the data value is to be returned to the main program, the procedure is

```
PROCEDURE Pop (VAR Start : DataPtr;
               VAR Number : integer);
  VAR
    P : DataPtr;
  BEGIN
    P := Start;              {  Use a temporary pointer       }
    Number := P^.Num;        {  Return value to main program  }
    Start := Start^.Next;    {  Move start to next node       }
    dispose (P)              {  Return P^ for later use       }
  END;  {  of PROCEDURE Pop  }
```

The next kind of deletion we examine is when the list is searched for a certain key value and the node containing this value is removed from the linked list. For example, if the list contains records for customers of a company, we might want to update the list when a former customer moves away. To illustrate the process, suppose the list is

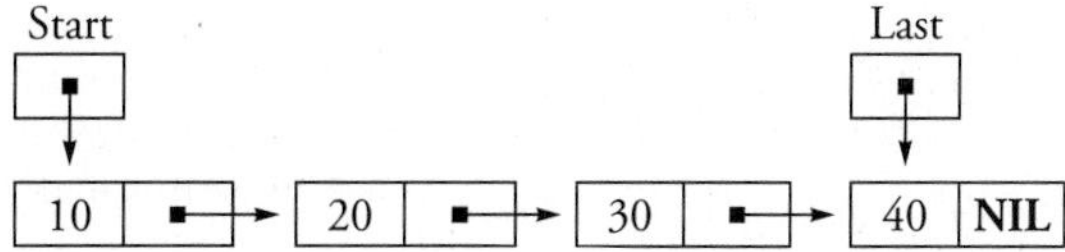

and we wish to delete

30	■

The new list is

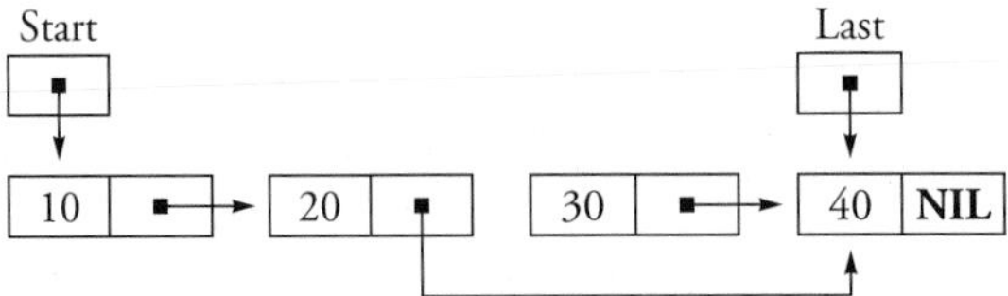

and the procedure **dispose** can be used to return the deleted node to the computer, producing

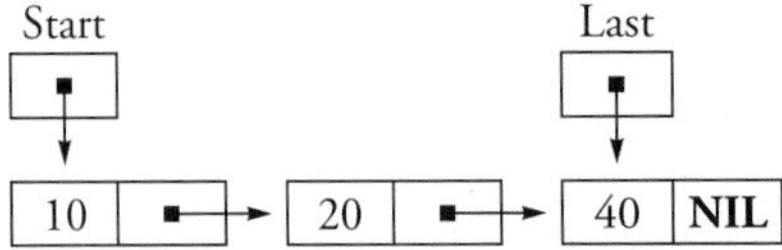

This method uses two temporary pointers. One pointer searches the list for the specified data value. Once it is located, the second pointer points to it, so we can use **dispose** to return it for subsequent use. If Before and P are the temporary pointers, the code is

```
BEGIN
  Before := Start;
  WHILE Before^.Next^.Num <> NewNum DO
    Before := Before^.Next;
  P := Before^.Next;
  Before^.Next := P^.Next;
  dispose (P)
END;
```

Now let's see how this segment of code deletes

30	■

A NOTE OF INTEREST

Using Pointers

Caution must be exercised when using pointers. Unless they are carefully described, it is easy to make a program hard to follow. Speaking to this point, Nazim H. Madhavji states: "It is often necessary to traverse deeply into the structure in order to access the required data, as can be seen in the following example, using pointers P1 and P2:

```
P1 := P2^.IDType^.ElementType^.Fields ...
```

Such 'spaghetti-like' directions get more cumbersome as SomeType gets more complex. Often, access paths of this kind are diagrammatically represented with no absolute certainty of their correctness." Madhavji continues, saying: "By raising the level of description of dynamic data structures, the visibility of these structures in programmed text can be increased."

from the previous list. First

```
Before := Start;
```

yields the list

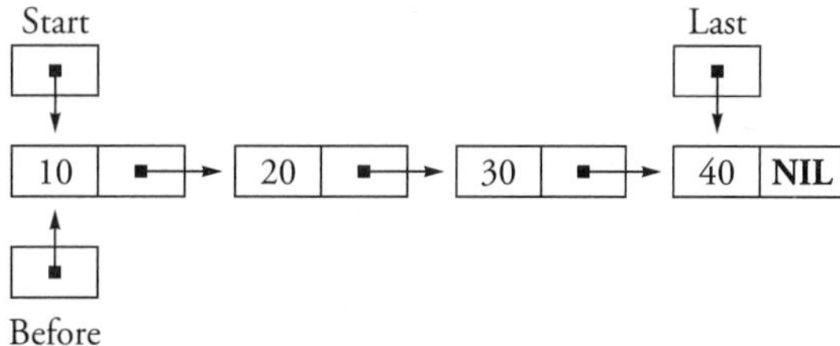

At this stage, NewNum is 30 and Before^.Next^.Num is 20. Since these values are not equal, the pointer Before is moved by

```
Before := Before^.Next;
```

and we have the list

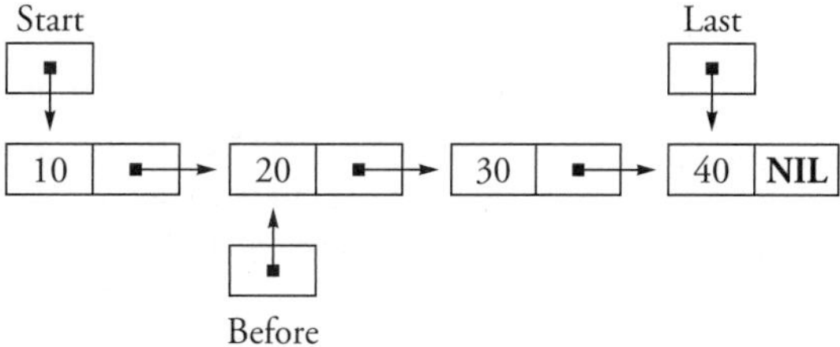

Now Before^.Next^.Num = NewNum (30), so the **WHILE** loop is exited and

```
P := Before^.Next;
```

produces the list

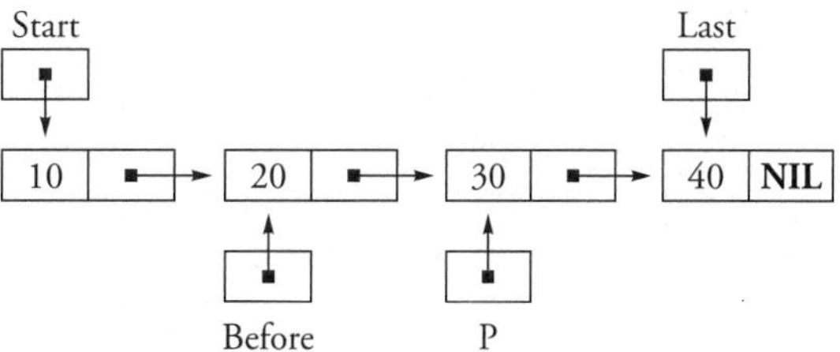

Now

```
Before^.Next := P^.Next;
```

yields the list

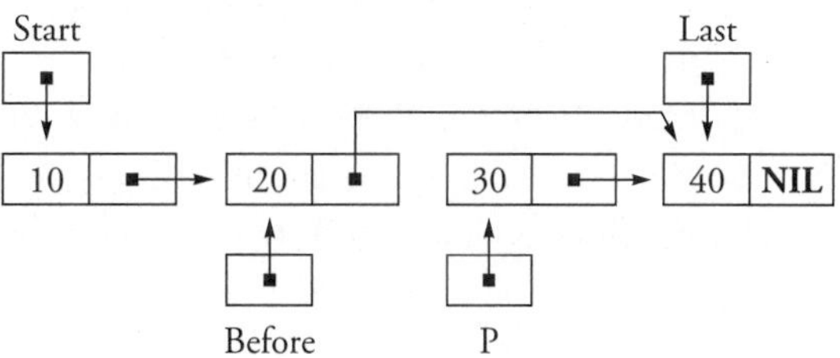

Finally, **dispose** (P) returns the node, resulting in the list

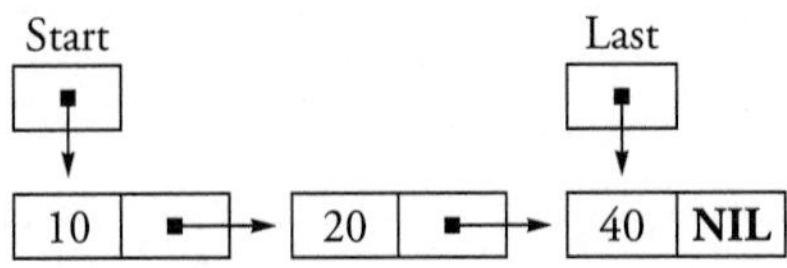

This process can be combined with deleting the first node to produce the following procedure.

```
PROCEDURE Delete (VAR Start : DataPtr;
                  Number : integer);
  VAR
    Before, P : DataPtr;
  BEGIN
    IF Number = Start^.Num THEN
      Pop (Start, Number)
    ELSE
      BEGIN
        Before := Start;
        WHILE Before^.Next^.Num <> Number DO
          Before := Before^.Next;
        P := Before^.Next;
        IF P^.Next = NIL THEN   {  Reset Last  }
          BEGIN
            Last := Before;
            Last^.Next := NIL
          END  {  of IF...THEN option  }
        ELSE
          Before^.Next := P^.Next;
        dispose (P)
      END  {  of ELSE option (not first node)  }
  END;  {  of PROCEDURE Delete  }
```

This procedure can now be used to delete any node from a linked list. However, it will produce an error if no match is found. A modification to protect against this possibility is left as an exercise.

EXERCISES 13.3

1. Illustrate how **PROCEDURE** Insert works when inserting a node in the middle of a linked list.
2. Write a test program to see what happens when Ptr is **NIL** and a reference is made to Ptr^.
3. Revise **PROCEDURE** Insert so it calls **PROCEDURE** Push if a node is to be inserted at the beginning of a list.
4. Modify **PROCEDURE** Delete to protect against the possibility of not finding a match when the list is searched.
5. Modify **PROCEDURE** Pop so no data value is returned when Pop is called.
6. Write a complete program that allows the user to do the following.
   a. Create a linked list of records where each record contains a person's name and an amount of money donated to a local fund-raising group. The list should be sorted alphabetically.
   b. Use a linked list to print the donor names and amounts.

   c. Read a name that is to be deleted, and then delete the appropriate record from the list.
   d. Print the revised list.
7. Modify **PROCEDURE** Delete to delete the *n*th node rather than a node with a particular data value.
8. Write a procedure to copy the integers in a linked list of integers into a file of integers.
9. Write a complete program that uses a linked list to sort a file of integers. Your program should create a sorted list, print the list, and save the sorted list for later use.
10. Write a procedure to delete duplicate records. Assume the list of records is ordered.

13.4 Other Dynamic Data Structures

OBJECTIVES

- to understand why a stack is a dynamic data structure
- to understand how to use a stack in a program
- to understand why a queue is a dynamic data structure
- to understand how to use a queue in a program
- to understand why a binary tree is a dynamic data structure
- to be able to create a binary search tree
- to be able to search a binary search tree

In this final section, we briefly examine some additional dynamic data structures: stacks, queues, and binary trees. All of these data structures have significant computer-oriented applications.

We used stacks in our earlier work with recursion in Section 8.4. Recall each recursive call adds something to a stack until a stopping state is reached. Stacks are also used when evaluating arithmetic expressions that contain parentheses; partial computations are put "on hold" until needed later in the process.

Queues are used when data do not arrive in an orderly manner. A typical setting is the allocation of priorities to computer users in a time-sharing system. Another example of a queue is a single waiting line for multiple service windows, as might be found at an airport or a bank.

Binary trees are used in programs in which a series of yes/no questions relate to the data. Examples include sorting, computer games, and data that can be stored in the form of a matrix.

The concepts behind stacks, queues, and binary trees and their elementary use are emphasized in this section, which serves as an introduction to these dynamic data structures. A suggested reading list is included for students who desire a more detailed development of these concepts.

Stacks

A *stack* can be implemented as a dynamic data structure in which access is made from only one end. Think of a stack as paper in a copying machine or trays in a cafeteria line. In both cases, the last one in will be the first one out; that is, items are put in, one at a time, at the top and removed, one at a time, from the top. This *last-in, first-out order* is referred to as LIFO; stacks are therefore often termed LIFO structures.

A stack can be envisioned

E
D
C
B
A

In this illustration, item E is considered the top element in the stack.

The two basic operations needed to work with stacks are the insertion of an element to create a new stack top (Push) and the removal of an element from the top of the stack (Pop). If a stack is represented by a linked list, Push and Pop are merely "insert at the beginning" and "delete from the beginning," respectively, as developed in Section 13.3.

To illustrate the use of a stack in a program, let's consider a program that checks an arithmetic expression to make sure parentheses are correctly matched (nested). Our program considers

```
(3 + 4 * (5 MOD 3))
```

to make sure the number of left parentheses matches the number of right parentheses. A first-level pseudocode for this problem is

1. Read a character
2. **IF** it is a "(" **THEN**
   Push it onto the stack
3. **IF** it is a ")" **THEN**
   Pop the previous "("
4. Check for an empty stack

The growing and shrinking of the stack is illustrated in Table 13.3.

◇ TABLE 13.3
Using a stack

Stack Before Read	Character Read	Stack After Character Processed
S	(	Stack top (S
(S	3ƀ+ƀ4ƀ*ƀ	Stack top (S
(S	(	Stack top ((S
((S	5ƀ**MOD**ƀ3	Stack top ((S
((S	)	Stack top (S
(S	)	Stack top S

ƀ represents a blank space

Two points need to be made concerning this program. First, since the stack is represented by a linked list, the illustration could be

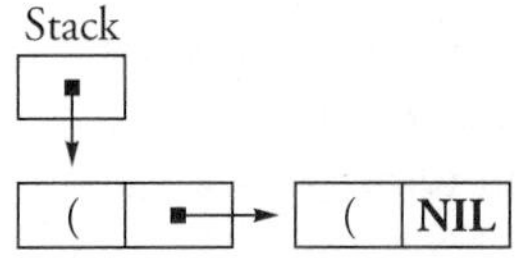

Second, before Pop is used on a stack, a check must be made to make sure the stack is not already empty. Thus, **PROCEDURE** Pop is replaced by **PROCEDURE** PopAndCheck, in which a suitable error message will appear if the user tries to pop an empty stack.

Now let's prepare code for the previous problem. The following definitions are used.

```
TYPE
  DataPtr = ^Node;
  Node = RECORD
           Sym : char;
           Next : DataPtr
         END;
VAR
  Stack : DataPtr;
```

The **PROCEDURE** Push is

```
PROCEDURE Push (VAR Stack : DataPtr;
                Symbol : char);
  VAR
    P : DataPtr;
  BEGIN
    new (P);
    P^.Sym := Symbol;
    P^.Next := Stack;
    Stack := P
  END;  {  of PROCEDURE Push  }
```

The **PROCEDURE** PopAndCheck is

```
PROCEDURE PopAndCheck (VAR Stack : DataPtr);
  VAR
    P : DataPtr;
  BEGIN
    IF Stack = NIL THEN      {  Check for empty stack  }
      writeln ('The parentheses are not correct.')
    ELSE
      BEGIN  {  Pop the stack  }
        P := Stack;
        Stack := Stack^.Next;
        dispose (P)
      END  {  of ELSE option  }
  END;  {  of PROCEDURE PopAndCheck  }
```

Given these two procedures, the main body of a program that examines an expression for correct use of parentheses follows.

```
BEGIN  {  Main program  }
  Stack := NIL;
  WHILE NOT eoln(Data) DO
    BEGIN
      read (Data, Symbol);
      IF Symbol = '(' THEN
        Push (Stack, Symbol);
      IF Symbol = ')' THEN
        PopAndCheck (Stack)
    END;
```

```
    {  Now check for an empty stack  }
    IF Stack <> NIL THEN
      writeln ('The parentheses are not correct.')
  END.  {  of main program  }
```

Several modifications of this short program are available and are suggested in the exercises at the end of this section.

Queues

A *queue* can be implemented as a dynamic data structure in which access is made from both ends. Elements are entered from one end (the rear) and removed from the other end (the front). This *first-in, first-out order* is referred to as FIFO; queues are termed FIFO structures. A queue is like a waiting line. Think of people standing in line to purchase tickets: each new customer enters at the rear of the line and exits from the front. A queue implemented as a linked list can be illustrated as

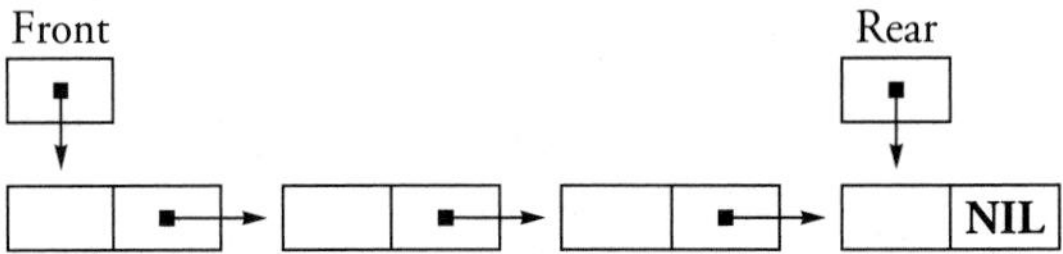

Two basic operations needed to work with queues are the removal of an element from the front of the list and the insertion of an element at the rear of the list. If we use the definitions

```
  TYPE
    DataPtr = ^Node;
    Node = RECORD
             Num : integer;
             Next : DataPtr
           END;
```

we can use variables declared by

```
  VAR
    Front, Rear : DataPtr;
```

when working with such a structure.

Removing an element from the front of a queue is similar to the use of **PROCEDURE** PopAndCheck with a stack. The only difference is that after an element has been removed, if the queue is empty, Rear must be assigned the value **NIL.** A procedure for removing an element from the front of a queue follows. It is assumed that the value of the element removed is to be returned to the main program via a variable parameter.

```
PROCEDURE Remove (VAR Front, Rear : DataPtr;
                  VAR Number : integer);
  VAR
    P : DataPtr;
  BEGIN
    IF Front = NIL THEN    {  Check for empty queue  }
      writeln ('The queue is empty.')
```

```
    ELSE
      BEGIN   {  Pop the queue  }
        P := Front;
        Front := Front^.Next;
        Number := P^.Num;
        dispose (P)
      END;  {  of ELSE option  }
    IF Front = NIL THEN  {  Set pointers for empty queue  }
      Rear := NIL
  END;  {  of PROCEDURE Remove  }
```

This procedure is called from the main program by

```
  Remove (Front, Rear, Number);
```

A procedure to insert an element at the rear of a queue (assuming there is at least one element in the queue) is similar to the procedure given in Section 13.3 for inserting an element at the end of a linked list. You are asked to write the code as an exercise at the end of this section.

Trees

A *tree* can be implemented as a dynamic data structure consisting of a special node called a root that points to zero or more other nodes, each of which points to zero or more other nodes, and so on. In general, a tree can be visualized as illustrated in Figure 13.4. The *root* of a tree is its first, or top, node. *Children* are nodes that are pointed to by an element, a *parent* is the node that is pointing to its children, and a *leaf* is a node that has no children.

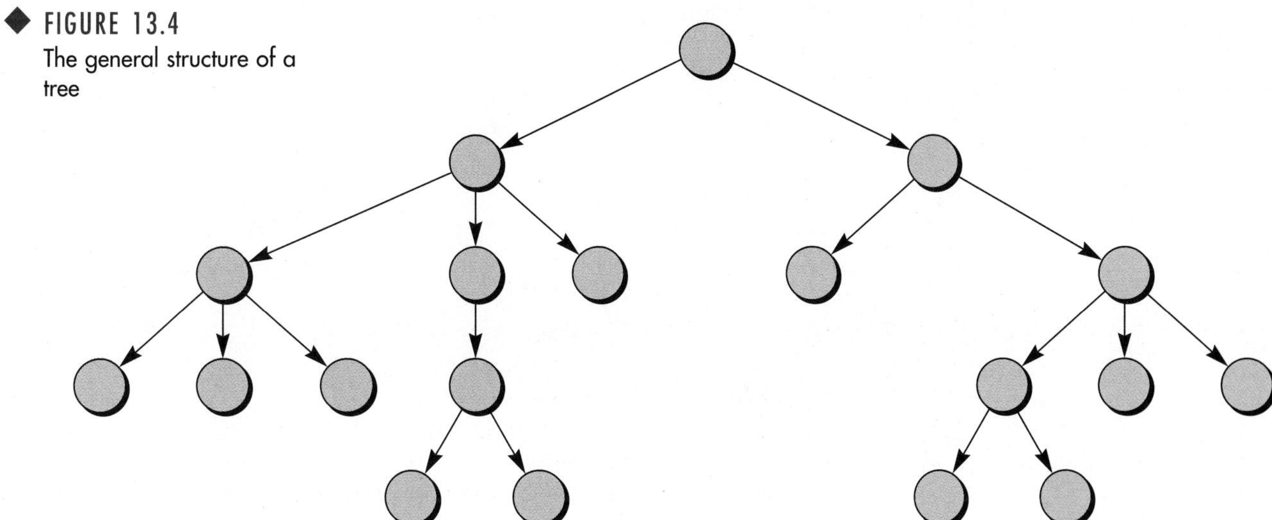

FIGURE 13.4
The general structure of a tree

Applications for trees include compiler programs, artificial intelligence, and game-playing programs. In general, trees can be applied in programs that call for information to be stored so it can be retrieved rapidly. As illustrated in Figure 13.4, pointers are especially appropriate for implementing a tree as a dynamic data structure. An external pointer is used to point to the root, and each parent uses pointers to point to its children. A more detailed tree is illustrated in Figure 13.5.

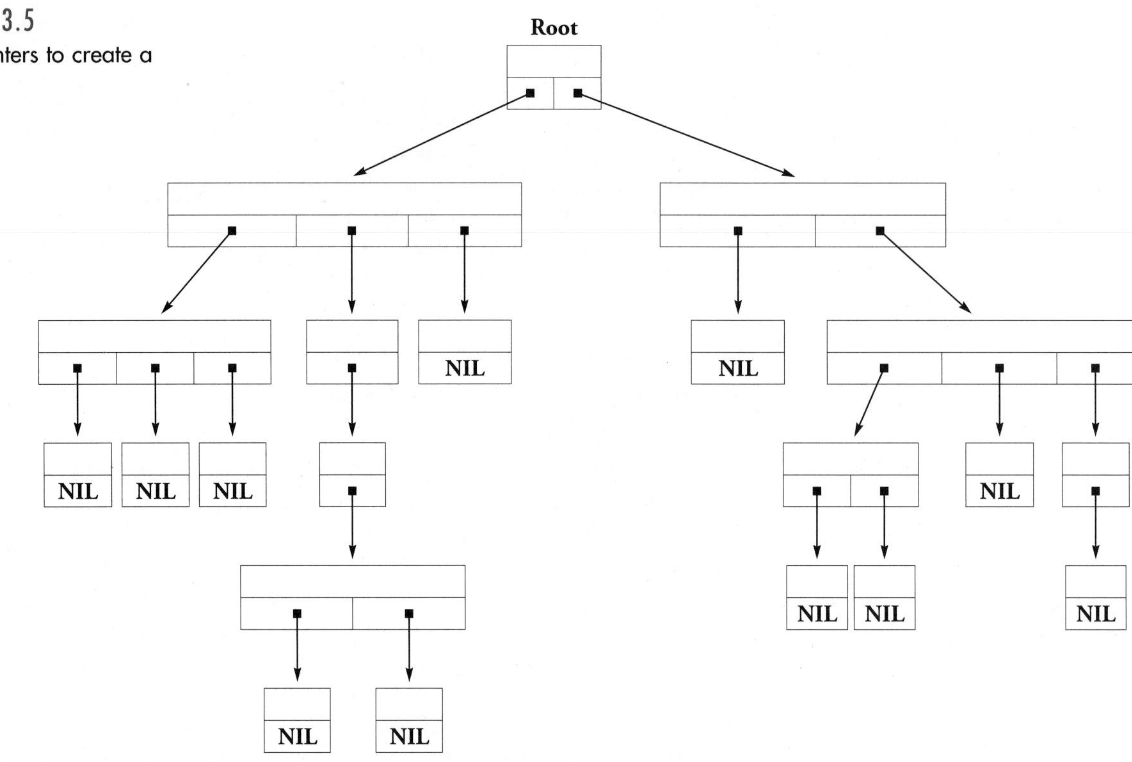

◆ FIGURE 13.5
Using pointers to create a tree

Binary Trees. From this point on, we will restrict our discussion of trees to binary trees. In a *binary tree,* each node can point to at most two children. A binary tree is illustrated in Figure 13.6.

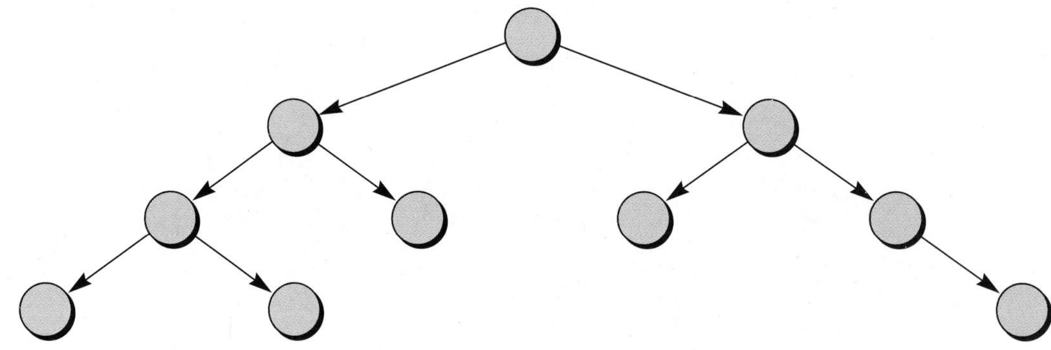

◆ FIGURE 13.6
A binary tree

If a binary tree is used to store integer values, a reasonable definition for the pointer type is

```
TYPE
  Pointer = ^TreeNode;
  TreeNode = RECORD
               Info : integer;
               RightChild : Pointer;
               LeftChild : Pointer
             END;
```

A particularly important kind of binary tree is a *binary search tree,* which is a binary tree formed according to the following rules.

1. The information in the key field of any node is greater than the information in the key field of any node of its left child and any children of the left child.
2. The information in the key field of any node is less than the information in the key field of any node of its right child and any children of the right child.

Figure 13.7 illustrates a binary search tree.

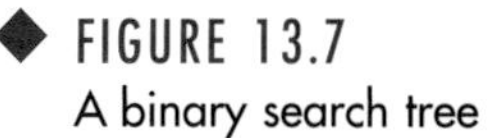

FIGURE 13.7
A binary search tree

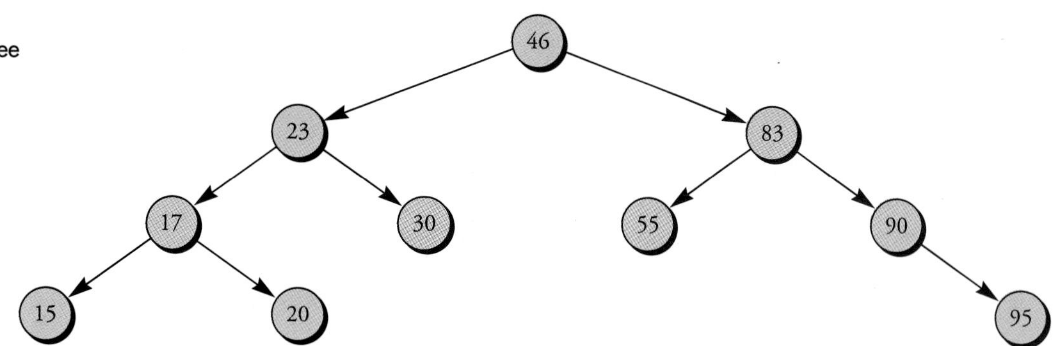

The reference to "search" is made because such trees are particularly efficient when we must search for a value. To illustrate, suppose we wish to see whether or not 30 is in the tree. At each node, we check to see if the desired value has been found. If it has not, we determine on which side to continue looking until either a match is found or the value **NIL** is encountered. If a match is not found, we are at the appropriate node for adding the new value (creating a child). As we search for 30, we traverse the tree via the path indicated by heavier arrows, as illustrated in Figure 13.8. Note that after only two comparisons (<46, >23), the desired value has been located.

FIGURE 13.8
Searching a tree for the value 30

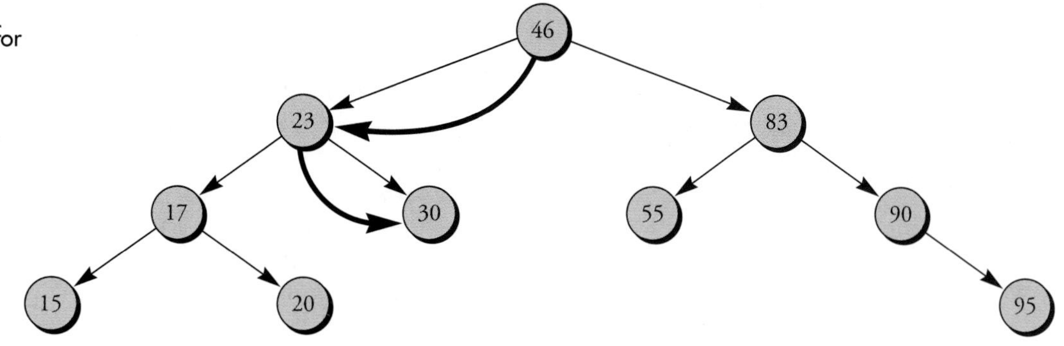

Now suppose we search the tree for the value 65. The path (again indicated by heavier arrows) is shown in Figure 13.9. At this stage, the right child is **NIL** and the value has not been located. It is now relatively easy to add the new value to the tree.

Binary search trees can be used to store any data that can be ordered. For example, the registrar of a university might want to access the record of a particular

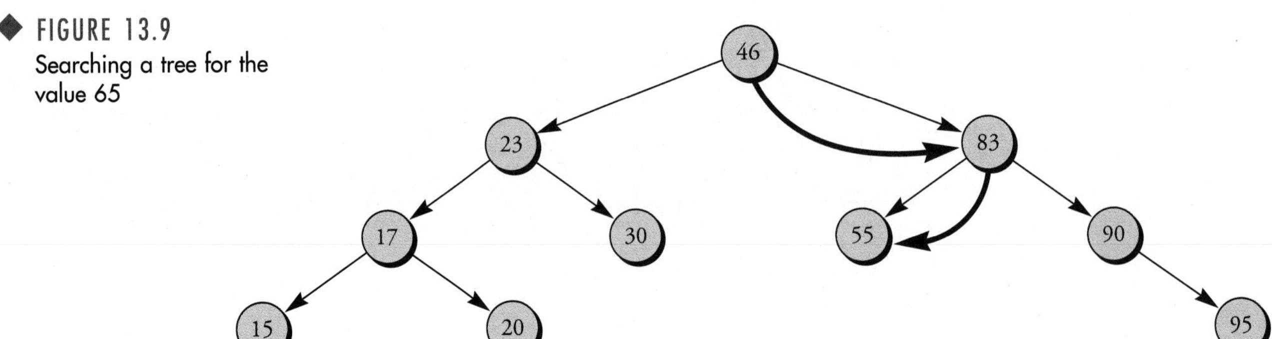

◆ **FIGURE 13.9**
Searching a tree for the value 65

student. If the records are stored alphabetically by student name in a binary search tree, quick retrieval is possible.

Implementing Binary Search Trees. We conclude this chapter with a relatively basic implementation of binary search trees: a program to create a binary search tree from integers in a data file. We print the integers in order, using a variation of the general procedure for searching a tree. The operations of inserting and deleting nodes are left as exercises at the end of this section.

Before we develop algorithms and write code for these implementations, we need to discuss the recursive nature of trees. (You may wish to reread Section 11.1 at this time.) When we move from one node to a right or left child, we are (in a sense) at the root of a subtree. Thus, the process of traversing a tree is

1. **IF** LeftChild <> **NIL THEN**
   traverse left branch
2. Take desired action
3. **IF** RightChild <> **NIL THEN**
   traverse right branch

Steps 1 and 3 are recursive; each return to them saves values associated with the current stage together with any pending action. If the desired action is to print the values of nodes in a binary search tree, step 2 is

2. Print the value

and when this procedure is called, the result is to print an ordered list of values contained in the tree. If we use the previous definitions

```
TYPE
  Pointer = ^TreeNode;
  TreeNode = RECORD
               Info : integer;
               RightChild : Pointer;
               LeftChild : Pointer
             END;
```

a procedure for printing is

```
PROCEDURE PrintTree (T : Pointer);
  BEGIN
    IF T = NIL THEN
      {  Do nothing  }
    ELSE
```

```
          BEGIN
            PrintTree (T^.LeftChild);
            writeln (T^.Info);
            PrintTree (T^.RightChild)
          END  {  of ELSE option  }
      END;  {  of PROCEDURE PrintTree  }
```

This procedure is called from the main program by

```
PrintTree (Root);
```

Notice how the recursive nature of this procedure provides a simple, efficient way to inspect the nodes of a binary search tree.

The process of creating a binary search tree is only slightly longer than the process of printing one. A first-level pseudocode is

1. Initialize root to **NIL**
2. **WHILE NOT eof DO**
   2.1 get a number
   2.2 add a node

A recursive procedure can be used to add a node. An algorithm for this is

2.2 add a node
   2.2.1 if the current node is **NIL,** store the value and stop
   2.2.2 if the new value is less than the current value, point to the left child and add the node to the left subtree
   2.2.3 if the new value is greater than the current value, point to the right child and add the node to the right subtree

Notice the recursive procedure to add a node adds only nodes containing distinct values. A slight modification (left as an exercise) allows duplicate values to be included.

A procedure for adding a node to a binary search tree is

```
PROCEDURE AddNode (VAR Node : Pointer;
                   Number : integer);
  BEGIN
    IF Node = NIL THEN  {  Add a new node  }
      BEGIN
        new (Node);
        Node^.Info := Number;
        Node^.LeftChild := NIL;
        Node^.RightChild := NIL
      END  {  of IF...THEN option  }
    ELSE IF Number < Node^.Info THEN
      AddNode (Node^.LeftChild, Number)   {  Move down left side   }
    ELSE
      AddNode (Node^.RightChild, Number)  {  Move down right side  }
  END;  {  of PROCEDURE AddNode  }
```

A complete program to read unordered integers from a data file, create a binary search tree, and then print an ordered list follows.

```
PROGRAM TreePrac (input, output);

{  This program illustrates working with a binary tree.  Note    }
{  the recursion used in AddNode and PrintTree.  Input is an     }
{  unordered list of integers.  Output is a sorted list of       }
{  integers that is printed from a binary search tree.           }
```

```
TYPE
  Pointer = ^TreeNode;
  TreeNode = RECORD
               Info : integer;
               RightChild : Pointer;
               LeftChild : Pointer
             END;  {  of RECORD TreeNode  }

VAR
  Root : Pointer;          {  Pointer to indicate the tree root  }
  Number : integer;        {  Integer read from the data file    }

{**************************************************************}

PROCEDURE AddNode (VAR Node : Pointer;
                   Number : integer);

  {  Given:   The root of a binary tree and a number            }
  {  Task:    Insert the number in the binary tree              }
  {  Return:  Nothing                                           }

  BEGIN
    IF Node = NIL THEN                         {  Add a new node  }
      BEGIN
        new (Node);
        Node^.Info := Number;
        Node^.LeftChild := NIL;
        Node^.RightChild := NIL
      END  {  of IF...THEN option  }
    ELSE IF Number < Node^.Info THEN       {  Move down left side  }
      AddNode (Node^.LeftChild, Number)
    ELSE
      AddNode (Node^.RightChild, Number) { Move down right side }
  END;  {  of PROCEDURE AddNode  }

{**************************************************************}

PROCEDURE PrintTree (Node : Pointer);

  {  Given:   The root of a binary tree                         }
  {  Task:    Print numbers in order from nodes of the binary   }
  {                tree                                         }
  {  Return:  Nothing                                           }

  BEGIN
    IF Node = NIL THEN
      {  Do nothing  }
    ELSE
      BEGIN
        PrintTree (Node^.LeftChild);
        writeln (Node^.Info);
        PrintTree (Node^.RightChild)
      END  {  of ELSE option  }
  END;  {  of PROCEDURE PrintTree  }
```

```
{****************************************************************}

BEGIN  {  Main program  }
  new (Root);
  Root := NIL;
  WHILE NOT eof DO
    BEGIN
      readln (Number);
      AddNode (Root, Number)
    END;  {  of WHILE NOT eof  }
  PrintTree (Root)
END.  {  of main program  }
```

When this program is run on the data file

the output is

```
-5
0
8
10
16
18
20
30
101
```

EXERCISES 13.4

1. Using the program for checking parentheses at the beginning of this section, illustrate how the stack grows and shrinks when the following expression is examined.

   `(5 / (3 - 2 * (4 + 3) - (8 DIV 2)))`

2. Write a test program to check an arithmetic expression for correct nesting of parentheses.
3. Modify the program in Exercise 2 so several expressions may be examined; then give more descriptive error messages. Finally, include a **SET** for the parentheses symbols "(" and ")".
4. Write a program that utilizes a stack to print a line of text in reverse order.
5. Stacks and queues can also be implemented using arrays rather than linked lists. With this in mind, do the following.
   a. Give appropriate definitions and declarations for using arrays for these data structures.
   b. Rewrite all procedures using array notation.
6. Write a procedure for inserting an element at the rear of a queue. Illustrate changes made in the linked list when such a procedure is executed.
7. Write a program that uses a stack to check an arithmetic expression for correct use of parentheses "( )", brackets "[ ]", and braces "{ }".
8. Indicate which of the following are binary search trees. Explain what is wrong with the ones that are not.

a.

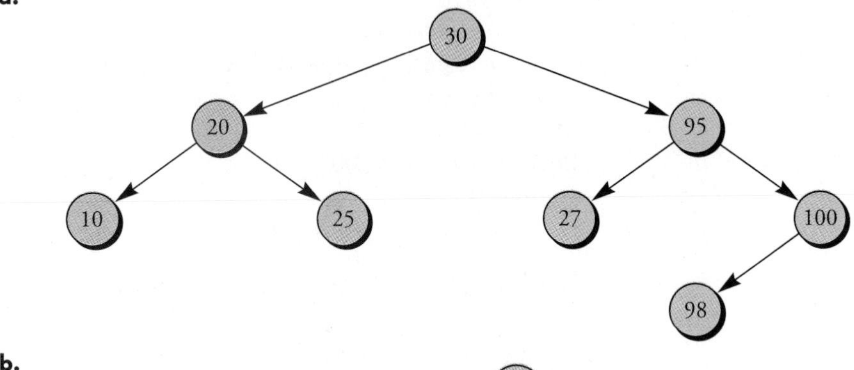
30
20
95
10
25
27
100
98

b.

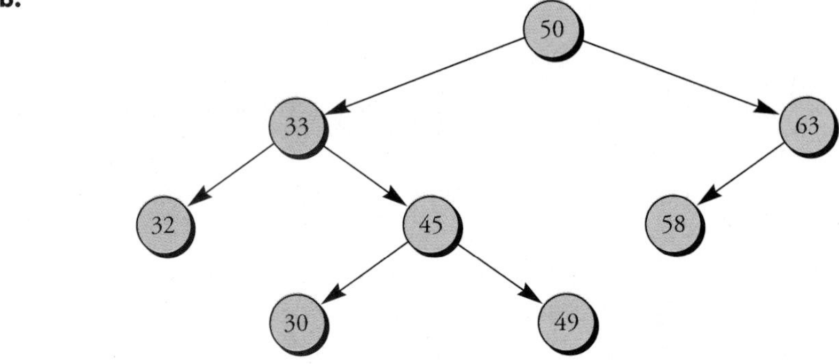
50
33
63
32
45
58
30
49

c.

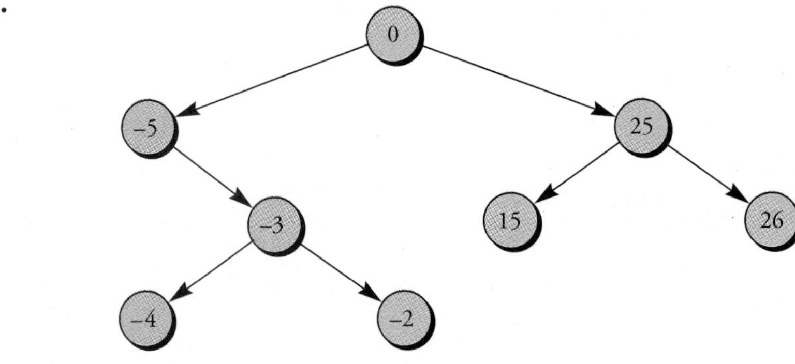
0
–5
25
–3
15
26
–4
–2

d.

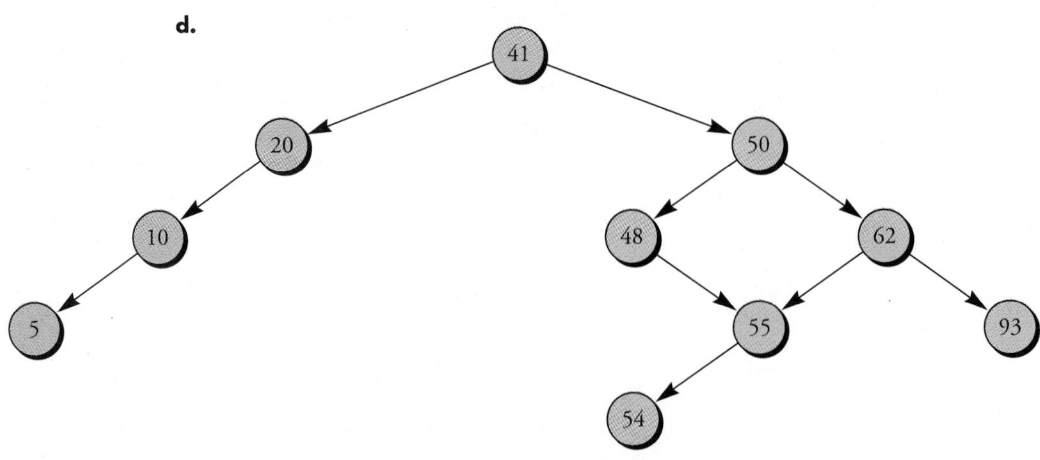
41
20
50
10
48
62
5
55
93
54

9. Modify **PROCEDURE** AddNode to include the possibility of having nodes of equal value.
10. Write a procedure that allows the user to insert a node in a binary search tree.
11. Write a function to search a binary search tree for a given value. The function should return **true** if the value is found and **false** if it is not found.
12. Write a procedure that allows the user to delete a node from a binary search tree.
13. Illustrate the binary search tree that is created when **PROGRAM** TreePrac is run using the data file

25	■	14	■	-3	■	145	■	0	■	98	■	81	■	73	■	85	■	92	■	56	■	21	■	■

RUNNING AND DEBUGGING HINTS

1. Be careful to distinguish between a pointer and its associated dynamic variable. Thus, if Ptr is a pointer, the variable is Ptr^.
2. When a dynamic variable is no longer needed in a program, use **dispose** so the memory location can be reallocated.
3. After using **dispose** with a pointer, its referenced variable is no longer available. If you use **dispose** (Ptr), then Ptr^ does not exist.
4. Be careful not to access the referenced variable of a pointer that is **NIL.** Thus, if the assignment

```
Ptr := NIL;
```

is made, a reference to Ptr^.Info results in an error.
5. When using pointers with subprograms, be careful to pass the pointer (not the referenced variable,) to the subprogram.
6. When creating dynamic data structures, be careful to initialize properly by assigning **NIL** where appropriate and to keep track of pointers as your structures grow and shrink.
7. Operations with pointers require that they be of the same data type. Thus, exercise caution when comparing or assigning them.
8. Values may be lost when pointers are inadvertently or prematurely reassigned. To avoid this, use as many auxiliary pointers as you wish. This is better than trying to use one pointer for two purposes.

SUMMARY

Key Terms

address (of a memory location)
binary search tree
binary tree
children
component (of a linked list)
dynamic structure
dynamic variable
first-in, first-out (FIFO) order
last-in, first-out (LIFO) order
leaf
linked list
node
parent
pointer variable
Pop
Push
queue
root
stack
static variable
tree
value (of a memory location)

Keywords

dispose
new
NIL

Key Concepts

- Values are stored in memory locations; each memory location has an address.
- A pointer variable contains the address of a memory location; pointer variables are declared by

```
TYPE
  AgeRange = 0..99;
VAR
  Ptr : ^AgeRange;
```

  where the caret (^) or up arrow (↑) is used before the predefined data type.
- A dynamic variable is a variable that is referenced through a pointer variable. Dynamic variables can be used in the same context as any other variable of the same type, and they are not declared in the variable declaration section. In the declaration

```
TYPE
  AgeRange = 0..99;
VAR
  Ptr : ^AgeRange;
```

  the dynamic variable is Ptr^ and is available after **new** (Ptr) is executed.
- Dynamic variables are created by

```
new (Ptr);
```

  and destroyed (memory area is made available for subsequent reuse) by

```
dispose (Ptr);
```

- Assuming the definition

```
TYPE
  AgeRange = 0..99;
VAR
  Ptr : ^AgeRange;
```

  the relationship between a pointer and its associated dynamic variable is illustrated by the code

```
new (Ptr);
Ptr^ := 21;
```

  which can be envisioned as

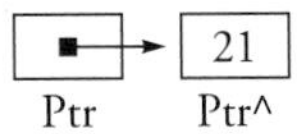

- The only legal operations on pointer variables are assignments and comparisons for equality.
- **NIL** can be assigned to a pointer variable; **NIL** is used in a Boolean expression to detect the end of a list.
- Dynamic data structures differ from static data structures in that dynamic data structures are modified during the execution of the program.
- A linked list is a dynamic data structure that is formed by having each component contain a pointer that points to the next component; generally, each component is a record with one field reserved for the pointer.
- A node is a component of a linked list.

- When creating a linked list, extra pointers are needed to keep track of the first, last, and newest component.
- When creating a linked list, the final component should have **NIL** assigned to its pointer field.
- Printing from a linked list is accomplished by starting with the first component in the list and proceeding sequentially through the list until the last component is reached; a typical procedure for printing from a linked list is

```
PROCEDURE Print (First : DataPtr);
  VAR
    P : DataPtr;
  BEGIN
    P := First;
    WHILE P <> NIL DO
      BEGIN
        writeln (P^.<field name>);
        P := P^.Next
      END  {  of WHILE loop  }
  END;  {  of PROCEDURE Print  }
```

- The insertion of a node in a linked list should encompass three cases: insertion at the beginning, in the middle, and at the end of a list.
- Inserting an element at the beginning of a linked list is a frequently used procedure, and is referred to as Push; one version of this procedure is

```
PROCEDURE Push (VAR Start : DataPtr;
                NewNum : integer);
  VAR
    P : DataPtr;
  BEGIN
    new (P);
    P^.New := NewNum;
    P^.Next := Start;
    Start := P;
    IF Start^.Next = NIL THEN
      Last := Start
  END;  {  of PROCEDURE Push  }
```

- Searching an ordered linked list to see where a new node should be inserted is accomplished by

```
Ptr := Start;
WHILE (Ptr <> NIL) AND (Ptr^.Num < NewNum) DO
  BEGIN
    Before := Ptr;
    Ptr := Ptr^.Next
  END;
```

- When deleting a node from a linked list, one can delete the first node, or search for a particular node and then delete it.
- Deleting the first node is referred to as Pop; one version of this procedure is

```
PROCEDURE Pop (VAR Start : DataPtr;
               VAR NewNum : integer);
  VAR
    P : DataPtr;
```

```
BEGIN
  P := Start;
  NewNum := P^.Num;
  Start := Start^.Next;
  dispose (P)
END;  {  of PROCEDURE Pop  }
```

- When a node is deleted from a linked list, it should be returned for subsequent use by the computer; this is done by using the standard procedure **dispose.**
- A stack is a dynamic data structure where access can be made from only one end; stacks are referred to as last-in, first-out (LIFO) structures.
- A queue is a dynamic data structure where access can be made from both ends; queues are referred to as first-in, first-out (FIFO) structures.
- A tree is a dynamic data structure consisting of a special node (called a root) that points to zero or more other nodes, each of which points to zero or more other nodes, and so on. Trees are represented symbolically as

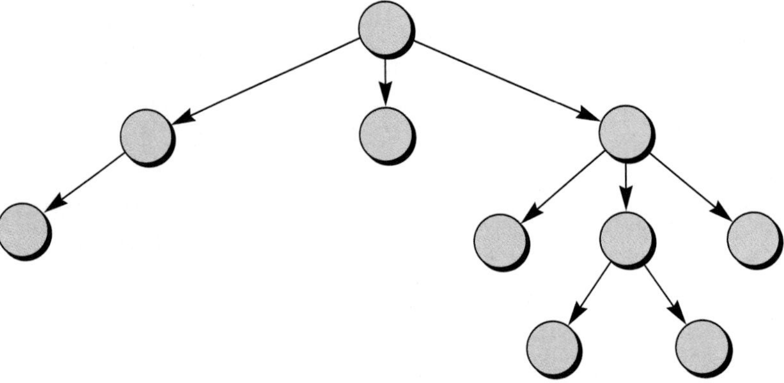

- A root is the first or top node of a tree.
- Trees are particularly useful in programs that use data that can be ordered and that need to be retrieved quickly.
- Binary trees are trees in which each node points to at most two other nodes; parent, right child, and left child are terms frequently used when working with binary trees. An illustration of a binary tree is

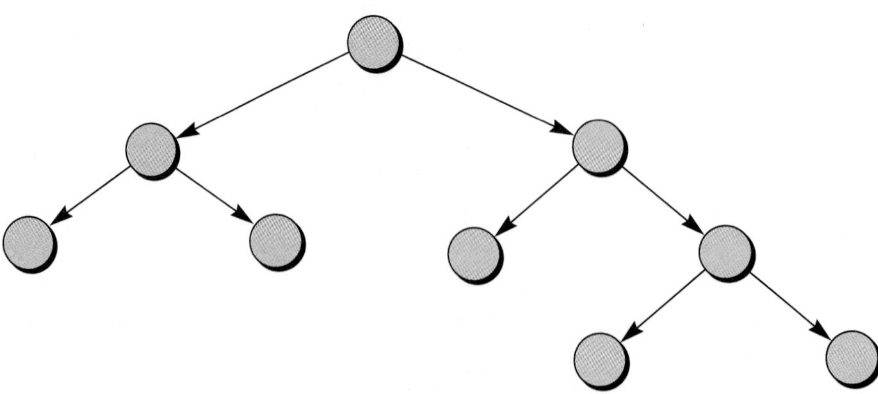

- Binary search trees are binary trees in which the information in the key field of any node is greater than the information in the key field of any node of its left child and any children of the left child; and the information in the key field of any node is less than the information in the key field of any node of its right child and any children of the right child. An illustration of a typical binary search tree is

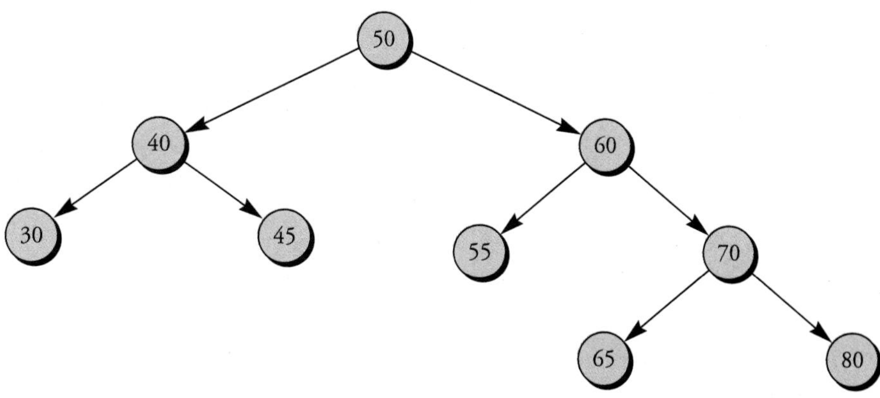

- Recursive procedures can be used when working with trees; to illustrate, the values in the nodes of a binary search tree can be printed (sequentially) with the procedure

```
PROCEDURE PrintTree (T : Pointer);
  BEGIN
    IF T = NIL THEN
      {  Do nothing  }
    ELSE
      BEGIN
        PrintTree (T^.LeftChild);
        writeln (T^.Info);
        PrintTree (T^.RightChild)
      END  {  of ELSE option  }
  END;  {  of PROCEDURE PrintTree  }
```

SUGGESTIONS FOR FURTHER READING

Nance, Douglas W., and Thomas L. Naps. *Introduction to Computer Science: Programming, Problem Solving, and Data Structures,* 3rd ed. St. Paul, MN: West Publishing Company, 1995.

Naps, Thomas L., and Bhagat Singh. *Program Design with Pascal: Principles, Algorithms, and Data Structures.* St. Paul, MN: West Publishing Company, 1988.

Naps, Thomas L., and Douglas W. Nance. *Introduction to Computer Science: Programming, Problem Solving, and Data Structures,* 3rd alternate ed. St. Paul, MN: West Publishing Company, 1995.

Naps, Thomas L., and George Pothering. *Introduction to Data Structures and Algorithm Analysis with Pascal.* St. Paul, MN: West Publishing Company, 1992.

Tenenbaum, Aaron M., and Moshe J. Augenstein. *Data Structures Using Pascal.* Englewood Cliffs, NJ: Prentice-Hall, 1981.

PROGRAMMING PROBLEMS AND PROJECTS

1. Creating an index for a textbook can be accomplished with a Pascal program that uses dynamic data structures and works with a text file. Assume that input for a program is a list of words to be included in an index. Write a program that scans the text and produces a list of page numbers indicating where each word is used in the text.
2. One of the problems faced by businesses is how best to manage their lines of customers. One method is to have a separate line for each cashier or station. Another is to have one feeder line where all customers wait and the customer at the front of the line goes to the first open station. Write a program to help a manager decide which method to use by simulating both options. Your program should allow for customers arriving at various intervals. The manager wants to know the average wait in each system, the average line length in each system (because of its psychological effect on customers), and the longest wait required.
3. Write a program to keep track of computer transactions on a mainframe computer. The computer can process only one job at a time. Each line of input contains a user's identification number, a starting time, and a sequence of integers representing the duration of each job. Assume all jobs are run on a first-come, first-serve basis. Your output should include a list of identification numbers, the starting and finishing times for each job, and the average waiting time for a transaction.
4. Several previous programming problems have involved keeping records and computing grades for students in some class. If linked lists are used for the students' records, such a program can be used for a class of 20 students or a class of 200 students. Write a recordkeeping program that utilizes linked lists. Input is from an unsorted data file. Each student's information consists of the student's name, 10 quiz scores, six program scores, and three examination scores. Output should include the following.
   a. A list, alphabetized by student name, that incorporates each student's quiz, program, and examination totals; total points; percentage grade; and letter grade
   b. The overall class average
   c. A histogram that depicts class averages
5. Modify the program you developed for the ReadMore Public Library (Problems 6 and 7, Chapter 9; and Problem 2, Chapter 11) to incorporate a dynamic data structure. Use a linked list to solve the same problem.
6. Mailing lists are frequently kept in a data file sorted alphabetically by customer name. However, when they are used to generate mailing labels for a bulk mailing, they must be sorted by zip code. Write a program to input an alphabetically sorted file and produce a list of labels sorted by zip code. The following data are on file for each customer.
   (1) Name
   (2) Address, including street (plus number), city, two-letter abbreviation for state, and zip code
   (3) Expiration information, including the month and year

   Use a binary tree to sort by zip code. Your labels should include some special symbol for all expiring subscriptions. (See Problem 1, Chapter 11.)
7. It is possible for a program to contain many more operations with stacks than we developed in this chapter. Write a complete program that includes the following stack operations.

(1) Flush: empties a stack
(2) Copy: creates a duplicate stack
(3) StackLength: returns the number of elements in a stack
(4) DisplayStack: displays the contents of a stack
(5) DisplayReverseStack: displays the contents of a stack in reverse order
(6) CompareStacks: compares two stacks and returns the boolean value **true** if the stacks are identical and **false** if they are not identical

Output from your program should demonstrate that all stack operations are functioning properly.

8. As a struggling professional football team, the Bay Area Brawlers have a highly volatile player roster. Write a program that allows the team to maintain its roster as a linked list alphabetically, ordered by player last name. Other data items stored for each player are

(1) Height
(2) Weight
(3) Age
(4) University affiliation

As an added option, have your program access players in descending order of weight and age.

9. Write a program that allows the input of an arbitrary number of polynomials as coefficient and exponent pairs. Store each polynomial as a linked list of coefficient-exponent pairs arranged in descending order by exponent. These pairs do not need to be entered in descending order; it is the responsibility of your program to arrange them that way. Your program should then be able to evaluate each of the polynomials for an arbitrary argument X and to display each of the polynomials in the appropriate descending exponent order. Make sure your program works for all "unusual" polynomials, such as the zero polynomial, polynomials of degree 1, and constant polynomials.

COMMUNICATION IN PRACTICE

1. Select a program from the *Programming Problems and Projects* section of this chapter that you have not yet worked. Construct a structure chart and write all documentary information for this program. Include variable definition, subprogram definition, required input, and required output. When you are finished, have a classmate read your documentation to see if it is clear precisely what is to be done.

2. Remove all documentation from a program you have written for this chapter. Exchange this modified version with another student who has done the same thing. Write documentation for the exchanged program. Compare your documentation with that originally written for the program. Discuss the differences and similarities with the other students in your class.

3. Linked lists, stacks, and queues can be presented by using either dynamic variables or static variables (arrays). Talk with a computer science instructor who prefers the dynamic variable approach and with one who prefers the static variable approach. List the advantages and disadvantages of each method. Give an oral report to your class summarizing your conversations with the instructors. Create a chart to use as part of your presentation.

Appendixes

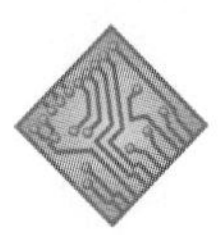

Appendix 1 Reserved Words

The following words have predefined meanings in standard Pascal and cannot be changed. Each of these, except **GOTO** and **LABEL,** have been developed in the text. These two statements are discussed in Appendix 7.

AND	**END**	**MOD**	**REPEAT**
ARRAY	**FILE**	**NIL**	**SET**
BEGIN	**FOR**	**NOT**	**THEN**
CASE	**FORWARD**	**OF**	**TO**
CONST	**FUNCTION**	**OR**	**TYPE**
DIV	**GOTO**	**PACKED**	**UNTIL**
DO	**IF**	**PROCEDURE**	**VAR**
DOWNTO	**IN**	**PROGRAM**	**WHILE**
ELSE	**LABEL**	**RECORD**	**WITH**

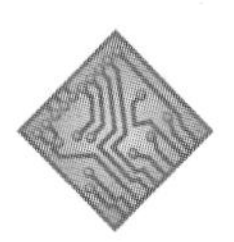

Appendix 2 Standard Identifiers

The standard identifiers for constants, types, files, functions, and procedures are set forth in this appendix. All have predefined meanings that could (but probably should not) be changed in a program. Summary descriptions are given for the functions and procedures.

Constants	*Types*	*Files*
false	**boolean**	**input**
maxint	**char**	**output**
true	**integer**	
	real	
	text	

Functions

Function	Parameter Type	Result Type	Value Returned
abs(x)	**integer**	**integer**	Absolute value of x
	real	**real**	
arctan(x)	**integer**	**real**	Arctangent of x
	real		(radians)
chr(a)	**integer**	**char**	Character with ordinal a
cos(x)	**integer**	**real**	Cosine of x (radians)
	real		
eof(F)	**file**	**boolean**	End-of-file test for F
eoln(F)	**file**	**boolean**	End-of-line test for F
exp(x)	**integer**	**real**	e^x
	real	**real**	
ln(x)	**integer** (positive)	**real**	Natural logarithm of x
	real (positive)		
odd(a)	**integer**	**boolean**	Tests for an odd integer a
ord(x)	nonreal scalar	**integer**	Ordinal number of x
pred(x)	nonreal scalar	same as x	Predecessor of x

Functions (Continued)

Function	Parameter Type	Result Type	Value Returned
round(*x*)	**real**	**integer**	Rounds off *x*
sin(*x*)	**integer** **real**	**real**	Sine of *x*
sqr(*x*)	**integer** **real**	**integer** **real**	Square of *x*
sqrt(*x*)	**integer** **real**	**real**	Square root of *x*
succ(*x*)	nonreal scalar	same as *x*	Successor of *x*
trunc(*x*)	**real**	**integer**	Truncated value of *x*

Procedures

Procedure Call	Purpose of Procedure
dispose (Ptr)	Returns variable referenced by Ptr to available space list
get (F)	Advances the file pointer for file F and assigns the new value to F^
new (Ptr)	Creates a variable of the type referenced by Ptr and stores a pointer to the new variable in Ptr
pack (U, J, P)	Copies unpacked array elements from U into the packed array P; copying starts with P[1] := U[J]
page (F)	Starts printing the next line of text F at the top of a new page
put (F)	Appends the current value of F to file F
read (F, <variable list>)	Reads values from file F into indicated variables; if F is not specified, **input** is assumed
readln (F, <variable list>)	Executes the same as **read** and then advances the file pointer to the first position following the next end-of-line marker
reset (F)	Resets the pointer in file F to the beginning for the purpose of reading from F
rewrite (F)	Resets the pointer in file F to the beginning for the purpose of writing to F
unpack (P, U, J)	Copies packed array elements from P into the unpacked array U; copying starts with U[J] := P[1]
write (F, <parameter list>)	Writes values specified by parameter list to text file F; if F is not specified, **output** is assumed
writeln (F, <parameter list>)	Executes the same as **write** and then places an end-of-line marker in F

Appendix 3
Syntax Diagrams

Syntax diagrams in this appendix are listed in the following order.

- Program
  - Identifier
  - File List
- Declarations and Definitions
  - Label Declaration
  - Constant Definition
  - Type Definition
    - Type
      - Enumerated Type
      - Subrange Type
      - Pointer Type
      - Array Type
      - Record Type
        - Field List
          - Fixed Part
          - Variant Part
            - Variant Description
      - File Type
      - Set Type
  - Variable Declaration
  - Procedure and Function Declarations
    - Formal Parameter List
- Body
  - Compound Statement
    - Statement
      - Assignment Statement
        - Expression
          - Term
            - Factor
              - Variable
              - Set Value

Boolean Expression
read or readln Statement
write or writeln Statement
Procedure Statement
IF Statement
CASE Statement
Case Label
WHILE Statement
REPEAT Statement
FOR Statement
WITH Statement
GOTO Statement
Empty Statement

Program

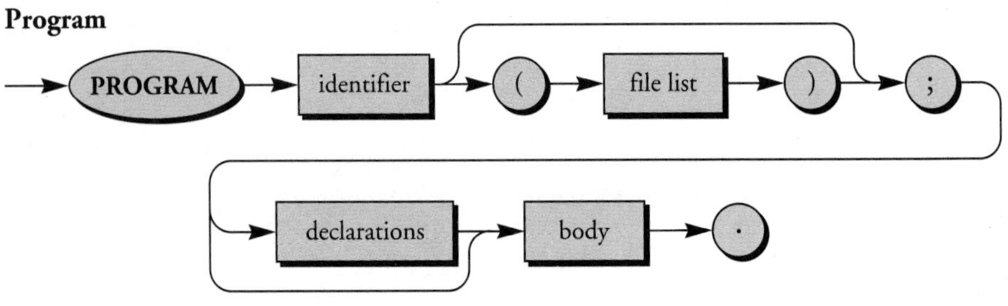

Identifier

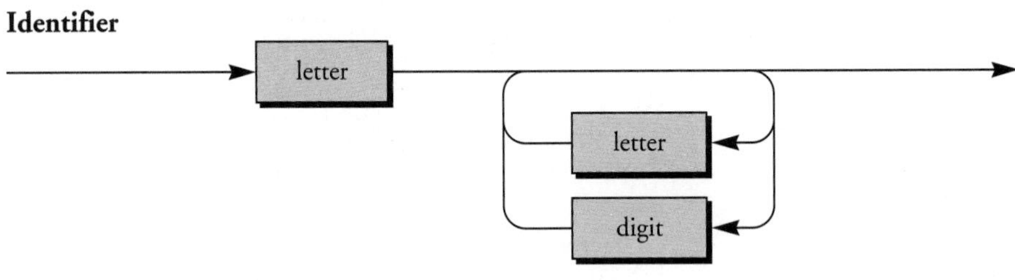

File List

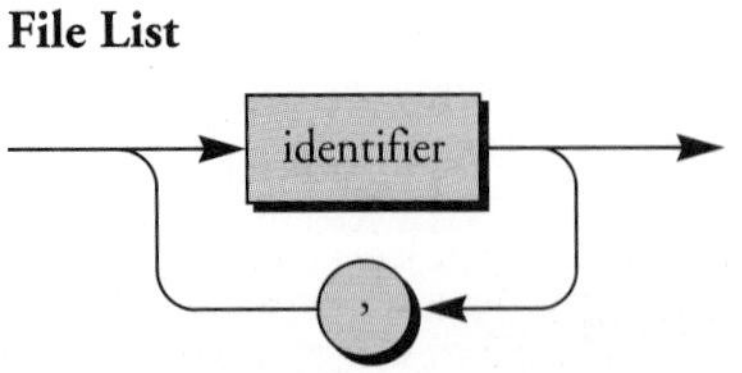

Declarations and Definitions

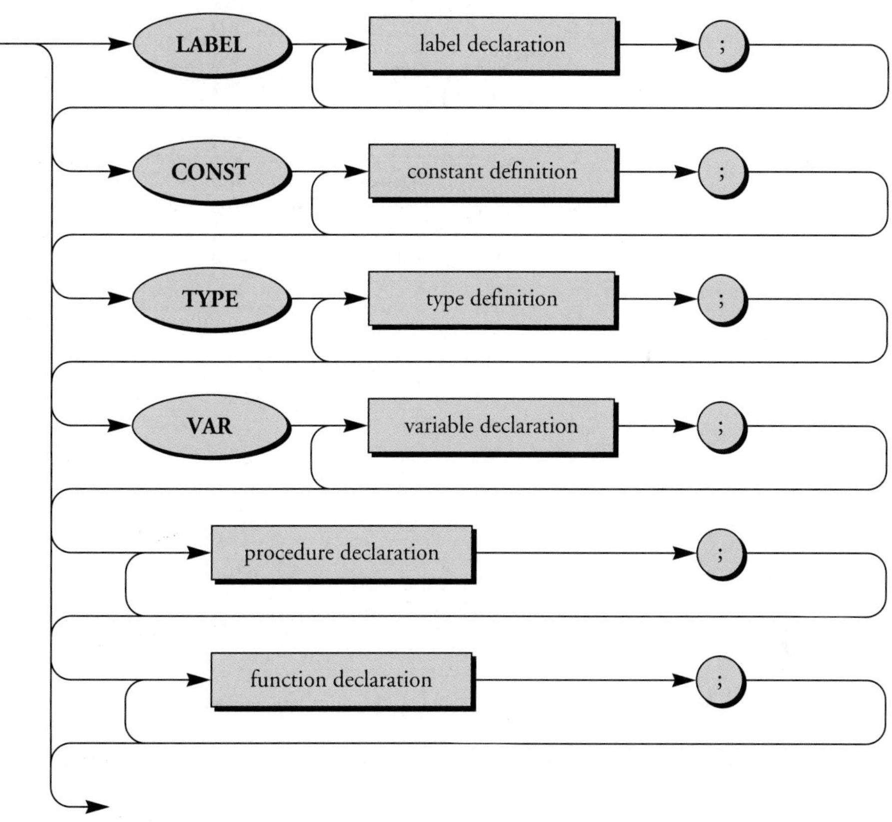

Label Declaration

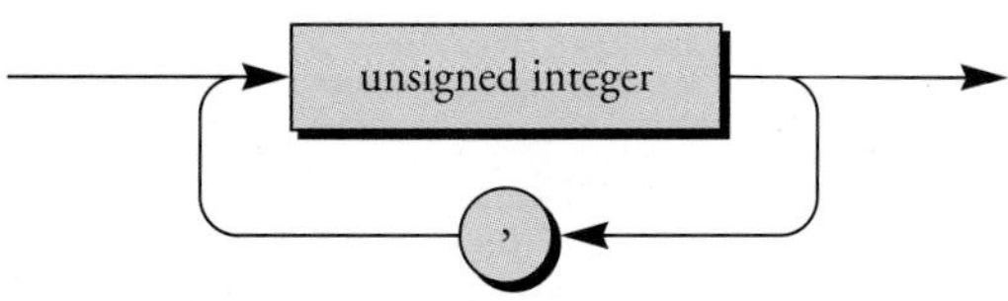

Constant Definition

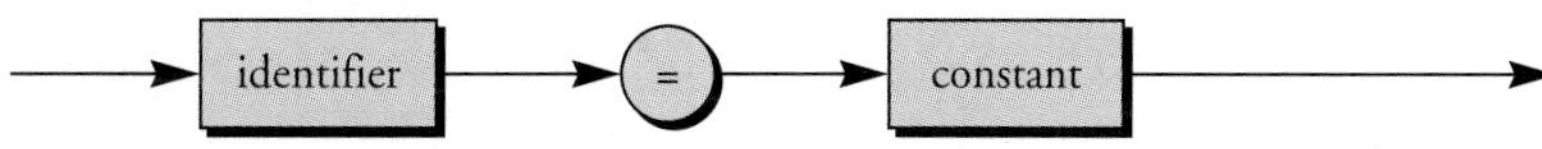

Type Definition

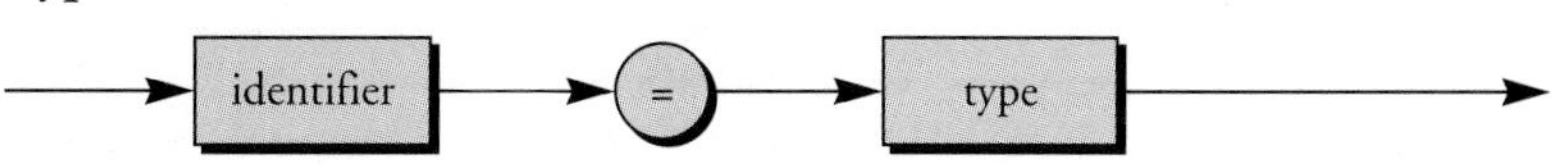

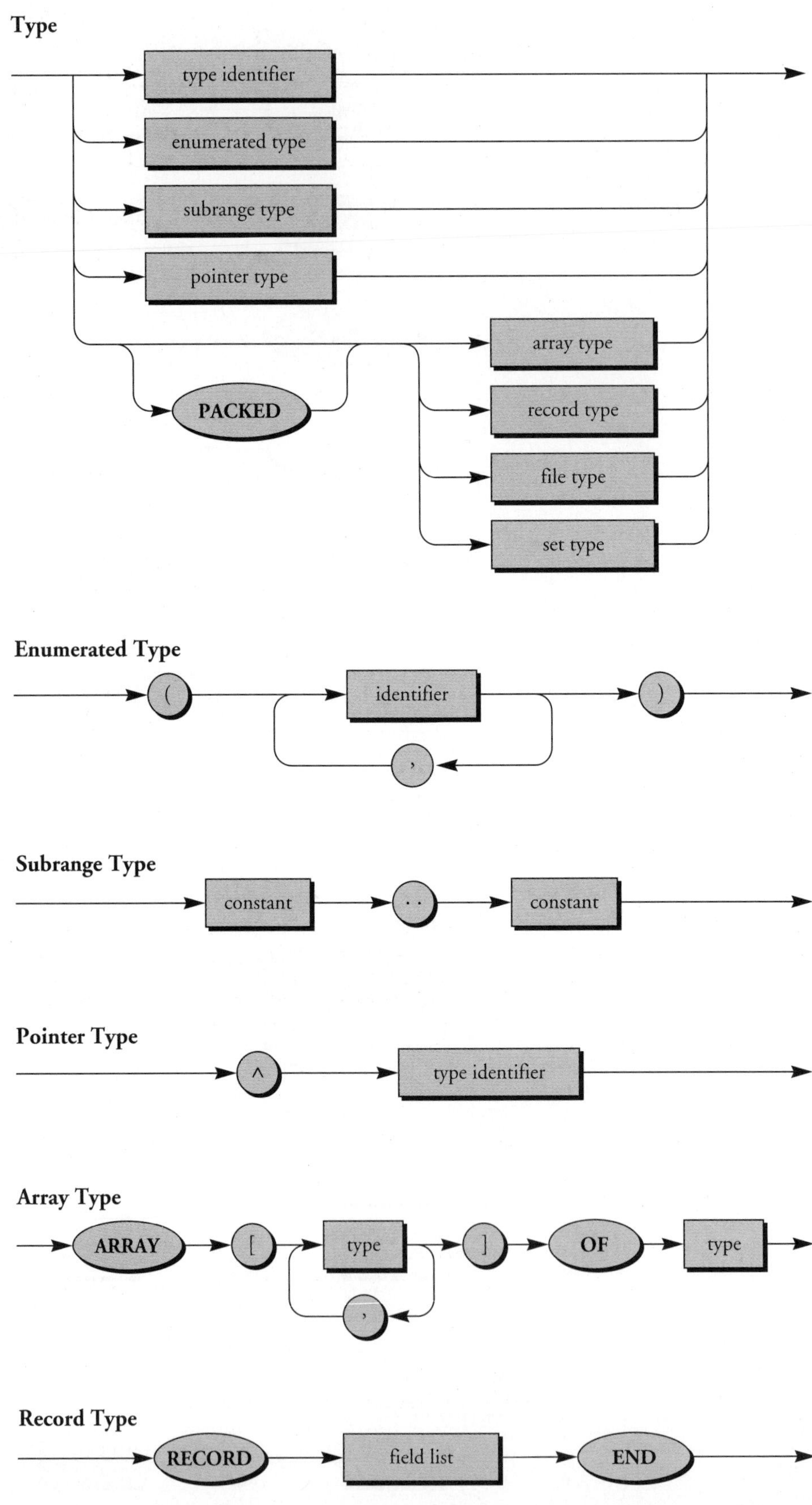
Type
type identifier
enumerated type
subrange type
pointer type
PACKED
array type
record type
file type
set type
Enumerated Type
(
identifier
,
)
Subrange Type
constant
..
constant
Pointer Type
^
type identifier
Array Type
ARRAY
[
type
,
]
OF
type
Record Type
RECORD
field list
END

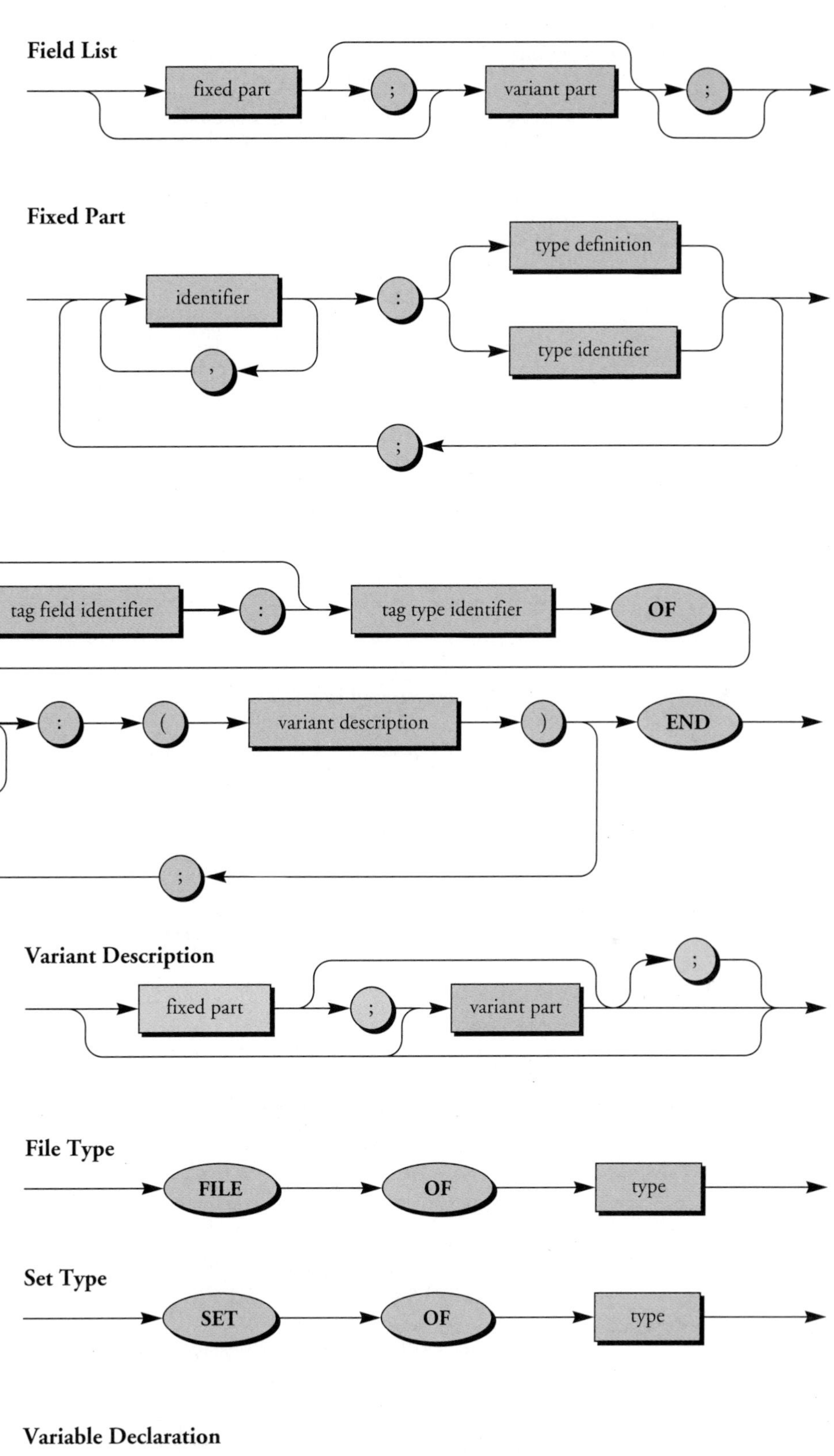
Field List
fixed part
;
variant part
;
Fixed Part
identifier
,
:
type definition
type identifier
;
Variant Part
CASE
tag field identifier
:
tag type identifier
OF
constant
,
:
(
variant description
)
END
;
Variant Description
fixed part
;
variant part
;
File Type
FILE
OF
type
Set Type
SET
OF
type
Variable Declaration
identifier
:
type

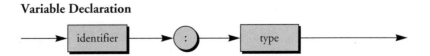

Procedure and Function Declarations

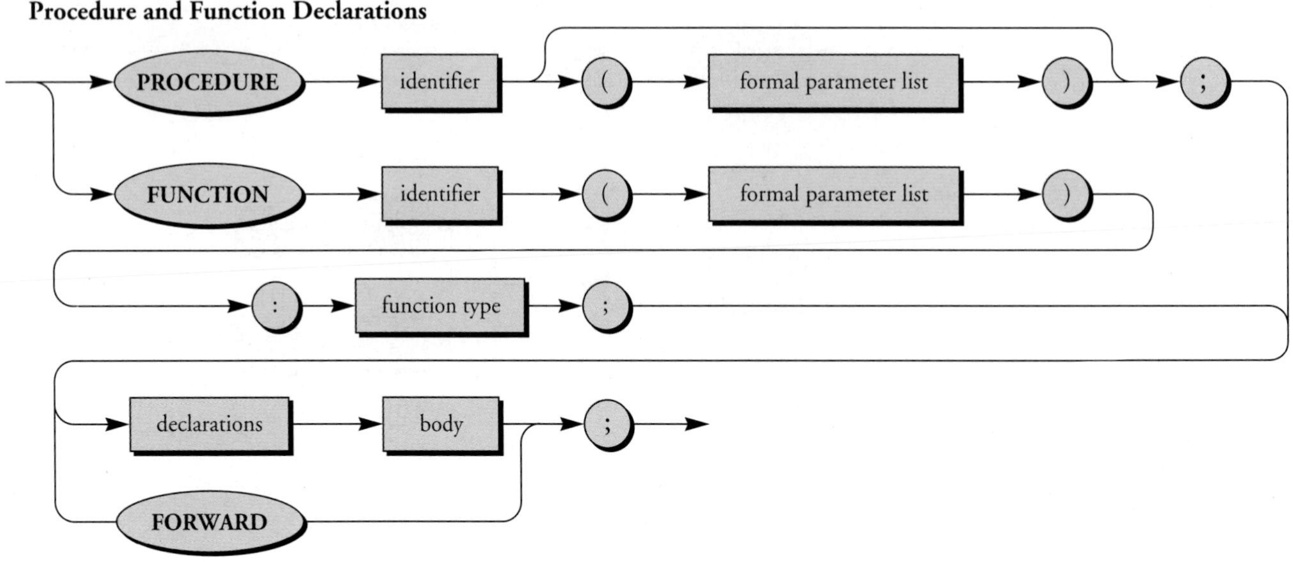

Formal Parameter List

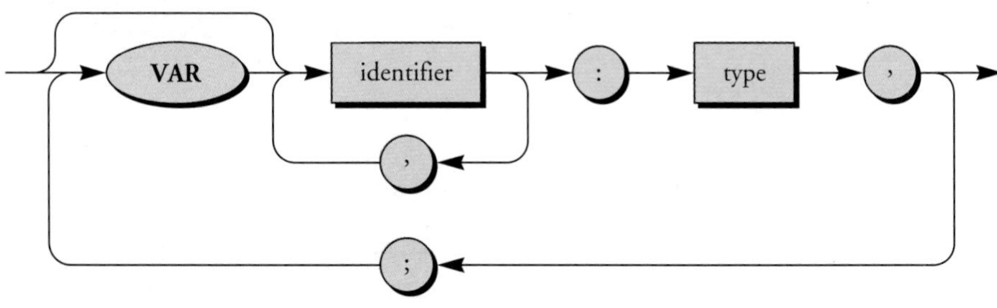

Body

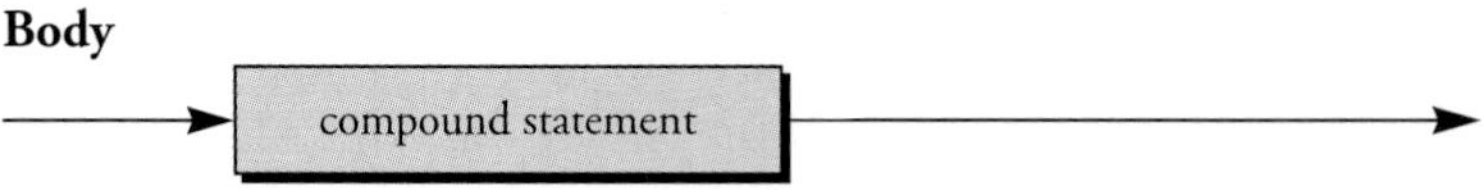

Compound Statement

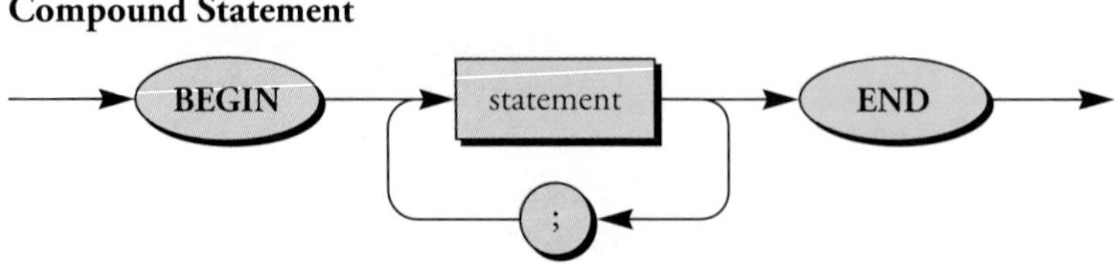

Statement

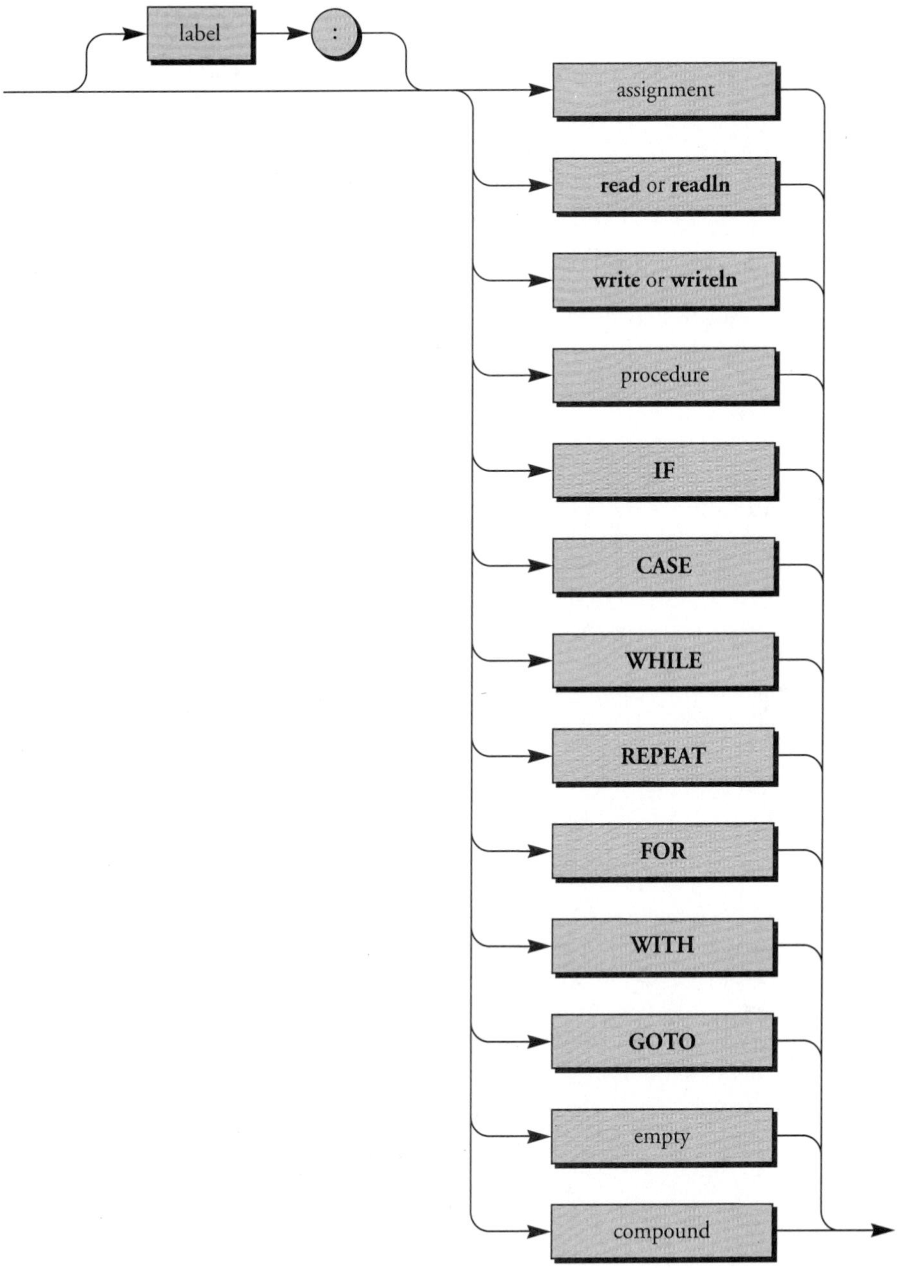

label
:
assignment
read or readln
write or writeln
procedure
IF
CASE
WHILE
REPEAT
FOR
WITH
GOTO
empty
compound

Assignment Statement

variable
function identifier
: =
expression

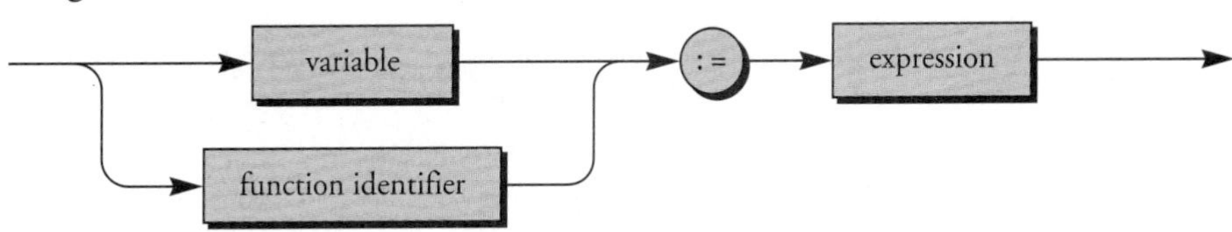

Expression

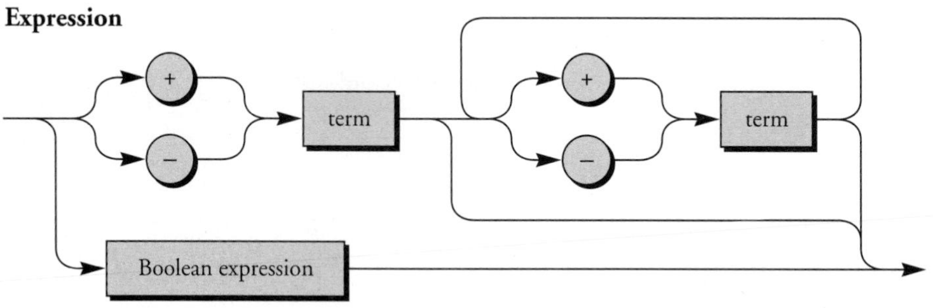

Term

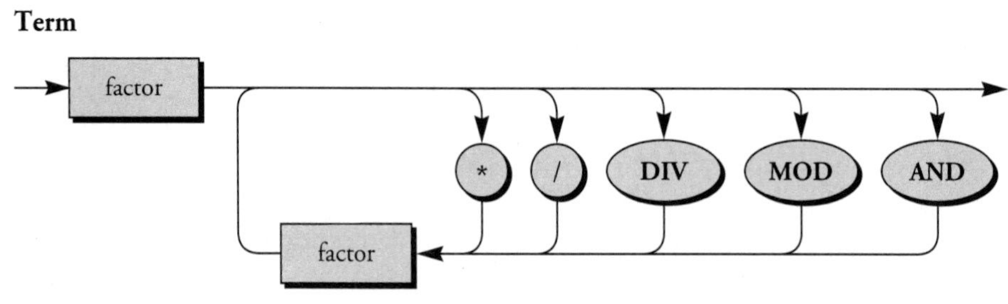

Factor

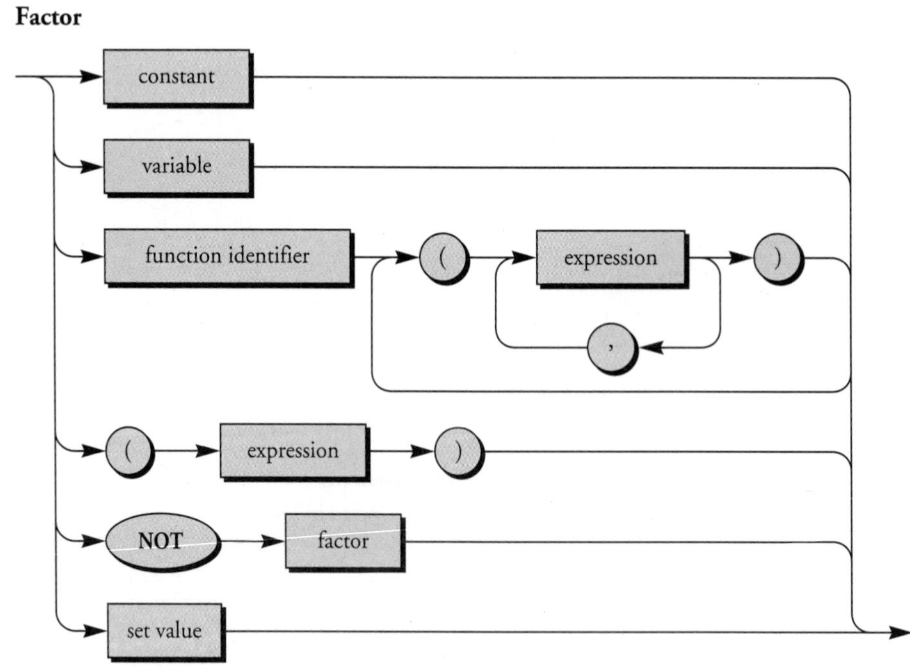

Variable

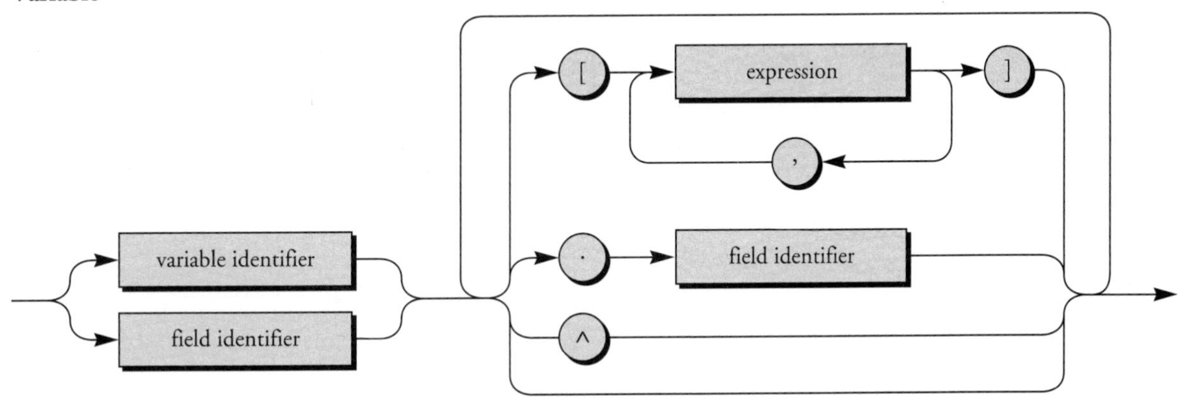

Set Value

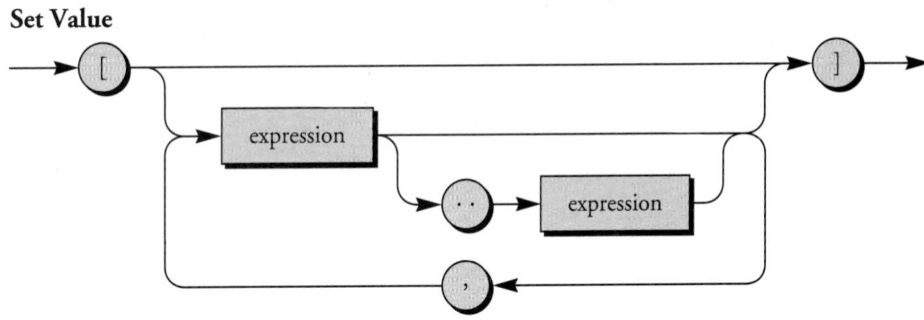

Boolean Expression

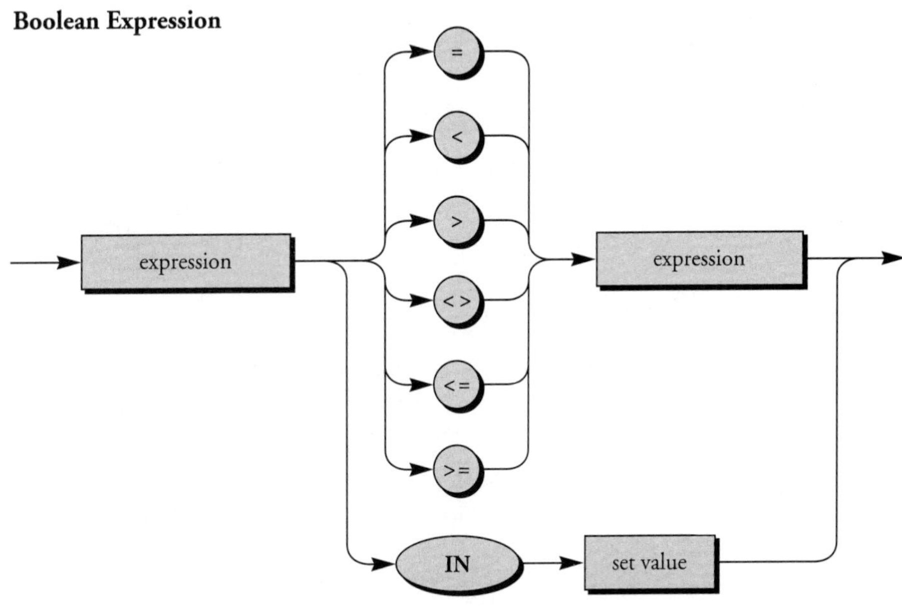

read or readln Statement

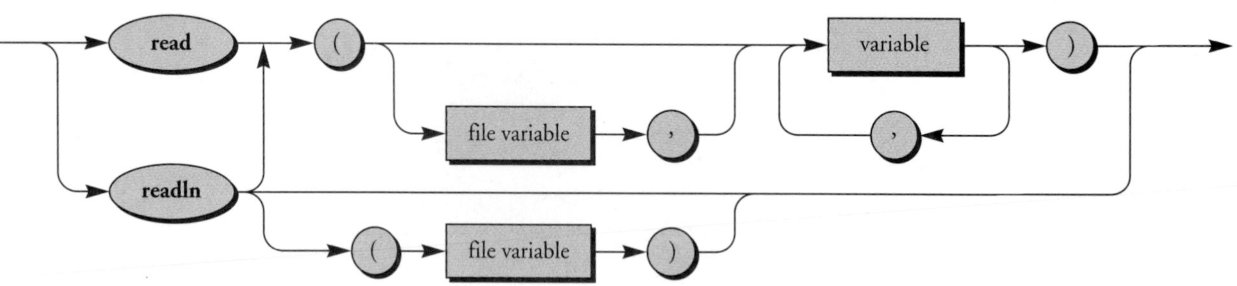

write or writeln Statement

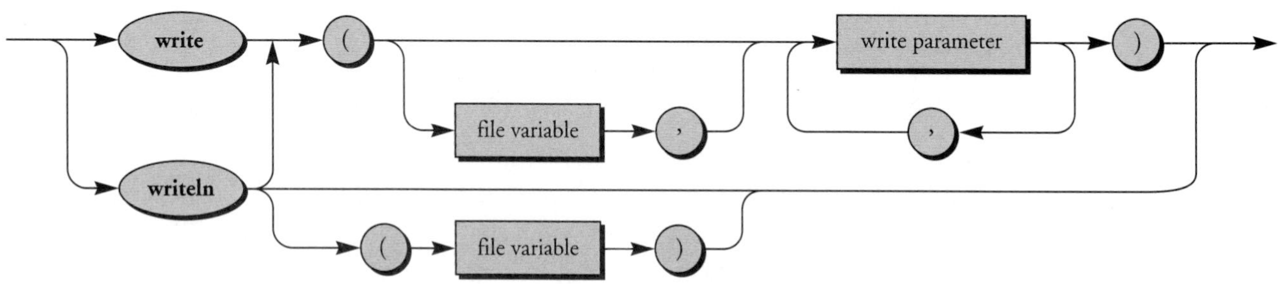

Procedure Statement

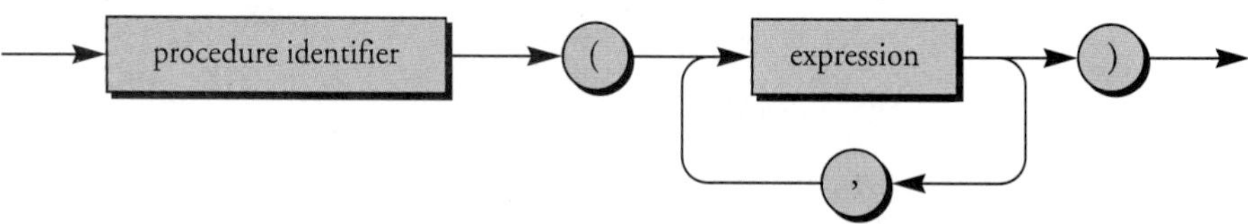

IF Statement

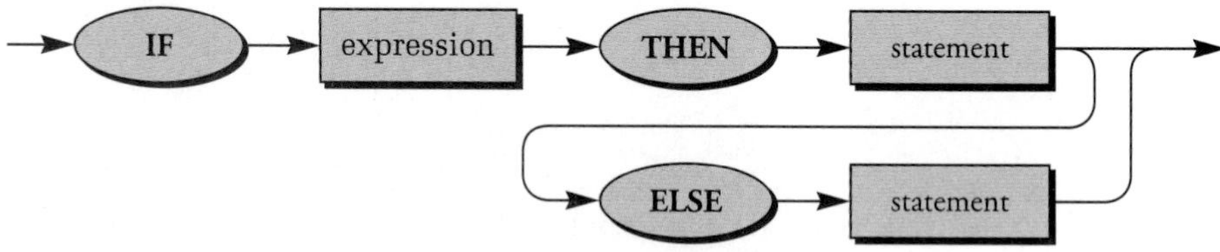

CASE Statement

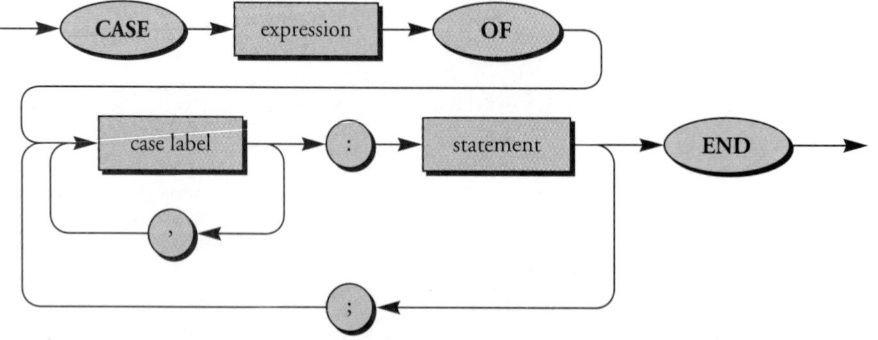

Case Label

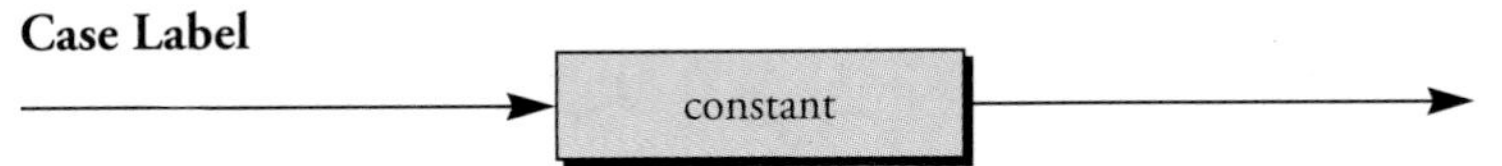

WHILE Statement

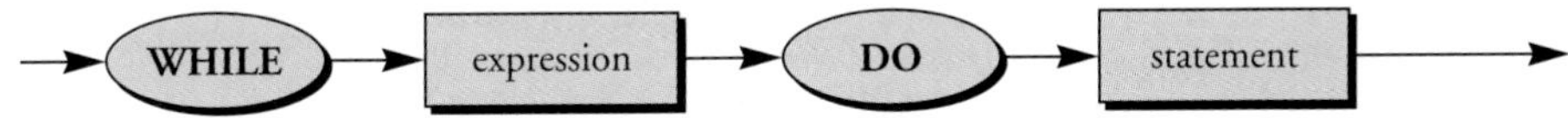

REPEAT Statement

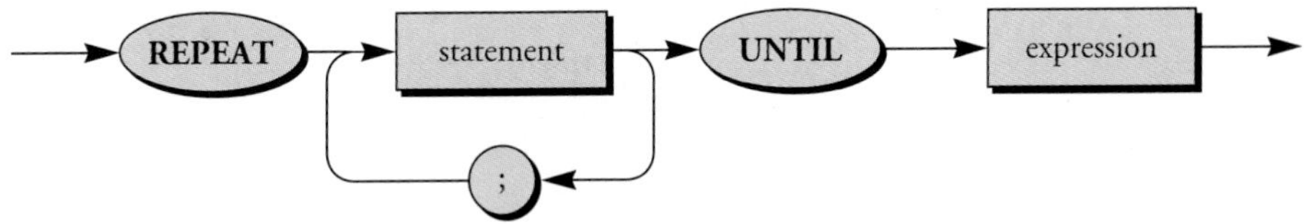

FOR Statement

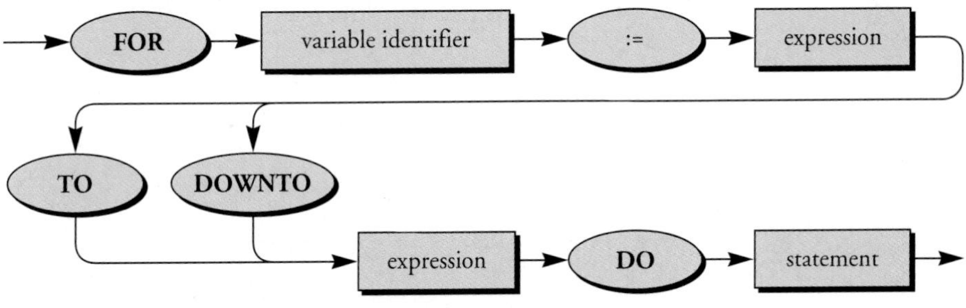

WITH Statement

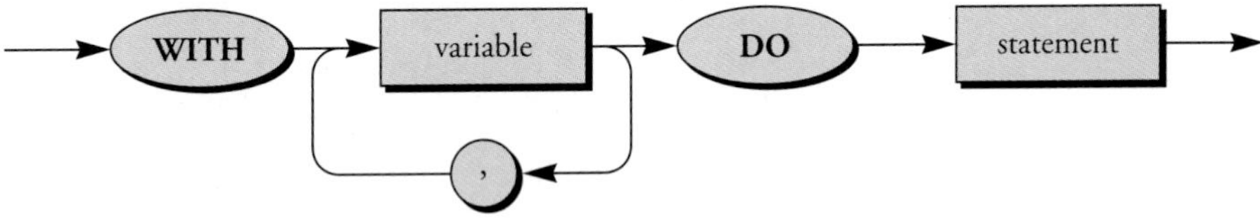

GOTO Statement

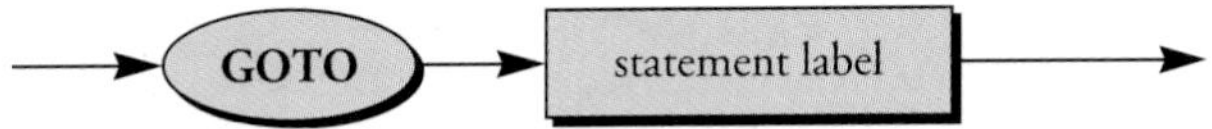

Empty Statement

Appendix 4
Character Sets

The two tables included here show the ordering of two common character sets. Note only printable characters are shown for each set. Ordinals without character representations either do not have standard representation or are associated with unprintable control characters. In each list, the blank is denoted by "ƀ".

The American Standard Code for Information Interchange (ASCII)

Left Digit(s)	Right Digit 0	1	2	3	4	5	6	7	8	9
3			ƀ	!	"	#	$	%	&	'
4	(	)	*	+	,	–	.	/	0	1
5	2	3	4	5	6	7	8	9	:	;
6	<	=	>	?	@	A	B	C	D	E
7	F	G	H	I	J	K	L	M	N	O
8	P	Q	R	S	T	U	V	W	X	Y
9	Z	[	\	]	^		`	a	b	c
10	d	e	f	g	h	i	j	k	l	m
11	n	o	p	q	r	s	t	u	v	w
12	x	y	z	{	|	}	~			

*Codes < 32 or > 126 are nonprintable.

The Extended Binary Coded Decimal Interchange Code (EBCDIC)

Left	Right Digit									
Digit(s)	0	1	2	3	4	5	6	7	8	9
6					ƀ					
7					¢	.	<	(	+	|
8	&									
9	!	$	*	)	;	¬		/		
10							^	,	%	
11	>	?								
12			:	#	@	'	=	"		a
13	b	c	d	e	f	g	h	i		
14						j	k	l	m	n
15	o	p	q	r						
16			s	t	u	v	w	x	y	z
17								\	{	}
18	[	]								
19				A	B	C	D	E	F	G
20	H	I								J
21	K	L	M	N	O	P	Q	R		
22							S	T	U	V
23	W	X	Y	Z						
24	0	1	2	3	4	5	6	7	8	9

*Codes not listed in this table are nonprintable.

Appendix 5
Compiler Error Messages

This list contains typical error messages used by a compiler to identify compilation errors. Such errors are identified by number with appropriate messages produced at the bottom of a compilation listing. Different compilers produce different error messages.

```
 1  ERROR IN SIMPLE TYPE.
 2  IDENTIFIER EXPECTED.
 3  'PROGRAM' EXPECTED.
 4  ')' EXPECTED.
 5  ' ' EXPECTED.
 6  UNEXPECTED SYMBOL.
 7  ERROR IN PARAMETER LIST.
 8  'OF' EXPECTED.
 9  '(' EXPECTED.
10  ERROR IN TYPE.
11  '[' EXPECTED.
12  ']' EXPECTED.
13  'END' EXPECTED.
14  ';' EXPECTED.
15  INTEGER CONSTANT EXPECTED.
16  '=' EXPECTED.
17  'BEGIN' EXPECTED.
18  ERROR IN DECLARATION PART.
19  ERROR IN FIELD-LIST.
20  ',' EXPECTED.
21  '..' EXPECTED.

40  VALUE PART ALLOWED ONLY IN MAIN PROGRAM.
41  TOO FEW VALUES SPECIFIED.
42  TOO MANY VALUES SPECIFIED.
43  VARIABLE INITIALIZED TWICE.
44  TYPE IS NEITHER ARRAY NOR RECORD.
45  REPETITION FACTOR MUST BE GREATER THAN ZERO.
50  ERROR IN CONSTANT.
```

51 ':=' EXPECTED.

52 'THEN' EXPECTED.

53 'UNTIL' EXPECTED.

54 'DO' EXPECTED.

55 'TO' OR 'DOWNTO' EXPECTED.

57 'FILE' EXPECTED.

58 ERROR IN FACTOR.

59 ERROR IN VARIABLE.

60 FILE TYPE IDENTIFIER EXPECTED.

101 IDENTIFIER DECLARED TWICE.

102 LOWBOUND EXCEEDS HIGHBOUND.

103 IDENTIFIER IS NOT OF APPROPRIATE CLASS.

104 IDENTIFIER NOT DECLARED.

105 SIGN NOT ALLOWED.

106 NUMBER EXPECTED.

107 INCOMPATIBLE SUBRANGE TYPES.

108 FILE NOT ALLOWED HERE.

109 TYPE MUST NOT BE REAL.

110 TAGFIELD TYPE MUST BE SCALAR OR SUBRANGE.

111 INCOMPATIBLE WITH TAGFIELD TYPE.

112 INDEX TYPE MUST NOT BE REAL.

113 INDEX TYPE MUST BE SCALAR OR SUBRANGE.

114 BASE TYPE MUST NOT BE REAL.

115 BASE TYPE MUST BE SCALAR OR SUBRANGE.

116 ERROR IN TYPE OF STANDARD PROCEDURE PARAMETER.

117 UNSATISFIED FORWARD REFERENCE.

119 FORWARD DECLARED; REPETITION OF PARAMETER LIST NOT ALLOWED.

120 FUNCTION RESULT TYPE MUST BE SCALAR, SUBRANGE, OR POINTER.

121 FILE VALUE PARAMETER NOT ALLOWED.

122 FORWARD DECLARED FUNCTION; REPETITION OF RESULT TYPE NOT ALLOWED.

123 MISSING RESULT TYPE IN FUNCTION DECLARATION.

124 FIXED-POINT FORMATTING ALLOWED FOR REALS ONLY.

125 ERROR IN TYPE OF STANDARD FUNCTION PARAMETER.

126 NUMBER OF PARAMETERS DOES NOT AGREE WITH DECLARATION.

127 INVALID PARAMETER SUBSTITUTION.

128 PARAMETER PROCEDURE/FUNCTION IS NOT COMPATIBLE WITH DECLARATION.

129 TYPE CONFLICT OF OPERANDS.

130 EXPRESSION IS NOT OF SET TYPE.

131 TESTS ON EQUALITY ALLOWED ONLY.

132 '<' AND '>' NOT ALLOWED FOR SET OPERANDS.

133 FILE COMPARISON NOT ALLOWED.

134 INVALID TYPE OF OPERAND(S).

135 TYPE OF OPERAND MUST BE BOOLEAN.

136 SET ELEMENT MUST BE SCALAR OR SUBRANGE.

137 SET ELEMENT TYPES NOT COMPATIBLE.

138 TYPE OF VARIABLE IS NOT ARRAY.
139 INDEX TYPE IS NOT COMPATIBLE WITH DECLARATION.
140 TYPE OF VARIABLE IS NOT RECORD.
141 TYPE OF VARIABLE MUST BE FILE OR POINTER.
142 INVALID PARAMETER SUBSTITUTION.
143 INVALID TYPE OF LOOP CONTROL VARIABLE.
144 INVALID TYPE OF EXPRESSION.
145 TYPE CONFLICT.
146 ASSIGNMENT OF FILES NOT ALLOWED.
147 LABEL TYPE INCOMPATIBLE WITH SELECTING EXPRESSION.
148 SUBRANGE BOUNDS MUST BE SCALAR.
149 INDEX TYPE MUST NOT BE INTEGER.
150 ASSIGNMENT TO THIS FUNCTION IS NOT ALLOWED.
151 ASSIGNMENT TO FORMAL FUNCTION IS NOT ALLOWED.
152 NO SUCH FIELD IN THIS RECORD.

155 CONTROL VARIABLE MUST NOT BE DECLARED ON AN INTERMEDIATE LEVEL.
156 MULTIDEFINED CASE LABEL.
157 RANGE OF CASE LABELS IS TOO LARGE.
158 MISSING CORRESPONDING VARIANT DECLARATION.
159 REAL OR STRING TAGFIELDS NOT ALLOWED.
160 PREVIOUS DECLARATION WAS NOT FORWARD.
161 MULTIPLE FORWARD DECLARATION.

164 SUBSTITUTION OF STANDARD PROCEDURE/FUNCTION NOT ALLOWED.
165 MULTIDEFINED LABEL.
166 MULTIDECLARED LABEL.
167 UNDECLARED LABEL.
168 UNDEFINED LABEL IN THE PREVIOUS BLOCK.
169 ERROR IN BASE SET.
170 VALUE PARAMETER EXPECTED.

172 UNDECLARED EXTERNAL FILE.
173 FORTRAN PROCEDURE OR FUNCTION EXPECTED.
174 PASCAL PROCEDURE OR FUNCTION EXPECTED.
175 MISSING FILE 'INPUT' IN PROGRAM HEADING.
176 MISSING FILE 'OUTPUT' IN PROGRAM HEADING.
177 ASSIGNMENT TO FUNCTION ALLOWED ONLY IN FUNCTION BODY.
178 MULTIDEFINED RECORD VARIANT.
179 X-OPTION OF ACTUAL PROCEDURE/FUNCTION DOES NOT MATCH FORMAL DECLARATION.
180 CONTROL VARIABLE MUST NOT BE FORMAL.
181 ARRAY SUBSCRIPT CALCULATION TOO COMPLICATED.
182 MAGNITUDE OF CASE LABEL IS TOO LARGE.
183 SUBRANGE OF TYPE REAL IS NOT ALLOWED.

198 ALTERNATE INPUT NOT FOUND.
199 ONLY ONE ALTERNATE INPUT MAY BE ACTIVE.

201 ERROR IN REAL CONSTANT DIGIT EXPECTED.
202 STRING CONSTANT MUST BE CONTAINED ON A SINGLE LINE.
203 INTEGER CONSTANT EXCEEDS RANGE.
204 8 OR 9 IN OCTAL NUMBER.
205 STRINGS OF LENGTH ZERO ARE NOT ALLOWED.
206 INTEGER PART OF REAL CONSTANT EXCEEDS RANGE.
207 REAL CONSTANT EXCEEDS RANGE.

250 TOO MANY NESTED SCOPES OF IDENTIFIERS.
251 TOO MANY NESTED PROCEDURES AND/OR FUNCTIONS.

255 TOO MANY ERRORS ON THIS SOURCE LINE.
256 TOO MANY EXTERNAL REFERENCES.

259 EXPRESSION TOO COMPLICATED.
260 TOO MANY EXIT LABELS.
261 TOO MANY LARGE VARIABLES.
262 NODE TO BE ALLOCATED IS TOO LARGE.
263 TOO MANY PROCEDURE/FUNCTION PARAMETERS.
264 TOO MANY PROCEDURES AND FUNCTIONS.

300 DIVISION BY ZERO.

302 INDEX EXPRESSION OUT OF BOUNDS.
303 VALUE TO BE ASSIGNED IS OUT OF BOUNDS.
304 ELEMENT EXPRESSION OUT OF RANGE.

350 ONLY THE LAST DIMENSION MAY BE PACKED.
351 ARRAY TYPE IDENTIFIER EXPECTED.
352 ARRAY VARIABLE EXPECTED.
353 POSITIVE INTEGER CONSTANT EXPECTED.

397 PACK AND UNPACK ARE NOT IMPLEMENTED FOR DYNAMIC ARRAYS.
398 IMPLEMENTATION RESTRICTION.

Appendix 6
Turbo Pascal Notes

This text is written using standard Pascal. The decision to use standard Pascal rather than some other version was made for three reasons.

1. Standard Pascal is still frequently used at many colleges and universities.
2. Although many different versions of Pascal are available, no single one is dominant.
3. Standard Pascal is the easiest version from which to adapt if some other version is being used.

Recently, however, Turbo Pascal has begun to grow rapidly in popularity due to the increasing use of personal computers, good compiler programs, and Turbo's relatively low cost. The third edition of this text has responded to the increasing use of Turbo Pascal by expanding this appendix. Here, reference is made to parts of the text where specific differences occur between standard and Turbo Pascal. Although Turbo references are to version 7.0, most comments apply to earlier versions. These differences are explained in some detail.

The remainder of this appendix consists of specific page references in bold type, followed by appropriate comments. Turbo logos (shown to the left) are used throughout the text to indicate a reference to this appendix.

T

Turbo Notes

Page 27: Additional reserved words in Turbo Pascal are

CONSTRUCTOR	**INTERFACE**	**USES**
DESTRUCTOR	**OBJECT**	**VIRTUAL**
IMPLEMENTATION	**PRIVATE**	**XOR**

Page 27: Standard identifiers in Turbo Pascal are

Data Types	*Constants*	*Functions*	*Procedures*	*Files*
boolean	**false**	**abs**	**dispose**	**input**
byte	**maxint**	**arotan**	**get**	**lst**
char	**true**	**chr**	**new**	**output**
comp		**cos**	**pack**	
double		**eof**	**page**	
extended		**eoln**	**put**	
integer		**exp**	**read**	
longint		**ln**	**readln**	
real		**odd**	**reset**	
shortint		**ord**	**rewrite**	
single		**pred**	**unpack**	
string		**round**	**write**	
text		**sin**	**writeln**	
word		**sqr**		
		sqrt		
		succ		
		trunc		

Page 29: Use of the underscore is allowed in Turbo Pascal. Thus, NumberOfTests could appear as Number_Of_Tests.

Page 30: Turbo does not require a file list with the program heading.

```
PROGRAM <name>;
```

is sufficient.

Page 37: The constant **maxint** is 32767. Most versions of Turbo also include the integer data types **byte, word, shortint,** and **longint.** For those versions, the constant **longmaxint** is 2147483647.

Page 38: Most versions of Turbo also include the real data types **single, double, extended,** and **comp:** the data type **single** is a floating point type with a range of $1.5 * 10^{-45}$ to $3.4 * 10^{38}$ (positive and negative); **double** is a floating point type with a range of $5.0 * 10^{-324}$ to $1.7 * 10^{308}$ (positive and negative); **extended** is a floating point type with a range of $3.4 * 10^{-4932}$ to $1.1 * 10^{4932}$ (positive and negative); and **comp** is an integral type with a range of $-9.2 * 10^{18}$ to $9.2 * 10^{18}$.

Page 39: string data types may be defined. For an explanation and illustration of declaring and using strings, see the note for page 465.

Page 39: Default output is to the monitor. Output can be directed to the printer by using lst (short for list) within a **writeln** statement. Thus

```
writeln ('Hello');
```

goes to the screen and

```
writeln (lst, 'Hello');
```

outputs to the printer.

In later versions of Turbo, the use of lst to send output to the printer is only available if you link a library procedure to your program. The standard file lst is defined in the unit Printer and is linked by

```
Uses Printer;
```

following the program header. Using lst, however, is not practical while debugging.

For ease in directing output between the CRT and the printer, Marilyn Jussel (Kearney State College) suggests a standard procedure that allows the user to select the output destination without changing code. While debugging, the output goes to the screen; otherwise, the output goes to the printer.

The version that requires the library unit CRT is

```
Uses CRT

PROCEDURE Output_To_Where;

  VAR
    OutFile : text;
    Choice : char;

  BEGIN
    writeln ('Do you want printer output?');
    write ('Please enter choice (Y or N)');
    readln (Choice);
    IF (upcase(Choice) = 'Y') THEN
      assign (OutFile, 'prn')
    ELSE
      AssignCRT (OutFile);  {  Procedure defined in Unit CRT  }
    rewrite (OutFile)
  END;  {  of PROCEDURE Output_To_Where  }
```

The second version does not require a library unit. The only change to the preceding segment of code is to convert the line following **ELSE** to

```
assign (OutFile, 'con');
```

The distinction should be made that on the screen, the command

```
writeln;
```

produces a blank line; on the printer, the programmer must include the output file name:

```
writeln (OutFile);
```

Page 41: The last line of output for Example 2.1 is

```
Pittsburgh, PA15238
```

Page 42: There is no default field width. Thus

```
writeln (100, 87, 95);
```

produces

```
1008795
```

Page 51: The **MOD** operator returns the remainder obtained by dividing its two operands; that is

```
i MOD j = i - (i DIV j) * j
```

The sign of the result of **MOD** is the same as the sign of *i*. An error occurs if *j* is zero. To better illustrate the difference, consider the expression –17 **MOD** 3. In standard Pascal, the result is 1; in Turbo Pascal, the result is –2.

Page 53: Turbo Pascal displays the error message

```
ARITHMETIC OVERFLOW
```

and halts execution.

Page 57: Numeric variables have a default setting of zero.

Page 65: The standard file **input** is not required as part of the heading. When omitted, the default input file is the keyboard.

Page 66: Interactive programs should use **readln** rather than **read.** In order for **read** to be used in an interactive program, a compiler directive ({$B–}) should be used. However, this directive restricts editing. For best results, use separate **readln**s for character data.

Page 69: Reading character data using **readln** presents no problems. However, if characters are mixed with numbers, each number must be followed by a blank, tab, or carriage return. Thus

```
23-A
```

is not allowed. It should be entered as

```
23 A
```

If you wish to symbolically enter the fraction 2/3, it would have to be 2 /3 or 2 / 3.

Page 70: See Turbo note for page 69.

Page 144: Output in Turbo is **true.**

Page 146: The logical operator **XOR** is available in Turbo Pascal. E1 **XOR** E2 is **true** whenever exactly one of E1 or E2 is **true**.

Page 183: Turbo Pascal does not include an **OTHERWISE** option for a **CASE** statement. However, an equivalent **ELSE** option is available. Syntax for the **ELSE** option is

```
CASE <selector> OF
   <label 1> : <statement 1>;
      .
      .
      .
   <label 2> : <statement n>
ELSE
   BEGIN
      <statement 1>;
        .
        .
        .
      <statement m>
   END {   of ELSE option   }
END {   of CASE statement   }
```

Page 207: In Turbo 7.0, the library procedure **continue** can be used to control loop iteration. It causes the innermost enclosing **FOR, WHILE,** or **REPEAT** statement to immediately proceed with the next iteration. For example, the following loop will skip processing all employees whose hours worked equal zero.

```
WHILE NOT eof(Data) DO
  BEGIN
    readln(Data, Hours, Payrate):
    IF Hours = 0 THEN
      continue;
    .
    .
    .
  END;
```

Check with your instructor before using the **continue** procedure since many programmers would criticize it as being unstructured in its logical control.

In Turbo 7.0, the library procedure **break** can be used to control loop iteration. It causes the innermost enclosing **FOR, WHILE,** or **REPEAT** statement to be exited immediately. For example, the following loop will terminate upon finding an employee whose hours worked equal zero.

```
WHILE NOT eof(DATA) DO
  BEGIN
    readln (Data, Hours, Payrate);
    IF Hours = 0 THEN
      break;
    .
    .
    .
  END;
```

Check with your instructor before using the **break** procedure since many programmers would criticize it as being unstructured in its logical control.

Page 210: All variables are initialized to zero as a default setting. When a loop has been exited, the loop index retains the last assigned value.

Page 219: See note for page 207.

Page 226: See note for page 207 .

Page 265: Text files are written using the Turbo editor. You can create a data disk by using the Turbo editor in the same way you would write a program. However, instead of program lines, you enter appropriate lines of data. When finished, you exit the editor and save the file on the disk by entering 'S'.

When the file is saved on the disk, it is listed in the directory as DATA1.PAS (unless some other designator is specified). You can then use the data file by declaring a file of type **text** in the variable declaration section. The file name does not have to be listed in the program heading. Thus, you could have

```
PROGRAM UseData;
VAR
  DataFile : text;
```

Within the program, you must then assign the file name on the directory to the declared file. This can be accomplished by

```
assign (DataFile, 'DATA.PAS');
reset (DataFile);
```

Notice DataFile is **reset** to guarantee the pointer is at the beginning of the file. At this stage, you can use **read** or **readln** to get input from the text file DataFile. You can accomplish this by including the file name in the **read** or **readln** command. Thus, you might have

```
WHILE NOT eof(DataFile) DO
  BEGIN
    readln (DataFile, Num);
    writeln (Num)
  END;
```

When you finish reading from a text file, you should close it with a **close** command. In the previous example, this would be

```
close (DataFile);
```

The Boolean flags **eoln** and **eof** can be used with text files. The text file must be included as an argument. Thus, you might have such statements as

```
WHILE NOT eof(Data);
```

or

```
WHILE NOT eoln(Data);
```

When reading from a text file, you must include the file name as an argument. Typical statements are

read (Data, <variables here>); or **readln** (Data, <variables here>);

Page 266: See note for page 265.
Page 341: A **string** data type is available in Turbo Pascal. Correct syntax is

```
VAR
  Name : string;
```

or

```
VAR
  Name : string[n];
```

for early versions of Turbo, where *n* specifies the string length (from 1 through 255). With this declaration, you can have a statement such as

```
readln (Data, Score, Name);
```

as part of a program. Several string functions and procedures are available in Turbo. They include **delete, insert, str, concat(+), copy, length, pos, val,** and **numstr.** Students working in a Turbo environment are encouraged to become familiar with each of these.
Page 342: All variables are automatically packed in Turbo. Thus, packed arrays need not be declared and procedures **pack** and **unpack** have no effect. (For a discussion of **pack** and **unpack,** see Appendix 8.)
Page 344: In Turbo, the length of a string variable is dynamic. The actual length is determined by the current string value assigned to that variable. Therefore, even though Name may be declared as string[20], if Name is assigned 'Sue', its length will be 3.

Page 387: Since **string** is a data type available in Turbo Pascal, packed arrays of characters are not needed. An array of **strings** can be thought of as a one-dimensional array.

Page 432: Loops are not needed for reading names when using a **string** data type. The code on page 433 could be replaced by

```
WITH Student DO
  BEGIN
    read (Data, Name);
    FOR J := 1 TO 3 DO
      read (Data, Score[J];
    readln (Data);
    Average := (Score[1] + Score[2] + Score[3]) / 3
  END;
```

Page 479: File names are not required as part of a program heading. If information is stored in a binary file named DATA, it is listed in the directory as DATA.PAS. Assuming such a file of integers exists, the following program illustrates how the data can be accessed.

```
PROGRAM UseData;
VAR
  DataFile : FILE OF integer;
  Num : integer;
BEGIN
  assign (DataFile, 'DATA.PAS');
  reset (DataFile);
  WHILE NOT eof(DataFile) DO
    BEGIN
      read (DataFile, Num);
      writeln (Num)
    END;
  close (DataFile)
END.
```

The effect of this program is to print the integers in DATA.PAS to the screen.

Page 481: Turbo Pascal permits random access of binary files. Using the procedure **seek,** a particular file component can be located by

```
seek (<file name>, <position - 1>);
```

The component can then be obtained by

```
read (<file name>, <component>);
```

Random access files can be opened for reading **(read)** and writing **(write)** at the same time. Thus, if you are updating a file, you reposition the pointer by

```
seek (<file name>, <position - 1>);
```

after processing a component and then **write** the updated component to the file by

```
write (<file name>, <component>):
```

When you are finished, you should close the file by

```
close (<file name>);
```

Page 483: Files in Turbo may be created in two ways. Files of type **text** are created by using the Turbo editor with an appropriately named data file. Both numeric and nonnumeric data may be entered in a text file. Both **read** and **readln** may be used to retrieve data from a text file.

Binary files must be created from a program by writing to a defined file. A sample program that creates a binary file of integers from a text file follows.

```
PROGRAM FilePrac;

VAR
  Num : integer;                 {  Integers moved between files  }
  NewFile : FILE OF integer;     {  Binary file of integers       }
  OldFile : text;                {  Existing text file            }

BEGIN
  assign (OldFile, 'INTDATA.PA S');
  assign (NewFile, 'NEWDATA.PA S');
  reset (OldFile);
  rewrite (NewFile);
  writeln ('OldFile', 'Values to NewFile':28);
  writeln ('-------', '-----------------':28);
  WHILE NOT eof(OldFile) DO
    BEGIN
      readln (OldFile, Num);     {  Read from the text file       }
      write (Num);               {  Display the number            }
      Num := Num * 10;
      writeln (Num:20);          {  Display the new number        }
      write (NewFile, Num)       {  Write to the binary file      }
    END;  {  of WHILE NOT eof(Old File)  }
  close (OldFile);
  close (NewFile);
  reset (NewFile);
  writeln;

  {  Now display contents of the binary file.                      }
  writeln ('Values from NewFile');
  writeln ('-------------------');
  WHILE NOT eof(NewFile) DO
    BEGIN
      read (NewFile, Num);
      writeln (Num)
    END;  {  of WHILE NOT eof(New File)  }
  close (NewFile)
END.  {  of main program  }
```

Output from this program is

```
OldFile             Values to NewFile
-------             -----------------
2                   20
4                   40
6                   60
8                   80
10                  100
```

```
Values from NewFile
-------------------
20
40
60
80
100
```

Page 484: get and **put** are not used in Turbo Pascal. All files are accessed using **read, readln, write,** or **writeln** statements. This simplifies working with files, since you no longer must work with file windows and buffer variables.

Page 488: There are no internal files in Turbo Pascal.

Page 496: The following program is a sample of creating a file of records in Turbo. Specifically, this program creates a file of records for Programming Problem and Projects number 9 in Chapter 10.

```
PROGRAM CreateDataFile;

TYPE
  Flight = RECORD
             FlightNumber : integer;
             ETA : 0..2400;
             ETD : 0..2400;
             Orig, Dest : string[15]
           END;  {  of RECORD Flight  }

VAR
  FlightFile : FILE OF Flight;
  FlightRec : Flight;
  MoreData : boolean;
  Continue : char;

BEGIN
  assign (FlightFile, 'NewFile.pas');
  rewrite (FlightFile);
  MoreData := true;
  WHILE MoreData DO     { Get one flight record }
    BEGIN
      WITH FlightRec DO
        BEGIN
          ClrScr;
          writeln ('Enter a data line');
          writeln ('Origin         *Destination    * ETA    ETD    Flight Num');
          readln (Orig, Dest, ETA, ETD, FlightNumber)
        END;  {  of WITH...DO  }
      write (FlightFile, FlightRec);    {  Write one record to the file }
      write ('Continue? y or n    ');
      readln (Continue);
      MoreData := (Continue = 'y') OR (Continue = 'Y')
    END;  {  of getting data  }
  close (FlightFile);
  reset (FlightFile);    { Print contents of the binary file }
```

```
  {  Display contents of the binary file  }
  WHILE NOT eof(FlightFile) DO
    BEGIN
      read (FlightFile, FlightRec);
      WITH FlightRec DO
        writeln (Orig:12, Dest:12, ETA:5, ETD:5, FlightNumber:5)
    END  {  of WHILE NOT eof  }
END.  {  of program  }
```

A sample run of this program produces the binary file

```
Detroit        Chicago          752  756  521
Chicago        Tampa           1157  857  911
```

Page 545: The maximum number of elements in a set is 256, and the ordinal values of the base type must be within the range of zero through 255.

Page 571: Turbo Pascal uses a caret (^) rather than an up arrow (↑) to indicate pointer variables.

Appendix 7
GOTO Statement

In your work with computers, you may have heard of a **GOTO** statement. This is another statement in Pascal that allows a programmer to transfer control within a program. The **GOTO** statement has the effect of making an immediate, unconditional transfer to an indicated designation. You should not use **GOTO** statements in a Pascal program, but for the sake of completeness, you should be aware of their existence and how they work.

Early programming languages needed a branching statement; therefore, both FORTRAN and BASIC were designed using a **GOTO** statement for branching. Subsequent languages, particularly Pascal, included more sophisticated branching and looping statements. These statements led to an emphasis on structured programming, which is easier to design and read. If you are a beginning programmer and have not used the **GOTO** statement in another language, you should continue to develop your skills without including this statement. If you have already written programs in a language that uses **GOTO** statements, you should still attempt to write all Pascal programs without **GOTO** statements.

One instance in which **GOTO** statements might be appropriate is in making a quick exit from some part of the program. For example, if you are getting data from somewhere within a program and you have a check for valid data, your design could include a program segment such as

```
read data;
IF (<bad data>) THEN
  BEGIN
    <Write error message>;
    GOTO <end of program>
  END
ELSE
  <Process data>
```

Keeping the previous admonitions against using **GOTO** statements in mind, we will now briefly examine the form, syntax, and flow of control for these statements.

GOTO statements require the use of numerically labeled statements. Thus, your program could contain

```
LABEL
  <label 1>,
  <label 2>;
      .
      .
      .
GOTO 100;
      .
      .
      .
100: <program statement>;
      .
      .
      .
```

All labels must be declared in a label declaration section that precedes the constant definition section in a program. Each label can only be used for a single program statement. The form for the label declaration section is

> **LABEL**
> <label 1>,
> <label 2>,
> .
> .
> .
> <label *n*>

The correct form for a **GOTO** statement is

> **GOTO** <numeric label>

where numeric label is an integer from 1 to 9999, inclusive. Declared labels are then used with appropriate statements in a program. Proper syntax for labeling a statement is

> <label> : <program statement>

Consider the fragment

```
BEGIN
  read (Num);
  IF Num < 0 THEN
    GOTO 100
  ELSE
    Sum := Sum + Num;
       .
       .
       .
  100: writeln ('Data include a negative number,':40)
END.
```

In this instance, when a negative number is encountered as a data item, an appropriate message is printed and the program is terminated.

GOTO statements permit you to immediately transfer out of any control structure. As stated, we recommend you avoid the use of this statement whenever possible. However, if you must use it, use it only to exit immediately from some point in the program; never use it to construct a loop in Pascal.

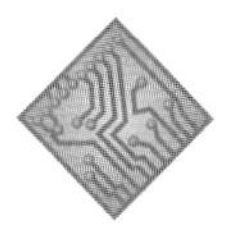

Appendix 8
Packing and Unpacking

The basic trade-off between working with arrays and packed arrays is that packed arrays require less memory but more time to access individual components. It is possible to facilitate working with packed and unpacked arrays (arrays that are not packed) by using assignment loops. For example, consider the following declarations.

```
TYPE
  String10 = PACKED ARRAY [1..10] OF char;
  Array10 = ARRAY [1..10] OF char;
VAR
  PakName : String10;
  UnpakName : Array10;
```

We now have reserved memory for

PakName

and

UnpakName

	UnpakName[1]
	UnpakName[2]
	UnpakName[3]
	UnpakName[4]
	UnpakName[5]
	UnpakName[6]
	UnpakName[7]
	UnpakName[8]
	UnpakName[9]
	UnpakName[10]

Now suppose UnpakName contains the name 'John Smith'.

UnpakName

'J'
'o'
'h'
'n'
'S'
'm'
'i'
't'
'h'

and we wish to put the characters into a packed array for storage, sorting, or writing. This can be accomplished by

```
FOR J := 1 TO 10 DO
  PakName[J] := UnpakName[J];
```

which produces

PakName

'J'	'o'	'h'	'n'	''	'S'	'm'	'i'	't'	'h'

This string can still be accessed as one packed array variable.

A **FOR** loop can also be used to transfer elements from a packed array to an unpacked array, but Pascal does provide standard procedures for both of these processes. An array can be packed by

```
pack (UnpackedArray, J, PackedArray);
```

which fills all of PackedArray with elements of UnpackedArray, starting with UnpackedArray [J]. An array can be unpacked by

```
unpack (PackedArray, UnpackedArray, K);
```

which copies all elements of PackedArray into UnpackedArray, putting the first element in UnpackedArray [K]. For these procedures, PackedArray and UnpackedArray do not have to be of the same length and K may be a constant or an expression. Unfortunately, **pack** and **unpack** are difficult to use. Therefore, since **FOR** loops can accomplish the same results and are about as efficient, you will do well to use them if you wish to transfer between packed and unpacked arrays.

Glossary

abstract data type (ADT) A form of abstraction that arises from the use of defined types. An ADT consists of a class of objects, a defined set of properties of those objects, and a set of operations for processing the objects.

accumulator A variable used for the purpose of summing successive values of some other variable.

actual parameter A variable or expression contained in a procedure or function call and passed to that procedure or function. *See also* **formal parameter.**

address An integer value that the computer can use to reference a location. Often called *address of a memory location. See also* **value.**

algorithm A finite sequence of effective statements that, when applied to the problem, will solve it.

applications software Programs designed for a specific use.

argument A value or expression passed in a function or procedure call. Also referred to as a *parameter.*

arithmetic/logic unit (ALU) The part of the central processing unit (CPU) that performs arithmetic operations and evaluates expressions.

array A structured variable designed to handle data of the same type.

array index The relative position of the components of an array.

array of records An array with record as its component type.

ASCII collating sequence The American Standard Code for Information Interchange ordering for a character set.

assembly language A computer language that allows words and symbols to be used in an unsophisticated manner to accomplish simple tasks. *See also* **high-level language** and **machine language.**

assertion Special comments used with selection and repetition statements to indicate what is expected to happen and when certain conditions will hold.

assignment compatible When an expression can be assigned to the variable.

assignment statement A method of putting values into memory locations.

batch input Input for a program being run in batch mode. Also referred to as *stream input. See also* **batch processing.**

batch processing A technique of executing the program and data from a file that has been created. User interaction with the computer is not required during execution. Also referred to as *stream input. See also* **batch input.**

BEGIN. . .END block The segment of code between **BEGIN** and **END** that, when a compound statement is executed within a program, is treated as a single statement.

binary digit A digit, either 0 or 1, in the binary number system. Program instructions are stored in memory using a sequence of binary digits. Binary digits are called *bits.*

binary file A file in which information is stored using binary representation for components.

binary notation The representation of data using binary digits.

binary search The process of examining the middle value of a sorted array to see which half contains the value in question and then halving until that value is located.

binary search tree A binary tree such that the information in the key field of any node (1) is greater than the information in the key field of any node of its left child and any of its children and (2) is less than the information in the key field of any node of its right child and any of its children.

binary tree A tree such that each node can point to at most two children.

bit *See* **binary digit.**

block A program in Pascal can be thought of as a heading and a block. The block contains an optional declaration part and a compound statement. The block structure for a subprogram is called a *subblock. See also* **subblock.**

Boolean expression An expression that has a value of either true or false. *See also* **compound Boolean expression** and **simple Boolean expression.**

bottom-up testing Independent testing of modules.

bubble sort Rearranges elements of an array until they are in either ascending or descending order. Consecutive elements are compared to move (bubble) the elements to the top or bottom accordingly during each pass. *See also* **index sort, insertion sort, quick sort,** and **selection sort.**

buffer variable The actual vehicle through which values are passed to or from a file component.

built-in function *See* **standard function.**

bus A group of wires imprinted on a circuit board to facilitate communication between components of a computer.

byte A sequence of bits used to encode a character in memory. *See also* **word.**

call Any reference to a subprogram by an executable statement. Also referred to as *invoke.*

cancellation error An error caused when numbers of substantially different sizes are used in an operation. *See also* **representational error.**

central processing unit (CPU) A major hardware component that consists of the arithmetic/logic unit (ALU) and the control unit.

character set The list of characters available for data and program statements. *See also* **collating sequence.**

children Nodes pointed to by an element in a tree.

code (writing) The process of writing executable statements that are part of a program to solve a problem.

cohesive subprogram A subprogram designed to accomplish a single task.

collating sequence The particular order sequence for a character set used by a machine. *See also* **ASCII** and **EBCDIC.**

comment A nonexecutable statement used to make a program more readable.

compatible *See* **assignment compatible, type identical,** and **type compatible.**

compilation error An error detected when the program is being compiled. A complete list of compilation error messages appears in Appendix 5. *See also* **design (logic) error, run-time error,** and **syntax error.**

compiler A computer program that automatically converts instructions in a high-level language to machine language.

component of a file One element of the file data type.

component of a linked list *See* **node.**

component of an array One element of the array data type.

compound Boolean expression The complete expression when logical connectives and negation are used to generate Boolean values. *See also* **Boolean expression** and **simple Boolean expression.**

compound statement The use of the reserved words **BEGIN** and **END** to make several simple statements into a single compound statement.

conditional statement *See* **selection statement.**

constant The contents of a memory location that cannot be changed in the body of the program.

constant definition section The section in which program constants are defined for subsequent use.

control structure A structure that controls the flow of execution of program statements.

control unit The part of the central processing unit (CPU) that controls the operation of the rest of the computer.

counter A variable used to count the number of times some process is completed.

data The particular characters that are used to represent information in a form suitable for storage, processing, and communication.

data abstraction The separation between the conceptual definition of a data structure and its eventual implementation.

data type A formal description of the set of values that a variable can have.

data validation The process of examining data prior to its use in a program.

debugging The process of eliminating errors or "bugs" from a program.

declaration section The section used to declare (name) all symbolic constants, data types, variables, and subprograms that are necessary to the program.

declaration statement A statement that defines types in the **TYPE** section, declares variables in the **VAR** section, and is used as the program heading.

decrement To decrease the value of a variable.

degenerate case *See* **stopping state.**

design error An error such that a program runs but produces unexpected results. Also referred to as a *logic error. See also* **compilation error, run-time error,** and **syntax error.**

difference The difference of set A and set B is A – B, where A – B contains the elements that are in A but that are not in B. *See also* **intersection, subset,** and **union.**

dynamic structure A data structure that may expand or contract during execution of a program.

dynamic variable A variable accessed by a pointer variable; frequently designed as Ptr^ or Ptr↑.

EBCDIC collating sequence The Extended Binary Coded Decimal Interchange Code ordering for a character set.

echo checking A debugging technique in which values of variables and input data are displayed during program execution.

effective statement A clear, unambiguous instruction that can be carried out.

element of an array *See* **component of an array.**

element of a set A value that has been assigned to a set.

empty set A set containing no elements. Also called a *null set.*

empty statement A semicolon used to indicate that no action is to be taken. Also referred to as a *null statement.*

encapsulation The process of hiding the implementation details of a subprogram.

end-of-file (eof) marker A special marker inserted by the machine to indicate the end of the data file. In this text, it is represented by a black square (■).

end-of-line (eoln) marker A special marker inserted by the machine to indicate the end of a line in the data. In this text, it is represented by a black column (▮).

entrance controlled loop *See* **pretest loop.**

enumerated data type A data type that is defined in the **TYPE** definition section by the programmer. Also referred to as *user-defined data type.*

error *See* **cancellation error, compilation error, design (logic) error, representational error, round-off error, run-time error,** and **syntax error.**

executable section Contains the statements that cause the computer to do something. Starts with the reserved word **BEGIN** and concludes with the reserved word **END.**

executable statement The basic unit of grammar in Pascal. Consists of valid identifiers, standard identifiers, reserved words, numbers, and/or characters, together with appropriate punctuation.

execute To perform a program step-by-step.

exit controlled loop *See* **posttest loop.**

exponential form *See* **floating point form.**

expression The combination of two or more values to produce a single value.

extended IF statement Nested selection in which additional **IF. . .THEN. . .ELSE** statements are used in the **ELSE** option. *See also* **nested IF statement.**

external file A file used to store data in secondary storage between runs of a program. *See also* **internal file.**

field A component of a record.

field selector When referring to fields in a record, the period that separates the record name from the field name.

field width The phrase used to describe the number of columns used for various output. *See also* **formatting.**

FIFO First-in, first out structure. *See* **queue.**

file A data structure that consists of a sequence of components that are all of the same type.

file window A term used in this text, although not designated by Pascal, to indicate an imaginary window through which the values of a file component can be transferred.

fixed part The part of a record structure in which the number and type of data fields are fixed for all records of a particular type. *See also* **variant part.**

fixed point form A method of writing decimal numbers where the decimal is placed where it belongs in the number. *See also* **floating point form.**

fixed repetition loop A loop used when it is known in advance the number of times a segment of code needs to be repeated. **FOR. . .TO. . .DO** is a fixed repetition loop. Also referred to as an *iterated loop.*

floating point form A method for writing numbers in scientific notation to accommodate numbers that may have very large or very small values. Exactly one nonzero digit must appear on the left of the decimal. *See also* **fixed point form.**

FOR loop A fixed repetition loop that causes a fragment of code to be executed a predetermined number of times. **FOR. . .TO. . .DO** and **FOR. . .DOWNTO. . .DO** are **FOR** loops.

formal parameter A variable, declared and used in a procedure or function declaration, that is replaced by an actual parameter when the procedure or function is called. *See also* **actual parameter.**

formatting Designating the desired field width when printing integers, reals, Boolean values, and character strings. *See also* **field width.**

forward reference A method by which a subprogram can call another subprogram that appears later in the declaration section.

function *See* **standard function** and **user-defined function.**

global identifier An identifier that can be used by the main program and all subprograms in a program. Also referred to as a *global variable.*

global variable *See* **global identifier.**

hardware The actual computing machine and its support devices.

higher-dimensional array An array of more than two dimensions.

high-level language Any programming language that uses words and symbols to make it relatively easy to read and write a program. *See also* **assembly language** and **machine language.**

identifiers Words that must be created according to a well-defined set of rules but that can have any meaning subject to these rules. *See also* **standard identifiers.**

increment To increase the value of a variable.

index *See* **array index** or **loop index.**

index sort Sorting an array by ordering the indices of the components rather than by exchanging the components. *See also* **bubble sort, insertion sort, quick sort,** and **selection sort.**

index type The data type used to specify the range for the index of an array. The index type can be any ordinal data type that specifies an initial value and a final value.

infinite loop A loop in which the controlling condition is not changed to allow the loop to terminate.

input Data obtained by a program during its execution. *See also* **batch input** and **interactive input.**

input assertion A precondition for a loop.

input device A device that provides information to the computer. Typical devices are keyboards, disk drives, card readers, and tape drives. *See also* **I/O device** and **output device.**

input statement A statement that uses **read** or **readln** to get input.

insertion sort Sorts an array of elements in either ascending or descending order. Starts with an empty array and inserts elements one at a time in their proper order. *See also* **bubble sort, index sort, quick sort,** and **selection sort.**

instruction A simple, elementary task performed by a computer.

integer arithmetic operations Operations allowed on data of type **integer,** which include addition, subtraction, multiplication, **MOD,** and **DIV** to produce integer answers.

integer overflow *See* **overflow.**

interactive input A method of getting data into the program from the keyboard. User interaction is required during execution.

interface A formal statement of how communication occurs between subprograms, the main driver, and other subprograms.

internal file A file, also called a *temporary* or *scratch file,* that is used for processing only and not saved in secondary storage. *See also* **external file.**

intersection The intersection of set A and set B is A * B, where A * B contains the elements that are in both A and B. *See also* **difference, subset,** and **union.**

invariant expression An assertion that is true before the loop and after each iteration of the loop.

invoke *See* **call.**

I/O device Any device that allows information to be transmitted to or from a computer. *See also* **input device** and **output device.**

iterated loop *See* **fixed repetition loop.**

keywords Either reserved words or predefined identifiers.

leaf In a tree, a node that has no children.

length of an array The number of components of an array.

LIFO Last-in, first-out structure. *See* **stack.**

linear search *See* **sequential search.**

linked list A list of data items in which each item is linked to the next one by means of a pointer.

local identifier An identifier that is restricted to use within a subblock of a program. Also referred to as a *local variable.*

local variable *See* **local identifier.**

logical operator Either logical connective **(AND, OR)** or negation **(NOT).**

logic error *See* **design error.**

loop index Variable used for control values in a **FOR** loop.

loop invariant An assertion that expresses a relationship between variables that remain constant throughout all iterations of the loop.

loop variant An assertion that changes in terms of truth between the first and final executions of the loop.

loop verification The process of guaranteeing that a loop performs its intended task.

loops Program statements that cause a process to be repeated. *See also* **FOR loop, REPEAT. . .UNTIL loop,** and **WHILE. . .DO loop.**

low-level language *See* **assembly language.**

machine language The language used directly by the computer in all its calculations and processing. *See also* **assembly-language** and **high-level language.**

main block The part of a program that consists of both the declaration and executable sections.

main driver The main program when subprograms are used to accomplish specific tasks.

mainframe computer A large computer typically used by major companies and universities. *See also* **microcomputer** and **minicomputer.**

main memory Memory contained in the computer. Also referred to as *primary memory. See also* **memory** and **secondary memory device.**

main unit The central processing unit (CPU) and the main (primary) memory of a computer, hooked to an input device and an output device.

master file An existing external file.

maxint The largest integer constant available to a particular system.

memory The ordered sequence of storage cells that can be accessed by address. The instructions and variables of an executing program are temporarily held here while the program is executed. *See also* **main memory** and **secondary memory device.**

memory location A storage cell that can be accessed by address. *See also* **memory.**

merge The process of combining lists; typically refers to files or arrays.

microcomputer A personal computer with relatively limited memory, generally used by one person at a time. *See also* **mainframe computer** and **minicomputer.**

minicomputer A small version of a mainframe computer that can be used by several people at once. *See also* **mainframe computer** and **microcomputer.**

mixed-mode expression An expression containing data of both **integer** and **real** types; the value will be given as a real, not as an integer.

modular development The process of developing an algorithm using modules. *See also* **module.**

modularity The property possessed by a program that is written using modules.

module An independent unit that is part of a larger development; usually a procedure or function. *See also* **modular development.**

module specifications Descriptions of data received, information returned, and logic used in the module.

negation The use of the logical operator **NOT** to negate the Boolean value of an expression.

nested IF statement A selection statement used within another selection statement. *See also* **extended IF statement.**

nested loop A loop that appears as one of the statements in the body of another loop.

nested record A record that appears as a field in another record.

nested selection Any combination of selection statements within another selection statement. *See also* **selection statement.**

node One data item in a linked list.

nonlocal identifier An identifier available outside a subblock. Also referred to as a *nonlocal variable.*

nonlocal variable *See* **nonlocal identifier.**

null set *See* **empty set.**

null statement *See* **empty statement.**

object code *See* **object program.**

object program The machine-code version of the source program. Also called *object code.*

opened for reading Positions a pointer at the beginning of a file for the purpose of reading from the file.

opened for writing Positions a pointer at the beginning of a file for the purpose of writing to the file.

opening a file Positions a pointer at the beginning of a file. *See also* **opened for reading** and **opened for writing.**

operating system A large program that allows the user to communicate with the hardware.

ordinal data type A data type ordered in some association with the integers; each integer is the ordinal of its associated character.

output Information that is produced by a program.

output assertion A postcondition for a loop.

output device A device that allows the user to see the results of a program; typically a monitor or printer. *See* **input device** and **I/O device.**

overflow In arithmetic operations, if a value is too large for the computer's memory location, a meaningless value may be assigned or an error message may result. *See also* **underflow.**

packed array An array in which data are placed in consecutive bytes. *See also* **unpacked array.**

parallel arrays Arrays of the same length but with different component data types.

parameter *See* **argument.**

parameter list A list of parameters (arguments). An actual parameter list is contained in the procedure or function call. A formal parameter list is contained in the procedure or function heading.

parent In a tree, the node that is pointing to its children.

passed by reference When variable parameters are used in subprograms.

peripheral memory *See* **secondary memory device** and **memory.**

pointer variable A variable that contains the address of a memory location; frequently designated as Ptr. *See also* **address** and **dynamic variable.**

pop A procedure to delete a node from a linked list.

postcondition An assertion written after a segment of code.

posttest loop A loop in which the control condition is tested after the loop is executed. **REPEAT. . .UNTIL** is a posttest loop. Also referred to as an *exit controlled loop.*

precedence rule The order of priority in which numeric operations are performed.

precondition An assertion written before a particular statement.

pretest condition A condition that controls whether or not the body of the loop is executed before going through the loop.

pretest loop A loop in which the control condition is tested before the loop is executed. **WHILE. . .DO** is a pretest loop. Also referred to as an *entrance controlled loop.*

primary memory *See* **main memory** and **memory.**

procedural abstraction The process of considering only what a procedure is to do rather than the details of the procedure.

procedure A subprogram designed to perform a specific task as part of a larger program. Procedures are not limited to returning a single value to the main program.

processing statement A statement that causes the computer to take action when a program is run.

program A set of instructions that tells the machine (the hardware) what to do.

program heading The first statement of any Pascal program; it must contain the reserved word **PROGRAM.**

programming language Formal language that computer scientists use to give instructions to the computer.

program proof An analysis of a program that attempts to verify the correctness of program results.

program protection A method of using selection statements to guard against unexpected results.

program walk-through The process of carefully following, using pencil and paper, the steps the computer uses to solve the problem given in a program. Also referred to as a *trace.*

prompt A marker on the terminal screen that requests input data.

protection *See* **program protection.**

pseudocode A stylized, half-English, half-code language that is written in English but suggests Pascal code.

push A procedure for adding a node to the beginning of a linked list.

queue A dynamic data structure in which elements are entered from one end and removed from the other end. Also referred to as a *FIFO (first-in, first-out) structure.*

quick sort A relatively fast sorting technique that uses recursion. *See also* **bubble sort, index sort, insertion sort,** and **selection sort.**

reading from a file Retrieving data from a file.

real arithmetic operations Operations allowed on data of type **real,** including addition, subtraction, multiplication, and division.

real overflow *See* **overflow.**

record A data structure that is a collection of fields that may be treated as a whole or as individual fields.

recursion The process of a subprogram calling itself. A clearly defined stopping state must exist. Any recursive subprogram can be rewritten using iteration.

recursive step A well-defined step that leads to the stopping state in the recursive process.

recursive subprogram *See* **recursion.**

relational operator An operator used to compare data items of the same type.

REPEAT. . .UNTIL loop A posttest loop thatexamines a Boolean expression after causing a fragment to be executed.

repetition *See* **loops.**

representational error An error caused by the way in which a real number is stored in memory. *See also* **cancellation error.**

reserved words Words that have predefined meanings that cannot be changed. Reserved words are highlighted in the text in capital boldface print; a list of reserved words in Pascal appears in Appendix 1.

return type The data type for a function name.

robust The state in which a program is completely protected against all possible crashes from bad data and unexpected values.

root The first or top node in a tree.

round-off error An error caused when a decimal is truncated or rounded off.

run-time error An error that is detected after compilation is complete, when an error message results instead of the correct output. *See also* **compilation error, design (logic) error,** and **syntax error.**

scope of identifier The largest block in which the identifier is available.

scratch file *See* **internal file.**

secondary memory device An auxiliary device for memory; usually a disk or magnetic tape. Also referred to as *peripheral memory. See also* **main memory** and **memory.**

selection sort A sorting algorithm that sorts the components of an array in either ascending or descending order. This process puts the smallest or largest element in the top position and repeats the process on the remaining array components. *See also* **bubble sort, index sort, insertion sort,** and **quick sort.**

selection statement A control statement that selects some particular logical path based upon the value of an expression. Also referred to as a *conditional statement. See also* **nested selection.**

self-documenting code Code that is written using descriptive identifiers.

sentinel value A special value that indicates the end of a set of data or of a process.

sequential algorithm *See* **straight-line algorithm.**

sequential search The process of searching a list by examining the first component and then examining successive components in the order in which they occur. Also referred to as *linear search.*

set A structured data type that consists of a collection of distinct elements from an indicated base type, which must be ordinal.

side effect An unintentional change in a variable that results from some action taken in a program.

simple Boolean expression An expression in which two numbers or variable values are compared using a single relational operator. *See also* **Boolean expression** and **compound Boolean expression.**

simple statement A single-action, executable statement.

software Programs that make the hardware (the machine) do something (word processing, data-base management, games, etc.).

software engineering The process of developing and maintaining large software systems.

software system life cycle The development, maintenance, and demise of a software system. Phases include analysis, design, coding, testing/verification, maintenance, and obsolescence.

sort-merge The process of repeatedly subdividing a long list, sorting shorter lists, and then merging them to obtain a single sorted list.

source program A program written by a programmer. *See also* **system program.**

stack A dynamic data structure that can be accessed from only one end. Also referred to as a *LIFO (last-in, first-out) structure.*

standard function A built-in function available in most versions of Pascal.

standard identifiers Words that have predefined meanings that can be changed if needed. Standard identifiers are highlighted in text in lowercase boldface print; a list of standard identifiers in Pascal appears in Appendix 2.

standard simple types The predefined data types **integer, real, char,** and **boolean.**

statement The basic unit of expression in Pascal. A program consists of a sequence of statements.

static variable A variable of a size (for example, array length) that is fixed at compilation time. A certain memory area is reserved for each variable, and this location is retained for the declared variable as long as the program or subprogram in which the variable is defined is active.

stepwise refinement The process of repeatedly subdividing tasks into subtasks until each subtask is easily accomplished. *See also* **structured programming** and **top-down design.**

stopping state The well-defined termination of a recursive process. Also referred to as *degenerate case.*

straight-line algorithm An algorithm that consists of a sequence of simple tasks. Also called *sequential algorithm.*

stream input *See* **batch input** and **batch processing.**

string An abbreviated name for a string constant.

string constant One or more characters used as a constant in a program. Also referred to as a *string.*

string data type A data type that permits a sequence of characters. The *string* data type is not available in standard Pascal but can be simulated using a packed array of characters.

structure chart A graphic method of indicating the relationship between modules when designing the solution to a problem.

structured programming Programming that parallels a solution to a problem achieved by top-down design. *See also* **stepwise refinement** and **top-down design.**

stub programming A no-frills, simple, and often incomplete version of a final program.

subblock A block structure for a subprogram. *See also* **block.**

subprogram A program within a program. Procedures and functions are subprograms.

subrange The defined subset of values of an existing ordinal data type.

subscript *See* **array index** and **loop index.**

subset Set A is a subset of set B if all the elements in A are also in B. *See also* **difference, intersection,** and **union.**

super computer A system capable of enormous operating speed due to parallel processing.

syntax The formal rules governing the construction of valid statements.

syntax diagramming A method used to formally describe the legal syntax of language structures; syntax diagrams appear in Appendix 3.

syntax error An error in the spelling, punctuation, or placement of certain key symbols in a program. *See also* **compilation error, design (logic) error,** and **run-time error.**

system program A special program used by the computer to activate the compiler, run the machine-code version, and cause output to be generated. *See also* **source program.**

system software The programs that allow users to write and execute other programs, including operating systems such as DOS.

tag field A field used in defining variant records. Values of the tag field determine the variant record structure.

temporary file *See* **internal file.**

test program A short program written to provide an answer to a specific question.

text file A file of characters that is divided into lines.

top-down design A design methodology for solving a problem whereby the problem is first stated and the main task is then subdivided into major subtasks. Each subtask is then subdivided into smaller subtasks. This process is repeated until each remaining subtask can be easily solved. *See also* **stepwise refinement** and **structured programming.**

trace *See* **program walk-through.**

transaction file A file containing changes to be made in a master file.

tree A dynamic data structure consisting of a special node (a root) that points to zero or more other nodes, each of which points to zero or more other nodes, and so on.

two-dimensional array An array in which each element is accessed by a reference to a pair of indices.

two-way merge The process of merging two sorted lists.

type *See* **data type.**

type compatible When variables have the same base type. *See also* **type identical.**

type identical When variables are declared with the same type identifier. A variable parameter and its argument must be of identical type. *See also* **type compatible.**

underflow If a value is too small to be represented by a computer, the value is automatically replaced by zero. *See also* **overflow.**

union The union of set A and set B is A + B, where A + B contains any element that is in A or that is in B. *See also* **difference, intersection,** and **subset.**

universal set Any set that contains all possible values of the base type.

unpacked array An array in which data are not in consecutive bytes. *See also* **packed array.**

user-defined data type *See* **enumerated data type.**

user-defined function A subprogram (function) written by the programmer to perform a specific task. Functions return one value when called.

user-friendly program An interactive program with clear, easy-to-follow messages for the user.

value The value of the contents of a memory location. Often called *value of a memory location. See also* **address.**

value parameter A formal parameter that is local to a subprogram. The value of this parameter is not returned to the calling program.

variable A memory location, referenced by an identifier, with a value that can be changed during a program.

variable condition loop A repetition statement in which the loop control condition changes within the body of the loop.

variable declaration section The portion of the declaration section in which program variables are declared for subsequent use.

variable dictionary A listing of the meanings of variables used in a program.

variable parameter A formal parameter that is not local to a subprogram. The value of this parameter is returned to the calling program.

variant part The part of a record structure in which the number and type of fields can vary. *See also* **fixed part.**

WHILE. . .DO loop A pretest loop that examines a Boolean expression before causing a fragment to be executed.

word A unit of memory consisting of one or more bytes. Words can be addressed.

writing to a file The process of entering data to a file.

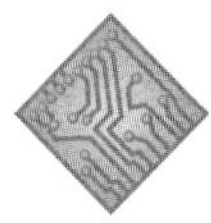

Answers to Selected Exercises

This section contains answers to selected exercises from the exercise sets at the end of each section in the text. In general, answers to odd-numbered problems are given.

CHAPTER 1

Section 1.3

1. **a.** and **c.** are effective statements.
   b. is not effective because you cannot determine when to perform the action.
   d. is not effective because there is no smallest positive fraction.
   e. is not effective because you cannot determine in advance which stocks will increase in value.
3. **a.** 1. Select a topic
      2. Research the topic
      3. Outline the paper
      4. Refine the outline
      5. Write the rough draft
      6. Read and revise the rough draft
      7. Write the final paper
   c. 1. Get a list of colleges
      2. Examine criteria (programs, distance, money, and so on)
      3. Screen to a manageable number
      4. Obtain further information
      5. Make a decision
5. **a.** First-level development
      1. Get information for first employee
      2. Perform computations for first employee
      3. Print results for first employee
      4.
      5. } repeat steps 1–3 for second employee
      6.

   Second-level development
   1. Get information for first employee
      1.1 get hourly wage
      1.2 get number of hours worked
   2. Perform computations for first employee
      2.1 compute gross pay
      2.2 compute deductions
      2.3 compute net pay
   3. Print results for first employee
      3.1 print input data
      3.2 print gross pay
      3.3 print deductions
      3.4 print net pay
   4.
   5. } repeat steps 1–3 for second employee
   6.

   Third-level development
   1. Get information for first employee
      1.1 get hourly wage
      1.2 get number of hours worked
   2. Perform computations for first employee
      2.1 compute gross pay
      2.2 compute deductions
         2.2.1 federal withholding
         2.2.2 state withholding
         2.2.3 social security
         2.2.4 union dues
         2.2.5 compute total deductions
      2.3 compute net pay
         2.3.1 subtract total deductions from gross pay
   3. Print results for first employee
      3.1 print input data
         3.1.1 print hourly wage
         3.1.2 print hours worked
      3.2 print gross pay
      3.3 print deductions
         3.3.1 print federal withholding
         3.3.2 print state withholding
         3.3.3 print social security
         3.3.4 print union dues
         3.3.5 print total deductions
      3.4 print net pay
   4.
   5. } repeat steps 1–3 for second employee
   6.
7. There are several ways to solve this problem, one of which follows:
   1. Get the numbers as input
   2. Put them in order (Small, Large)
   3. Check for a divisor
      3.1 **IF** Small is a divisor of Large
         THEN
         3.1.1 GCD is Small
         ELSE
         3.1.2 Decrease Small until a common divisor is found

14. Print the results

3.1.2 can be further refined as

3.1.2 Decrease Small until a common divisor is found

3.1.2.2 **REPEAT**

IF GCDCandidate is a common divisor **THEN**

GCD is GCDCandidate

ELSE

Decrease GCDCandidate by 1 **UNTIL** a common divisor is found

Section 1.4

3. **a.**, **b.**, and **e.** are valid; however, a semicolon must be used between the heading in **a.** and the next line of code.

   c. does not begin with the reserved word **PROGRAM.**

   d. is missing an identifier for the program name.

   f. and **g.** use improper identifiers for the program name.

5. A combined constant definition statement is

```
CONST
  Name = 'Julie Adams';
  Age = 18;
  BirthDate = 'November 10, 1976';
  Birthplace = 'Carson City, MI';
```

Section 1.5

1. **a.**, **d.**, **e.**, **g.**, and **h.** are valid.
   b. has a decimal.
   c. has a comma.
   f. is probably larger than **maxint.**
   h. use of E causes **real** data type.

3. **a.** 1.73E2
   b. 7.43927E11
   c. -2.3E-8
   d. 1.4768E1
   e. -5.2E0

5. **a.** and **d.** are type **integer.**

   b., **c.**, and **g.** are type **real.**

   e. and **f.** are string constants.

7. **a.**
```
writeln ('Score':14);
writeln ('-----':14);
writeln (86:13);
writeln (82:13);
writeln (79:13);
```

CHAPTER 2

Section 2.1

1. **a.** 11 **f.** 63
   b. -41 **g.** 48
   c. 3 **h.** 140
   d. 24 **i.** 1
   e. 126 **j.** 7

3. **a.** and **b.** are valid (type **integer).**

   c., **e.**, **f.**, **g.**, **h.**, and **i** are valid (type **real).**

   d. and **j.** are invalid.

5. Output will vary according to local implementation.

Section 2.2

1. **a.**, **b.**, **e.**, **f.**, and **h**, are valid assignment statements.

   c. is invalid. A real cannot be assigned to an integer variable.

   d. is invalid. An operand cannot be on the left of an assignment statement.

   g. is invalid. IQ / 3 is a real.

3.

	A	B
a.	3	-5
b.	26	31
c.	-3	-5
d.	9	9

5. **a.** d := r * t;
   c. S = n * (n - 1) / 2;

7.
```
Gender        M
Age           23
Height        73 inches
Weight        186.5 lbs
```

9. column 11

```
********************************
*                              *
*   Name      Age      Gender  *
*   ----      ---      ------  *

*   Jones      21        M     *
*                              *
********************************
```

11. column 10
↓
```
        This  reviews string formatting.
When a letterAis used,
        Oops! I forgot to format.
        When a letter A is used,
        it is a string of length one.
```

Section 2.3

a.

83	95	' '	100.0
Num1	Num2	Ch	Num3

b.

83	95	'.'	0.0
Num1	Num2	Ch	Num3

c.

83	-72	' '	93.5
Num1	Num2	Ch	Num3

d.

83	-72	' '	93.5
Num1	Num2	Ch	Num3

e. Error. Not enough values.

f.

70	73	'–'	80.5
Num1	Num2	Ch	Num3

g.

91	92	' '	93.0
Num1	Num2	Ch	Num3

h.

-76	-81	'–'	16.5
Num1	Num2	Ch	Num3

Section 2.4

3.

```
     CPS 150                TEST #2
  ---------------------------------

     Total points               100
     My score                    93
     Class average             82.3
```

Section 2.5

1. a. 15.2 d. 36
   b. 14 e. -4.5
   c. 0 f. -11.98
3. a. `sqrt(A * A + B * B)`
   b. `(-B + sqrt(B * B - 4 * A * C)) / (2 * A)`
   and
   `(-B - sqrt(B * B - 4 * A * C)) / (2 * A)`
5. `(round(10 * X)) / 10.0`
7. a. `-4.30 4.30 -4 -4`
   b. **4** (depends upon character set—;65 in ASCII)
   c. Depends upon character set
9. a. `Uppercase := chr(ord(LowerCase) - ord('a') + ord('A'));`
   b. `IntValue := ord(Digit) - ord('0');`

CHAPTER 3

Section 3.2

3. a. A and B are variable parameters.
   X is a value parameter.
   b. A and X are variable parameters.
   B and Ch are value parameters.
   c. X, Y, and Z are variable parameters.
   A, B, and Ch are value parameters.

5. a. **Prob5 (Num1, Num2, Letter);**
   b. **PrintHeader;**
   c. **FindMax (Num1, Num2, Max);**
   d. **Switch (Num1, Num2);**

7. b.
```
PROCEDURE MaxAndAver (X, Y, Z : real;
                      VAR Max, Aver : real);
BEGIN
  Max := X;
  IF Y > Max THEN
    Max := Y:
  IF Z > Max THEN
    Max := Z;
  Aver := (X + Y + Z) / 3.0
END;
```

Section 3.3

7. Identifiers for this program are represented schematically by the figure at right.

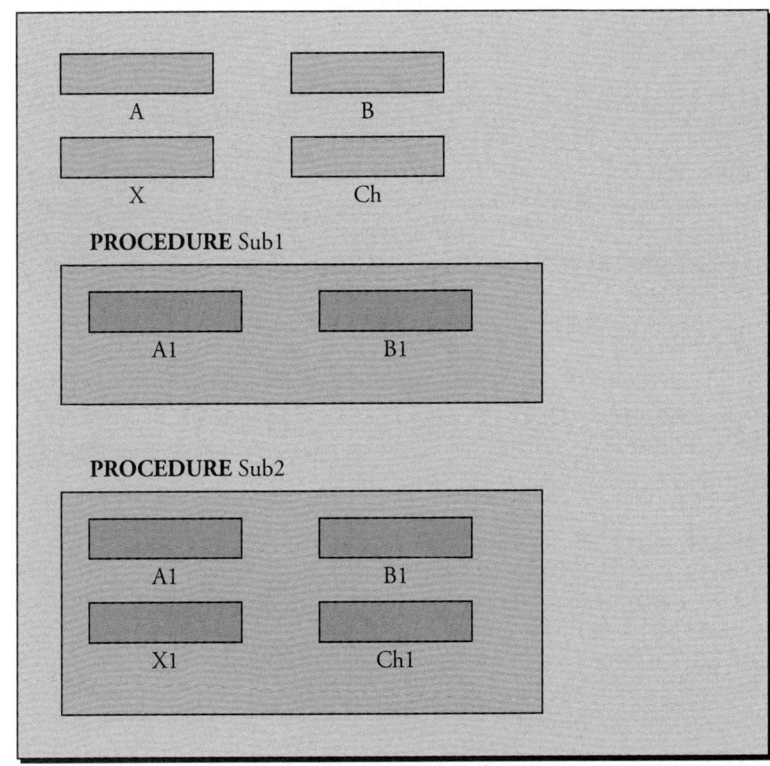

9.
```
10
20
10
30
30
```
11. a. Average cannot be used as a procedure name since it has already been declared as an identifier with scope that includes that procedure.
    b. No errors. The variables declared in the procedure heading are local to it.
    c. No errors.
13. The main program is trying to access an identifier that is not available. The line
    writeln (X1:20:2);
    in the main program is inappropriate because the scope of X1 is **PROCEDURE** Sub1.

Section 3.4

3. **c.** and **d.** are valid.

   a. is invalid. The data type for what will be returned to the calling program must be listed.

   FUNCTION RoundTenth (X : real) : real;

   b. is invalid. Data types must be listed for X and Y.
   e. is invalid. The comma following **char** should be a semicolon.

CHAPTER 4

Section 4.1

1. `true true  false`
   `false`
3. Only **c.** and **f.** are valid.
5. **a., b., d.,** and **g.** are **true.**

   c., e., and **f.** (which compare as reals) are **false.**
7. **a., b.,** and **c.** are **true.**

   d. and **e.** are **false.**

Section 4.2

1. a. `10    5`
   b. No output
   c. `5`   B has no value.
   d. `10    5`
   e. `15    4`
      `15    4`
   f. `10    5`
3. a. should be

```
IF A = 10 THEN ...
```

   b. `3 < X < 10`
   cannot be evaluated. This should be
   `(3 < X) AND (X < 10)`

   c. This expression needs **BEGIN** and **END** to be consistent with indenting. It should be

```
IF A > 0 THEN
  BEGIN
    Count := Count + 1;
    Sum := Sum + A
  END;
```

   d. `IF Ch = 'A' OR 'B' THEN`

   should be

```
IF (CH = 'A') OR (CH = 'B') THEN
```

5. Yes
9.

```
BEGIN
  readln (Num1, Num2, Num3);
  Total := Total + Num1 + Num2 + Num3;
  writeln (Num1:5, Num2:5, Num3:5);
  writeln;
  writeln (Total)
END;
```

11.

```
read (Ch1, Ch2, Ch3);
IF (Ch1 <= Ch2) AND (Ch2 <= Ch3) THEN
  writeln (Ch1, Ch2, Ch3);
```

This can also be written as

```
read (Ch1, Ch2, Ch3);
IF Ch1 <= Ch2 THEN
  IF Ch2 <= Ch3 THEN
    writeln (Ch1, Ch2, Ch3);
```

Section 4.3

1. a. `-14    14`
   b. `50    25`
      `1    75`
   c. `10    5`
      `5    0`

3. a. Since the intent appears to be a statement that counts characters other than periods, a **BEGIN . . . END** block should be included in the **IF . . . THEN** option.

```
IF Ch <> '.' THEN
  BEGIN
    CharCount := CharCount + 1;
    writeln (Ch)
  END  { of IF...THEN option }
ELSE
  PeriodCount := PeriodCount + 1;
```

b. The semicolon between **END** and **ELSE** should be omitted.

c. Technically this fragment will run. However, since it appears that OldAge := OldAge + Age is to be included in the **ELSE** option, the programmer probably meant

```
ELSE
  BEGIN
    OldCount := OldCount + 1;
    OldAge := OldAge + Age
  END;
```

Section 4.4

	X	Y
1. a.	38.15	763.0
b.	-21.0	21.0
c.	600.0	1200.0
d.	3000.0	9000.0

3. a.
```
IF Ch = 'M' THEN
  IF Sum > 1000 THEN
    X := X + 1
  ELSE
    X := X + 2
ELSE IF Ch = 'F' THEN
  IF Sum > 1000 THEN
    X := X + 3
  ELSE
    X := X + 4;
```

b.
```
read (Num);
  IF Num > 0 THEN
    IF Num <= 10000 THEN
      BEGIN
        Count := Count + 1;
        Sum := Sum + Num
      END
    ELSE
      writeln ('Value out of range':27)
  ELSE
    writeln ('Value out of range':27);
```

c.
```
IF A > 0 THEN
  IF B > 0 THEN
    writeln ('Both positive':22)
  ELSE
    writeln ('Some negative':22)
ELSE
  writeln ('Some negative':22);
```

d.
```
IF C <= 0 THEN
   IF A > 0 THEN
     IF B > 0 THEN
       writeln ('Option one':19)
     ELSE
       writeln ('Option two':19)
   ELSE
     writeln ('Option two':19)
ELSE
  writeln ('Option one':19);
```

5.
```
IF Average < 90 THEN
   IF Average < 80 THEN
     IF Average < 70 THEN
       IF Average < 55 THEN
           Grade := 'E'
       ELSE Grade := 'D'
     ELSE Grade := 'C'
   ELSE Grade := 'B'
ELSE Grade := 'A' ;
```

This could be written using sequential **IF . . . THEN** statements. For example

```
IF (Average <= 100) AND (Average >= 90) THEN
  Grade := 'A' ;
IF (Average < 90) AND (Average >= 80) THEN
  Grade := 'B' ;
        .
        .
        .
```

The disadvantage of this method is that each Boolean expression for each statement will always be evaluated. This is relatively inefficient.

7.

8	13	104
A	B	C

Section 4.5

3.
```
IF ((Age DIV 10) > 10) OR ((Age DIV 10) < 1) THEN
   writeln ('Value of age is', Age)
ELSE
   .
   .  (CASE statement here)
   .
```

5. a. `5          3          125`
   b. `You have purchased   Super Unleaded gasoline`
   c. `3         -3`
   d. `5         10          -5`

7. Assume there is a variable ClassType. The design of the fragment to compute fees is

```
read (ClassType);
CASE ClassType OF
  'U' :
  'G' :   (list options here)
  'F' :
  'S' :
END;  {  of CASE  }
```

CHAPTER 5

Section 5.2

1. a.
```
*
 *
  *
   *
    *
     *
```
b.
```
 1 :    9
 2 :    8
 3 :    7
 4 :    6
 5 :    5
 6 :    4
 7 :    3
 8 :    2
 9 :    1
10 :    0
```
c.
```
**   2
**   3
**   4
**   5
**   6
**   7
**   8
**   9
**  10
**  11
**  12
**  13
**  14
**  15
**  16
**  17
**  18
**  19
**  20
```
d.
```
 1
 2
 3
 4
 5
 6
 7
 8
 9
10
11
12
13
14
15
16
17
18
19
20
21
```

3. a.
```
FOR J := 1 TO 4 DO
  writeln ('*':10);
```
b.
```
FOR J := 1 TO 8 DO
  writeln ('***':J + 5);
```
c.
```
writeln ('*':10);
FOR J := 1 TO 3 DO
  writeln ('*':10 - J, '*':2 * J);
writeln ('**** ****':14);
FOR J := 1 TO 2 DO
  writeln ('* *':11);
writeln ('***':11);
```
d. This is a "look ahead" problem that can be solved by a loop within a loop. This idea is developed in Section 5.6.
```
FOR J := 5 DOWNTO 1 DO
  BEGIN
    write (' ':(6 - J)); {  Indent a line  }
    FOR K := 1 TO (2 * J - 1) DO {  Print a line  }
      write ('*');
    writeln
  END;
```

5. a.
```
FOR J := 1 TO 5 DO
  write (J:3);
FOR J := 5 DOWNTO 1 DO
  write (6 - J:3);
```
b.
```
FOR J := 1 TO 5 DO
  writeln ('*':J);
FOR J := 5 DOWNTO 1 DO
  writeln ('*':(6 - J));
```

7.
```
FOR J := 2 TO 10 DO
  writeln (12 - J:12 - J);
```

9. The key loop in this program will be something like
```
FOR FACTOR := -10 TO 10 DO
  BEGIN
    Num := 5 * FACTOR;
    writeln (Num:10, Num * Num:10, Num * Num * Num:10)
  END;  {  of printing the chart  }
```

Section 5.3

3. a.
```
 1
 2
 3
 4
 5
 6
 7
 8
 9
10
```
b.
```
1        0
2        1
3        2
4        1
5        2
```
c.
```
54       50
```
d.
```
The partial sum is      1
The partial sum is      3
The partial sum is      6
The partial sum is     10
The partial sum is     15
The count is     5
```
e.
```
     96.00       2.00
```
5. a.
```
WHILE Num > 0 DO
BEGIN
  writeln (Num:10:2);
  Num := Num - 0.5
END;
```

Section 5.4

1. A pretest loop tests the Boolean expression before executing the loop. A posttest loop tests the Boolean expression after the loop has been executed.

3. a.
```
1   9
2   8
3   7
4   6
5   5
6   4
```
b.
```
  2
  4
  8
 16
 32
 64
128
```
c.
```
 1
 2
 3
 4
 5
 6
 7
 8
 9
10
```
d.
```
1   0
2   1
3   2
4   1
5   2
```
5. a.
```
IF Num > 0 THEN
   REPEAT
     writeln (Num:10:2);
     Num := Num - 0.5
   UNTIL Num <= 0;
```

Section 5.6

1. a.
```
FOR K := 1 TO 5 DO
  BEGIN
    write (' ':K);
    FOR J := K TO 5 DO
      write ('*');
    writeln
  END;
```
c.
```
FOR K := 1 TO 7 DO
  IF K < 5 THEN
    BEGIN
      FOR J := 1 TO 3 DO
        write ('*');
      writeln
    END
  ELSE
    BEGIN
      FOR J := 1 TO 6 DO
        write ('*');
      writeln
    END;
```
3.
```
4  4  4  4
5  5  5  5
6  6  6  6
7  7  7  7

5  5  5
6  6  6
7  7  7

6  6
7  7
```

Section 5.7

1. a. This is an infinite loop.
   b. The loop control variable K is unassigned once the **FOR . . . TO** loop is exited. Thus, the attempt to use K in the expression K **MOD** 3 = 0 may result in an error.
5. We will assign the first number to both Small and Large, and then identify the smallest and largest numbers from the list.
```
{  Assign the first number in the list  }
{  to both Small and Large              }

readln (Num);
Small := Num;
Large := Num;

{  Now read the rest of the list and identify  }
{  the smallest and largest numbers            }

REPEAT
  readln (Num);
  IF Num > Large THEN
    Large := Num:
  IF Num < Small THEN
    Small := Num;
UNTIL eof;
```

CHAPTER 6

Section 6.1

3. The variables should be formatted so the integers will be separated by blanks. You should check your answers to Exercises 5–7 on your computer due to possible differences in reading text files.

11.
```
PROGRAM DeleteBlanks (input, output, NoBlank);
VAR
  NoBlank : text;
  Ch :char;
BEGIN
  rewrite (NoBlank);  {  Open for writing  }
  WHILE NOT eof DO
    BEGIN
      WHILE NOT eoln DO
        BEGIN
          read (Ch);
          IF Ch <> ' ' THEN
            write (NoBlank, Ch)
        END;  {  of WHILE NOT eoln  }
      readln;
      writeln (NoBlank)
    END  {  of WHILE NOT eof  }
END.  {  of main program  }
```

Section 6.2

3. **a.** Jane is listed in both type Names and type People.
   b. Red is listed twice in type Colors.
   c. Parentheses are needed around the values:

```
TYPE
  Letters = (A, C, E);
```

5. **a.**, **d.**, and **e.** are valid.
   b. is invalid; Tues + Wed is not defined.
   c. is valid (but a poor choice).
   f. is invalid; you cannot **write** user-defined values.
   g. is invalid; you cannot **read** user-defined ordinals.
   h. is invalid; the operation Tues + 1 is not defined.

Section 6.3

1. **a.** The definition is invalid; 10 . . 1 is not a subrange of an existing ordinal data type.
   b. Bases and Double are valid. Score is invalid because Second . . Home is not a subrange.
   c. All definitions and declarations are valid. However,

```
Hue := Blue;
```

   is an invalid use because Blue is not in the subrange defined for Stripes.
   d. The definitions are invalid because the type Days must be defined before the subrange Weekdays.
   e. All definitions and declarations are valid, but

```
Score2 := Score1 + 70;
```

   will produce a run-time error because the intended value is not in the defined subrange.

3. **a.** Dependents usually refers to the number of single-family dependents for tax purposes; 20 is a reasonable maximum.
   b. Assuming hours worked are in one week, 0 to 60 is a reasonable range.
   c. The subrange was chosen for a maximum score of 10. This would vary for other maximum scores.
   d. The subrange could be used if the total points were a maximum of 700. This might be used in some grading programs.

5. **a.** and **b.** are compatible. The base type is ChessPieces.

   c. and **f.** are incompatible.

   d. and **e.** are compatible. The base type is **integer.**

Section 6.4

1. **a.** Oak
   b. Cotton
   c. 2
   d. Invalid
   e. 3
   f. Invalid
   g. 0
3. **a.** 'D'
   b. 75
   c. 'H'
   d. Invalid; addition of characters is not defined.
   e. Invalid; **pred**('K') is a character, so the operation '+' is not defined.
   f. 'Z'
5. **a.**
```
Weekend
Weekday
Weekday
Weekday
Weekday
Weekday
```
   b. For a **WHILE** loop, you could use the Boolean expression **WHILE** Day < Sat **DO:**
```
Day := Sun;
WHILE Day < Sat DO
  BEGIN
     .
     .     (body of loop here)
     .
  END;  {  of WHILE loop  }
```
   A **FOR** loop could be controlled by the Boolean expression
```
FOR Day := Sun TO Fri DO
  BEGIN
     .
     .     (body of loop here)
     .
  END;  {  of FOR loop  }
```
   c. This can be accomplished by using ordinal values. For example, if OrdValue has been declared, the loop could be
```
OrdValue := 0;
  REPEAT
    CASE OrdValue OF
      0         :  (action here)
      1,2,3,4,5 :
    END;  {  of CASE OrdValue  }
    OrdValue := OrdValue + 1
  UNTIL OrdValue = 6;
```
   d. The last value (Sat) is not being considered. This could be altered by using a **FOR** loop and including Sat or by using a variable control loop and adding a **writeln** statement such as
```
writeln ('Weekend':20);
```
   outside the loop.

7. Assuming the variables MonthNum and Month have been appropriately declared, a function could be

```
FUNCTION Month (MonthNum : integer) : MonthName;
  BEGIN
    CASE MonthNum OF
      1  : Month := Jan;
      2  : Month := Feb;
           .
           .
           .
      12 : Month := Dec
    END  {  of CASE MonthNum  }
  END;  {  of FUNCTION Month  }
```

CHAPTER 7

Section 7.1

1. a.
```
TYPE
  ScoreList = ARRAY [1..35] OF integer;
VAR
  Score : ScoreList;
```
   b.
```
TYPE
  PriceList = ARRAY [1..20] OF real;
VAR
  CarCost : PriceList;
```
   c.
```
CONST
  NumQuestions = 50;
TYPE
  AnswerList = ARRAY [1..NumQuestions] OF char;
VAR
  Answer : AnswerList;
```
   Note: It is possible to use an array of element type **boolean** here.

   d.
```
TYPE
  GradeList = Array [1..6] OF char;
VAR
  Grade : GradeList;
```
3. a. There is no error if Hours has been defined as a constant.
   b. No error
   c. No index range has been given for the array.
   d. The index range should be [1 . . 10] rather than [1 **TO** 10].
   e. The index range is not appropriate; something like **ARRAY** [<index range>] **OF boolean** should be used.
   f. [1 . . . 5] should be [1 . . 5].
5. a.
```
TYPE
  LetterList = ARRAY [1..100] OF 'A'..'Z';
VAR
  Letter : LetterList;
```
   b.
```
TYPE
  Name = ARRAY [1..30] OF char;
VAR
  CompanyName : Name;
```
   c.
```
TYPE
  ScoreList = ARRAY [30..59] OF real;
VAR
  Score : ScoreList;
```

7. a. Money

183.25	Money[1]
10.04	Money[2]
17.32	Money[3]

b. Money

10.04	Money[1]
19.26	Money[2]
17.32	Money[3]

c. Money

19.26	Money[1]
10.04	Money[2]
2.68	Money[3]

Section 7.2

1. a. List

0	List[1]
0	List[2]
1	List[3]
1	List[4]
1	List[5]

b. List

5	List[1]
6	List[2]
7	List[3]
8	List[4]
9	List[5]

Score

1	Score[1]
2	Score[2]
2	Score[3]
2	Score[4]
3	Score[5]

c. Answer

false	Answer[1]
true	Answer[2]
false	Answer[3]
true	Answer[4]
false	Answer[5]
true	Answer[6]
false	Answer[7]
true	Answer[8]
false	Answer[9]
true	Answer[10]

d. The contents of this array depend upon the character set being used.

3. The section counts the number of scores > 90.

5.
```
TYPE
  ListOfLetters = ARRAY [1..20] OF char;
VAR
  Letter : ListOfLetters;
```

A **FOR** loop could be used as follows:

```
FOR J := 1 TO 20 DO
  read (Letter[J]);
```

7.
```
FOR J := 1 TO 100 DO
  A[J] := 0.0;
```

9. a. **JOHN SMITH**
   b. **SMITH, JOHN**
   c. **HTIMS NHOJ**

11.
```
writeln ('Test Number', 'Score':10);
writeln ('-----------', '-----':10);
writeln;
FOR J := 1 TO 50 DO
  writeln ('<':4, J:2, '>', TestScore[J]:11);
```

Section 7.3

1. a. After one pass: After two passes:

After one pass	After two passes
-20	-20
10	-2
0	0
10	10
8	8
30	30
-2	10

b. Three exchanges are made.

3. A high to low sort is achieved by changing

```
IF A[K] < A[Index] THEN
```

to

```
IF A[K] > A[Index] THEN
```

Section 7.4

1. **a.** is valid; it can be called by

```
NewList (List1, Aray);
```

b. is invalid; a semicolon instead of a colon should appear after Row.
c. is invalid; an array declaration cannot be included in the heading.
d. is valid; it can be called by

```
NewList (List1, List2);
```

e. is invalid; Column cannot be used as a variable name.
f. is invalid; an array declaration cannot be included in the heading.
g. is invalid; Name is not a data type.
h. is valid; it can be called by

```
Surnames (Name1, Name2);
```

i. is invalid; Name is not a data type.
j. is valid; it can be called by

```
Table (List1, List2);
```

3. **a.** `PROCEDURE OldList (X : Row; Y : Column);`
b. `PROCEDURE ChangeList (X : Row; N : String20; D : Week);`
c. This call is inappropriate because the data type for A and B has not been defined in the **TYPE** section.
d. This call is inappropriate because the argument String20 is a data type rather than a variable.

5. **a.**

List1	List2
1	0
4	0
9	0
16	0
25	0
36	0
49	0
64	0
81	0
100	0

Section 7.5

1. **a.**, **c.**, **d.**, and **f** are valid (**true**);
b. and **e.** are invalid (**false**).

3. **a.** `To err is human. Computers do not forgive.`
b.

```
To err is human. Computers do not forgive.
There are 15 blanks.
```

c.

```
To err is human. C                    **********
```

↑ (position 20) (20 blanks)

d.

```
To err is human. Computers do not forgive.
        .evigrof ton od sretupmoC .namuh si rre oT
```

(8 blanks)

5.
```
MCount := 0;
FOR J := 1 TO 100 DO
  IF Message[J] = 'M' THEN
    MCount := MCount + 1;
```

Section 7.6

1.
```
FOR J := 1 TO Length DO
  IF Num = A[J] THEN
    writeln (Num, ' is in position', J:5);
```

3. The value of Index in the loop can be used as a counter.

5. a. **Num = 18**

	First	Last	Mid	A[Mid]	Found
Before loop	1	5	Undefined	Undefined	**false**
After first pass	1	2	3	37	**false**
After second pass	1	2	1	18	**true**

c. **Num = 76**

	First	Last	Mid	A[Mid]	Found
Before loop	1	5	Undefined	Undefined	**false**
After first pass	4	5	3	37	**false**
After second pass	4	3	4	92	**false**

Since First > Last, the loop will be exited and an appropriate message should be printed.

7. Algorithmic developments for this problem follow.

a.
1. Copy file components into an array
2. Get number to look for
3. Search sequentially for a match

c.
1. Copy file components into an array
2. Get new number
3. Use a binary search until Last < First
4. Assign First to Position
5. Move array components ahead one from Position to the end of the list:

```
FOR J := Length DOWNTO Position DO
  A[J + 1] := A[J];
```

6. Assign new number to

```
A[Position];
```

9. There will be a maximum of five passes.

CHAPTER 8

Section 8.1

1. a.
```
DrugPrice = ARRAY [1..4, 1..5] OF real;
DrugPrice = ARRAY [1..4] OF ARRAY [1..5] OF real;
```
b.
```
Grade = ARRAY [1..20, 1..6] OF char;
Grade = ARRAY [1..20] OF ARRAY [1..6] OF char;
```
c.
```
QuizScore = ARRAY [1..30, 1..12] OF integer;
QuizScore = ARRAY [1..30] OF ARRAY [1..12] OF integer;
```

3. a.

ShippingCost

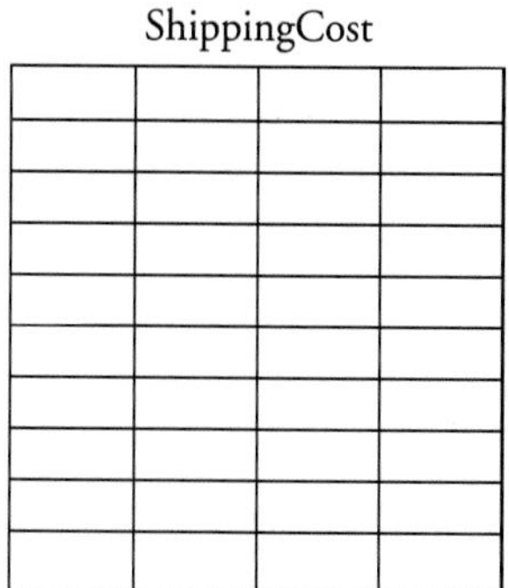

40 locations available

GradeBook

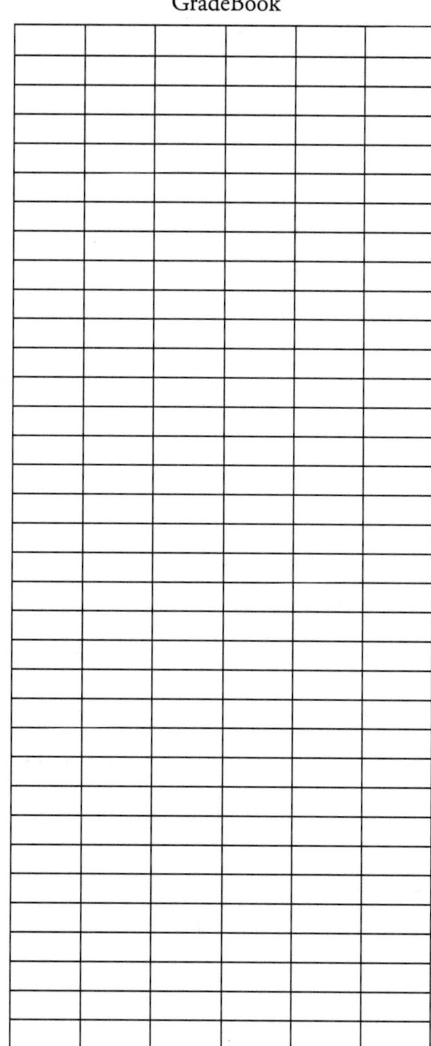

210 locations available

b. A

15 locations available

c. Schedule

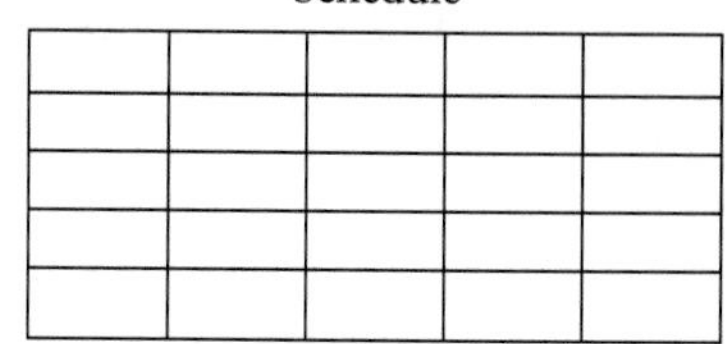

25 locations available

d. AnswerSheet

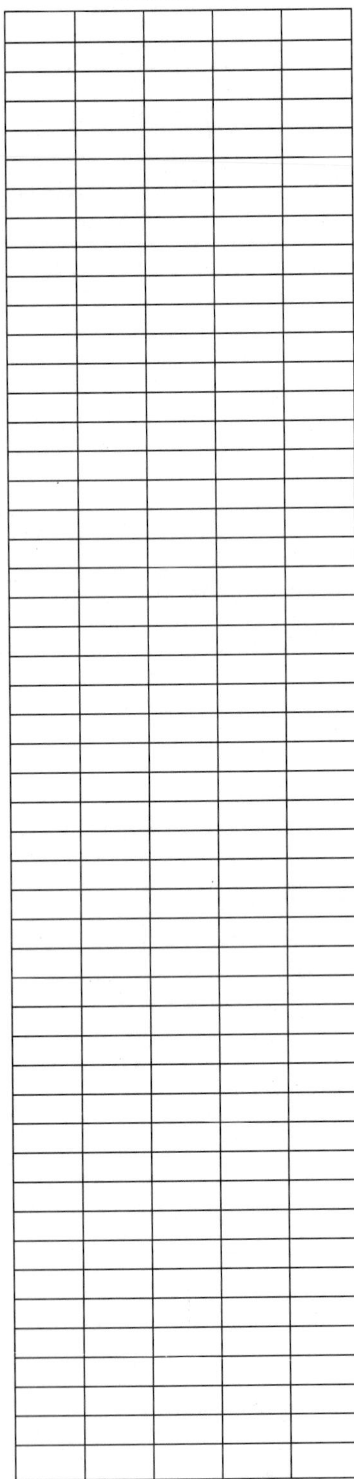

250 locations available

5\. a.
```
FOR J := 1 TO 3 DO
  FOR K := 1 TO 6 DO
    A[J,K] := 2 * J + K;
```
b.
```
FOR J := 1 TO 3 DO
  FOR K := 1 TO 6 DO
    A[J,K] := 0;
```
c.
```
FOR J := 1 TO 3 DO
  FOR K := 1 TO 6 DO
    A[J,K] := 2 * J;
```
7\.
```
TYPE
  String20 = PACKED ARRAY [1..20] OF char;
  NameList = ARRAY [1..50] OF String20;
VAR
  Name: NameList;

FOR J := 1 TO 50 DO          {  Loop to get data  }
  BEGIN
    FOR K := 1 TO 20 DO      {  Read one line  }
      read (Name[J,K)]);
    readln
  END;  {  of FOR loop  }
```
9\. a.
```
FOR J := 1 TO 4 DO
  BEGIN
    MinRow[J] := Table[J,1];
    FOR K := 2 TO 5 DO
      IF Table[J,K] < MinRow[J] THEN
        MinRow[J] := Table [J,K]
  END;  {  of FOR loop  }
```
c.
```
Total := 0;
FOR J := 1 TO 4 DO
  FOR K := 1 TO 5 DO
    Total := Total + Table[J,K];
```
11\. a.
```
TYPE
  Table = ARRAY [1..3, 1..8] OF integer;
```
b.
```
PROCEDURE Replace (VAR A : Table);
  VAR
    J, K : integer;
  BEGIN
    FOR J := 1 TO 3 DO
      FOR K := 1 TO 8 DO
        IF A[J,K] < 0 THEN
          A[J,K] := 0
  END:  {  of PROCEDURE Replace  }
```
c. **PROCEDURE** Replace in **b.** could be called by

```
Replace (Table3X5);
```
13\. a. How values are read into matrices A and B depends upon how data are arranged in the data file.

b.
```
FOR Row := 1 TO M DO
  FOR Column := 1 TO P DO
    BEGIN
      {  Compute partial products down a column  }
      Sum := 0;
      FOR InnerDimension := 1 TO N DO
      Sum := Sum + A[Row, InnerDimension] *
             B[InnerDimension, Column] ;
      C[Row, Column] := Sum
      END;  {  of summing down one column  }
```

Section 8.2

1. a. This prints an alphabetical listing of the states that begin with the letter O.
   b. This prints every fifth state in reverse alphabetical order.
   c. This lists the first two letters of each state.
   d. This counts all occurrences of the letter *A* in the names of the states.
3. Assume the number of data lines is in NumLines.

a.
```
FOR J := 1 TO NumLines DO
  BEGIN
    read (Name[J,1]);
    K := 1;
    WHILE Name[J,K] <> '*' DO
      BEGIN
        K := K + 1;
        read (Name[J,K])
      END;  { of WHILE loop }
    Length := K;
    FOR K := Length TO 20 DO
      Name [J,K] := ' ';
    readln
  END;  { of FOR loop }
```

c.
```
FOR J := 1 TO NumLines Do
  BEGIN
    FOR J := 1 TO 20 DO
      read (Name[J,K]);
    readln
  END;  { of FOR loop }
```

Section 8.3

1. a. These declarations are not appropriate because Names is an array of 10 elements but Amounts is an array of 15 elements.
   b. These declarations are appropriate because both Table and Names represent arrays of size 12 × 10.
3. b. Assume an array type is defined as

```
TYPE
  GradeCount = ARRAY ['A'..'E'] OF integer;
```

If Count is a variable of type GradeCount, the frequency of each grade can be determined by

```
FOR Ch := 'A' TO 'E' DO  { Initialize }
  Count[Ch] := 0;
FOR J := 1 TO ListLength DO
  CASE Grade[J] OF
    'A' : Count['A'] := Count['A'] + 1;
    'B' : Count['B'] := Count['B'] + 1;
    'C' : Count['C'] := Count['C'] + 1;
    'D' : Count['D'] := Count['D'] + 1;
    'E' : Count['E'] := Count['E'] + 1
  END;  { of CASE Grade[J] }
```

Section 8.4

1. a. `2 * 3 * 10 = 60`
   b. `6 * 3 * 4 = 72`
   c. `3 * 2 * 11 = 66`
   d. `4 * 10 * 15 = 600`
3.
```
TYPE
  Floor = 1..4;
  Wing = 1..5;
  Room = 1..20;
  FloorPlan = ARRAY [Floor, Wing, Room] OF char;
VAR
  RoomType : FloorPlan;
```

5. There are 10 schools, 12 sports, and two genders. Thus, there are 10 *12 *2 = 240 memory locations reserved.

7. a.
```
{ Initialize to zero }
FOR School := 'A' TO 'J' DO
  NumGrants[School] := 0;
FOR School := 'A' TO 'J' DO  { Consider each school }
  FOR Sport := Baseball TO Wrestling DO  { Consider each sport }
    FOR Gender := Male TO Female DO  { Consider each gender }
      NumGrants[School] := NumGrants[School] +
                           Grants[School, Sport, Gender];
```

CHAPTER 9

Section 9.1

5. a. Employee

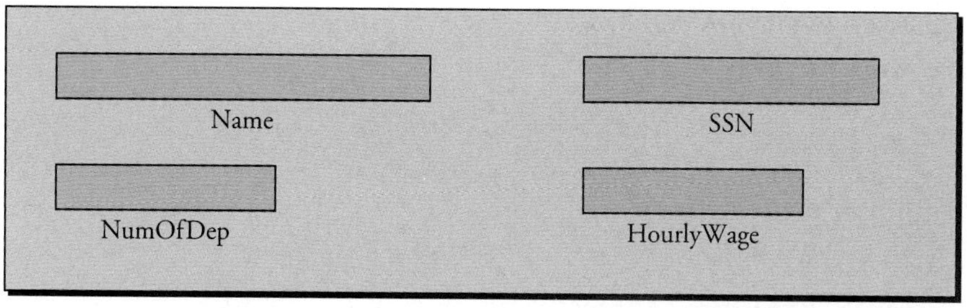

Name

SSN

NumOfDep

HourlyWage

b. House

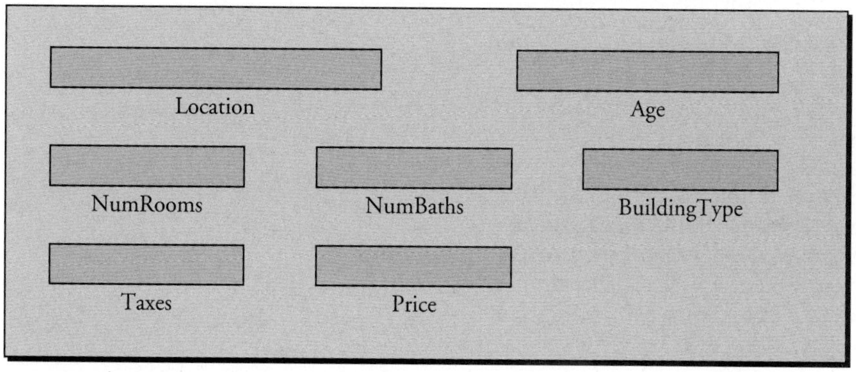

Location

Age

NumRooms

NumBaths

BuildingType

Taxes

Price

c. PhoneListing

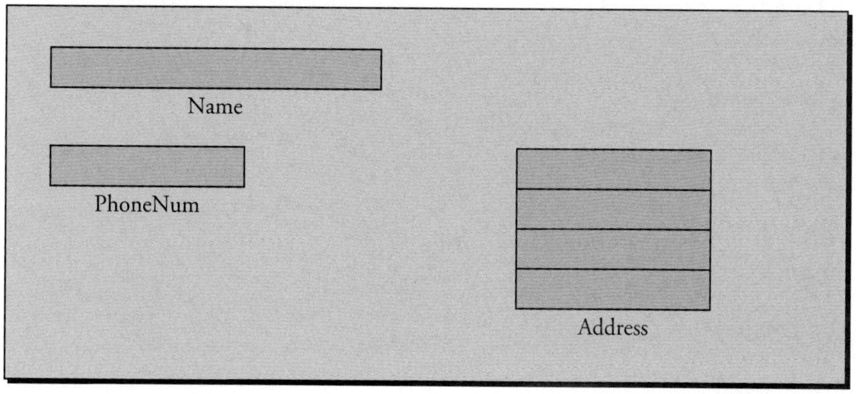

Name

PhoneNum

Address

7. **a.**

```
Info : RECORD
```

should be

```
Info = RECORD
```

and

```
Name = PACKED
```

should be

```
Name : PACKED
```

b. Member is used as both a variable and a data type.

c.

```
IQ = 50..200
```

should be

```
IQ : 50..200
```

Section 9.2

1. **a.**, **c.**, and **d.** are valid.

   b. is invalid; Cust2 and Cust3 are not of identical type.

   e. is valid but demonstrates a poor practice. For better readability, you should always determine precisely which fields are being used.

3. **a.** The three different methods you could use are

(1)
```
Employee2 := Employee1;
```

(2)
```
WITH Employee2 DO
  BEGIN
    Name := Employee1.Name;
    SSN := Employee1.SSN;
    Age := Employee1.Age;
    HourlyWage := Employee1.HourlyWage;
    HoursWorked := Employee1.HoursWorked;
    Volunteer := Employee1.Volunteer
  END;  {  of WITH...DO loop  }
```

(3)
```
WITH Employee1 DO
  BEGIN
    Employee2.Name := Name;
    Employee2.SSN := SSN;
    Employee2.Age := Age;
    Employee2.HourlyWage := HourlyWage;
    Employee2.HoursWorked := HoursWorked;
    Employee2.Volunteer := Volunteer
  END;  {  of WITH...DO loop  }
```

b. Consider

```
WITH Employee2 DO
  BEGIN
    Temp := HoursWorked;
    Employee2 := Employee1;
    HoursWorked := Temp
  END;  {  of WITH...DO loop  }
```

5.
```
FUNCTION Grade (Pts : integer) : char;
  VAR
    Percent : real;
  BEGIN
    Percent := Pts / 5;  {  Compute percent  }
    IF Percent < 60 THEN
      Grade := 'E'
    ELSE IF Percent < 70 THEN
      Grade := 'D'
    ELSE IF Percent < 80 THEN
      Grade := 'C'
    ELSE IF Percent < 90 THEN
```

```
      Grade := 'B'
    ELSE
      Grade := 'A'
  END;  {  of FUNCTION Grade  }
```

This function can be called by

```
With Student DO
  LetterGrade := Grade(TotalPts);
```

Section 9.3

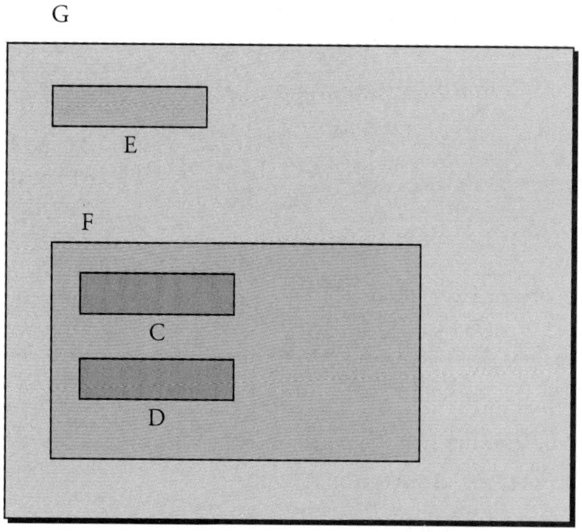

1. **a.** See figure at right.
   b. **i.**, **iii.**, **iv.**, **viii.**, **ix.**, and **x.** are valid references **ii.**, **v.**, **vi.**, and **vii.** are invalid references

3.
```
TYPE
  String20 = PACKED ARRAY [1..20] OF char;
  Status = ('S', 'M', 'W', 'D');
  NumKids = 0..15;
  FamilyRec = RECORD
                MaritalStatus : Status;
                Children : NumKids
              END;  {  of RECORD FamilyRec  }
  AddressRec = RECORD
                 Street : String 20;
                 City : String20;
                 State : PACKED ARRAY [1..2] OF char;
                 ZipCode : integer
               END;  {  of RECORD AddressRec  }
  CustomerInfo  = RECORD
                    Name : String20;
                    Address : AddressRec;
                    SSN : PACKED ARRAY [1..11] OF char;
                    AnnualIncome : real;
                    FamilyInfo : FamilyRec
                  END;  {  of RECORD CustomerInfo  }
VAR
  Customer : CustomerInfo;
```

5.
```
CONST
  SquadSize = 15;
TYPE
  String20 = PACKED ARRAY [1..20] OF char;
  AgeRange = 15..25;
  HeightRange = 70..100;
  WeightRange = 100..300;
  PlayerInfo = RECORD
                 Name : String20;
                 Age : AgeRange;
                 Height : HeightRange;
                 Weight : WeightRange;
                 ScoringAv : real;
                 ReboundAv : real
               END;  {  of RECORD PlayerInfo  }
  PlayerList = ARRAY [1..SquadSize] OF PlayerInfo;
VAR
  Player : PlayerList;
```

7. a.

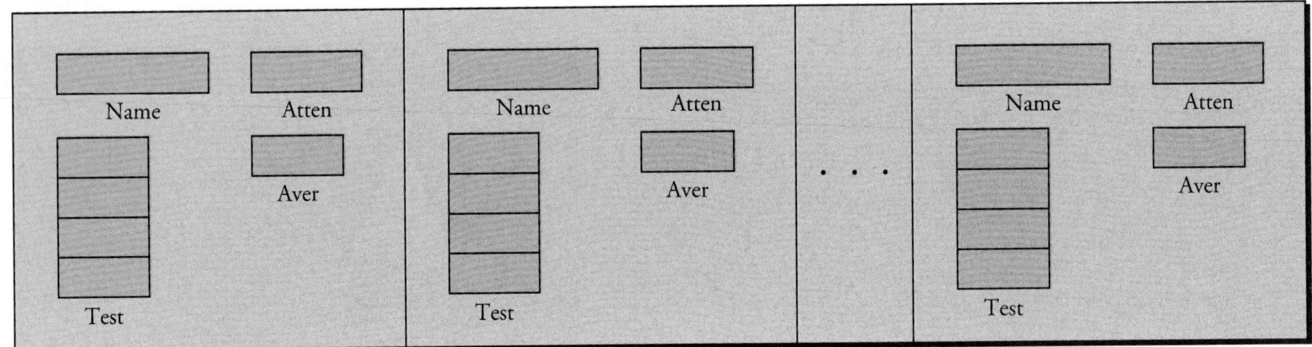

b. This function computes the test average for one student. It could be called by

```
WITH Student[K] DO
  Aver := GuessWhat(Test);
```

c. Format and headings will vary according to personal preference. However, your procedure should include

```
WITH St DO  {  Printout for St  }
  BEGIN
    .
    .
    .
    write ('Your attendance was ');
    CASE Atten OF
      Excellent : writeln ('excellent.');
      Average   : writeln ('average.');
      Poor      : writeln ('poor.')
    END;  {  of CASE  }
    .
    .
    .
  END;  {  of WITH...DO loop  }
```

Section 9.4

3. a. The type TagType for the tag field Tag has not been defined.
   b. There is no value listed for the C of the tag field.
   c. There is a syntax error. A semicolon is needed between **boolean** and **CASE.** A type has not been given for the tag field. It should be

```
CASE Tag : TagType OF
```

   d. Only one variant part can be defined in a record.

5. a.

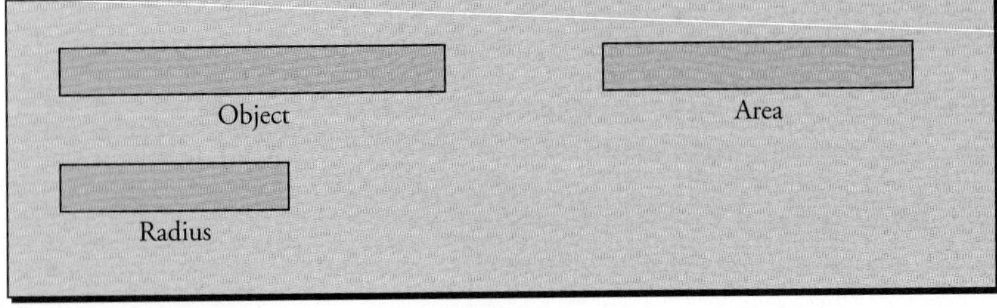

b.

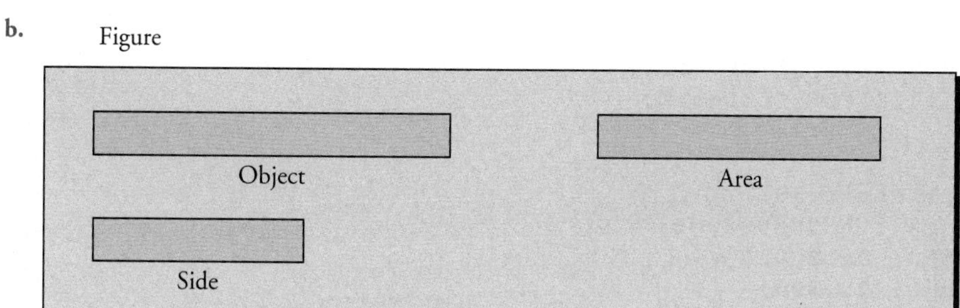

c.

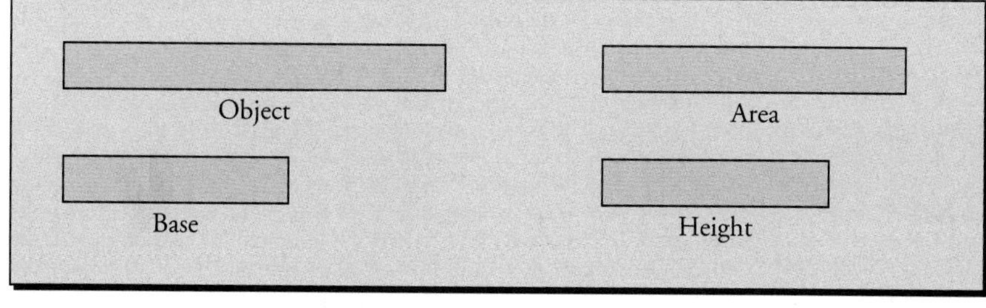

7.
```
PubType = (Book, Article);
DataRange = 1600..2000;
PublicationInfo = RECORD
                    Author : String30;
                    Title : String30;
                    Date : DataRange;
                    CASE Pub : PubType OF
                      Book    : (Publisher : String30;
                                 City : String30);
                      Article : (JournalName : String30;
                                 VolumeNumber : integer)
                  END;  {  of RECORD PublicationInfo  }
```

CHAPTER 10

Section 10.1

3. **a.** is valid; the component type is an integer in the subrange 0 . . 120.

   b. is invalid; no file type has been defined.

   c. is invalid; the component type for a file cannot be another file.

   d. is invalid; the expression
   FILE[1 . . 100] has no meaning.

   e. is valid; the component type is **integer.**

5.
```
TYPE
  String20 = PACKED ARRAY [1..20] OF char;
  AddressType = ARRAY [1..3] OF String20;
  GenderType = (M, F);
  PatientInfo = RECORD
                  Name : String20;
                  Address : AddressType;
                  Height : 0..200;
                  Weight : 0..300;
                  Age : 0..120;
                  Gender : GenderType;
                  InsuranceCo : String20
                END;  { of RECORD PatientInfo }
  PatientFile = FILE OF PatientInfo;
VAR
  Patient : PatientFile;
```

Section 10.2

3.
```
TYPE
  FileType = FILE OF 0..100;
VAR
  SevenMult : FileType;
```

A fragment of code for this problem is

```
rewrite (SevenMult);  { Open the file }
Num := 1;
Sevens := 7;
WHILE Sevens < 100 DO
  BEGIN
    SevenMult^ := Sevens;
    put (SevenMult);
    Num := Num + 1;
    Sevens := 7 * Num
  END;  { of WHILE loop }
```

5. Using **get** we have

```
reset (FivesFile);
A := FivesFile^;
get (FivesFile);
B := FivesFile^;
get (FivesFile);
C := FivesFile^;
get (FivesFile);
D := FivesFile^;
```

Using **read** we have

```
reset (FivesFile);
read (FivesFile, A);
read (FivesFile, B);
read (FivesFile, C);
read (FivesFile, D);
```

7. The **reset** procedure opens a file so values may be read from it. The contents of the file are not altered by this command. When **reset**(<file name>) is executed, the value of the first component is copied into the buffer variable.
The **rewrite** procedure opens a file so values may be written to it. When **rewrite**(<file name>) is executed, any previous contents are lost.

9. a. The **reset** procedure opens the file for reading from the file; and **put** is used to write to the file. It appears that

```
reset(File1);
```

should have been

```
rewrite(File1);
```

b. No errors

c. The buffer variable is not properly written.

```
File1 := 10 * J;
```

should be

```
File1^ := 10 * J;
```

d. This loop will execute, but nothing happens. In order to put the values into File1, the loop should be

```
FOR J := 1 TO 5 DO
  BEGIN
    File1^ := J * 10;
    put (File1)
  END;
```

e. The files are mixed up. It appears the intent is to copy the contents of File1 into File2.

f. No errors. This is a correct version of a problem similiar to the one posed in Example 13.4.

11. The output is

```
-17
-4
```

The files contain the following values.

8	-17	0	-4	21

OldFile

8	0	21

NewFile

Section 10.3

1. b.
```
TYPE
  String20 = PACKED ARRAY [1..20] OF char;
  BookInfo = RECORD
               Author : String20;
               Title : String20;
               StockNumber : integer;
               Price : real;
               Quantity : 0..500
             END;  {  of RECORD BookInfo  }
  BookFile = FILE OF BookInfo;
VAR
  Book : BookFile;
```

3. a.
```
TYPE
  String20 = PACKED ARRAY [1..20] OF char;
  QuizList = ARRAY [1..10] OF 0..10;
  TestList = ARRAY [1..4] OF 0..100;
  StudentRec = RECORD
                 Name : String20;
                 Number : integer;
                 Quiz : QuizList;
                 Test : TestList
               END;  {  of RECORD StudentRec  }
  StudentFile = FILE OF StudentRec;
VAR
  Student : StudentFile;
```

b.
```
PROCEDURE GetData (VAR St : StudentFile);
  VAR
    J : integer;
  BEGIN
    rewrite (St);        {  Open St for writing  }
    WHILE NOT eof(input) DO
      BEGIN
        WITH St^ DO  {  Get data for one student  }
```

```
        BEGIN
          FOR J := 1 TO 20 DO
            read (Name[J]);    {  Get a name  }
          read (Number);      {  Get student ID  }
          FOR J := 1 TO 10 DO
            read (Quiz[J]);    {  Get quiz scores  }
          FOR J := 1 TO 4 DO
            read (Test[J])  {  Get test scores  }
        END;  {  of WITH...DO  }
      readln;
      put (St)   {  Move data to file  }
    END  {  of WHILE NOT eof  }
  END;  {  of PROCEDURE GetData  }
```

c. The basic design for this task is to

1. Transfer records to an array
2. Sort the array
3. Transfer records from the array back to the file

Assuming suitable definitions and declarations have been made, a procedure for this is

```
PROCEDURE SortFile (VAR St : StudentFile);
  VAR
    Temp : StudentRec;
    J, K, Length, Index : integer;
    TempList : ARRAY [1..MaxSize] OF StudentRec;
  BEGIN
    reset (St);
    J := 0;
    WHILE NOT eof(St) DO  {  Copy to array  }
      BEGIN
        J := J + 1;
        TempList[J] := St^;
        get (St)
      END;  {  of WHILE Not eof  }
    Length := J;

  {  Now sort the array  }
    FOR J := 1 TO Length - 1 DO
      BEGIN
        Index := J;
        FOR K := J + 1 TO Length DO
          IF TempList[K].Name < TempList[Index].Name THEN
            Index := K;
        IF Index <> J THEN
          Swap (TempList[Index], TempList[J])
      END;  {  of one pass  }

  {  Now copy back to the file  }
    rewrite (St);
    FOR J := 1 TO Length DO
      BEGIN
        St^ := TempList[J];
        put (St)
      END  {  of FOR loop  }
    END;  {  of PROCEDURE SortFile  }
```

CHAPTER 11

Section 11.1

1.
```
PROCEDURE InsertionSort (VAR NumList : List;
                         VAR NewLength : integer);
  VAR
    Num, Temp, K : integer;
    Done : boolean;
  BEGIN
    readln (Num);
    List[1] := Num;
    NewLength := 1;
    WHILE NOT eof DO
      BEGIN
        NewLength := NewLength + 1;
        readln (Num);
        Temp := Num;
        K := NewLength;
        Done := false;
        WHILE K >= 2 AND NOT Done DO
          IF Temp < List[K - 1] THEN
            BEGIN
              List[K] := List[K - 1];
              K := K - 1
            END  {  of IF...THEN option  }
          ELSE  {  Temp >= List value  }
            Done := true;
        List[K] := Temp
      END  {  of WHILE NOT eof  }
END;  {  of PROCEDURE InsertionSort  }
```

3. Rewrite the sort as
```
BEGIN
  Count := 0;
  FOR Index := 2 TO ListLength DO
    BEGIN
      Temp := List[Index];
      Count := Count + 1;       {  Increment counter  }
      Done := false;
      WHILE (K >= 2) AND (NOT Done) DO
        IF Temp < List[K - 1] THEN
          BEGIN
            List[K] := List[K - 1];
            Count := Count + 1;    {  Increment counter  }
            K := K - 1
          END  {  of IF...THEN option  }
        ELSE
          Done := true;
      List[K] := Temp;
      Count := Count + 1     {  Increment counter  }
    END  {  of FOR loop  }
END;  {  of PROCEDURE InsertionSort  }
```

5. The bubble sort modification is

```
BEGIN  {  Exchange values  }
  Temp := A[J];
  A[J] := A[J + 1];
  A[J + 1] := Temp;
  ExchangeMade := true;
  Count := Count + 3  {  Counter here  }
END;  {  of exchanging values  }
```

9. Assume the arrays are A and B. The bubble sort change is then

```
BEGIN  {  Exchange values  }
  TempA := A[J];
  TempB := B[J];
  A[J] := A[J + 1];
  B[J] := B[J + 1];
  A[J + 1] := TempA;
  B[J + 1] := TempB;
  ExchangeMade := true
END;  {  of exchanging values  }
```

If you use a sort that calls **PROCEDURE** Swap, the appropriate change is

```
BEGIN
  Swap (A[J], A[J + 1]);
  Swap (B[J], B[J +, 1])
END;
```

Section 11.2

1. Modify the code for a bubble sort by using

```
FOR J := 1 TO Length DO
  BEGIN
    Count := Count + 1;  {  Counter here  }
    IF A[ J] > A[J + 1] THEN
      BEGIN
        .
        .
        .
      END;  {  of IF...THEN option  }
```

CHAPTER 12

Section 12.1

1. **a.** **real** is not an ordinal data type.
   b. **integer** will exceed the maximum size for a set.
   c. : should be =.
   d. Brackets should not be used.
   e. No errors
3. a. `A := ['J', 'I', 'M'];`
   b. `A := ['P', 'A', 'S', 'C', 'L'];`
   c. The elements are 'T', 'O', and 'Y'. The eight subsets are [ ], ['T'], ['O'], ['Y'], ['T', 'O'], ['T', 'Y'], ['O', 'Y'], ['T', 'O', 'Y']
5. **a.** Brackets are needed:

   ```
   A := ['J'..'O'];
   ```

   b. No errors
   c. Single quotations marks are needed:

   ```
   B := ['A'..'Z'];
   ```

   d. 'E' and 'I' are listed more than once.
   e. [ ] is not a set variable.
   f. Since 'S' is in the subrange 'A' .. 'T', it is listed more than once.

7. a.
```
TYPE
  Hues = (Red, Orange, Yellow, Green, Blue, Indigo, Violet);
  RainbowSet = SET OF Hues;
VAR
  Rainbow : RainbowSet;
```
c.
```
Type
  SomeFruits = (Apple, Orange, Banana, Grape, Pear, Peach,
                Strawberry);
  FruitSet = SET OF SomeFruits;
VAR
  Fruit : FruitSet;
```

Section 12.2

1. No; when A = B, both A >= B and A <= B are **true.**
3. a. A + B = [–3..4, 7..10]
   A * B = [0,1,2,8,10]
   A – B = [–3,–2,–1]
   B – A = [3,4,7,9]
   c. A + B = B
   A * B = A
   A – B = A
   B – A = B
5. All of these are **true.**
7. Code for this is

```
VowelsUppercase := ['A', 'E', 'I', 'O', 'U'];
VowelCount := 0;
WHILE NOT eof DO
  BEGIN
    read(Ch);
    IF Ch IN VowelsUppercase THEN
      VowelCount := VowelCount + 1
  END;  {  of WHILE NOT eof  }
```

Section 12.3

3. Modify **PROGRAM** Delete-Blanks presented in Example 9.4 (Section 9.) by changing

```
IF Ch = '' THEN
  Ch := '*';
```

to

```
IF Ch IN Vowels THEN
  write '*'
ELSE
  write (Ch);
```

7.
```
FUNCTION AllOddDigits (Num : integer) : boolean;
  TYPE
    Digits = SET OF 0..9;
  VAR
    EvenDigits : Digits;
    NumDigits, J, Digit : integer;
  BEGIN
    EvenDigits := [0,2,4,6,8];
    IF Num DIV 1000 = 0 THEN  {  Num < 1000  }
      IF Num DIV 100 = 0 THEN  {  Num < 100  }
        IF Num DIV 10 = 0 THEN  {  Num < 10  }
          NumDigits := 1
```

```
        ELSE NumDigits := 2
      ELSE NumDigits := 3
    ELSE NumDigits := 4;
    AllOddDigits := true;
    FOR J := 1 TO NumDigits DO
      BEGIN
        Digit := abs(Num MOD 10);
        IF Digit IN EvenDigits THEN
          AllOddDigits := false;
        Num := Num DIV 10
      END  {  of FOR loop  }
  END;  {  of FUNCTION AllOddDigits  }
```

CHAPTER 13

Chapter 13.1

3. [■]→[Blue] [■]→[Red]

Ptr1 Ptr1^ Ptr2 Ptr2^

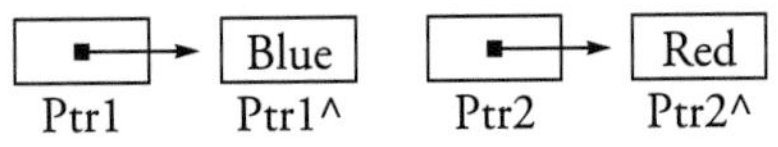

5. **c.**, **f.**, and **h.** are valid.

   a. is invalid; IntPtr1 + 1 is not allowed.

   b. is invalid; pointers cannot be used with **writeln.**

   d. is invalid; < is not a valid comparison for pointers.

   e is invalid:

   ```
   BoolPtr NOT NIL
   ```

   should be

   ```
   BoolPtr2 <> NIL
   ```

   g. is invalid; BoolPtr2 is not a Boolean expression.

Section 13.2

3. Assume the file name is Num. A procedure is then

```
PROCEDURE PrintNumbers (First : DataPtr);
  VAR
    P : DataPtr;
  BEGIN
    P := First;
    WHILE P <> NIL DO
      BEGIN
        writeln (P^.Num);
        P := P^.Next
      END  {  of WHILE loop  }
  END;  {  of PROCEDURE PrintNumbers  }
```

This procedure is called by

```
PrintNumbers (Start);
```

5. a.
```
TYPE
  String20 = PACKED ARRAY [1..20] OF char;
  TestList = ARRAY [1..4] OF 0..100;
  QuizList = ARRAY [1..10] OF 0..10;
  DataPtr = ^StudentInfo;
  StudentInfo = RECORD
                  Name : String20;
                  Test : TestList;
                  Quiz : QuizList;
                  Average : real;
                  Grade : char;
                  Next : DataPtr
                  END;  {  of RECORD StudentInfo  }
VAR
  Student : DataPtr;
```

b. The pointer variable is Student. The pointer type is DataPtr.

c. i. Assume Start, Ptr, and Last have been declared to be of type DataPtr. Data for the first student can then be obtained by

```
new (Start);
Ptr := Start;
Last := Start;
WITH Start^ DO
  BEGIN
    FOR J := 1 TO 20 DO
      read (Name[J]);
    FOR J := 1 TO 4 DO
      read (Test[J]);
    FOR J := 1 TO 10 DO
      read (Quiz[J]);
    Next := NIL
  END;  {  of WITH...DO  }
readln;
```

ii. Data for the second student can be obtained by

```
new (Last);
Ptr^.Next := Last;
Ptr := Last;
WITH Last^ DO
  BEGIN
    FOR J := 1 TO 20 DO
      read (Name[J]);
    FOR J := 1 TO 4 DO
      read (Test[J]);
    FOR J := 1 TO 10 DO
      read (Quiz[J])
  END;  {  of WITH...DO  }
readln;
Ptr^.Next := NIL;
```

7. a. Working from the original

```
 A          B          C
[■]        [■]        [■]
 |          |          |
 v          v          v
[1 | ■]--->[2 | ■]--->[3 | NIL]
```

each time, we get

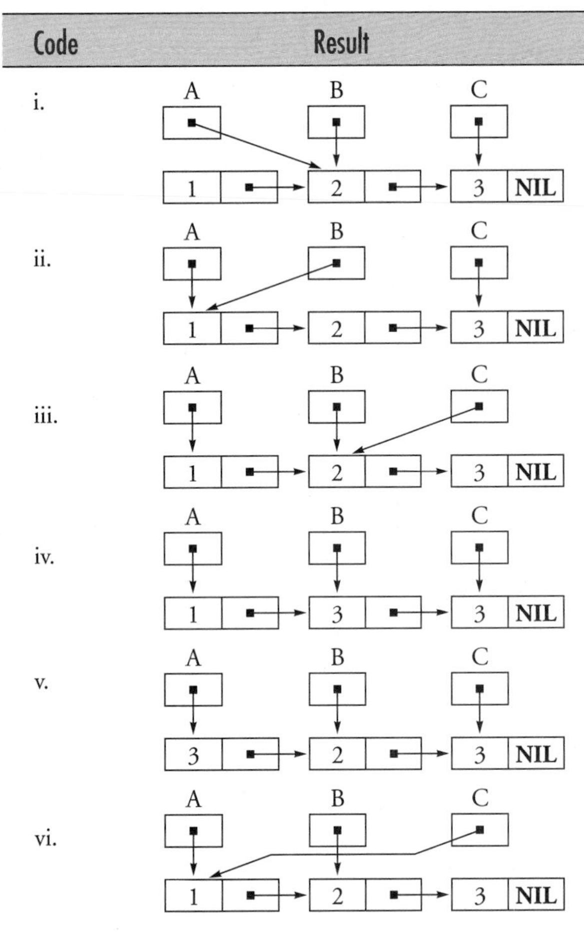

b.
```
A^.Next^.Next := B;
```

9. Assume the linked list has been declared and values have been read into the field Num for each component of the list. Further assume Start is the pointer to the first node. A function for summing is then

```
FUNCTION Sum (First : DataPtr) : integer;
  VAR
    Total : integer;
    P : DataPtr;
  BEGIN
    Total := 0;
    P := First;
    WHILE P <> NIL DO
      BEGIN
        Total := Total + P^.Num;
        P := P^.Next
      END;  {  of WHILE loop  }
    Sum := Total
  END;  {  of FUNCTION Sum  }
This can be called by
  ListTotal := Sum(Start);
```

Section 13.3

1. Assume the original list is envisioned as

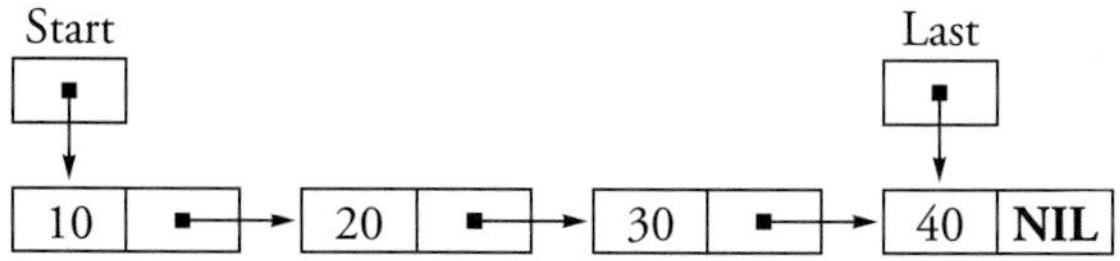

and you wish to insert 25 into it. The initialization produces

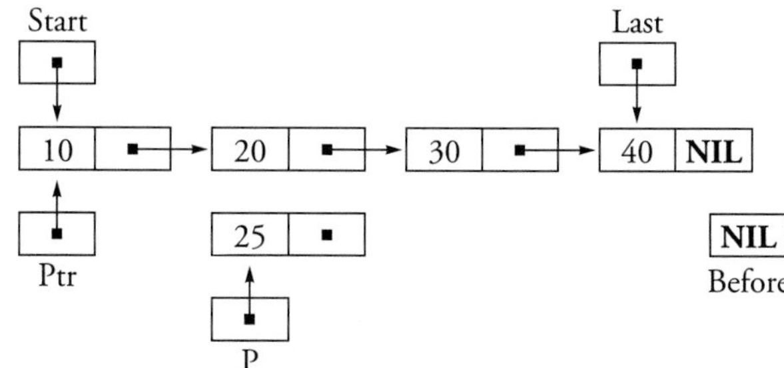

Since the loop is not empty, the
WHILE loop will be executed until the result is

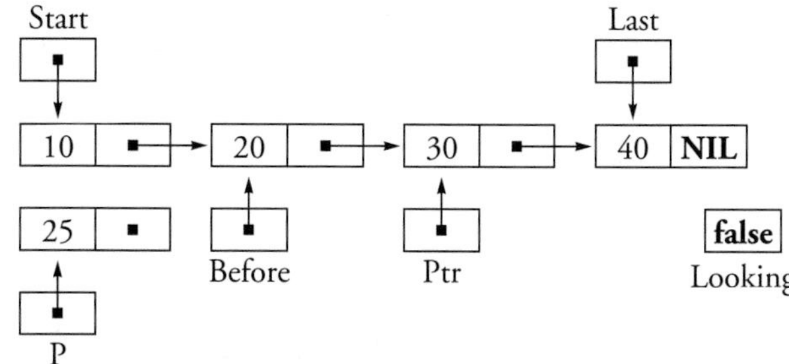

The pointers are then moved to obtain

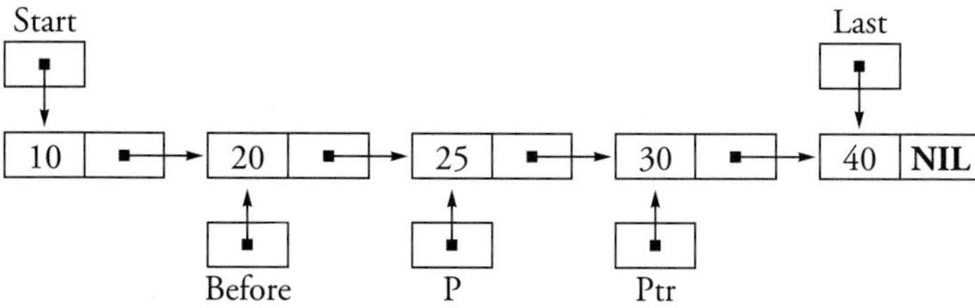

3. The new code is

```
IF Before = NIL THEN
  Push (Start, NewNum)      {  Call to Push  }
ELSE
  Before^.Next := P;
```

5. The heading becomes

```
PROCEDURE Pop (VAR Start : DataPtr);
```

and the line

```
NewNum := P^.Num
```

should be deleted.

7.
```
PROCEDURE Delete (VAR Start : DataPtr;
                      Position : integer);
  VAR
    Before, P : DataPtr;
  BEGIN
    IF Position = 1 THEN
      Pop (Start, Start^.Num)
    ELSE
      BEGIN
        Before := Start;
        FOR J := 1 TO (Position - 2) DO
          Before := Before^.Next;
        P := Before^.Next;
        Before^.Next := P^.Next;
       dispose (P)
      END  {  of ELSE option  }
  END;  {  of modified PROCEDURE Delete  }
```

Section 13.4

1. Illustrating only the parentheses, you get

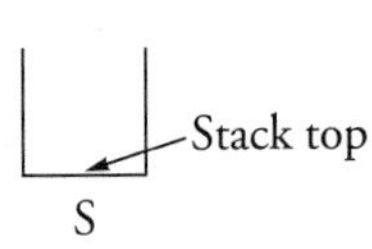

Character Read	New Stack
"("	(
"("	((
"("	(((
")"	((
"("	(((
")"	((
")"	(
")"	(empty)

5. a.
```
CONST
  MaxStack = <value>;
TYPE
  Stack = RECORD
            Item : ARRAY [1..MaxStack] OF <data type>;
            Top : 0..MaxStack
          END;  {  of RECORD Stack  }
VAR
  S : Stack;
```

b. Push becomes

```
PROCEDURE Push (VAR S : Stack;
                X : integer);
  BEGIN
    IF S.Top = MaxStack THEN
      writeln ('Stack overflow')
    ELSE
      BEGIN
        S.Top := S.Top + 1;
        S.Item[S.Top] := X
      END  {  of ELSE option  }
  END;  {  of PROCEDURE Push  }
```

PopAndCheck becomes

```
PROCEDURE PopAndCheck (VAR S : Stack;
                       VAR X : integer;
                       VAR Underflow : boolean);
BEGIN
  IF Empty(S) THEN  {  Check for empty stack  }
    Underflow := true
  ELSE
    BEGIN
      Underflow := false;
      X := S.Item[S.Top];
      S.Top := S.Top - 1
    END  {  of ELSE option  }
END;  {  of PROCEDURE PopAndCheck  }
```

9. Change the **ELSE** option to

```
ELSE IF Num = Node^.Info THEN
  writeln (Num, 'is a duplicate value.')
ELSE IF Num < Node^.Info THEN
  AddNode (Node^.LeftChild, Num)
ELSE
  AddNode (Node^.RightChild, Num)
```

11.
```
FUNCTION Search (Node : Pointer;
                 NewNum : integer) : boolean;
  VAR
    Found : boolean;
    Current : Pointer;
  BEGIN
    Current := Node;
    Found := false;
    WHILE (Current <> NIL) AND NOT Found DO
      IF Current^.Num = NewNum THEN
        Found := true
      ELSE IF Current^.Num < NewNum THEN
        Current := Current^.RightChild
```

```
      ELSE
        Current := Current^.LeftChild;
    Search := Found
  END;  {  of FUNCTION Search  }
```

13.

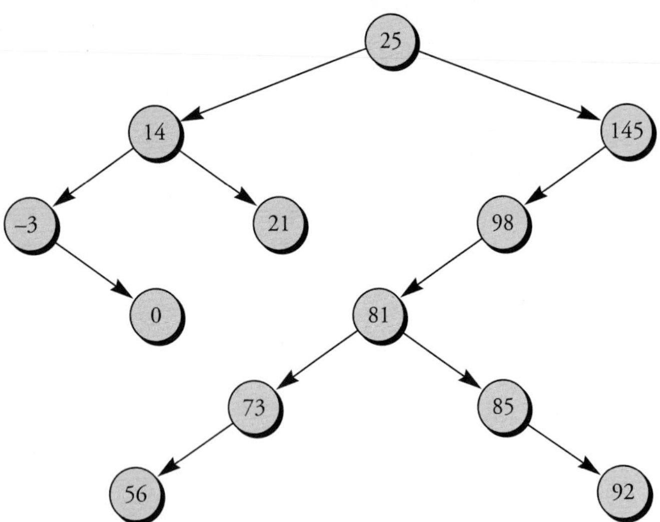

Index

Credits

PHOTOS

Figures 1.4, 1.5a, 1.5b, 1.5c, 1.6a and 1.6b: Courtesy of IBM Corporation.

Figure 1.5d: Courtesy of Apple Computer, Inc.

Figure 1.8: Robert Barclay.

NOTES OF INTEREST

Page 4: Ethics and Computer Science

From the *Minneapolis Star/Tribune,* October 14, 1990, The Washington Post. Reprinted with permission.

Page 8: Advances in Computing Technology

Page 12: Data Loss on Floppy Disks

Reprinted with permission from *Information Systems in Business: An Introduction,* p. 230, by James O. Hicks, Jr. Copyright © 1990 by West Publishing Company. All rights reserved. Permission for figure is credited to Verbatim Corporation, 1200 W WT Harris Blvd., Charlotte, NC 28213.

Page 16: Why Learn Pascal?

Reprinted with permission from "Pascal," by T. Woteki and A. Freiden, published in the September 1983 issue of *Popular Computing* magazine. © McGraw-Hill, Inc., New York. All rights reserved.

Page 20: Software Verification

From Ivars Peterson, "Finding Fault: The Formidable Task of Eradicating Software Bugs," SCIENCE NEWS, February 16, 1991, Vol. 139. Reprinted with permission from SCIENCE NEWS, the weekly newsmagazine of science. Copyright © 1991 by Science Services, Inc. Photo courtesy of Ontario Hydro.

Page 28: Object-Oriented Programming (OOP), Part 1

Page 35: Blaise Pascal

Adapted from William Dunham, *Journey Through Genius: The Great Theorems of Mathematics,* John Wiley & Sons, 1990. Photos: Courtesy of IBM Corporation.

Page 61: Herman Hollerith

Reprinted by permission from *Introduction to Computers with BASIC,* pp. 27–28, by Fred G. Harold. Copyright © 1984 by West Publishing Company. All rights reserved. Photos courtesy of IBM Corporation.

Page 70: Communication Skills Needed From P. Jackowitz, R. Plishka, J. Sidbury, J. Hartman, and C. White, ACM Press *SIGCSE Bulletin* 22, No. 1, (February, 1990). Copyright 1991, Association for Computing Machinery, Inc. Reprinted by permission of Association for Computing Machinery, Inc.

Page 73: Defined Constants and Space Shuttle Computing, *Communications of the ACM* 27, No. 9 (September 1984); 880. Copyright 1984, Association for Computing Machinery, Inc. Reprinted by permission of Association for Computing Machinery, Inc.

Pages 80 and 86: Debugging or Sleuthing

From J. Bentley, *Communications of the ACM* 28, No. 2 (February 1985): 139. Copyright 1985, Association for Computing Machinery, Inc. Reprinted by permission of Association for Computing Machinery, Inc.

Page 91: Structured Programming

Page 112: Computer Ethics: Hacking and Other Intrusions

Reprinted by permission from *Computers Under Attack: Intruders, Worms, and Viruses,* pp. 150–155, edited by Peter J. Denning, Article 7, "The West German Hacker Incident and Other Intrusions," by Mel Mandell. Copyright 1990, Association for Computing Machinery, Inc.

Page 123: Program Documentation—EDS Style

Page 125: Niklaus Wirth

Adapted from Nicklaus Wirth, Programming Language Design to Computer Construction, 1984 Turing Award Lecture, *Communications of the ACM,* 28, No. 2 (February 1985).

Page 148: George Boole

Adapted from William Dunham, *Journey Through Genius: The Great Theorems of Mathematics,* John Wiley & Sons, 1990. Photo: The Bettmann Archive.

Page 153: New Legal Research Uses Plain English

Page 163: Artificial Intelligence
Reprinted by permission from *The Mind Tool,* Fifth Ed., pp. 394–398, by Neill Graham. Copyright © 1989 by West Publishing Company. All rights reserved.
Page 185: A Software Glitch
From Ivars Peterson, "Finding Fault: The Formidable Task of Eradicating Software Bugs," SCIENCE NEWS, February 16, 1991, Vol. 139. Reprinted with permission from SCIENCE NEWS, the weekly newsmagazine of science. Copyright 1991 by Science Services, Inc.
Page 215: Charles Babbage
Reprinted by permission from *Introduction to Computers with BASIC,* pp. 24–26, by Fred G. Harold. Copyright © 1984 by West Publishing Company. All rights reserved. Photos courtesy of IBM Corporation.
Page 222: Ada Augusta Byron
Reprinted by permission from *Introduction to Computers with BASIC,* pp. 26–27, by Fred G. Harold. Copyright © 1984 by West Publishing Company. All rights reserved. Photo: The Bettmann Archive.
Page 242: IBM and Apple = Pinstripes and T-shirts
Page 276: Inspections: Debugging in the 1990s
Page 282: Career Opportunities in Computer Science
From Carol Wilson, Western Kentucky University, Bowling Green, Kentucky, 1991.
Page 291: Computer Ethics: Viruses
From Philip J. Hilts, Science Lab, in *The Washington Post National Weekly Edition,* May 23–29, 1988. Reprinted by permission of The Washington Post.
Page 311: Monolithic Idea: Invention of the Integrated Circuit
Adapted from T. R. Reid, "The Chip," *Science,* February 1985, pp. 32–41.
Page 318: Impact of Computers on Art
From Dana J. Lamb, "The Impact of the Computer on the Arts," *Academic Computing,* April, 1989, pp. 22–24. Reprinted by permission from Academic Computing.
Page 325: Too Few Women in the Computer Science Pipeline?
From Carol Wilson, Western Kentucky University, Bowling Green, Kentucky, 1991.
Page 395: Computer Ethics: Worms
Reprinted by permission from *Computers Under Attack: Intruders, Worms, and Viruses,* pp. 191 and 265, edited by Peter J. Denning, Article 9, "Computer Security in the Business World," by Maurice V. Wilkes; and Article 16, "The 'Worm' Programs—Early Experience with a Distributed Computation," by John F. Shoch and Jon A. Hupp. Copyright 1990, Association for Computing Machinery, Inc.
Page 439: Using Key Fields in Records
From David Gifford and Alfred Spector: "The TWA Reservations System: An Interview with Carol Flood and Ted Celentio," *Communications of the ACM* 17, No. 7 (July 1984): 650–657, Copyright 1984, Association for Computing Machinery, Inc. Reprinted by permission of Association for Computing Machinery, Inc.
Page 449: Computer Insecurity
From *The Chronicle of Higher Education,* by David L. Wilson, February 16, 1994. Reprinted by permission.
Page 462: Artist of Interface
From Ron Wolf, "Artist a Go-Between for Users, Computers," *The Chicago Tribune,* June 10, 1990. Reprinted by permission from Knight-Ridder Tribune News.
Page 483: Relational Databases
From William D. Nance, Management Information Systems, San Jose State University, San Jose, California, 1991.
Page 490: Backup and Recovery of Data
From William D. Nance, Management Information Systems, San Jose State University, San Jose, California, 1991.
Page 500: History Stuck on Old Computer Tapes
From the *Minneapolis Star/Tribune,* "30 Years of History Stuck on Old Computer Tapes," January 2, 1991. Reprinted by permission of the Associated Press.
Page 533: Gene Mapping Computer Scientists Examine Problems of Genome Project
From *The Chronicle of Higher Education,* May 9, 1990. Reprinted by permission of The Chronicle of Higher Education.
Page 546: Fractal Geometry and Benoit Mandlebrot Figure from *Integrated Computer Graphics,* p. 128, by Bruce Mielke. Copyright © 1991 by West Publishing Company.
Page 555: Object-Oriented Programming–Part 2
Adapted from "Starting with the Basics of Object-Oriented Programming Using Turbo Pascal 5.5," by Captain Byron B. Thatcher, in *Interface: The Computer Education Quarterly* 12, Issue 4 (1990): 15–18.
Page 573: When Will Object Technology Meet Its Potential?
Reprinted by permission of Sigs Publications, Inc. Copyright © 1992.
Page 594: Using Pointers
From Nazim H. Madhavji, "Visibility Aspects of Programmed Dynamic Data Structures," *Communications of the ACM* 27, no. 8 (August 1984): 766. Copyright 1984, Association for Computing Machinery, Inc. Reprinted by permission of Association for Computing Machinery, Inc.